Human Sexuality

McGraw-Hill Book Company

New York St. Louis San Francisco Auckland Bogotá Hamburg
Johannesburg London Madrid Mexico Montreal New Delhi
Panama Paris São Paulo Singapore Sydney Tokyo Toronto

Human Sexuality

E. R. Mahoney

Professor of Sociology
Western Washington University

Human Sexuality

1 2 3 4 5 6 7 8 9 0 DOCDOC 8 9 8 7 6 5 4 3

ISBN 0-07-039650-7

See Photo Credits on pages 623-624.
Copyrights included on this page by reference.

This book was set in Helvetica by Black Dot, Inc.
(ECU). The editors were Patricia S. Nave and
David Dunham; the designer was Merrill Haber;
the production supervisor was Dennis J. Conroy.
The photo editor was Linda Gutierrez.
R. R. Donnelley & Sons Company was printer
and binder.

Cover photograph by Duane Michals, with
permission of dancers of the Ohio Ballet, Akron,
Ohio; Artistic Director, Heinz Poll.

Library of Congress Cataloging in Publication Data

Mahoney, E. R.
    Human sexuality.

    Bibliography: p.
    Includes index.
    1. Sex (Psychology)   2. Sex (Biology)
3. Sex—Social aspects.   I. Title.
BF692.M278   1983   306.7   82-12708
ISBN 0-07-039650-7

TO THE LEADER OF THE BAND

Contents in Brief

Contents

Chapter 3
Reproductive Anatomy and Processes   45

Chapter 4
Becoming Sexual   83

Chapter 7
Sexuality and Youth

Chapter 8
Traditional Marriage and Sexuality

Chapter 9
Heterosexual Alternatives to Traditional Marriage   263

Chapter 14
The Sex Business

Chapter 15
Prostitution

Chapter 16
Sexually Transmitted Diseases

Chapter 17
Health, Sexuality, and Treatment

Preface

Every author of a college text has some specific reasons for undertaking such a project. I suspect that in most cases a major reason is the feeling that one can write a text which is better than those which already exist. I am no different. This text was written to fill what I see as gaps in existing human sexuality texts.

These gaps concern my view of what the study of human sexuality is and is not. The study of human sexuality is not for the purpose of telling students how they or other people should conduct their sexuality. A text should provide knowledge which stands on its own, independent of notions concerning right or wrong, good or bad, better or worse that are applied to the subject matter. The study of human sexuality is multidisciplinary. In order to adequately encompass its subject matter, one must pull together work from such disciplines as psychology, sociology, anatomy-physiology, biochemistry, public health, medicine, history, and anthropology. The knowledge we have about human sexuality from these diverse fields is obtained through research, which is cumulative. This means that in an adequate text in human sexuality for college-level courses the content must be a summary and a synthesis of the accumulation of research findings from a number of disciplines.

This text is thus intended to be multidisciplinary, research-based, and explanatory as well as descriptive. After the text was completed, I made a content analysis of the bibliographies of the existing human sexuality texts. Compared with existing texts, this text has far fewer sources from popular magazines and newspapers, more sources from professional sociology, psychology, and medical journals, and more sources from such disciplines as anthropology, history, public health, and epidemiology. There are not only more sources, but the proportion of material from the major disciplines in the study of human sexuality is more evenly balanced than in any existing text.

WHAT THIS TEXT IS

In addition to explaining why I wrote this text, I should point out that a number of my basic beliefs have influenced its form and content. Since I think it is important that you understand as much about me and what I have done here as possible, I will briefly describe these beliefs and how they have influenced what you are going to read.

1. *You have a right to expect accurate and ample information.* Texts are powerful. When you read something written by an "authority" such as

an author, you are most likely to believe that it is the truth. It should be. I have thus taken special care to make certain that the content of this text is based on established scientific research findings or on a considerable amount of accumulated evidence. You will find many citations in this text. These are the sources of my information and are available for you to check the material and to read more about it. That is your right and my obligation. Additionally, you should have plenty of material to underline. Since texts are expensive, they should not ramble on and on and not tell you very much. I have therefore attempted to pack information into the pages while at the same time keeping the amount of information within the limits of practical learning.

2. *I assume students want to know.* I have assumed that if you were not interested in the subject matter, you would not be reading this book. Therefore, I have not used tricky gimmicks or have not placed chapters in some special order to entice you to read them.

3. *I assume that students are intelligent.* This may sound silly, but it seems to me that many texts assume that students are not capable of understanding what we really know about human sexuality. I have frankly found many texts to be insulting to the student's intelligence since they reveal so little of what we know about human sexuality. While I have not assumed that you have a doctoral degree, I have assumed that you are capable of digesting a considerable amount of material and of dealing with complex concepts and research findings from the whole range of disciplines constituting human sexuality. If you wanted to take a Mickey Mouse course, you would probably have signed up for underwater basketweaving. After all, part of a college education is being intellectually stimulated and challenged.

4. *You should have fun.* A text should not only supply you with ample material and push you at times, but it should also be fun to read. There is absolutely nothing wrong with enjoying yourself while learning. I have thus attempted to write this text in much the same manner as I give my course. There are sections of the text which are mainly humorous, rather than instructional, in content. I have also attempted to write in a manner such that you can come along with me. I really enjoyed writing this text, moving from idea to idea and topic to topic. I have attempted to convey this excitement to you and to write in a manner whereby you and I cover the material together rather than merely lecture to you as the author.

5. *A text should be honest.* Absurd as it may sound, many texts are not honest. They simply do not reveal all aspects of human sexuality as they really are. All too often the socially acceptable and desirable aspects of a particular form of sexuality are discussed in living detail, but the student is not told about those aspects which are socially unacceptable, unpleasant, or not erotic. It is dishonest to avoid these topics of sexuality (and there are not all that many) just because they might disturb some readers who only want to read about the "nice sex" or do

not want to know that certain things actually happen. We discuss it all. I do not do so to shock or to titillate, but to inform. After all, we *are* studying human sexual behavior. If we are not going to study it as it exists, why bother?

6. *I should facilitate your learning.* Given all the above, I very strongly believe that a text should not make learning a struggle. I should do what I can to help you obtain the end result—more knowledge about the subject when you are finished with your course than when you started. Apart from the method of writing, I have included a number of elements to facilitate your learning. The text includes many tables and figures, which are very useful learning tools since they present a point graphically as well as in words. There are special boxed inserts throughout. These boxes contain examples from everyday life, questionnaires for you to fill out and score to measure your own attitudes about sexual topics, interesting historical pieces about selected topics, and descriptions of behavior patterns in other cultures. Finally, a Study Guide is included at the end of every chapter. These guides provide you with concepts to review, two self-tests with answers, suggestions for additional reading, and topics for group or class discussion. All these elements are designed to aid you in learning the material. I hope you enjoy the educational experience this text provides.

ACKNOWLEDGMENTS

When you sit down and think about all the people who have had some significant impact on a project such as this, you begin to realize how much influence and aid other people have provided. To the following people for the following reasons, "thanks, thanks very much"! My friends for letting me disappear from life for longer than I realized; my colleagues for listening to me being consumed by a single task, for providing ideas, and for tolerating my sometimes foul moods; Clive Davis for the most profound and unselfish editorial comments I have ever seen—which have had many positive influences on this text; David Dunham for taking on a project of great magnitude and not only doing it well but remaining calm, clear, sophisticated, and pleasant despite my many personal quirks and authorship bullheadedness; the many students from whom this text originated and to whom it ends; and to that very special person who has not only helped me but has tolerated, remotivated, inspired, and encouraged me—thanks, Judy.

E. R. Mahoney

Human Sexuality

Chapter 1
Our Sexual Ancestors

Most of us generally like to think that what we are doing today sexually is largely our own generation's invention and that it is much different from the sexual behavior of any generation in the past (Box 1-1).

In some ways this is true, because patterns of sexual values, attitudes, and behaviors do change. However, contemporary sexuality has its roots firmly planted in a stream of sexual history. In a very real sense, we cannot truly understand sexuality today unless we understand what our ancestors have passed down to us and how this has shaped our present sexual attitudes, values, and behaviors.

In this chapter, we shall review the history of sexuality in Western culture and discuss some of the ways in which these past patterns of sexuality influence us today. As you read through this chapter, you should try to think about contemporary sexual attitudes, values, and behaviors that you see and how they have a close resemblance to those of a particular historical period.

ANCIENT EGYPT

Among the Egyptians, sex and religion were closely connected. Sexual symbols played an important part in religious rituals and the Egyptian gods were clearly sexual beings (Figure 1-1).

In the male-oriented Egyptian culture, the male phallus was greatly admired, phallic statues being a central part of religious festivals. Intercourse was at times a sacred act with great importance attached to female virginity. With female virginity viewed as the gateway to future generations, a woman was often expected to change from her virgin status in a ritual manner. Often this involved the aid of a temple priest, a stranger, or an artificial penis (Sussman, 1976).

THE ANCIENT HEBREWS

The early Hebrews were never a powerful people and were thus frequently under the threat of being taken over by other groups. Hebrew sexual codes seem to have swayed back and forth with the amount of threat present. In times of danger, Hebrew sexual attitudes were restrictive, while in more relaxed times, sexual attitudes were more permissive (Bullough, 1976).

About the seventh century B.C., the Jews rejected the connection between sexuality and

BOX 1-1

COLLEGE STUDENTS' PERCEPTION OF PARENTS' SEXUAL BEHAVIOR

Pocs and Godow (1977) asked 646 college students if they thought their parents had ever engaged in various sexual behaviors. The researchers compared the students' estimates of their parents' behavior with the findings of Kinsey on the sexual behaviors of the parents' generation. As shown below, both daughters and sons dramatically underestimated parental sexual behavior. Not only did this underestimation appear for past behaviors, but the students said they thought their parents engaged in intercourse with each other an average of four times a month; the actual frequency was between eight and nine times a month.

Sexual Behavior	Daughters Thinking Their Mothers Had Ever Engaged In Behavior (%)	Mother's Generation Who Had Engaged in Behavior (%)	Sons Thinking Their Fathers Had Ever Engaged in Behavior (%)	Father's Generation Who Had Engaged in Behavior (%)
Premarital petting	63	99	81	89
Premarital intercourse	10	50	45	92
Extramarital intercourse	2	26	12	50
Oral-genital Sex	25	49	34	59
Masturbation	31	62	73	93

Source: Pocs and Godow (1977), tables 1 and 2.

religion, which had begun in Egypt. The Jewish god Yahweh had no sexual interests or characteristics. The sexual view of the Hebrews came to be centered on the idea that the primary reason for sexual activity was procreation. The scriptures said to go forth and multiply, and any form of sexual behavior which did not lead to conception was not exactly popular. Masturbation and celibacy were thus equally undesirable. Marriage was expected, the younger the better, and sexual intercourse before marriage was viewed in a very negative light.

Hebrew society was also male-dominated and the male penis praised for its generative power.[1] As among the Egyptians, male phalli were taken as war trophies. David, upon bring-

[1]Consistent with the low status historically given women, it has been common to think of the female as simply a passive receptacle in reproductive behavior, including coitus and actual conception. The male was seen as the active agent, with even his sperm being active in bringing about conception inside the female reproductive tract. As we shall see in Chapter 3, this is in error. In fact, the male is rather passive in the reproductive processes and the female reproductive system is truly the active agent in reproduction.

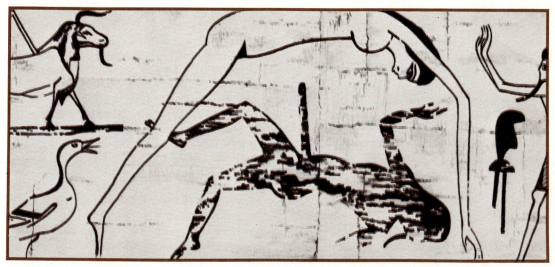

Figure 1-1 This reproduction of an ancient Egyptian drawing demonstrates the extent to which sexuality was seen as part of religion by the ancient Egyptians. In this drawing the sky god Nut and the earth god Geb are about to engage in intercourse.

ing the foreskins of 200 slain Phillistines to King Saul, was given the king's daughter in marriage (Bullough, 1976). The status of women was far from that of equality. Women were male property and sexually treated as such. Intercourse before marriage, for example, was reacted to by the guilty male's either paying the woman's father for making her "used property" or by his marrying the woman. Moreover, women were seen as sexually troublesome. The "sex drive" of women was thought to be more powerful than that of men, and female sexuality was frequently blamed for male corruption. Eve, through her sexuality, lured Adam away from his perfect union with God.

Sex was not to be without pleasure, but pleasure came in a poor second to reproduction. The emphasis on marriage and reproduction was evident in the practice of levirate marriage. That is, if a husband died without heirs, it was the duty of his nearest male relative to take his place and provide his widow with children. This is where Onan got into trouble. He properly had intercourse with his slain brother's wife, but while doing so, he "spilled his

seed upon the ground" (he withdrew his penis prior to ejaculation). He thus failed to carry out God's will and the Lord took his life. Onanism has come to refer to masturbation, but the original sin was simply nonprocreative ejaculation (withdrawal).

As a group, the ancient Jews were unique in their time. They developed what was then a rigid sexual code, they separated sexual activity from religious activity, and they did not encourage sex for the sake of enjoyment alone.

ANCIENT GREECE

It is in the views of the Greeks combined with those of the ancient Hebrews that we find many of the origins of contemporary American sexual attitudes.

At the peak of Greek civilization, sensuality and an open expression of sexuality were common in Greek life. The Greeks valued all things human and placed particular emphasis upon sex and beauty as human qualities. They also separated the sexual from the sacred, but, unlike the ancient Hebrews, they saw sexuality as a joyous human expression and an activity over which the gods had no moral concern.

Considerable emphasis was placed on erotic and sensual behaviors. Kissing took many different forms as an affectional and erotic activity, and the female breast was seen as highly erotic. Intercourse was practiced in a variety of positions and oral sex was a common prelude to intercourse. Nudity was common in many public places; the Greek word *gymnasium* came from *gymnos,* meaning "being nude or dressed in a tunic."

Women were clearly inferior in the Greek view, serving as wives and mothers—preferably of sons. While strong emphasis was placed on the beauty of the human body, it was the male body that was considered the most beautiful. Male homosexuality was seen largely in a spiritual, rather than a physical, light and was described by some as the true form of human love. Male homosexuality was tolerated and perhaps encouraged as long as it did not interfere with the foundation of Greek society—the family (Bullough, 1976). Female homosexuality was, like women in general, of little significance and most often associated with prostitutes.

As Greek society started to decline, the view of sex began to change. As groups such as the Romans became increasingly powerful, a small cult known as the Orphic religion increased in influence. A central belief in this religion was that it was possible to be immortal by being pure (a reasonable set of beliefs when the decline of the great Greek civilization was apparent). Humans were seen in the Orphic religion as having two basic natures. On the one hand was the mind, which was spiritual, intellectual, and good. On the other hand was the body, which was material, more akin

The Greek view of sex as a joyous, erotic activity is illustrated in this ancient Greek painting. Many everyday utensils were decorated with erotic art. This painting appeared on the bottom of a drinking cup so that it was seen only after the last drink had been taken.

to lower animals, and bad. The soul or mind was locked inside the body as a punishment for sin. The soul was thus a higher form of existence, possibly immortal, locked inside a mortal body—a mortal body governed by evil passion.

As the Orphic view became increasingly popular, hostility toward the principal passion of the body (sex) increased. The most influential person in this increasing hostility was the philosopher Plato. Plato rejected the cultlike aspects of the Orphic religion and applauded the philosophical dimensions. His ideas have passed down to us the concept of *Greek dualism* (Bullough and Bullough, 1977). This concept basically says that we have a dual nature: the mind and the body. Matters of the mind are intellectual and spiritual, while matters of the body are material and physical. In Plato's view, matters of the mind are clearly superior to matters of the body; sex, as one of the supreme bodily passions, only serves to reduce humans to the level of animals.

THE ROMANS

The sexual attitudes and behaviors of ancient Rome contrasted sharply with those of the Greeks. The Romans never adopted the Greek view of the beauty and spiritual nature of sex. They viewed sex in a purely physical fashion. Rather than a form of ultimate beauty, the body was an instrument of sex (Sussman, 1976).

The Romans were rather matter-of-fact about sex, having the view that one should have a good time while the having was possible (Sussman, 1976). Appropriate sites for sexual activity were limited only by convenience and their being somewhat removed from public view. The arches beneath the great aqueducts became a popular location for prostitutes—so popular that the Latin word for arches *(fornices)* became the name for Roman houses of prostitution and was changed to the verb *to fornicate.* This very physical view of sex has come down to us in the form of many

Latin-based words for sexual activity, such as *cunnilingus* (oral stimulation of the female genitals), *fellatio* (oral stimulation of the male genitals), *masturbation, prostitution,* and *pornography.*

Removing sex from the notions of beauty and joyous human expression, the Romans frequently placed an emphasis upon its cruel and sadistic use. This was especially the case in the late years of the Roman Empire. The bloody arenas and their activities took on strong sexual overtones, and prostitutes waited outside for aroused customers following the performance. Many of the events themselves included sexual activity. It was not uncommon for couples to be forced to engage in intercourse before the crowds, and women were known to be raped by animals for the pleasure of the throngs. Even though some historians have questioned the extent to which the portrayals are true, it is clear that many of the late Roman emperors were notorious for their sexual interests and activities. Caligula, for example, was delighted with those who could perform the most bizarre of sexual acts for his viewing pleasure. Women in Roman society were expected to be sexually active, and Messalina, the young wife of the aging emperor Claudius, did not hesitate to exceed this expectation. Apart from taking a full-time lover into the palace, she frequently forced women of nobility to have intercourse with strangers while their husbands were compelled to watch (Sussman, 1976). Messalina also made it a pastime to sneak out of the palace at night and secretly occupy a bed as a prostitute (Bullough and Bullough, 1978).

THE MIDDLE AGES

The period from the fall of the Western Roman Empire (A.D. 476) until the Renaissance about a thousand years later is known as the Middle Ages. During this period, the Roman Catholic Church moved into the vacancy created by the passing of Roman civilization. In doing so, the Church attempted to establish a new set of values, including a negative view of sex.

This 1475 book illustration depicts the common view of sex during the Middle Ages. Sex is the work of the devil, and sexual enjoyment results in nuisances for the individual. This human weakness of being unable to resist sexual temptation brings joy to the devil and his workers.

Church doctrine defined celibacy as the prime virtue, and the only justification for having intercourse was procreation. Sex was seen as an animal lust and nothing more. Intercourse could lose some if its sinful qualities when conducted in marriage,[2] but lifelong virginity was the preferred condition and marriage was really a crutch for those who could not cope. Given the reality of people engaging in intercourse, the Church strongly recommended the man above and the woman below as the only proper intercourse position. Many theologians argued that any other position was the work of the devil. Oral and anal sex were, of course, particularly despised. Strongly opposed to erotic pleasure per se, the Church advocated high-fashion nightwear in the form of the *chemise cagoule* (Sussman, 1976). This was a nightshirt with one strategically placed hole through which the husband could impregnate his wife with an absolute minimum of body contact.

Official Church doctrine continued to be, however, largely wishful thinking. Among the population at large, as well as within the clergy itself, there remained a strong interest in sex. While the extent of clerical sexual activity varied from place to place, clerical celibacy was not the order of the day (Sussman, 1976).[3]

[2]This approval of sex in marriage was a clear compromise between a set of strict religious ideals set forth by Saint Augustine and the reality of what people did. Making sex in marriage sanctified in the eyes of the Church made it possible for people to "serve two masters": their own sexual interests and behaviors and the wishes of the Church.

[3]This also appears to be somewhat the case today. In the only research I know of on the subject, Halstead and Halstead (1978) surveyed 126 former nuns and priests on sexual behaviors before, during, and after they became nuns or priests. In this sample, they found that only 46 percent had been celibate before, and only 32 percent celibate during the time they were priests or nuns. Before becoming priests or nuns, 47 percent had masturbated, 11 percent had engaged in intercourse, 9 percent had engaged in oral-genital sex, and 11 percent had had homosexual experience. During the time they were priests or nuns, 57 percent masturbated, 15 percent engaged in intercourse, 5 percent engaged in oral-genital sex, and 21 percent had a homosexual experience. It must be kept in mind, however, that this sample was of *former* nuns and priests. Therefore, these data are not generalizable to any population. Additionally, the respondents were not broken down by gender, so we do not know how these behaviors were distributed between nuns and priests.

Sexuality during the Middle Ages can be accurately described as the result of the Church's failure to make its restrictive and dismal views of sex popular.

During the Middle Ages, the low status of women remained unchanged, as did the notion that women were lustful, passion-ridden, and often the cause of male troubles. During the fourteenth century, this view of women was put into action by attacks on witchcraft. There was almost no understanding of many natural phenomena and the unexplainable was accounted for in supernatural terms. Everything from mental illness and male problems with erection to the Black Death (which killed almost half the European population in 1348) was attributed to supernatural evils. Topping the list of suspected agents of the devil were women, many of whom were tortured and killed for the alleged practice of witchcraft.

THE RENAISSANCE

Beginning in fifteenth-century Italy, human living took on a new meaning. Life became more highly valued, the concept of individualism grew popular, and there was a sharp turn away from notions of faith and devoutness. With all this came a relaxation of the rules against sexual expression. As the values of ancient Greece were praised, sexual expression as an individual quality came to be enjoyed in its own right. Extravagance, individuality, and sensuality became common.

The party was, however, to be soon interrupted by an unwelcome visitor. Syphilis hit Europe in massive proportions and developed into a major social and health problem. The dreaded disease served as a fuel for those who wanted to reform society's evil ways.

THE REFORMATION

It was clear that the Church had failed to implement its view of sexuality. The widespread syphilis infection of the population and the very high rates of illegitimacy provided ammunition for religious reformers such as John Calvin and Martin Luther.

Calvin argued that syphilis was the wrath of God for the sexual license which the Church had failed to control. Under the influence of Calvin and others, the revolt known as the Reformation took place. It split Christianity into Protestant and Catholic camps, the latter emphasizing more restrictive sexual codes.

A major figure in the Reformation, Calvin held that humans were sinless in their original state. The Fall of Man came with the expulsion of Adam and Eve from the Garden of Eden. From that point on, humans were totally sinful and could be redeemed only by the grace of God. Calvin was not certain, however, who had received the grace of God, but he was convinced that you could tell by a person's actions. The proof came to be in the pudding. If you worked hard to overcome your inherent sinfulness and the weakness of sexuality, it was obvious that you had been chosen. Such a view, needless to say, resulted in more restrictive sexual views than those which were popular during the Renaissance.

THE ELIZABETHAN ERA

Even though, by 1600, Queen Elizabeth I had been known for forty-two years as the Virgin Queen, the population of England refused to be impressed. Sex was an enjoyable part of life, as clearly demonstrated in the works of one William Shakespeare. He made no effort to dampen the sexual element in his works. Even while the bawdy Shakespearian plays remained very popular, a small group of religious reformers appeared on the horizon. The Puritans, as they were called, took as their goal many of Calvin's ideas. They became increasingly disturbed with governmental indifference and hostility to their views. When the New World became a possible place to live, the Puritans found an open territory to establish a new and pure society—the American colonies.

COLONIAL AMERICA

The colonies were diverse in occupations, languages, and ethnic groups. The Puritans themselves were not a single group, but consisted of three separate religious denominations. All this diversity in the new land was tied together, however, by a common set of sexual and religious attitudes. It was the spirit of Puritanism that established the first colonies.

The essence of Puritan thought was a closely regulated lifestyle. One was expected to be rational, industrious, free of passion, and most important, always mindful of God. Among all things in life, thoughts of God came first. Anything that distracted one from such thoughts was frowned upon. Passion, of which sex was the most severe, was definitely a diversion from this primary duty.

A strong emphasis was placed on marriage by the Puritans, but marriage was a rational, not a romantic, choice. It was further seen as making the sex act clean, since marriage and procreation were God's will. Everyone was expected to marry, and sex that could not rightfully lead to procreation was strongly disapproved. Thus, premarital sexual activity was constantly guarded against. Among the New England Quakers (a Puritan group), a couple had to submit to an investigation of their past by a church committee. If a young man came from another community, he was expected to bring with him a certificate of good moral character (Bullough, 1976).

Dating in groups was common in colonial America, but when a young man and woman wished to get to know each other seriously, he called upon her at her home. With few beds and even less firewood, the Puritans were not night people. One means of courtship was therefore *bundling,* in which the young man and woman spent the night together in her bed, but separated by a variety of ingenious devices. The woman would be "bundled" in a string-drawn sacklike gown, or a *bundling board* would be placed down the center of the bed. Bundling was also commonly practiced as a matter of hospitality. If a visiting male stayed overnight, he would use the husband's side of the bed while the husband slept on the floor.

To enforce their rigid sexual views, the Puritans established harsh penalties for homosexuality, adultery, premarital sex (fornication), and sexual contacts with animals (bestiality).

Premarital intercourse was either noted by a keen observer out behind the barn or seen when a married couple had a child "too soon" after marriage. In either case, the original punishment for fornication was public whipping. Adultery, homosexuality, and bestiality were to be punished by hanging.

Regardless of these strong penalties, there was rather widespread disregard for the laws. Premarital intercourse, prostitution, the sexual use of servants, slaves, and Indians, and male intercourse with farm animals were all far from rare (Oaks, 1978).[4] In the face of the continuing inability to shape sexual behavior by law, the penalties for sexual transgressions were gradually lessened. For example, the punishment for fornication went from public whipping to fines, with offenders being given their choice of paying through the pocketbook or the back. The last recorded execution for bestiality was that of Benjamin Goad, who was hanged in 1673 for having intercourse with a horse. This punishment raised such a furor that the last case of this sort, in 1681, resulted in much less severe punishment. A Thomas Sadeler was whipped, forced to sit in the gallows with a rope around his neck, branded on the forehead with the letter P (for pollution), and banished from the colony (Oaks, 1978).

THE VICTORIAN ERA

In the United States, the years 1865 through 1918 are marked as the Victorian period. Carrying over Puritan thought from colonial times, humans were still seen as spiritually weak and physically base. In Victorian thought, however, one could rise above this miserable condition to the heights of success if one practiced hard work, thrift, and stern self-control. This view was reflected in the economic outlook. This was a period of rapid industrial growth. The

---

[4]A major factor contributing to the occurrence of these sexual activities, particularly sexual activity with animals, was the presence of many more men than women. The early colonies were very unbalanced in the proportion of men and women. Thus, acceptable sexual partners through marriage were simply not available for a large proportion of the males.

power and vitality of the economy were important concerns and individual success was an important goal. Ideas about sexuality are seldom divorced from the larger social situation, and this was certainly true in the Victorian period. Ideas about sexuality were strongly related to these economic notions. The sexual pitfalls of wasting, rather than saving, became an important part of Victorian sexual ideas (Barker-Benfield, 1978).

Male Sexuality and the Dangers of Sexual Excess

One of the popular spokespersons for a dominant Victorian view of sexuality was a prominent physician named William Acton. In Acton's thinking, true virility was the ability to control one's sexual passions. In the ideal Victorian male, every passion was held in absolute control by a strong will. Not to do so was to be less of a man.

Holding one's passion in control was not easy because males were seen as naturally lusty creatures. However, such control was essential if one were to keep all kinds of terrible things from happening. Sex was seen as a constant energy which was part of one's vital life force. This vital life force was further seen as limited. One was thought to have only so many orgasms, and when one used these up, one was thought to shrivel like a prune. Acton and many others adopted the view that ejaculation was (note the analogy to money) a "lavish expenditure of the vital fluid semen." It was not at all uncommon to hear "experts" note that the "loss" of 1 ounce of semen was equal to the loss of 40 ounces of blood. This idea was first popularized by the Swiss physician Tissot, who published a book in 1760 entitled *Onanism, or a Treatise upon the Disorders Produced by Masturbation.* Although Tissot's work was not published in the United States until 1832, his ideas were found in the writing of Benjamin Rush, the dominant medical person in the United States at the end of the 1700s. Rush was a signer of the Declaration of Independence, an advocate for the emancipation of slaves and abolition of the death penal-

ty, and a proponent of sexual reform based on the idea that all diseases were due to a single cause. This cause was the weakening and shocking of the nervous system. Rush argued that sexual activity contributed greatly to this deterioration. This concern with using up a limited resource is clear in the Victorian term for ejaculation—"to spend," a rather dramatic contrast to the present-day term "to come," which suggests that one has arrived at a desirable goal. Excessive sexual activity was thus seen as a real danger to life, limb, mind, and the very fabric of society. Of course, what constituted "excessive" was a matter of opinion. One expert advised marital intercourse no more than twelve times a year or insanity would surely result. Others recommended different frequencies of intercourse depending on one's occupation.

Even more dreaded than marital sexual activity was the sexual activity of youth in the form of masturbation. Acton's description of the young male who masturbates reflects a common view of the period.

> The frame is stunted and weak, the muscles undeveloped, the eye is sunken and heavy, the complexion is sallow, pasty, or covered with spots of acne, the hands are damp and cold, and the skin moist. The boy shuns the society of others, creeps about alone, joins with repugnance in the amusements of his schoolfellows. He cannot look anyone in the face, and becomes careless in dress and uncleanly in person. His intellect has become sluggish and enfeebled, and if his evil habits are persisted in, he may end in becoming a drivelling idiot. . . . (Murstein, 1974:252)

These dangers were to be avoided at all costs, and therefore many remedies were offered to curb the sexual urges of the naturally lusty male and to protect male youths from masturbating or erecting themselves into certain ruin. Diets of "calm" food were suggested. Sylvester Graham advocated eating his unbolted wheat flour—which we know today in the

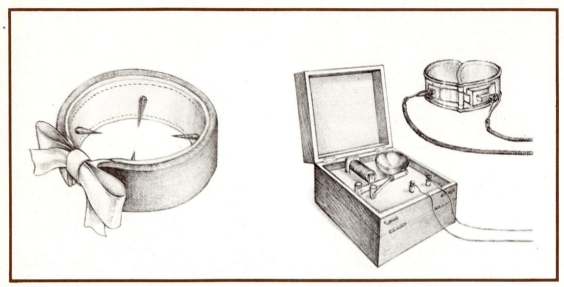

Figure 1-2 These two devices were invented during the Victorian period to prevent adolescent males from having erections during their sleep. The device on the left, with its sharp points, is simple in both purpose and design. It was placed around the young male's penis when he went to bed. If he had an erection the results are obvious. The device on the right is more complicated. The box contained a small battery that supplied current through the two wires to the metal ring. This ring was split and was placed around the young male's penis when he went to bed. On the box was a spring steel bar that was held against the two poles as long as electrical current flowed through the two wires. If the male had an erection, the flow of current was broken by the metal ring expanding and breaking contact. This loss of electrical current resulted in a loss of magnetism in the two poles. As a result, the spring bar flew forward, struck the bell, and thus woke up his parents.

form of the graham cracker.[5] Other suggestions and practices were more severe. Several devices were patented which were designed to discourage an erection during sleep (Figure 1-2). In extreme cases, Acton recommended inserting an instrument into the tip of the penis and flushing the organ with silver nitrate, a highly caustic substance which could easily result in permanent damage.

Female Sexuality

While the male was seen as naturally sexual, female sexuality was viewed quite differently.

[5]Another prominent figure of the time was John Harvey Kellogg. From his Battle Creek sanatorium, he suggested that sexual activity, especially orgasm, caused a dangerous shock to the nervous system that could result in insanity. Kellogg's brother is known today for bringing breakfast food into the American diet.

Females were pictured as weak, ethereal, fragile, delicate, pure creatures who were, above all else, passionless. As Acton put it:

> . . . the majority of women (happily for society) are not much troubled with sexual feelings of any kind. What men are habitually, women are only exceptionally. It is too true, I admit, as the Divorce Court shows, that there are some few women who have sexual desires so strong that they surpass those of men, and shock public feeling by their consequence. I admit, of course, the existence of sexual excitement terminating even in nymphomania, a form of insanity that those accustomed to visit lunatic asylums must be fully conversant with; but with these sad exceptions, there can be no doubt that sexual feeling in the female is in

the majority of cases in abeyance, and that it requires positive and considerable excitement to be aroused at all; moderate compared with that of the male . . . love of home, of children, and of domestic duties are the only passions they (females) feel. (Murstein, 1974: 253)[6]

Given this view of female sexuality, female masturbation was seen as even more terrible than male masturbation and was thought to result in all forms of ailments, many of which would affect reproduction. Even though less attention was given to the possibility of female masturbation during adolescence (since women were considered to have little interest in sex), the remedies were equal in severity to those for males. Mutilation and removal of the clitoris were not unknown during this period.[7]

These Victorian views were largely those of the influential middle class, a growing segment of the population in an increasingly industrial society. Chastity and purity were thus the mark of the proper middle-class woman. Given the obvious difficulty of checking to see if one were chaste and pure, appearances became of prime importance. A proper middle-class "lady" was not to dress in a revealing or provocative manner, she would not use vulgar language, and her mind was to remain free of any sensual thought. The proper female never mentioned the miscarriage of justice and always nibbled the bosom or neck of the chicken —never the breast. Dresses were an inch off the ground with long sleeves and skirts which bloomed outward with numerous petticoats. The bustle appeared in gigantic form, jutting out from the back of the dress some 3 feet at a near right-angle to the body. Inside, the body was firmly encased in a corset complete with metal stays and tight strings. The effect of

Typical middle-class female attire of the Victorian era.

such attire was to assure immobility, fragility, and a nonfunctional nature. Musically, women did not pucker their lips, part their legs, flex their muscles, or muss their dress and hair. They played the piano (Murstein, 1974).

Marriage was seen as transforming and purifying male lust. While prior to marriage the male could sow his wild oats, women in mar-

[6]These were not just the views of a few resident crazies. William Hammand, then Surgeon General of the United States, wrote much the same thing about female sexuality. For an excellent discussion of the origin of this view of the passionless female, see Cott (1978).

[7]The clitoris is located slightly above the vaginal opening and is the principal organ of sexual sensation in the female (see Chap. 3).

riage tamed the lusty male. This served to elevate women to a pedestal as guardians of the
moral fiber of society. There was also at this
time an increasing emphasis upon insulating
children from the adult world. With increasing
industrialization, the home became less of a
location for economic activities and more of a
refuge. It was in the home that children were
to be protected from the adult male world.
Women, "obviously" the "natural" guardians of
children, should then be isolated as well. Motherhood became a special calling and women
were raised even higher on a pedestal. The
home also came to be a haven for the male
returning from the rigors of industrial life outside, a haven where the "good wife" catered
to his every need.

Not all women were, however, middle-
class. There were also women to whom the
male should go to engage in those sexual acts
he would never do with a proper woman (wife).
These women were prostitutes and represented the polar opposite of the proper woman.
There were thus two distinct types of women in
Victorian thought. "Good" women were frail,
wan mothers and wives, and above all else—
passionless. At the other extreme were "bad"
women, who were not frail or wan, were not
mothers or wives, and were, above all, sexual.
The prostitute was, of course, the ideal bad
woman.

In order to assure that nothing resembling
the activity of "bad" women was brought before the family, several precautions were
taken. Statues were covered with fig leaves
where there had been genitals. Piano legs,
since they resembled human anatomy, were
covered with skirts. Many literary works underwent revision. The most diligent worker here
was Thomas Bowdler (the origin of the term
"to bowdlerize") who produced *The Family
Shakespeare,* in which all phrases and words
unsuited for family reading were removed. Just
for good measure, Bowdler also polished up
the Bible. It was also suggested by some that
a book written by a male and a book written by
a female should not be placed next to each
other on the shelf unless, of course, the authors were married to each other.

SEXUAL DISSENT

Even in the presence of such views of sexuality, there was a strong undercurrent of sexual
dissent. A substantial minority of vocal individuals saw sex as natural and healthy. Writers
such as Thoreau, Emerson, and Alcott questioned the tone of the times and advocated a
return to nature, romantic love, and the development and appreciation of human relationships, including sexuality. Organized communal marriage experiments had already taken
place and had won some popularity. The wom-
en's movement was gaining strength and many
of its members were attacking the sexual repression of women. Staunch advocates of contraception had emerged and gained popularity,
even in the face of strong opposition. By the
1890s, the seeds of change to occur in the
twentieth century had been firmly planted.

CHANGES IN THE TWENTIETH
CENTURY

The changes that came during the twentieth
century cannot be precisely dated since they
were the result of a series of evolving events.
However, it is possible to note the general
form of change that occurred during various
periods.

1910–1930

During these decades, the Victorian attitude
toward sex was mortally wounded. While it is
impossible to isolate exactly why sexual attitudes changed, most scholars agree that certain factors made a definite contribution.

Wars always seem to bring about a relaxation of traditional moral values. World War I
revealed to many Americans that all they held
dear was vulnerable. As Murstein (1974) discusses, that war appeared to leave many
Americans with a "live for today" attitude.

Good old American know-how had brought
us to a powerful political and economic position in the world. Science, education, and
knowledge thus came to be highly regarded

and intellectuals were held in great esteem. Although Sigmund Freud visited America only once, his ideas found a welcome home in the United States. They became very popular and served as a direct (but partial) assault on Victorian views of sexuality. Freud rejected the belief that children were sexual innocents who could be protected from the evils of sexuality. He also rejected the view that sex was found only in the bedroom and the genitals. In Freud's view, sexuality was a major fact of all human existence from birth onward. Sexuality, according to him, crept into, and affected, every aspect of life. More important, he argued that personality disorders were caused by how one's sexuality was treated. While Freud contended that repression of the "sexual instinct" often led to positive outcomes (such as music and art), he thought it more frequently the case that repression of this instinctual human urge was harmful. In Freud's words:

> It may be asserted . . . that the task of mastering such a powerful impulse as that of the sexual instinct by any other means than satisfying it is one which can call for the whole of man's forces. Mastering it by sublimation, by deflecting the sexual instinctual forces away from their sexual aim to higher cultural aims, can be achieved by a minority, and then only intermittently . . . .Most of the rest become neurotic or harmed in one way or another. . . . (Freud, 1959:237)

These ideas were taken by many as a justification for reducing restrictions on sexuality. The sexual instinct and the dangers of its repression were not reserved for men only. Freud argued that women were as innately sexual as men. In this sense, Freudian ideas served to partly change Victorian concepts of women as asexual.

On the subject of female sexuality, Freud's ideas were, however, strongly influenced by the Victorian period of which he was a product. Much more important than allowing that women were sexual, Freud put forth a set of ideas which were widely accepted in American society and which had profoundly negative effects on views of female sexuality. He argued that the child passes through three stages of development. In each stage, different areas of the body become the focus of attention and sexual energy. The first stage was said to last from birth to 1 year. In this oral stage, the child's chief source of pleasure is the mouth and lip region. The second stage, occurring during the second year of life, is the anal. Here the child's attention is focused on elimination. The third stage, the phallic, lasts from age 3 to 6. The focus here is on the genitals. The nature of this focus is, however, very different for males and females, according to Freud. He argued that the girl realizes that she has no penis. After the initial trauma of this discovery, she feels cheated and suffers from penis envy. She concludes that she once had a penis but that it was cut off. From the time of this conclusion onward, the female spends most of her life trying to compensate for this obvious genital deficiency. Settling for the next best thing, the woman desires to be impregnated by the male penis, with pregnancy making up for the lack of such an important appendage. Her personality is basically self-oriented, in large part because of her feelings of sexual inferiority. She is typically ashamed in her general attempt to hide her genital deficiencies. She is intellectually inferior because her thoughts are inhibited by sexual repression. This restriction explained to Freud why, as he saw it, women had not played a major role in human affairs. He did allow, however, that women have made one contribution to civilization. In weaving and sewing, he said, women are subconsciously attempting to duplicate pubic hair (which serves the function of covering their grossly inadequate genitals).

Freud's view of women in general, and of female sexuality in particular, was that they are simply imperfect men. His view of sexuality was that males proudly parade their protrusion while females live in shame and horror of their mutilated genitals. The widespread acceptance of Freud's ideas had the effect of raising generations of women (and men) with a Victorian view of female sexuality. This result is perhaps nowhere more apparent than in Freud's *dual orgasm theory,* which existed unchallenged and intact well into the 1960s.

Freud argued that there are two types of female orgasm: vaginal and clitoral. Healthy, normal female development involved moving away from the clitoris to the vagina as the center of sexual pleasure. A failure to transfer the focus from the clitoris to the vagina was defined as a lack of maturity. Thus, the clitoral orgasm was said to be an immature response and the vaginal orgasm a mature response. Given the scientific fact that the clitoris is the center of sexual sensation and that the majority of women experience orgasm from stimulation of the clitoris and not through vaginal penetration alone, generations of women were convinced that something was wrong with them because they could not reach orgasm from vaginal stimulation alone. Of course, what Freud's dual orgasm theory really did was to argue that the male is not only sexually superior, but that women are dependent upon a male penis inserted in a vagina for a "mature" sexual response. He thus justified the necessity of the male for female sexuality (Freud also classified masturbation as a sign of sexual immaturity and ill health, thus ruling out the possibility of masturbation for women as well).

The effects of Freud's ideas on Americans' view of sexuality were thus mixed. His ideas served as the intellectual basis for arguing that sexual repression is harmful, thus legitimizing sexuality. His concept of the universal sexual instinct also aided somewhat in his presentation of women as sexual beings. More important, however, his ideas "kept women in their place"—a place which had been defined by Victorian thought as being inferior to that of men. The importance of Freud's concepts was in his argument that the very basis of this inferiority is sexual.

The early part of the twentieth century also saw rather pronounced increases in the rights of women, at least compared with the past. By 1920, women were granted the right to vote and the women's movement was very active. The "new woman" of the Jazz Age also appeared in America. The "red hot babies,"

The flapper of the 1920s symbolized in dress the changes taking place in women's roles and sexuality.

the "flaming youth," and the "flappers" of the 1920s were replacing the Victorian image of women. Bustles, long skirts, petticoats, fragile hairstyles, and binding corsets were cast aside. The young woman now wore flimsy, long-waisted, knee-length dresses, short hair, lipstick, perfume, and flesh-colored stockings. The "in" female image among youth became the devil-may-care, cigarette-smoking, dynamic, sexy playmate who frequented the nightclubs and speakeasys.[8]

1950–1960

While today the 1950s may not seem to have been very dynamic sexually, they consisted of the establishment of a greater openness to sexuality which was yet to come.

In 1948, Alfred Kinsey and his associates published *Sexual Behavior in the Human Male,* followed in 1953 by the volume on the female. Kinsey's struggles to do his research, have it funded, and get it published reflected perhaps the last effective attack against the discussion and examination of sexual matters. The acceptance of Kinsey's research by the public reflected the existing interest in sexual matters.

In 1953, the public presentation of sex appeared in another form. Hugh Hefner published the first issue of *Playboy* magazine. The rapid rise in the magazine's popularity was indicative of the public's acceptance of sex. Hefner brought sex and nude photographs to take their place on American newsstands alongside the most respectable periodicals. In an aspiring post-war America, he connected sex with success and upward mobility. Hedonism and sexuality were no longer the mark of sure ruin, but the symbols of social and economic achievement. In *Playboy,* sex was unrealistic, but it was clean, wholesome, all-American fun.

The music of the time also reflected an increasing acceptance of sex and sensuality. Rock and roll was here to stay and the sensu-

ality of Elvis Presley brought uninhibited screams of delight from female teenagers across the land. But resistance was still evident. *Playboy* only slowly revealed the female nipple and always covered the pubic region. Regardless of his popularity, Presley's first television appearance on the Ed Sullivan show involved only views from the waist up; the sensuality of the young singer was still a bit much for the majority of Americans.

1960–1970

The 1960s saw a massive erosion of the "waist-up–only" mentality. A large, young adult population from the World War II baby boom arrived on the scene. This population frequently, loudly, and visibly challenged the established values of American society—including sexuality. The sexual attitude changes of the sixties were reflected in many ways. The sexual attitudes of college students became more liberal, the percentage of college-age women with coital experience increased rapidly, and Rudi Geinreich introduced the topless bathing suit. The pill became popular and available, and Masters and Johnson published their research on human sexual response which involved directly observing people engaged in masturbation and coitus. Terms such as "swingers" (couples who exchange sexual partners) and "groupies" became part of our vocabulary; sexually explicit motion pictures made their way into legitimate theaters and middle-class cocktail conversation. The San Francisco sex shows became a must stop on any vacation. Women began to define their own sexuality by discussing the errors of Freudian thought, demanding contraceptive availability, and fighting for the legalization of abortion on the basis of women's rights.

The peace, love, and "hang-loose" ethic of the late 1960s youth movement filtered down rapidly into the larger population, affecting everything from middle-class male hairstyles to sexual attitudes. At the same time, the widespread questioning of traditions and authority came into being. At the heart of tradition and authority in American society was the issue of

---

[8]These changes, especially in female sexuality, were greatly affected by a change in economic atmosphere from saving to consuming. For an excellent discussion of these changes, see Ryan (1979, chap. 5).

sex. Attacks on and changes in traditional sexual attitudes and values were symbolic of an attack on "the system." While most Americans were not going to march against the war in Vietnam or speak out for women's rights, a more liberal sexual climate had a little something for both watchers and doers. For all the social turmoil of the 1960s, it was increased sexual liberalism and tolerance that most publicly sifted into the 1970s.

The 1970s

In the 1970s, the beginnings of the more open attitude toward sexuality found in the 1960s became well established. The women's movement initiated a forceful and effective assault on traditional definitions of women, including female sexuality. Abortion was legalized by the Supreme Court. The topics of homosexuality and rape became public and political issues. Sexual therapy developed as a new and legitimate occupation. A major figure in women's professional tennis was a person who had had sex-change surgery. Sex manuals emphasizing pure enjoyment became best-sellers. Sex surveys and advice appeared in most major women's magazines. *Playboy,* in meeting the competition from *Penthouse,* revealed that females (and males) do have genitals. Popular magazines that aimed at a female audience showed male nudes. Pornography became readily available for public consumption in almost every city, developing as a major industry. The slick new porn emerged in the form of the movie *Deep Throat,* which gained legitimacy by being seen by millions, reviewed by the most respectable of magazines, and featured as the subject of middle-class cocktail conversation. Group-sex clubs opened in major cities. The up-down movement of female breasts came to prime-time, top-rated television shows. Vaginal douches (in flavors) and sprays entered the marketplace, waterbeds became common fare, Sears Roebuck sold vibrators shaped suspiciously in the form of a male appendage, and male strippers delighted female audiences. In the 1970s, sex literally came out into the open.

THE PAST AND THE PRESENT

How things have changed! Or have they? While it is certainly true that in many ways the status of sexuality in American society today bears little resemblance to the Victorian period or before, this is not the total picture. Americans entered the twentieth century with four major sexual inheritances. While the changes that have taken place in this century, and even in the last ten years, have been great, we still have a strong sexual tie to our past in the form of these four sexual themes.

What Is, and What Is Supposed to Be

Throughout history, there has been a gap between what is supposed to take place sexually and what is really happening in the population at large. Up through Victorian times, this gap was generally (but not always) in the direction of society's sexual behavior being more liberal than what official moralists and the media said it should be. Today, we still have a chasm between the ideal and the actual. While the media, popular writers, and contemporary moralists (both the very liberal and the very conservative) would have us believe that sexual freedom and lack of inhibition or restraint are everywhere, most Americans hardly live this way. For the average American, the 1960s and 1970s brought a verbal revolution in which people came to talk more about sex. Actual changes in behavior have not quite matched the talk. This gap between what the media say people are doing sexually and what people really are doing has consequences for how people feel about their sexuality. In Victorian times, one was most likely to feel inferior if one were sexually active; today, one is most likely to feel inferior if one is not.

Sex Is Good—Sex Is Bad

Beginning with Greek dualism, Western culture has always had mixed feelings about sex. While it may feel great, it is a pleasure of the body and so is somehow less a virtue than activities of the mind. We still have this approach-avoidance feeling about sex. Despite its widespread use and approval, some psychologists still object to the use of masturbation in sexual therapy. Even though they would really like to try it, many people worry about the rightness and wrongness of such activities as oral-genital sex. We are convinced that birth control is a good thing, but still have difficulty making it available to sexually active teenagers. We have legalized abortion, but the laws are much clearer than people's attitudes. Casual sex is the kind most arousing to people, but not the most approved. National Football League teams hire cheerleaders to dress in titillating outfits to reveal as much breast, leg, buttock, and stomach as television will permit, but fire them if they pose for *Playboy*.[9] Television prime-time shows are organized around large breasts jiggling across the screen, but the same networks sexually censor major motion pictures in order to "protect" their viewing audience. Clearly, while we have come to accept sexuality's being more visible in society, we are still not sure whether it should be.

Sex as Biologically Based

Throughout history, sexuality has been viewed as arising from biological sources rather than from learning or culture. Humans have consistently been seen as having "natural" sexual urges. In some periods, this "natural" sexual urge was to be repressed; in other periods, it was to be let free. Sometimes only men had it; at other times women were more possessed of it than men. In more modern times, biological differences between males and females have served as the basis of the argument of fundamental differences in their sexuality.

Today this biological bias is still very much with us. We are still arguing over the difference in male and female sexuality on the basis of differences in anatomy. The medical profession, despite the grossly inadequate training of

physicians in the area of sexuality, still remains the keeper of sexual expertise and advice (Hunt, 1979). Research funds for the study of human sexuality are still granted only if social scientists couch the research in terms of some medically relevant problem such as marital fertility, adolescent pregnancy, or venereal disease. Despite growing evidence to the contrary, many scientists still argue that one can learn about human sexual behavior by studying other animals which share a common biology.

Patriarchal Dominance

Last but not least, we entered the twentieth century with a long tradition of male dominance; in this tradition, men are viewed as superior, make the rules, and establish the definition of who is what. In defining the sexuality of women, men came to different conclusions at different points in history. For the ancient Hebrews, and Christianity in general, women were highly sexual. For the Greeks, Puritans, and Victorians, women were asexual. Regardless of the time, the outcome was for and by men (Laws and Schwartz, 1977). We brought with us from the nineteenth century the concept that men are naturally sexual and that the expression of this sexuality is the essence of biologically being male. Since men are naturally sexual, they need sex. Since women are naturally asexual, they do not. The social rules about who should be able to do what sexually were based on this logic. The *sexual double standard* was established and accepted as part of this tradition. Men could engage prostitutes and have extramarital and premarital intercourse. Women were arrested for prostitution and not allowed to engage in extramarital or premarital sex.

While the double standard has been dealt some severe blows in the last fifty years, it still remains a significant part of our view of sexuality. As women have begun to establish the definitions of female sexuality, they have met with solid resistance. Abortion still remains a hotly debated (and political) issue; rape is still viewed as somehow being related to the wom-

[9]It is worth more than a passing thought that in 1978 the television movie which drew the single largest audience was the *Dallas Cowboys Cheerleaders*.

an's "enticement" of the natural male lust which needs somehow to be expressed. Birth control remains a female responsibility and foreplay (before insertion of the penis) is as popular as the "goal" of orgasm.

In a very real sense, the sexual revolution of the sixties and seventies has perhaps placed women in an even more difficult position than before. With the new sexual liberalism, women are expected to be ready, willing, and able for sex. While in the past women were expected to be asexual, today they are expected to be all sexual; neither definition was created by women.

While sexuality today is undoubtedly very much different from what it was a hundred years ago in this society, the sexual heritage of the past remains with us. We often slip into the narrow perspective of the present and think that not only are we much different from people in the past, but that the past has little bearing on our behavior today. In terms of dominant themes of sexuality in Western culture, we are the past. This fact will repeatedly be apparent as we review contemporary sexual patterns in American society.

STUDY GUIDE: HOW TO USE IT

In writing this text, I decided at the beginning to make it as complete as possible. Consequently, there is a lot of material in each chapter and the material is not always simple. To aid you in learning the material—and in preparing for the inevitable examination—I looked at a number of different types of study guides in various subjects and finally settled on this form. I think you will find that if you use the study guide at the end of every chapter, you will do much better in learning the material than if you skip over it. With the "Terms to Know" (and in this chapter only, "Names to Know"), you should be able to give a brief description of what the term means and why it is important in this chapter. Do not just memorize some definition, but be able to explain the term to a friend who is not taking this course.

The "True-False" and "Multiple-Choice" self-tests are for you to test yourself for your general understanding of the material. Each answer generally has an explanation for why that is the answer. This is the key to the questions. It is not enough to be able to get the answer right. You should also be able to say why this is the answer and why the question is important. The "Topics for Discussion" are intended as food for thought or for group discussion or study activity. They are designed so that you can use the material in the chapter to discuss a certain issue and thus put what you have learned to work.

The "Suggested Readings" are included for those of you who may want to examine the subject matter of the chapter in more depth. Another way to get a list of suggested readings is to find a part of the chapter that interests you and to look up the original works that are cited in that part of the chapter. These citations can be found in full in the Bibliography at the end of the text.

STUDY GUIDE

TERMS TO KNOW

Orphic religion	Puritanism	Dual orgasm theory
Greek dualism	Bundling	Patriarchal dominance
Chemise cagoule	Muscular Christianity	Sexual double standard

NAMES TO KNOW

Alfred Kinsey	Messalina	Thomas Bowdler
William Shakespeare	John Calvin	Sigmund Freud
Plato	William Acton	Hugh Hefner
Caligula	Tissot	NFL cheerleaders

SELF-TEST

Part I: True-False Statements

1. Sex was a central part of the religious practices of ancient Greece.
2. Ancient Hebrew society was male-dominated.
3. The Greeks and the Romans viewed sex as a joyous human activity associated with beauty, sensuality, and the erotic.
4. The essence of Puritan thought was that one must always be mindful of God.
5. The ideal Victorian male was one who could hold all passion in control by strong will.
6. During the Victorian era in America, sex was seen as a constant energy which was limited and part of the body's vital life force.
7. In Victorian thought, males and females were seen as naturally lustful creatures.
8. Freud argued that even though sexuality was a part of all aspects of life, the sexual instinct must be repressed in order for an individual to develop a healthy personality.
9. In Freud's view, women were simply imperfect men.
10. The sexual double standard is based on the idea that, biologically, males have a greater need for sex than do females.

Part II: Multiple-Choice Questions
Select the best of the three alternatives.

1. The concept that matters of the mind are more highly valued and less "animalistic" comes to us from (a) Plato and the Orphics, (b) the Middle Ages, (c) the Victorians.
2. The thought of Sigmund Freud served to change American sexual attitudes in the early twentieth century by (a) liberalizing them, (b) making them more conservative, (c) liberalizing them in some ways and in others maintaining existing Victorian ideas.
3. The ancient Romans viewed sex in a very (a) romantic, (b) physical, or (c) repressive manner.
4. Among the ancient Greeks, attitudes about homosexuality reflected (a) the status of males and females in Greek society, (b) the physical view of sex held by the Greeks, (c) some influences from the ancient Hebrews.
5. In the Middle Ages, sex was seen as (a) a joyous human expression, (b) the work of the devil, (c) a part of the animalistic side of humans.
6. During the Victorian period, the proper middle-class woman was seen as (a) a sexy playmate, (b) a social and sexual equal to the male, (c) passionless.

7. Freud's dual orgasm theory basically argued that *(a)* a mature female sexual response needs masturbation, *(b)* a mature female sexual response needs a male and his penis, *(c)* a mature male sexual response needs a female.
8. The idea that hedonism and sexuality were not the marks of certain ruin but the symbols of social and economic achievement was clearly put forth in the 1950s by *(a)* Alfred Kinsey and his research, *(b)* Hugh Hefner and *Playboy, (c)* William Acton.

TOPICS FOR DISCUSSION

1. At the end of this chapter, there is a brief discussion of how certain parts of the history of sexuality in Western culture are very much with us today. Think of other examples of how some aspects of sexual attitudes, values, or behaviors today reflect prior periods in history such as those of the Greeks, Hebrews, etc.
2. Construct an imaginary society today on the basis that the only influence on that society has been one single historical period. Describe what the sexual attitudes and behaviors of that society would be.

SUGGESTED READINGS

Bullough, V. L., *Sexual Variance in Society and History.* New York: John Wiley & Sons, 1976.
This is an exceptional review of disapproved sexual practices throughout the history of both Western and Eastern cultures, written by one of the foremost scholars in the history of sexuality. Even though the focus is on sexual variance, and especially homosexuality, each chapter contains an excellent discussion of the dominant sexual attitudes and behavior patterns of the time and place.

Bullough, V., and B. Bullough, *Sin, Sickness, and Sanity: A History of Sexual Attitudes.* New York: Meridian, 1977.
This paperbook book, of much shorter length than the above, focuses on major themes in sexual attitudes in Western culture rather than on dominant sexual patterns in particular cultures.

Murstein, B. I., *Love, Sex, and Marriage Through the Ages.* New York: Springer, 1974.
The single best discussion of the history of love, sex, and marriage.

For some firsthand looks at sexual attitudes in recent history, there are a number of relatively easy and interesting sources to contact:

Go to your library and look up any ''Manual for Young Boys'' or ''Advice to Young Marrieds'' published in the late 1800s or early 1900s. You will find some interesting reading.

Go to your library (probably the microfilm section) and browse through the 1954, 1955, or other dates of *Playboy* magazine. Note the sexual tone of the period, including the topics discussed and the nature of the photographs. Pay particular attention to the language and the images of women and sex that are portrayed. *Caution:* Be prepared for missing pages. It is rather commonplace for people to cut out portions of even microfilm from this magazine.

Go back to *Time* and *Newsweek* magazines between 1948 and 1954 and look up articles on Kinsey and his research. They will give you a good idea of the sexual atmosphere of the period. The best way to find these articles is to check Kinsey's name in the *Readers' Guide to Periodical Literature* in the library.

KEY TO SELF-TEST QUESTIONS

Part I: True-False Statements

1. F (The Greeks saw sex as no business of the gods.)
2. T (It was a strong patriarchal society.)
3. F (Only the Greeks, not the Romans.)
4. T (This tenet explained why the passion of sex was considered a problem.)
5. T (The emotionless, self-controlled male was highly admired.)
6. T (This was the reason for so much concern with "excessive" sexual activity.)
7. F (Only males were thus seen; females were thought to be passionless unless something was wrong.)
8. F (He argued that repression of the sexual instinct could be harmful.)
9. T (Also, he said, they spend most of their psychological lives trying to overcome this.)
10. T (Males have a "natural urge" but females do not. Therefore, went the reasoning, the sexual norms should be different.)

Part II: Multiple-Choice Questions

1. *a* (The concept of Greek dualism.)
2. *c* (Liberalizing them by pointing out the dangers of sexual repression and the fact that males and females both have the "sexual instinct," but Freud maintained Victorian ideas in his description of female sexuality.)
3. *b* (Note the Latin terms we inherited from the Romans and the sexual spectacles.)
4. *a* (To the Greeks, the highest beauty was male beauty and sex and beauty went together; female homosexuality was associated with prostitutes.)
5. *b* (Note the fifteenth-century wood carving in the text.)
6. *c* (But males were naturally lustful creatures.)
7. *b* (Because he argued that "vaginal" orgasm was the mark of maturity.)
8. *b* (Compare this idea with the Victorian belief about the dangers of sexual excess and the Calvinist notions about who are the "chosen.")

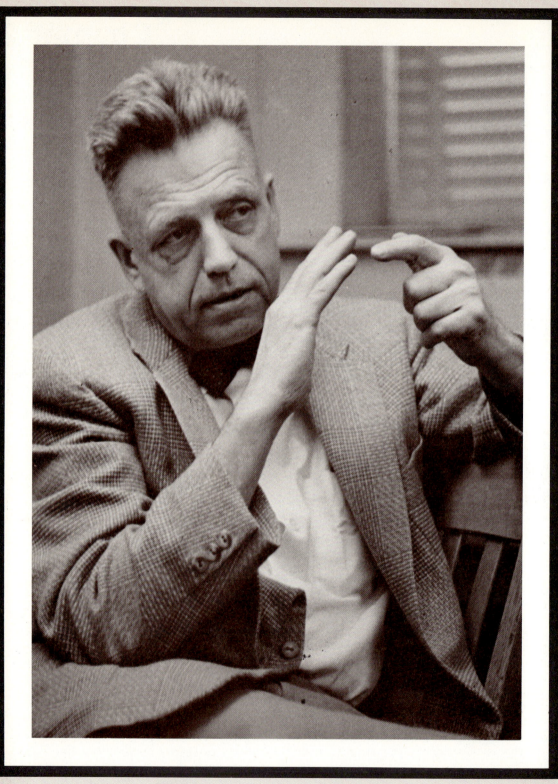

Chapter 2
The Study
of Human Sexuality

SEXUALITY: WHAT IS IT WE ARE STUDYING

You would think that since we have accumulated enough knowledge about human sexuality to offer college courses and textbooks on the subject, we would have a neat, precise, and widely acceptable definition of *human sexuality*. Such is not (embarrassingly enough) the case. In fact, if you look through most books, you will not find any definition of sexuality. In the rest, the different definitions have little in common.

How is it, then, that we can study something we cannot define? In actuality, people working in the area of sexuality do have a vague sort of definition. We all "sort of" know what we mean by the term *sexuality,* but we find it difficult to put in precise terms. Generally, this is the case in a new field, such as the study of sexuality, and this vagueness usually works well enough for a time. Such definitional sloppiness works because we share a general notion of what falls under the label "sexuality" and what does not. The problems start when we do not all agree that a subject is properly considered to be an aspect of sexuality. For example, is the study of rape part of the study of human sexuality? It involves behaviors and

parts of the body generally thought of as sexual, but the motivation of the rapist may be to engage in violence, not lust or erotic activity.

I have no solution to this problem of defining sexuality because such definitions evolve over time (see Haeberle, 1978: 124–128) as a field of inquiry ages. Professionals grapple with the fringes and some topics become part of the study of sexuality while others do not. No one person sits down and specifies what is and what is not part of what is called sexuality. This will only come in time.

To provide a general definition of sexuality for our purposes, *sexuality is any aspect of human thought or behavior that has sexual meaning.* Thus, what is sexuality to one person may not be so to another. This is true because what I may see as having sexual meaning may not have the same meaning for you, and vice versa.

PERSPECTIVES IN THE STUDY OF HUMAN SEXUALITY

The study of human sexuality is found in many different disciplines, including biology, anthropology, psychology, and sociology. For the student, this means that human sexuality is viewed from many different perspectives, depending upon which discipline is doing the viewing.[1] These various perspectives on the same subject can, on the one hand, be confusing but, on the other hand, offer diversity and depth in understanding.

How different disciplines view human sexuality is analogous to watching a football game from different locations in the stadium. Each discipline that studies human sexuality is sitting in a different location and thus has a slightly different perspective on the same subject. Having a particular discipline's perspective simply means that one will probably place greater emphasis on some aspects of human sexuality than on others. For example, a psychologist may typically focus on individual learning, perception, personality, and thought processes as related to sexuality. Sitting in the biology section of the stadium means that you will probably pay more attention to anatomy, physiology, and body chemistry. The sociologist, on the other hand, is typically interested in how an individual's social environment influences sexuality and how patterns of sexuality differ among various social groups and categories. The anthropologist is most likely to emphasize the diversity of human sexuality by studying and describing differences across many cultures.[2]

Why Perspectives Are Important
These are very different perspectives or ways of looking at human sexuality. These perspectives are important because sexual behavior is not all psychological, all biological, or all social. Human sexuality is a combination of all these elements. Some aspects of human sexu-

ality are influenced more by psychological processes while other aspects are influenced more by social process and yet others by biological processes. In order fully to understand human sexuality, we must examine the view from all these perspectives, rather than simply viewing from one vantage point.

THE DIMENSIONS OF HUMAN SEXUALITY

There are three dimensions to human sexuality: the social, the psychological, and the biological. None of these three dimensions is any more or less important than the others. In understanding human sexuality, we are not involved in a popularity contest to see which dimension is "the best." We can understand human sexuality only by examining all three of its dimensions and how they are related to one another.

The Biological Dimension
The biological dimension of human sexuality is diverse. In a general sense, it consists of bodily structure and processes. It includes everything from the structure of the sex organs to the workings of the nervous system. The importance of the biological dimension is obvious. The structure and operation of basic sexual equipment set limits on the possibilities of one's sexuality. For example, if a male does not have an erection, there are limits to what his sexual activities will be.

On the other hand, we must be careful not to place too much emphasis on the biological dimension. One of the amazing aspects of humans is their ability to learn. As a consequence, human sexuality takes an almost infinite variety of forms. While one's body is important in this variety, it by no means dictates one's sexual destiny.

The Social Dimension
Human sexuality involves a great deal more than body parts and their action or even body

[1]The term "student" is used here is a general sense. All of us who are interested in learning are students. Thus, these comments apply to those of you who are enrolled in a course as well as your professor and myself.

[2]In the study of human sexuality, anthropology is the forgotten discipline. Generally, people who study human sexuality pay little attention to a rather large literature on sexual patterns in other cultures. As we shall see, simply looking at humans other than those residing in the United States can aid us greatly in understanding human sexuality.

chemicals and their effects. What is sexual and how one engages in sexuality are not totally or automatically dictated by the nature of one's biology.

As far as we know, the basic biological equipment of sex has remained unchanged since the dawn of civilization. However, what humans have defined as sexual and the ways in which sexuality has been conducted vary tremendously over time and across cultures. This variation is due to the social dimension of human sexuality, that is, to the social and cultural environment in which an individual lives. It is one's culture and historical period that define what sexuality is and how one engages in sexual activity.

We shall review many examples of how sexuality differs from one culture to another, but an example of how sexuality differs over time in American society is useful here. In nineteenth-century America, masturbation was considered a personal and social evil. Parents, medical experts, religious leaders, and adolescents were convinced that all kinds of terrible things resulted from masturbation. Today, masturbation is viewed as an integral part of sexual learning and is a central ingredient of much highly respected sexual therapy. That behavior, once thought to result in warts and worse, is now viewed as not only normal, but beneficial.

The social dimension of human sexuality also appears in a form other than differences' over time and across cultures. Within any society at any given time, there are differences between social groups and categories in sexuality. What is sexual and how the sexual act is done differ in American society today because of such factors as gender, social class, ethnicity, age, and religion. These differences appear because, as a member of a particular social group, an individual learns the particular view of sexuality held by that group.

Thus, within a diverse society such as that of the United States, part of our sexuality is shaped by the larger culture and part is shaped by the particular social groups and categories to which we belong.

The Psychological Dimension

Human sexuality is shaped not only by the biological and social factors, but by individual psychological processes as well. In any given culture and any given social group, there are individual differences in sexuality. An individual's sexuality is not merely the result of being stamped out of a neat little culture or social group mold. Each individual has a unique personal style of psychological processes in the form of thinking and perceiving. Each of us has an individual personality. Each of us also has a personal history of learning experiences. All these factors have an effect upon our sexuality. In order to understand human sexuality fully, we must understand how these individual psychological processes affect sexuality.

It must be kept in mind, however, that while these psychological processes are individual processes (*you* think, *you* perceive, *you* learn), many of us share the same individual characteristics. Many of us have very similar learning experiences, personality characteristics, and ways of viewing the world. It is important to remember that each individual is unique in terms of who he or she is as a total person, and at the same time, that many individuals share certain psychological characteristics. In the study of human sexuality, we are interested in both aspects: how individuals who have in common a certain psychological characteristic behave or think in a certain manner, and how each individual as a unique combination of psychological characteristics is uniquely different sexually.

WHAT AND HOW WE KNOW ABOUT HUMAN SEXUALITY

Anything we know has two dimensions: content and method. Content refers to what we know and method refers to how we come to know it. While this may seem rather simpleminded, it is very important for the student of sexuality. Anything presented as knowledge must be considered in the light of how that knowledge was obtained.

Facts and Opinions

In any area which is important to people, you will find an abundance of opinions. Such is the case with human sexuality. Personal opinions are significant. They not only are one of the mainstays of a free society, but they also represent and generate thought and discussion. Personal opinions are not necessarily, however, facts. In the area of human sexuality, the problem arises when facts and opinions are confused or not clearly distinguished. Since sexuality has traditionally been a matter of morality, we often find people presenting their personal opinions on sexuality as if they were facts.

There are serious ethical issues involved here. Sexuality is seldom a topic in which people have no interest. Often this interest is in terms of a personal concern about sexuality: "Am I different?" Students of human sexuality should gain knowledge from their study. The importance of this knowledge (apart from the fact that knowledge is worthwhile in itself) is that ignorance is the absence of options. In making personal decisions about our own sexuality as well as that of others, it is far better to have accurate knowledge than to operate on the basis of fear, myth, rumor, or just plain not knowing.

The scientist studying human sexuality, as well as anyone writing on the subject, has an ethical obligation to provide either knowledge or personal opinion, but not opinion disguised as knowledge. On the other hand, making personal decisions about sexuality is just that, a personal matter and not the business of the scientist or teacher. What you or I *should* do as individuals is not a scientific question, but a matter of personal opinion about "right" and "wrong." Questions of right and wrong are matters of individual morals, not questions of knowledge.[3]

[3]This is not to say that scientists and teachers do not or should not have opinions. As a member of both categories, I have plenty and have a perfect right to them. However, as a teacher and a scientist, I have an ethical obligation to students to clearly distinguish facts from opinions, particularly since the role of scientist-and-teacher may be very powerful in the eyes of some students, and therefore what that person says may be taken very seriously.

Moral Values

Before the study of human sexuality became a concern of scientists, "knowledge" about sex was frequently based on moral values. Given any set of moral values that one holds, there are certain things which *must* be true. For example, if one believes that any type of sexual activity that is not intended for the production of offspring is immoral, then there are a series of "truths" which must follow. Masturbation, nonmarital sex, and plain old passion are simply bad. The danger in knowing on the basis of moral values is that the knowledge is almost certain to support the moral values. For example, if you morally know that masturbation is bad, you will probably never discover that masturbation aids human sexual development. Rather, you are likely—as was the case in the nineteenth century—to "discover" solid evidence "proving" that masturbation causes everything from warts to the destruction of society.

We all have our own moral values. However, we must be careful that our personal views of right and wrong, good and bad, do not generate "knowledge" about human sexuality. What *is* is one thing; what we morally think *should* be is quite another.

On the surface, this discussion may appear to be a little absurd. After all, if you look at the facts, how could your moral values influence what the facts indicate. "Easily," is the answer, and it comes to even the most reputable of scientists. In being a person of your discipline seeking knowledge about some phenomenon, you are at the same time an individual—one who has attitudes, values, and preferences. To keep one's personal moral values from sneaking into one's interpretation of, and attention to, facts is very difficult. For example, we have massive amounts of data on the proportion of adolescents with intercourse experience. From these data, it would seem simple to state whether or not there have been changes here in the last twenty-five years. However, what we find is that what one wishes had happened influences what one sees as having happened. What one person sees as massive increases in adolescent intercourse, another sees as the same pattern that has been around for years.

Common Sense

Someone once said that the problem with common sense is that it is so common. As members of a society, we learn that certain things are just common sense. However, what we all know as a matter of common sense is usually either a gross oversimplification or out-and-out incorrect. Knowledge is not democratic. We do not establish knowledge by finding out how many people think this or that is true. What makes up common sense is usually a series of ideas or beliefs in a society which have been passed down from generation to generation. As such, these commonsense ideas may or may not be correct.

The history of thought on human sexuality is filled with commonsense notions that were later proven incorrect. Often, these commonsense ideas are the basis of fear, anxiety, and the mistreatment of people. The Victorian concept that masturbation results in mental and physical illness was common sense at the time. It also had the effect of making millions of people worry about the probability of their keeling over, going insane, or sprouting hair on their palms. Even more serious, unknown numbers of young males and females had their genitals medically mutilated in the name of "curing" masturbation. The idea that women were asexual was also common sense in its time. The effect of this bit of wisdom was to dehumanize, demean, and depress the sexuality of one half the population.

Scientific Knowledge

Today, we do not establish knowledge about human sexuality by means of authority, opinion, moral values, or common sense. Rather, we come to know by means of *scientific inquiry*. Scientific inquiry involves a strict set of rules about how one comes to know something. These rules are based on two fundamental principles: *objectivity* and *public access*. Objectivity refers to the way in which things come to be known. Basically, scientific knowledge is obtained objectively in that what one finds out has nothing to do with one's personal values, attitudes, or beliefs about the phenomenon. If the rules of objectivity are followed, you are just as likely to discover something that fits with your personal preferences as you are to discover something which runs directly counter to the way you wish things were. Public access refers to the fact that scientific knowledge is obtainable by any other scientist. That is, when I say I have found something, I must have found it by using techniques that can be used by any other scientist. The importance of this is that what I found can be checked; it is open to public scrutiny and is not a purely private experience. Knowledge obtained through visions, divine insight, or other such private experience is not open to scrutiny and cannot be checked by anyone else.

Types of Research in the Scientific Study of Sexuality

One of the pieces of advice consistently given me while I was writing this text was not to discuss *research* too early. Following most other texts, the reasoning here is that students are (1) not interested in something as boring as sex research, and (2) that you must do something cute to keep students' attention before you present research. Quite frankly, I do not agree with this reasoning. I think the assumptions behind these thoughts sell students short and foster an image of them that is both incorrect and demeaning. We are going to discuss sex research now because this is the point at which it is the most valuable for your learning to discuss the topic. There are some things you should know before you proceed in order that you may get the most out of this text. I further assume that you are studying the subject because you want to learn and that you do not have to be tricked or enticed by a bunch of silly gimmicks to make your way through the material. I also feel very strongly that an author has an obligation to students not to make the reading a demonstration of bravery or dedication. The material should not only be accurate and informative, but should read easily and be as much fun as it can be.

Scientific observations can be made and conclusions drawn in various ways. While we frequently associate science with a person wearing a white lab coat locked away in a room filled with complicated equipment, there are actually many ways in which scientific research is conducted. These ways of conducting research are called *research methods.* In the area of sex research, four basic research methods are commonly used: *case studies, observational studies, survey research,* and *experimental research.*

Case studies   The case study method has never been especially popular among sociologists or experimental psychologists, but it is a valuable means of obtaining data on human sexuality. This method is most often used by practicing clinicians and involves an in-depth analysis of one or a few individuals. For example, a physician or a sexual therapist may report the detailed characteristics of a particular case which yields information about some facet of human sexuality.

The major problem with the case study method is that one never knows how repre-

BOX 2-1

AN EXAMPLE OF A SERIES OF QUESTIONS FORMING A SCALE

Below is the Index of Sexual Satisfaction developed by Hudson et al. (1981). This scale produces a single score for each person who fills it out. This score provides a measure of the magnitude of a problem in the sexual part of a two-person relationship as seen by the respondent (Hudson et al., 1981:159).

You can answer the questions if you want and then, when you have finished, you can score yourself according to the instructions at the end.

This questionnaire is designed to measure the degree of satisfaction you have in the sexual relationship with your partner. It is not a test, so there are no right or wrong answers. Answer each item as carefully and accurately as you can by placing a number beside each one as follows:

1 = Rarely or none of the time
2 = A little of the time
3 = Some of the time
4 = A good part of the time
5 = Most of the time

Please begin:

1. I feel that my partner enjoys our sex life. _____
2. My sex life is very exciting. _____
3. Sex is fun for my partner and me. _____
4. I feel that my partner sees little in me except for the sex I can give. _____
5. I feel that sex is dirty and disgusting. _____
6. My sex life is monotonous. _____
7. When we have sex it is too rushed and hurriedly completed. _____
8. I feel my sex life is lacking in quality. _____
9. My partner is sexually very exciting. _____

sentative the people are who make up the cases. For example, one is always in danger of drawing conclusions about all rapists from observations made on a few atypical rapists. In the early studies of homosexuality, this in fact was done. A few people, generally those who were having severe problems of living in a heterosexual society, would be examined in detail and conclusions drawn about all homosexual persons. As a result, we had some very misleading ideas about homosexuality.

Additionally, the case study method seldom uses a *control* or *comparison group.* One may conclude, for example, that "gay" males have certain characteristics that, actually, are characteristics of males in general and not just gay ones. If a group of heterosexual males had been used for comparison, such an error would not have arisen.

The case study method is, however, valuable. One major benefit is that it is in depth and it may give the researcher insightful hunches which would not be obtained without an in-depth examination of a few cases. For example, we are beginning to rethink our ideas about the nature of male orgasm on the basis of a recent case study which questions the view that males are biologically capable of only one big orgasm in a short period. In-depth probing about in a few selected cases often reveals things about sexuality one would not otherwise see.

10. I enjoy the sex techniques that my partner likes or uses. _____
11. I feel that my partner wants too much sex from me. _____
12. I think that sex is wonderful. _____
13. My partner dwells on sex too much. _____
14. I feel that sex is something that has to be endured in our relationship. _____
15. My partner is too rough or brutal when we have sex. _____
16. My partner observes good personal hygiene. _____
17. I feel that sex is a normal function of our relationship. _____
18. My partner does not want sex when I do. _____
19. I feel that our sex life really adds a lot to our relationship. _____
20. I would like to have sexual contact with someone other than my partner. _____
21. It is easy for me to get sexually excited by my partner. _____
22. I feel that my partner is sexually pleased with me. _____
23. My partner is very sensitive to my sexual needs and desires. _____
24. I feel that I should have sex more often. _____
25. I feel that my sex life is boring. _____

How to score: First, you must have answered all items. If you did not, the responses cannot be scored. Second, you have to rescore some of the items because they are worded in a different direction than the rest. To do this, change the scores for items 1, 2, 3, 9, 10, 12, 17, 19, 21, 22, 23. Change these scores as follows: An answer of 5 is changed to 1; a 4 is changed to 2; a 3 remains 3; a 2 is changed to 4; a 1 is changed to 5. Third, add these scores for all 25 items and, from the total, subtract 25. This is your total score.
What the scores mean: The possible scores range from 0 to 100. A low score indicates little or no sexual problem in your relationship with this person, while a high score indicates the presence of a sexual problem.

Observational research   Observational research takes many forms. *Participant observation* involves becoming an actual member of a group and observing its activities. For example, studies of "swinging" (the exchange of sexual partners in a group setting) have been done using participant observation. Observational research may also take the form of *nonparticipant observation,* an example being observing behavior patterns in a gay bar or "singles only" club without actually being a participant. Observational research may also be very structured and may involve detailed observation with sophisticated scientific equipment. The classic example here is the work of Masters and Johnson (1966) in which human sexual response was studied in the laboratory by detailed observation of bodily changes during intercourse and masturbation.

Good observational research involves making detailed observations which are not biased by the observer's own values and which are capable of being duplicated by another observer in the same situation. The weakness in observational research is that often these criteria are not met. It is difficult, for example, to take on-the-spot detailed notes that are purely objective if one is a participant observer in group sex.

A limitation in observation research is that you must have something to observe. You cannot observe people's attitudes by merely watching their behavior, and you cannot follow people around to observe how they have intercourse in their homes.[4]

The value of most observational research is that it provides insights into behaviors and forms of living which cannot be gained by any other means. For example, you cannot find out much about bodily changes during sexual arousal by asking people because most of us don't pay much attention to the dilation of our blood vessels while in the heat of passion.

Survey research   In studying the social and psychological dimensions of human sexuality, one of the two most frequently used research methods is *survey research.* Primarily used by sociologists, it consists of collecting data about people's attitudes and behaviors by asking them questions. The questions may be very direct ("How many times in the last four weeks have you engaged in intercourse?") or may be in the form of a series of questions which form a scale (Box 2-1). The questions may be asked by means of either face-to-face interviews, telephone interviews, or questionnaires.

The strength of survey research is that the questions are not asked of just anyone who happens to be wandering along the street. Rather, the questions are asked of a sample of people who represent some large population. Ideally, the sample is selected from the larger population by means of sophisticated techniques known as *probability sampling.* In probability sampling, the researcher knows the exact chance of anyone in the population (for example, all persons in the United States over the age of 16) being included in the sample. If you know this, you can calculate exactly how accurately your sample represents the larger population. Using such techniques, it is possible to draw very accurate conclusions about the larger population from a very small sample.

The drawbacks to survey research can be severe. Survey research is, first of all, expensive. Taking a probability sample of never-married women between 15 and 19 years of age in the United States and using face-to-face interviews takes a lot of lunch money. Second, all the accuracy in your sample can be lost if a large proportion of the subjects selected refuse to participate or complete a questionnaire. The major weakness, however, is that you are limited in the kinds of conclusions you can draw. You can take all your data and find out what behavior is related to what other behavior in your sample. You can never, howev-

---

[4]It is interesting to note the things that researchers are and are not allowed to do in observational research. While it is generally considered unethical to invade the privacy of persons engaged in approved sexual activity (for example, marital sexuality), it is not generally considered unethical to invade the privacy of those persons engaged in nonapproved sexual activity. For example, observational research on the sexual activity of gay persons and swingers is common. Doing the same thing through the bedroom windows of heterosexuals is called "peeping" and will likely result in arrest.

er, say what *causes* what behavior. Unfortunately, questions of cause and effect are often the most interesting and exciting.

Let us take an example of this problem. Say we are interested in how marital sexual satisfaction is related to marital happiness. We select a sample and administer a questionnaire. We do our data analysis and find that happily married couples have glorious sex lives and unhappily married couples live in sexual despair. We can conclude that marital happiness and sexual satisfaction are related. But the burning question is what causes what. Does marital happiness lead to sexual satisfaction or does sexual satisfaction lead to marital happiness? Perhaps both. Perhaps neither. Maybe there is a third factor, such as the amount of time that two people spend with each other which causes both marital happiness and sexual satisfaction. Survey research cannot answer these questions of causality.[5]

Experimental research While survey research is the typical method of sociologists, experimental research is one of the major tools of the psychologist and the biological scientist. The essence of experimental research is that one can study whether and how one thing has a causal effect upon another. This is made possible by being able to tightly control what takes place in the research situation. Let us say we are interested in how sexual arousal affects how close males and females sit to one another. We would form perhaps three groups of subjects. One group might be highly sexually aroused by some visual means; a second group might be mildly sexually aroused; and a third group would not be aroused at all. We would then ask each subject to take a seat in a room where there was a person of the other sex and observe how seating distance differed between the three arousal groups. We would probably compare the average seating distances for the high, mild, and no-arousal groups with one another. If there was a significant difference in

the seating distance between the three groups, we would conclude that sexual arousal affects seating distance.

We can make this statement because of several characteristics of experimental research. First, we know that the arousal took place before anyone sat down. It is quite likely that seating distance itself affects arousal and, had we done this study with survey research, we would have observed a relationship but would have been unable to tell what caused what. Second, when we placed people in the different arousal groups, we did so by means of *random assignment.* That is, the group in which each person was placed had nothing to do with the subject or the researcher, but was assigned on a purely random basis (for example, whether the subject drew a red, blue, or yellow marble from a box). This is important in that when people are randomly assigned to an experimental group, we know that all the groups are the same in every possible way except one—in this case, the amount of sexual arousal. If we then observe differences among the groups in seating distance, we know they are due to only one thing: the differences among the three groups in sexual arousal.

Experimental research may sound like the last word in sex research since you can draw conclusions about cause and effect. However, things are never quite this easy. There are many questions which cannot be answered by experimental research. In our marital happiness and sexual satisfaction question, how would we study this using experimental research? You certainly cannot take a sample of people who are about to get married and randomly assign them to a life of either sexual bliss or utter desperation and watch to see what happens to their marriage in the next ten years. Even if you were able to manipulate sexuality in this way, there are quite obvious ethical issues involved. Another major problem in experimental research is that subjects volunteer to participate and you almost never have a probability sample of any population. Consequently, the generalization of your findings is somewhat limited. This problem can be dealt with, however, by doing the experi-

---

[5]There are ways in which you can very closely approximate the answer to what causes what in survey research through the use of sophisticated statistical techniques in the analysis of data, e.g., *path analysis.*

ment over and over with different kinds of people each time. If you always find the same results, you can feel fairly confident about the generality of the findings.

Experimental research is frequently criticized for being "unreal" since it is a contrived situation which takes place in the laboratory. This criticism, however, involves a misconception about the nature of scientific research. In one sense, experimental research is not meant to be real. The everyday world is a mishmash of innumerable things taking place all at once. As two people lie in bed about to engage in intercourse, the dog barks, the phone rings, and the worries of the day may be zipping through either his or her head. To attempt to study sexual arousal in this very real situation is virtually impossible because so many things are happening at once. In experimental research, we purify the situation so that we can observe the effects of one variable or a few tightly controlled ones. Unless we reduce the situation to a simpler form, we can never obtain any idea about what affects what. This simplification is "unreal." It is unreal because it is pure. In this pure situation, we can become increasingly complex and actually introduce (as we have done) distractions and see how they affect sexual arousal. By systematically studying the behavior experimentally, we can eventually arrive at a very accurate description of what affects sexual arousal. If we just wade into the "real" situation, we emerge with little more than a great deal of confusion.

Which Method Is Best?

There is no one best research method. All methods have their strong and weak points. Some methods are better than others for specific research questions.[6]

---

[6]In the ideal research situation, we use all four methods to answer a given set of questions. We attempt to approach the research question from a number of different angles. If you obtain the same answers regardless of the method, you are really starting to accumulate an understanding of the topic. In a textbook, it is impossible to discuss in detail how solid every research finding is. However, where a given finding has been repeated through a variety of methods, this solidity will be noted.

As scientists, we generally feel pretty smug about our favorite research method, sometimes claiming that those who use other methods have not yet seen the light. Actually, all four methods are important. In doing survey or experimental research, you first have to have a clear idea of what the questions are. It is very difficult, for example, to do a survey of prostitutes' attitudes about their lifestyle if you do not have the slightest idea of what a prostitute's lifestyle is. This is something you are likely to learn only through case study or observational research. Experimentally, the same rule applies. It was not until the detailed observational research of Masters and Johnson (1966) that we were able to do sophisticated experimental research on sexual arousal. Before that time, we just did not have sufficient knowledge of the physiology of sexual response to develop sensitive and accurate measurements of sexual arousal (Zuckerman, 1971).

Thus, no one research method is going to provide all the answers and there is no single best method. The real question is that of connecting the most appropriate method with one's research question.

SEX RESEARCH: HOW GOOD ARE THE ANSWERS?

Questions are frequently raised about how much faith one can place in the findings of sex research. The answer to this question depends on two things: the method itself and the user of the method.

The Characteristics of the Method

Many of the questions that are raised about sex research focus on characteristics of the method being used and whether it is possible to get valid data when studying human sexuality.

Who volunteers for sex research?

All participants in any research (with the exception of the U.S. census, which requires participation by law) do so on a voluntary basis. It is commonly argued that people who volunteer for sex research are somehow different, and that the conclusions drawn are therefore likely to be very limited. There are some differences between volunteers and nonvolunteers for sex research, but the differences are small. Volunteers tend to have less guilt about sexuality, less fear of sex, a wider range of past sexual experiences, and more liberal sexual attitudes (Diamont, 1970; Farkas et al., 1978; Kaats and Davis, 1971). These differences, however, are not peculiar to sex research. Rather, they are differences between research volunteers and nonvolunteers in general (Barker and Perlman, 1975).

Will people tell you the truth about sex? A second major question is whether people will give the researcher honest answers about their sexual attitudes and behavior. The evidence indicates that people do give honest answers and that, in this regard, sex research is no different from any other kind of research (Udry and Morris, 1967; DeLamater and Mac-Courquodale, 1975).

Do you have to be especially careful in sex research? Many people think that since sex is something special in this society, special research skills and cautions are required to obtain good data. In general, more concern is given to questioning the validity of sex research data than is warranted. For example, recent research has found that the failure of people to complete or return questionnaires about their sexuality is not related to their sexual attitudes or behaviors. When one is doing survey research, people's answers to questions have also been found not to differ whether obtained in personal, face-to-face interviews or in anonymous questionnaires. The answers also do not appear to be influenced by the sex of the interviewer, the phrasing of the questions, when the sexual questions appear, whether the interviewers are competent or incompetent, or whether the interviewers are experienced or inexperienced in interviewing (DeLamater and MacCourquodale, 1975; DeLamater, 1974; Johnson and DeLamater, 1976; Kaats and Davis, 1971).

In summary, sex research is not a special

kind of research, requiring extraordinary caution or tricky methods. The problems appear to be the same types of problems faced in any social-psychological research (Barker and Perlman, 1975; Johnson and DeLamater, 1976).

The User of the Method

Sex research does face, however, some special problems: Who does the research and why he or she does it. Sex is a topic that sells. Recently, a great deal of "research" has been conducted which had as its primary goal making money rather than a scientific contribution. Almost anyone can go through the motions of doing survey research. But scientific research involves more than writing out a list of questions, running a ditto machine, and handing out sheets of paper to people who pass along the sidewalk. The problem of entertainment being passed off as scientific research is an ethical one. The trained scientist can easily distinguish between good research and garbage. The untrained person cannot. The ethical issue is that thousands of people read these "research" reports which are put forth as valid fact and what they say is taken as truth. Since these studies frequently contain serious research errors, unsuspecting people are being ripped off in an area in which they may have many questions and may be looking for answers.

ETHICAL ISSUES IN SEX RESEARCH

Apart from the serious ethical issue of passing off poor research as science, there are ethical questions involving the people who participate in sex research.

Any research involving humans must follow certain basic ethical guidelines. Specifically, all participants must be fully informed about what they will be doing in the research and they must be guaranteed that no physical or psychological harm will be done as a result of their research participation.

Again, most people feel that these issues are much more important in sex research than other research areas. It is commonly thought that sex research participants are especially concerned about remaining anonymous and that their participation will cause them personal distress and psychological discomfort. These fears are generally unfounded. Abramson (1977) found that college students participating in experiments on sexual behavior liked the participation, would participate for no reward, were not particularly concerned about remaining anonymous, and saw their participation as constructive and void of negative aftereffects.

SEX RESEARCHERS AND THEIR WORK

The study of the sexual dimension of human existence dates back to ancient times. Greek physicians such as Hippocrates made inquiry into reproduction. The famous anatomical drawings by Leonardo da Vinci in the sixteenth century reveal his investigation into sexual response, intercourse, and conception.

Sex research as we know it today did not commence until around 1900. From these unsure and meager beginnings early in this century, sex research has progressed dramatically in both its acceptability and sophistication.

General Trends in Sex Research

Early sex research was often as much a feat of bravery as of science; examining the sexual aspect of human existence was not acceptable. If employed as a college professor, one was likely to place his or her job on the line by venturing into this forbidden ground. In the 1930s, two college professors were fired for doing what was described then as "smut sociology." This threat and fear were still present in the 1940s. Dr. Alfred Kinsey faced public and private threats, highly organized attempts to stop his research and its publication, and he was given the choice of either staying out of the classroom (so he would not have contact with students) or ceasing his research (Pomeroy, 1972).

As a consequence of not being an acceptable activity, early sex research most often took the form of investigating a medical or social problem which incidentally involved sexual behavior. This was not particularly difficult since many forms of sexual behavior were considered social and medical problems.

In the late 1930s, the study of sexuality began slowly to emerge as a topic worthy of study in its own right. Bromley and Britten published research on college students and psychologist Louis Terman studied sexuality in marriage. Kinsey, however, was the landmark figure in this development; he blazed the way for sex research to emerge later as a respectable activity.

In the 1960s, sex research came into its own. Not only had Kinsey set the precedent and fought the battles, but attitudes about sexuality were becoming more liberal. Especially important was a verbal sexual revolution in which talking about sex became more acceptable. Also opening the door for an increasing amount of sex research was the fact that all the talk about a "sexual revolution" among youth gained the attention of social scientists. As a consequence of this greater freedom and interest, studies of the sexual attitudes and behaviors of college students burst forth in the professional social science journals.

Still, in the 1960s the quality of sex research was certainly not high by scientific standards, a condition that still remains somewhat with us today. The problem here was that sex research has never been a prestigious activity. While you could always impress your friends and relatives by saying you were a biochemist or an experimental psychologist, you were likely to draw snickers or suspicious glances if you said you were a sex researcher. This, of course, tells us something about how we think about sex in American society. As a consequence of its traditionally low status, sex research has only recently been able to attract the attention of many highly competent scientists.

Even though the quality of present-day sex research is sometimes not as high as we would wish, the 1970s were a period of refine-

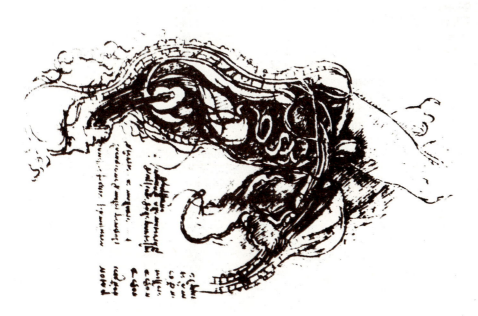

Anatomical drawings by Leonardo da Vinci.

ment. It was now legitimate to do sex research. As a consequence, several important developments took place. President Johnson commissioned a massive study of the effects of pornography, and several major studies of adolescent and adult female sexuality were federally funded. It is worth clearly noting, however, that this government funding still had strong shades of the early days. The federal government has yet to fund a major research project on sexual behavior per se. The massive research on obscenity and pornography, published in 1970, was funded because pornography was seen as a social ill. When the report failed to conclude that pornography had a negative impact upon individuals and society, it was promptly tossed aside by President Nixon. The studies of adolescent and adult intercourse behavior were not studies of sexual behavior. In the adolescent case, they were studies of what was defined as a social problem—adolescent pregnancy. In the adult case, the interest was in marital fertility. In both these federally funded projects, we learn about sexuality only because intercourse happens to be involved in conception and pregnancy.

The 1970s also saw social psychologists enter the scene. The value of their increasing interest in sex research is difficult to overemphasize. Prior to this time, the vast majority of persons doing sex research came to the subject matter with either a psychoanalytic or a medical orientation. As a result, research questions took a very narrow form. Previously, most persons involved in sex research had not brought solid research training with them. Social psychologists, however, entered the field of sex research by framing research questions as questions of human behavior. It was reasoned that if we already know that certain factors affect human behavior in the nonsexual sphere, then there is no reason why these same factors should not be important in the sexual sphere. With this reasoning, the understanding of sexual behavior as sexual behavior made a giant leap forward. Since most social psychologists are required to be highly trained in research methods, statistics, and data anal-

ysis, the new kids on the block not only started to ask questions about sexual behavior which had never been asked before, but they had the research skills to answer these questions through sophisticated scientific research. Both the asking of the questions and the seeking of the answers dramatically influenced the direction and quality of sex research.

During the 1970s, sex research became both popular and profitable. With the increasing acceptability of talking about sex (the verbal sexual revolution), popular magazines provided funding for sex research. *Playboy* funded Morton Hunt's study *Sexual Behavior in the 1970's,* which was serialized in the magazine. *Redbook* funded and published the *Redbook Report on Female Sexuality,* which appeared in serial form in the magazine and book form in 1977 (Tavris and Sadd, 1977), and in 1980 *Cosmopolitan* conducted a major study of sexuality.[7]

Sex research during the seventies also took the form of a political tool and debate with the appearance of the best-selling *Hite Report* in 1977. While Hite's report contained some interesting ideas, the research itself not only suffered major flaws but also took on strong political tones of the then-raging male-versus-female debate. The *Hite Report* (referred to by some critics as the "Hype Report") was followed by what was heralded as yet another landmark study. Peitropinto and Simenauer (1978) published *Beyond the Male Myth,* in which little effort was made to hide the attempt to refute almost everything Hite had said about male sexuality. In the case of both these publications, the battle is interesting, but the research sorely lacks scientific merit.

Sex research in the 1980s has emerged as a relatively sophisticated and respectable endeavor. Given the improved quality of sex research in this decade, we, as students, are very lucky. The student of human sexuality literally stands in the middle of a knowledge revolution as she or he studies the subject. Al-

---

[7]The value of these research efforts varied widely. While the Hunt research suffered some glaring ailments, the *Redbook* research, conducted by sociologist Robert Bell and psychologists Carol Tavris and Susan Sadd, was a major contribution.

most every three to four months, a major research finding appears in the field which makes a major contribution to or modification of our current state of understanding. In a very real sense, this makes human sexuality a very exciting field of study, and this pattern is likely to continue for some time.

Some People Worth Knowing

Any field of inquiry has its giants; on their shoulders the rest of us stand and look about. What you see from these shoulders depends on the height of the giants and what they have provided as a view of the terrain.

Richard von Krafft-Ebing (1840–1902) Krafft-Ebing was not a sex researcher, but a writer who put forth a set of views on human sexuality which dramatically influenced thought on the subject for some time. Specializing in forensic psychiatry, Krafft-Ebing was considered an expert witness in sex-crime cases. His major work was a large volume entitled *Psychopathia Sexualis,* published in 1886. This volume became immensely popular and contributed a great deal to the view of sex as disgusting.

During his time, "normal" sex consisted of a man and a woman meeting, being attracted, getting married, and living in eternal dispassionate bliss. Infrequently, the early years of the marriage would involve the man's inserting his penis in the woman's vagina for the purpose of procreation. He would have a quick orgasm and she would gaze at the ceiling. Krafft-Ebing attempted to convince his readers that any variation from this pattern of marital bang, bang, pop was a sexual aberration in either the early or late states of development. All behaviors which did not fit this pattern, including masturbation, frequent intercourse, oral sex, fetishes, sexual activity among the elderly, and homosexuality, were located somewhere on the continuum of sexual perversions. If unchecked in their early stages, they would surely lead to the most disgusting of sex crimes.

The early chapters of *Psychopathia Sexualis* begin with detailed case histories of the most lurid, lust-crazed, rape-torture murderers one can imagine. Krafft-Ebing then sets out to work backward and show how these are related to lesser "deviations" taking place earlier in life (e.g., to masturbation).

The impact of these views is difficult to estimate, but as late as 1965 two editions of the work appeared in print with introductions by reputable psychiatrists. While the introductions noted that Krafft-Ebing was a little dated, no comment was made about the fact that the pages were filled with absolute nonsense. Today, the work still appears, selling as pornography.

The essence of Krafft-Ebing's view was that sex is sick and is to be viewed with fear and disgust, since any deviation from the accepted "normal" pattern is a sure sign of a deep-seated perversion.

Havelock Ellis (1859–1939) Ellis was not a sex researcher in the sense that we have discussed research. Rather, he was a scholar and thinker who put forth many ideas which turned out to be far ahead of their time.

Ellis was dedicated and prolific in his work. He began writing about sex in the 1890s and continued his work until his death. His work was at first banned, but later came to be gradually accepted. As a child, Ellis was shy and sensitive. His father was a sea captain and much of his childhood was spent with his mother. From her interest in urination, he developed a fetish for this act. His mother offered that it was good for the skin and Ellis recalled how, as a youngster, he stood guard while she stood urinating when they went to an outdoor fair.

Accepting a popular idea of the time, Ellis feared that because he did not have an interest in sex, he was physically wasting away owing to not using his sexual organs. He became intellectually preoccupied with sex, particularly unusual sexual activities. As a teenager, he decided that he would devote his life to the study of sex.[8]

---

[8]For an excellent and interesting biography of this exceptional person, see Phyllis Grosskurth, *Havelock Ellis: A Biography.* New York: Alfred A. Knopf, 1980.

Havelock Ellis.

Ellis was a scholar ahead of his time. From his accumulation of massive amounts of information on sexual practices in other cultures, he developed many ideas about sexuality, including:

- Masturbation is common in both males and females of all ages.
- Homosexuality and heterosexuality are not polar opposites but matters of degree.
- Homosexuals are not perverts, but humans who should be treated with the respect given any person.
- The absence of female sexual desire is a myth.
- Male and female orgasms are quite similar.
- Women have multiple orgasms.
- Sexual disorders are largely psychologically based.

- "Normal" sexual development is very diverse and may take many different forms that should not be viewed as abnormal.
- Marriage is a private, personal, psychological relationship between two people and not the business of the state.
- Jealousy is not a useful emotion. Marital partners should freely communicate with each other and be free to have an open marriage involving other sexual partners.

It is interesting to note that Ellis stood in strong disagreement with the ideas of Sigmund Freud. As history would have it, Freud's ideas became much more popular than those of Ellis. However, not only have Ellis's views of sexuality survived and surfaced today, but he himself was very much what we would call a modern, liberated, nonsexist man.

Alfred C. Kinsey (1884–1956) The mark Kinsey left upon the field of human sexuality is difficult to overestimate. His work not only exemplified the scientific approach to understanding human sexuality, but made a significant contribution to the public's knowledge of sex.

Kinsey's work is important to the scientific community because he broke the barriers of research on sexuality. In doing so, he faced opposition and obstacles which few other people could have overcome. The outcome of his efforts was that sex research was made reasonably acceptable. The lumps had been taken and the precedent set. Even though there have been many criticisms of Kinsey's research, his work still remains the major study of human sexuality today and has served as a base on which much subsequent research has been founded.

Kinsey also brought sex out of the closet and into public view. In doing so, he provided Americans with the facts of people's sexual existence, and in these facts people found data which demolished many of the myths and reduced many of the fears of the past. In a very real sense, Kinsey's research was a cultural event. Even though both volumes, *Sexual Behavior in the Human Male* (1948) and *Sexu-*

(b)

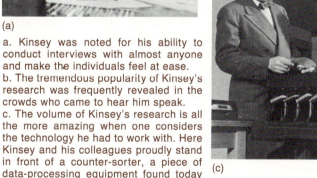

(a)

a. Kinsey was noted for his ability to conduct interviews with almost anyone and make the individuals feel at ease.
b. The tremendous popularity of Kinsey's research was frequently revealed in the crowds who came to hear him speak.
c. The volume of Kinsey's research is all the more amazing when one considers the technology he had to work with. Here Kinsey and his colleagues proudly stand in front of a counter-sorter, a piece of data-processing equipment found today only in museums.

(c)

al Behavior in the Human Female (1953), were filled with charts, tables, and graphs and were written in scientific form, they became instant best-sellers. Kinsey and sex were a topic of public discussion, and with this discussion came a new openness toward talking about, learning about, and dealing with sexuality.

For all this Kinsey paid a high price. He was a scientist in the finest tradition. He held strict standards for his research, demanded and put in long hours, and was dedicated to acquiring scientific knowledge about human sexuality. As reward, he faced both public and private opposition in its most severe of forms. Church and civic leaders publicly denounced his moral character and some members of the scientific community went to great effort to point out the statistical weakness of his research. While today we see the enormous contribution Kinsey made to the study of sexuality, he died before his work was accepted by his colleagues.[9]

[9]For a complete compilation of the statistical criticisms of Kinsey, see W. G. Cochran et al. (1954).

William Masters and Virginia Johnson   Just as Kinsey broke new ground, so did this famous research team. The contribution of Masters and Johnson was also twofold. On the one hand, they made major breakthroughs in our knowledge of human sexual response, and, on the other hand, their work was a public event.

The scientific contribution of Masters and Johnson appeared in the 1966 publication of *Human Sexual Response*. This volume provided new insights into the physiological processes in sexual arousal and orgasm. Perhaps it is difficult to imagine today, but up to that time our knowledge about these fundamental sexual processes was severely limited. Even though the climate was far less repressive, the research activities of Masters and Johnson were controversial. Detailed observation of the physiological changes during sexual arousal and response were made with humans while they engaged in intercourse and masturbation in a laboratory setting. Not only did the knowledge obtained from these studies constitute a scientific revolution of sorts, but also blazed the trail for future research of this nature.

As in the case of Kinsey, the work of Masters and Johnson was a cultural event. Discussion of their research and its findings was everywhere. Sex was again a media topic which people were talking about. This time, however, they were not focusing on people's answers to questions, but on the observations which had been made of real people engaging in real sexual activity.

Masters and Johnson's research also found its way into social and political issues. In their findings on female orgasm, they demolished the Freudian myths of female sexuality.

These scientific data served as the basis for a new wave of women's defining their own sexuality in female, not male, terms. Masters and Johnson's work continued, also serving as the basis for development of sexual therapy as a respectable field. We could now not only talk about sexual problems, but their treatment became acceptable as well.

THE PRESENT AND FUTURE

As noted earlier, this is a very exciting time to be a student of human sexuality because one rarely has the chance to be on the ever-changing brink of new knowledge. Today, the professional research on human sexuality is largely of high scientific quality. More important, however, is the fact that with many more highly qualified people working in the field, we are discovering new knowledge almost every month. It is not uncommon to pick up a professional journal and find a research article which dramatically changes the state of knowledge in the field. This is the stuff of which scientific and intellectual excitement is made. (It is also the thing which drives you crazy if you are trying to write a textbook that is totally up to date with the latest findings from sex research.)

The future offers even more of the same. We are still (as a public) somewhat fascinated with the whole topic. I suspect, however, that the newness of public discussion of sex will wear off. Scientific research will continue and our knowledge will increase. It is very likely that you will look back and notice that you took this course when the field was on the ground floor.

STUDY GUIDE

TERMS TO KNOW

The dimensions of human sexuality

Case study

Observational studies

Survey research

Experimental research

Probability sampling

Random assignment

NAMES TO KNOW

da Vinci

Alfred Kinsey

Krafft-Ebing

Psychopathia Sexualis

Havelock Ellis

SELF-TEST

Part I: True-False Statements

1. Most of the people who work in the field of human sexuality agree upon a clear definition of sexuality.
2. Having a particular perspective (biological, sociological, or psychological) in studying sexuality means that you will have better answers to questions than someone else who has a different perspective.
3. There are three dimensions to human sexuality: the social, psychological, and clinical.
4. The case study method involves sampling a large number of people.
5. The one major problem with experimental research is that one cannot make any assumptions about cause and effect.
6. Research has shown that people who volunteer to participate in sex research are very different from people who volunteer for other types of research.
7. One of the problems faced in sex research is that people tend to not tell you the truth about their sexual attitudes and behaviors.
8. Published reports of sex research increased significantly in the 1960s, and the quality of this research was high.
9. Social psychologists' growing interest in sex research in the 1970s was important because they were generally trained researchers and saw human sexual behavior as human behavior.
10. The work of Krafft-Ebing portrayed human sexuality as a normal, healthy aspect of human behavior.

Part II: Multiple-Choice Questions
Select the best of the three alternatives.

1. Havelock Ellis was a person *(a)* who viewed sex as a potentially dangerous part of human existence, *(b)* whose views on human sexuality were far ahead of his time, *(c)* who conducted the major piece of sex research in the 1940s.
2. One of the important aspects of Masters and Johnsons' *Human Sexual Response* research was that *(a)* they made it possible to conduct sex research, *(b)* their work was a media event, *(c)* they did an in-depth analysis of attitudes toward sexuality.
3. The primary weakness of survey research is that *(a)* usually only one or two individual cases are examined in great detail, *(b)* there are some instances where you simply cannot bring people into the laboratory, *(c)* you can say that two things are related, but cannot make any assumptions about what causes what.
4. In the 1960s, one of the problems with the quality of sex research was that *(a)* it was difficult for the field to attract many highly competent people, *(b)* there was no public interest in the subject, *(c)* massive federal funding of sex research did not start until the 1970s.
5. Krafft-Ebing argued that sex crimes were *(a)* linked to earlier patterns of "deviant" sexual behavior such as masturbation, *(b)* not related to forms of sexual behavior earlier in life, *(c)* widespread among the American public.
6. Kinsey's research was *(a)* immediately accepted by most of his colleagues before his death, *(b)* the work which broke the barriers against studying human sexuality in American society, *(c)* largely kept from public consumption.

TOPICS FOR DISCUSSION

1. Some things change and some remain very much the same. Review the discussion of Krafft-Ebing, Ellis, Kinsey, and Masters and Johnson in this chapter and then think about examples of their kind of work or viewpoint in current discussions of sexuality on television, in newspapers, or in your own community. Whose position is most common today?
2. Go through a popular newspaper column that frequently discusses sexuality. It is best if several of you get several different columns ("Dear Abby" is a good one). Look through them and see what perspective on human sexuality is being used in each one. Discuss how this perspective tends to lead the writer to see some aspects of human sexuality and miss others.

SUGGESTED READINGS

Pomeroy, W. B., *Dr. Kinsey and the Institute for Sex Research.* New York: Harper & Row, 1972.
This biography of Kinsey and history of his work is excellent. It is written by one of the persons who worked with Kinsey and is filled with little bits of inside information and knowledge of the person and his work that comes only from being a close colleague. This is fun reading and gives some good insight into the times.

This is a good point in your study of human sexuality to become acquainted with the professional journals in the field (be in the know and refer to them as "journals," not "magazines"). They can be easily located in the periodicals section of your library by going through the master index or card catalog for the location of journals. Sometimes this can be a bit puzzling since some of these journals may be in social sciences, others in health sciences, and still others in the medical library. (This diversity of classification itself is worth thinking about because it tells you the perspective of human sexuality used by your library to locate the journals). The major journals you should just sit and browse through (and you probably will get strange looks from others) are:

Journal of Sex Research—Today's leading journal in the study of human sexuality. The most recent issues contain the most interesting topics and the highest-quality research.

Archives of Sexual Behavior—One of the major journals in the field that tends to lean toward a biological perspective.

Journal of Sex and Marital Therapy—Note that even the title of this journal tells us something about the traditional view of sexuality in our society. Contains many articles on therapy.

In addition to these journals, many others frequently contain work in the area of human sexuality. To locate a particular topic, use the *Social Science Citation Index,* the *Science Citation Index,* or *Index Medicus.* Your library staff will probably be glad to show you how to use these valuable reference sources.

KEY TO SELF-TEST QUESTIONS

Part I: True-False Statements

1. F (We all "know" what the word means but have no agreed-upon precise definition.)
2. F (A perspective does not provide you with necessarily better answers, just a different point of view.)
3. F (Social, psychological, biological.)
4. F (A case study generally involves very few cases examined in great detail. The survey method involves large samples.)
5. F (This is one of its major strengths. It is a weakness of survey research.)
6. F (Research shows that they tend to be very similar.)
7. F (This is largely a myth.)
8. F (Published reports of sex research increased but the quality was very often low.)
9. T
10. F (Quite the opposite.)

Part II: Multiple-Choice Questions

1. *b* (Although never very popular [compared with Freud], his ideas were much more in line with todays' thinking.)
2. *b* (Like the work of Kinsey, one of the major aspects of their work was that it was widely known, publicized, and discussed.)
3. *c* (This is one of the reasons experimental research is so important.)
4. *a* (There was still a very strong stigma attached to being a sex researcher.)
5. *a* (This was the thrust of his arguing for the danger of any "deviant" patterns of sexual behavior, such as masturbation.)
6. *b* (His work set the precedent by being quality work, widely published, and frequently discussed regardless of the furor it raised.)

Chapter 3
Reproductive Anatomy and Processes

When I asked for suggestions in the writing of this text, many persons advised that a discussion of anatomy either be eliminated entirely or justified very clearly. The reasoning behind these suggestions was that either a discussion of biology is inappropriate since human sexuality is so social, or that students are bored by anatomy and physiology.

I do not believe either justification to be correct. First, we must understand the structure of those parts of the body that are commonly labeled sexual. Human sexuality is a constant interplay between social definitions of what is sexual and biological capacity. A person who does not have a basic understanding of the parts of the body commonly called "sexual" really does not have a well-rounded understanding of human sexuality. Second, I have found that students have a very real interest in anatomy and physiology. The human body is a fascinating system and the intricate ways in which it functions are true marvels. If discussed in a manner not designed to reduce insomnia, anatomy and physiology are thrilling to learn about. There are also many myths about how the "sexual" parts of the body work. To be informed about human sexuality is to replace myth and guessing with knowledge about anatomy and physiology.

THERE IS NO SEXUAL ANATOMY

You have perhaps noticed that this chapter is titled "Reproductive Anatomy and Processes" —not "Sexual Anatomy." This is a major difference between this text and many others in which you will commonly find a discussion of something called "sexual anatomy."

The reason we will not discuss "sexual" anatomy is that there is no such thing. In the evolution of the human species, a complex anatomical system came to be developed around the necessary function of reproduction. There is no such anatomical system serving the function of human sexual activity and expression.

Today we have a set of behaviors and body parts that are, in contemporary American society, called "sexual." Many of these parts of the human anatomy have reproductive functions as part of the reproductive system. The reason, however, that these parts of the body are labeled sexual is social, not biological. Therefore, we cannot discuss as an anatomical system something that is a matter of social definition. For example, what is the "sexual anatomy"? Most of us would probably agree that the penis (how about the scrotum?), the vagina, the clitoris, and the vaginal lips are part of the "sexual anatomy." How about the female breasts? The male breasts? What about very "sexual" parts of the body such as the inside of the thighs, the lips, the earlobes, the skin of the abdomen? These are certainly parts of the body which many people would consider sexual, but they are not part of a single anatomical system.

There is also the problem of whose opinion and personal preference we might use to identify "sexual anatomy." Within any society, there are vast differences in what parts of the anatomy are given sexual meaning, and as we move from one culture to the next, these differences become even greater. If we are going to discuss "sexual anatomy," we must be able to discuss a set of anatomical features, the list of which does not vary according to personal opinion or cultural differences. Can you imagine what utter confusion would result if the nature of the digestive system or nervous system differed depending on social definition and not on biological function? This is, of course, why you will not find a discussion of "sexual anatomy" in college anatomy textbooks.

Therefore, in this chapter we shall discuss *reproductive* anatomy. Many of the parts of the reproductive system, as well as many of the functions of this system, have been given sexual meaning in this culture. The biology of the reproductive system is, however, designed around reproduction, not sexuality.

It is extremely important that the biological structure of humans not be confused with social definitions of "right" and "wrong" in terms of behavior. The mere fact that many parts of the body to which we attach the label "sexual" are biologically designed for reproduction is irrelevant for morals or social rules about behavior. The biological function of human anatomy is biologically determined. The social meaning attached to parts of the anatomy and their biological function is purely social. There is no such thing as "natural" or "unnatural" human behavior as prescribed by what certain parts of the body are biologically designed to do. For example, the social definition that homosexuality is unacceptable is a purely social definition. There is nothing *inherently* natural or unnatural about homosexuality. The fact that same-sex sexual activity cannot result in reproduction does not mean that the social behavior of same-sex sexual activity is "naturally" wrong. What the biological system does is one thing and what social definitions develop about sexual behavior is quite another. The same applies to contraception, masturbation, or sexual intercourse past the age of reproduction.

MALE REPRODUCTIVE STRUCTURE

The major male reproductive functions are the manufacture of sperm cells and the transport of sperm to the female reproductive system. Some of the male reproductive anatomy is responsible only for the production of sperm cells, some is responsible only for the delivery of those sperm cells, and some is responsible for both production and delivery (Figure 3-1).

Penis

The penis (pronounced pee-nis) is an erectile organ, meaning that it is capable of erection because of its structure. Externally, the penis consists of the *shaft* or *body,* the *glans,* and the *prepuce* (pree'-pus) or *foreskin.*

The shaft consists of the external part of the penis extending from the body wall to the glans. The glans is a mound of tissue which is rich in sensory receptors and thus highly sensitive to touch (tactile) stimulation. The glans is covered with a fold of skin called the prepuce or foreskin. When the penis is flaccid (not erect), the prepuce covers the glans. When the penis becomes erect (tumescent), the increase in its length moves the glans out from under the foreskin and it is fully exposed. In many Western cultures, the foreskin or prepuce is frequently removed shortly after birth by the operation called *circumcision.* There is no difference in the sensitivity of a circumcised and an uncircumcised penis. The removal of the prepuce by circumcision does, however, reduce the possibility of infection. Under the foreskin are sweat glands called Tyson's glands. These glands secrete a substance

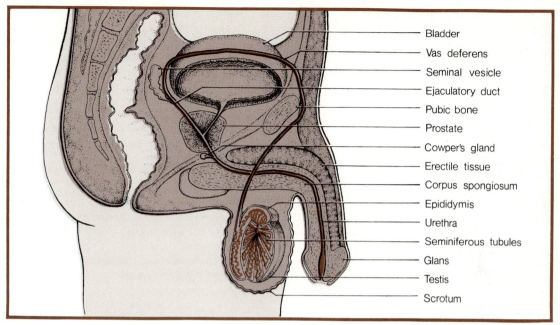

Bladder
Vas deferens
Seminal vesicle
Ejaculatory duct
Pubic bone
Prostate
Cowper's gland
Erectile tissue
Corpus spongiosum
Epididymis
Urethra
Seminiferous tubules
Glans
Testis
Scrotum

Figure 3-1 A cutaway side view of the male reproductive system.

called *smegma.* Proper hygiene includes cleansing this area to remove smegma in an uncircumcised penis. The rim of the glans is called the *corona* or *coronal ridge,* and this area is particularly sensitive to touch. On the underside of the penis is the *frenulum,* which connects the glans to the foreskin. In a circumcised penis, the frenulum appears as a thin dark line.

Internally, the penis consists of three parallel cylinders of tissue. These have the capability of becoming engorged with large amounts of blood and thus of increasing in size in the process of erection. The erection process is simply one in which the flow of blood into these erectile tissues exceeds the flow of blood outward. The result is that they become engorged with blood and the penis swells in size. These three erectile tissues consist of the paired *corpora cavernosa* (sing. corpus cavernosum) in the top of the penis and running the length of the organ and the *corpus spongiosum*, running the length of the penis below the cavernosa (Figure 3-2). The urethra,

(yoo-ree'-thra), which carries urine and semen outside the body, passes through the spongiosum to the *meatus* (mee-ay'-tus), the urethral opening. The cavernosa end near the glans area of the penis while the spongiosum is enlarged at the tip of the penis to form the glans (Figure 3-2). The penis enters the body wall forming the *root of the penis,* and at this point these three columns of erectile tissue separate. The two diverging parts of the cavernosa are called the *crura* and are attached to the pubic arch (a main skeletal structure of the pelvis). The spongiosum becomes enlarged inside the body wall as the *bulb of the penis* and runs between the crura (Figure 3-2).

The average length of the penis in the flaccid (not erect) state is slightly over 4 inches and slightly over 6 inches when erect (Gebhard and Johnson, 1979). There is, however, considerable variation in both the size and shape of the penis from person to person. While rare, penises smaller than 3 inches and as long as 13 inches are not unknown. The diversity among males in penis size is greater

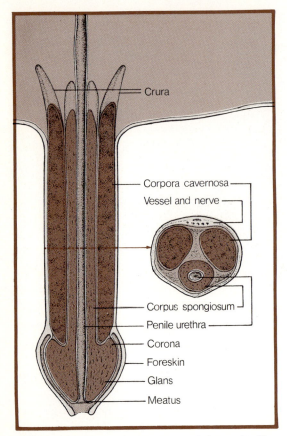

Crura

Corpora cavernosa

Vessel and nerve

Corpus spongiosum

Penile urethra

Corona

Foreskin

Glans

Meatus

Figure 3-2 The internal structure of the penis. The illustration on the left shows a cutaway view of the length of the penis from the crura inside the body wall to the meatus or urethral opening. The illustration on the right is a cross-section view of the shaft, or body, of the penis.

in the flaccid than the erect state. This is because a smaller penis increases proportionately more in size when erect than does a larger penis.

The size and shape of the penis are not related to race, ethnicity, body build, or the size of other body parts. An analysis of the original Kinsey data from Gebhard and Johnson (1979) reveals that in the Kinsey samples, white males had an average flaccid penis length of 4.0 inches compared with 4.3 inches for black males. White males had an average

erect penis length of 6.2 inches compared with 6.4 inches for black males. The average white male penis circumference was 3.7 inches, and the average black male penis 3.8 inches.[1]

Contrary to popular advertisements in many men's magazines, you cannot make the penis larger by exercise or the use of some contraption. The penis is an erectile organ and is thus composed of erectile tissue, not muscle. Muscle tissue can be enlarged by exercise, erectile tissue cannot.

Scrotum

The *scrotum* (scroe'-tum) is a pouch of skin that hangs from the lower abdominal region below the penis (Figure 3-1). The wall of the scrotum contains a layer of smooth muscle fiber called the *dartos muscle.* This muscle aids in the regulation of temperature within the scrotal sac. This temperature regulation is important since sperm cannot be produced in the testes of the scrotal sac if the temperature is that of the internal body temperature. With the scrotum, and thus the testes, actually being outside the body cavity, the temperature of the testes can be regulated by the body. When the outside temperature is cold, the dartos muscle pulls the scrotum up close to the body wall, thus increasing the temperature. When the outside temperature is high, the dartos muscle relaxes and the scrotum hangs away from the body wall, thus reducing the temperature.

Testes

The scrotum is divided into two chambers, each of which contains a testis (plural, testes). Each testis (tes-tis) is suspended in the scrotum cavity by a *spermatic cord* which contains blood vessels, nerves, and the vas deferens

---

[1]These figures were obtained by computing the means from the Kinsey data presented in Gebhard and Johnson (1979). The white sample exceeded 2000 while the black sample numbered only 59. Both the black and white samples were of college-educated males who had never been convicted of a crime (these factors are not known to influence penis size), and the data are self-measurements directed by written instructions.

BOX 3-1

PENIS CURVATURE, OR EVERYTHING YOU ALWAYS WANTED TO KNOW BUT. . . .

In the erect state, most male penises are not pushed straight out from the body. The majority (66 percent) of erections are up from horizontal but not completely vertical. Only 12 percent are vertical or near-vertical, and 5 percent and fewer are horizontal. The erection most often does not go right or left. In erection, 65 percent are straight out, but 29 percent are to the left while only 6 percent are to the right. The erect penis is usually not curved (51 percent), but 28 percent curve up and 11 percent curve to the left, while only 2 percent curve right and 6 percent curve down. The reason for the tendency of the erect penis to curve to the left more often than to the right is, as far as I know, not known. Interestingly, Kinsey found that most males placed the penis on the left side of the trouser seam.

These data are from the Kinsey data on white males (Gebhard and Johnson, 1979: 121, 122, 123).

(which we shall discuss) (Figure 3-3). Each testis is an egg-shaped structure about 2 inches in length and 1.25 inches in diameter. Within the scrotum, each testis is surrounded by a sturdy, fibrous white capsule called the *tunica albuginea* (too'-ni-ka al-boo-jin'-i-ya) (white tunic). From this protective capsule, thin sheets of connecting tissue extent inward and divide each testis into 200 or more spaces or lobules (lob'-yules). These sheets of connective tissue forming the lobules are called *septa* (sing. septum) and they join at the back of each testis to form a thick mass of tissue (Figure 3-3).

Each of these lobules or spaces within the testis is tightly packed with between one and three coiled *seminiferous tubules* (sem-i-nif'-er-us too'-byules). Each seminiferous tubule is about 3 inches long and each testis contains about one-third mile of seminiferous tubules.

The seminiferous tubules of each testis are united in the back of the testis to form a complex network of channels called the *rete* (ree'tee) *testis.* A series of ducts drain the rete testis and enter the beginning of the epididymis (sing. ep-i-did'-i-mis, plural, ep-i-did'-i-me-deez), which we shall discuss shortly.

Descent of the testes In the male fetus, the testes originate in tissue located behind the abdominal cavity near the kidneys. About one month before birth, they descend to

Figure 3-3 A cutaway side view of the internal structure of a testis.

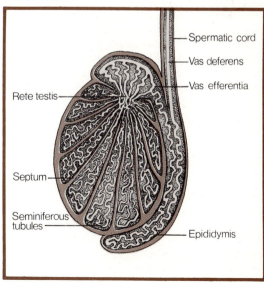

the lower abdominal cavity and into the scrotum. The exact nature of this process is not well understood, but it is aided by a muscular cord called the *gubernaculum.* The gubernaculum is attached to the inside of the scrotal sac and the developing testis. As the testes descend, they follow this cord and carry with them vasa deferentia, blood vessels, and nerves which form the spermatic cord. The descent of the testes is important since internal body temperature is too high for the production of sperm cells. If the testes do not descend, sterility will result. Correcting undescended testes is done ideally before age 5 by either hormone treatment or surgery. As the testes move into the scrotum, the point of entry closes around the spermatic cord. If this closure does not take place, the intestine may slip through into the scrotal area. This is called an *inguinal* (in-gui'-nal) *hernia,* since the canal between the body wall and the abdominal cavity through which the descending testes travel is the *inguinal canal.*[2] An inguinal hernia can be easily corrected by surgery a few months after birth.

Epididymis

The *epididymis* (ep-i-did'-i-mis) is a tightly coiled tube about 20 feet in length. Its diameter is barely microscopic in size and the entire structure is enclosed in a fibrous case of tissue. The epididymis begins after the rete testes and emerges from the testis at the top. Eventually the epididymis becomes the vas deferens. The epididymis functions to transport, store, and nourish sperm cells.

Vas Deferens

The *vas deferens* (sing. def'-er-ens, plural, *vasa deferentia*) is a muscular tube about 1.75

inches long which emerges from the epididymis of each testis and ends behind the urinary bladder. Near its end, and behind the bladder, a segment of the vas deferens is enlarged, forming an area called the *ampulla.* The vas deferens becomes smaller again and connects with the duct from the seminal vesicle. At this juncture with the duct from the seminal vesicle is the *ejaculatory duct* (Figure 3-1). The ejaculatory ducts empty into the urethra.

Seminal Vesicles

The *seminal vesicles* (sem'-in-al ves'-i-cals) are a pair of glands which drain into the vasa deferentia at the ejaculatory ducts. Each seminal vesicle is a saclike structure about ¼ inch long. It is attached to the vas deferens near the base of the bladder. The seminal vesicles contain a fluid which is secreted into the vas deferens and aids in the regulation of the acid-base balance of the ejaculate as the sperm are carried out of the body. This fluid is also rich in nutrients and is thought to provide the sperm with their energy source. Sperm have a high energy requirement, but little actual space to store energy. They can therefore not survive without some type of life-support system external to their structure. As we shall see, some parts of the sperm do contribute to this energy source as well. The seminal vesicle fluid also contains prostaglandins, which are thought to stimulate muscle contractions in the female reproductive tract. These aid the movement of the sperm through the tract toward the female egg cell. The contents of the seminal vesicles enter the vas deferens at ejaculation and this fluid, combined with sperm cells and other secretions, forms the *seminal fluid* or *semen* (see'-men).

Prostate Gland

The prostate gland is located just beneath the urinary bladder and is approximately ½ inch in diameter and ⅓ inch thick, being shaped somewhat like a doughnut. The urethra passes through the prostate and into the penis. The prostate actually contains many glands that

[2]The mother's smoking during pregnancy is associated with moderate anomalies or abnormalities in the child at birth. This increase in incidence of birth anomalies is mainly, however, among male children. One of them is inguinal hernia, which is significantly more likely in male children whose mothers smoked 20 or more cigarettes a day than in male children whose mothers never smoked (Christianson, 1980).

are separated by fibrous tissue and smooth muscles. All the ducts from these various glands open into the urethra from the prostate.

When ejaculation takes place, the prostate secretes a thin, milky fluid into the urethra. This fluid makes up most of the total ejaculation and tends to neutralize the acidity of the semen (the acidity is mainly due to the waste products from the sperm cells) and the female vaginal canal. This neutralizing of acidity enhances the life chances of the sperm cells as they exist in both the male ejaculate and the female reproductive system.

The prostate gland is small in children and increases in size during adolescence. As males age, it often enlarges, resulting in a squeezing of the urethra and thus retarding or even stopping urine passing from the body. If medication does not reduce the swelling of the prostate, the gland must be removed by surgery. Removing the prostate does not necessarily alter a male's sexual functioning.

Bulbourethral Glands
The *bulbourethral* (bul'-boe-yoo-re'-thral) *glands* (Cowper's glands) are two glands the size of peas located below the prostate. They are filled with numerous tubes, the linings of which secrete a mucouslike fluid which is released in response to sexual stimulation. It is commonly stated that the function of this secretion is to lubricate the tip of the penis in preparation for intercourse. This may have been the function many millions of years ago, but it certainly does not serve this function in humans today. The secretion does not pass outside the body until late in the plateau stage of arousal. This means that vaginal penetration would have to be very short indeed and actually follow considerable sexual stimulation. Second, the amount of fluid secreted is so small as to be useless as a vaginal lubricant in coitus. The important function of the secretion of the Cowper's glands is neutralization of the acidity in the male urethra prior to the passage of semen through the urethra in ejaculation. This is a kind of flush-out system clearing the way of acid for the male reproductive cells.

THE PRODUCTION AND TRANSPORTATION OF SPERM

Spermatogenesis (sper'-mah-toe-jen'-e-sis), or the production of sperm cells, is carried out within the internal structure of the testes. The maturing and effective transportation of the sperm cells to the female reproductive system involve the entire male reproductive system in a complex orchestration of events.

The Production of Sperm Cells
The *seminiferous tubules* are the sperm cell factories of the male reproductive system. Each seminiferous tubule is filled with cells and surrounded by a membrane. Those outermost cells which provide contact with the membrane are called *spermatogonia* (sper'-mah-toe-go'-nee-a). They undergo cell division, and some of the newly formed cells move away from the membrane and increase in size, becoming *primary spermatocytes* (sper-ma-toe-sites). The primary spermatocytes each divide, forming two *secondary spermatocytes.* These in turn divide, forming two *spermatids* (sper'-ma-tids). The spermatids then mature into *spermatozoa* or *sperm.*

This entire process of cell division resulting in sperm cells requires about 72 days. Each day a male produces several million sperm.

After the process of cell division from spermatogonia to sperm, the sperm remain in the seminiferous tubules. From here they pass through the rete testis and into the epididymis and the vas deferens. Movement of the sperm cells through the rete testis is not carried out by the sperm cells themselves, since they are not self-propelling at this time. Rather, movement is accomplished by two methods. First, the pressure created by the continuous formation of sperm cells and fluid in the seminiferous tubules pushes the sperm through the rete testis. Second, there is a peristaltic-like action of the smooth muscle cells in the rete testis which moves the sperm along.[3]

---

[3]Peristalsis (pair-is-tal'-sis) or peristaltic action is a wavelike movement of muscles in a tubular organ. This process takes place in many parts of the human body.

The sperm's excursion through the epididymis to the beginning of the vas deferens takes about 9 to 14 days. During this time, the sperm mature and become somewhat motile (capable of self-movement). The sperm are then stored in the epididymis and the first part of the vas deferens in preparation for ejaculation to take place. If ejaculation does not take place, the sperm cells are simply absorbed by the body.

The Structure of Sperm

Sperm are actually single cells and are among the most highly specialized in the human body. A sperm cell consists of three basic parts: the *head, body* or *middlepiece,* and *tail* (Figure 3-4). The head region is oval in outline and consists almost entirely of a cell nucleus. This nucleus is densely filled with DNA, which carries the genetic information of the male. The tip of the sperm head is covered with the

acrosome. This is a protein-filled material containing enzymes that allow the sperm to gain entry into the female egg cell in the process of fertilization. Below the head are the *centrioles* (sen'-tree-oles). These are two small cylindrical bodies composed of twenty-four *microtubules.* Microtubules are extremely small hollow tubes filled with protein. All cells, including sperm cells, contain two centrioles located near the nucleus. The body or middlepiece of the sperm is thought to be responsible for the transport of oxygen to the tail of the sperm through molecules (aerobic activity). This oxygen provides the energy supply for the movement of the tail. The tail consists of contracting filaments that produce a spiral motion (not a whiplike one). This spiral action of the tail partially propels the sperm through the female reproductive tract after ejaculation. The most important function of the tail movement is, however, forcing the sperm through the surface of the female egg cell once contact has been made. The ability of sperm to actually move themselves through the female reproductive tract is minimal.

Figure 3-4 The male sperm.

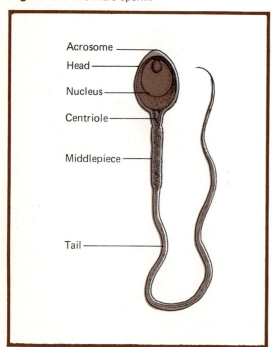

Acrosome

Head

Nucleus

Centriole

Middlepiece

Tail

The Transportation of Sperm

The mature sperm from the epididymis and first part of the vas deferens are transported to the outside of the male body through the process of ejaculation. *Ejaculation* is the expulsion of semen from the urethra. Ejaculation generally accompanies orgasm, but orgasm and ejaculation are two separate physiological processes and need not always take place at the same time. (We shall discuss orgasm and ejaculation in detail in Chapter 5.) Ejaculation is the result of a nerve reflex action which takes place in the *ejaculation center* (a nerve connection) in the lumbar and sacral region of the spinal cord (approximately in the small of the back). As a result of this nerve reflex action, impulses are sent to the smooth muscles in the walls of the epididymides (ep-i-did'-i-mides), vasa deferentia, and ejaculatory ducts. These nerve impulses cause peristaltic contractions in the walls of these organs. At the same time, nerve impulses create rhythmic contractions in the seminal vesicles, prostate gland, and muscles at the base of the erectile tissues in the penis.

This complicated series of responses during ejaculation consists of a well-timed sequence. First, the bulbourethral glands secrete. This is followed by the prostate gland's secreting, then the sperm moves through the vas deferens. Then the seminal vesicles join along, and finally the accumulated seminal fluid is expelled from the penis through the urethra. The seminal fluid thus consists of the contribution of all these glands as the sperm rush out of the body in ejaculation. Its content is about 60 percent prostate gland secretions, 30 percent secretions from the seminal vesicles, 5 percent or less secretions from the bulbourethral glands, and 5 percent fluid and sperm from the testis and epididymides.

The process of ejaculation takes place in two stages which can be felt by the male. With the muscular contractions of the prostate, vasa deferentia, and seminal vesicles, the male has the feeling that ejaculation is inevitable. This is the case because the ejaculatory response has started with nerve impulses from the ejaculation center. This first stage involves the emptying of the contents of the ducts and glands into the urethra. This is called *emission.* The second stage is the expulsion of the seminal fluid from the penis and is accompanied by intensely pleasurable sensations.

In the process of ejaculation, the opening from the bladder into the urethra closes. This stops the ejaculate from going into the bladder and the urine from leaving. It is at this point that the function of the urethra and penis changes from transporting waste materials (urine) to transporting reproductive cells. If this opening does not close, the ejaculate may be forced into the bladder instead of out through the penis. This is called *retrograde ejaculation.*

HORMONAL PROCESSES IN MALE SEXUAL DEVELOPMENT

At puberty, an unknown brain mechanism causes the hypothalamus to release *GRH*

(gonadotropin-releasing hormone). The GRH enters the blood vessels leading to the pituitary gland and the pituitary releases FSH (the follicle-stimulating hormone) and LH (the *luteinizing hormone*). The LH causes the testes to secrete a group of male sex-related hormones called *androgens* (an'-dro-jens). The most important of them is *testosterone* (testos'-te-ron).

The secretion of testosterone by the testes results in development of the secondary sexual characteristics (the external differences between males and females which are not directly involved in reproduction). There is a development of body hair, especially on the face and pubic region. The larynx (voice box) enlarges and the vocal cords thicken, resulting in a lower pitch to the voice. Testosterone is also responsible for the characteristic male muscle structure, skeletal shape, and fatty tissue distribution of wider shoulders and narrower pelvic region. The pelvic width is, of course, directly related to reproduction since the wider female pelvic area is conducive to the birth process. Testosterone is also responsible for changes in the genitals associated with reproductive capacity. Specifically, the penis and the scrotum enlarge. As the testes grow, they secrete even larger amounts of testosterone. This secretion rate is kept in check by the hypothalamus being sensitive to the amount of testosterone. When the level becomes too high, the hypothalamus shuts off GRH to the pituitary, which shuts off LH, which slows down the secretion of testosterone from the testes.

If the testes are removed prior to puberty (castration), the male becomes a *eunuch.* The sex organs do not develop and secondary sexual characteristics do not appear. If castration takes place after puberty, there is some loss of secondary sexual characteristics, but it is thought that most of these remain because of androgen secretions from the adrenal glands.

It is important to note that the changes that take place during puberty signal the beginning of *reproductive* capacity, not *sexual* capacity. Males and females are capable of sexual activity before puberty. The changes occurring in the body are the result of hormonal processes responsible for reproductive capability. Note that the secretion of FSH at puberty results in the production of mature sperm cells by the testes and these other body changes are connected to this reproductive capacity. We often confuse reproductive capacity and sexual capacity in this society just as we confuse reproductive anatomy and sexual anatomy. This is the primary reason we think that adolescence is a prime sexual period (see Chapter 4).

FEMALE REPRODUCTIVE STRUCTURE

The reproductive functions of the female anatomy are more complex than those of the male. They include the production of egg cells, the transport of these egg cells through the reproductive system to the point of fertilization, the transport of male sperm through the female reproductive system to the point of fertilization, the transport of the fertilized egg cell, the maintenance of the fertilized egg cell through the transformation into a human fetus, the maintenance of the developing fetus, and the delivery of the fully developed fetus through the process of birth.

There are thus many anatomical structures, physiological processes, and biochemical exchanges which take place in the female reproductive system.

Vulva

The *vulva* or *pedendum* is the name given to the *external female genitals*. The vulva consists of the mons pubis, labia majora, labia minora, clitoris, and vestibule (Figure 3-5).

Mons Pubis

The *mons pubis* is a mound of fatty tissue which covers the pubic bone (see Figure 3-7

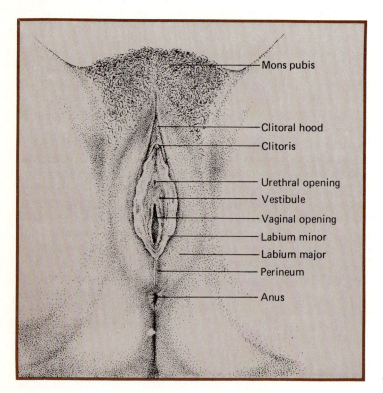

Figure 3-5 External genitals of the female.

Mons pubis

Clitoral hood

Clitoris

Urethral opening

Vestibule

Vaginal opening

Labium minor

Labium major

Perineum

Anus

for location of pubic bone). At puberty, this area becomes covered with coarse pubic hair. The mons contains many touch receptors and is thus sensitive to tactile stimulation.

Labia Majora

The *labia majora* (large lips) are two folds of skin running from the mons pubis to behind or, as shown in Figure 3-5, below the vaginal opening. The labia majora meet and fold together, forming protection for the genitals. The labia majora are covered with pubic hair and are rich in touch receptors.

Labia Minora

The *labia minora* are two smaller folds of tissue which lie just within the labia majora (Figure 3-5). The labia minora (sing. labium minor) join at the top, forming a hood over the clitoris (clitoral hood). The labia minora are without hair and are rich in touch receptors and blood vessels, the latter making for their reddish coloration. In both the labia majora and the labia minora, the size and shape vary greatly from one person to the next. Figure 3-5 is drawn for clarity and thus does not represent the individual variations in genital structure.

Clitoris

The *clitoris* (klit'-o-ris) originates from the same embryonic tissue as does the penis and is the center of sexual sensation and stimulation in the female. It is composed of erectile tissue consisting of two columns of *corpora cavernosa*. As in the erection of the penis, these tissues become engorged with blood during sexual arousal, resulting in the clitoris becoming erect. As in the penis, the cavernosa form *crura* within the body wall and are attached to the pubic arch. The clitoris does not contain a column of spongiosum as in the penis, and the urethra does not run through the clitoris, but opens to the outside of the body between the clitoris and the vaginal opening (Figure 3-5). Externally, the clitoris consists of a *shaft* or *body* and a sensitive tip

called the *glans,* which is richly supplied with touch receptors. The size of the clitoris and the degree to which it projects from under the clitoral hood vary greatly from person to person, as do all genital structures.

Vestibule

The *vestibule* is that space enclosed by the labia minora. Within the vestibule are two openings: the vaginal opening and the urethral opening (Figure 3-5).

Hymen

The *hymen* is a thin ring of tissue covering the vaginal opening. Historically, a great deal of myth has surrounded this small bit of tissue— myth based on different cultures' fascination with the concept of female virginity. The hymen usually contains an opening in some form. Thus, the absence of a hymen indicates nothing regarding a woman's intercourse experience. In actuality, there is no such thing as the absence of a hymen. It is always present; it just has different types of opening structures (Figure 3-6). Rarely, a female will be born with a hymen which has no opening (imperforated hymen). This type of hymen completely blocks the vaginal opening and must be surgically opened so that menstrual flow may exit from the uterus and vagina at puberty.

Perineum

The *perineum* (pair-i-nee'-um) is the skin-covered muscular region between the vaginal opening and the anus (Figure 3-5). This is an important support structure for the vagina and uterus (this is clear in Figure 3-7). Frequently, childbirth may result in an uneven tearing of this tissue. For this reason, an incision is often made from the bottom of the vaginal opening through the perineum during childbirth (a procedure called an *episiotomy*) so that the tissue is not damaged by tearing. Following childbirth, the incision is closed and the tissue heals back to its original state within two weeks (Mims and Swenson, 1980).

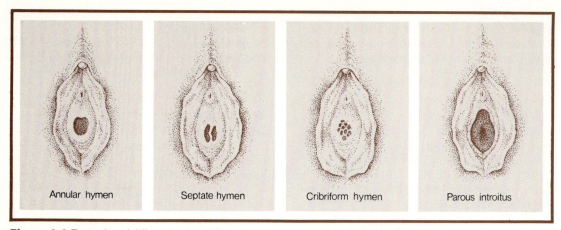

Annular hymen   Septate hymen   Cribriform hymen   Parous introitus

Figure 3-6 Examples of different types of hymen structure. At birth the female may have any one of many different types of hymen in terms of closure or opening. As is evident, the presence of an open hymen is not proof of intercourse experience since many women are born with the hymen partially or fully open to the degree it would be after coital experience. If the hymen is fully closed at birth, it must be surgically opened before the first menstrual flow to allow material to move out of the vagina.

Figure 3-7 A cutaway side view of the female reproductive system.

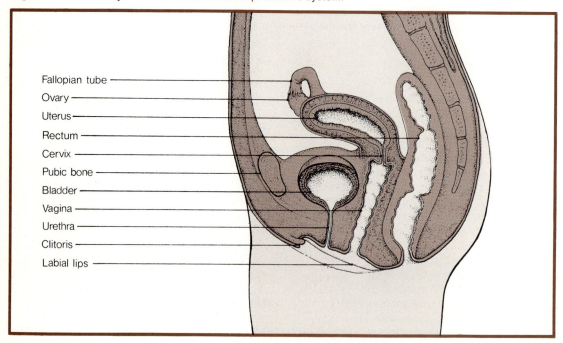

Fallopian tube

Ovary

Uterus

Rectum

Cervix

Pubic bone

Bladder

Vagina

Urethra

Clitoris

Labial lips

Vestibular Glands

On each side of the vaginal opening are two small glands which correspond to the bulbourethral glands in the male. These *Bartholin's glands* secrete a mucus during sexual excitement which insignificantly aids in the lubrication of the vaginal opening.

Ovaries

The organs responsible for male sperm cells and female egg cells are homologous (similar in origin). While male sperm are produced in the testes, the female egg cells are produced in the *ovaries*.

The ovaries are two solid, egg-shaped structures about 2.75 inches in length, 1.5 inches wide, and ⅓ inch thick (Figure 3-8). One ovary is located on each side of the pelvic cavity and each ovary is attached by a suspending ligament to the body musculature and by an *ovarian ligament* to the uterus.

The tissue structure of the ovary is divided into two regions which, while not physically distinct, differ in basic composition. The inner *medulla* region of the ovary consists of blood vessels and nerve fibers. The outer *cortex* region consists of more compact tissue in the form of *ovarian follicles*. The ovarian follicles are tiny masses of cells which have a general granular appearance. The outer surface of each ovary is covered with a large layer of cells called the *germinal epithelium* (ep-i-thee'-lee-um). It is the germinal epithelium which produces female egg cells.[4] The ovaries contain approximately 500,000 ova (egg cells) at birth, and no more are produced during the woman's life span. Most of these ova die and are not used in ovulation.

Oviducts

The *oviducts* (named for their function of carrying mature ova) are also called *fallopian*

[4]Like the testes, the ovaries descend to their final location shortly before birth.

Figure 3-8 The internal reproductive organs of the female.

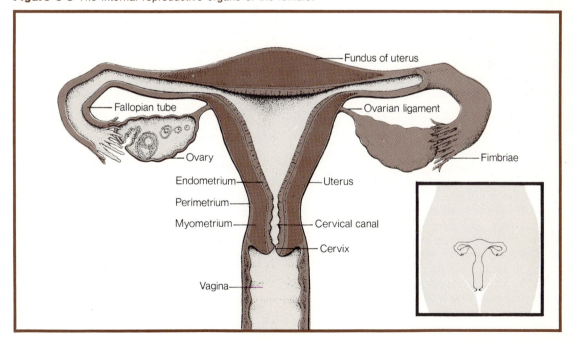

tubes (after the Italian anatomist Fallopius) or *uterine tubes* (because they are attached to the uterus). The oviducts carry egg cells toward the uterus and sperm cells toward the egg cell, and are the location for the fertilization of a female egg cell by a male sperm cell.

Each oviduct enters the uterus near the top and on the side and extends outward and downward, having a total length of about 4 inches and a diameter of about 3/16 inch.

Near each ovary, each of the oviducts becomes larger and funnel-shaped, forming the infundibulum (in-fun-dib'-u-lum). The infundibulum has a number of branched extensions called *fimbriae* (fim'-bree-eye). These finger-like fimbriae encircle, but, with one exception, usually do not touch, the ovary. One of the larger fimbriae (the *ovarian fimbria*) is attached to the ovary.

The wall of the oviduct is composed of three layers; an inner mucus layer, a middle muscular layer, and an outer covering. The inner mucous layer is lined with hairlike fibers of tissue called *cilia* (si'-lee-ya). This layer of the oviduct secretes mucous and the cilia beat a flowing motion in the direction of the uterus. This motion carries the egg cell toward the uterus.

Uterus

The *uterus* (yoo'-te-rus) is a hollow, muscular organ shaped somewhat like an upside-down pear. It is about 3 inches in length, 2 inches wide at the widest point, and 1 inch thick. One of the magnificent pieces of body architecture, the uterus increases in size dramatically during the process of pregnancy.

The upper two-thirds of the uterus (the body) is rounded and dome-shaped (Figure 3-7). The oviducts enter here at the widest part of the uterus. Above the oviducts, the uterus bulges slightly, forming the *fundus* of the uterus. The lower one-third of the uterus is composed of the tubular-shaped *cervix*. (Figure 3-7). The cervix extends downward to join the *vagina* (va-jy'-na) at a right angle.

The wall of the uterus is composed of three different layers of tissue. The innermost

layer is the *endometrium*, which consists of a mucus membrane. The middle layer, the *myometrium*, is a thick, muscular layer consisting of smooth muscles which run in longitudinal, circular, and spiral patterns and provide the uterus with not only great strength but the ability to expel a fully developed fetus. These muscles are thickest and most powerful in the fundus region and thinnest in the cervix region. This variation allows the fundus to contract with force pushing the fetus downward toward the cervix and permits the cervix to be stretched in the process of birth. The outer layer of the uterus is the *perimetrium*, consisting of ligament which covers only the upper body of the uterus and none of the cervix. This specialized structure further adds to the strength of the upper part of the uterus and the flexibility of the cervical area.

Vagina

The vagina is a tubular structure about 3.5 inches in length which extends from the cervix to the vestibule where the vaginal opening is formed. The vagina is actually a potential space since, in a nonaroused state, the walls of the vagina touch each other. Only during sexual arousal or the introduction of something like a penis into the vagina does the potential space become an open tubular space.

The vagina extends up and back from the vaginal opening and is located between the urinary bladder and the rectum (Figure 3-7). It is attached to both the bladder and the rectum by connecting tissue. The upper 25 percent of the vagina is separated from the rectum.

The upper portion of the vagina surrounds the cervix in such a way that the cervix protrudes into the vaginal canal. Thus small recesses, called fornices (for'-ni-seez), exist between the wall of the vagina and the cervix, and are important in physical examinations. The fornices allow the internal abdominal organs to be indirectly touched.

The vaginal wall consists of three layers of tissue similar to that of the uterus: an inner mucous layer, a middle muscular layer, and an outer fibrous layer.

BOX 3-2

ALTERATION OF THE GENITALS

Throughout many cultures of the world, genital alteration is common. Male circumcision, in which the foreskin or prepuce is removed, is quite common as a status passage from boyhood to manhood. *Subincision,* which involves a slit being made in the underside of the penis and through the urethra for the length of the organ, is less common.

It is estimated (Morgan and Steinem, 1980) that some 30 million women in the world are today subject to genital alteration in one of three forms: *circumcision,* involving the removal of the prepuce or clitoral hood but none of the clitoris; *clitoridectomy,* involving removal of all or part of the clitoris; and *infibulation,* which involves joining the labia majora together, usually following some other form of genital alteration.

Such procedures very frequently result in severe health problems as well as physical trauma and the loss of all sexual sensation. Infibulation often results in repeated "surgery," since the vulva has to be cut open for intercourse and even more so for childbirth.

In the nineteenth century in the United States, various forms of "sexual surgery" were performed on women with some regularity (Barker-Benfield, 1975). Such operations were prescribed for a variety of stated reasons. Medical wisdom held that a woman's sexuality was responsible for mental disorders and the basis of the problem was thought to be her genitals. Operations were also performed to stop female masturbation, and the frequency of surgery generally accompanied the rise of the specialty of gynecology as male physicians came to the rescue of society by curing the ills of womanhood through various forms of female sexual surgery. Much of this surgery had to do not only with the low status of women, but with women's being blamed for what was seen as the degeneration of society after the Civil War (Barker-Benfield, 1975).

Clitoridectomy was first performed in the United States in the late 1860s and continued to be practiced until perhaps as late as 1925. It was largely replaced by circumcision, which was performed until at least 1937. These were common "cures" for what was thought to be an increase in female masturbation. Other procedures were also part of this mentality. Female castration or *oophorectomy* (oh-off-oh-rek-toh-mee) was invented in Rome, Georgia, in 1872 and was popular between 1880 and 1910. This procedure (removal of the ovaries) was performed as a cure for female psychological disorders until 1946 in the United States. The recent concern over unnecessary hysterectomies (removal of the uterus) may be new, but the basis of the concern is not. The first successful hysterectomy in the United States was performed in 1853 and evidently became a popular part of the surgical procedures of the new field of gynecology from the middle to the late 1800s (Barker-Benfield, 1975).

FEMALE EGG CELL PRODUCTION

While male sperm cell production begins at puberty and continues throughout adulthood, female egg cell production begins before the female's birth and ceases in her middle age.

During the development of the female fetus, small groups of cells grow inward from deep in the germinal epithelium and form *ovarian follicles*. Through a process of cell division, the ovarian follicles contain cellular bodies called *oocytes* (oh'-oh-syts). The ovarian follicles and their oocytes remain unchanged in the ovaries throughout childhood. At puberty, mature egg cells are produced in the ovaries.

Ovulation

Ovulation is the process of producing a mature egg cell. At puberty, this initial production is called *menarche* (me-nar'-key). Throughout the woman's reproductive years, each month results in the production of one mature egg cell from one of the ovaries. The cycle of events which occurs in the female reproductive system each month is the *menstrual cycle*.

When menarche takes place, an unknown process causes the hypothalamus in the brain to release the gonadatropin-releasing hormone (GRH). The GRH stimulates the pituitary gland to secrete the follicle-stimulating hormone (FSH) and the luteinizing hormone (LH). FSH is so named because of its action on the ovarian follicles that have been sitting in the ovaries since infancy. LH will be discussed in detail shortly. FSH acts on the ovary to stimulate the maturation of a follicle and the process of ovulation begins. With this hormonal stimulation, some of the ovarian follicles increase in size as they mature over a period of fourteen days (in the first menstrual cycle, the ovaries also increase in size). When a follicle has completely matured, it appears on the surface of the ovary as a blisterlike bulge. At this point, the luteinizing hormone (LH) is released in a large amount from the pituitary gland, an action that apparently causes the mature follicle to rupture. As this rupture takes place, the follicle oozes from the ovary and the process of

ovulation has occurred as the fluid in the follicle and the mature egg cell leave the ovary and enter the open space between the ovary and the opening of the oviduct. When the egg cell leaves the ovary, it is swept up by the fimbriae which sweep across the surface of the ovary. Since the egg cell spends some time out of the ovary and not yet in the oviduct, it is actually in the body cavity and can be fertilized by a sperm cell. This, however, is rare.

Only one egg cell is produced in each menstrual cycle, and the ovaries alternate in releasing egg cells. In 1 to 2 percent of all menstrual cycles, two egg cells will be produced. This event is the most common cause of multiple births (fraternal twins when both egg cells are fertilized by separate sperm cells).

The process of the follicle's maturing to the point where a mature egg cell is released in ovulation takes approximately fourteen days. It is generally stated that these fourteen days are to be counted from the end of the menstrual flow for purposes of contraception (calendar rhythm method). However, unless one has a perfect twenty-eight-day menstrual cycle, this is not the case. As we shall see, this fact makes the calendar rhythm method fairly unreliable.

Menstruation

While menstruation has traditionally been viewed and dealt with socially as an unclean process to be handled with great caution and finesse, it is an integral part of the complex process of reproduction.

When the follicle in the ovary begins to mature, it releases the hormone estrogens (a general name for a group of female sex-related hormones). These estrogens cause the inner layer of the uterus (the endometrium) to begin preparation for a fertilized egg cell to arrive. This preparation takes the form of an increase in the thickness of the endometrium. After ovulation, the space left in the follicle by the departed egg cell and follicular fluid fills with blood and forms a clot. At this time, the cells of the follicle increase greatly in size and form a new structure called the corpus luteum.

The *corpus luteum* acts during the last half of the menstrual cycle to produce large amounts of the hormones progesterone and estrogen. The progesterone causes the endometrium of the uterus to become even more engorged with blood and glandular tissue, thus increasing considerably in thickness. The corpus luteum stops functioning if the egg cell released in ovulation is not fertilized by a sperm cell. When the corpus luteum ceases to function, the levels of estrogen and progesterone decrease rapidly. With this decrease, the blood vessels of the endometrium are restricted. This restriction shuts down the supply of oxygen and nutrients to the tissues of the endometrium, and these tissues soon disintegrate and fall away. When they do so, blood escapes from the capillaries of the endometrium, owing to damage in the process of disintegration.

The disintegrated endometrium tissues and this blood from the damaged capillaries pass out of the uterus through the cervix and out of the body through the vagina as the *menstrual flow*.[5] This flow usually lasts for three to five days, and the beginning of the flow marks the first day of a new menstrual cycle. Following the complete shedding of the tissues and blood from the endometrium, the process begins all over again. These changes through the menstrual cycle may be summarized as shown in Figure 3-9.

Menopause From the time of the first menstrual cycle on, ovulation takes place at relatively regular intervals until middle age. In the middle to late forties, menstrual cycles become irregular, and in a few months to years,

[5]It takes approximately thirty-six hours for menstrual fluid to travel from the uterus to the outside of the vagina.

BOX 3-3
MENSTRUAL SYNCHRONY

One of the interesting, and as yet not understood, characteristics of menstruation is that females who are in frequent interaction with one another rather rapidly become synchronized in the timing of their cycles (McClintock, 1971). Graham and McGrew (1980) studied female college students over a period of four months. It was found that closest female friends developed synchrony in their menstrual cycles in a period of three months. At the beginning of the study, pairs of women averaged eleven days apart in their cycles, but after only three months, they were six days apart. The major factor in the amount of ensuing menstrual synchronization was closeness of friendship and the amount of time spent together. This synchronization takes place regardless of knowledge of one another's cycles. In the Graham and McGrew study, only 16 percent of the women knew their closest friend's cycle. The reason that such synchronization takes place remains unknown, but it is assumed that it has something to do with olfactory (smell) processes. For example, Russel et al. (1977) had female subjects place an extract of perspiration on their upper lip (it had no detectable odor to the subject) for a period of four months. The extract was taken from a female donor who had regular menstrual cycles. Over the four-month period, the subjects' menstrual cycles came closer and closer to that of the donor, while a control group of women who applied a placebo substance on their lips showed no menstrual synchrony with the donor.

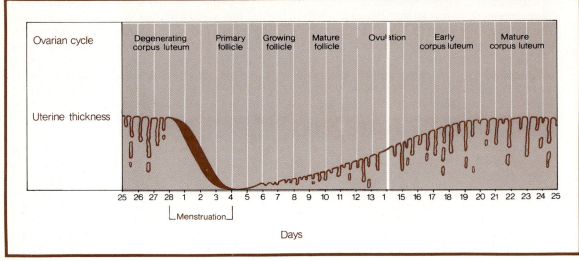

Figure 3-9 Ovarian cycles and changes in the lining (endometrium) of the uterus during the menstrual cycle.

they cease. This period of life is called *menopause.*

Menopause appears to be caused by the aging of the ovaries. After producing one mature egg cell approximately each month for some thirty-five years, the ovarian follicles become fewer and fewer in number and eventually disappear. When there are no follicles to mature, ovulation no longer occurs and the blood level of estrogen is thus reduced. As a result of this reduction in estrogen, certain physical changes take place which are really the opposite of those we shall see appear at puberty. The vagina, uterus, oviducts, and external genitals decrease in size. Pubic and general body hair becomes thinner and the breasts become smaller. Other common physical symptoms of menopause are "hot flashes," dizziness, headaches, heart palpitations, and soreness of the joints. It generally takes one to two years for menopause (the stopping of menstruation). Menopause occurs early in the *climacteric,* that period lasting fifteen to twenty years in which the body readjusts to the absence of the menstrual cycle.

Social status of menstruation
Throughout history, menstruation has been shrouded in suspicion, ignorance, and mystery, and has served as a basis for discriminating against women. Many preliterate societies view women as contaminated and made impure by menstruation. A common result is restriction to a menstrual hut for the protection of others, since menstrual discharge is seen as damaging to everything from crops to human health. Western culture has a long history of this attitude. The Bible quite clearly states that menstruating women and everything they touch is unclean (Leviticus 20:19 and 15:4). The early Christians thought that menstruation was a curse put on women for the sins of Eve. Thus the term the "curse" became an abbreviation of the "curse of Eve." Even today, orthodox Judaism prescribes a cleansing process for women after menstruation. The stigma attached to menstruation as an unmentionable is no more evident than in the criminal case of Lizzie Borden, who allegedly hacked her parents to death with an ax. Although the crime was popularized in song, film, and even TV movies, it is not commonly known that she was probably acquitted because of the unmentionable nature of menstruation. In her trial in 1892, her alibi was that she was washing out her menstrual rags at the time of the murders. (This was before the de-

velopment of the disposable sanitary napkin and women wore something resembling a diaper to absorb the menstrual flow.) The judge and attorneys in the case felt that it would be improper to mention what the defendent was supposedly doing, and this piece of evidence never became widely known. The parties also apparently agreed that no woman would tell of washing her menstrual rags unless she was really doing so, and no evidence presented by the prosecution was strong enough to override this assumption (Bullough and Bullough, 1977: chapter 8).

Perhaps the factor which most strongly affects the timing of heterosexual intercourse in the United States is the taboo on menstrual sex. Recent studies (Erickson-Paige, 1977; Pietropinto and Simenauer, 1977) reveal that approximately half of all married couples refrain from sexual activity during menstruation. This taboo is more common among older persons, couples having a traditional view of marriage, and those who are more religiously traditional (Erickson-Paige, 1977). Still, even the most sexually liberal of writers adhere to a menstrual sex taboo. The author of the *Joy of Sex* recommends activities other than coitus during menstruation and *The Sensuous Woman* suggests avoiding group sexual activity at this time.

The menstrual taboo is worldwide and is generally associated with a number of other pollution beliefs which a society holds. While the exact form of the restrictions placed on women during menstruation vary greatly from one culture to the next, the limitations are commonly sexual in nature and focus on the concept of contamination. In reality, intercourse or any other sexual activity is perfectly safe and clean during menstruation. The only process that is taking place is the sloughing off of the lining of an organ; such a normal body process occurs in thousands of other locations in and on the body every day.

Bullough and Bullough (1977) have also suggested that one of the major reasons women wore so many petticoats and other clothes prior to the twentieth century was in an attempt to hide the "curse." In the late nineteenth century, there were many attempts to

devise some method of dealing with menstrual flow other than the use of rags. Between 1854 and 1914, there were at least twenty patents for devices ranging from napkins and sacks to menstrual receivers. Not only did they not work very well, but marketing them was a major problem. In 1896, the Johnson and Johnson Company developed a disposable cotton sanitary napkin but withdrew it because of a lack of sales.

In 1920, Kimberley Clark Company rather accidentally invented Kotex, a product that was to have profound effects. The company had been left with large quantities of cellulose wadding used for bandage material in World War I. The wood fibers of the material were much more absorbent than cotton. Upon discovering that army nurses had been using the material for sanitary napkins, the company developed Kotex. This was the first manufacture of an effective sanitary napkin. Marketing, however, was difficult. Stores thought that public display of the product was improper, and in some cases the public demanded removal of the display. Magazines were also unenthusiastic about accepting Kotex advertisements, and it was not until 1924 that the first magazine ad for sanitary napkins appeared (in the *Ladies Home Journal*). In 1926, Montgomery Ward finally listed Kotex in its catalog. The retail price was quite high at 60 cents apiece, a fact that restricted early adoption to middle- and upper-class women. In a short time, however, advertisements and sales were nationwide and women were able to wear less restrictive clothing without anxiety (Bullough and Bullough, 1977; Bullough, 1980).

The myths of menstruation have also been put forth to systematically discriminate against women. In 1875, an article, published in the *American Journal of Obstetrics,* argued that menstruation was a pathology and that intercourse during menstruation was not only dangerous, but resulted in gonorrhea. This general attitude appeared rather commonly in the medical profession. Dr. Clark, a Harvard medical professor, wrote in 1873 that the body could not do two things at once. It was impossible, he argued, for a woman to use her brain in higher education and have her reproductive

BOX 3-4

TAMPON USE RISKS

While toxic shock syndrome (TSS) received a great deal of public attention in 1981, the association between toxic shock infection and tampon use remains ambiguous and not clearly understood. Cases of toxic shock were recorded many years before tampons became popular—and recorded for females not using tampons, females who had not yet reached menarche, and even males. It is possible, but by no means clearly established, that tampons allow bacteria to build to an infectious point in the vagina; for this reason, there appeared to have been more TSS cases associated with "superabsorbent" tampon use. On the other hand, gynecologists not uncommonly report rare cases of women who have worn a tampon so long that it became imbedded in the vaginal lining, without TSS taking place. Changing tampons with extreme frequency or "roughness" is also associated with a few cases of vaginal ulcerations. The ulceration occurs because of "drying" of the vaginal wall in a specific spot. Tampon abuse is also associated with infrequent cases of changes in the vaginal mucous before ulceration develops (Friedrich, 1981).

system develop. This was clearly evidenced, Clark contended, by menstrual disorders among women college students. The consequence of menstruating and having one's reproductive system develop at the time one is engaging in intellectual or learning activities, he held, is an overload on the central nervous system and a dwindling of reproductive ability. Clark concluded that since women are obviously meant to be primarily reproductive creatures, they should not be educated. He was also not excited about women's working, but this was not as bad as mental activity.

Although Clark's ideas met with criticism, they were not unique within the medical profession. In 1900, the president of the American Gynecological Society stated that school officials should provide rest periods for menstruating women in order to avoid damage during this period of weakness. In 1905, the president of the Oregon Medical Society stated that studying not only diminished a woman's beauty and took away her sexual desire, but caused at least five reproductive-related diseases. Even in 1931, a very popular sex manual written by a progressive physician stated that women were ill during menses and should rest

for at least two days and not engage in any physical exercise.

While such attitudes have changed rather dramatically over time, scientists and the public alike are still concerned with the mental and physical declines in women during menses, thereby reflecting these prior attitudes but in a "modern" way. It should be recalled that as recently as 1970, Hubert Humphrey's physician stated that women could not fulfill leadership roles because of their mental processes during menstruation. (Bullough and Bullough, 1977, chapter 8). It was not until March 24, 1973, that *All in the Family* broke the taboo of mentioning menstruation on television.

HORMONAL PROCESSES IN FEMALE SEXUAL DEVELOPMENT

At puberty, the hypothalamus and the pituitary function in the same manner in both sexes. The release of LH from the pituitary causes the ovaries in the female to begin secreting estrogen (a general name given to a group of female sex-related hormones). This increased estrogen secreted from the ovaries results in breast development, enlargement of the vagina, uterus, oviducts, ovaries, and external genitals. There is also an increase in the amount of fatty tissue, mainly in the breasts, thighs, and buttocks. Androgens (male sex-related hormones) are also secreted in the female by the adrenal glands (also somewhat by the ovaries). The relative lack of androgen in the female is responsible for the characteristic female skeletal configuration of narrow shoulders and wider hips than the male. Females with higher androgen levels have more malelike muscle, fatty tissue, and skeletal features.

CONCEPTION

After sperm cells are deposited in the vaginal tract of the female, they begin their journey to perhaps meet an egg cell. The first thing which must happen, however, is that the sperm must make their way into the cervix. This entry is aided by a very interesting and often ignored aspect of the female anatomy. At the peak of sexual arousal, the uterus is no longer in a forward-leaning position, as shown in Figure 3-7. Rather, it is upright and has actually pulled up the top of the vagina, thereby making the vaginal canal taller and more spacious. Directly under the opening of the cervix into the vagina, a small recess has formed in the vagina. This recess collects the deposited seminal fluid if the female is lying on her back. As arousal declines, the uterus settles downward and the cervix lowers to be directly over or in the pool of seminal fluid. Nothing could be more conducive in aiding the entry of

BOX 3-5
PAINFUL MENSTRUATION AND TREATMENT

Painful cramps during menstruation are part of a large complex of symptoms of physical menstrual distress. Painful menstruation is more than an individual problem; it also has large economic costs. Dysmenorrhea (painful menstruation) is often said to cause 140 million lost work hours a year. This figure is probably a dramatic underestimate, since it was computed in 1945 by J. O. Haman when not nearly so many women were in the labor force as are working today. Painful menstruation, involving cramps, nausea, and other discomforts to the point of being unable to perform normal daily activities, is relatively common. Svanberg and Ulmsten (1981) found that in a sample of Swedish teenage women, 43 percent had occasional to consistent menstrual pain, and between 12 and 26 percent (depending on age) had menstrual pain severe enough to prevent their performing normal activities.

The cause of menstrual cramps is the presence of large amounts of the prostaglandin hormones inducing severe contractions and thus cramping in the uterus as the lining sheds. This can be easily treated by prescribing medications that inhibit prostaglandin and thus decrease the severe uterine contractions. The most often prescribed are mefenamic acid (under the trade name of Ponstel), which is 84 to 94 percent effective; ibuprofen (under the trade name of Motrin), which is 61 to 100 percent effective, and naproxen and sodium salts (popularly known as Anaprox), said to be 67 to 86 percent effective (Dingfelder, 1981). Motrin was the first prostaglandin inhibitor approved for use, but, while there have been few comparative studies of these various drugs, Anaprox appears to have the advantage of rapid onset and long duration.

sperm cells to the cervix from the vagina.

Once the sperm cells enter the cervix, they are filtered by the mucus in the cervix. This filtering process selects out and destroys abnormally shaped sperm cells (Perry et al., 1977; Hanson and Overstreet, 1981). For example, 50 percent of the sperm cells have the normal oval shape when the ejaculate enters the vagina. By the time the sperm cells get through a portion of the cervical mucus, this proportion of normal, oval-shaped sperm has increased to 80 percent by the destruction of abnormally shaped sperm (Hanson and Overstreet, 1981).

The cervical mucus also keeps sperm out of the female reproductive tract by blocking the passage of sperm into the cervix during those periods of the menstrual cycle when conception is not likely. When ovulation is about to occur and shortly after it has taken place, the cervical mucus changes in such a way as to facilitate the passage of sperm from the vagina into the cervix. At this point, the cervical mucus exercises some selection in which sperm cells are allowed to pass (Hanson and Overstreet, 1981).

Once in the female reproductive tract, sperm cells need all the help they can get, since their own means of transportation is not very effective. The tail of the sperm moves in a spiral motion, which is not sufficient to propel the sperm fully through the cervix, into and through the uterus, and down an oviduct where fertilization of an egg may take place. The principal means by which sperm move through the uterus and oviducts is thought to be by muscle contractions of these organs. What controls these muscle contractions remains unknown, but the chemical content of the seminal fluid is believed to be important.

Not only are the sperm cells moved along the uterine tube, but the egg cell is moved toward the sperm cell as well. As the egg cell escapes the surface of the ovary at ovulation, it is encircled by the fimbriae and moves into the infundibulum of the oviduct. The cilia of the oviduct then help move the egg in the direction of the uterus. This movement toward the uterus is also aided by the peristaltic action of the muscular layer of the oviduct.

With the peristaltic action and the beating of the cilia in such a manner as to move the egg cell toward the uterus, the sperm cell is fighting an uphill battle, since everything is moving in the opposite direction to that the sperm has to travel. Here again, the female reproductive system comes to the aid of the sperm. When the estrogen in the female body is high, the mucus in the oviducts is thick and the cilia are many in number. However, when the estrogen level drops (as it does when ovulation is triggered), the mucus in the oviducts becomes thin and the cilia fewer in number. These changes aid in the sperm's not being pushed backward in the oviduct while on their way to meet an egg cell (Jansen, 1980).

An additional problem confronts sperm cells. At ovulation, only one ovary produces an egg cell, and that egg cell travels down the oviduct nearest that ovary. Sperm cells do not, of course, know which oviduct contains the egg cell, so half of them start off down the wrong oviduct when leaving the uterus.

These problems of sperm transport are balanced by raw numbers. In a single ejaculation, as many as 300 to 500 million sperm cells are present. Only a few hundred of these ever make contact with an egg cell, and only one will actually fertilize the egg cell.

Fertilization

When a sperm cell reaches the egg, it is usually in the portion of the uterine tube nearest the ovary. Movement from the point of ejaculation to contact with the egg takes approximately one hour. The sperm reaches the egg cell by means of random movement; there is no evidence that any "attraction" process takes place.

Once a sperm cell makes contact with the egg, the acrosome covering its tip releases an enzyme that breaks down the cellular tissue of the egg surface and allows passage of the sperm. Although there may be other sperm cells nearby, only one sperm cell enters the egg. This is accomplished by a blocking process. When the sperm cell and the egg cell membranes come together, the surface of the egg releases molecules. Some of the mole-

Figure 3-10 Changes in a fertilized female egg cell from the point of ovulation to implantation in the uterus.

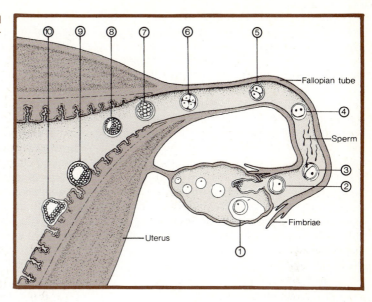

1. A follicle in the ovary preparing to release an egg cell.
2. An egg cell has been swept into the fallopian tube (oviduct) by the fimbriae.
3. Fertilization takes place when the sperm cell penetrates the egg cell.
4. The nucleus of the egg cell and the sperm cell resides within the egg cell structure. This structure is now called a *zygote*.
5. Cell division begins with two cells being formed by segmentation.
6. Cell division continues with four cells being formed.
7. Cell division has now created a cluster of sixteen cells called a *morula*. The zygote reaches the uterus about three days after fertilization.
8. Six days after fertilization, the cells form a hollow ball called a *blastocyst* which floats free in the uterus.
9. At the end of the sixth or the beginning of the seventh day after fertilization, the blastocyst begins to implant in the endometrium of the uterus.
10. By the ninth or tenth day after fertilization, implantation is complete and the endometrium, or lining of the uterus, is closed over the point where the blastocyst entered. (Adopted from Haeberle, 1978:70.)

cules prevent other sperm from breaking down the sites on the egg cell surface where the sperm must begin entry, and other molecules are thought to cause the egg cell to become impenetrable. Not only does the egg cell stop other sperm from entering after one has made entry, but the female reproductive tract provides sperm with the ability to enter the surface of the egg. Even though sperm cells become mature in the epididymis, they are not able to break through the egg surface until they have been in the female reproductive tract for some time. As the sperm pass through the cervical mucus, they undergo *capacitation;* that is, the acrosome obtains the ability to release enzymes that allow the sperm cell to enter the egg cell (Overstreet et al., 1980).

The ability of sperm cells to fertilize an egg cell (male fertility) is, given the random nature of coming into contact with the egg cell, largely a matter of numbers. Fewer than 50 million sperm cells per milliliter of seminal fluid usually means that fertilization of an egg will not take place. Other factors are also important, including the size, shape, and ability of the sperm to move through the surface of the egg.

When a sperm cell reaches the egg and makes its way through the surface, the egg and sperm unite in the same common membrane. The tail of the sperm has been primarily responsible for the sperm's entering the egg and the tail has by now been lost in the process. The head of the sperm remains and swells to form a nucleus. The egg cell now undergoes cell division, which forms a mature egg cell and a secondary cellular body, the latter of which is expelled from the common membrane. The nucleus of the egg cell and the nucleus of the sperm cell meet in the center of the egg cell. The respective membranes coating each disappear, the chromosomes of the egg and sperm unite, and the process of fertilization is complete (Figure 3-10).

Early Embryo Development

The process of fertilization normally takes place in the uterine tube near the opening to the ovary (Figure 3-10). Following fertilization, the egg continues toward the uterus. This movement into the uterus usually takes about three days.

During this movement down the uterine tube following fertilization, important processes are taking place. The union of sperm and egg in fertilization results in a newly formed structure called a *zygote* (zī′-gote). The zygote begins the process of *segmentation* through a series of divisions collectively called *cleavage*. The single zygote first divides into two cells. Each of these then divides, forming four cells, and so forth. This first cell division takes place approximately twenty-four hours after fertilization. By the time the zygote reaches the uterus (approximately three days after fertilization), it consists of a tiny cluster of sixteen cells called a *morula* (mor′-yoo-la).

By the sixth day following fertilization, the future embryo is floating free in the uterus. During this floating-free period, the cells have arranged to form a hollow ball called a *blastocyst.* While the blastocyst is floating free in the uterus, the lining of the original egg cell begins to disintegrate. Toward the end of the sixth or seventh day following fertilization, the blastocyst attaches itself to the lining of the uterus and begins to implant itself in the endometrium. This is accomplished by the outermost cells of the blastocyst (called the *trophoblast*) secreting enzymes that simply erode away a small area in the endometrium. By the ninth or tenth day following fertilization,

the embryo has completed implantation in the lining of the uterus and the opening through which it entered is closed over. This closure is first formed by a blood clot and then by a regeneration of the endometrium. After this occurs, all development of the embryo and, later, of the fetus takes place within the wall of the uterus.

Hormonal processes in implantation   In a normal menstrual cycle, the egg cell leaves the ovary and a corpus luteum is formed within the ovary. The corpus luteum secretes large amounts of progesterone and estrogen hormones, a process that results in the lining of the uterus becoming prepared for a fertilized egg. When the corpus luteum disintegrates, the estrogen and progesterone levels fall off rapidly, the endometrium sloughs off, and the menstrual flow begins. If this happens after implantation or while a fertilized egg cell is in the uterus before implantation, the embryo is lost. This loss is prevented by the cells of the trophoblast secreting a hormone that signals the corpus luteum not to disintegrate. The corpus luteum thus continues to secrete progesterone and estrogen and the endometrium of the uterus remains intact because the estrogen and progesterone levels inhibit the secretion of FSH and LH and thus inhibit the normal menstrual cycle. This additional estrogen, now continuing to be secreted by the corpus luteum, also stimulates the growth of the muscular layer of the uterus in preparation for fetal growth and stretching of the uterus as well as birth.

The corpus luteum continues to secrete hormones throughout pregnancy. After the first three months, however, the placenta takes over this function.

Abnormal implantation   Infrequently, an embryo will become implanted in other than the uterus (the uterine tube, ovary, cervix, or abdominal cavity outside the entrance to the uterine tube). The result is an *ectopic pregnancy.*[6] Most commonly, ectopic pregnan-

---

[6]Approximately 1 out of every 130 pregnancies is ectopic; approximately 41,000 ectopic pregnancies a year occur in the United States. In 1977, however, there were only 39 deaths due to ectopic pregnancies (Ory and Women's Health Study, 1981).

cy takes place in the uterine tube (a tubal pregnancy). In a tubal pregnancy, the enlargement of the developing embryo can rupture the uterine tube, causing severe pain and bleeding. The proper treatment involves prompt surgery to remove the embryo and the damaged uterine tube.

Twins The inner cells of the blastocyst give rise to the embryo itself, while the outer cells (the trophoblast) give rise to processes which maintain the developing embryo and fetus. At times, the inner cell mass of the blastocyst divides to form two separate groups of cells, each of which may develop into a separate fetus. Since fertilization has already taken place between one egg and one sperm, the two sets of cells have identical genes and develop into *identical twins.* Rarely, these two groups of cells fail to separate completely and remain joined at some point on their surface. As they develop into separate fetuses, they remain joined and at birth the result is *cojoined twins* (Siamese twins). Where they are joined depends upon where the developing cell masses were joined and what part of the future human body that tissue will become.

Fraternal twins result when two egg cells are produced at ovulation and each is fertilized by separate sperm cells. Since each zygote has formed a unique genetic structure (separate sperm cells and separate egg cells), fraternal twins are not identical and may even be of different sex. Triplets and other multiple births, while more rare, result from the same processes and may be either fraternal or identical.

Fetal Membranes and Placenta

There are four membranes which develop to protect the embryo, supply food and oxygen, and eliminate waste material. These membranes are not part of the embryo itself but surround the embryo and are discarded at birth (Figure 3-11).

Yolk sac Even though there is no yolk in the human egg cell, a yolk sac forms as a small outcropping on the embryo between the second and sixth weeks of embryonic development in the uterus. The walls of the yolk sac

serve as a temporary center for the development of blood cells.

Chorion The chorion is a membrane that develops from the trophoblast. At implantation, the trophoblast develops a thin membrane over its surface called the *chorion* (ko'-ree-on). From the chorion, projections, called *chorionic villi,* extend into the rich blood cavities of the endometrium. These villi become concentrated on the side of the trophoblast nearest the endometrium, and this mass of tissue formed by the intrusion of the villi into the endometrium becomes the placenta.

Placenta The placenta is the organ of exchange between the mother and the fetus. The placenta provides nutrients and oxygen from the mother's bloodstream and removes wastes from the fetus in the same manner. There is, however, no direct connection between the blood supply of the mother and that of the fetus. As the embryo develops, blood vessels extend from the embryo to the chorionic villi through the umbilical arteries and veins in the umbilical cord. Blood from the fetus flows into the chorionic villi and exchanges nutrients, oxygen, and wastes with the maternal blood through the membrane of the chorion. The maternal and fetal blood supplies do not have contact with each other, since all exchange takes place through this membrane of the chorion. The placenta also serves the important function of secreting certain hormones during pregnancy.

Amnion The amnion is a membrane which surrounds the entire embryo and begins to develop early in embryonic life. Between the amnion and the embryo is the *amniotic cavity*, which is filled with a clear *amniotic fluid.* This fluid is extremely important in that it keeps the embryo moist and acts as a shock absorber.

FETAL DEVELOPMENT

Pregnancy normally lasts for 40 weeks (280 days) when counted from the beginning of the last menstrual cycle. This period of *gestation* (pregnancy) is generally divided into three equal periods called *trimesters.* From the second to the eighth week following fertilization, the organism is called an embryo. From the second month until birth, the organism is a fetus. It is useful to review and summarize the development of the organism in terms of the processes which take place in each trimester.

The First Month

Very early in the first month, the basic cell structures of the embryo are forming. They consist of three basic cell layers: an innermost *endoderm,* a middle *mesoderm,* and an outer *ectoderm.* These cell layers give rise to the complex structure of the human fetus. During this time the fetal membranes and the placenta are also developing.

At four weeks, the embryo is about 0.2 inch long. Even though it is extremely small compared with the fetus, at birth it has already grown to be 10,000 times heavier than the zygote which made its way into the uterus. The head region of the embryo grows much faster than other regions and is overly large at this stage. By this time, the three primary regions of the brain have differentiated and the eyes, ears, and olfactory (smell) organs have started to develop. Limb buds, which will eventually become arms and legs, have just begun to develop. The gastrointestinal tract is developing and the liver, pancreas, and gallbladder are evident as small outgrowths from a primitive embryonic gut.

The Second Month

At two months, the embryo is about 1.2 inches long and weighs about 0.04 ounce. During the second month, the face forms with a prominent nose, lips, eyelids, cheeks, and ears (which at this stage of development are located in the neck region). Arms and legs are evident and fingers and toes are developing (Figure 3-11). A thin tail develops in the fifth week but soon lags behind the rest of the embryo in growth. The liver becomes large and the small intestine begins to take a coiled shape. Major blood vessels are in their final fetal position and the heart takes on its final shape. Muscles are in the process of developing and the brain begins

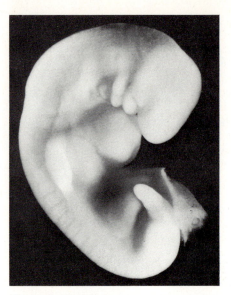

The embryo at 28 days.

to send impulses in the regulation of other organs during the second month. Some simple reflexes are also apparent during this period. The beginnings of external genital structures are evident but sex cannot be identified externally at this time.

The Third Month

By the third month, the embryo is usually called a *fetus.* By the end of this month, it is almost 2.2 inches long and weighs approximately 0.5 ounce. In this period, the external genital structures differentiate as male or female and the ears and eyes approach their final positions. Some of the bones become distinct and the fetus engages in breathing movements by pumping amniotic fluid in and out of the lungs.

The Second Trimester

By five months of development, the fetus weighs an average of 1 pound and is 10 inches long. The heart is beating at 150 beats per minute and can be heard with a stethoscope. The fetus is moving in the amniotic cavity, and during the fifth month, the mother becomes aware of this movement.

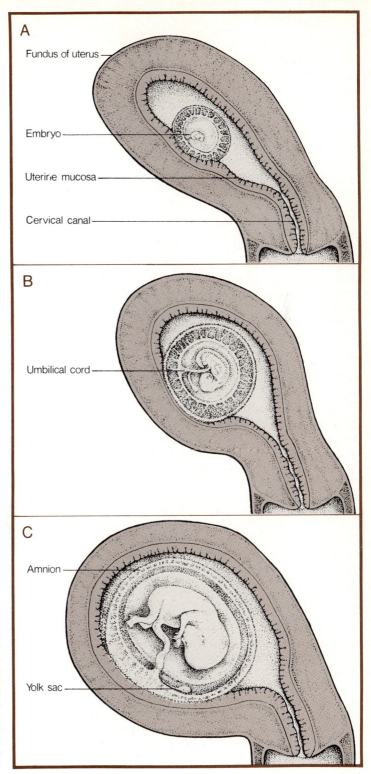

Figure 3-11 The development of the fetus, fetal membranes, and placenta. The embryo and membranes are the actual size shown, and the uterus is within the average size range. *(a)* Three weeks after fertilization. The embryo is implanted in the endometrium of the uterus (uterine mucosa). *(b)* Five weeks after fertilization. *(c)* Eight weeks after fertilization. (Based on Vander et al., 1980:507, figure 16-25.)

BOX 3-6

THE FETUS AS A FOREIGN BODY

The fetus and the placental unit are actually foreign bodies in the mother as far as the immunological system is concerned. Thus, the mother's body must go through some process in which the fetus is not rejected when implantation occurs or when the fetus begins to grow in the uterus. This is thought to take place at fertilization, and the protection element that protects the fetus against being regarded as a foreign element and being spontaneously aborted is believed to be contained in the trophoblast. It is thought that the immunological factors of the male (in the sperm) and the female (in the egg) react to form an "infection." This infection reaction is then seen as leading to the production of various substances that appear to dampen the mother's immune system from responding to the "foreign elements" from the male reproductive system. The fetus thus becomes an immunologically privileged tissue. It may be that if the male and female share certain antigens (foreign proteins to which the immune system reacts) spontaneous abortion results. It is thought that immunizing a woman before pregnancy with the male partner's blood may overcome this problem (Beer et al., 1981).

The Third Trimester

The last three months of gestation is a period of rapid growth and development. The final formation of the tissues and organs takes place. In the sixth month, the skin has a wrinkled appearance that will later diminish with fat deposits. If the fetus is born during the sixth month, it will almost certainly not survive because the brain has not developed enough to sustain such vital body functions as breathing. During the seventh month, the brain grows rapidly, the sucking and grasping reflexes are apparent, and the fetus may suck its thumb. Most of the body is covered with a downy hair called *lanugo* (la-noo'-go), which is usually shed before birth. During the last part of the third trimester, fat is deposited in the skin tissue and the wrinkled appearance is mostly lost. At birth, the full-term fetus weighs about 7 pounds and is about 20 inches long.

Sexual Differentiation

This section will probably take two readings to really understand. On the first reading, you will get an overall view; on the second time through, the gaps will be filled and the information will be clear.

Until the sixth or seventh week of embryonic development, the organism is not *sexually differentiated* in terms of anatomy and physiology. While the genetic sex of the fetus has already been determined by chromosome composition at the point of fertilization, the primitive gonad has not yet differentiated into male or female.

The gonad of the embryo has two connections to two separate systems of ducts; the *Wolffian ducts* that are a part of the developing urinary system, and the *Mullerian ducts*. If the early gonad differentiates into a testis, the Wolffian duct remains and develops into part of the male reproductive system. If the gonad develops into an ovary, the Mullerian duct system develops and forms a female reproductive system. As Money (1977:59) points out, "There is no doubt about it that nature's first disposition is to make a female." For a female reproductive structure to form, it is not necessary to have fetal gonads which will release hormonal secretions.

However, for a male reproductive system

to develop, it is absolutely essential to have fetal gonads which will release these hormonal substances, and these fetal gonads must be testes. In order for the fetus to develop a male reproductive structure, fetal testes must be present and they must release a so-called Mullerian-inhibiting substance which keeps the Mullerian duct from developing. This *prevents* the development of an oviduct and the uterus on that side (left or right). These fetal testes must also release a male hormonal substance that stops the Wolffian ducts from regressing, thus assuring the development of the male reproductive structures. Thus, something must happen to the fetal gonads for the formation of a male reproductive system and this something is the formation of fetal testes. If this does not happen, the natural path of development is the formation of a physiological female. It is quite accurate to say that in the process of sexual differentiation, the formation of a male reproductive system requires an alteration. Without that alteration taking place, the natural formation of the reproductive structures will produce a physiological and anatomical female.

Given that the early gonad is undifferentiated (is neither male nor female), the male and female reproductive structures come from the same embryonic tissues. As shown in Figure 3-12, the primitive external genital structure consists of a genital tubercle, a labio-scrotal swelling, a urogenital groove, and a urethro-labial fold. In the female, the genital tubercle becomes the clitoris. In the male, it becomes the penis. The labio-scrotal swelling becomes the labia majora in the female and the scrotum in the male. In the female, the urethro-labial fold remains open and becomes the labia minora; in the male, they close and become the penile urethra. Table 3-1 shows the exact homologous nature of male and female reproductive anatomy. The left-hand column lists the adult female anatomy and the right-hand column the adult male anatomy, which originates from the same embryonic tissue source.

Incomplete Differentiation

The development of fetal testes is not yet fully understood, but involves a process taking place in the short arm of the Y chromosome (chromosomally, males have a Y chromosome while females do not). If this process of differentiating the embryo into a male is not com-

TABLE 3-1

Adult male and female anatomical structures that develop from the same embryonic tissue.

Adult Female	Adult Male
Ovary	Testis
Vagina (upper portion)	Vagina musculina
Uterus	Prostatic utricle
	Appendix testis
Canals and ducts of Gartner	Seminal vesicles
	Vas deferens
	Epididymis
Bladder	Bladder
Urethra	Prostatic urethra
Vestibule	Penile urethra
Labia majora	Scrotum
Labia minora	Urethral tube of penis
Clitoris	Penis
Vestibular glands	Cowper's glands
Prostate gland	Prostate gland

Source: Sevely and Bennett (1978, table 1, p. 6).

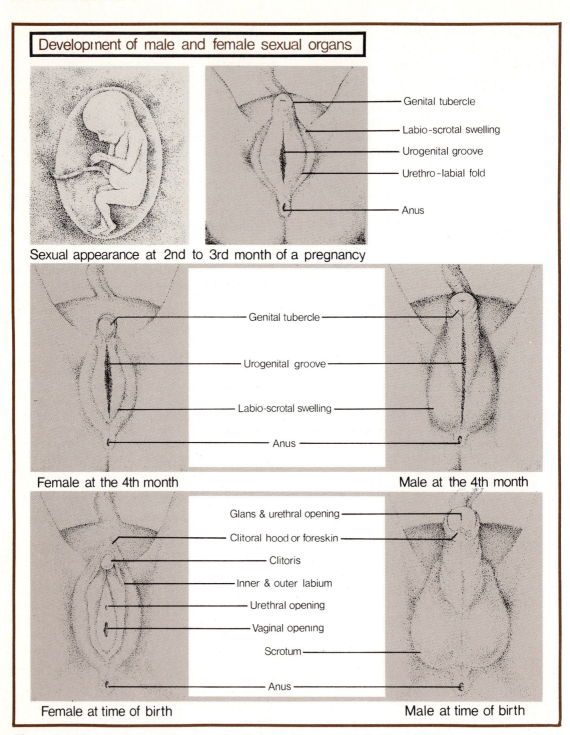

Development of male and female sexual organs

Sexual appearance at 2nd to 3rd month of a pregnancy

- Genital tubercle
- Labio-scrotal swelling
- Urogenital groove
- Urethro-labial fold
- Anus

Female at the 4th month   Male at the 4th month

- Genital tubercle
- Urogenital groove
- Labio-scrotal swelling
- Anus

Female at time of birth   Male at time of birth

- Glans & urethral opening
- Clitoral hood or foreskin
- Clitoris
- Inner & outer labium
- Urethral opening
- Vaginal opening
- Scrotum
- Anus

Figure 3-12 The development of male and female "sexual" organs up to the time of birth through the process of sexual differentiation.

pleted when the embryo is chromosomally a male (has a Y chromosome), the person will be born with some reproductive structure abnormality. These abnormalities may take many different forms as a result of many different sexual differentiation derangements. However, hermaphroditism and pseudohermaphroditism are perhaps the best known.

Hermaphroditism A true hermaphrodite is a person who has both ovarian and testicular tissue. In one-third of the cases of hermaphroditism, there is an ovary on one side (usually the left) and a testis on the other side. In 20 percent of the cases, the structures for the production of reproductive cells (sperm or egg) are mixed ovaries and testes (ovotestes) on both sides. In the remaining cases, there is an ovotestis on one side and an ovary *or* testis on the other. When an ovary is present, it is usually in the normal position and may even ovulate. A uterus is almost always present and is usually well developed. When a testis is present, it may be located in the scrotum, inguinal canal, or abdominal cavity. In true hermaphrodites, the external genitals are highly variable, ranging from rudimentary female external genitals to a mixture of male and female to rudimentary male genitals (Lev-ran, 1977). Classification of sex is most often made on the basis of genital appearance; this assessment sometimes does not match the person's chromosomal sex. We shall discuss the implications and outcomes of this in greater detail in Chapter 4.

Pseudohermaphroditism Pseudohermaphroditism is not true hermaphroditism, as the name implies. There are at least eleven different types of pseudohermaphroditism, depending on the exact cause. The defining characteristic of male pseudohermaphroditism is the presence of testicle tissue. Generally there is a partly or completely feminine body build with testes on both sides and XY chromosomes. Female pseudohermaphroditism is characterized by the presence of ovarian tissue. There are usually two ovaries, XX chromosomes, and normal development of the internal reproductive structures in conjunction with ambiguous (male or female?) external genitals (Lev-ran, 1977).

THE BIRTH PROCESS

As *parturition* (the birth process) approaches, the body does several things to prepare. After the seventh month, the placental secretions of estrogen increase. One of the results of this is that the contracting ability of the uterus is increased. A second effect is the enlargement of the vagina and a relaxation of the ligaments in the pelvic region.

As the fetus develops, the uterine walls are stretched. This stretching of uterine tissues is thought to cause the hypothalamus in the brain to send signals to the pituitary gland to release the hormone *oxytocin.* Oxytocin is an important factor in the stimulation of uterine contractions associated with the beginning of labor. *Labor* is the process of muscular contractions forcing the fetus through the birth canal (the cervix and vagina). Once labor begins, there are rhythmic contractions which start at the top of the uterus and travel downward, forcing the fetus toward the cervix. The fetus is normally in a head-down position, meaning that the head of the fetus is forced against the cervix. This pressure causes the cervix to stretch, an action thought to cause a reflex that stimulates even stronger uterine contractions. This process is aided by the dilation of the cervix, which is thought to create an increase in the release of oxytocin, causing increased contractions of the uterus.

Oxytocin stimulates the production of prostaglandins. These prostaglandins stimulate contractions of the uterus and cervix (recall our discussion of menstruation). Before oxytocin can stimulate the production of prostaglandins in the beginning of the birth process, the uterus and cervix must be sensitized to oxytocin. How this sensitizing occurs is not clearly understood. It does appear, however, that oxytocin in the birth process originates from both the fetus and the mother (Husslein et al., 1981; Fuchs et al., 1981).

We have already noted that the muscle structure of the uterus is unique in that muscle tissue runs in all directions so as to provide contractions in the pattern necessary for birth to take place. These muscle contractions must, however, be highly coordinated so as to push the fetus downward and out of the uterus. This coordination is aided by the presence of *gap junctions* in the muscle fibers of the uterus.

Gap junctions are contacts between cells and are the sites of low electrical resistance in the flow of electrical current between cells (all muscle contractions are due to the flow of electrical current or signals). When the cervix is closed (has no dilation) and there are few uterine contractions, there are few gap junctions in the uterus. As labor proceeds, the number of gap junctions increases. The appearance of these gap junctions with labor is thought to lead to effective termination of the pregnancy by allowing electrical events to occur throughout the uterine muscles. The increase in gap junctions is believed to result in muscle contractions throughout the uterus and cervix that are highly synchronized in such a manner as to effectively push the fetus out of the uterus and cervix (Garfield and Hayashi, 1981).

About ten to fifteen minutes after birth, the placenta separates from the uterine wall and is expelled through the birth canal. This is the *afterbirth,* and it is accompanied by bleeding due to the vascular damage in its separation from the uterus. This bleeding is minimized, however, by continuing contractions of the uterus that result in a restriction of the blood vessels.

The next several weeks following pregnancy result in the uterus returning to its normal size and the endometrium sloughing off and being discharged. Following this, the lining of the uterus returns to its condition prior to pregnancy.

THE MAMMARY GLANDS

The *mammary glands* are accessory female reproductive organs in that, even though not directly involved in reproduction itself, they are specialized to secrete milk following pregnancy.

The mammary glands are located in the

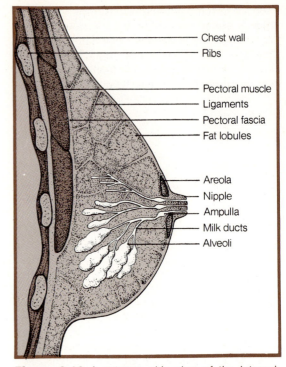

Figure 3-13 A cutaway side view of the internal structure of the female breast. The top half of the illustration shows the appearance of the breast when the woman is not pregnant. The bottom half of the illustration shows the appearance of the breast during pregnancy and while lactation continues. Note the enlargement of the alveoli when milk is being produced.

breasts, which are elevations that lie over the pectoral muscles and extend from the second to the sixth ribs. A *nipple* is located at the tip of each breast and is surrounded by a circular area of darker-colored skin called the *areola* (Figure 3-13).

The adult female mammary glands largely consist of masses, or lobules, of fat tissue. The amount of this fatty tissue determines the size of the breasts. Within each mammary gland are fifteen to twenty lobes, each containing *alveolar glands* which are tube-shaped and a *milk duct* which leads to the nipple. Near the nipple, these ducts are enlarged to form *ampulla.* These lobes are separated by connective tissue and fat lobules. The mammary glands are suspended from the chest wall by ligaments that extend from the skin of the breasts. The connective tissues also act as a support mechanism, being attached to the fascia of the pectoral muscles.

Development of the Breasts

Before puberty, the breasts of males and females are quite similar. As puberty is reached, the male mammary glands fail to develop and the female mammary glands are stimulated to growth by the secretion of hormones from the ovaries. In this breast development process, the alveolar glands and ducts enlarge and fat is deposited in the breasts.

Lactation

Lactation is the production of milk by the mammary glands. During pregnancy, high concentrations of estrogen and progesterone produced by the placenta stimulate the development of the glands and ducts in the mammary glands. Estrogen is responsible for the growth of the ducts (and the deposit of additional fat), while progesterone is responsible for the development of the alveoli (al-vee'-o-lee). During pregnancy, the mammary glands become capable of secreting milk but actually produce no milk. The reason is that even though the estrogen and progesterone stimulate gland and duct development, they also inhibit the hypothalamus. The inhibited hypothalamus in turn suppresses the secretion of the hormone prolactin on the part of the pituitary. It is prolactin which is responsible for the production of milk in the mammary glands. Following birth, the levels of estrogen and progesterone in the mother decline rapidly. The hypothalamus is no longer inhibited, and it sends a message to the pituitary to release prolactin, and the mammary glands begin producing milk. This hormonal effect takes place two or three days after birth. In the meantime, the glands in the breasts secrete a substance called *colostrum* which contains some of the nutrients in mother's milk but lacks fat.

The release of oxytocin is also controlled by the higher brain centers. Thus, a nursing mother may leak milk from the breasts when she hears her baby cry or some other psycho-

BOX 3-7
WET NURSES

Closely associated with the development of techniques for the vulcanization of rubber was the development of the infant feeding nipple. Since breast feeding of an infant is somewhat confining for the nursing mother, there were always wet nurses in Europe and America who were used by upper-class families. The wet nurses were women who were producing milk, usually because they had their own infant, and would sell their nursing services. In the late 1800s, wet nursing declined sharply and disappeared in the United States and Europe. The reason was twofold. First was the pasteurization of milk, which made it possible to give infants other than human milk without the danger of disease transmission. The second reason was the technology to deliver the nonhuman milk to the infant made possible by the vulcanization of rubber. From almost the time rubber was first vulcanized, rubber nipples appeared. The first American patent for a rubber nipple was granted on August 4, 1845, to Elijah Pratt. It was followed by numerous other patents, including nipples with long tubes and a pear-shaped bottle with an imitation breast worn by the mother (Bullough, 1980:66).

logical stimulation is present. Owing to this psychological effect, any number of sociopsychological factors can inhibit a woman's ability to nurse.

As long as milk is removed from the mammary glands, prolactin and oxytocin continue to be released by the pituitary. Milk thus continues to be produced and released. This process may continue for a number of years. Milk production ceases shortly after nursing stops.

Another significant hormonal action in lactation is that the suckling reflex action on the hypothalamus inhibits ovulation. This occurs, however, for only a short period of time and in only about 50 percent of all women. Lactation is therefore not an effective means of birth control.

The milk produced in the breasts does not simply flow out through the duct system. Because of the structure of the ducts, the infant cannot suck milk out of the alveoli. The milk must first be moved from the alveoli into the ducts, from which it can be sucked by the in-fant. This process is called *milk let-down* and works in the following manner. The alveoli are surrounded by specialized cells, called *myoepithelial cells.* These cells contract and force milk from the alveoli into the milk ducts. The contraction of these cells and the consequent ejection of milk into the ducts are the result of a reflex action. This reflex takes place when the breast is sucked or the nipple or areola is stimulated. The stimulation results in a sensory impulse being sent to the hypothalamus, which in turn signals the pituitary gland to secrete the hormone oxytocin. The oxytocin travels to the breasts through the bloodstream and stimulates the contraction of the epithelial cells. Milk is then ejected into the milk ducts. This process takes less than a minute from the beginning of stimulation. Since this reflex may be initiated by breast stimulation, milk may be ejected into the ducts with sexual arousal, and at orgasm, it may be released in squirts from the nipple (Mims and Swenson, 1980).

STUDY GUIDE

TERMS TO KNOW

Sexual anatomy	Septa	Emission
Penis	Rete testis	Retrograde ejaculation
Glans	Gubernaculum	Vulva
Prepuce	Inguinal canal	Mons pubis
Circumcision	Epididymis	Labia majora
Coronal ridge	Vas deferens	Labia minora
Frenulum	Seminal vesicles	Clitoris
Corpora cavernosa	Semen	Clitoral hood
Corpus spongiosum	Prostate gland	Vestibule
Crura	Ejaculation	Hymen
Scrotum	Bulbourethral glands	Perineum
Dartos muscle	Spermatogenesis	Bartholin's glands
Testis	Spermatogonia	Ovaries
Tunica albuginea	Acrosome	Uterine tubes

Fimbriae	Menopause	Alveolar glands (alveloi)
Ovarian fimbria	Climacteric	Lactation
Uterus	Ectopic pregnancy	Colostrum
Cervix	Identical twins	Milk let-down
Layers of uterus	Fraternal twins	Gap junctions
Vagina	Cojoined twins	Prostaglandin inhibitors
Ovulation	Placenta	Morula
Menarche	Sexual differentiation	Blastocyst
Menstrual cycle	Oxytocin	Implantation
Corpus luteum	Mammary glands	Capacitation

SELF TEST

Part I: True-False Statements

1. The penis and clitoris are both erectile organs.
2. The corpora cavernosa form the crura inside the body wall.
3. The gubernaculum serves to regulate the temperature of the testes.
4. Sperm are manufactured in the vas deferens.
5. The fluid of the seminal vesicles is actually sperm.
6. Spermatogenesis takes place in the seminiferous tubules.
7. Testosterone results in the secondary sexual characteristics of males.
8. Like the penis, the clitoris contains three columns of erectile tissue.
9. No part of the uterine tube touches the ovary.
10. The vagina is an open, tubular-shaped space.
11. Between one and three egg cells are produced in each menstrual cycle.
12. Menstrual flow begins because the corpus luteum dies owing to an egg cell's not being fertilized.
13. The sperm cell is unable to penetrate the egg cell at the time of ejaculation.
14. Fraternal twins result when two egg cells are produced at ovulation and each is fertilized by separate sperm cells.
15. There is a direct connection between the blood supply of the mother and that of the fetus through the placenta.
16. Male and female genitals develop from the same embryonic tissue.
17. The same tissue may become either a male penis or a female clitoris.
18. The high levels of estrogen and progesterone during pregnancy result in the production of milk in the mammary glands.
19. Milk continues to be produced in the mammary glands as long as it is removed from the glands.
20. Lactation is an effective means of birth control.

Part II: Multiple-Choice Questions
Select the best of the three alternatives.

1. The penile urethra runs through the *(a)* corpora cavernosa; *(b)* corpus spongiosum; *(c)* crura.

2. Most of the ejaculate or seminal fluid is made up of secretion from the *(a)* seminal vesicles; *(b)* testes; *(c)* prostate.
3. The entire process of cell division which results in sperm cells takes about *(a)* 30 days; *(b)* 12 days; *(c)* 72 days.
4. That part of the sperm responsible for secreting the enzyme that makes possible the penetration of the egg cell is *(a)* the acrosome; *(b)* the nucleus; *(c)* the centriole.
5. In ejaculation, the emptying of the contents of the ducts and glands into the urethra is *(a)* retrograde ejaculation; *(b)* lactation; *(c)* emission.
6. The physical changes which take place at puberty signal the *(a)* beginning of reproductive capacity; *(b)* beginning of sexual capacity; *(c)* beginning of sexual differentiation.
7. Protection of the female genitals is provided by the *(a)* labia majora; *(b)* labia minora; *(c)* perineum.
8. The glans is located on the tip of the *(a)* clitoris; *(b)* penis; *(c)* both the clitoris and penis.
9. An important support structure for the vagina and uterus is the *(a)* perineum; *(b)* dartos muscle; *(c)* ovarian ligament.
10. The lower one-third of the uterus is the *(a)* frenulum; *(b)* fundus; *(c)* cervix.
11. Female egg cell production begins *(a)* at puberty; *(b)* before birth; *(c)* shortly after birth.

TOPICS FOR DISCUSSION

1. Make a list of the four or five things you learned in this chapter that most surprised or impressed you. Then the males in your class should each read off their lists and the females in the class should each read off theirs. Compare the things listed by males and females; see whether any things were commonly listed by many people; discuss how the males' and females' lists differ, where they are the same, and why you think these differences and similarities exist in our society.
2. Make a list of the things you learned in this chapter that you previously had misconceptions about. In the beginning of the chapter, I said that one of the reasons we should understand anatomy is that knowledge of anatomy affects our sexual interaction. Think about how your misconceptions could have, or have, influenced your sexual interaction with another person (or even your own thoughts and actions about your own sexuality).

SUGGESTED READINGS

The best additional reading is in the form of some good college anatomy textbooks. They will supply you with more detailed discussion of many of the topics covered in this chapter. Some well-written and solid chapters are available in:

Vander, A. J., J. H. Sherman, and D. S. Luciano, *Human Physiology: The Mechanisms of Body Function.* New York: McGraw-Hill, 1980.

Solomon, E. P., and P. W. Davis, *Understanding Human Anatomy and Physiology.* New York: McGraw-Hill, 1978.

Hole, J. W., Jr., *Human Anatomy and Physiology.* Dubuque, Iowa: Wm. C. Brown, 1978.

KEY TO SELF-TEST QUESTIONS

Part I: True-False Statements

1. T (Both are composed of erectile tissue and become erect during arousal.)
2. T (This is the case in both the penis and clitoris.)
3. F (The dartos muscle does this. The gubernaculum is thought to move the testes to their final location when they descend.)
4. F (They are manufactured in the seminiferous tubules.)
5. F (The fluid of the seminal vesicles aids in nutrition for the sperm and in neutralizing the acidity of the female reproductive tract.)
6. T
7. T
8. F (The clitoris contains two, the penis three. The penis contains the corpus spongiosum, through which runs the penile urethra.)
9. F (One of the fimbriae does touch the ovary.)
10. F (It is a potential space but becomes an open space only when the walls move apart.)
11. F (One egg cell is produced in each menstrual cycle. In rare occasions, two will be produced. What happens then?)
12. T (When the corpus lutuem continues to survive, high estrogen levels are maintained and the lining of the uterus continues to be supplied with a rich flow of nutrients so that implantation can take place.)
13. T (Sperm cells are not capable of penetrating the egg cell until they are capacitated by some unknown process supplied by the female reproductive system.)
14. T (See answer 11 above. They are fraternal and not identical twins because of two sperm cells and two egg cells. How are identical twins produced?)
15. F (They each have their own separate blood supply and only share nutrient and waste exchange through the placenta.)
16. T (Whether the fetus will be male or female in terms of genital structure is the process of sexual differentiation.)
17. T
18. F (The production of milk in the mammary glands is the result of prolactin.)
19. T
20. F (It may have this function, but is simply not effective or dependable as a contraceptive technique.)

Part II: Multiple-Choice Questions

1. *b* (Two cavernosa as in the clitoris and one spongiosum not in the clitoris.)
2. *c* 3. *c* 4. *a*
5. *c* (This is the first of two stages in ejaculation.)
6. *a* (Sexual capacity takes place much, much earlier and has nothing to do with reproductive capacity in an anatomical or a physiological sense.)
7. *a* (The outer lips of the vagina fold over the internal genital structure.)
8. *c* (Again, more similarities than differences exist between males and females.)
9. *a* (A major support structure.)
10. *c* (Frenulum is the underside of the circumcised penis and fundus is the upper portion of the uterus.)
11. *b* (Unlike the male, the female begins egg cell production before birth. Egg cells do not mature and result in the process of ovulation until puberty. What is menarche?)

Chapter 4
Becoming Sexual

How is it that people come to have an interest in sex and develop patterns and preferences of sexual behaviors? Further, why is there diversity among people in both the level of sexual interest and the types of sexual conduct? In short, how is it that people become sexual beings of a certain form?

BECOMING SEXUAL: NATURE OR NURTURE

If there is any single issue which can be called "the debate" about human behavior, it is the question of nature versus nurture. The basic question in this debate is whether human behavior is determined more (and to what extent) by biological factors, or nature—or by learning, or nurture. Currently, this argument is raging full steam in the field of human sexuality. While some argue that sexuality stems from biological forces within the individual, others contend that sexuality is the result of learning.

Sexuality as Biologically Determined
The view that sexuality is driven or directed by some *natural biological force* has been popular in Western culture for centuries. It is thus

not surprising that this view finds widespread acceptance today. Throughout history, however, opinions have differed about the nature of this biological sexual force.

Who has it? There has frequently been disagreement over time about who, if anyone, has the most of this biological sexual force. The early Hebrews thought that females were innately more sexual than males, while the Victorians left us with the notion that males are naturally more sexual than women.

What does it do? There have also been changes over the years in opinions about the effect of this natural biological force. In many periods in history, this natural sexual urge was thought to push one down a path of perversion, degradation, or at least undesirable forms of behavior. Today, the popular view is that one's natural sexuality is an expression of an essential human quality, and is thus good and healthy. Whether this natural biological sexual urge is seen as resulting in positive or negative outcomes depends, of course, upon the large view of sexuality in society.

Where is it? Ideas about the exact location of this natural biological force have also varied over time. The most popular and influential statement of sexuality as biologically determined was that of Freud. Freud argued that the sexual instinct was just that, an instinctual force common to all humans. This instinctual force, he said, takes the form of sexual or libidinal energy inside the individual which has to be expressed in some manner (the analogy of a steam engine is appropriate here). The way in which this sexual energy is expressed and reacted to determines virtually all aspects of human existence, in Freud's view, including individual personality, individual behavior, and the shape of civilizations. Freud, however, never discussed the exact location of this powerful biological force. If this sexual force is a basic aspect of a human's innate makeup, it must be located somewhere in the body. It must be observable. As in the case of all instinct theories, however, Freud never concerned himself with this issue. Rather, the vague concept of a sexual instinct was used to account for behaviors which he observed. As such, the concept of a sexual instinct—or any instinct—remains a mythical creature, a sort of sexual hobgoblin scurrying around inside the individual, never to be observed or measured.

The contemporary view Today, the location of the biological force thought to be responsible for human sexuality is somewhat more specific than in Freud's theories. The natural biological sexual force is now said to be hormones which influence sexual interest and behavior through the body chemistry.

Hormones are argued to influence human sexuality in two ways. First, absolute amounts of a hormone are assumed to determine the absolute amount of "sex drive" of an individual. In this view, individuals with high levels of certain hormones are thought to have a stronger "sex drive" than individuals with lower levels of these hormones. A cautious modification of this concept is that there is a certain minimum hormone level that must be present in an individual's body for the person to have sexual interest and engage in sexual behavior. Second, hormones are thought to influence human sexuality in a fluctuating manner. As the level of certain hormones fluctuates on a day-to-day or hour-to-hour basis, the sex drive

of the individual is believed to fluctuate accordingly. One popular form of this fluctuating hormone view is that sexual desire in females is assumed to vary over the menstrual cycle as the level of certain hormones changes (discussed in detail later in this chapter).

Sex As Learned

The view that sexuality is learned takes a variety of forms. Some argue that biological factors account for the individual's general level of sexual interest, but that learning determines the way in which that interest is expressed. In this view, learning is seen as a kind of tinting or directing of a biologically determined sex drive. At the other extreme of the learning argument are those who contend that biological factors have nothing to do with what we call "sex drive" or the direction any level of sexual interest takes. Rather, both the level of a person's interest in sex and the behavioral direction that interest takes is learned. From this standpoint, the only aspects of sexuality which are biologically determined are anatomical. In order to engage in penile-vaginal intercourse, a penis must be placed inside a vagina. If, how, why, and how often these organs come together is seen as determined by learning.

What Is the Answer?

Quite honestly, we do not for certain know the answer. We simply do not yet have enough scientific data to be able to say with certainty whether biology or learning is more important. Actually, the question is not even this simple. It is really one of how much which biological factors influence what aspects of sexuality, and how much learning affects which aspects of sexuality.

Biological Evidence

The evidence relating to biological factors affecting sexuality comes from two general types of studies; those conducted on animals other than humans and those conducted on humans.

Nonhuman animal studies There are

many studies which reveal that certain parts of the brain are responsible for controlling certain hormone levels in both nonhuman and human animals. There is also a fair amount of data indicating that these hormone levels directly affect sexual activity in nonhuman animals. The very important question is, What is done with these nonhuman findings? To leap from *observations of monkeys and rats* to *statements about humans* is a *very risky leap* for a number of reasons.

1. Even the studies on the effects of sex hormones on primates leave a great many unanswered questions (Davidson, 1978). When these unanswered questions are considered, it is apparent that the extent and manner in which hormones influence primate sexual behavior are not as clear as some writers would have you believe.

2. Many of the studies of nonhuman animals fail to find the same hormone effects in all mammals. For example, many of the effects hormones are observed to have on the sexual behavior of rats are not duplicated in monkeys. Thus, it appears that it is even difficult to make accurate generalizations from one nonhuman species to another, let alone from nonhumans to humans.

3. It is clear that sexual activity in nonhuman primates is largely (but by no means totally) a reflex process. That is, a given stimulus (for example, hormone level or scent) somewhat automatically produces a given sexual response. Human behavior in general involves fewer reflex processes and many more complex thought processes. In general, we find that as we move up the evolutionary ladder toward humans, reflex becomes less important and learning becomes more important, owing to the increasing dominance of those parts of the brain responsible for thought. It may well be that few, if any, of the findings about the sexual behavior of primates or rats apply to human conduct for this reason alone.

Human studies The most damaging evidence for the idea that hormones control human sexual behavior comes, however, from direct studies of humans. Despite frequent popular reports of how scientists have isolated this or that hormone which determines sexual interest and activity, the most recent research consistently reveals that hormone levels are not related to human sexuality. Some examples of recent research illustrate the general nature of these findings.

Benkert et al. (1979) divided a group of twenty-nine males who were unable to get an erection into two groups. To one group they administered daily doses of testosterone (a male sex hormone), and to the second, daily doses of a placebo. At the end of the study period, the "cure" rate for the two groups was not significantly different.

Brown et al. (1978) measured the naturally occurring level of testosterone in a sample of males and plotted this measurement against sexual interest and activity for one week. Over this time, there was no significant relationship between hormone level and either sexual interest or activity.

Persky et al. (1978b) examined the level of estradiol (es-tra-dy'-ol), the principal female estrogen hormone produced in the ovaries, in a sample of married women twice a week for three consecutive menstrual cycles. Several measures of sexual interest, arousal, and activity were also obtained twice weekly. The results revealed no relationship between estradiol levels and any of the measures of sexual interest, arousal, or activity.

In a similar study, Persky et al. (1978a) obtained twice-weekly measures of progesterone and estradiol hormone levels from married women and testosterone levels in women and their husbands. Examination of the relationship between these hormone levels and several measures of sexual interest, arousal, and activity over three menstrual cycles failed to reveal any relationship for either males or females.

Evan and Distiller (1979) tested the actual effects of the luteinizing-releasing hormone (a chemical that occurs naturally in the brain and that is known to activate certain sex hormone levels) on the sexual arousal of males. Males were injected with luteinizing-releasing hormone, and their sexual arousal was measured physiologically while they were viewing an erotic film. Although the luteinizing-releasing hormone did, in fact, alter the level of certain sex hormones in the men, it had no effect on sexual arousal. Abplanalp et al. (1979) obtained precise measures of estrogen levels several times a week and examined them in relation to both the frequency and the enjoyment of heterosexual activities. No relationship was found. Scheiner-Engel et al. (1981) examined the relationship between estradiol, progesterone, and testosterone and two different measures (self-report and physiological) of sexual arousal in women when shown sexual stimuli. They found no significant relationship between any of the hormone levels and either measure of sexual arousal.

These studies all deal with fluctuating or circulating hormone levels. It may be the case that certain absolute levels of hormones are required for sexual interest and activity to be present, and that beyond this minimal level, the amount of hormone is irrelevant. However, there is also no convincing support for this idea either. For example, Heim (1981) found that 73 percent of a sample of rapists who had been castrated (had their testes, and thus the source of the hormone testosterone, removed) still masturbated and engaged in intercourse. While it is reported periodically that injections of testosterone in males create sexual interest and activity, these reports are suspect in light of more carefully controlled studies. The same evidence is available in the case of females. Repeatedly, recent studies have reported (see Chapter 16) that removing women's ovaries (and thus the source of estrogen) does not necessarily result in a decline in either sexual interest or activity. In fact, many of these studies find an increase in sexual desire and activity after such surgical procedures.

Thus, even though the idea that sexual interest and activity are biologically determined is part of a long tradition in Western culture (Chapter 1), there is simply no consistent support for such a notion.

Evidence for Learning

The evidence that the amount and direction of one's sexual interest are the result of learning is overwhelming. In fact, this evidence will be reviewed from topic to topic throughout most of this text. It is thus not possible in the space of a few pages to pull together all the research on the effects of learning on sexuality. However, the rest of this chapter will discuss two major aspects of sexual learning. The first is how learning in general takes place. The second is an overview of major characteristics of sexual learning in American society. Throughout the rest of the text, we shall see numerous examples of these two discussions as we move from one aspect of human sexuality to another.

SEXUAL LEARNING

What we learn (sexually or otherwise) is a function of two basic factors: (1) the nature of the *social environment* in which we live; and (2) the *specific learning experiences* we have in that social environment. The social environment is important for sexual learning because it determines what is likely to be learned. It makes a great difference whether you live in Dani, Mangaian, or American society simply in terms of the content of sexual learning available. The individual's specific learning experiences are important because they determine what particular aspects of all that is available in a culture will actually be learned. Not everyone in a society learns everything.

The Social Environment

The way in which the social environment affects what we learn sexually is more clearly understood if we understand the social environment at three different, but related, levels: the *society* in which we live, the *groups and social categories* to which we belong, and our *unique individual learning history*.

Society Every individual is a member of a society. In that society, there is a set of rules and definitions (some unwritten, some written in the form of laws or religious principles) concerning proper sexuality. Each society has what can be considered its own definition of what sexuality is and how it is done. A very large part of our sexual learning is acquired by learning sexuality as defined in the society of which we are a member.

It is often very difficult to stand back and look objectively at sexuality in our own culture since we have learned what our society defines as proper sexuality so well that sexuality as we do it seems natural or "the only way." It is thus helpful to examine sexuality in other cultures much different from our own. In doing so, we gain some perspective on our own patterns of learned sexuality and we clearly see how much being a member of a certain society determines what one will do sexually.

The Grand Valley Dani of Indonesia (Heider, 1976) have what most Americans would see as little interest in sexual activity. Intercourse does not take place before marriage and usually does not occur in marriage until two years after the couple establish their own residence. After a woman has given birth, a married couple will not have intercourse for a period of four to six years. During this period, they do not engage in any other form of sexual activity. We look at this pattern of sexual frequency and probably think that the Dani must either have some very strong enforcement procedures or, like the ideal Victorian male, have an abundance of will power. This, however, is not the case. The Dani do not see their behavior as involving a lack of sex and do not experience stress, anxiety, tension, or other reactions. They behave this way because they have learned to behave this way and thus see their behavior as perfectly normal. Having learned something different about how frequently a person is supposed to "need" sex and what happens if one goes without sex for six years, most American adults probably see the Dani as a little strange.

At the other end of the sexual activity continuum are the Mangaia of Polynesia, for whom sex is a very enjoyable and frequent part of life. Beginning in early adolescence, males and females take an avid interest in intercourse. Women always orgasm during intercourse and demand that males be able to maintain contin-

uous coital activity for an extended time. To meet this social expectation, it is not unusual for males to engage in intercourse three or four times a night, five or six nights a week, with orgasm in each intercourse session (see Box 4-1).

Why these vast differences among cultures? These different peoples are all human beings. As far as we know, there are no brain-structure or hormone differences between middle-class Americans, the Grand Valley Dani, and the Mangaia which would explain the differences in their sexual interest and behavior. The way in which these peoples do differ is that they are members of different cultures that have different definitions of appropriate and expected sexual interest and activity. These peoples differ because they have learned to behave sexually in different ways. The Grand Valley Dani have not learned to "repress a natural sexual urge," nor have the Mangaia "let a natural sexual urge run free." Rather, different cultures have developed and transmitted to each generation a particular set of expectations for what is regarded in that culture as normal sexual behavior. Such diversity from one culture to the next strongly suggests that sex is not a biological force, but that human beings are incredibly adaptable in their behavior as a function of learning that certain patterns of sexual behavior are "the way." As we shall see, there is also great diversity in American society—diversity which can be linked to different learning experiences.

Given these differences among cultures and the differences among individuals within a culture, it becomes apparent that the concept of sex drive as some mysterious biological force within the individual is not an accurate representation of why humans have differing levels of sexual interest and activity. While biological factors such as absolute minimum levels of certain hormones may be somewhat important, the vast diversity in human sexual behavior appears to be a result of learning.

Social groups and categories   Even though, as Americans, we are all members of American society, we are also members of particular social categories and groups which are part of the large society. We may be black,

BOX 4-1
TOO MUCH IN RHODE ISLAND

What is perfectly normal and expected behavior in one culture is perfectly abnormal and problematic in another. Perhaps the clearest example I have seen of this was a case reported in the *Journal of The American Medical Association* in 1979 (Volume 242: 284–285). In the question-and-answer section of the *Journal* where physicians with problem cases write in and ask for advice from experts, a physician from Rhode Island reported on a young married man with an "insatiable sexual drive." This 29-year-old man suffered intense pain in his left testicle if he did not engage in intercourse at least two or three times a day. The inquiring physician reported that he had tried several drug treatments and that examination by a psychiatrist and an internist had not been helpful.

In the advice given by two responding physicians, we see several aspects of the American view of sex relative to that in Mangaia. Both physicians who gave advice clearly felt that the man's behavior was pathological; he was assumed to have some yet undiscovered physical "problem" or some psychological disturbance. Neither physician suggested that the man's behavior was due to learning. Rather, his frequency of sexual intercourse was seen as "abnormal" and some "abnormal" physical or psychological condition was assumed to be the cause. One advising physician suggested an elaborate series of tests for physical disorders and then recommended that if they revealed nothing, "more exhaustive psychiatric study" was probably needed. He noted that "such states" most commonly represent "a disturbed emotional situation stemming from factors" which are "latent" and "hidden" (even though one cannot find anything wrong, it must be there because his behavior was seen as so abnormal). The second advising physician immediately assumed that the couple's frequency of intercourse was associated with marital conflict and that the man's behavior represented aggression and hostility. The patient is described by this adviser as directing hostility in the form of sex against his wife. In Mangaia, this married man would be seen as simply doing what he was expected to do, and any less frequent sexual activity on his part might well be interpreted as "directing hostility toward his wife."

white, or Hispanic; male or female; Catholic, Jewish, or Protestant; rich or poor; young or old. Even though each of these social categories and groups is a part of the larger society, each is distinguished by its own definitions of how and what sexuality is. Generally, these are slight variations within the larger societal view of sexuality, but they are very important variations nonetheless. Being raised female results in learning a view of sexuality which has much in common with the male view, but also results in very different sexual learning. As we shall see in the next few pages, the single most important social group or category of membership in American society as far as sexuality is concerned is gender. Western culture has a long tradition of defining male and female sexuality as different. As a result, the patterns of sexual learning for males and females differ greatly. Consequently, patterns of sexual behavior, attitudes, and values differ for males and females in American society.

Individual learning history Each of us also has a unique individual learning history which is not directly a function of being a member of a particular society or subgroup within that society. Two individuals, for example, may both be members of American society, be of the same sex, age, ethnicity, religion, and social class, and yet have somewhat different individual learning histories which result in very different patterns of sexual attitudes and behaviors.

The content of sexual learning for individuals is thus a function of the individual's social learning environment. This consists of being a member of a certain society, belonging to certain groups and social categories in that society, and having unique individual sexual learning histories. This means that there is much sexual learning which all Americans share by virtue of being members of the same society. It also means that there is much sexual learning they do not share by virtue of being members of different social groups and categories. Last, it means that even if two individuals in the same society are virtually identical in their membership in social groups and categories, their sexualities will not be identical because they will have experienced somewhat different and unique learning histories.

Sexual Scripts

In understanding the sexual learning which a person acquires as a member of a society and of particular social groups and categories within that society, the concept of sexual script is of central importance (Gagnon, 1974; Gagnon and Simon, 1973; Gagnon, 1977).

A sexual script is analogous to the script for a play or movie. It is the overall blueprint of what sexuality is and of how it is practiced in a society or subgroup. Sexual scripts are much simpler than actual behavior because they are stated in general form and seldom take into account the wide range of differences in individuals and situations. Sexual scripts thus serve as the general guideline for sexuality, but not as a detailed roadmap showing all the detours, potholes, and delightful experiences along the way.

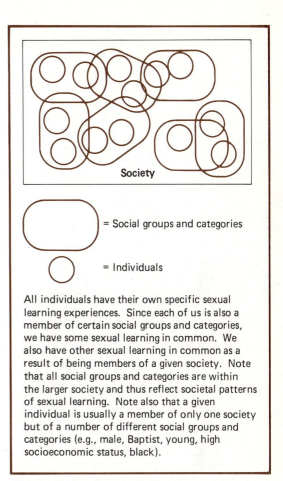

All individuals have their own specific sexual learning experiences. Since each of us is also a member of certain social groups and categories, we have some sexual learning in common. We also have other sexual learning in common as a result of being members of a given society. Note that all social groups and categories are within the larger society and thus reflect societal patterns of sexual learning. Note also that a given individual is usually a member of only one society but of a number of different social groups and categories (e.g., male, Baptist, young, high socioeconomic status, black).

Figure 4-1 Levels of sexual learning.

Some aspects of the sexual script are not obvious. As members of a particular society, most people learn their culture's sexual scripts quite well. Consequently, we seldom see our sexual behavior in the objective and removed fashion as would a person from another culture. As members of a society, we believe in and follow the dominant sexual script and are usually not even aware of its existence unless called upon to take an objective look at what our sexual behavior is all about—such as we do in a human sexuality class.

A large part of sexual learning for individuals is thus learning the sexual script of the society and subgroup of which they are members. A very large part, in fact, of becoming an acceptable member of a society is learning what that society defines as proper sexuality and behaving accordingly.

Parts of the Sexual Script

The sexual script designates the whom, what, when, where, and why of sexuality (Gagnon, 1977).

Whom   As members of a society, we learn *whom* one does and does not do sexual things with. In American society, the dominant sexual script presently contains such "whom" designations as a person of the other sex, who is about the same age, and who has certain marital, ethnic, social class, and blood relationship characteristics (Gagnon, 1977). The whom we do sexual things with also depends on what those sexual things are. One may appropriately talk about one's past sexual experiences with a person of the same sex but not with a first date or with one's parents. A married man may go to a Nevada house of prostitution with a group of his male friends, but he does not have sex with his wife when these same friends are present. Sexual scripts are not engraved in stone—they do change. One of the apparent changes is in the age of partners. In recent years, the restrictions on age differences between sexual partners have declined somewhat.

What   The sexual script also designates the *what* of sexuality. Many individual characteristics and behaviors which are defined as sexual in our culture are not seen as such in other cultures, and vice versa. Not all cultures share the American enthusiasm for female breasts, and while we emphasize hugging and kissing as taking place prior to genital activity, many cultures see such activities as unimportant or downright funny.

When   The *when* of the sexual script has a more powerful influence on sexual behavior than we often realize. Part of the when of our culture's sexual script designates when in the life cycle one is supposed to be a "sexual

person." In the traditional sexual script in American society, one is not supposed to be sexually active before puberty or in the period we call old age. Actual sexual behavior is dramatically influenced by these social definitions of when sexuality should take place. As we shall see, there is no biological reason why persons do not engage in intercourse before puberty. Most Americans do not do so, however, because they have learned the when of the sexual script very well. Again, we see changes in the sexual script with the recent emphasis on the appropriateness of sexual activity for elderly persons. The when of the sexual script also defines other dimensions of the timing of sexual activity. For example, how many times should a male and a female college student go out before they engage in intercourse? Even more specifically, the sexual script designates the daily timing of sex. How frequently are people expected to want to have intercourse? One is supposed to engage in sex at certain times of the day, and sex at other times generally contains a strong element of excitement.

Where   The *where* of sexuality is also an important part of the sexual script. In American society, sexual activity is closely associated with the concept of privacy. A male would never consider having intercourse with a female in the presence of her parents (even if they should approve), and sexual activity is typically confined to private places such as bedrooms. Among the Mangaia, however, unmarried men and women engage in intercourse in the same room as the one where her parents are supposedly sleeping. Locations for sexual activity are also designated in the where of the sexual script. Intercourse is possible in almost any physical setting. In American society, however, a bed is considered more appropriate than the front lawn or the dining room table.

Why   The *why* of the sexual script is perhaps one of the most fascinating aspects of sexual learning. The why involves the learned reasons for engaging in various forms of sexual conduct. Since most of us have learned our culture's sexual script well, we are likely to suggest that learning why one is interested in sex is nonsense. We all know why. You are either horny or sharing deep emotional expression and communication in the form of love. Many cultures, however, find these reasons simply silly. The Mangaia, for example, cannot understand what liking someone has to do with intercourse since they make no connection between sexual activity and affection. In fact, the Mangaia would probably argue that we are a little confused on what comes first, sex or love. In Mangaian society, one would never think of liking someone of the opposite sex unless one had first engaged in intercourse with her or him. Even in our own culture, the learned reasons for engaging in sex vary across social categories and groups. Males, for example, are much more likely to state that a "need" for sex is a reason, while females are much more likely to state that the expression and symbolizing of love are why one wants sexual activity.

The Individual in Society and Society in the Individual

At first glance, we might feel that the concept of a sexual script is removed from the individual and how he or she personally feels about sexuality—that the sexual script refers to something "out there," while the important location of sexuality is the individual. This is not what the concept means. Not only are we in society, but society is in us. As members of a particular society, we learn our society's sexual script and the sexual scripts of the social groups and categories of which we are members. We do not just learn this script, however, the way we learn bus schedules. We learn bus schedules as a matter of necessity. We do not believe in them in the sense that we think they are the only right bus schedules in the world and that to not have this kind of schedule is a moral issue.

When we learn the sexual script, however, we do feel this way. As members of a society, we learn that how our society defines sexuality is the *one* way sexuality is really supposed to be. We believe in the sexual scripts, we internalize them. They become—through learning— *our* way of doing sexuality, not just a set of

bus schedules out there to which we conform with reluctance and necessity. We learn that the sexual script is the right way to do sexuality and we internalize this idea so strongly that deviations from the script may often result in feelings of guilt (about our own behavior) or feelings of moral indignation and disgust (about others' behavior). For example, most of us react with no small amount of bad feeling when we read (Chapter 15) about 11-year-old male and female prostitutes. Even less extreme examples illustrate the point. Since the dominant sexual script in American society is heterosexual, visualize clearly in your mind two males engaged in sexual activity and think about how you feel, or think about your reaction to an 18-year-old female college student who has intercourse with two males at once. These reactions are due to the fact that you have been socialized into American society and have internalized a certain sexual script. This script is not universal among all peoples of the world and even differs slightly from one person to another in this culture (not all of you had the same reaction to these examples). The sexual script is not simply something out there. It is something which exists before we get here and which becomes a central part of us as we learn to be members of this society and of particular groups and social categories within this society.

How We Learn

We do not acquire sexual learning by, at age 13, picking up a copy of *The Sexual Script* at our local newstand and reading the "How to Be a Sexual Person in American Society" chapter. Rather, sexual learning takes place through the same specific learning processes by which we learn anything.[1] These processes are in the form of types of learning.

[1] Actually, with the greater discussion of sex since the 1970s, this has become more of a possibility. For example, almost monthly, *Cosmopolitan* has at least one article on sex. The problem with such media communications is that they often serve the function of entertainment for the reader and, in doing so, fail to provide an accurate representation of what most Americans consider appropriate. For example, group sex may make for good reading but is not going to find wide acceptance throughout most of society.

Instrumental or operant learning

A major learning process occurs when we are reinforced for engaging in certain behaviors and not reinforced, or even punished, for engaging in other behaviors. If we are reinforced for engaging in a behavior, we are likely to repeat that behavior. This is more than a matter of pigeons pecking a button to get more corn. Reinforcement makes people feel good. It creates positive feelings about yourself, about the behavior, and about the person who provides the reinforcement. Thus, through instrumental learning, reinforcement (so called because engaging in the behavior is instrumental in getting the reinforcement) not only creates a greater chance that you will repeat the behavior, but you come to like the behavior as well.

For example, a young male makes a comment to his male peers about the appearance, actions, or physical characteristics of a female. His male friends reinforce him for this behavior by means of agreeing with him or accepting him as "one of the guys." It is likely that not only will he say such things in the future, but that he will like saying such things and like the characteristics of females to which he is referring. In this repeated process, he is learning what female characteristics are sexually attractive. Much the same process takes place in dating. Through sexual interaction in dating, one learns what behaviors are part of "proper" sexuality and learns to develop a liking or disliking for these behaviors, depending on whether our partner gives reinforcement or punishment. The nature of the reinforcement and punishment in these situations is, it should be noted, generally subtle in the form of cues which indicate approval or disapproval.

Imitation and observational learning

We do not have to engage in any overt behavior to learn about sexuality. We learn a considerable amount about sexuality merely by observing others. In one form of learning by observation, we learn by imitating. We observe what others do, and if they are people we admire or want to be like, we may imitate their behavior. In this case, the mere imitation of the behavior is rewarding because we are being like someone we admire. We may also learn by observing the behavior of others and noting that it is reinforced. For example, we watch television or the movies or read advertisements and note that people with certain behavior patterns or characteristics are valued or directly reinforced. We are learning that these are sexually valuable and important characteristics, not through our own behavior but by observing the behavior of others and the reinforcement of that behavior.

Classical conditioning

Sexual learning also takes place by means of classical conditioning. In this learning process, something that has no sexual meaning is consistently paired with something that does have sexual meaning. After repeated pairing, that which had no sexual value comes to take on the sexual value attached to the other object or event, even in the absence of the original object or event that had sexual meaning. In this manner, people may learn to be sexually aroused by things which are not normally considered sexual and would thus not produce reinforcement from others for responding to them in a sexual manner. For example, bearskin rugs do not create sexual arousal in most people, and it is very unlikely that your parents or peers are going to reinforce you for being sexually aroused by a bearskin rug. Assume, however, that you have a series of delightful sexual experiences on a bearskin rug. After continual pairing of the bearskin rug with the pleasurable sexual experience, it is likely that the bearskin rug may come to elicit mild sexual arousal on your part. It is in this way that people probably come to be sexually aroused by anything from pain to shoes (Rachman, 1966; Rachman and Hodgson, 1968).

Stimulus generalization

Learning to think of something as sexually appropriate, sexually arousing, or sexually meaningful may also take place without one's ever having been in contact with that particular object or event. When we learn to attach sexual meaning to something, be it an object or event, we also generalize that sexual meaning to similar stimuli. An example of stimulus generalization is provided in a study of classical conditioning by Rachman (1966). This researcher conditioned males to be sexually aroused by shoes. He did so by pairing pictures of shoes with erotic slides, and after repeated pairing, the shoes alone were accompanied by sexual arousal. This learned response to pictures of shoes did not, however, take place for only shoes, but for all shoelike apparel. The response was generalized to similar stimuli.

Trials and intensity   In all these learning processes, the certainty of the learning is influenced by two factors: the *number of learning trials* and the *intensity of the experience.* In most cases, it is unlikely that much learning will take place with one incident (one trial). If, however, the same experience occurs time after time, the learning of a particular piece of information is quite likely. The intensity of the learning experience also influences learning. A mere passing observation of some behavior may result in no learning at all, while having one's total existence momentarily encompassed in a particular situation of high intensity results in considerable learning. In fact, a one-trial learning experience of high intensity can result in a very powerful learning experience. As we shall see, rape is such an experience. Even though a person may experience only one incident of rape, the intensity of the classical conditioning which takes place in the rape situation results in learning that is difficult to overcome readily.

The Structure of Sexual Learning

So far, this discussion may sound as though sexual learning is highly structured, that it takes place in the form of a neat, almost sterile package. Such a view is not appealing to most people because it suggests that people are simply rats or pigeons. Human learning is, however, far more complex and less controlled than that of the laboratory rat. A second misconception about sexual learning is that it develops in some *developmental sequence* or straight-line manner. It has been popular since Freud's time to think of learning, particularly

Imitation is an important form of learning for children.

sexual learning, as taking place in *developmental stages.* In this view, the child learns a certain thing in stage 1 and then something else in stage 2, and so on. While this is a nice clean model of how learning might occur, it does not match what really happens.

Learning takes place in bits and pieces, and the bits and pieces do not necessarily follow a neat progression in which this bit of learning is added to that bit of learning. Rather, we learn this little bit here and another little bit there. Some of these pieces fit together nicely, while others may not fit together at all.

Learning takes place at different times for different individuals. Owing to the differences in our learning environments and experiences, one person may learn at age 5 what another person learns at age 10. A very large part of the differential sexual outlooks of people is simply due to the differences between individuals in sexual learning opportunities because of different social environments.

In any learning, including sexual learning, the individual is not just a passive receptacle, but an active agent. Prior learning affects later learning. By the mere fact that you have certain learning experiences, you are more or less likely to stay away from, or actively attempt to be involved in, certain sexual learning situations. These decisions on your part have a strong impact on what you are likely to learn. Also, you and I may both learn the same seven pieces of sexual information, but this is not the end of the sexual learning process. The important aspect is how we may put these seven pieces together to construct a view of what sexuality is all about. It is very unlikely that you and I will put these pieces of information together in exactly the same way.

Sexual learning is thus often ambiguous, haphazard, unclear, and full of a wide range of alternatives. While we can identify certain types of learning experiences which *tend* to produce very similar sexual attitudes and behaviors, no two individuals are ever identical. Thus, many of us share many similarities because of similar sexual learning experiences, but at the same time each of us is a unique person sexually.

CHILDHOOD SEXUAL LEARNING

While sexual learning is not developmental in the sense that it proceeds in a straight line through distinct stages, it is also not totally chaotic. Given the fact that in American society we define certain large periods of an individual's life as appropriate for certain forms and degrees of sexual involvement, sexual learning in childhood is of a certain nature. Likewise, certain general patterns of sexual learning are also present during adolescence.

It is thus important to note that, at least in American society, there are general periods in life in which certain types of sexual learning take place. It must be kept in mind that (1) these are not human universals in that all humans everywhere learn the same things at the same periods in life, and (2) that even in American society, there is great diversity among individuals in terms of what is learned and when. The following descriptions of childhood and adolescent sexual learning are thus general patterns that prevail in American society. They are not, however, descriptions of the sexual learning experiences of every individual. Some people learn in adulthood what others learn as children or adolescents. These are, however, general patterns which characterize the sexual learning experiences of most individuals in American society.

The most important characteristic of sexual learning in childhood is that much is learned by the attempt to not teach. In American society, childhood is a period of life when one is not supposed to be a sexual being. Therefore, parents either do not engage in teaching children about sexual matters or, in the more extreme case, actively attempt to keep children from learning about sexuality as it is viewed by adults. The consequence of this tactic is, however, really teaching the child a great deal.

The Content and Processes of Sexual Learning in Childhood

Three major processes characterize what parents communicate to children about sexuality (Gagnon, 1977; Simon and Gagnon, 1973). These processes are largely attempts to "protect" children from a certain segment of the adult world—sexuality. Given this protective orientation of parents in their children's sexual learning, sexual learning on the part of the child is largely prohibitive and unintended.

Judging without naming Parents judge acts without naming them. For example, they often react negatively to children's touching their genitals. The reaction, however, seldom involves a name for the prohibited act. "Don't do that" is much more common than "Don't masturbate" or "Don't play with your genitals." This prohibitive attitude toward such acts as placing one's hands upon one's genitals is generally an outcome of adults' attributing adult meanings and motivation to children. Children randomly engage in hand movements which adults define as SEXplay. The touching of one's genitals frequently takes the form of simple hand wandering. These touches may begin as a chance encounter between fingers and genitals. Since this contact may feel good, it is likely to be self-reinforcing and repeated.[2] Parents see this activity from the point of view of adults as SEXplay. The child, however, has no conception of the behavior as either sex or play. Children not only do not have a concept of "sex," but are a long way from being able to look at fingers touching genitals as masturbation, let alone develop a complex motivational concept for the activity—"I think I will masturbate." The child *does* have a conception, however, of what parents communicate in their prohibition. The child probably (there is no way of telling for certain) realizes that the prohibitive response of the parents vaguely has something to do with "down there." What that "down there" is, what one has actually done, and why this unnamed act with these unnamed parts of one's body is frowned upon by these important people remain a mystery.

Undefined words Children learn words without learning the acts or objects to which they refer. Sounds, including sexual words, float around in the child's world. These words become part of the child's vocabulary through imitating what others say. What is missing in this imitation, however, is what the word means and what it stands for. When children

TABLE 4-1
Accuracy of initial sex information.
Thornburg (1981) obtained data from over 1100 teenagers on their first source of sexual information and the characteristics of that information. The degree of accuracy of that initial information is shown below by sexual topic.

Topic	Quality of Initial Information (in percent)	
	Accurate	Distorted
Abortion	95	5
Menstruation	85	15
Prostitution	85	15
Conception	84	16
Intercourse	83	17
Petting	81	19
Venereal disease	80	20
Masturbation	77	23
Homosexuality	76	24
Ejaculation	67	33
Contraception	67	33
Seminal emissions	66	34

Source: Thornburg (1981), p. 276, table 3.

verbalize a "sexual" word, they are most likely to be admonished by adults not to say that word. Here again, the lesson is prohibitive and mysterious. Children know that the word means something that adults don't like to hear them say, but what it means remains a mystery to them. Later, when the child learns from peers what the word does refer to, the connection between the sexual and the prohibited will be made complete.

Mislabeling Parents routinely mislabel acts and objects of a sexual nature. The child is likely to learn that she or he has a wee-wee, not a penis or vagina; that children come about because "Mommy and Daddy love each other," not because of sexual intercourse. Out of this mislabeling, the child begins to accumulate "knowledge" about what will later be learned to be sexual matters. This knowledge is at best misleading and often colors the view the young person has of sexuality for some time to come. A classic example is the young

[2]This contact feels good just as does the tactile stimulation of other highly sensitive parts of the body (due to high concentrations of nerve endings). Adults, however, pay much less attention to the tactile stimulation of these other areas (mouth, bottoms of the feet, hands) because these parts carry no special meaning, as genitals do. Stimulation of the mouth in the form of thumb sucking is interesting here in that "expert" and public opinion have swayed back and forth on the healthfulness of this activity. While thumb sucking was once considered to result in any number of psychological disasters, it seems today to be regarded as more of a "natural" behavior, and therefore it should not be suppressed.

Childhood sexual learning often involves knowing that the "something" called sex is off limits and something adults make a big fuss about, but the child does not understand why—that is, how adults actually *do* view sexuality.

woman who, late in her childhood, had been informed by her mother that one gets pregnant by sleeping with a man. On a long bus trip with her parents, she sat next to a young soldier, and in the long hours of the night accidentally fell asleep. Upon awaking, she waited anxiously for the signs of pregnancy to appear, since she had in fact "slept with a man" who was seated next to her (Petras, 1973:136–137).

The Outcome of Childhood Sexual Learning

These sexual learning processes in childhood have two major consequences which play an

important role in later sexual learning (Simon and Gagnon, 1973).

First, fantasy overruns the sexual ideas of the child. In the absence of concrete information but in the presence of the mystery which has been created, the child knows that something is going on. What that something is is not clear. The sexual picture is fragmented and somewhat confused and is not even sexual in the child's mind. What fills in the gaps in the mystery—and the attention adults have paid to these matters has clearly shown that the mystery is important—is the child's imagination. Thus, children construct delightfully inaccurate images of the sexual—images which are based on small bits of information and a profound ability to imagine. (See Table 4-1.) Aiding in this process of constructing an imaginary view of the sexual are peers, who obtained their sexual information in the same way. As Simon and Gagnon (1973) point out, peers continue the sexual learning process begun by parents by systematically misinforming one another about sexuality.

Second, the primary descriptions given to parts of the body which will later take on sexual meaning is "dirty" and "prohibited." The only really solid piece of information most children obtain about their genital area is that it is associated with elimination. The child also learns that "pee-pee" and "number two" are less than *socially* desirable activities. For females, this learning appears to be even more common than for males. The first real communication many women receive about their genitals is centered on menstruation, a process which is still clearly defined as unclean and to be hidden or disguised. Many times, the notion that the genitals are associated with things publicly unmentionable may be quite confusing to the child. On the one hand, parents may praise the child for "doing a good job" in using the potty. On the other hand, when the child bursts into a living room full of guests and announces his or her bathroom achievement, the parents' reaction of embarrassment may be clearly communicated.

This general association of the genitals with something dirty is further enhanced by the dirty joke—a term which speaks for itself since the content of the humor is most often sexual. As children near adolescence, they hear and exchange stories which they vaguely understand as dealing with sexual matters. The stories are traded between peers and accompanied by laughter. Even though the reason for the humor is often unclear, it is obvious to the child that the stories deal with something called sex, that they are dirty, and that they are to be hidden from adult ears as well as from the child's peers of the other sex.

The dirty joke is not an isolated part of the child's sexual learning. The basic content of what the child learns is that sexual matters are generally prohibited, viewed with scorn, placed in the context of shame, and generally disapproved of—but yet valued—by the adult world. The dirty joke is only a part of the general nature of sexual conversation among children, conversation which is clandestine and secret in nature (Simon and Gagnon, 1973). Such is the nature of sexual learning in this period of life.

Learning by Doing

Childhood sexual learning also involves engaging in "sexual" activity. Elias and Gebhard (1969) studied the sexual experience of 432 white males and females between the ages of 4 and 14. Of the males in this age group, 52 percent had experienced homosexual activity, 34 percent heterosexual activity of some type, and 56 percent had stimulated their genitals for the purpose of pleasure. The average age of engaging in homosexual and heterosexual activity was 9 years. (This average age is much higher for all individuals, since this average age of 9 years is based on only those who have been active before age 14). Among females between the ages of 4 and 14, 35 percent had engaged in homosexual activity, 37 percent in heterosexual activity, and 30 percent in masturbation.

These sexual activities must, however, be seen with caution. They predominantly involve "playing around" rather than engaging in coitus or oral or anal sexual activity. Further, it is not at all clear that they are seen by all the participants as sexual in the adult sense of the term. They are more likely to be pleasurable play activity which involves the genitals. These activities do, however, influence sexual learning. They are sporadic and not clearly sexually motivated behaviors in which the vague meanings learned in early childhood infrequently come together with some vaguely defined behaviors.

In all the sexual learning of childhood, very little has been learned about the personal or interpersonal aspects of sexuality. In adolescence, these are the issues which become important. As such, childhood sexual learning does little to prepare one for adolescent sexual concerns.

ADOLESCENT SEXUAL LEARNING

During adolescence, the individual emerges into a sexual world more akin to adult conceptions of what sexuality is all about. Not only does the adult conception of sexuality start to become clear, but this meaning is developed and expanded upon in the context of emerging sexual activity and heterosexual relationships. The individual brings into this period of sexual exploration and developing interpersonal relationships the learning of childhood—learning which does not outfit one very well for dealing with interpersonal sexuality and the development of sexual expression. This is not to say that childhood sexual learning determines one's sexuality for life. This is certainly not true. What is the case is that childhood sexual learning has an impact upon sexual learning as an adolescent and young adult. (See Table 4-2.) The impact is that a considerable amount of childhood sexual learning must be overcome or replaced. The classic example here is nudity. Since children generally learn that nudity in the presence of the other sex is inappropriate, the very act of completely disrobing in full view of the other can, the first few times, produce no small amount of anxiety and discomfort (Gagnon, 1977).

In this vein, Simon and Gagnon (1973) have described adolescent and young adult sexual learning as learning to deal with guilt.

TABLE 4-2
When sexual concepts are first learned.
In Thornburg's study (1981), individuals were asked how old they were when they first learned different sexual concepts. The percentages of those learning different sexual concepts or topics at different ages are shown below.

Concept	Percentages of Those Learning of Concept			
	Before age 9	Age 9–11	Age 12–13	Age 14 and Over
Abortion		26	56	17
Conception	21	43	35	2
Contraception	3	30	46	21
Ejaculation	1	26	53	20
Homosexuality	1	28	59	12
Intercourse	5	40	47	8
Masturbation	1	25	59	14
Menstruation	6	48	37	9
Petting	5	30	56	9
Prostitution	1	31	53	14
Seminal emissions	1	18	51	30
Venereal disease	1	20	61	18

As is evident, most sexual concepts are first learned by most people between the ages of 9 and 13, with the peak between 12 and 13. Adolescence is thus that period in which one learns specific sexual concepts, while childhood is where the individual learns the general meanings (positive or negative) to attach to what will be discovered in adolesence to be the sexual.
Source: Thornburg (1981), p. 276, table 2.

One of the main things that have been learned as a child is that sex is bad. As the young adolescent begins to engage in sexual activity, she or he (more she than he) must grapple with putting together the badness of sex with the goodness of self (Laws and Schwartz, 1977). The extent to which childhood sexual learning has resulted in a close connection between guilt and sex is evident in the personality characteristic of *sex guilt* (Mosher, 1961; 1966; 1968).

As a personality characteristic, *sex guilt is a general expectation that an individual has to experience self-induced punishment for approaching or thinking about sex.* The personality characteristic of sex guilt is not to be confused with plain, old feeling guilty. As a personality characteristic, sex guilt is stable across time and situations. Feeling guilty is a situational reaction to a specific situation or event. Individuals who are high on sex guilt are very likely to punish themselves with feelings of anxiety when they approach or think about

approaching the sexual. Individuals who are low on sex guilt are unlikely to do so (Figure 4-2).

Of all the personality characteristics examined in the study of sexuality, sex guilt appears to be the single most important. The personality characteristic of sex guilt is a learned view of the sexual dimension of life, and its effect on the individual demonstrates the powerful impact of childhood and early adolescent sexual learning on late adolescent and adult sexual behavior (Abramson et al., 1977b). This personality characteristic appears to result from childhood and early adolescent sexual learning experiences which emphasize the prohibitive and dirty view of the sexual (Abramson et al., 1977a). Needless to say, sex guilt has a dramatic influence on individual sexual behavior.

Research has revealed a number of important findings about high sex-guilt individuals: They have less sexual experience and less variety of sexual experiences (Abramson and Mosher, 1975; D'Augelli and Cross, 1975;

Figure 4-2 The reactions of high and low sex guilt individuals when they approach or think about approaching sexual stimuli.

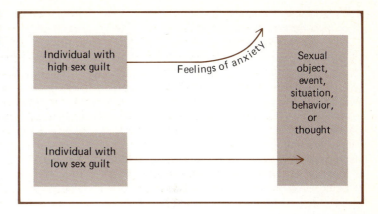

Gerrard, 1977; Langston, 1975; Mendelsohn and Mosher, 1979); they have more traditional moral and sexual standards (D'Augelli and Cross, 1975); they are more condemning of casual premarital sex (Mendelsohn and Mosher, 1979); they are less likely to expose themselves to sexually explicit materials, and when they do they spend less time looking at the material (Schill and Chapin, 1972). It was also found that they have less appreciation of sexual humor (Schwartz, 1972), see erotic materials as less sexually stimulating (Ray and Walker, 1973), and are more likely to feel guilty after looking at erotic material (Mosher and Abramson, 1977; Pagano and Kirscher, 1978). Research has further shown that high sex-guilt individuals are less likely to perceive sexual meaning in something (Schill and Chapin, 1972; Galbraith and Mosher, 1968; Galbraith and Mosher, 1970).

High sex-guilt persons also experience less sexual arousal when they have erotic thoughts, and when they have such thoughts, they experience greater feelings of guilt, shame, distress, fear, disgust, and anger as well as less enjoyment (Mosher and White, 1980). High sex-guilt males and females are less interested in heterosexual interaction (Mosher and White, 1980). High sex-guilt males are also less willing to administer pleasure to a female (Janda et al., 1981). Sex guilt also affects sexual learning itself, since sexual learning involves coming into psychological

contact with the subject of sex. High sex-guilt males and females believe more sexual myths than do those with low sex guilt (Mosher, 1979), and they retain less information about birth control from lectures on the subject (Schwartz, 1973a).

As sexual values, attitudes, and behaviors change over time, the sexual learning environment in a society changes. As this environment changes, differences in individuals from one generation to another appear. This is the case for sex guilt. Not only is sex guilt strongly related to age, with younger persons more likely to be low in sex guilt (DiVasto et al., 1981), but sex-guilt scores of college students have even declined since the late 1960s (Abramson et al., 1977).

The powerful effect of sex guilt on behavior clearly indicates a very important point about sexual learning: Much, if not most, sexual learning is indirect. A person does not have to learn to respond this or that particular way to a given situation. Rather, he or she may develop a certain personality pattern through learning. This personality pattern then determines how the individual will respond to a wide variety of situations that he or she has never directly encountered in previous learning experiences.

Genitals and Gender

From early adolescence onward, the most important factor in sexual learning is gender. It is important here to make a distinction between biological sex and gender. The biological sex of an individual is most often denoted by the male's having 46 XY chromosomes, a certain genital structure, and secondary sexual characteristics, and by the female's having 46 XX chromosomes, a certain genital structure, and certain secondary sexual characteristics. These are biological characteristics and are used to label the biological sex of an individual. Gender refers to socially and psychologically being male or female in terms of what the society defines as masculine and feminine characteristics. Biological sex is thus biological in nature, while gender is social.

Biological sex is socially defined   Even biological sex is not biologically determined. Whether one is biologically a male or female is determined by two factors: (1) what biological characteristics we agree to use to classify a person as male or female, and (2) whether a person has these characteristics. In most cultures, these biological characteristics are the nature of the genitals, the nature of secondary sexual characteristics, and chromosome composition. Most often we use secondary sexual characteristics and genitals to classify a person's sex. These, however, may not necessarily match a person's chromosome composition or even match each other. When such instances arrive, we become very confused (see Box 4-2). It is not totally clear what one's chromosomes look like by examining their genitals. In some cases, the genital structure of the newborn may not be clear as to being male or female, and a sex classification may be made which does not match the chromosome composition.

Genitals do not determine gender   In these cases where persons are identified as being a certain sex on the basis of their genitals and their chromosomes reveal they are another sex, we can obtain some idea of whether sex equals gender. In instances where the newborn appears to be male but actually has an enlarged clitoris, or in cases where the newborn's penis is accidently removed by faulty circumcision, the person behaves as appropriate to the gender he or she is raised to be, not to the gender we would expect from the person's biological makeup. Thus, one becomes the gender one learns to become regardless of chromosomes (Money and Delery, 1976; Green, 1979a).

AGS: Hormones do not equal gender   A great deal of research has been done in cases where the child has some hormone abnormality prior to birth. One such abnormality is adrenogenital syndrome (AGS). In this situation, an abnormal amount of androgens from the brain affect the fetus around the third month of pregnancy. The result is a female fetus whose external genitals have been masculinized before birth because of the unusually high level of androgens. If not treated by the injection of cortisol after birth, the masculinization will continue after birth and at early puberty.

Two sets of studies have examined children with AGS. Money and his colleagues at Johns Hopkins University Hospital have studied fifteen females whose AGS was detected and treated early (Ehrhardt et al., 1968a; 1968b; Lewis et al., 1968; Money and Lewis, 1966). Another group of scientists have studied seventeen females whose AGS was also treated early (Baker and Ehrhardt, 1974; Ehrhardt, 1973; 1975; Ehrhardt and Baker, 1973; 1975). The researchers generally conclude that gender is determined by hormones in that these AGS females behave differently from females not having AGS. The primary way in which they are described as being different is that they are more "tomboyish" in their behavior. For example, AGS females are described as having little or no interest in dolls, preferring clothes such as shorts and shirts and blue jeans, and liking to play with boys. These behaviors are taken as indicating that AGS female children, whose early external genital structure was masculinized by hormones before birth, are *less female* in gender behavior than non-AGS females. If these data can be taken as actually showing this assumption, they would provide strong support for the notion that gender behavior is determined by hormones.

BOX 4-2

PERSON OF UNCERTAIN SEX SENTENCED TO WOMEN'S JAIL

San Jose, Calif. (AP)—A seemingly male office clerk with a mustache is serving time for vehicular manslaughter in a women's jail because officials say he is a female from the waist down.

"He really doesn't fit anyhere," Judge John McInerny said of Paul Becerra, who began a 90-day sentence on Tuesday. "This is the most difficult sentencing case I've had. He looks like a man, talks like a man and acts like a man."

Becerra, 41, had pleaded guilty to vehicular manslaughter after the car he was driving while drunk smashed into a truck last February, killing his 2-year-old daughter.

Because of his previous drinking record, the Santa Clara County district attorney's office urged that he serve a one-year prison term.

He was then ordered to Vacaville state prison for a routine diagnostic study, officials said. It was there, during a strip search, that his sex became unclear.

Prison doctors said they found Becerra has a "functional vagina" and therefore cannot be admitted to a men's prison.

A further investigation revealed that Becerra was born a female in San Francisco and underwent a sex change operation 10 years ago. But he ran out of money and was never able to complete the transformation.

Officials said that he married and became a father when his wife was artificially inseminated. That child was the one killed in the crash.

"We felt he—or she—should go to the state women's prison at Frontera," said Phil Guthrie of the Department of Corrections.

The district attorney's office then decided to withdraw its recommendation of a prison sentence because of the unusual nature of the case and Judge McInerny ordered Becerra to serve 90 days in the women's jail in San Jose.

He also fined Becerra $3,750, put him on probation for 10 years and ordered his driver's license forfeited.

"It might seem like a lenient sentence," Judge McInerny said. "But he's getting more punishment than the ordinary person would suffer in a year."

Jail officials said they had no plans to make a special arrangements at the women's jail for Becerra.

"As far as we are concerned, he is a woman," said a spokesman, who asked not to be named.

Source: *The News Tribune*, Tacoma, Wash., Jan. 23, 1980, p. A-8.

There are, however, some very serious questions to be raised about these findings. First, it is assumed that these behaviors are masculine. There are serious doubts about this classification. What are dolls, for example? The Incredible Hulk? No, this is a boy's toy, not a doll! What is masculine about shorts, shirts, and jeans? What is masculine about playing with boys? The point is that the behavior of male and female children is more similar than different, and one of the major things which makes it different is looking at things boys do as "boy things" (playing with the Incredible Hulk is not seen as playing with dolls) and seeing things girls do as "girl things." Rather than see these behaviors as "tomboyish," I can look at them and conclude that these AGS females were actually thrust forward in their *female* gender development to age 16. For example, 16-year-old females do not play with dolls, they like to wear shorts, shirts, and blue jeans, and they like to be around boys. What is to keep us from concluding that the actual effects of the hormones is to make these females *more feminine* than we would expect them to be for their age? In this same vein, it should be pointed out that none of the AGS females had any doubt about whether she was a female.

Second, even the existence of these behaviors is to be questioned. The reports of these behaviors were made by parents. These parents not only knew of the child's hormone and genital structure problem, but were also probably informed as to what the researchers thought would be the child's behavior (more masculine). It is very clear that what you tell a person about another influences that person's perception of the other's behavior. For example, Condry and Condry (1976) placed an infant behind a one-way mirror (you can see in, but not out). The child was then exposed to a jack-in-the-box as well as other stimuli. Half of a large group of observers were told that the infant's name was David. The other half were told that the child's name was Dana. The observers then rated the infant's reaction to the jack-in-the-box. Those who rated David's behavior described "his" reaction as anger. Those who rated Dana's behavior described "her" reaction as fear. Other ratings also followed the same pattern of perceiving the same behavior much differently on the basis of the assumed sex of the infant. What is to say that parents of AGS children did not simply describe what they expected to see: a female child with more masculine behavior and interests because they knew she had masculinized genitals?

Even though the AGS studies are often cited as evidence in support of the notion that the hormones that determine genital structure are responsible for gender, they fall far short of providing such evidence. If we are left with the AGS studies to argue that gender behavior is determined by biological sex, we do not have much of an argument.

Effects of progestin on gender Another group of studies has examined children whose mothers received progestin treatment to prevent spontaneous abortion (Money and Ehrhardt, 1972). Here the progestin-masculinized female children were described as tomboys because they liked to compete with boys, were self-reliant, assertive, and independent, and preferred slacks to dresses. Nothing need really be said about this classification except that if these studies were done in 1982, one wonders if these females would still be called tomboys, or would they be seen as modern women? It is important to note here that in one study (Zussman, cited in Dalton, 1976), male and female children who had been exposed to large doses of progesterone before birth were compared with children who had not been exposed on standardized measures of masculinity-femininity. No significant differences were found between the exposed and nonexposed children among either males or females.

But genitals do determine gender The connection between one's genitals and one's gender is clear. One's genitals do determine one's gender in most cases. The connection is not biological, in which case you are destined to develop a typical "masculine" behavior pattern if your genitals are largely protruding, and are destined to develop a typical "feminine" behavior pattern if your genitals are largely not protruding. Rather, one's genitals are most often used at birth to identify who is male and who is female; once this definition is established, the process of teaching that person to be one gender or the other begins. Genitals determine gender only inasmuch as we label a person as biologically a male or female on the basis of that person's genital appearance at birth (sometimes this is "wrong" in comparison with the chromosomes). Then, on the basis of this label, we teach the person to be of the male or female gender.

Gender and Sexuality

It is common to encounter the idea that males are somehow different sexually from females because of the biological fact that they are males. It is common in Western culture to entertain the notion that males and females "naturally" differ in sexuality because of the biological characteristics that make them male or female. As we have seen, these biological characteristics have (1) no demonstrated relationship to levels of sexual interest or activity, and (2) no demonstrated relationship to those behaviors we think are associated with male or female gender.

Gender, however, is perhaps the single most important factor in determining the pattern of one's sexuality. The reason is that males and females learn different patterns of sexuality. This difference in male and female sexual learning is the result of two major factors. First, males and females specifically learn different views of sexuality as a direct result of explicit sexual learning. Second, learning to be male or female has a powerful indirect effect on one's approach to sexuality. The very nature of male and female gender roles involves learning things which will indirectly affect how one approaches, views, and deals with sexuality.

We shall first examine how overall characteristics of male and female gender learning result in different orientations to sexuality on the part of males and females. Next we shall turn to specific male and female differences in learning directly about sexuality. These differences in sexual learning are very significant. We shall see examples of these differences in learning appear again and again in everything from adolescent sexuality to marriage to homosexuality to rape to prostitution to sexuality and chronic illness. The importance of gender differences in sexual learning is inescapable.[3]

Goals and success An integral part of the traditional male role is to achieve. Having clear goals and reaching them is a central feature of learning to be male in American socie-

ty. In sexuality, this aspect of the traditional male role has been reflected in males' placing more emphasis on "getting somewhere" sexually than do females. For example, males are more likely to see kissing as leading to some other behavior, while females are more likely to see kissing as an enjoyable activity in and of itself (Houston, 1981). Traditionally, this goal orientation has led males to place great emphasis on the number of sexual "conquests." While the more modern male role (Gross, 1978) has changed this somewhat, sexual goals are still stressed. Males are expected to bring the female to orgasm by being a competent sexual performer. The content of the goal has thus changed, but the emphasis remains the same: reaching a sexual goal by being competent or hardworking.

Control and power Another central feature of the traditional male role is to have power and be in control. Most males in American society learn very early that there are few fates worse than being a "wimp" or "sissy." These are terms describing a male who does not have power and who is not in control—characteristics assigned to the traditional female role. Sexually, this dimension of the traditional male role is reflected in many ways. Males initiate sexual activity and are expected to lead the flow of events. Clear evidence of the degree to which this is a reflection of traditional male role learning is that those males who are less sex-typed in their gender behavior (more likely to combine traditional male and female behaviors) are less likely always to be the initiator in sex (Allgeier, 1981). This traditional male expectation to be in control places considerable pressure on males to initiate sexual activity when they may not want to (Komarovsky, 1976; Hass, 1979). This control and power aspect of the traditional male role also plays an important part in the existence and nature of sexual assault of females by males (Chapter 13). Once a male has initiated sexual activity, he is expected to maintain control of the situation; that is, he has the responsibility to make everything work out the way it should. These are responsibilities and pressures which many males would (although not

---

[3]For a detailed discussion of the male role and sexuality in American society, see Gross (1978).

admittedly) rather not have. This aspect of the male role also means that female sexual initiation of sex may be difficult for many males to deal with—not because it is undesirable, but because it offends one's masculinity. Many males thus react negatively to female sexual initiation (Komarovsky, 1976). Being expected to be in control also means that men well trained in this aspect of the male role may have trouble letting the woman take the lead in sexual activities or even suggesting that certain activities or variations may be enjoyable. In the most extreme case, males may be sexually turned off by such events.

Male control and power also have important implications for female sexual learning. While males are being trained in assertiveness, control, and power, females are being trained in passivity and docility. The outcome is that adolescent female hetrosexual activity often takes place under male direction. However, the male's actual knowledge of what is satisfying and pleasurable from the female's perspective is unlikely to be clearly communicated, since she is not allowed to be in control. The male thus learns about female sexuality from his own imagination, the tales of his peers, the media, or pornography, but not directly from the only truly reliable source: females themselves.

Knowledge and wisdom   On top of being capable of success in reaching goals and doing so by being in power and control, the male is supposed to be all-knowing and wise. This is particularly the case in sexual matters since it is readily assumed that males are much more sexual than females. This expectation, held of and by males, often results in males being unable and unwilling to reveal their lack of knowledge, particularly about female sexuality and particularly to their female partner.[4] This results, of course, in a sensitive sexual situation in which attempts on the female's part to inform must be approached with

extreme caution. Further, this produces an often less-than-satisfactory sexual situation for the female, since a lack of infinite sexual wisdom on the male's part cannot be easily broached even though the result might be a better sexual experience for both.

The Peer Group

During all of adolescence, a great deal of interaction takes place with one's peers. This interaction is, in early adolescence, largely homosocial (with the same sex). In middle and later adolescence, peer interaction becomes more and more heterosocial.

In sexual learning, the peer group plays an important part, particularly given the nature of parental sexual teaching in both childhood and adolescence. By adolescence, most children cannot openly discuss sexuality (especially those issues which may be of greatest interest) with their parents. Peers, however, are more than willing to discuss the increasingly important subject of sex. Also, adolescence is a period in which parents in American society become less important for the young person and peers become more important. In general, adolescence involves a movement away from parents and toward peers as the influential reference point in one's daily life.

The peer group thus becomes an increasingly significant source of sexual learning during adolescence. During this period, many important aspects of sexual learning take place which influence adult sexuality. While some of them are very similar for males and females, many aspects of this adolescent learning differ greatly by gender. It is these patterns of adolescent sexual learning that explain many of the differences found between male and female sexuality.

Sexual myths   While parents have generally tended to misinform their children during childhood, peers often tend systematically to misinform during adolescence. They do so by communicating sexual myths and exaggerations as available facts. As a consequence of parental lack of informing and peer misinforming, a rather large percentage of college stu-

---

[4]One of the better indicators of this is the number of informational articles on sex which you will find in the popular women's and men's magazines. If your class is like most, you are also likely to find that the women are more likely to ask questions than are the men.

dents today believe many sexual myths, with males holding more myths than females (Mosher, 1979). The effect of holding these myths on sexual interaction during adolescence and young adulthood has not been investigated, but it is interesting to note that the amount of one's sexual experience is not related to how many sexual myths one believes (Mosher, 1979). This obviously means that much sexual activity during this period of life takes place in the context of, and is even based on, mythical beliefs about sexuality.

Quantity versus quality In general, during adolescence males learn to view sex in a quantitative manner while females learn to view sex in a qualitative manner. Perhaps one of the earliest sources of this learning to view sex differently lies in early adolescent masturbation. Males tend to start masturbating at a slightly younger age than do females, but, more important, they masturbate more frequently (Hass, 1979). This difference persists between the ages of 13 and 15 and disappears at later ages (Hass, 1979). In general, there is greater support for masturbation among the male than the female peer group. For example, how many terms can you think of for male masturbation, compared with how many exist for female masturbation? Right! And these terms and what they refer to are readily communicated among males, thus implying at least the existence, if not the approval, of the activity. What males learn through this communication is not quality (how good it is supposed to feel) but quantity (getting an erection and "achieving" ejaculation). In the not uncommon male group-masturbation situation in early adolescence, one is not reinforced for having the best feeling orgasm or taking the longest time to ejaculate. Rather, quantity is reinforced; the most acclaim goes to the male who can ejaculate the fastest, farthest, and most often.

In cross-sex sexual interaction, the same male peer approval for quantity remains. The important characteristic of sexual experience in the eyes of the adolescent male peer group is likely to be experience. The young male quickly learns that the desirable thing is to "score" or "get a little." Romantic and interpersonal experiences are not the stuff of adolescent male peer approval. These are merely means to the end of obtaining sex in quantity, not quality.

Among adolescent females, the peer approval situation is quite different. Peer approval for females rests not upon how much sexual experience one gets but upon interpersonal involvement and emotional bonds in cross-sex relationships. Sex in the female peer group is approved as an indicator of an interpersonal relationship, not as an end in itself. There is no female equivalent of the stud, only the easy lay, the promiscuous woman, or, worst of all, the whore. Rather than being reinforced for the quantity of their sexual experience, females are punished. Reinforcement for females comes from properly playing the "gatekeeper" role, that is, placing one's sexual activity in the proper interpersonal context.

These differences in the male and female peer groups are evident in a number of studies. For example, Carns (1973) found that among college students, males are not only more likely to tell their male friends about their initial intercourse experiences than are females to tell their female friends, but that males tell their friends sooner after the event and tell more people than do females. Further, Carns found that males were much more likely than females to receive praise from peers, while females were much more likely than males to receive condemnation. A study by Mendelsohn and Mosher (1979) underlines the male-female difference in the interpersonal context of sexual activity. Female college students were found to be much more likely to condemn a peer who began her intercourse career with a physically attractive male than with a peer who had her first coital experience with a loved fiancé. Males, on the other hand, were more likely to praise a male who had his first intercourse with a physically attractive female than one who had his first coitus with a loved financée. Quite clearly, males learn sex first and interpersonal relationships second, while females learn interpersonal relationships first and sex second (Simon and Gagnon, 1973). It is not difficult to understand why most adolescents experience male-female conflict of some intensity on the topic of sex.

Physical and interpersonal sexuality Closely related to the difference in male and female sexual learning in terms of quantity versus quality is the issue of physical versus interpersonal sexuality. Among male peers, females are frequently discussed in terms of their physical-sexual characteristics rather than their social and psychological attributes. Among females, much less attention is given to the purely physical attributes of males and much more attention is directed toward interpersonal characteristics. Part of this male emphasis on the physical side of sexuality tends to come from early masturbation experience. Masturbation is generally not an interpersonal experience, but a physical one. Males, having slightly earlier and much more frequent masturbation activity than females, thus obtain much more learning that sex is physical. Compared with males, females are much more likely to have the first sexual experience in the interpersonal situation of petting. Thus, in general, males are more likely to learn to place an emphasis on the physical aspects of sex, while females are more likely to learn to emphasize the interpersonal aspect.

This difference is also seen in male and female experiences in masturbation. The widespread existence of male magazines containing photographs of nude or partially nude women provides males with female physical features to look at while masturbating. Such experiences on the part of adolescent females are unlikely. Thus, during adolescence, males learn to view sex in a much more physical sense than do females, while females are more likely to learn to place sex in an extended interpersonal context. Language clearly reflects this difference. Females are much more likely than males to use the phrase "make love" when referring to intercourse, while males are much more likely to use physical (and aggressive-dominant) words such as "bang" and "fuck" (Walsh and Leonard, 1974).

Genital sex and diffuse sex Since males experience much more of their early ad-

olescent sexual activity in the form of masturbation than do females, they tend to locate sexuality in the genitals. Females, on the other hand, are much more likely to have their early intense sexual experience in the form of petting rather than masturbation. Heterosexual petting generally involves stimulation of a number of areas of the female body and not the genitals alone. Females are thus much more prone than males to physically locate sex in areas other than the genitals—to see sex as physically diffuse. The male genital orientation and the female diffuse orientation are further aided by males placing greater emphasis on the purely physical aspects of sexual interaction, while females learn to place greater emphasis on the interpersonal (whole person) aspects. These male and female views of the physical location of sexuality are further supported by the media. Look through any series of major advertisements in popular magazines and you will note that many areas of the female body are given sensual emphasis, while little of the male body is so portrayed.

The sequence of sex Through both more extensive masturbation experience and a goal orientation toward sexual activity, males learn a clear sequence of what one does sexually. One becomes aroused to the point of erection, continues stimulation until orgasm, and then quits. In this sequence, males learn that there is a goal (orgasm) and a sequence of activities which are engaged in for the purpose of reaching that goal. Females, however, do not become so committed to this sequence. When males and females enter sexual interaction together, they are thus likely to have very different views of the nature of the sequence of behaviors, the importance of orgasm, and the speed with which one should reach it.

Orgasm Only recently has attention been given to the importance of masturbation in learning orgasm. As we shall see in our discussion of sexual therapy, this discovery has led to effective treatment techniques for women who have difficulty with orgasm response.

In masturbation, males learn much more

about orgasm than do females. At first, ejaculation usually takes place with a few seconds of manual stimulation. When the novelty wears off, orgasm takes longer. Regardless, through masturbation males learn exactly what orgasm is, what the feelings are that are associated with arousal to that point, and what to do to "achieve" orgasm. Males have no doubt when they have had an orgasm. There is physical evidence in the form of ejaculation. One sees what has happened and can easily associate the observed event with sensations and actions.

For females, however, orgasm is less likely to be experienced in masturbation in early or middle adolescence, and they are less likely than males to have their first orgasm experience in masturbation. Also, for purely physiological reasons, females are not as clear about what orgasm is. There is no concrete, observable event (ejaculation) which can be associated with subjective feelings or stimulating behaviors. In Hass's 1979 study of adolescents, 33 percent of the females did not know whether they had ever had orgasm. The outcome of this male-female difference is that males learn to "achieve" orgasm much more readily and regularly than do females.

Viewing the world erotically Not only does the mass media supply males with many more examples of what is erotic than it does females, but these images are put to use by males and connected directly with one's sexual activity in the form of masturbation. Through the media (movies, television, magazines), males have a good idea of what kinds of stimuli are sexual turn-ons. During masturbation, fantasy is typically employed by adolescent males and the images in the fantasy are connected directly to the sexual activity. While masturbating, the adolescent male frequently fantasizes about the girl next door, movie stars, and actual pictures of nude women. This masturbation activity, with the aid of these sexual stimuli, solidifies the male's image of what is sexual about females.

These images come from the larger society's perspective. For example, the *Playboy*

centerfold represents what "good sex" is all about. What this "good sex" consists of is most likely to be physical characteristics and the imagined physical activities which one would do with this person. These images of "good sex" which adolescent males are constructing while looking at the *Playboy* centerfold and masturbating do not commmonly contain such elements as romance, love, and interpersonal involvement. In a very real sense, adolescent males are thus learning to define sexuality as certain desirable female physical characteristics, certain physical-sexual activities, and certain sequences of these activities focused toward the goal of orgasm. This is a rather different sexual picture than that being learned by adolescent females.

Another important aspect of the adolescent male's learning to view the world erotically while the adolescent female is not is a wide gap between males and females in the meaning attached to certain things. It is very commonplace for males to see certain female actions or dress as highly erotic and sensual, while the female who is performing the actions or is dressed in a certain way does not see her behavior as having these qualities at all. Even college-age females tend to select, for example, certain fashions because they are popular or cute. Males, on the other hand, may see these fashions as erotic and attribute erotic motivations to their wearers. I have frequently noted that many males construct images of the sexuality of certain females purely on the basis of their appearance, only to have this image destroyed by the female's actual attitudes and behavior. This gap between males and females in the extent to which they attach erotic meaning to their environment tends to exist throughout adulthood and, as we shall see, has important implications. For example, males with a very strong interest in sex tend to be less interpersonally sensitive to their female partner (Murstein, 1974b).

Who One Views Erotically

Storms (1981) has recently presented a convincing theory describing how individuals learn to view persons of either the same or other sex as erotic. This theory is based on, and summarizes, a vast amount of established research. In preadolescence the individual's strongest emotional attachments are to persons of the same sex. As we shall see, the majority of males and almost half of all females have a same-sex sexual experience before reaching adolescence. If individuals develop clear sexual feelings before adolescence they are likely to see persons of the same sex as more erotic than persons of the other sex (homosexual orientation). If, as is most often the case, individuals develop clear sexual feelings in adolescence, when strong emotional attachments have shifted to persons of the other sex, they are likely to see persons of the other sex as more erotic than persons of the same sex (heterosexual orientation).

ADULT SEXUAL LEARNING

Learning does not stop at age 18, but continues throughout one's life. Traditionally, social scientists have adopted a psychoanalytic model of behavior (largely a la Freud) which states that all important learning and personality formation take place in childhood. This is simply not the case.

While we have discussed how sexual learning does not take place in nice, neat stages which never vary, it is also true that certain types of learning experiences and content are more likely at some periods than at others.

It is also true that previous sexual learning affects later sexual learning. What one learns in adolescence, for example, influences the kinds of learning experiences and environments one is likely to confront as an adult.

The major changes that occur in adult sexual learning involve the circumstances encountered as one moves through the life cycle. What happens on this journey (marriage, divorce, widowhood, illness, the pregnancy of a teenage daughter, an extramarital affair, physiological aging) involve a wealth of sexual learning experiences.

These later learning experiences not only take place on top of what one has learned earlier in life, but they are the result of another important factor. As social change brings with it changes in sexual attitudes and behaviors, one may find that one's adolescent and young adult sexual learning is out of step with contemporary patterns. For example, you grew up during the recent "sexual revolution," but your parents experienced these changes as adults.

SEX EDUCATION

Learning about sex also takes the form of sex education: *formalized* or *planned learning about sex.* Such education may be acquired in a variety of situations, including the home, school, church, or specialized groups and organizations (Scales, 1979).

Where Does It Take Place?

The primary source of sex information during childhood and adolescence is same-sex friends (Figure 4-3) and independent reading.[5] For males, parents play a minor role as a source of sex information, but for females, mothers are an important source. For both males and females, the school is unlikely to be the primary source. Box 4-3 illustrates these findings.

These sources of sex information in childhood and adolescence have changed very little over time. Gebhard (1977b) compared the primary sources of sex information for respondents in 1938 through 1960 with the sources for college students in 1975. Few differences were apparent, with the exception that for males, same-sex friends had declined in importance and the media had increased. For females, there were no significant changes over time in the sources of sex information.

[5]A recent form of this independent reading may well be the much discussed Judy Blume novels which have become very popular among preadolescents and young adolescents. (See Chap. 10 for a more complete discussion.)

Figure 4-3 Primary sources of sex information as reported by male and female college students. (Source: Spanier, 1977:78, Table 1.)

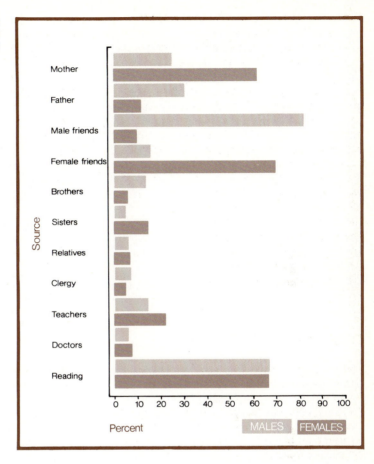

Is There a Need for Sex Education in the Schools?

The answer to this question depends on where and how you think children should obtain information about sex, how much information you think they should obtain at what age, and how effective various sources of sex information are in transmitting knowledge.

Even though only 31 percent of the parents questioned in a 1977 General Mills survey of the American family said that there was a need for some agency other than the family to "teach children about sex," parents do not appear to be doing much in this regard. Parents in general do not seem eager to discuss sex with their children. Many wait until the time is "right" and then find that such a discussion is more "too little, too late" than anything else. It is not surprising that in Hass's 1979 study, 65 percent of the adolescents said that they did not feel that they could be open about sex with their parents. Parents tend to agree. Curley and Hoff (1974) found that 72 percent of the parents and 61 percent of the children studied said that parents did not supply enough information about sex. Also, parents today (given the history of sex education in the United States) are quite likely to have insufficient information themselves.

Peers are not well equipped as sex educa-

BOX 4-3

LEARNING ABOUT SEX IN ISRAEL

Lancet et al. questioned 16- and 17-year-olds in Israel regarding their main sources of sex information. The results were as follows:

Main source	Males (%)	Females (%)
Friends	39	41
Books	52	38
Mother	7	21
Doctor	14	15
Pamphlets	13	7
Teacher	8	4
Father	6	3
Films	9	9

Source: Lancet et al. (1978: 1086, table 5).

As in the United States, books and friends are the most common source of sex information. Doctors are more important than in the United States. The mother is important for females but not males, and the father is just not important.

tors since they have little accurate knowledge about sex (Thornburg, 1975; Schwartz, 1968). Even though peers are willing to talk about sex, such discussion is most often the systematic exchange of misinformation. Thornburg (1981) found, in a large sample of high school students, that the least accurate sex information held was that most likely to have been learned from peers.

Monge et al. (1977) found that in a sample of ninth graders, the knowledge level concerning reproduction and childbearing was rather low (Table 4-3). Similar findings have also been reported by Walters et al. (1979). Even among college students, knowledge of many aspects of sexuality is lacking. In a recent study of college students, 55 percent of the males and 43 percent of the females thought that humans can get stuck together when they have intercourse; 40 percent of the males and 24 percent of the females incorrectly thought that pregnancy is more likely if the male and female have orgasm in intercourse at exactly the same time; and 47 percent of the males and 23 percent of the females did not know

that it is the male who determines the biological sex of the child (Mosher, 1979).

It is clear that the level of knowledge about sex is not high among adolescents and young adults. It is also clear that sexual activity among teenagers exceeds knowledge. Thus, many adolescents today are engaging in behavior about which they have little concrete knowledge. In a recent study of high school students, Thornburg (1981) found that contraception was the sexual topic on which teenagers received the most distorted information.

The Extent of Sex Education in the Schools

In 1928, Usilton and Edson wrote a report on sex education in high schools in the United States as of 1927 (U.S. Public Health Service, 1928). At that time, only 45 percent of the high schools had any form of sex education and most of it was in the context of some other course, such as biology or social science. Only 16 percent of the schools had what was then called "emergency" courses. These were not

TABLE 4-3

Ninth graders who knew certain aspects of reproduction and childbearing (in percent).

What was known	Percentage who knew*
Seminal vesicles are part of the reproductive system	55
Meaning of the word "menstruation"	38
Fallopian tubes are part of the reproductive system	30
Meaning of the word "menopause"	27
Meaning of the word "coitus"	14
Meaning of the word "scrotum"	13

*These percentages do not reflect the proportion of respondents who knew about the act or process to which these words refer. These are technical words and reflect perhaps scientific knowledge, but not "street knowledge."
Source: Monge et al. (1977).

"Boy, that sure is a relief! I was planning to tell him the facts of life next week."

complete courses, but a special presentation on sex education, most frequently in the form of a lecture. Moreover, the existence of any type of sex education differed greatly from state to state. For example, 84 percent of the high schools in Massachusetts, 83 percent in Louisiana, and 80 percent in Georgia had no sex education of any kind, while only 16 percent in the District of Columbia had no sex education. The topics covered under the label of sex education were also quite limited in 1927 (Table 4-4).

It is a good thing this situation has changed today. Right? Wrong. Currently, only three states require some form of sex education in the schools and the other forty-seven either have no specification or let local districts decide (*Family Planning Perspectives,* November–December 1980). Although no states prohibit sex education (Louisiana changed its law in 1979), six states discourage any discussion of birth control and twelve require parental consent or allow students to be excused from sex education classes. Exact estimates of the proportion of schools having sex

education programs differ, but generally point to the same conclusion. In 1974, the National Education Association found that out of 800 public school systems sampled, approximately 70 percent had *some* form of sex education. Only 10 percent, however, provided a sex education program (Scales, 1979). In a more recent study, only 35 percent of the schools sampled offered a separate sex education course (Scales, 1979).

Sex education in schools is still most frequently a small segment of another course and

TABLE 4-4

Major sex education topics covered in United States high schools offering sex education courses in 1927.

Topic	Schools Covering Topic (%)
Eugenics and heredity	78
Reproduction	69
Social aspects of sex	51
Venereal diseases	34
Internal secretion	25
Menstruation	25
Seminal emissions (wet dreams, ejaculation)	10

Source: United States Public Health Service (1928:10, table 9).

BOX 4-4
SEX EDUCATION IN THE SOVIET UNION

The sources of information about sex are essentially the same for young people in the Soviet Union as they are in the United States. In a recent survey of 300 Moscow students age 15 to 17, only 21 percent said that they first learned of sex in family or school. The vast majority obtained their first sexual knowledge from cheap novels, peers, and older friends.

As with many types of information, sexual materials are soundly banned by Soviet censors. There is, however, an active black market for *Playboy* and *Hustler* magazines, and X-rated movies are smuggled into the country from nearby Scandinavia.

In general, the level of exposure to sources of sexual information appears to be quite low in the Soviet Union. One Soviet doctor has reported that he has to explain sexual intercourse and birth control to adult men and women, many of whom are married. This is not particularly surprising, given the fact that it was not until 1974 that the first sex manual was released in Russia. Entitled *Female Sexual Problems,* it was an instant best-seller even though the contents were naive and often inaccurate.

This interest in sex in the context of the repression of information is evident among teenagers. More than 70 percent of the teenagers in a recent Moscow study said that nothing was wrong with premarital sex, an attitude which is quite inconsistent with the way sexual matters are dealt with by the government. Sex education programs do exist in almost all schools and there is even a recent effort to remove these from biology and gear the content to the age level of the students. Still, however, the content of these courses would strike most American youth as somewhat old-fashioned. In courses designed for 16- and 17-year-old students, there is frequently sex segregation; typical topics include "Friendship and Comradeship," "Female Honor and Male Dignity," "First Step in Love," "The Art of Interpersonal Relations," "Personal Hygiene," and "Let's Talk about Fashion and Cosmetics."

Source: *Seattle Post-Intelligencer,* Oct. 14, 1979.

the content of this education varies a great deal. In a survey of state boards of education and state guidelines for sex education, Kirby and Scales (1979) found that contraception, abortion, masturbation, and homosexuality were the topics *least* likely to be covered. Venereal disease, the anatomy of reproduction, and family roles and responsibilities were the topics *most* likely to be discussed. Evidently, the content of sex education in schools has not changed much since 1927.

The topics which are most likely to be covered are of the least interest to students and those least likely to be covered hold the most interest. Many courses place a strong emphasis on "family living." Students, however, find this emphasis irrelevant to their interests and often resent the school's attempting to push traditional values of sex equaling marriage. Students are most frequently interested in the here-and-now problems of teenage living, such as contraception. However, in 1978 only 31 percent of all 13- to 18-year-olds (72 percent of those who had taken a sex education course) had received any course instruction in contraception (Gallup, 1978). It is not surprising that only 36 percent of all teenagers who have had a sex education course said it was "very helpful," even though 46 percent said that such a course was "fairly helpful." Course ratings increase when birth control is discussed, but the fact remains that many sex education courses are history lessons in which the teacher tells students about things they have already done as if they had not. Predominantly, sex education courses consist of what adults think teenagers should know, not what teenagers want and need to know.

The Sex Education Interests of Children and Adolescents

McCormick (1980) recently examined the questions and situations children put before their parents concerning sex. While these questions do not differ for males and females either in adolescence or before, they do vary with the age of children. Overall, preadolescents present their parents with more questions and situations dealing with sex than do adolescents.[6] Specific topics which are less likely to arise in adolescence than preadolescence are modesty and nudity, female development and menstruation, fetal development at birth, intercourse, genitals, and sexual experimentation. Topics which are more often raised by adolescents than preadolescents are abortion, sexual molestation and assault on self, contraception, and dating (Table 4-5). This change in sexual questions from preadolescence to adolescence represents a transition in interests from concern with one's own body to concern with the interpersonal aspects and possible consequences of sexuality and sexual behavior.

Developing Sex Education Programs in Schools

Currently in the United States, sex education is offered by a wide range of organizations other than schools. Many youth-oriented agencies such as the YMCA, Red Cross, Future Homemakers of America, Parent-Teachers Associations, and youth church groups are involved in health fairs, training of youth and adult education teams, information dispersal, and meetings (Scales, 1979).[7] Still other national organizations serve in the capacity of promoting quality sex education. The Sex Information and Education Council of the United States (SIECUS) and the American Association of Sex Educators, Counselors, and Therapists are two such prominent organizations.

By far the most potentially important organization is, however, the school. It is here that the battle of sex education has been, and is, fought in America. For decades, communities across the country have become embattled in the issue of sex education in the public schools. For a review of these notorious, and often bitter, exchanges, see Hottois and Milner (1975), Haims (1973), and Breasted (1970).

The nature of these controversies is interesting. Parental objection to sex education in schools is generally minor. Rather than oppose sex education, parents are more likely to resist it (Clawar, 1977), and the vast majority of adults in the United States support the concept of sex education in the public schools (Table 4-6). Parental resistance to sex education usually centers around three issues (Scales, 1979:26):

- Qualifications, behavior, and methods to be employed by the teacher
- The content and focus of the course, particularly concern that children will be stimulated into engaging in sexual activity

---

[6]This is a good example of the outcome of childhood sexual learning. By the time one enters adolescence, one has likely learned that sex is dirty, prohibited, or both, and is something one does not talk to one's parents about.

[7]The conservative attack on sex education in the schools by Moral Majority may soon change all these activities, and such an effort will be aided by the budget cutbacks in federal funding at the local and state levels, which the United States will experience at least through 1984.

TABLE 4-5
Sexual topics raised in the home by preadolescents and adolescents.

Sexual Topics Raised by Preadolescents	
Frequently	**Infrequently**
Modesty, nudity	Breast feeding
Female development, menstruation	Masturbation
Fetal development, birth	Abortion
Intercourse	Sexual molestation, assault of
Genitals	others
Love, marriage, sex	Sexual molestation, assault of
Homosexuality	self
Dirty words, jokes	Contraception
Petting, premarital sex	Conception
Experimentation, exploration	Infant siblings
	Sex education material
	Dating

Sexual Topics Raised by Adolescents	
Frequently	**Infrequently**
Abortion	Modesty, nudity
Homosexuality	Breast feeding
Dirty words, jokes	Female development, menstruation
Petting, premarital sex	Fetal development, birth
Sexual molestation, assault of	Intercourse
self	Genitals
Contraception	Masturbation
Dating	Sexual molestation, assault of
Love, marriage, sex	others
	Conception
	Infant siblings

Source: McCormick (1980).

• Fears of dealing with children's increased knowledge about sexuality

Considering all individuals who are opposed to sex education in the schools, it has been found that these persons tend to have a traditional orientation toward the family and women's roles (they agree with the statement, "A woman's place is in the home"), and they are against premarital sex. These factors are important in that individuals who are against sex education in the schools see the educational system intruding into traditional family authority and feel that they are isolated from what they see as a massive urban educational system (Richardson and Cranston, 1981). Sex education is thus symbolic of social change which they find threatening, and they react to it in a political effort.

As Mahoney (1979:274) has pointed out, sex education is not a political issue which winds up in the moral arena but a moral issue which winds up in the political arena. When the debates over sex education arise, sex education rapidly becomes a public political issue. Frequently, political fervor is incited by the op-

TABLE 4-6
Percentage of persons age 18 and over favoring sex education in U.S. public schools.

Year	Percent
1974	82
1975	79
1977	77

Source: Davis (1980).

ponents' calling up conservative religious and political feelings ("It's a Communist plot" to "breed rampant sex among youth"). When these opponents are successful in defeating a sex education program—as they often are—they perhaps feel better because they have won a small battle in preserving what they see as the traditional authority of the family against the onslaught of the public education system. They have also created serious negative consequences for many young people, however.

When such antisex education efforts are successful, it is generally owing to mismanagement on the part of school administrators. Rather than this vocal minority of opponents convincing the majority of the community of the moral rightness of their views, defeat usually comes when the community conflict gets out of hand (Hottois and Milner, 1975; Scales, 1979). Sex education programs are usually suggested by school superintendents. Then public meetings follow. These meetings evoke the wrath of the anti–sex education segment, whose outrage gets plentiful media coverage because of its sensationalism (Hottois and Milner, 1975). The issue is thus made political and the probability is increased that the idea will be dropped. When such dissent is managed, rather than battled, by school officials, the outcome tends to be free of political or moral sensationalism and the program goes into effect. If fact, when such minority dissent

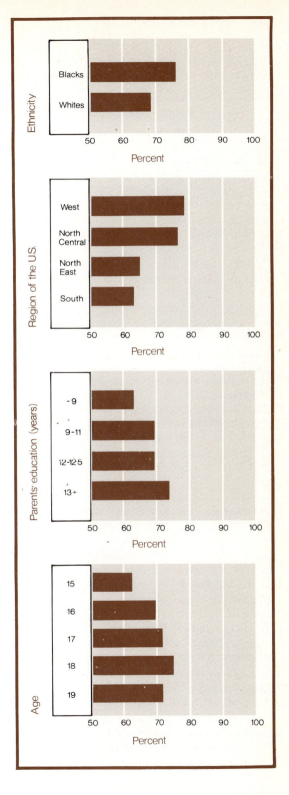

Figure 4-4 The proportion of 15- to 19-year old never-married females in the United States who have had a sex education course by various social characteristics. (Source: Zelnik, 1979.)

is managed judiciously, existing programs are likely to expand rather than decline (Scales, 1979).

How Many Teenagers Have Had Sex Education?

Sixty-nine percent of all 15- to 19-year-old never-married females in the United States have had formal sex education instruction (Zelnick, 1979), as shown in Figure 4-4; only 43 percent of all 13- to 18-year-olds have had a sex education course (Gallup, 1978). Blacks, students in the western and north central United States, and students whose parents are higher in socioeconomic status are more likely than others to have received formal sex education (Zelnick, 1979). (See Figure 4-4.)

The Effectiveness of Sex Education Programs

Does sex education in the schools work? The evaluation of sex education courses and programs is only now getting started in this country, and a central question here is what one uses as a measure of the success of such instruction.

One such measure is knowledge of sexual functioning and reproduction. Nationally, sex education does not fare well in this regard. In a recent national study of 15- to 19-year-old females who had never been married, only 63 percent of those who had a course in sex education said they knew what time of the month was the highest in pregnancy risk. Of these who said they knew, only 57 percent actually did (36 percent of all those who had had a course) (Zelnick, 1979). This apparently differs considerably from program to program. Monge et al. (1979) found that ninth graders who had taken a specific course showed a significant improvement in knowledge in a number of areas. Thinking back to our previous discussion on the male role and sexual learning, it is interesting to note that females learned more than males.

Sex Education and Sexual Behavior

A common fear of sex education is that it will spur preadolescents and adolescents into immediate sexual activity they would not otherwise experience until much later.[8] This "knowing is doing" assumption is not only incorrect, but it involves a rather naive view of the real sexual behavior patterns of adolescents today. As we shall see, actual sexual activity among teenagers today far exceeds their knowledge of sex and sexuality (Chapter 7).

In general, having received sex education does not influence sexual behavior (Spanier, 1976; 1977). The occurrence of such behavior, however, depends on the source of the information other than a sex education course. Among females, sexual behavior appears to occur less frequently when the primary source of information is the mother and more frequently when the primary source is male friends or independent reading. Among males, sexual behavior seems to occur less often when the primary source of information is a person in the clergy and more often when the source is male or female friends or independent reading (Spanier, 1977).

Taking a college course in human sexuality also appears to influence sexual attitudes, but not behavior. Students who have had such a course are more accepting of both their own and others' sexual behavior after the course. This greater acceptance is present for at least two years after the course has been completed and involves such behaviors as masturbation, homosexuality, intercourse, oral-genital sex, sex observed by others, group sex, multiple sex relations, female sexual aggressiveness, erotic stimuli, and intercourse during menstruation (Story, 1979).

SUMMARY

In Chapter 1, we discussed the concept of Greek dualism and referred to Western culture's inheritance of the Greek concept of a

---

[8]For an excellent review of the effects of sex education, see Kilmann et al. (1981).

separation of mind and body. In the question of how individuals become sexual beings, this question of mind versus body appears again. This time, the debate is whether sexual interest is determined by biological factors (body) or learning (mind).

While the view exists that biological factors determine sexual interest, there is no substantial evidence for this argument. Rather, the weight of the evidence suggests the importance of learning.

The nature of the individual's sexual learning experiences is determined by his or her social environment. This social environment consists of the society of which one is a member, the social groups and categories to which one belongs, and one's unique learning history. A central aspect of sexual learning is learning the sexual script of one's society. In learning the sexual script, the individual is not only in society, but society comes to be within the individual. We learn the sexual script with such conviction that, for us, it becomes the right way sexuality is done.

This is the content of what is learned. This learning takes place by means of the same processes through which we learn anything: instrumental or operant learning, imitation and observational learning, and classical conditioning.

The individual, unlike the laboratory rat, is not just a passive being in this learning. Rather, the individual actively participates by putting together the bits and pieces of sexual learning into a whole which consists of an overall view of sexuality.

Sexual learning does not take place in neat packages at the same time for everyone. Individuals differ greatly in not only how readily they learn, but how they put pieces of learning together to form a whole picture.

Certain periods of life are characterized by certain types of learning experiences and content. Childhood sexual learning is framed around parents attempting not to teach. In the process, they teach a great deal, most of which focuses on sex as dirty and somehow not really socially desirable. In all these childhood learning experiences, including actual sexual activity, the child very rarely develops a crystal-clear picture of sexuality, at least as it appears from the adult point of view. Adolescent sexual learning involves bringing the content and experiences of childhood sexual learning into the realm of social sex, that is, of interpersonal sexuality. Here sexual learning is clearly different for males and females, and sexual learning centers on male and female gender learning.

Sexual learning continues through adult life, involving the learning experiences which come about as one passes through the life cycle. Also important in adult learning are social changes in sexuality.

Sex education involves formalized or planned learning about sex. In real life, little sexual information is acquired in this manner. Peers in American society always have been, and still are, the most important source of sex information.

Sex education in the schools still remains very similar in both scope and content to what it was in 1927. Consistently, the content of courses focuses on those aspects of sexuality which are of the least interest to the students. However, as long as we remain with the view discussed in Chapter 1 that "sex is bad—sex is good," it is unlikely that much will be done to improve the quality of sex education. While the effectiveness of sex education courses differs greatly, overall, students appear to learn very little. Given the sexual activity characteristics of adolescents that we shall examine in Chapter 7, this is not surprising. Students do not find the content of sex education courses of much interest (and it is difficult to learn something you are not interested in) because sexual activity among teenagers exceeds both their own knowledge and that presented in the classroom.

STUDY GUIDE

TERMS TO KNOW

Nature versus nurture

Society/groups and categories/unique individual learning

Sexual script

The individual in society/society in the individual

Instrumental or operant learning

Imitation and observational learning

Classical conditioning

Stimulus generalization

Judging without naming

Undefined words

Mislabeling

Sex guilt

SELF TEST

Part I: True-False Statements

1. The contemporary view of a biological force determining or influencing sexuality is that human sexual activity is instinctual.
2. The nonhuman animal studies on the influence of hormones on sexual activity provide weak or no evidence for the argument that human sexuality is strongly influenced by hormone levels.
3. In studies of hormones and sexual activity in humans, we find no consistent evidence of a relationship.
4. Sex is a natural human behavior or interest.
5. A single learning experience may be a powerful one.
6. Sexual learning takes place in a developmental sequence in which there are a series of developmental stages.
7. Sex guilt is when you feel guilty about doing something sexual.
8. Defining a person as male or female has nothing to do with social definitions.
9. The chief sources of sex information in childhood and adolescence have not changed significantly in the last forty years.
10. Both males and females of college age report that the opposite-sex parent was the major source of sex information for them.
11. In sex education courses in schools, we find that the topics most likely to be covered are those of least interest to the students.
12. The majority of teenagers in the United States who have had a sex education course describe it as "very helpful."
13. Preadolescent children present their parents with more questions about sex than do adolescents.
14. Teenagers who have had a sex education course appear to be significantly more knowledgeable than teenagers who have not had such a course.
15. Most states require sex education in the schools.

Part II: Multiple-Choice Questions
Select the best of the three alternatives.

1. For females, sexual behavior appears to be lessened when the primary source of sex information is____, and increased when the primary source is____or____.

(a) independent reading/mother/sex education course, (b) mother/male friends/independent reading, (c) clergy/male friends/female friends.

2. The Grand Valley Dani (a) learn to have what we Americans would call little interest in sex; (b) repress their sexual interests; (c) see the lack of sex their culture imposes on them as distressing.

3. Sexual scripts are (a) more complex than actual sexual behavior; (b) general guidelines for what is sexually appropriate; (c) more important for females than for males.

4. The certainty of a learning experience resulting in learning is influenced by what two factors? (a) Stimulus generalization and intelligence; (b) classical conditioning and gender; (c) intensity and trials.

5. In their sexual learning, children in American society (a) imagine a great deal when they themselves fill in the gaps in the sexual information they are provided; (b) learn to see sex as natural and clean; (c) clearly distinguish sexual meanings from the meanings of elimination as far as their genitals are concerned.

6. Sex guilt (a) is when you feel guilty about sex; (b) is a general expectation to experience self-induced punishment for approaching, or thinking about approaching, sexual stimuli; (c) has no effect on sexual learning.

7. Whether your genitals are those of a male or female is (a) important in biologically determining your gender behavior; (b) irrelevant for gender behavior biologically, but important in labeling you a male or female; (c) closely tied to your being tomboyish if you are a female with AGS.

8. In 50 percent of the 186 cultures studied by Broude and Greene, females either "always" initiated sexual activity or males and females initiated sexual activity with equal frequency. This finding strongly suggests that (a) male and female patterns of sexual behavior are influenced by gender in that, biologically, males and females differ in their level of sexual interest; (b) male and female patterns of sexual behavior are learned; (c) males tend to have a stronger sex drive than females because of hormone levels.

TOPICS FOR DISCUSSION

1. In this chapter we have discussed how male and female patterns of sexual behavior differ owing to how male gender and female gender are defined in American society. For example, we discussed the male emphases on goals and knowledge and wisdom. What these interests indicate is that much sexual learning takes place which is not directly intended to be sexual learning or is not explicitly sexual learning. Discuss examples of how this occurs for males and females in childhood and adolescence from your own experience or observations.

2. The concept of sexual script is an extremely important one in the study of human sexuality. Each person in your class should write down the sexual script as he or she sees it for some particular form of sexual interaction. The best way to do this is for the teacher to select a form of sexual interaction (e.g., a male and female adolescent engaging in petting on a date) and then to have each person write down twenty behaviors or actions that will take place and the sequence in which they will occur. Be sure that you list who is doing each behavior (e.g., "He does x," "She does y"). When all the students have finished their lists, compare them. Note the extent to which there is agreement on the sexual script, whether males agree with one another more than they do with females and vice versa, whether there are significant differences in the scripts given by males and females, and where the greatest amounts of agreement and disagreement exist and the implications of these differences for male-female interaction.

SUGGESTED READINGS

Laws, J. L., and **P. Schwartz,** *Sexual Scripts: The Social Construction of Female Sexuality.* Hinsdale, Ill.: The Dryden Press, 1977.
Although this appears to be a monograph, it is actually a set of chapters written by different people. This is an exceptional excursion into the female sexual script in American society and will make you think. You should be cautioned, however, that many of the statements are not supported by actual research findings. Nonetheless, this book is important reading.

Katchadourian, H. A. (Ed.), *Human Sexuality: A Comparative and Developmental Perspective.* Berkeley: University of California Press, 1979.
This work promises to integrate information from a variety of different disciples, but falls far short of that goal by simply having different chapters on this or that discipline's view of human sexuality. Of importance, however, are the chapters in Parts I and II, since they discuss the evolutionary and biological perspectives.

Gagnon, J. H. and **W. S. Simon,** *Sexual Conduct: The Social Sources of Human Sexuality.* Chicago: Aldine, 1973.
This is the classic work in the concept of sexual scripts and is very valuable reading on sexual learning content and processes.

Gagnon, J. H., "Scripts and the Social Coordination of Sexual Conduct," in J. K. Cole and R. Deinstbier (Eds.), *Nebraska Symposium on Motivation.* Lincoln: University of Nebraska Press, 1974.
The concept of sexual scripts has far-reaching implications for the notion that people engage in certain behaviors because of internal motivations to do so. This is a good, clear statement of how the concept of sexual scripts pertains to the idea of motivation and a good discussion of coordinated activity in sexual interaction.

For an excellent recent discussion of sex education in the United States, see the entire issue of *Journal of School Health,* April 1981, vol. **51,** No. 4.

KEY TO SELF-TEST QUESTIONS

Part I: True-False Statements

1. F (This was the view of the past, but today the common view is that hormones determine or influence sexuality.)
2. T
3. T (The consistency we do find suggests that there is no relationship in humans.)
4. F (Evidence within American society and across other cultures reveals that having an interest in sex is learned.)
5. T (The clearest example of this is the devastating effects of rape.)
6. F (There are general forms and content of learning at certain ages, but it is not clearly developmental.)
7. F (Sex guilt is a personality characteristic, not a matter of feeling guilty.)
8. F (We use certain criteria to define a person as male or female, and these criteria are socially accepted definitions not determined by some ultimate biological law.)
9. T (The main information sources are still one's peers.)
10. F (For females, but not males, the same sex parent is important.)
11. T (Those topics students are most interested in are the least likely to be covered.)

12. F (For the above reason.)
13. T
14. F (There is a very small difference.)
15. F (Only three do so.)

Part II: Multiple-Choice Questions

1. *b*
2. *a*
3. *b*
4. *c*
5. *a*
6. *b*
7. *b*
8. *b*

Chapter 5
Sexual Arousal

Sexual arousal is a fascinating and highly informative dimension of the human being. In the study of sexual arousal, one cannot help but appreciate the intricacy and complexity of human behavior.

Human sexual arousal involves a series of social, psychological, physiological, and neurological processes which are related to one another in exciting, yet not fully understood, ways. Sexual arousal involves psychological processes primarily through learning and thought processes. This learning, however, is based on social definitions of appropriate and inappropriate sexuality, and what is learned is affected by the very history and structure of society. Sexual arousal is also physiological in that it involves a complex set of changes in the body—changes which are activated by what one has learned as a member of a society. Last, what goes on in the head is connected to what goes on in the genitals by means of an inadequately understood set of neurological (brain and nervous system) processes. No one of these processes (social, psychological, physiological, neurological) is any more important than any other. Rather, we must understand sexual arousal as a process which is the result of a rather complex set of relationships among all four of these processes.

PHYSIOLOGICAL PROCESSES: THE SEXUAL RESPONSE CYCLE

In their landmark research, Masters and Johnson (1966) identified and described the changes which take place in the body as one moves from an unaroused state through increasing sexual arousal, orgasm, and back to an unaroused state. For the sake of analysis and description, Masters and Johnson divided this entire process into four stages which describe the sexual response cycle: *excitement, plateau, orgasm* and *resolution*.[1]

These stages are sequential in that they occur in this order, but they are not so distinct that one jumps from one stage to the next. Rather, the four stages describe the *flow* of events which take place, after "effective sexual stimulation." These stages do not describe the exact changes which take place for all people all the time. The physiological processes in each stage are typical, but they do vary from

[1]Kaplan (1974), in her approach to sexual therapy, views sexual response as having two phases. The first is genital vasocongestion resulting in male erection and female vaginal lubrication and swelling. The second is the muscular contraction during orgasm. In 1979 she revised this view somewhat to include sexual desire, sexual excitement, and orgasm as three stages in arousal and response.

individual to individual and from time to time for the same individual. Last, these stages do not describe *why* sexual arousal takes place. Masters and Johnson began at the point of "effective sexual stimulation" and thus the stages describe what happens physiologically *when* sexual arousal does take place.

Vasocongestion and Myotonia

Two basic physiological processes take place in sexual arousal: vasocongestion and myotonia. *Vasocongestion* is the engorgement or overfilling of blood vessels. During sexual arousal, this is most pronounced in the genital and pelvic regions, but it occurs in other areas of the body as well. In a nonaroused state, the flow of blood into an organ or area through the system of arteries is equal to the outflow through the veins. In sexual arousal, nerve impulses are sent to the muscle fibers in the small arteries in certain organs and areas. These nerve impulses cause the small arteries to dilate or become larger. As the small arteries dilate, more blood flows in than can flow out, creating a congestion of blood. With this

vasocongestion the organ swells, hardens, and changes color.

Myotonia is increased muscle tension. As in the case of vasocongestion, myotonia is widespread during sexual arousal and results in specific bodily changes throughout the sexual response cycle. The most important of these changes take place in the genital region. While muscle tension has not received much attention as a process taking place during sexual arousal, recent research reveals that myotonia is the most important physiological process involved in orgasm. It might be suggested that perhaps one of the reasons much more attention has been given to vasocongestion is that, as we shall see, it is central to male erection. Once we began to examine myotonia in arousal, we began to understand more about female sexual response, particularly orgasm.

Stages of the Sexual Response Cycle

Excitement The beginning of the sexual response cycle is the excitement stage, characterized by the onset of vasocongestion and myotonia.

BOX 5-1
ERECTIONS DURING SLEEP

From adolescence through late adulthood, it is normal for males to have erections while sleeping (Karacan et al., 1972; 1978). Whether the erection is partial or full, the average male has several erections during a normal night's sleep (Marshall et al., 1981). Nocturnal erections tend to be associated with periods of rapid eye movement (REM) (dream periods) (Fisher et al., 1965; Kahn and Fisher, 1969). Recent research (Marshall et al., 1981) has found that the lack of nocturnal erections is associated with impotence (the inability to obtain an erection sufficient for vaginal penetration). Impotence generally falls within one of two categories, based on its assumed cause. Psychogenic impotence is caused by some psychological factor, while organic impotence is caused by some physiological factor. Interestingly, Marshall et al. (1981) found that males with psychogenic impotence almost invariably had erections during their sleep, averaging four erections per night. Males with organic impotence had fewer and smaller nocturnal erections than males with psychogenic impotence, but they also frequently had them. Females also experience nocturnal vaginal vasocongestion during REM periods (Abel, 1979).

Figure 5-1 Changes in male genitals from nonaroused state through excitement, plateau, and orgasm.

Due to this initial vasocongestion, the most obvious physical change in males is erection or tumescence of the penis. As vasocongestion in the penis takes place, the organ swells, becomes harder, and moves from a flaccid to an erect state (Figure 5-1). The development of erection during the excitement stage is often fragile and may be inhibited or impaired by nonsexual distractions. During excitement, the scrotal skin of the male contracts and thickens and the scrotum becomes tighter. The testes are lifted up toward the body wall by the tightening of the scrotum and the shortening of the spermatic cords.

In females, several obvious changes occur during excitement. Owing to vasocongestion, the clitoris hardens and increases in size. This tumescence of the clitoris is not always observable to the naked eye and its extent varies from individual to individual. Regardless of its visibility, this process always takes place, resulting in the glans of the clitoris coming into closer contact with the surrounding tissue. The labia majora flatten and separate from the vaginal opening during excitement. Because of vasocongestion, the breasts enlarge, a rashlike coloration (more pronounced in the female) appears on the chest region, and the labia minora increase in size. Myotonia also creates erection of the nipples.

Several significant changes appear in the vagina during the excitement stage. Vasocongestion results in an action like sweating (not yet fully understood) on the vaginal walls, producing vaginal lubrication. This is the first physiological evidence of sexual arousal, usually beginning within 10 to 30 seconds from the onset of excitement. In the inner two-thirds of the vagina, myotonia causes the normally collapsed vaginal walls to expand. This expansion results in the vaginal canal becoming longer and wider. At the same time, the uterus begins to elevate, producing a tenting effect (similar to pulling up the top of a collapsed tent) (Figure 5-2).

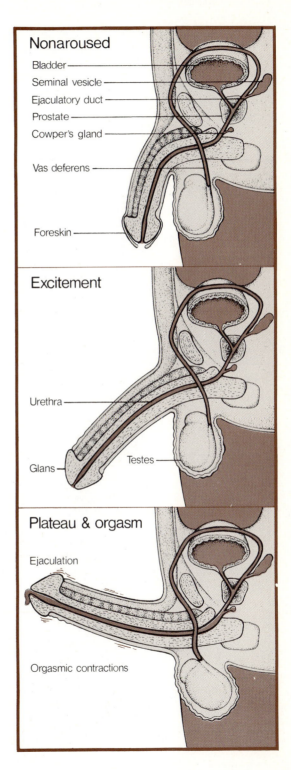

Nonaroused

Bladder
Seminal vesicle
Ejaculatory duct
Prostate
Cowper's gland
Vas deferens
Foreskin

Excitement

Urethra
Glans
Testes

Plateau & orgasm

Ejaculation
Orgasmic contractions

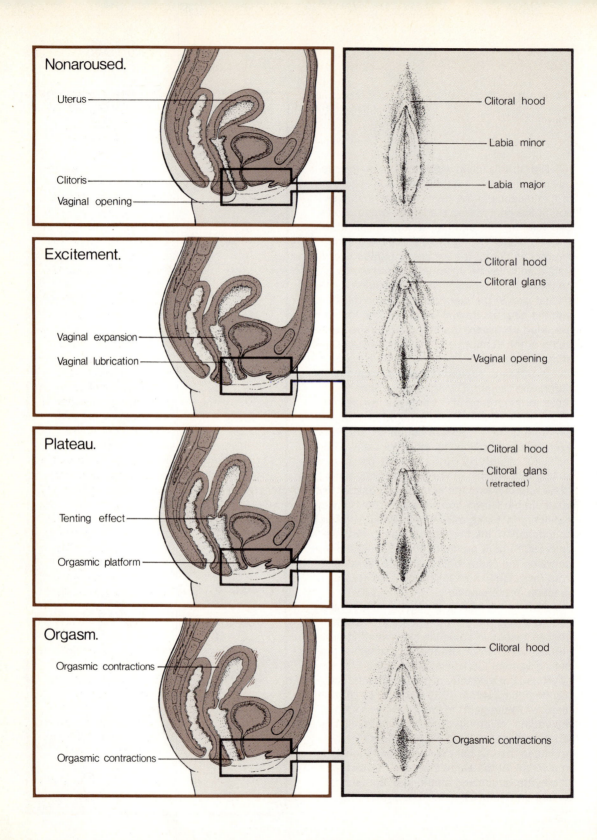

Nonaroused.

Uterus

Clitoris

Vaginal opening

Clitoral hood

Labia minor

Labia major

Excitement.

Vaginal expansion

Vaginal lubrication

Clitoral hood

Clitoral glans

Vaginal opening

Plateau.

Tenting effect

Orgasmic platform

Clitoral hood

Clitoral glans
(retracted)

Orgasm.

Orgasmic contractions

Orgasmic contractions

Clitoral hood

Orgasmic contractions

Figure 5-2 Changes in the female reproductive anatomy in the stages of sexual arousal from nonaroused state through orgasm. The illustrations on the left show a side view of the internal changes which take place in each stage and the illustrations on the right detail the changes which take place in the clitoris, vaginal opening, and labia.

Plateau During the plateau stage, vasocongestion reaches its peak. For males, this means that the penis is fully erect and erection is unlikely to be lost because of distractions. The size of the penis in the erect state is related to its size in the flaccid state; however, the relative increase in size during erection is greater for smaller organs. Thus, while there is considerable individual variation in flaccid penis size, this individual variation is somewhat less in the erect state. The coronal ridge of the penis swells during plateau and becomes darker in color. The testes enlarge and continue to elevate until they are resting against the body wall (Figure 5-1).

In females, vasocongestion continues in the breasts. The resulting increase in their size (up to 25 percent larger than in the nonaroused state) may make the nipples appear to retract. Rather, the breast is swelling around the erect nipple. The tenting effect and expansion of the vaginal walls increase, resulting in the vagina's being almost twice as long and one-third again as wide as in a nonaroused state. An important change in the vagina during plateau is formation of the *orgasmic platform* through vasocongestion in the outer third of the vagina. Owing to this vasocongestion, this portion of the vagina swells, often creating a noticeable decrease in the size of the vaginal opening (Figure 5-2). Lubrication of the vagina now slows considerably. The clitoris continues to become congested with blood, and in the latter part of the plateau stage, it becomes elevated and retracts under the clitoral hood, with the shaft becoming about 50 percent shorter (Figure 5-2). The uterus enlarges during plateau, as do the labia minora, and as orgasm approaches, the labia minora increase in reddish color.

Even though "stages" suggests that movement through excitement and plateau is a smooth, ever-increasing process, this is not necessarily so. During both excitement and plateau, there may or may not be a steady increase in arousal. Plateau, for example, frequently involves a series of peaks and valleys of sexual arousal before the point of orgasm is reached.

Orgasm Orgasm is characterized by the massive release of muscle tension which has built up during excitement and plateau; this release is accompanied by very pleasurable sensations.

Orgasm in the male consists of two stages. The first is a preliminary or "get-ready" stage in which one has the feeling that ejaculation is inevitable, as indeed it is. In this stage, the vas, seminal vesicles, and prostate contract and force the ejaculate into the bulb at the base of the urethra. This is called *emission*. The second stage consists of the urethral bulb, urethra, and penis contracting rhythmically, forcing the ejaculate from the urethral bulb through the urethra and out of the penis. The degree of force with which the ejaculate is expelled from the penis varies with each individual and with other factors, such as age and time since last ejaculation. These contractions are generally accompanied by very pleasurable sensations and usually consist of three to four pulsations of the penis at 0.8 second intervals. Slower and less forceful pulsations continue for a few seconds. While the amount of ejaculate is usually about a teaspoonful, there is also individual variation as well as variation due to time since last ejaculation and age.

Female orgasm consists of a series of rhythmic contractions in the vagina, uterus, and anus, the most pronounced being in the orgasmic platform (Figure 5-2). These contractions occur at about 0.8 second intervals and may be few in number or prolonged, depending on the "strength" of orgasm. Usually three to four such contractions take place in a single orgasm.

Physiologically, male and female orgasms are identical processes, the only difference being in anatomy. This physiological identity is reflected in what orgasm feels like. If men and women write descriptions of how an orgasm feels and these descriptions are given to others (with the anatomical references deleted), the accounts written by males cannot be distinguished from those written by females. This is the case regardless of the gender or professional expertise of the reader (Vance and Wagner, 1976).

Male and female orgasms also do not differ in the sense that males ejaculate and females do not. First of all, ejaculation and orgasm are separate physiological processes.

Orgasm is a neuromuscular release of built-up sexual tension which peaks in the late plateau stage. Ejaculation is the muscular contraction of certain tissues in the body which transports ejaculate. Ejaculation in males generally accompanies orgasm but need not. Males may experience orgasm without ejaculating (Robbins and Jensen, 1978). Usually males learn that orgasm equals ejaculation, and thus orgasm and ejaculation almost always go together in actual behavior. Some males, however, learn to distinguish the orgasm response from the ejaculation response and can thus have one or more orgasms without any ejaculation.

BOX 5-2
A NOTE ON FEMALE EJACULATION

The "fact" that females do not and cannot ejaculate is so ingrained in the medical and biological communities that many professionals simply refuse to believe the existing research. When this book was being reviewed prior to publication, several reviewers, commenting on this section of the manuscript, wrote that they "simply did not believe the research findings." The following letter, written to the *Journal of Sex Research,* delightfully reveals these feelings and their demise as viewed by a physician. I suspect that Dr. Weisberg's honest and revealing letter will become a classic in the history of sex research.

I'm confused. A board-certified obstetrician gynecologist, who is also a certified sex educator and therapist, ought to know whether or not a woman ejaculates.

I first learned about female ejaculation at an American Association for Sex Educators, Counselors, and Therapists meeting. The presentation was full of foreign-sounding phrases like Grafenberg spots and female ejaculation.

"Bull," I said. "I spend half of my waking hours examining, cutting apart, putting together, removing or rearranging female reproductive organs. There is no prostate and women don't ejaculate."

After the presentation, I, along with two other physicians and a registered nurse (all sex therapists), challenged the presentors. "Show us," we said. And they did.

Strange as it sounds, the whole group went up to a room in the hotel and had the opportunity of examining one of the subjects about whom the paper was written. The vulva and vagina were normal with no abnormal masses or spots. The urethra was normal. Everything was normal. She then had her partner stimulate her by inserting two fingers into the vagina and stroking along the urethra lengthwise. To our amazement, the area began to swell. It eventually became a firm 1×2 cm oval area distinctly different from the rest of the vagina. In a few moments the subject seemed to perform a Valsalva maneuver (bearing

It is also possible to ejaculate without orgasm. Nocturnal emissions ("wet dreams") involve this process. Ejaculation, but without orgasm, may also take place by electrical stimulation of certain nerve centers.

As we shall see, orgasm and ejaculation involve entirely different nervous system processes. It has long been thought that females do not ejaculate. Perhaps because of western culture's attitude that males and females "really are different," female ejaculation was taken as a myth. In fact, when women would report the expulsion of fluid from the vaginal area during orgasm, they were typically told that

this was uncontrollable urination on their part. (It is no wonder that females do not know they ejaculate, since we have convinced them that they cannot and told them that what they experience is a very undesirable urinary behavior.) Through recent research, we now know that some females have the physiological capacity for ejaculation and do ejaculate. In males, the ejaculate consists mostly of fluid secreted from the prostate gland. It has long been considered medical fact that females do not have a prostate gland. This now appears to be an error. As we noted in Chapter 3, the genital and reproductive systems of males and females

down as if starting to defecate) and seconds later several ccs of milky fluid shot out of the urethra. The material was clearly not urine. In fact, if the chemical analyses described in the paper are correct, its composition was closest to prostatic fluid.

Okay, the Grafenberg spot is there. But what is it? Is it erectile tissue around the urethra? Is it merely vasocongestion in normal tissue? Is it edema? Is it some embryological anomaly?

I remembered that epithelial buds, which arise from the primitive female urethra and the urogenital sinus are the homologues of the prostate. What I didn't remember, but subsequently found in an embryology book, was that the lower glands occasionally hypertrophy and make a "female prostate."

I was really confused. I checked with several anatomists, all of whom thought I was crazy. But my patients didn't think I was crazy. A few told me that they ejaculate. Some knew about the erotic area around the urethra. And *everyone* who went home to experiment found the Grafenberg spot.

I still have no explanation for this, but I can attest to the fact that the Grafenberg spot and female ejaculation exist.

Years from now I am sure that a medical school lecturer will joke about how it wasn't until 1980 that the medical community finally accepted the fact that women really do ejaculate.

Martin Weisberg, MD
Assistant Professor
Obstetrics and Gynecology and
Psychiatry
Thomas Jefferson University Hospital
Philadelphia, Pa.

Source: *The Journal of Sex Research*, 1981, **17,** 90–91.

come from the exact same tissues. It is only in the process of sexual differentiation during fetal development that these tissues form male or female anatomical characteristics. In the male, the tissue which forms the prostate gland and various related ducts is highly developed. In females, the research indicates, while this tissue is not as highly developed as in males, it is present and functional in many women (Perry and Whipple, 1981).

The rudimentary female prostate may take the form of what is called the *Grafenberg spot*. This is an area which—like the male prostate—lies along the urethra. If one inserts a finger into the vagina, the Grafenberg spot can be manually stimulated by gently pressing upward (12:00 direction). If the Grafenberg spot is manually stimulated, it swells to 3 or 4 times its normal size, and women who do ejaculate identify this spot as the "trigger" for their ejaculation (Perry and Whipple, 1981). Researchers have only begun to explore female ejaculation, but it is clear that many females do ejaculate and the ejaculation (as in males) can be separated from orgasm. The amount of the female ejaculate varies, but some females ejaculate an easily measurable amount of fluid that may spurt as far as 3 feet from the urinary opening (Addiego et al., 1981). The research to date suggests that this fluid is chemically very similar to the secretion of the male prostate gland, a finding which leads researchers to suggest that the Grafenberg spot is simply a "less developed" female prostate. It is assumed that the fluid from the prostate in the female is secreted into the urethra in much the same manner as in males. As we shall see, female ejaculation appears to be closely related to the process of myotonia.

Types of orgasm   As discussed in Chapter 1, Freud argued that there are two types of female orgasm: the "mature" vaginal orgasm and the "immature" clitoral orgasm. When Masters and Johnson published their research in 1966, their work was seen as demolishing the idea of two types of female orgasm. They reported that, physiologically, there is only one type of female orgasm. This report was based on the observation that regardless

of how, where, or why sexual stimulation takes place on the body, the clitoris is the center of sexual sensation. Of course, Freud's distinction between vaginally oriented and clitorally oriented orgasms as mature and immature was a value judgment and not a scientific observation. However, it now appears that when we accepted the Masters and Johnson conclusion that there is only one type of female orgasm, we made a serious error. Following Masters and Johnson, most experts in sexuality agreed that regardless of where or how sexual stimulation takes place for females (vagina, clitoris, breasts, hair, teeth, or eyebrows), orgasm sensations and responses are centered in the clitoris.[2]

It was further argued that the most or only "effective" sexual stimulation (meaning the most likely to create arousal to orgasm) for females is direct stimulation of the clitoris. On the basis of this assumption, it was argued that intercourse with a penis moving in and out of a vagina is ineffective in female stimulation. The reasoning here was that in most intercourse positions, there is very little contact between the penis and clitoris, and that the only way the clitoris is stimulated by coitus is that the penis moves the labia minora back and forth and they in turn rub over the top of the clitoris. The assumption here was that the vaginal walls contain too few nerve endings to be highly sensitive to the penis.

These assumptions now appear to have been wrong. Very clearly, there is not one type of female orgasm and not all women respond to only clitoral stimulation.

Women have for years said that an orgasm by means of only clitoral stimulation (such as by masturbation) feels different from an orgasm by means of intercourse. In 1973, Fisher, in this extensive research on female orgasm, found that women did describe orgasm found that women did describe orgasm by these two types of stimulation differently. Fisher's findings were generally branded as an attempt to revitalize the old Freudian concept of

[2]Kinsey et al. (1953) found that some women experienced orgasm by having their eyebrows stroked, their hair gently blown, or mild pressure applied to their teeth.

dual orgasm. However, as more research has accumulated and researchers have begun to listen to women describe *their* orgasm experiences, it is clear that some women have orgasm by stimulation of the clitoris alone and other women have orgasm by deep penetration of the vagina by a penis (Ellison, 1980). These two types of orgasm do in fact feel different. Orgasm by means of clitoral stimulation is typically described as very intense, sharp, electric, and ecstatic, while orgasm by means of deep vaginal penetration is described as more internal, deep, warm, soothing, full, and subtle (Robertiello, 1970; Singer and Singer, 1972; Fisher, 1973; Butler, 1976; Bentler and Peeler, 1979; Ellison, 1980).

There is a solid physiological basis for two types of female orgasm in terms of the type of stimulation that brings about the response. The body contains two nerve pathways to the genitals. One involves the *pudendal* nerve, which runs from the spinal cord to the majority of muscles in the outer third of the vagina and the clitoris. The second involves the *pelvic* nerve, which runs from the spinal cord to about one-third of the muscles in the outer third of the vagina, the bladder, and the uterus and cervix. Probably, those women who have orgasm by deep vaginal penetration are highly sensitive in the pelvic nerve pathway. Thus, pressure against the cervix, uterus, and inner part of the vagina is sexually stimulating. Those women who have orgasm by clitoral stimulation alone are probably more sensitive along the pudendal nerve pathway to the clitoris and orgasmic platform.

These nerve pathways and different types of female orgasm are also related to differences in muscle strength, which is in turn related to female ejaculation. Women who ejaculate have stronger muscles in the outer one-third of the vagina and uterus than women who do not ejaculate (Perry and Whipple, 1981). Perry and Whipple found that the strength of muscle contractions in the uterus are 136 percent greater for women who ejaculate than for women who do not, and vaginal muscle contractions are 49 percent stronger. Graber (1981) and Huey et al. (1981) further found

that women who have never experienced orgasm have the lowest vaginal and uterine muscle strength, that women who have had orgasm only by means of clitoral stimulation have moderate vaginal and uterine muscle strength, and that women who have orgasm through either clitoral or vaginal stimulation have the greatest muscle strength.

These various research findings fit together to provide us with a picture of the two types of female orgasms. Clitoral orgasm is associated with lower vaginal, and especially uterine, muscle strength and a dominance of the pudendal nerve pathway. Vaginal orgasm, or orgasm through deep vaginal penetration and thus pressure stimulation on the inner part of the vagina, the cervix, and the uterus, is associated with greater muscle strength in the vagina, and especially the uterus, the dominance of the pelvic nerve pathway, and the probability of ejaculation. The reason ejaculation is more likely in this case is that the pelvic nerve is the nerve which serves the male prostate gland. It is almost certain that it serves the female prostate gland as well (the Grafenberg spot).

It is unclear to what extent these differences are fixed. It is clear that the probability of orgasm in a woman can be increased by learning to voluntarily control the vaginal musculature and by strengthening these muscles.[3]

It is interesting to note that in all the debate about types of female orgasms, the poor male orgasm has been ignored. I suggest that we will find the same two types of male orgasm to be similarly well based on the same nerve pathways and muscle strength differences, and that these male types will center on such processes as being able to voluntarily control orgasm, ejaculation, and multiple orgasm.

There are several reasons for suggesting this. The first is anatomical. There is no anatomical reason why males should not have different kinds of orgasm response such as we have described in females. The second is ob-

---

[3]For a review of female vaginal musculature and its relationship to sexual functioning, see Graber (1981).

BOX 5-3

MUSCLE CONTRACTIONS DURING ORGASM

Mould (1980) has reviewed the neuromuscular processes which are most likely involved in orgasm in a discussion of female orgasm response. He quite reasonably argues that the evidence suggests that physical sensory information (physical stimulation) is combined with cognitive information (the interpretation of the sensory information) to result in vasocongestion. The vasocongestion is proposed by Mould to have two effects relevant to actual orgasm. First, the pelvic muscles stretch with vasocongestion. Second, these muscles reach a threshold at which the actual musculature process of orgasm can take place. This process is called *clonic contraction,* in which repetitive, involuntary contractions of the muscles occur. This clonic contraction is an abnormal response in all parts of the body except the pelvic muscles in orgasm. As these contractions take place, vasocongestion decreases. This decrease is perhaps why orgasmic contractions become less intense as orgasm continues, and it may account for the fact that women with stronger pelvic muscles are more likely to have multiple orgasm. Since a certain level of tension reached in the muscles is necessary for the clonic contractions of orgasm to occur, this may also account for the fact that greater pelvic muscle strength appears to be related to a greater likelihood of orgasm. It may also explain why, if psychological factors inhibit a high level of arousal and thus vasocongestion, orgasm is not experienced, since the necessary level of muscle tension for clonic contractions to take place is not reached. (For a good review of the nature and role of vaginal muscles in female sexual response, see Graber (1981).)

servational. As noted earlier, Vance and Wagner (1976) found that the descriptions of orgasm given by males and females could not be distinguished by independent judges. If there are two types of female orgasm which feel different, there must then be two different descriptions of male orgasm, or Vance and Wagner would have found that judges could tell a female orgasm description from a male orgasm description. I suspect that if we were to ask males about orgasm, we would find that an orgasm brought about by stimulation of the shaft of the penis feels like a female orgasm only by means of deep vaginal penetration, and an orgasm by means of stimulation of the glans of the penis feels like a female orgasm brought about only by stimulation of the clitoris.

Resolution While orgasm may be the high point of the sexual response cycle, there

is more yet to come. Regardless of the physiological identity of male and female orgasm, there is thought to be one difference—a difference found in the resolution stage. Following orgasm, both males and females go through the resolution stage. This involves a reversal of those physiological changes that took place during excitement and plateau. There is a relaxation of muscle tension throughout the body and a release of blood from the congested vessels. Observable changes during resolution for females include a reduction in breast size, the clitoris emerging from under the clitoral hood, a loss of tumescence of the clitoris, and a gradual disappearance of the sexual flush coloration of the chest region. The orgasmic platform subsides, the tenting effect reverses as the uterus lowers, the color of the vaginal walls returns to a lighter hue, and the vaginal walls return to their original collapsed position. In males, the most obvious physical change is the loss of erection with the reversal of vasocongestion. This occurs in two stages. First, there is a rather rapid flow of blood from the penis and thus a rapid decline in erection. This is only a partial reversal of vasocongestion. The second stage consists of the vasocongestion gradually reversing fully over a period of minutes and the penis thus returning to its nonarousal size and shape.

Masters and Johnson (1966) reported that a, if not the, major difference between males and females is that males have a *refractory period* following orgasm while females do not. During this period, males are not capable of further arousal and thus not capable of further orgasm. The length of this period was reported by Masters and Johnson to vary a great deal from one person to the next and from one sexual encounter to the next. They argued that since females had no such refractory period as in the case of males, they had the physiological potential of *multiple orgasm,* a series of complete and separate orgasm responses one after the other and each separated by mere seconds. In actuality, only about 13 percent of all females ever experience multiple orgasm.

It now appears, however, that Masters and Johnson were wrong. One of the major problems with their 1966 work is that they confused orgasm and ejaculation. It is very clear that males (and probably females as well) are not capable of multiple ejaculation. However, male multiple orgasm is not only possible, but is known to take place. Kinsey et al. (1948) reported that 10 percent of the males 25 years of age had multiple orgasm now and then. This assertion was considered absurd by most readers and simply ignored (just as we ignored the reports of women about ejaculation). Recently, Robbins and Jensen (1978) studied thirteen males aged 22 to 56 who reported that they experienced multiple orgasms prior to ejaculating. Physiological measures taken on one of these subjects confirmed these reports. This subject exhibited three separate orgasms in a matter of seconds and a fourth upon ejaculating. If this topic is raised in your class, you will find more males who will tell you that they have multiple orgasms. It is presently unclear to what the refractory period described by Masters and Johnson applies. It is obvious, however, that it does not apply to the inability of males to have multiple orgasms, each of which is separate from ejaculation. Perhaps because Masters and Johnson confused orgasm and ejaculation when talking about males (think about that one for a minute) but not about females, the refractory period refers to the time required for a male (and probably a female as well) to ejaculate a second or third time.

THE NERVOUS SYSTEM AND SEXUAL AROUSAL

Sexual arousal involves much more than the dilation of blood vessels and increasing muscle tension. The brain, spinal cord, and a complex nervous system all play a central role in sexual arousal and response. It is this incredibly complex aspect of the human body which is the least understood in terms of sexual arousal.

Erection and Ejaculation Centers in the Spinal Cord

In males, erection and ejaculation may take place without any sensation of sexual stimulation or pleasure. The erection center is located in the lower part of the male spinal cord (Figure 5-3). It is a nerve center that controls nerve impulses sent to the penis. These nerve impulses go to the muscles of the arteries and cause dilation of the muscular walls of the arteries, the result being vasocongestion. Erection may take place as a simple reflex action, as in a knee jerk when the knee is tapped with a rubber hammer. The process works as follows. Sense organs which detect touch (in this case located in the penis or genital region) transmit the message of touch to the nerve centers in the spinal cord. The nerve centers receive the message and send out a signal to tissues which produce a physiological response, in this instance the muscles in the arteries of the penis. This process can take place without the brain's ever hearing about it, and if this is so, no sensation is experienced even though erection occurs.

Many men with damaged or completely severed spinal cords have erections but do not feel anything simply because this reflex action can operate as a self-contained system (Higgins, 1979). This same reflex action takes place in ejaculation through the ejaculation center located somewhat higher in the spinal cord (Figure 5-3). It is assumed that females have similar centers, but their existence and the responses they control are not known.[4]

Erogenous Zones

Many people believe that touching certain areas of the body automatically produces sexual arousal ("Blow in my ear, I'll follow you anywhere"). Such thinking can result in approaching sexual arousal in much the same manner as one approaches the buttons on an elevator. The sexual result is quite likely to be about as exciting as the ride.

What we call erogenous zones (penis, clitoris, labia minora, breasts, nipples, between the anus and genitals, mouth, lips, buttocks, thighs, etc.) are areas which are rich in nerve endings and thus sensitive to touch. The touch to which they are sensitive, however, is *any* touch. There are no special sexual touch receptors anywhere in the body. All touch receptors throughout the body are the same and the only information they relay is touch. Thus, the touch of a physician or nurse is the same as that of a lover. What makes a certain area of the body sexually sensitive is that the brain interprets a touch as sexual. This interpretation involves not only where the body is being touched, but also the how, who, why, and when of the touch. Lips are very sensitive to sexual stimulation, but when was the last time you became sexually aroused while eating pizza or having your teeth cleaned? What

makes any part of the body an erogenous zone in any situation is that sexual meanings are attached to that part of the body, and then that part is touched in what is defined as a sexual manner. A significant part of learning that certain areas are erogenous zones is that such areas are usually touched only in sexual situations (Gagnon, 1977).[5]

Erogenous zones are thus not physiologically determined except in the sense that they are rich in nerve endings. Rather, erogenous zones are social and personal creations. Any part of the body can have erotic meaning, and what is a highly erogenous zone for one individual may be a source of irritation for another. Erogenous zones differ dramatically from one culture to another and, as Gagnon (1977) points out, tend to rise and fall in popularity. Male nipples have been receiving a lot of attention lately and are rapidly on their way to becoming a new erogenous zone. Some areas of the body also physiologically qualify, but never quite make it. Hands, for example, are very sensitive to touch, and even though they receive a great deal of tactile stimulation in sexual interaction, they are not considered an erogenous zone (Gagnon, 1977).

The Power of Positive Thinking

It should now be obvious why it is frequently said that the most important sexual organ is located between the ears. It is in the brain that the interpretation is made that any stimulus (sight, sound, smell, touch) is sexual. Without this interpretation process in the brain, there is nothing. By themselves, without the interpretive processes performed in the brain, these sexual stimuli are not sexual stimuli.

Making the entire process of sexual arousal even more fascinating, of course, is the fact that the brain need not receive any message of sensation from any sense organ. Imagination alone is sufficient for the brain to send the message of sexual excitement to other parts of

---

[4]For a detailed discussion of vascular processes in erection, see Tordjman et al. (1980). For a review and discussion of the work in this area, see Mould (1980).

[5]This is why gynecological examinations are much more socially and psychologically complex situations than dental examinations.

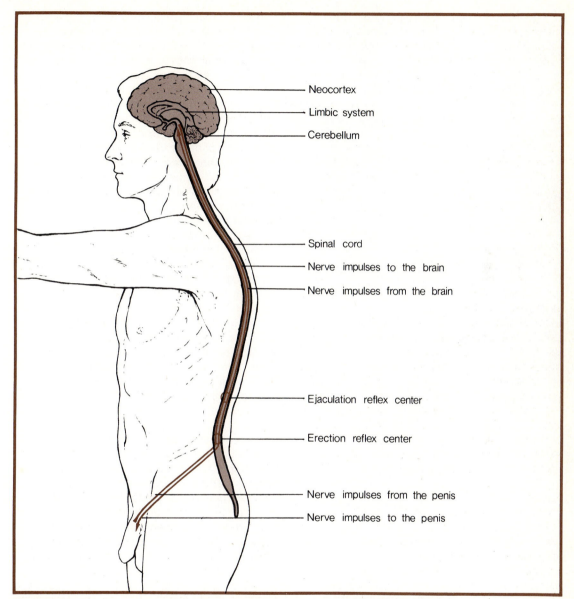

Neocortex
Limbic system
Cerebellum

Spinal cord
Nerve impulses to the brain
Nerve impulses from the brain

Ejaculation reflex center

Erection reflex center

Nerve impulses from the penis
Nerve impulses to the penis

Figure 5-3 The nervous system processes in male sexual arousal and response. Nerve impulses of touch or other sensations in a part of the body (in this example the penis) are sent to the spinal cord, through which they travel to the brain. Messages are sent back through the spinal cord and out the nerve system to the penis, creating physiological changes in the form of erection.

What are considered erogenous zones are in some situations merely parts of the body.

the body. As we shall see, imagination is perhaps the most powerful of all sexual stimuli.

The Interplay of Mind and Body

It is important to keep in mind that regardless of what happens in the brain, a fully functioning physiological system must be operating for sexual arousal and response to take place. For males or females with severe spinal cord injuries, for example, the brain may be spinning with sexual thoughts but no genital reactions develop since these messages from the brain cannot get through the spinal cord to the genitals.

With normal aging, certain physiological changes affect sexual arousal and response.

In males, penile sensitivity declines with age, reflecting a general decline in sensitivity to touch (Edwards and Husted, 1976; Thornbury and Mistretta, 1981). Erection also takes longer to obtain and ejaculation is less forceful. Resolution is more rapid and erection disappears a few seconds after orgasm in a single, rather than two, stages. In females, vaginal lubrication takes longer and is less prolific, the tenting effect of the vaginal walls does not develop fully, and orgasmic contractions are fewer and less intense. Even though clitoral responsiveness remains unchanged with age, resolution is more rapid. The vaginal walls also become thinner, frequently resulting in a burning sensation during urination after intercourse because of indirect irritation of the bladder by the penis (Katchadourian and Lunde, 1975). As disastrous as these changes may sound, none of them means that highly satisfying sexual arousal and response are not possible with increasing age. They are simply changes that call for adjustments in sexual activity patterns. As we shall see, information stored in the brain through learning has the most effect on sexual activity with increasing age; for example, one may learn that sexuality and youth go together in this society, while sexuality and old age do not.

Certain diseases also have an effect on certain physiological processes so that arousal is impaired. These may be changes in the brain or nerves, changes in musculature, or changes in the veins and arteries, all of which can alter both vasocongestion and myotonia. Certain drugs and medications can also alter the responses of the central nervous system, the muscles, or the veins and arteries as well as other physiological processes related to sexual arousal.

It would be ideal if we could draw a diagram indicating how much sexual arousal is a function of psychological processes and how much it is a function of physiological processes. At the present time, that is not possible with our limited knowledge. However, as research accumulates, the overwhelming importance of psychological processes emerges. This fact becomes most clear in the study of sexuality and chronic illness. In general, we find that among the chronically ill, psychological processes play a much more influential role in sexual desire, arousal, response, and activity than do physiological processes. This is often true even when the physiological damage from the chronic illness or its treatment is major. We shall discuss this in detail in Chapter 16. At that time, you may wish to turn back to sections of this chapter.

While we tend to place a great deal of emphasis on the existence and nature of body parts labeled "sexual," these parts are not necessary for sexual arousal and response. Large amounts of genital tissue can be removed without affecting sexual response. For example, the penis can be amputated without affecting either arousal or orgasm (Money, 1977). Females who have had radical surgery on the vulva or whose clitoris has been surgically removed still experience orgasm (Money, 1977). The important factor here is not the existence of the organ, but the functioning of the relevant nerve pathways.

INFORMATION STORED IN THE BRAIN

The central information stored in the brain is what the individual has learned is sexually arousing. As noted earlier, no touch, smell, sight, or sound is automatically arousing to humans. What is sexually arousing is what one has learned is sexually arousing.

Learning as a Member of a Culture: Different Strokes

What we learn is sexually arousing is limited only by circumstance. Anything you can think of has the potential to be sexually arousing if it has been given that sexual meaning.

As we examine what turns people on, we find, however, a great deal of agreement within a society. While there are certainly individual exceptions, most people in a society are aroused by much the same things. This is so not because most people in a society are "normal," but because most of what we learn is

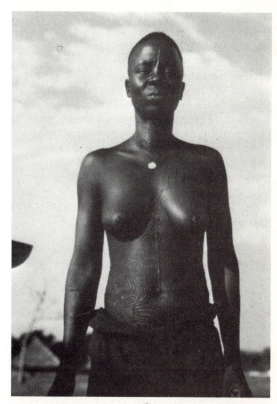

What constitutes beauty differs from culture to culture. This Bakuba woman from Zaire is adorned with intricate keloid markings which are regarded as highly beautiful and erotic. The scars are made before adolescence by pinching a small amount of skin between the fingers and slicing it with a razor blade. Charcoal is then rubbed in the incision, leaving a slightly discolored scar when the skin heals.

sexually arousing comes from our culture's definition of what is erotic. Within any society, there are rather clear cultural definitions about what is and is not considered sexual and erotic. Most members of society learn these definitions well—so well, in fact, that they believe that what their culture defines as sexually arousing is only "natural" and anything else is somehow "not normal." Learning this definition and feeling this way is a large part of what being an acceptable sexual member of a society is all about.

What is sexually arousing, then, has nothing to do with what is incorrectly called "natural" human behavior. What is highly arousing in one society may be downright disgusting in another. Most males in American society find female breasts very arousing. Many cultures, such as the Mangaia of Polynesia, could care less about this aspect of the female anatomy. While our culture places great emphasis upon slimness as being sexually appealing, obese women in Old Hawaii were considered to be highly erotic. In East Bay in Melanesia, the inside of a female thigh is very erotic, especially if adorned with a tattoo. The same part of a woman's thigh is of sure interest to most males in our culture, but the presence of a "born to lose" tattoo is not likely to create a lot of sexual arousal in most males.

The vast majority of individuals in American society define affection, tenderness, caressing, and foreplay as highly erotic and essential components of appropriate sexual activity. Not all cultures share this view. Among the Mangaia, foreplay is often viewed as a waste of time and prolonged foreplay before coitus is simply in bad form.[6] The cultures of Romonum Island in Truk associate pain and frustration with sexual arousal, and lovers frequently inflict pain on each other during foreplay. The Sciriono find it highly arousing to scratch and pinch each other on the neck and chest, as well as to poke fingers in each other's eyes. As orgasm approaches, Sciriono lovers often scratch each other to the point of bleeding and emerge wounded; one is proud of one's sexual scars (this is not so different,

---

[6]Some aspects of sexuality in American society are very different from the patterns in other cultures, while others are very similar in ways we often overlook. For example, a male in our culture who does not engage in foreplay is considered crude and a poor lover: A Mangaian male, however, who spends "too much" time in foreplay will be called a "limp penis" by his female partner, who does not hesitate to publicly announce his lack of sexual technique. We might think that biting is unusual, but it is apparently more common in American patterns of sexual activity than we might think. For example, Kinsey found that of the college-educated white adults studied, 34 percent of the males and 38 percent of the females reported biting their partner during sexual activity, and 44 percent of the males and 42 percent of the females reported being bitten. Of those who had been bitten, most of both males and females said that the bite was sexually arousing (Gebhard and Johnson, 1979).

mind you, from a male's often proudly reported rug burns on the knees or scratches on the back in American society). Choriti women commonly engage in the highly erotic act of spitting in their partner's face during intercourse, and Arinaye women frequently bite off pieces of their lover's eyebrows and spit them aside with some enthusiasm.

Learning at the Individual Level

Learning what is sexually arousing takes place on the individual level in each individual's learning experience. A very large number of these individual learning experiences are determined by the culture in which one lives; not many Americans are heavily into erotic eyebrow biting. Within any culture, however, there is individual variation in what people have learned is sexually arousing; the variation comes about through unique individual learning experiences.

In Chapter 4, we discussed the various types of learning and will not describe them again here. It is useful, however, to indicate some of the ways in which we learn what is sexually arousing at the individual level.

Operant or instrumental conditioning plays a role in sexual arousal in that we are positively reinforced for being seuxally aroused by the same things others find sexually arousing. It is largely in this manner that we learn what is culturally appropriate or inappropriate as a sexual stimulus. While definitions of what is sexually arousing differ by gender, social class, race, religiosity, sexual preference, and many other social dimensions, peers play a vital role in this process of sexual learning. The male who is positively reinforced by his peers for saying "Look at her boobs!" is learning sexual arousal through operant or instrumental conditioning. So is the adolescent who receives negative reinforcement from peers for saying something to the effect that he or she is really turned on by people who never brush their teeth.

Modeling and observational learning also play a central role in learning what is sexually arousing. It does not take much in the way of keen insight to observe what one's older peers regard as sexually arousing. Mass media are very important in this regard. Television, movies, advertising, and magazines all convey clear images of what is sexually arousing in this society.

Learning what is sexually arousing also is acquired through classical conditioning. It is perhaps through this form of learning that people come to be sexually aroused by such things as rubber, leather, pain, fuzzy rugs, and urination. For example, if one of these objects or events is accidently paired with something that is sexually arousing, the person may develop a sexual response to this object or event through the process of classical conditioning.

Learning what is sexually arousing does not have to take place for every single object and event that turns a person on. Through *stimulus generalization,* we may have learned a response to all stimuli with a certain characteristic in common. Recall that Rachman, for example, conditioned males to be sexually aroused by shoes. This sexual arousal was not limited to the shoes used in the experiment, but was generalized to all shoelike apparel.

WHAT IS SEXUALLY AROUSING?

Given that what one responds to sexually is learned and that what is learned is largely dictated by cultural definitions, what do members of American society generally find sexually arousing?

Fantasy

Sexual fantasies range from a passing thought in daydreaming (Mednick, 1977; Giambra and Martin, 1977) to complex, vivid, and full-color thoughts of sexual activities (Carlson and Coleman, 1977). While only a few years ago many members of the psychiatric profession argued that women's sexual fantasies represented deep-seated sexual conflict and maladjustment, today we know that this is not true. Approximately 60 percent of all males and fe-

males have sexual fantasies during coitus (Hariton and Singer, 1974; Sue, 1979). However, the vast majority of people who do fantasize during coitus do not do so all the time. For example, in a study of college students' sexual fantasizing, only 5 to 6 percent of the males and females always fantasized during intercourse (Sue, 1979).

The question of male-female differences in the content of sexual fantasies during coitus remains somewhat confused. Since researchers have only recently given sexual fantasies any concerted attention, there is some disagreement as to male-female differences. As shown in Table 5-1, males have been found to fantasize more about imaginary lovers than do females. Other research has found, however, that males tend to fantasize more about what is happening at the moment and about real sexual experiences in their past while females tend to fantasize more about imaginary lovers (McCauley and Swann, 1976).

One difference in the content of male and female sexual fantasies does appear to be clear. Whether these fantasies are part of daydreaming, masturbation, or coitus, males and females tend to fantasize along the lines of traditional male and female sexual roles. Males tend to fantasize that a female is the recipient of their sexual advances, while females tend to fantasize that they are the recipients of male sexual advances (Mednick, 1977). In this vein, females are more likely to fantasize that they are being forced to engage in sexual activity (see Table 5-1).

"Submissive" sexual fantasies on the part of females are a reflection of traditional definitions of the female role (being passive and swept away by a strong, virile male). It is thus not surprising that they are more common in older and more sexually traditional women (Hariton and Singer, 1974; Moreault and Fallingstad, 1978).

The fact that females have submissive fantasies is seen by some as indicating that women subconsciously want to be sexually dominated and perhaps even forced into sexual activity. This assumption is simply not so and is a misunderstanding of the nature of fan-

TABLE 5-1
Male and female college students reporting various sexual fantasies during intercourse.

Content of sexual fantasy	Males (%)	Females (%)
A former lover	43	41
An imaginary lover	44	24
Oral-genital sex	61	51
Group sex	19	14
Being forced or overpowered into a sexual relationship	21	36
Others observing you engage in sexual intercourse	15	20
Others finding you sexually irresistible	55	53
Being rejected or sexually abused	11	13
Forcing others to have sexual relations with you	23	16
Others giving in to you after resisting at first	37	24
Observing others engaging in sex	18	13
A member of the same sex	3	9
Animals	1	4

Source: Sue (1979, table 3).

tasies. Sexual fantasies are carefree sexual excursions which increase arousal. The very essence of why fantasies are sexually exciting is not that they are something we would really do if we had the chance, but something we can do in our minds with all the exciting elements present and all the negative elements absent. Women no more want to be forced into sex in real life than men want to go out and force. Real life is real, sexual fantasies are only fun.

The uses of sexual fantasies
Primarily, sexual fantasies serve to increase arousal. This does not mean that sexual fantasizing occurs only when other aspects of the sexual situation are not arousing, but that the fantasy adds something to the situation. Often, sexual fantasies are used to spice up, or make more attractive and interesting, a sexual situation which is not quite up to one's expectations or desires (Table 5-2).

The use of sexual fantasies to enhance a sexual experience is more common on the part of females (Sue, 1979; McCauley and Swann,

1980). They are also more likely to use sexual fantasies during coitus to decrease anxiety about the sexual experience. Males, on the other hand, are more likely to use fantasies to control and direct their sexual activity (McCauley and Swann, 1980).

Individual differences Sexual fantasies do not occur with the same frequencies for all individuals, nor do all people have equally rich and complex sexual fantasies. In general, males and females fantasize with equal frequency, but females are more likely than males to be physiologically aroused by their fantasies and tend to have more vivid and complex fantasy images (Carlson and Coleman, 1977).

Not only does sexual fantasizing reflect a creative personality (Hariton and Singer, 1974), but for both males and females more frequent and rich sexual fantasies tend to be associated with more sexual experience, more interest in sex, more exposure to visual erotic stimuli, and more general daydreaming activity (Brown and Hart, 1977; Carlson and Coleman,

"I think you're being silly. Would you like it better if I was thinking of *you* and sleeping with Robert Redford?"

1977). Among females, liberal attitudes toward women's roles are also associated with more frequent fantasizing (Brown and Hart, 1977).

Physical Characteristics

Whether we like it or not, people are "sex objects" and constitute collections of sex stimuli in the sense that we regard various aspects of others, such as their gender, anatomical structures and physical appearance, features as relevant to sexuality. (Griffitt, 1979: 295.)

Overall physical attractiveness

Physical attractiveness itself is often sexually arousing. Both males and females not only see physically attractive persons of the other sex as more sexually warm and responsive

TABLE 5-2
The purpose of sexual fantasies during coitus as reported by male and female college students.

Purpose of sexual fantasies	Males (%)	Females (%)
To facilitate sexual arousal	38	45
To increase my partner's attractiveness	30	22
To imagine activities that my partner and I do not engage in	18	13
To relieve boredom	3	5
Uncertain	10	15

Source: Sue (1979, table 4).

BOX 5-4
MEASURING SEXUAL AROUSAL

The scientific measurement of sexual arousal takes two forms. The simplest method is the person's report of how aroused he or she is (self-report). In this method, individuals usually indicate the amount of sexual arousal they are experiencing by means of a paper-and-pencil technique. For example, one may circle a number of a scale from 1 to 7 where 1 = no arousal and 7 = high arousal. A more sophisticated type of self-report is a psychophysical measurement in which the person does something physical in proportion to the amount of arousal he or she experiences psychologically (hence, the name psychophysical). An example here is squeezing a handgrip or moving a lever in proportion to the amount of arousal experienced.

The second major method of measuring sexual arousal is direct physiological measurement. Since vasocongestion accompanies sexual arousal, a technique which accurately measures the amount of vasocongestion in the genitals provides a measure of sexual arousal. For males, this is done by means of a penile strain gauge that consists of a rubber tube placed around the penis. The inside of the tube is filled with mercury and a small electric current is fed through the mercury. As the penis enlarges, the tube stretches and the column of mercury in the tube decreases in diameter. Since the resistance of the mercury to the electrical current is a direct function of the diameter of the mercury column, changes in the diameter of the penis can be measured by charting the electrical current conducted through the mercury in the rubber tube. For females, the method is somewhat more complex. Here, a vaginal photoplethysmograph is employed. It consists of a cylinder approximately the size and shape of a tampon which is inserted into the vagina. A light source in the cylinder shines light against the vaginal wall and a photoelectric cell at the other end of the cylinder detects how much of this light is reflected back off the wall. Since the amount of reflected light is directly related to the amount of blood in the tissues, vasocongestion can be measured by the amount of this light.

While the direct physiological measures in the form of the penile strain gauge and vaginal photoplethysmograph sound superior to self-report techniques, they are not necessarily infallible. There are a number of technical and conceptual problems with both physiological measures (see Hatch, 1979; Farkas et al., 1979). Additionally, the relationship between self-report and physiological measurement of arousal is quite high, given the complexity of what is being measured, but is by no means perfect (Briddell et al., 1978). This raises the central question of whether sexual arousal is what one experiences psychologically or physiologically. While there is a general correspondence between the two, they do not always perfectly match.

than unattractive persons (Dion et al., 1972), but also as more desirable sexual partners.

Pretty not only pleases, it also creates arousal. Merely looking at a physically attract-ive person of the other sex creates erotic pleasure for many individuals, including erection and vaginal lubrication (Mathes and Edwards, 1978).

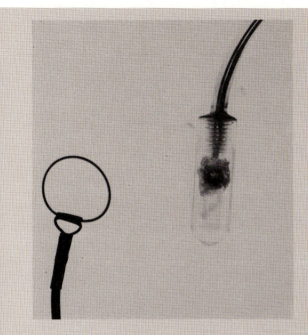

The penile strain gauge (left) and the vaginal photoplethysmograph (right.)

Very recently, Abramson et al. (1981) have devised what appears to be the most promising physiological measurement of sexual arousal by means of a photographic technique known as *thermography*. Thermography is a means of measuring heat generation from an object via a photograph. Since vasocongestion and myotonia are both associated with increased heat in the specific areas of the body where they occur, thermograms provide a direct measure of the extent and location of sexual arousal. One of the major advantages of this method over other physiological techniques is that it is used for both males and females, and thus measurement is directly comparable. This is not possible with the plethysmograph and strain gauges. Also, the entire body, not just the genitals, can be measured for signs of sexual arousal. Last, the measurement is not intrusive. Rather than having something inserted in the vagina or something placed around the penis, the subject merely stands behind a screen that has a hole for a remote-control camera to shoot through. Thermogram measures of sexual arousal also correlate strongly with self-reported sexual arousal for both males and females.

Body characteristics Apart from physical attractiveness, people also have clear preferences in terms of body shapes, sizes, and features. Most males in American society ascetically prefer a moderate female figure (in terms of size of bust, buttocks, and legs) and have some dislike for either a thin or a heavy female figure, especially the latter (Wiggins et

An ad for a bust enlarger from a Sears, Roebuck catalog, circa 1890.

al., 1968). Females also have certain preferences for male body sizes. Most women prefer a male figure composed of small buttocks and a moderately large chest (toss out the barbells because Atlas types are not the most preferred) (Beck et al., 1976). Females also tend to prefer a moderate-sized male body and to dislike a small male body size more than a large one (Beck et al., 1976).

Various parts of the anatomy differ in the extent to which they are sexually stimulating. Wildman et al. (1976) asked female college students whether the male penis, legs, buttocks, or chest was the most sexually stimulating to them. Chests won, going away with 51 percent of the votes, followed by the penis (23 percent), buttocks (9 percent), and legs (1 percent). Males were asked whether the female

bust, buttocks, genitals, or legs were the most sexually stimulating. Even though the bust was the most popular (38 percent), males tend to like everything. Buttocks got over 24 percent of the votes, genitals 21 percent, and legs 18 percent.

These preferences of males not only are widely reflected in the media, but are the basis of a major sexual attractiveness industry. Women here are caught in a catch-22 with regard to male enthusiasm for female breasts. Not only do large-busted women have to live with a particular set of experiences to which males are often very insensitive but, while males tend to prefer a large bust, they (and females) tend to stereotype large-busted women. Kleinke and Staneski (1980) conducted a careful series of experiments on first impressions of women on the basis of their bust size. They found that *both* male and female observers thought that females with large busts were less intelligent, competent, moral, and modest than females with small busts, who were seen as highly intelligent, competent, modest, and moral. It is not difficult to understand why adolescent females view breasts as the most important female secondary sexual characteristic (Collins, 1981).

Dress, Places, and Sexual Aids

Dress may be one of the more frequently employed aids to sexual arousal in American society. In Tavris and Sadd's 1977 study of 10,000 American women, 66 percent said they liked to dress in erotic clothing as a stimulus to lovemaking. The most popular articles were lingerie or lacy feminine clothing (mentioned by 40 percent of these women), followed by black or obviously "suggestive" clothing (mentioned by 20 percent). Anyone doubting the importance of dress for sexual arousal should note the fact that Fredericks of Hollywood—a firm specializing in "sexy" clothes—is a multimillion-dollar business. Also noteworthy is the volume of designer jeans sold in the United States; this article of clothing is advertised by models who are chosen and posed to communicate other than the durability of the product.

Places can also be sexually arousing. Some 76 percent of Tavris and Sadd's respondents said they varied the location of their sexual activity to enhance arousal. The most popular variations were some room other than the bedroom (49 percent mentioned), a hotel or motel (23 percent), and outdoors (19 percent).

Advertising for sexual aids to enhance arousal have recently become quite common and Tavris and Sadd's data suggest why. Of the *Redbook* readers in their sample, 21 percent said they used some object or substance as a sexual aid. Of these women, 39 percent reported the use of vibrators; 19 percent, penis-shaped objects; 25 percent, oils; 2 percent, feathers; and 16 percent, miscellaneous. Of those who had tried sexual aids, 97 percent said they were usually or always pleasurable.

Behaviors

Physical activites associated with sexual activity perhaps come to mind when many people think about "what is sexually arousing." In the next chapter, we will address specific sexual behaviors in detail and their relationship to sexual arousal, satisfaction, and pleasure. We will also explore sexually arousing behaviors throughout the rest of the text as we discuss such sexualities as homosexuality, adolescent sexual behavior, sex in marriage, aging and sex, and a number of variations in sexuality ranging from group sex to transvestism.

COGNITIVE PROCESSES IN SEXUAL AROUSAL

Sexual arousal would be a reasonably simple process if all that took place were the activation of what the individual had learned was sexually arousing. Psychologically, however, human behavior is more complex than finding some one piece of information which has been stored in the brain. Rather, human psychological processes involve *cognition,* or mental processes that transform and manipulate input from all senses. While all the cognitive processes at work in sexual arousal are not yet understood, certain mental processes are central to sexual arousal.

The Labeling of Emotions

In the early part of the excitement stage, certain general physiological changes begin to appear, such as increased heart rate, respiration, and temperature. These changes are, however, not peculiar to sexual arousal. Rather, they are changes which indicate a state of *generalized physiological arousal* (GPA) in the body. GPA occurs in physical exercise and in a variety of emotional states, such as anger, joy, fear, anxiety, disgust, and sexual arousal (Hoon et al., 1976). The nonspecific character of GPA is demonstrated in an experiment by Adamson et al. (1972). On eleven separate physiological measures, women had the same reactions to films of explicit sexual activity as they did to films of Nazi concentration camp atrocities.

Few of us would argue that sexual arousal feels the same as getting mad at your roommate or running around the block. What makes the very early stages of sexual arousal different from these other emotional states is that, even though the same kind of GPA takes place, the beginning of sexual arousal is labeled as a distinct emotional experience. The kind of emotional label we attach to the GPA is due to the cues present in the particular situation. Most of the time that we experience sexual arousal (or any other emotional state), the cues in the situation have themselves created the arousal. If a person scares you or turns you on, you experience GPA *because* that person jumped out of the closet (a fear cue) or stroked your navel (a sexual cue). However, if you experience some degree of GPA with no immediate cues indicating the appropriate emotional state, the emotion that will be experienced will be sexual arousal *if sexual cues are made available.* This is most likely to take place when the level of GPA has declined from a previously high state but is still present in the form of *residual excitation.* In situations such as this, the cues as to why the residual excitation is present have been removed from the situation and other cues can be introduced.

An example is an experiment by Cantor et al., (1975). Male subjects engaged in vigorous physical exercise and after a five-minute period—during which the level of GPA decreased and the cues indicating the reason for the remaining GPA were not readily apparent—they were exposed to erotic photographs. Exposure to these photos after the five-minute interval resulted in greater sexual arousal than did exposure immediately after exercise or exposure to a group of subjects who had not first engaged in exercise. Arousal did not take place immediately after the exercise because the subjects clearly understood why they were breathing hard and their hearts were pounding. Arousal was higher after the five-minute period because there was still some residual GPA, and when the sexual cues were presented, subjects quickly labeled this residual GPA as sexual arousal. Arousal was less for those subjects who had not exercised because there

was no residual GPA to be labeled as sexual arousal when the sexual cues in the form of the photos were presented.

Other emotional states increasing sexual arousal It has commonly been argued that certain emotional states, such as fear and anxiety, inhibit sexual arousal (Masters and Johnson, 1970). Much sexual therapy has, in fact, been guided by such an assumption. Recent research indicates, however, that such emotional states as fear and anxiety may actually *increase,* rather than decrease, sexual arousal owing to increasing GPA and to this GPA's being labeled as sexual arousal when sexual cues are presented.

A number of experiments have demonstrated that creating the emotion of mild fear in individuals leads to greater sexual arousal when presented with sexual cues than when mild fear has not been experienced (Dutton and Aron, 1974; Roviaro and Holmes, 1980).

Two very clear experiments have also demonstrated that the emotion of anxiety increases the amount of sexual arousal experienced when sexual stimuli are presented. Hoon et al., (1977) found that women whose anxiety level was increased by watching vivid films of automobile accidents were more sexually aroused by erotic films they viewed immediately afterward than were women who had not first seen the accident films. Wolchik et al. (1980) have found the same effect of anxiety on sexual arousal for males.

It is important to note here that it is the *emotion* of anxiety which is influential in increasing sexual arousal and not the stimulus which creates the anxiety. Thus, while one type of stimulus may increase anxiety in one person, the same stimulus may not do so in another person. The consequence would be that one person would experience increased sexual arousal and the other would not. For example, Wolchik et al. (1980) found that films of automobile accidents created depression in men and that this depression decreased sexual arousal. In previous research (Hoon et al., 1977), automobile accident films created anxiety, not depression, in women, and thus arousal was subsequently increased.

The emotional state of depression is generally found to decrease sexual arousal. When we discuss the relationship between sexuality and chronic illnesses, we shall see the close relationship between depression and sexual arousal.

Using Physiological Cues to Interpret the Onset of Sexual Arousal

To a considerable extent, we use physiological changes taking place in the body as cues that we are becoming sexually aroused. If we are in a sexual situation and our hearts start to beat a little faster, we are likely to interpret this increase as meaning that we are getting sexually excited.

This process of using physiological changes as cues of sexual arousal has important implications. Females, for example, have greater difficulty than do males in detecting genital changes during sexual arousal (Heiman, 1975). Since the psychological experience of sexual arousal somewhat depends on being able to detect and label subtle physiological changes in the sexual response cycle, one of the reasons females are less likely to experience orgasm is that they are less likely to perceive these subtle physiological changes. One of the factors that distinguishes women who do and those who do not orgasm with ease is awareness of the perception of such bodily changes (Wincze et al., 1976; Hoon and Hoon, 1978). In the treatment of female orgasm difficulty, teaching women to become sensitive to physiological changes during sexual arousal has thus proven an effective technique (Kaplan, 1974; LoPiccolo and Lobitz, 1972).

This difference between males and females in the perception of physiological changes during sexual arousal is the result of both learning and anatomy. On the learning side, the much earlier, more common, and more frequent masturbation activity of adolescent males means that they get much more practice in becoming sensitive to genital and other physiological changes in sexual arousal. On the anatomy side, it is difficult to not notice an erection, but vaginal lubrication is much less obvious.

Heightened Self-Awareness and Nonarousal

Too much of a good thing is always a possibility. Self-awareness, if too intense, actually inhibits sexual arousal. When one person is self-aware, one's attention tends to focus on that aspect of self which is the most important at the time. This focusing initiates self-evaluation in which the individual attempts to bring that important aspect of self into line with whatever behavior standards the individual holds (Wicklund, 1975). If a person has lofty standards for sexual performance ("I really want to be a sensational lover tonight"), increased self-awareness is likely to result in anxiety and impaired, rather than improved, sexual arousal. Farkes et al. (1979), for example, found that when they told males that most people found an erotic film highly arousing, their level of sexual arousal (measured by erection) while watching the film was significantly less than when they were told that most people did not find the film very erotic. This very subtle *demand for performance* ("Everyone is really turned on by this film, so we know you will be too") increased self-awareness and reduced sexual arousal. Similar processes affect female sexual arousal as well (Wilson and Lawson, 1978).

Personality and Sexual Arousal

While there is little research on personality factors that influence sexual arousal, two personality characteristics are important: *sex guilt* and *authoritarianism*.

Sex guilt   The personality characteristic of sex guilt has considerable influence on a wide range of sexual behaviors, including arousal. *Sex guilt is the general expectation for self-administered punishment for violating or anticipating violating one's own standards for sexual behavior* (Mosher, 1961; 1966; 1968). Individuals who are high in sex guilt tend to experience self-induced anxiety and negative feelings when they approach, or think about approaching, sexual stimuli. For example, persons with high sex guilt have less sexual experience and less exposure to erotic material, and they learn less from a lecture on birth control than do individuals with less sex guilt. The reason is that when a person with high sex guilt approaches, or thinks about approaching, a sexual situation, he or she begins to feel anxiety. To avoid this anxiety, the person escapes from the situation (either physically or mentally).

Sex guilt is a personality characteristic and should not be confused with the emotional state of "feeling guilty." Feeling guilty is a fleeting response to one situation or another. Sex guilt is a personality characteristic and is thus stable for an individual across both time and situations.[7] It is not surprising, then, that individuals who are high in sex guilt are less aroused by sexual stimuli (Ray and Walker, 1973; Gibbons, 1978; Griffitt and Kaiser, 1978; Mosher and White, 1980). This effect of sex guilt on sexual arousal is especially strong when self-awareness is increased. In situations where an individual focuses attention on what he or she is doing, the individual's personal standards for conduct become much more salient and the impact of sex guilt becomes greater (Gibbons, 1978). The reason is that sex guilt is specific to *one's own personal sexual standards* rather than to the sexual standards of others.

Sex anxiety   Closely related, but yet quite different, is sex anxiety. A person who is high on sex anxiety has a general expectation to be punished for the violation of others' sexual standards (Janda and O'Grady, 1980). People with high sex anxiety have a clear view of what they think others in general hold as sexual standards. If they violate or think about violating these sexual standards, they anticipate (through anxiety) being punished for this violation. The essential difference between sex guilt

and sex anxiety is that sex anxiety refers to the sexual standards of others. Although there has not been any direct research on how sex anxiety influences sexual arousal, it is probably an important personality characteristic influencing arousal, since high sex anxiety reflects discomfort in social situations where sexuality is implied, anxiety about socially unacceptable forms of sexual behavior, and anxiety over sexual behavior in private (Janda and O'Grady, 1980).

Authoritarianism   Authoritarianism refers to an individual's tendency to see the world in black and white, as right and wrong or good and bad, with no gray area in between. Authoritarians (compared with nonauthoritarians) also tend to have an exaggerated concern with sexual matters. The outcome of this exaggerated concern is that male authoritarians (we do not know about female ones) are apt to overemphasize or pay more attention to the sexual attributes of females (Rothstein, 1960). Perhaps for this reason authoritarians tend to be more aroused by erotic stimuli (Byrne et al., 1974). The catch here is that when they are sexually aroused, authoritarians are likely to have their feelings of arousal accompanied by disgust and dislike for the sexual stimulus which creates the arousal.

This obvious conflict between good feelings (sexual arousal) and bad feelings (disgust with the sexual stimulus) is nicely illustrated in an incident which happened to a friend of mine in the San Juan Islands. For a group of visiting males on a boat tour of the islands, one of the must sites is the local nude beach. Pulling into the cove near the beach, many of the men remarked—as they peered intently through their binoculars—how disgusting it was that people would sit around with no clothes on.

APHRODISIACS

Throughout written history, humans have sought, and reported to have found, substances which create or increase sexual arousal. The list of so-called aphrodisiacs is almost endless. Such common foods as oysters and

---

[7]It is well to note that between 1968 and 1978, sex-guilt scores of college students changed in the direction of less guilt (Abramson and Handschumacher, 1978). This change suggests changes in sexual learning in American society (see Chap. 4).

exotic delicacies like raw bull's testicles (prairie oysters) and powdered rhinocerous horn have all been praised for their sexual effects. Many supposed aphrodisiacs apparently obtained their reputation through the "doctrine of signatures" applied to various foods. The notion here is that anything which resembles the genitals must contain substances of sexual power.

There is, however, no known substance which increases the responsiveness of the genitals or automatically increases sexual desire (Kaplan, 1974). Some substances that have been applauded as aphrodisiacs irritate the genitourinary tract, causing dilation of the nearby blood vessels and, thus, genital sensations which can be mistaken for sexual arousal. One such infamous substance is cantharides, better known as "Spanish fly." This is a drug derived from a beautiful beetle of southern Europe. The insect is heated until it turns to powder and is then eaten. Rather than sexual arousal, large doses may result in quite the opposite: serious illness and death. Another infamous drug is yohimbine, extracted from the bark of the yohimbe tree. While reputed to have aphrodisiac qualities, its only effect is to stimulate the erection center in the spinal cord, a process involving, not sexual arousal, but a reflex action due to stimulation of the nervous system.

Today, drugs perhaps top the list as the most widely reputed enhancers of sexual arousal and response. In this area we have not even begun to explore the questions. So, while there may very well be some truth to popular folklore, its real value remains to be seen.

Marijuana has the most widespread reputation for enhancing sexual enjoyment and arousal. In repeated surveys, approximately half the respondents reported that marijuana in small doses increases sexual desire and enjoyment. There are a number of possible reasons why this may in fact be so (Jarvik and Brecher, 1977). Marijuana may relax inhibitions, making sexual arousal more likely and enjoyment greater. The drug may increase one's focus on sensuous elements. Marijuana may alter one's perception of time and thus

make the flow of sexual events more enjoyable. The drug is also commonly used in situations that are perhaps conducive to sexual arousal: sitting down, relaxing, and forgetting the day's worries in a mellow mood. Last is the drug's sexual reputation. If one believes it will increase arousal, it may very well do just that. The reported effects of marijuana on sexuality differ for males and females—a fact reflecting the psychological impact of the drug. Females are much more likely to report that marijuana increases their sexual desire, while males are more likely to report that it increases their sexual enjoyment (Koff, 1974). The reason for the variation is probably that marijuana reduces inhibitions for females and reduces performance anxiety for males. In both cases, the effect is due to relaxation, not any chemical effect of the drug.

Amyl nitrate has also become popular, particularly among male homosexuals (Goode and Troiden, 1979). "Poppers," as they are called, were originally intended for the quick treatment of chest pain. They are frequently inhaled at the moment of orgasm, with the reported effect of dramatically enhancing and prolonging the orgasm sensations (Everett, 1975). This effect may be due to the sudden drop in blood pressure caused by the drug. The known results of such use include dizziness, severe headache, and some cases of death (Kaplan, 1974).

Cocaine has gained a wide reputation for enhancing sexual arousal and response. It appears, however, that many users also report that it results in a decrease in sexual arousal (Mims and Swenson, 1980). Cocaine stimulates the central nervous system and thus may result in the more efficient transmission of messages through the nerves. Its euphoric effects may also change one's perception of sexual events. On the other hand, mood elevation is then followed by depression. The prolonged use of cocaine may result in central nervous system damage sufficient to decrease sexual functioning (Mims and Swenson, 1980).

Amphetamines are also central nervous system stimulants. Men often report that these drugs have a positive effect on sex by prolonging erection, delaying ejaculation, and increasing the ability to reach orgasm repeatedly. These results are most likely due to the blocking of distractions in the environment and stimulation of nerves throughout the entire body with the drug (Mims and Swenson, 1980). Women, on the other hand, are more likely to report negative sexual effects from amphetamines. The reason for this difference is not known (Mims and Swenson, 1980).

Heroin as a major narcotic has received considerable attention for its effects on sexual arousal and response. For men, heroin appears to result in less sexual interest, difficulty in reaching orgasm, and less satisfying orgasm sensations. For women, initial use may be accompanied by a loss of inhibition, which may enhance sexual feelings, but prolonged use is usually accompanied by reports of less sexual desire, sexual sensation, and orgasm (Mims and Swenson, 1980).

One chemical which has received considerable attention in recent years is vitamin E. Reputed to do wonders for one's sexual life, vitamin E sales have increased dramatically. In actuality, this vitamin has no effect on any aspect of male or female sexual desire or functioning (Herold et al., 1979).

There are interesting behavior patterns in drug use related to sexuality. Those who prefer sedative drugs (which sedate you) tend to be higher in sex guilt than those individuals who use stimulants (Ugerer et al., 1976). Perhaps sedation allows one to escape from the normal sex-guilt pattern. Also females are more likely than males to take drugs which have a disinhibiting effect (Mitchell et al., 1970); this pattern is clearly related to what we have discussed about male and female sexual learning.

There are also many therapeutic drugs used to treat medical conditions of various kinds. With very few exceptions, these drugs have an adverse effect on sexual arousal and response by affecting the central nervous system, muscle response, or psychological state (Mims and Swenson, 1980).

SEX AND SMELL

By associating a particular odor with a memorable sexual experience, we can later be aroused by that scent. We also learn to perceive certain types of odors as sexually arousing by being continually exposed to this message in advertising.

We seem to have a great deal of faith that the sexual behavior of lower animals will somehow tell us something about human sexuality. It is therefore popular to suggest that humans have an instinctual sexual reaction to pheromones. Pheromones are chemical substances (copulins) which are secreted by the female and which act as a sexual attractant to the male. While such chemical processes of sexual attraction are clearly identified in other mammals, including primates, they have not been found in humans. The same fatty acid materials which are found in the vaginal secretions of female primates and which act as sexual attractants in primates are found in human vaginal secretions (Michael et al., 1974).

However, leaping from this observation of chemical similarity to the suggestion that humans are sexually attracted or aroused by these vaginal secretions requires ignoring the existing research. Doty et al. (1975) had male and female subjects smell vaginal secretions from four females which had been sampled over several ovulatory phases. While the intensity and pleasantness of the vaginal odors varied over the menstrual cycle, across subjects, and across the female donors, there was no evidence at all that some odors were more attractive than others.

It could be the case, however, that while the human vaginal secretions are not perceived as attractive, they sexually attract anyway. This assumption would follow from the behavior of primates. In a sound piece of experimenal research, Morris and Udry (1978) tested the sexual attraction characteristics of pheromones by isolating fatty acids from human female vaginal secretions. They gave one group of married couples a substance made from vaginal secretions and a second group of married couples a water substance. Both substances were odorless and the subjects had no idea which substance they had been given. The female placed a small amount of the substance on her body each night and the couple kept a daily sexual activity-and-interest diary. The results revealed no differences between the water and vaginal secretion groups in either sexual desire or activity for the experimental period.

ALCOHOL AND SEXUAL AROUSAL

It provokes the desires but takes away the performance. (Shakespeare, *Macbeth,* Act II, scene iii, line 34.)

The Psychological Effects of Alcohol on Arousal

Alcohol is commonly thought to increase sexual arousal and to lessen inhibition. While this idea is a bit too simple, alcohol does clearly influence sexual arousal by means of certain psychological processes—specifically, the *expectancy effect.* Wilson and Lawson (1976) led males to believe that the drink they consumed contained either vodka and tonic or tonic alone. For half the subjects in each of these two groups (group 1 were told they had vodka and tonic, group 2 were told they had tonic alone), the drink really did contain vodka and for the other half it contained only tonic. Measures of the males' penile erection while they subsequently viewed erotic films revealed that the *subjects who thought they drank vodka were more sexually aroused than were subjects who thought they drank only tonic, regardless of the actual content of their drink.* This expectancy effect (if you expect it to happen, it does) is another example of cognitive processes affecting sexual arousal. These expectancy effects are not present, however, for females (Wilson and Lawson, 1978). This dif-

ference is most likely due to gender differences in the cognitive control of physiological sexual arousal. It is clear, for example, that males can exert considerable cognitive control over such responses as erection. When presented with erotic stimuli, they can voluntarily increase or decrease erection (Laws and Rubin, 1969; Rubin and Hensen, 1975). Males can also increase the size of an erection by merely "thinking big" (Rosen et al., 1975).

While much less research has been done on the female's cognitive control of physiological sexual arousal, it does appear that even though females can voluntarily control the amount of vasocongestion in the vagina, they are better able to lower vasocongestion than to increase it (Cerny, 1978). Males seem to be equally effective at cognitively controlling both increases and decreases in vasocongestion. This gender difference reflects male and female differences in sexual learning. Females are much more likely than males to learn to be gatekeepers or not to get "too aroused."

This expectancy effect reflects the fact that behavior while drinking is largely learned behavior and not some automatic reaction to alcohol in the blood. Society provides us with very clear definitions of how one behaves when one drinks. Since we have been socialized as members of this society, we have learned these definitions—and learned them so well that we do not even realize (or perhaps are not even willing to believe) that our behavior while drinking is governed by the very same types of social rules that govern our behavior while sitting in a classroom lecture.

These social definitions of how one is to behave when drinking center on "getting loose." A major part of this getting loose when drinking is not being responsible for one's behavior, including sexual behavior. This is dramatically illustrated in a number of studies of sexual behavior and drinking. Sexual behaviors that an individual would not normally engage in are more likely when the drinking role is activated. For example, males who *think* they have consumed alcohol are significantly more aroused by sexual stimuli depicting rape and sadism than are males who think they have not consumed alcohol (Briddell et al., 1978).

The tendency of individuals to engage in self-exoneration ("I am not responsible for what I do") in the drinking role is very clear in the research on sex guilt and drinking. As we have noted, persons high in sex guilt are less likely to approach sexual stimuli because, when they do, they punish themselves with anxiety for violating their own sexual standards. Lang et al. (1980) found that when high sex-guilt males *thought* they had consumed alcohol, the sexual behavior we would expect from their high sex guilt vanished. Specifically, when given the opportunity to look at erotic slides, high sex-guilt males who *thought* they had consumed alcohol (but actually had not) spent significantly more time looking at the slides than low sex-guilt males who thought they had consumed alcohol. The high sex-guilt males would have normally spent much less time looking at the slides than the low sex-guilt males. However, since they thought they had consumed alcohol, they were able to activate the drinking role and declare themselves not responsible for their otherwise unacceptable (to themselves) behavior. This conclusion is further supported by the research of Lansky and Wilson (1981). It was found that the expectancy effect of alcohol was strongest when the sexual stimuli were highly deviant or the individual was high in sex guilt.

The Physiological Effects of Alcohol on Sexual Arousal

Males Shakespeare was almost correct. For males, a low level of alcohol in the blood slightly increases the maximum size of an erection relative to the size when no alcohol is present (Farkas and Rosen, 1976). This fact is due to two factors. First, alcohol causes a psychologically exaggerated response to one's environment and to the sexual response as well (Kalin, 1972). Second, a low level of alcohol in the blood causes dilation of the blood vessels

in the penis, resulting in slightly increased retention of blood and thus a larger erection.

As the level of alcohol in the blood increases, however, the sexual outcome becomes far less exciting. Increasing amounts of alcohol have a depressant effect on the central nervous system and messages to and from the brain and erection center become impaired. The result is not only that one feels less arousal, but also an erection takes longer to obtain and when (or if) obtained, the maximum length and diameter of the penis are less (Farkas and Rosen, 1976) (Figure 5-4). The depressant effect of alcohol on the central nervous system does, however, have what might be viewed as a positive effect. The impairment of messages in the central nervous system results in the male's taking longer to reach orgasm (Malatesta et al., 1979). Intercourse can thus be prolonged and may result in greater sexual satisfaction in the female partner.

Females For females, the physiological effects of alcohol on sexual arousal are somewhat different. While low levels of alcohol slightly increase physiological sexual arousal in males, they do not do so in females. For females, the level of physiological sexual arousal steadily declines with increasing levels of alcohol in the bloodstream (Wilson and Lawson, 1978).

Even more interesting is the fact that for females, this steadily declining physiological sexual arousal does not coincide with self-reported sexual arousal (Wilson and Lawson, 1978). As the level of alcohol in the blood increases, females report that they feel more sexually aroused even though, physiologically, sexual arousal is declining.

This rather notable difference between males and females in the correspondence between what is happening in the genitals and what is happening in the mind is more than slightly intriguing. Perhaps this difference is a result of two factors. First, women are generally less likely than males to accurately perceive physiological changes taking place in the early stages of sexual arousal. Second, males and females differ in their beliefs about the effects

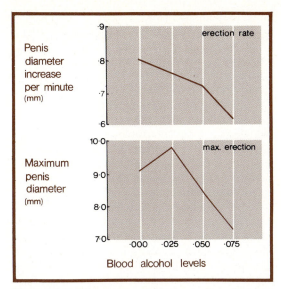

Figure 5-4 Changes in erection rate (how fast one gets an erection) and the maximum size of erection with various levels of alcohol in the blood. *Top:* As the level of alcohol in the blood increases, it takes longer to get an erection. *Bottom:* A small amount of alcohol in the bloodstream increases the maximum size of the erection (penis diameter), but then increasing amounts of alcohol result in a rapidly decreasing penis size at maximum erection. (Source: Farkas and Rosen, 1976, Figure 2.)

of alcohol on arousal. Women are more likely than men to report that they drink to feel warm, sexy, and romantic (Wilsnack, 1974) and that alcohol increases sexual pleasure (Athanasiou et al., 1970). The belief that alcohol has positive sexual effects, combined with less accuracy in perceiving physiological changes during arousal, is quite likely to result in the female's reporting greater sexual arousal with increased alcohol consumption while quite the opposite is taking place in the genitals. Males, on the other hand, tend not only to more accurately perceive what the genitals are or are not up to, but have all heard—if not experienced—that the latter is likely when more than a little alcohol has been consumed.

THE IMMEDIATE SOCIAL AND PSYCHOLOGICAL EFFECTS OF SEXUAL AROUSAL

In addition to the physiological changes occurring during sexual arousal, there are also a number of equally important social and psychological effects.

Perception of the Other Sex

When we are sexually aroused, our sensitivity to the sexually relevant characteristics of others is increased (Griffitt, 1977). This increased sensitivity to the sexually relevant qualities of the other sex applies to both their positive and negative qualities. For example, not only do sexually aroused males and females spend more time looking at the other sex (Griffitt et al., 1974), but what they see is different from what they see when not aroused. Sexually aroused males and females see physically attractive persons of the other sex as even more attractive and see unattractive persons of the other sex as even more unattractive (Kaiser and Griffitt, 1981; Weidner et al., 1979). This sexually accentuated perception of the other sex also applies to other sexually relevant features, such as body and personal characteristics. Sexually aroused males are more likely to see an attractive female as having a sexually attractive body, including a larger bust and more positively evaluated waist and genitals. Likewise, sexually aroused females perceive a male as having more attractive hips and genitals. Additionally, sexually aroused males perceive females as more sexually receptive, feminine, sophisticated, amorous, careless, and nasty, and as better dating, marriage, and sexual partners (Stephan et al., 1971; Kaiser and Griffitt, 1981).

When sexually aroused, both males and females tend to focus their perception of the other sex on those characteristics which are sexually relevant. What is sexually relevant differs somewhat, however, for males and females. When sexually aroused, females tend to view a male in an overall more positive vein across a wide range of personal characteristics, including the sexual. When males are sexually aroused, they tend to view females in a more positive vein on just sexually relevant characteristics. This difference, while not widely investigated, perhaps reflects a basic gender difference in sexual learning. Females are more likely than males to see a close connection between sex and an interpersonal relationship, while males are more likely than females to see sex as independent of the overall interpersonal relationship between two people. This is not to suggest that males make no connection between sex and interpersonal relationships. This is clearly not the case. Males, in fact, directly connect sex and love, and when sexually aroused, they feel greater love (but not liking) for a female they have been dating (Dermer and Pyszczynski, 1978). The connection between sex and affection is, however, greater on the part of females (see Chapters 4, 6, and 7).

If I'm Turned On, You Must Be Too: Projecting Arousal to Others

Sexual arousal also affects males' perception of the sexual arousal of a female. When viewing erotic slides, the more sexually aroused males are, the more they think females are aroused by the same material. While males tend to project their level of arousal to females, females are less likely to return the projection. Rather, females generally tend to overestimate the degree to which males are sexually aroused; this tendency is not unexpected, given our culture's traditional view of males as lusty creatures (Griffitt, 1973; Veitch and Griffitt, in press).

THE FRAGILE NATURE OF SEXUAL AROUSAL

Sexual arousal in the excitement stage is a very fragile state. It is a condition which is neither highly stable over time nor resistant to outside influences. Males become rather quickly satiated when exposed to sexually arousing stimuli repeatedly. Howard et al., (1971) exposed male college students to 90 minutes of erotic movies, pictures, magazines, and novels each day for ten days. Each day the amount of sexual arousal experienced consistently declined (Figure 5-5) owing to increasing satiation with the once novel material.

Sexual arousal in the excitement stage can also be easily interrupted or blocked by other stimuli which compete for the individual's attention (Farkas, Sine, and Evans, 1979). Geer and Fuhr (1976) had four groups of males wear earphones, through which, on one channel, they heard a tape recording erotically describing a sexual encounter between a man and a woman. Through the other channel, they heard a series of numbers being read aloud. One group of subjects only listened to the numbers while at the same time listening to the erotic tape recording. A second group had to write down the numbers they heard. A third group had to copy the numbers down in pairs, and a fourth group had to classify pairs of numbers as being odd or even and adding to less or more than 50. Not unexpectedly, as the numbers task became more complicated, the sexual arousal brought about by the erotic tape declined dramatically (Figure 5-6). Even though sexual arousal is a strong emotional state, it is quite easily disrupted by distraction in the excitement stage. As sexual arousal rises, however, the surrounding environment becomes increasingly blocked out of the individual's perception and disruption of arousal by distraction is less likely.

SUMMARY

Sexual arousal consists of psychological, social, physiological, and nervous system processes, all of which are closely connected. Physiologically, the changes which take place during sexual arousal may be described by the four stages of sexual response: excitement, plateau, orgasm, and resolution. While many changes occur in males and females over these stages, the major processes consist of vasocongestion and myotonia. Although differ-

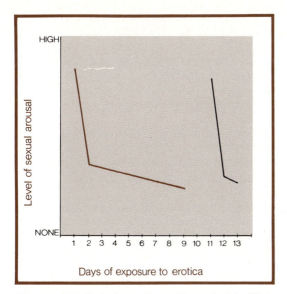

Figure 5-5 Satiation with erotic material. When males viewed the same erotic material each day for ten straight days, sexual arousal to the material drastically declined. This decline in sexual arousal was due to being satiated. When new material was introduced on the eleventh day, arousal was again high and then rapidly declined on day 12 as satiation with this material also took place. (Source: Howard et al., 1971:117.)

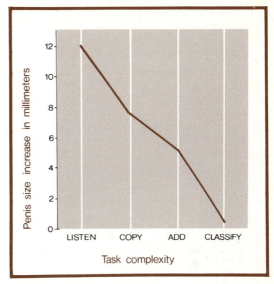

Figure 5-6 The effects of distraction on sexual arousal. Males listened to an erotic recording while performing one of four different cognitive tasks. The more complex the cognitive task, the less the sexual arousal (measured by increase in penis size) to the recording. (Source: Geer and Fuhr, 1976.)

ences between males and females do exist during sexual arousal, the physiological similarities far overshadow the differences, even in the case of orgasm and ejaculation.

Neurological, or nervous system, processes are also central to sexual arousal. While certain physiological signs of sexual arousal take the form of reflex actions, sexual arousal itself is a psychological process involving the subjective feeling of being aroused. This subjective feeling of arousal is dependent upon processes of interpretation taking place in the brain. While in lower animals, brain-controlled hormone levels affect sexual response, this does not appear to be the case for humans because of the massive role played by learning and abstract thought in human behavior.

Erogenous zones reflect this powerful effect of learning. Physiologically, there are no special sexual touch receptors in the body, and any part of the body can become an erogenous zone. A touch of any part of the body becomes sexual when it is defined, on the basis of learning, as sexual.

The primary information stored in the brain which affects sexual arousal is what we have learned is sexually arousing. The content of this learning differs from culture to culture and from individual to individual. Within any culture, there is, however, rather strong agreement about what is sexually arousing, since the specific learning histories of individuals are limited and defined by the culture of which each individual is a member.

Fantasy is an important part of sexual arousal and reflects gender role learning as well as creativity and one's general sexual attitude.

Physical characteristics of others are also arousing, including physical attractiveness, body shape and size, and certain body parts.

Sexual techniques and equipment are frequently thought to be central in sexual arousal, a view which reflects the American tendency to work hard at having fun. Almost any equipment will do, and the equipment and technique that are necessary for sexual arousal depend on what the partners define as sexually arousing.

Sexual arousal is also facilitated by places, modes of dress, and sexual aids, all of which are employed by a substantial number of Americans in their sexual activities.

Cognitive processes also play an important part in sexual arousal in the form of the labeling of emotions, the transfer of arousal from one emotional state to another, and the use of physiological cues to interpret that sexual arousal is taking place.

Aphrodisiacs, while popular for ages, have not been scientifically shown to exist. Several drugs may have some effect on sexual arousal, but not through direct chemical properties. Alcohol has the general effect of dramatically dampening physiological sexual arousal. For males but not for females, alcohol has an influential expectancy effect in which sexual arousal is increased if one thinks one has consumed alcohol.

Sexual arousal also has immediate social and psychological effects on behavior, including perceiving the opposite sex, projecting arousal to the opposite sex, and influencing interpersonal aggression.

Regardless of the effect of sexual arousal, both psychologically and behaviorally, this apparently powerful emotional response is fragile and can be easily diminished by distraction or satiation.

STUDY GUIDE

TERMS TO KNOW

Sexual response cycle	Residual excitation	Stimulus generalization
Excitement stage	Labeling of emotions	Vaginal photoplethysmograph
Plateau stage	Emission	Penile strain guage
Resolution	Keloid markings	Orgasmic platform
Refractory period	Heightened self-awareness	Tenting effect
Vasocongestion	Sex guilt	Multiple orgasm
Myotonia	Aphrodisiacs	Ejaculation
Grafenberg spot	Anaphrodisiacs	Thermograms
Generalized physiological arousal (GPA)	Expectancy effect	

SELF-TEST

Part I: True-False Statements

1. Vasocongestion and myotonia are the two basic physiological processes which take place during sexual arousal.
2. While the male penis becomes erect during sexual arousal, the female clitoris does not.

3. Both males and females ejaculate, but in females the organs of ejaculation may not be developed to the point of being capable of ejaculation.
4. Orgasm is the massive release of blood from several organs and areas in the body.
5. Males and females differ to the extent that females have the physiological potential for multiple orgasm while males do not.
6. The rudimentary female prostate gland is thought to be the Grafenberg spot.
7. Studies of female orgasm reveal two types of orgasm, clitoral and vaginal.
8. Women who ejaculate have stronger vaginal and uterine muscles than women who do not.
9. One of the apparent errors made by Masters and Johnson in their research on the differences between males and females in orgasm response was that they confused male orgasm and ejaculation.
10. Those special areas of the body which have special sexual touch receptors are called erogenous zones.
11. In males, the sensitivity of the penis to stimulation tends to decline with age.
12. Sexual fantasies during sexual activity are primarily used by people to increase their sexual arousal.
13. When we examine the types of things that are sexually arousing to humans, we find that what turns people on is very similar from culture to culture.
14. Both males and females tend to have a negative first impression of a woman with a large bust.
15. The generalized physiological arousal during the very early stages of sexual arousal occurs only for sexual arousal.
16. Heightened self-awareness, regardless of its level, increases sexual arousal.
17. There is no known food or drink that automatically increases sexual arousal.
18. Research indicates that while pheromones do serve as sexual attractants for other animals, they do not serve this function for humans.
19. Low amounts of alcohol in the blood tend to increase sexual arousal in males, while high alcohol levels decrease this arousal.
20. Sexual arousal has no effect on the perception of the sexually relevant characteristics of others.

Part II: Multiple-Choice Questions

Select the best of the three alternatives.

1. Vaginal lubrication begins in the____stage and decreases or may even stop in the____stage of arousal and response: *(a)* orgasm, excitement *(b)* excitement, plateau *(c)* excitement, resolution.
2. Orgasm is characterized by *(a)* the massive release of muscle tension; *(b)* ejaculation; *(c)* myotonia.
3. Masters and Johnson argued that males have____period while females do not, and that the existence of this period is the reason males do not have the capacity for multiple orgasm: *(a)* an excitement *(b)* a resolution *(c)* a refractory.
4. Erogenous zones are *(a)* determined by the location of sexual touch receptors in the skin; *(b)* determined by social and cultural definitions; *(c)* the same from one society to the next.
5. Males and females both tend to have sexual fantasies *(a)* that reflect deep-seated psychological problems; *(b)* along the lines of traditional definitions of male and female behavior; *(c)* in most of their intercourse experiences
6. Compared with males, females tend to have sexual fantasies which *(a)* are more vivid and complex; *(b)* are more frequent; *(c)* are more "kinky."

7. Generalized physiological arousal refers to changes which take place in the body *(a)* only when sexual arousal takes place; *(b)* only when anxiety is experienced; *(c)* when any of a number of emotional experiences occurs.

8. Owing to the nature of generalized physiological arousal (GPA), sexual arousal may be increased or more likely if the person first experiences *(a)* physical exercise; *(b)* anxiety; *(c)* anything which increases GPA.

9. The term *expectancy effect* refers to the fact that *(a)* low levels of alcohol increase sexual arousal for males; *(b)* if males think they have consumed a small amount of alcohol, their sexual arousal increases; *(c)* if one is required to perform sexually, one's level of sexual arousal may decline.

10. For females, an increasing amount of alcohol in the blood is accompanied by *(a)* a steady decline in actual physiological indicators of sexual arousal and an increase in feeling sexually aroused; *(b)* a steady decline in the actual physiological indicators of sexual arousal and a decline in feeling sexually aroused; *(c)* an increase in the physiological indicators of sexual arousal and an increase in feelings of sexual arousal.

TOPICS FOR DISCUSSION

1. Go through a few of the more popular men's and women's magazines and look for advertisements which use sex to sell the product. As you look, note the following: the type of product, how sex is communicated, who is the target, what is used to communicate sexuality (what body part, posture, look, or saying). After you complete this examination, compare notes on what is presented in men's and women's magazines. Discuss how the things you have noted are related to Chapter 5 on sexual arousal.

2. In a group of males and females, discuss the kinds of changes that men and women in the group would have to make in terms of learning about and experiencing sexual arousal if each person were suddenly transformed into a person of the other sex.

SUGGESTED READINGS

Federation of Women's Health Centers, *A New View of a Woman's Body.* New York: Simon & Schuster, 1981.
A new perspective based on current research on the functioning and structure of the female body. A good, solid discussion of sexual arousal and response at the physiological level.

Marshall, D. S., and **R. C. Suggs,** *Human Sexual Behavior.* Engelwood Cliffs, N.J.: Prentice-Hall, 1971.
This is the classic collection of anthropological studies of the diversity of human sexual behavior. Not giving serious consideration to these studies is not studying human sexual behavior.

Masters, W. H., and **V. Johnson,** *Human Sexual Response.* Boston: Little Brown, 1966.
The classic Masters and Johnson study. Even though it is technical and somewhat boring reading, this is the original source, a fact which makes it worth reading by itself. Of particular interest is the rather mechanical approach to sexual arousal employed by Masters and Johnson. This is a result of their medical orientation and concentration on physiological processes.

KEY TO SELF-TEST QUESTIONS

Part I: True-False Statements

1. T (The accumulation of blood and increased muscle tension are the two processes.)
2. F (Both the penis and the clitoris become erect during sexual arousal and for the same reason—vasocongestion.)
3. T (Male and female genitals and reproductive organs are generated from the same tissue, but the female ejaculation system may not develop sufficiently actually to function in ejaculation.)
4. F (Orgasm is the massive release of muscle tension. Following orgasm, there is a reversal of vasocongestion.)
5. F (Masters and Johnson thought so, but more recent research reveals that both males and females have this potential. The Masters and Johnson error appears to be due to their confusion of orgasm and ejaculation.)
6. T (See 3 above.)
7. T (Masters and Johnson argued that all female orgasm is centered in the clitoris and that the vagina is not sensitive to touch. We now know that the vagina is sensitive and that "vaginal" and "clitoral" orgasm feel different and are probably associated with different nerve structures and muscle strengths.)
8. T (They are also more likely to reach orgasm through vaginal stimulation.)
9. T (While noting that male orgasm and ejaculation are different processes, they used the terms interchangeably, a fact which apparently resulted in a number of errors in comparing males and females.)
10. F (All touch receptors in the body are the same. There are not special *sexual* touch receptors.)
11. T (So does the sensitivity to touch throughout the body.)
12. T
13. F (Since what is sexually arousing is learned, it may differ greatly from one culture to the next, and it often does.)
14. T (Large-busted women are seen by both males and females as less intelligent, competent, moral, and modest than small-busted women.)
15. F (Generalized physiological arousal refers to physiological changes in the body which are not specific to any emotion.)
16. F (A low to moderate level of heightened self-awareness increases arousal because of increasing sensitivity to bodily changes. A higher level of self-awareness actually decreases arousal.)
17. T
18. T
19. T (Note that the same pattern does not hold for females.)
20. F (Sexual arousal has a strong effect, but it differs for men and women in some ways.)

Part II: Multiple-Choice Questions

1. *b*	**6.** *a*
2. *a*	**7.** *c*
3. *c*	**8.** *c*
4. *b*	**9.** *b*
5. *b*	**10.** *a*

Chapter 6
Sexual Pleasure and Technique

Even though almost any form of behavior can and does result in sexual pleasure for humans, the range of pleasurable sexual activities found in any society is much more limited than what is humanly possible. This is because, as members of a society, we learn what activities are defined as sexually pleasurable and appropriate.[1] In American society, the dominant forms of sexually pleasurable activities fall into the categories of masturbation, intercourse, oral-genital stimulation, and touching and caressing.

MASTURBATION

The history of masturbation is stormy. Originating in the ancient Hebrews' negative view of all nonprocreative sex, masturbation has long been treated with disapproval, scorn, and disgust. In the 1700s and 1800s, popular and medical thought held that masturbation led to both medical and physical illness and even death. This widely accepted medical view was largely the result of the traditional Christian view of masturbation and the lack of medical knowledge about many forms of illness, particularly diseases affecting children and adolescents (Neuman, 1975).[2] Even in the early part of the twentieth century, some major hospitals made it a practice to parade people who had undiagnosed illnesses before medical students to demonstrate the evil consequences of masturbation (Miller & Lief, 1976). While this view on the part of the medical profession has obviously changed, it has not totally disappeared. In one recent study of over 4000 medical students, 14 percent thought that masturbation leads to physical and mental disturbances (Miller & Lief, 1976).

Today, the status of masturbation is considerably higher than in the past. Rather than

---

[1]As we shall see, what are defined as sexually pleasurable activities change over time. Social changes in sexual pleasuring are most often the result of individual variations on the dominant sexual script becoming popular. This has taken place with many sexual activities and has the general tendency of middle-class sexual behavior patterns becoming popular among lower socioeconomic groups (Weinberg, 1980).

[2]This was a firm belief held by many in the medical profession. It was not uncommon to attribute childhood and adolescent deaths which were actually from yet-undiagnosed diseases (e.g., tuberculosis) to self-abuse. In addition to the moral climate of the period, attributing such deaths to masturbation eased the conscience of parents, doctors, and patients since they "knew" what caused the death. Not rarely, adolescents confessed on their death beds that they had masturbated (Neuman, 1975).

being viewed as the source of problems, masturbation is increasingly seen as the remedy. No small part of this change is due originally to Kinsey's research. The Kinsey research provided the public with not only their first concrete information about the fact that others masturbated too, but also data to dispel the myths about warts, hairy palms, and insanity. The research of Masters and Johnson (1966) more recently added greatly to the new status of masturbation. They reported that female orgasm was more intense through masturbation than through intercourse. Following this finding (which many women knew all along but nobody paid any attention to), masturbation became an important issue in the changing definitions of women's roles and female sexuality. Masturbation was widely discussed as not only a safe, convenient, and male-free form of sexual pleasure, but a means for learning about one's body and sexual responses. More recently, masturbation has come to be employed as a central technique in sexual therapy. Masturbation has proven an effective method for teaching women to orgasm and males to control ejaculation. Even in sexual therapy, the past, however, remains. As recently as 1978, clinical psychologists debated the morality of using masturbation as a therapy technique (see the *Journal of Clinical and Consulting Psychology,* Vol. **46,** 6).

One-Person Masturbation

Although the term masturbation is generally used to refer to physical *self-stimulation,* this definition is difficult to defend. For example, manual stimulation by another person can also be considered masturbation since the same activities are engaged in; the hand just belongs to someone else.

Self-stimulation is the most common form of masturbation. Kinsey found that 92 percent of all males and 62 percent of all females had engaged in masturbation. For the American public in general, these figures appear to have changed little over time. Hunt (1974) reported that 94 percent of all males and 63 percent of all females studied had engaged in masturba-

TABLE 6-1

Age at first masturbation as reported by male and female college students.

Age at First Masturbation	Percentage*	
	Males	**Females**
5–8	15	20
9–12	42	32
13–16	40	32
17–21	5	16

*Includes only those with masturbation experience: 89 percent of the males and 61 percent of the females.
Source: Arafat and Cotton (1974).

tion; these figures are in agreement with other more recent studies.

Regardless of age, males are more likely to masturbate than females. For example, in a 1975 study of college students, Abramson and Mosher found that 92 percent of the males and 72 percent of the females had masturbated. Hass (1979) found that 75 percent of the males and 52 percent of the females age 15 and 16 had masturbated.

The initial experience   Not only are males more likely to masturbate than females, but on the average, they begin at a younger age (Table 6-1).

Generally, one's first masturbation experience is accompanied by somewhat mixed feelings of pleasure, anxiety, excitement, and curious, unsure exploration. One is likely to have heard about masturbation, but what it is and how it is done is seldom clearly communicated.

> "I guess I discovered it on my own. I had heard the word, but didn't know exactly what it meant," said a 15-year-old female (Hass, 1979:87).

> "When I was 11, my brother told me about it, then one night in the shower I tried it myself. I had an orgasm and it scared the shit out of me. I knew what it was but I hadn't known what it would feel like," a 17-year-old male reported (Hass, 1979:92).

TABLE 6-2
Frequency of masturbation by black and white male and female college students.

Frequency of Masturbation	Males (%)		Females (%)	
	Blacks	Whites	Blacks	Whites
Very frequently	54	4	11	3
Frequently	2	11	11	7
Sometimes	5	49	13	25
Almost never	24	34	66	65

Source: Houston (1981).

Most comonly, females first experience masturbation as an accident, and males first experience it accidentally or from peers.

> "I discovered on the uneven parallel bars in gymnastics that if I leaned against the bar in a specific way in which my vagina was pressured, it would feel pleasant," said a 16-year-old female (Hass, 1979:89).

> "I was in the shower washing myself and fantasizing about this girl. I discovered the soap felt good against my penis. I then started to masturbate and eventually achieved orgasm," said a 16-year-old male (Hass, 1979:89).

> "My friend showed me. We were sitting there one day and he showed me by doing it himself," according to a 16-year-old male (Hass, 1979:90).

Frequency of masturbation The frequency of masturbation varies greatly according to such characteristics as age, attitude toward masturbation, the amount of pleasure one obtains from masturbation, ethnicity, gender, marital status, and other types of sexual activity in which one engages. As Kinsey pointed out, there is great individual diversity in masturbation, as in all sexual behavior. Among college students, the frequency of masturbation ranges from "never" to "several times a day" (Abramson and Mosher, 1975; Arafat and Cotton, 1974).

Males masturbate more frequently than females (See Table 6-2) and black males and females both masturbate more frequently than white males and females (Table 6-2). The difference in masturbation frequency between males and females also differs by ethnicity. The male-female difference is greater among blacks than whites (Table 6-2).

Single and divorced individuals masturbate more frequently than do married and cohabiting persons (Huey et al., 1981). The frequency of masturbation among females is also related to the type of stimulation which is most likely to create arousal to the point of orgasm for a person. Since it appears that most females obtain more stimulation from clitoral stimulation than deep vaginal pressure stimulation, masturbation is the most reliable sexual technique for orgasm for most women (Clifford, 1978). Masturbation also has the characteristic of one's being able to administer the stimulation in the exact physical manner most preferred (Clifford, 1978). For this reason, those females who experience orgasm through masturbation but not coitus masturbate the most frequently (Huey et al., 1981).

While masturbation is typically thought of as an adolescent activity (usually in a sense that puts down both masturbation and adolescents), it is a source of sexual pleasure for many married adults. Hunt (1974) found that 72 percent of the married men age 20 to 40 masturbated an average of twenty-four times a year, and 68 percent of the married women masturbated an average of ten times a year. Tavris and Sadd (1977) found that two-thirds of the married women studied in a large sample had masturbated since they were married: 16 percent "often" and 52 percent "occasionally."

Reasons for masturbating The old notion that the only reason people masturbate is that they have no other form of sexual activity is misleading. Most adolescents and young adults who masturbate do so because it feels good and they feel horny (Table 6-3).

BOX 6-1
ATTITUDE TOWARD MASTURBATION

Below is a scale, developed by Abramson and Mosher (1975), which measures attitude toward masturbation. You may complete this questionnaire by indicating the degree to which you agree or disagree with each of the statements. The method of scoring your answers and interpreting your score is given on page 165.

	Agree strongly	Agree	No opinion	Disagree	Disagree strongly
1. People masturbate to escape from feelings of tension and anxiety.	( )	( )	( )	( )	( )
2. People who masturbate will not enjoy sexual intercourse as much as those who refrain from masturbation.	( )	( )	( )	( )	( )
3. Masturbation is a private matter which neither harms nor concerns anyone else.	( )	( )	( )	( )	( )
4. Masturbation is a sin against yourself.	( )	( )	( )	( )	( )
5. Masturbation in childhood can help a person develop a natural, healthy attitude toward sex.	( )	( )	( )	( )	( )
6. Masturbation as an adult is juvenile and immature.	( )	( )	( )	( )	( )
7. Masturbation can lead to homosexuality.	( )	( )	( )	( )	( )
8. Excessive masturbation is physically impossible, so it is a needless worry.	( )	( )	( )	( )	( )
9. If you enjoy masturbating very much, you may never learn to relate to the opposite sex.	( )	( )	( )	( )	( )
10. After masturbating, a person feels degraded.	( )	( )	( )	( )	( )
11. Experience with masturbation can potentially help a woman become orgiastic in sexual intercourse.	( )	( )	( )	( )	( )
12. I feel guilty about masturbating.	( )	( )	( )	( )	( )
13. Masturbation can be "a friend in need" when there is no "friend in deed."	( )	( )	( )	( )	( )
14. Masturbation can provide an outlet for sex fantasies without harming anyone else or endangering oneself.	( )	( )	( )	( )	( )
15. Excessive masturbation can lead to problems of impotence in men and frigidity in women.	( )	( )	( )	( )	( )
16. Masturbation is an escape mechanism which prevents a person from developing a mature sexual outlook.	( )	( )	( )	( )	( )

Masturbation is also a means of reducing tension and feelings of loneliness. More and more frequently, young women masturbate to learn more about their bodies and to explore their sexual responses and feelings. In a sample of college women, Clifford (1978) found that 54 percent masturbated for this purpose. Women are much more likely than men to masturbate for this reason (Abramson and Mosher, 1975). Among married women, Tavris and Sadd (1977) found that 38 percent masturbated when their husband was absent, 18 percent

17. Masturbation can provide harmless relief from sexual tensions. ( ) ( ) ( ) ( ) ( )
18. Playing with your own genitals is disgusting. ( ) ( ) ( ) ( ) ( )
19. Excessive masturbation is associated with neurosis, depression, and behavioral problems. ( ) ( ) ( ) ( ) ( )
20. Any masturbation is too much. ( ) ( ) ( ) ( ) ( )
21. Masturbation is a compulsive, addictive habit which, once begun, is almost impossible to stop. ( ) ( ) ( ) ( ) ( )
22. Masturbation is fun. ( ) ( ) ( ) ( ) ( )
23. When I masturbate, I am disgusted with myself. ( ) ( ) ( ) ( ) ( )
24. A pattern of frequent masturbation is associated with introversion and withdrawal from social contacts. ( ) ( ) ( ) ( ) ( )
25. I would be ashamed to admit publicly that I have masturbated. ( ) ( ) ( ) ( ) ( )
26. Excessive masturbation leads to mental dullness and fatigue. ( ) ( ) ( ) ( ) ( )
27. Masturbation is a normal sexual outlet. ( ) ( ) ( ) ( ) ( )
28. Masturbation is caused by an excessive preoccupation with thoughts of sex. ( ) ( ) ( ) ( ) ( )
29. Masturbation can teach you to enjoy the sensuousness of your own body. ( ) ( ) ( ) ( ) ( )
30. After I masturbate, I am disgusted with myself for losing control of my body. ( ) ( ) ( ) ( ) ( )

Scoring: For each statement score 1 for "Strongly agree," 2 for "Agree," 3 for "No opinion," 4 for "Disagree," and 5 for "Strongly disagree." Except for items 3, 5, 8, 11, 13, 14, 17, 22, 27, 29, score your answers in reverse. That is, 1 for "Strongly disagree" and 5 for "Strongly agree." After you have written the score next to each of your answers, total the number of points. There are no right and wrong answers as such. Rather, the answers you gave reflect your feelings. Your feelings, regardless of what they are, are just as valid as anyone else's and no better or worse than anyone else's. For your total score, a low score indicates a negative attitude and a high score indicates a positive attitude toward masturbation. The lowest possible score is 30 and the highest 150. In a sample of 96 male and 102 female undergraduate students at the University of Connecticut in 1975, the average score for both males and females was 72. Among females, a negative attitude toward masturbation is related to amount of sexual experience, frequency of masturbation per month, and maximum frequency of masturbation per day. Among males, a negative attitude toward masturbation is related only to the frequency of masturbation per month (Abramson and Mosher, 1975).

TABLE 6-3
Reasons for masturbating as reported by 20 to 22-year-old males and females.

Reason	Males (%)	Females (%)
Feels "horny"	47	39
For pleasure	21	24
Loneliness	12	16
Frustration and mental strain	11	9
Absence of mate	8	11

Source: Arafat and Cotton (1974).

when intercourse was not satisfying, 16 percent for sexual experimentation, and 14 percent because it was a pleasant habit developed before marriage.

Feelings about masturbating Even though adolescents and young adults most frequently feel physical satisfaction immediately after masturbating (68 percent of the males and 57 percent of the females report this response), the fears and anxieties of the past are still with us. In Arafat and Cotton's (1974) research with college men and women, 13 percent of the males and 10 percent of the females reported feelings of guilt; 5 percent of the males and 1 percent of the females, feelings of being perverted; and 3 percent of the males and 7 percent of the females, fears of becoming insane. Masturbation also results in considerable sexual pleasure, especially for women. Reflecting the earlier findings of Masters and Johnson, Arafat and Cotton found that among college students, one-third of the women reported that orgasm is more intense in masturbation than in intercourse. This was reported by only 9 percent of the males.

Techniques of masturbation Not only does masturbation have the advantage of your not having to dress up for the occasion, but everything you need is carried with you. While males may use equipment ranging from toilet-paper rolls, overripe melons, and gadgets one plugs into the cigarette lighter while driving to work (the number of sales of which are unknown), and females may use anything from vibrators (uncommon) to zucchini (also uncom-

mon) and washing machines (very uncommon) (Hite, 1977), most people use their hands.[3]

Male masturbation techniques tend to be less varied than female techniques. Most commonly, males grasp the penis between the thumb and a few fingers and stroke up and down with light to moderate pressure while touching the glans on the up motion. The penis may also be held with the entire hand (depending on the size of both), and lubrication may also be used to alleviate irritation and enhance the sensation. Most men avoid directly stimulating the glans for extended periods since, as in the case of the clitoris, rough treatment here is more likely to produce irritation than pleasure.

Female masturbation techniques frequently involve other than genital manipulation, a relatively rare practice among males (Table 6-4). This difference is primarily due to the more genital focus males learn in their definition of sexuality (Chapter 4). Female masturbation techniques also often involve methods other than using the hands. One-third of the college women studied by Clifford used muscle

TABLE 6-4
Areas of body stimulated by females in masturbation.

Area of Body	Percentages of Females
Clitoris	73
Around clitoris	65
Labia and vaginal extrance	65
Breasts and vaginal interior	49
Hips and thighs	27
Stomach	19
Entire body	12

Source: Clifford (1978:567), random sample of college women.

[3]Although not used for masturbation by the majority of the female population, vibrators have become recognized and have gained respectability for this purpose. Most major vibrator manufacturers market vibrators designed for "tender areas" and "ultimate sensation of localized areas." In 1983, the vibrator industry expects sales of some 3 million units and sexual aids such as vibrators make up a significant portion of the world of commercial sex.

tension and thigh movement, and 15 percent used running water over the genitals.

Whether females use frequent or only occasional stimulation of the clitoris, it is through such stimulation that orgasm occurs most frequently in masturbation. Most women use short, rhythmic strokes or long, slow strokes. Pressing down steadily on the clitoris or fluttering the fingers or gently pulling the clitoris are also common techniques. Most females masturbate for less than ten minutes at one time (47 percent, less than five minutes). However, fully 14 percent report masturbating for periods from sixteen minutes to two hours at a time (Clifford, 1978).

In perspective Masturbation might well be considered our most basic form of sexual activity (Dodson, 1974). In a very real sense, it is the only form of overt sexual activity that does not involve interaction with another person. As such, it is a relatively (but hardly totally) simple form of sexual stimulation and source of pleasure. Masturbation, as we have seen in Chapter 4, also serves an important function in sexual learning. In the past, this exploration and learning about one's sexual responses through masturbation have been the stronghold of males. As attitudes about masturbation have changed and as masturbation has been discussed and advocated among women, this learning opportunity is being explored by more and more women. In this same spirit, female masturbation has taken on some sexual-political overtones, representing a form of sexual activity and pleasure which is free from the traditional "necessity" of a male and his penis. Nevertheless, the vast majority of males and females feel that what masturbation provides in pure genital pleasure it lacks in interpersonal involvement, closeness, and communication. This missing element in self-stimulation makes one-person masturbation come in a poor second to coitus in most people's view of good sexual experiences.

Two-Person Masturbation

Masturbation also takes the form of one person's stimulating another. This might well be considered simply a form of caressing activity except that it is conducted in such a manner as to duplicate self-stimulation and is viewed by the participants themselves as masturbation.

Masturbation of one partner by another may be engaged in prior to coitus, after coitus, during actual coitus, or just as an activity in and of itself. Fisher (1973), for example, found that 63 percent of the married women studied generally had orgasm with their husbands by his first manually stimulating her clitoris and then having intercourse. Another 20 percent generally had orgasm by intromission followed by their partner's giving manual stimulation. Tavris and Sadd (1977) found that 31 percent of the married women used masturbation as an additional form of stimulation during intercourse and that 9 percent masturbated while their husbands watched with enjoyment.

It usually requires some practice and sensitivity to the responses of the other person when partner, or mutual, masturbation is first tried. Generalizing from one's own masturbation experiences may lead to techniques which are not at all stimulating to one's partner. As in all things sexual, there are no substitutes for communication and guidance in a nonthreatening manner.

COITUS

Coitus (ko'-eh-tus, coming from the Latin meaning "to go together") can take many different forms in terms of positions, accompanying activities, duration, speed, and other conditions. Generally, the term *coitus* is used to refer to insertion of the penis in the vagina. Even though this is the use of the term here, elsewhere it may refer to any form of penile insertion involving parts of the body other than the vagina and a partner other than female.

Coital Positions

When we think of different types of coitus, we usually think of different positions. The number of coital positions that are humanly possible is

These Oriental playing cards reveal not only the sex-positive view of Eastern cultures in general but also some of the endless possibilities in coital positions.

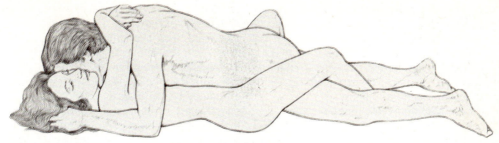

Figure 6-1 The male-on-top, face-to-face coital position ("missionary" position).

limited only by imagination, attitude, and athletic ability. Most of the hundreds of positions described at some time in history are derived from some basic position.

Face-to-face with male on top The traditional "missionary" position with the male on top and both partners lying facing each other is the most commonly used coital posture in American society (Figure 6-1).[4] There are many variations to this position. The male may support his weight with his hands or elbows while making thrusting movements with the hips, or he may relax his weight on his partner. Many men are concerned about crushing their partner, but this is not likely unless there are vast differences in size and weight. In any event, the way to find out is to ask. The full body contact is often an additional form of stimulation, providing closeness and intimacy as well as ease of subtle communication. On the other hand, it may be highly stimulating to both partners to have no other body contact than genital. In this case, the male supports himself with his hands and feet.

Thrusting movement of the penis in the vagina is not the only form of stimulation in this position. Given that straight movement of the penis in and out of the vagina results in little direct stimulation of the clitoris (although this varies depending on female anatomy and

how the male positions himself), some couples find it highly stimulating to press close together. The female pushes her body downward and the male his body upward. Such movement creates not only slow, deep penetration but also steady pressure of the male's pubic area against the clitoral region.

People vary greatly in not only speed with which they prefer thrusting movements, but the depth of penetration as well. As a general rule, jumping up and down like a rabbit does not result in much sensual pleasure for the female (unless, of course, that is what she prefers) and deep penetration should be made slowly.

Although Figure 6-1 shows one of the more common variations of this position, what the woman does with her legs provides many other possibilities. She may keep her legs tightly together (providing maximum clitoral stimulation but also requiring ample vaginal lubrication), or she may place her legs wide apart. She may keep her legs straight, bend them slightly, or place them around the male's waist or over his shoulder (providing deep penetration).

If the male is supporting his own weight with both hands, he has no opportunity to provide manual stimulation. A slight variation of this position involves the woman's placing her legs over the male's shoulders while he kneels in front of her. This allows slow or rapid thrusting motions during coitus, and both partners have their hands free to manually stimulate each other. Maximum visual communication and stimulation are also provided.

---

[4]This position is reputed to have acquired its name when, to the amazement of Polynesian women, missionaries would have coitus only in this position. The truth of this assertion remains to be proven.

Face-to-face with female on top

This position (Figure 6-2) not only provides the female much more freedom of movement and the opportunity to position herself for maximum clitoral stimulation, but allows the male to take less of a "director" role (something many males appreciate and enjoy).

There are also many variations on this basic position. The female can manually stimulate the male's genitals by reaching around her back, manually stimulate her own genitals, stimulate her breasts, have her breasts and/or clitoris manually stimulated by her partner, or have her breasts orally stimulated during coitus.

In this position, the female can also control the depth of penetration and amount of clitoral stimulation. She can move up and down or rock back and forth or lean forward while the male makes thrusting movements. In this forward leaning posture, she can control the angle of penetration and the amount of clitoral stimulation. This position also allows for oral stimulation of the breasts. She may also lean backward, thus changing the focus of stimulation within the vagina to the Grafenberg spot. This position also provides deep vagina-pressure stimulation—stimulation which can be enhanced by the male's pressing with his hand on that part of the female's abdomen where the penis is on the vagina. This position is also that in which the male is least likely to reach orgasm rapidly. Thus, partners may more closely coordinate their arousal to the point of orgasm if they find this desirable.

Side-by-side This position (Figure 6-3) allows both partners to feel next to each other in a relaxed manner without either partner's doing most of the "work" or controlling most of the action (whichever way you view it). This position allows touch and verbal communication and is a pleasing form of coitus following orgasm. If the male has partially lost erection, this position allows basic coital activity. Addi-

Figure 6-2 The female-on-top, face-to-face coital position.

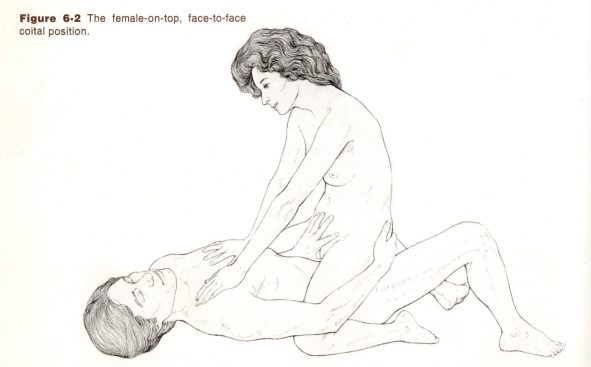

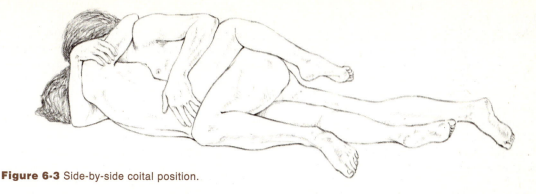

Figure 6-3 Side-by-side coital position.

tionally, it permits partial freedom of the hands
and allows partners to kiss. It may be experienced as an interlude between periods of male
orgasm and renewed arousal to full erection.
Some caution is required not to cut off circulation in each other's legs.

Rear entry This position (Figure 6-4)
involves inserting the penis in the vagina while
facing the female's back. There are again
many variations. The female may be on her
hands and knees or on her stomach. Both
partners may also be on their sides, although
full insertion is sometimes difficult in this posture. With the male behind the female in a
kneeling position, his hands, as well as one of

hers, are free to stimulate her back, hips,
breasts, or genitals. Many find this position
pleasurable since the sensations for both partners are different with the penis rubbing

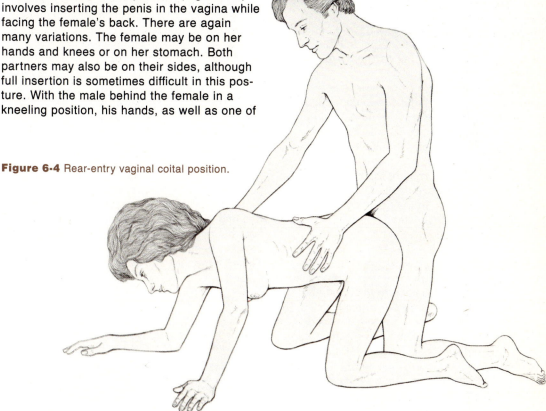

Figure 6-4 Rear-entry vaginal coital position.

TABLE 6-5
Changes over time in the use of coital positions by married couples.

Positions Frequently Used in Marital Coitus	Percentage of Married Couples by Decade of Respondent's Birth			
	Before 1900	1900–1909	1910–1919	1920–1929
Male on top, only position used	16	10	7	6
Male on top	100	100	100	100
Female on top	35	38	48	52
Side by side	27	31	34	29
Rear entry	10	12	18	16
Sitting	6	9	9	10
Standing	4	4	5	4

Source: Kinsey et al. (1953, table 101, p. 400).

against what would otherwise be the bottom of the vaginal canal and the penetration being deep. When the woman is on her stomach, the stimulation is also different from that of other positions. On the other hand, many do not care for this position because they feel that it is rather impersonal when the partners are not facing each other.

Other variations From these basic positions, the use of certain household furniture can provide infinite variety. Partners may engage in rear-entry or face-to-face coitus with the man sitting in a chair and the woman, on top, on his lap. The woman may sit on the edge of a table, bed, counter top or whatever while in the face-to-face position with the male standing or kneeling. In the absence of furniture, both partners may stand.

Coital Position Changes over Time
Historically, the male on top in the face-to-face position (missionary) has been the most approved. As shown in Table 6-5, the exclusive use of the missionary position has declined over time and other positions have gained popularity, particularly those with the female in the top position.

Today there is much greater variation in coital positions used among the population in general than in Kinsey's time. Hunt (1974)

found that of the married couples studied, 75 percent occasionally used the female-on-top position, 50 percent the side-by-side position, 25 percent the sitting position, and 80 percent rear entry vaginal coitus.[5]

As we might expect, these changes have not spread throughout all society. Older persons practice less positional variation—even allowing for lessened athletic ability—than do their younger counterparts (Hunt, 1974). Adolescents also have less experience with different coital positions than adults. Even among college students age 18 and 19, Mahoney (1979a) found that while 75 percent of the males had engaged in coitus in the missionary position, only 44 percent had experienced rearentry coitus. Among females, 64 percent had engaged in coitus in the missionary position, but only 38 percent in the rear-entry coital position. Similar findings were also noted by Kinsey (Gebhard and Johnson, 1979).

---

[5]The use of different coital positions was found by Kinsey to differ significantly by social class (as measured by educational level). College-educated males and females utilized more different coital positions than did those with less than a college education (Gebhard and Johnson, 1979). This difference may or may not be present today, but, as in the time of the Kinsey research, attitudes toward sexuality differ by social class and individuals with higher levels of education show greater acceptance of experimentation.

Coital Position Preferences

Within the last few years, there has been an increasing current of discussion about the extent to which various positions are enjoyed by women. As a result of the rising attention to female sexuality, and popularized by the *Hite Report* (Hite, 1977), it has become a common assumption that most women do not find much sexual satisfaction in many coital positions, especially the missionary position. A recent study by Swieczkowski and Walker (1978) suggests, however, that this is not so. It was found that the order of preference married women listed for coital positions (from most to least preferred) was male on top, female on top, side by side, prone rear entry, sitting face to face, kneeling rear entry, and sitting rear entry. This order of preferences mirrored almost exactly the frequency of using these positions as well as the frequency of orgasm by different positions. At least in this sample of women, position preference and practice correspond almost identically. In fact, the only disparity between preference and practice was that these women preferred to have coitus more often in all the positions. The dissatisfaction was not with how coitus took place, but how much of all kinds took place.

Female college students prefer the male-on-top position more than do males because it provides feelings of emotional intimacy (Allgeier, 1981). Even though much has been written about the political implications of who is on top, preference for the male-on-top position by women is not related to their being traditional or liberal in general female role behavior (Allgeier, 1981).

Allgeier and Fogel (1979) found, in fact, that most college females had a negative view of the female-on-top position. College-student males and females viewed slides showing a man and a woman having coitus in either the woman-above or woman-below position. While males did not differ in attitude toward these two positions, females disliked the woman-above position much more than that with the woman below. Further, females (but not males) evaluated the woman in the female-above position as less respectable, dirtier, less

moral, and less capable of being a wife and mother than the woman in the female-below position.

Interpersonal Processes in Position Experimentation

Variation in coital positions plays an important part in the development of sexual behaviors in a relationship. As Gagnon and Simon (1973:85) point out, positional variation is perhaps the most frequent form of sexual experimentation. While few couples give whips, rubber sheets, or olive oil much consideration, many people attempt to try different coital postures. The popularity of trying different coital positions is evident in what married males say they would like to do more often in their sexual activity. In one study, the single most popular wish was to use different coital positions, chosen by 53 percent of the men (Pietropinto and Simenauer, 1977). Oral sex ranked a poor second with 22 percent of the votes.

The processes involved in initiating and accomplishing such experimentation are interesting. Most frequently, new ideas are not discussed between partners. Pietropinto and Simenauer asked married males if they told their coital partner what they like to do. Only 8 percent said they discuss such things before or after having sex, and only 28 percent said they mention such things during sexual activity.

> The problem here, as it is in initiating or maintaining all forms of sexual variety, is that the novel behavior must normally be accomplished without speaking. In order for this to be successfully managed, the female (or male) must usually give signs that the change in position is a source of sexual pleasure. Commonly, this is done through either having orgasm or making the noises that are conventionally associated with sexual excitement. (Gagnon and Simon, 1973:85)

The processes involved here reveal how a relatively simple physical maneuver can be a complex social and psychological activity. Not only must subtle cues be exchanged (usually nonverbal), but all the processes must take place in the heat of passion and in a manner that will not interrupt the flow of erotic and sexually meaningful events. Decisions must be made as to the probable reaction to a suggestion and to what will happen if there is a rejection of the idea.

The diversity of sexual activities within a relationship is also related to how much the partners enjoy sex and the frequency of their sexual activity (Nowinski et al., 1981). A wider range of sexual behaviors in a relationship is also related to a desire to please one's partner and the perception that one's partner enjoys a wide range of sexual behaviors (Nowinski et al., 1981). What accounts for the diversity of sexual behaviors in a couple differs, however, for males and females. The best predictor of the diversity of sexual behaviors practiced by females in heterosexual relationships is enjoyment of sex followed by thinking that their partner's pleasure is associated with more diverse sexual activities. For the male, diversity is best predicted by his thinking that his partner's pleasure is associated with more diverse sexual activities, with his own enjoyment of sex the second best predictor (Nowinski et al., 1981). These patterns of what is first and second in importance in determining one's diversity of sexual activities are reflections of gender roles in sexual interaction (the male learns to do what pleases his partner and the female learns to be a gatekeeper and thus her own enjoyment is important).

Any introduction of a new sexual activity, including coital positions, must also be backed by its legitimacy as an erotic activity. That is, each act must already be, or come to be, defined as sexually appropriate and erotic. The extent to which such definitions are created and maintained between two people depends on the flexibility of each person's definitions of appropriate erotic activity. Such individual definitions generally, however, are the result of some wider societal definitions. Popular magazines, sex manuals, and, to a lesser extent,

erotic films do a great deal not only to suggest possibilities, but also to place a stamp of acceptability and eroticism on various forms of sexual conduct.

Human Diversity

The coital positions used and considered pleasurable differ greatly from one culture to the next. Among the Trobriand Islanders, the male typically squats in front of the female and holds her thighs under his arms with his hands on the ground. Among the Bala, the conventional intercourse position is the male on his right side and the female on her left, facing each other. The Bala also use the missionary position, but the female on top is considered very strange and apparently never used. The Inis Beag (a pseudonym for an Irish folk community) use only the missionary position and never remove their underclothes during coitus (Kinsey noted that only 67 percent of the women in the United States born before 1900 often had coitus in the nude). Among the Mangaia of Polynesia, the most frequent and preferred coital position is missionary (they must have changed their minds). The second most common position is the female standing and bending over with rear entry. The Mangaia also use a number of nonvaginal coital positions. Placement of the penis between the breasts (now popular in American erotic films), thighs, feet, and armpits is a common form of sexual activity. On Romonum Island and in East Bay, the most usual form of coitus is *striking*. The penis stimulates the clitoris without entering the vagina. When both partners are about to orgasm (simultaneous orgasm is highly valued), the penis is inserted in the vagina.

ORAL-GENITAL STIMULATION

Running a close second to anal sexual activity in the list of traditionally taboo sexual topics is oral-genital sex. Kinsey was the first to present Americans with data showing that if oral sex is a perversion (as was commonly argued in Victorian times), there are a lot of perverts and their numbers are on the increase.

Cunnilingus

Cunnilingus (kun-eh-lin′-gus) is oral stimulation of the female genitals (from the Latin *cunnus,* meaning "vulva," and *lingere,* meaning "to lick"). Many consider the mouth to be a perfect part of the anatomy for sexual stimulation. Not only does one have perfect control of this part of the anatomy, but it is warm, smooth, and wet.

Most commonly, the clitoris is the focus of oral stimulation, either by stroking with the tongue in darting or slow licking movements or by gently sucking. Sensually pleasurable activities also include kissing and licking the navel, thigh, and genital areas. A good clean shave helps the male here, so that one is not felt as steel wool with a tongue. Manual manipulation of the genitals can also accompany oral stimulation, often with the insertion of a finger in the vagina simulating coital movement. Many women also find body caressing (hips, stomach, thighs, breasts) highly pleasurable during cunnilingus, since sexual sensations then spread over the entire body. Some women find, however, that such activities distract from the oral stimulation itself.

Some males hesitate to engage in cunnilingus for a variety of reasons. Frequently, males have little familiarity with the appearance of the female genitals and may have carried over from adolescence misconceptions about the smell and cleanliness of the vagina. The association of female genitals with menstruation (seen in our culture as "dirty") does not aid in reducing these notions. Actually, the genitals contain fewer bacteria than the mouth and are as clean as, or cleaner than, other parts of the body.

Fellatio

Fellatio (fel-ay′-she-oh) is oral stimulation of the male genitals, the term coming from the Latin *fellare,* meaning "to suck." The partner can lick the glans of the penis or the testicles, or, more commonly, take the penis in the mouth and use an in-out motion while gently stimulating it with the lips and tongue. Some minor caution must be taken relating to the teeth, but many women worry about this more than necessary. The male should not become too enthusiastic in pelvic movement, since most women prefer to control the depth to which the penis moves into the mouth. Regardless of the popularity some years ago of the movie *Deep Throat,* a gag reflex takes place when anything, including a penis, touches the throat region of the mouth. Considerable practice is required to avoid this reflex by muscle relaxation.

Fellatio is also combined with manual stimulation of the penis. While oral stimulation takes place, stroking of the penile shaft is generally considered highly pleasurable.

If fellatio is continued to the point of male orgasm, the male may signal such an occurrence and the penis may be withdrawn, with manual stimulation continued to orgasm. The woman may also continue oral stimulation through orgasm, since there is nothing harmful or inherently distasteful about ejaculate. It has a slightly salty taste and resembles slightly cooked egg white in appearance and consistency. Since some may find fellatio to orgasm unpleasant, one must remember that this, as any sexual activity, is a matter of personal taste, not sexual necessity.

Mutual Oral-Genital Stimulation

Both partners may orally stimulate each other's genitals at the same time (known as "69" because of the position of the partners' heads during this activity). This technique (Figure 6-5) may provide strong feelings of intimacy and mutual involvement. One partner may not want to be on the bottom and thus lying on the side may be preferred. Most commonly, the woman prefers to be on top, since she can then control the depth of the penis in the mouth. Many people feel, however, that mutual

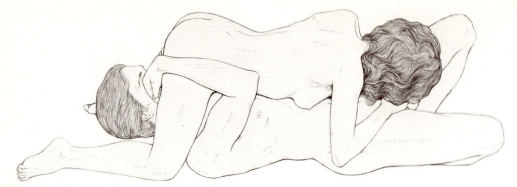

Figure 6-5 Mutual oral-genital stimulation (commonly referred to as "69").

oral-genital stimulation is too involved to be able to concentrate on the pleasure of the moment and still effectively stimulate one's partner.

The Acceptance of Oral-Genital Sexuality

While married females born before 1900 were very likely in Kinsey's time to have engaged in manual stimulation of a male's genitals (80 percent) or manual stimulation of their genitals by a male (88 percent), cunnilingus was experienced by only 42 percent of these women and fellatio by only 29 percent. From this generation on, however, oral-genital sexuality became more common. Among those women born between 1920 and 1929, cunnilingus was experienced by 57 percent and fellatio by the same proportion (Kinsey, 1953). More recently, Tavris and Sadd (1977), in their nationwide sample of married women, found that 97 percent had engaged in fellatio and 91 percent in cunnilingus. Today, in fact, the proportion of 16-year-olds who have oral-genital experience exceeds that of women born before 1900 (35 percent of both 16-year-old males and females, Hass, 1979).

Oral-genital activity is today practiced with some regularity in marriage. Among Tavris and Sadd's sample of women, approximately 40 percent engaged in both cunnilingus and fellatio "often" and another 45 to 48 percent, "occasionally."

While other forms of sexual activity have undergone some changes over time, oral-genital activity wins the popularity contest hands down. Its increasing acceptability has been strongly encouraged by popular magazines and even television. The discussion in 1978 on *Saturday Night Live* of Colonel Ingus and his licking-good chicken contains and reveals the kind of acceptability necessary for such changes to take place.

Better to Receive or Give?

While the mutuality of oral-genital activity is apparent in the relative frequency of cunnilingus and fellatio, it is evidently better to receive than to give. In Tavris and Sadd's study, cunnilingus is described as very enjoyable by 62 percent of the women, but only 34 percent were equally enthusiastic about fellatio. Males evidently feel the same. In Pietropinto and Simenauer's sample (1977), only 53 percent of the married men said they enjoyed cunnilingus. Another 21 percent said they did not mind doing it but did so to please their wives, and 9 percent said they regarded it as unpleasant, boring, or downright unnatural.

Social Variations in Oral-Genital Activity

Both the incidence and frequency of oral sex vary across certain social categories and groups. Oral-genital sex is more common among young than older marrieds (Hunt, 1974; Tavris and Sadd, 1977), the less religious (Bell, 1974; Tavris and Sadd, 1977), and the more highly educated (Hunt, 1974). Even these differences, however, are small. While only 7 percent of the Tavris and Sadd sample of married women had never tried cunnilingus, this "never" category rose to only 16 percent among women over age 40. Even though oral-genital activity is less common among the devout, fully 87 percent of the highly religious married women in Tavris and Sadd's study had experienced oral sex. While college-educated males and females today are still more liberal in this regard than grade school and high school educated adults, oral sexual activity has gained popularity among this latter segment of society. Kinsey described less educated males as viewing oral sex with suspicion and aversion, but Hunt (1974) and Pietropinto and Simeneaur (1977) found such attitudes eroding.[6]

Oral sexual attitudes and behaviors also differ by ethnicity, the reasons for such not being clear. Staples (1973:63), a black sociologist, argues that black males and females have a less accepting view of oral sex than whites. Staples (p. 63) goes so far as to state that among blacks, ". . . any sexual act other than simple and direct coitus is considered a perversion." While this state ent may be a biㄊm strongly worded, it is true that oral sex is less popular among both black males and females. In Pietropinto and Simenaur's research (1977), 14 percent of the white males and 33 percent of the black males said they did not engage in cunnilingus. Further, while 57 percent of the white males said they enjoyed cunnilingus, only 30 percent of the black males felt this way and almost twice as many blacks as whites had a strong negative reaction to cunnilingus. This pattern is not new. Kinsey (Gebhard and Johnson, 1979) found the same ethnic differ-

ences in oral sexual behavior. This pattern is also not merely a function of educational differences between blacks and whites in American society. Rather, it appears to be a true ethnic difference in learning of sexuality. Kinsey (Gebhard and Johnson, 1979) found that 78 percent of the college-educated black males had never engaged in cunnilingus, while 47 percent of the college-educated white males had never done so.

Situational factors are also important in the frequency of oral sexual activity. During the last three months of pregnancy, most couples decrease their frequency of intercourse. One of the activities which replaces coitus is oral-genital stimulation (Tolar and DiGrazia, 1976).

ANAL STIMULATION

Purely in terms of both attitudes and behavior, anal sexual stimulation is one of the last heterosexual frontiers in American society. While many taboos have dwindled away from the heterosexual scene over time, there has been little change in the meaning attached to anal sexual activity.

All forms of sexual activity involve a complex set of perceptions and meanings in order to take place and be enjoyed. No behavior is automatically sexual or erotic. Anal sex is an excellent example of this point. Unlike vaginal coitus or oral sex, anal sexual activity involves overcoming and replacing with sexual meanings a set of meanings which generally have no sexual connotation at all in this society (Gagnon and Simon, 1973:91).

In actuality, there is nothing unclean or repulsive about the anal region if normal hygiene practices are employed. Anal intercourse does require more caution and tenderness than vaginal intercourse. The anus has no natural lubrication and, unlike the vagina, does not expand with sexual arousal. Lubrication such as K-Y jelly (vaseline should be avoided) or saliva should be used, and the penis should be inserted only after ample relaxation and stimulation.

---

[6]This negative attitude toward oral-genital sexual activity on the part of adults with lower levels of education was also apparent in actual behavior. Kinsey (Gebhard and Johnson, 1979) found that college-educated males and females were much more likely than those without a college education to engage in both cunnilingus and fellatio.

Not unexpectedly, people vary greatly in their attitudes about anal intercourse. While some find it out-and-out disgusting, others revel in the experience. The anus is generally much tighter than the vagina and may provide strong penile stimulation. Many women orgasm with anal intercourse, especially if accompanied by clitoral stimulation.

Certain health precautions are necessary. The penis should not be inserted in the vagina after anal intercourse unless thoroughly washed. The rectum contains many bacteria which, if transported to the vagina, can cause vaginitis.

Another less common form of anal stimulation is *anilingus,* or oral stimulation of the anus. Here, the meanings attached to the anal region being combined with those attached to the mouth and face make the activity much more psychologically complex. The anal region, particularly the area between the anus and genitals (perineum), is highly sensitive and may be a source of strong sexual pleasure. This sexual stimulation can also be experienced by manual stimulation of the anal region as well as digital insertion into the anus.

Social Patterns of Heterosexual Anal Stimulation

Even though heterosexual anal stimulation is still repugnant to many, it is not rare today. Of the married women in Tavris and Sadd's sample, 43 percent had tried anal intercourse at least once. The frequency of anal intercourse remains, however, limited. Only 2 percent of all the married women in Tavris and Sadd's sample engaged in anal intercourse "often." Another 19 percent did so "occasionally," and 22 percent had tried it only once. The majority of these women were not especially enthusiastic. Of those who had tried anal intercourse at least once, only 10 percent thought it "very enjoyable," and 59 percent felt that it was either neutral, unpleasant, or repulsive. However, 31 percent did describe the experience as "somewhat enjoyable."

There is a distinct tendency of younger women to be more willing to try anal intercourse, and it is a more common activity among those women who are generally more excited about the quality of their marital sex.

Males have the same less-than-enthusiastic attitude about anal intercourse. When asked what they would like to do more often, only 4 percent of Pietropinto and Si menaur's married male sample mentioned anal intercourse.

Even with the generally negative attitudes toward anal coitus today, the popularity of this behavior has increased over time. Kinsey found that approximately 7 to 8 percent of the females and 5 percent of the males had *ever* engaged in anal coitus, and most of these individuals had done so only a few times. (Gebhard and Johnson, 1979).

Anal coitus is much more popular and common among homosexual males, whose behaviors we shall discuss later.

TOUCHING AND CARESSING

The essence of sexual interaction involves touching and caressing behaviors. Therefore it is difficult to discuss such techniques apart from other sexual activities.

Generally, such behaviors fall under the category (as if everything had to be in a "category") of what are called "foreplay" activities. This is a term worthy of some discussion itself. As Laws and Schwartz (1977) point out, the term "foreplay" reveals something about heterosexual activity. First, the "fore" suggests that such behaviors take place only before something else, that something else being coitus. Traditionally, such behaviors were discussed as techniques used to "get" the female ready for the big event. Second, the term "play" implies that these behaviors are not really serious sexual activities, but are only a kind of "messing around" until one gets down to serious sex. On both counts, foreplay comes off as secondary in importance to coitus. This, however, is perhaps more of a traditional male than a female view of sexuality; it may reflect a male's learning that the sequence of sexual activities is: Get ready, do it, orgasm, stop. Females tend not to be as committed to this sequence as are males, and they are more

likely to prefer foreplay before, during, and after coitus or orgasm.

We have repeatedly noted that Kinsey found many differences in heterosexual behavior by level of education. In general, it was found that college-educated males and females engaged in more diverse sexual activities than did males and females with less than a college education. This difference by level of education was readily apparent in touching and caressing activities. For example, among whites, those with a college education were twice as likely as those without a college education to engage in deep or tongue kissing in marriage (Gebhard and Johnson, 1979).

SEXUAL AIDS AND GUIDES

We Americans work hard at having fun. This is part of our work ethic, which tells us that anything worth doing is worth doing right. Doing anything right is assumed to involve training, the right equipment, the right technique, and practice. This work ethic applied to sex has paved the way for an entire industry which provides everything from sexual advice to paraphenalia.

Sexual Advice

Giving "expert" sexual advice has become an occupation. We have always been blessed with those who make a living from telling others what is best for them sexually. While such advice can be very beneficial when provided by professionals, it can be disastrous when the adviser is not a qualified professional. One popular writer in the 1970s, for example, proclaimed the joys of douching with carbonated water, actually a very dangerous activity.

Over time, the most popular of sexual advice has come in the form of "marriage manuals," later to be called "sex manuals" as we came to accept sex other than in marriage. These volumes have always been popular, even in the 1800s. Herein contains the problem. They have always been popular because a lot of people have always had a lot of questions about sex. This popularity means that there is the potential to make a great deal of money. While no doubt the intentions of most authors are honorable, one is always playing with fire when one mixes monetary aspirations and the very real needs of people.

Historically, such guides have reflected, in an exaggerated form, the sexual values of the period in which they were written. Nineteenth-century publications warned of the many dangers of sexual activity and excess (Walters, 1974). In the 1950s and 1960s, we were told of the effort necessary to awaken female sexual interest and how one must work hard at "obtaining good sex," but that one must not be frivolous about sexuality (must not enjoy it too much) (Lewis and Brissett, 1967). In the 1970s, America's preoccupation with *self* in the *me* generation became the dominant tone of sexual advice books. One was to cast off his or her cultural heritage as a silly burden of social constraint and redo one's self along any of a variety of sexual lifestyle choices. Sex was described as not only the avenue to personal development and fulfilment, but the cure-all for almost every social and personal problem. Sex was said to stop compulsive eating, keep one's weight down, keep one physically fit, make one's sex organs work better, make one's eyes clearer and one's expression more relaxed, and even cure some illnesses. Sexual happiness would also bring you a higher paying job and a nicer house.

In order to reap the much sought after sexual ecstacy described in these manuals, one still had to place an emphasis on performance. Performance now, however, was not so much getting in physical shape, but expanding one's sexuality into new realms. Readers were advised to shave their pubic regions, lasso a penis with their hair, and play rape, prostitution, and various costume games. The variety of physical activities was emphasized, including intermammary and armpit coitus, not using your hands (fish-fashion), and stimulation of the clitoris with the big toe (the latter, conducted in a restaurant under the table, was de-

scribed as very advanced sex). Orality and masturbation were strongly encouraged (including armpit kissing). Sexual aids were also big, ranging from ice cubes, bathtubs full of Jell-O, and beads inserted in the anus to vibrators, dildos, oils, lights, and cameras. Places were not overlooked, ski slopes being recommended for oral genital sex and airplanes for all-around fun (an idea stolen perhaps from the popular French film *Emanuelle*). Overall, sexual liberation in the manuals of the 1970s became sexual necessity. In this almost panic search for the ultimate sexual experience, sexuality was not only exalted, but it also became mechanized (Brissett and Lewis, 1979).

There is no doubt that many of these guides have been of value to many people. However, there is another side. One may compare one's sex life to that described or suggested and feel that one comes off quite poorly. Since, as we shall see, sexual enjoyment and satisfaction have almost nothing to do with technique itself, simply following a set of instructions is not likely to turn one's sex life into uncontrollable ecstacy. Perhaps, many people attempt to solve what is a serious personal and interpersonal sexual problem by buying this or that self-help book, which basically presents sexual interaction as a plumbing problem. If an interpersonal relationship is satisfactory, changes in the physical dimension of sex may be rewarding. If the problem is interpersonal, mechanical modifications are unlikely to be of any value.

Sexual Aids

In perhaps the search for the ultimate orgasm (and no doubt allowed by a greater openness in presenting and discussing sexual matters), the 1970s saw the rise of another major industry. Even the most middle-class of popular magazines carry articles urging one to send away for a wide range of devices designed to enhance one's sexual activity. Such devices range from joy jell and vibrators to french ticklers and underwear one would hope mother never accidentally pulls from the clothes hamper.

Sexual aids of various types are now relatively available to adults in the United States.

The mundane still head the list of sexual extras. Of the married women in Tavris and Sadd's research, 70 percent said they liked to dress in sexy lace and lingerie. The use of erotic pictures is also not uncommon among married couples. Of these same women, 40 percent reported "occasionally" using pictures or movies as an addition to marital lovemaking (Levin and Levin, 1975). Further, fully 21 percent of these women had at some time used such items as dildos, oils, feathers, and vibrators for increasing sexual pleasure (Tavris and Sadd, 1977). Sexual aids have apparently become voguish enough that some best-selling magazines have found it worthwhile to provide readers with "road tests" on some devices (*Playboy*, 1978).

LIMITATIONS OF TECHNIQUE

So far, we have discussed the physical aspects of various sexual techniques. It is important to end this discussion with some comment on the limitations of sexual technique.

In a very real sense, there is no such thing as the "right" and the "wrong" technique. Definitions of arousing and pleasurable sexual activities are not to be found in a recipe for sexual success. What is good sexual technique is what is arousing and enjoyable for both partners, and for that there is no list guaranteed always to please. A "skilled lover" is one who does things which highly arouse and please one's partner. What these might be depends on one's partner. You can know ninety-nine different coital positions and forty-two different ways of engaging in oral sex, be the only one on your block to know the old handkerchief trick, and still be a sexual flop if your partner is perfectly satisfied with one coital position, is not into oral sex, and could care less what you do with your handkerchief. What makes for satisfying sex is sensitivity to, and communication with, each other regardless of technique.

As far as sexual equipment is concerned, the same principles apply. The crucial factor is not the equipment, but the operator. Males, having learned that bigger is better, often worry about their penis size. Research reveals that men think penis size is more important to a woman's sexual satisfaction than women say it is (Tavris, 1977). For all but very, very few males, what they have will do just fine. Sex, unlike baseball, is not a game of inches. Females often worry about the attractiveness of their bodies, including the size and shape of such anatomical structures as legs, hips, and breasts. If only the beautiful, taut, and heavily endowed could experience high levels of sexual arousal and satisfaction, most of the world would be permanently stuck at the excitement stage. If, however, sexual partners like each other as persons, they will find that their sexual equipment works very well. On the other hand, there is nothing wrong with being more sexually aroused by large or small breasts, fat or skinny bodies, or large or small penises. It is just that these attributes do not mean the same thing to all people, and what is a turn-on to one person will not even gain the attention of another.

There is certainly no harm, and in fact probably considerable benefit, in being informed about such things as sexual techniques and equipment. However, being concerned about such things can not only lead to fear of being a failure in sexual performance, but is likely to miss the mark in terms of what we know are the essential elements of sexual pleasure and satisfaction: interpersonal communication, understanding, and sensitivity.

ORGASM

With the possible exceptions of heart disease and the Super Bowl, never have a series of blood flows and muscle contractions received so much attention in American society. Most of the attention which has been given to orgasm in recent years has been directed toward female orgasm, the stalking of which has sometimes taken the appearance of a national effort.[7]

This is not to say that orgasm is not an important and highly pleasurable part of sexual interaction. Rather, we should place this attention in perspective. Viewing orgasm as a goal and not having orgasm as a problem can lead to less, rather than more, sexual satisfaction and enjoyment.

The Frequency of Orgasm in Coitus

Compared with studies of female orgasm, we have almost no data on male orgasm frequency (the percentage of sexual encounters in which orgasm is experienced). It seems to be assumed that male orgasm is an automatic response to sexual stimulation and thus always occurs with the dependability of the rising sun. Such, however, is not quite the case. In coitus, 8 percent of married males over age 45 do not have orgasm anywhere from "occasionally" to "most of the time." Of married males age 25 to 44, 7 percent do not have orgasm at least one-quarter of the time they have coitus, and fully 15 percent of married males under age 25 do not have orgasm one-quarter or more of the time (Hunt, 1974).

As shown in Table 6-6, orgasm in coitus is far less frequent among females than males. Regardless of the study or when it was con-

[7]The term "frigidity" is commonly associated with a lack of female orgasm. This is a term which totally lacks any meaning. Rosen et al. (1972:180) define frigidity, for example, as ". . . a partial or complete inability of the female to be aroused sexually or to achieve orgasm." Apart from the temperature connotation and the term only applying to females, the definition is so global as to refer to almost anything.

TABLE 6-6
Percentage of intercourse experiences in which orgasm occurs, as reported by male and female college students.

Coitus in Which Orgasm Occurs (%)	Males (%)	Females (%)
90–100	88	20
70–80	9	39
50–60	2	17
30–40	0	8
10–20	0	11
Never	0	16

Source: Mahoney (1979).

ducted, the same answer appears. The female orgasm frequencies reported by Kinsey in 1953 are very close to those in more recent research (Bell, 1974; Tavris and Sadd, 1977). Approximately 15 percent of all married women always, and 7 percent of the same group never, orgasm in coitus. Among unmarried female college students, the only difference appears to be a slightly higher "never" experience (16 percent, Mahoney, 1979a).

Factors Related to Female Orgasm in Coitus

While we do not have any solid knowledge of the range of factors related to male orgasm frequency, we do have a rather clear understanding of what is related to female orgasm.

Bodily characteristics   Since orgasm is a physiological response, we might think that physiology plays a major role in female orgasm frequency. For the majority of women, bodily characteristics are not related to the frequency of orgasm, including breast, thigh, and general body touch sensitivity, breast size, age at first menstruation, menstrual characteristics, height, weight, or rate of maturation during adolescence (Fisher, 1973). There are, however, physiological characteristics which are important in orgasm. For males and females, a high level of vasocongestion must be obtainable so that the muscles involved in sexual arousal can reach that level of tension necessary for

orgasmic clonic contractions to take place (see Chapter 5). For females, the amount of strength in the pelvic muscles is also important for orgasm response.

Sexual technique   Often female orgasm is viewed as dependent upon male genital skills. This is really a somewhat antique view of sexuality wherein males are assigned the responsibility for bringing the female to orgasm. This view gained renewed popularity after the 1977 *Hite Report* appeared.

While what a male partner does in terms of sexual activities is without doubt important for female sexual arousal to orgasm, the importance of sexual technique is greatly exaggerated. Both Terman (1951) and Kinsey (1953) clearly found that male sexual technique had little relationship to female orgasm. More recent research reveals that the amount of time spent in foreplay, time taken for the male to reach orgasm, the duration of coitus, the elaborateness of sexual stimulation techniques, and the number of different coital positions used all have no relationship to female orgasm frequency in heterosexual activity (Fisher, 1973; Huey et al., 1981).

There are exceptions, however. In the case of extremes in a very wide range of sexual techniques, the likelihood of female orgasm remains the same. Gebhard (1966), for example, found that while penile insertion in intercourse lasting less than one minute was generally not sufficiently stimulating for female orgasm, 27 percent of the women had orgasm in 90 to 100 percent of their coitus when the husband's duration of penile intromission was less than one minute. Further, penile intromission anywhere between one and sixteen minutes resulted in the same frequency of female orgasm in coitus (Gebhard, 1966).

There are two major reasons why genital skills have little to do with female orgasm response. First, arousal to orgasm is highly dependent on psychological status, psychological status having to do with the personal and personality characteristics of the woman and with the nature of the interpersonal relationship itself. Second, sexual interaction is interaction. It is, for the majority of people, a process which involves mutual adaptation and adjustment. If the male partner reaches orgasm after only one minute of coital stimulation, the couple most likely adjusts their sexual activity to this.

The interpersonal relationship The likelihood of female orgasm in coitus increases as the interpersonal relationship with one's partner continues in time. For example, Kinsey (1953) found that in the first year of marriage, 25 percent of the women never had orgasm in coitus. By the fifth year of marriage this percentage had dropped to 17 percent, and by the twentieth year, to 11 percent. This effect is apparent even within the first year of marriage. In Kinsey's research (1953), 49 percent of the married women experienced orgasm in the first month of marriage, 55 percent by the second month; and 69 percent by the eleventh month.

Unfortunately, there have been no recent studies which have examined female orgasm in the first few months of marriage. It is very likely that these patterns noted by Kinsey do not exist for many newly married women today, since the vast majority of males and females now enter marriage with considerable sexual experience and sexual experience with each other. Today, "honeymoon sex" generally takes place some time before marriage.

The increase in orgasm with the duration of a relationship has been termed a "practice effect" (Fisher, 1973). There is more to it, however, than practicing to have orgasm. As relationships continue, they develop interpersonally. Increased familiarity, closeness, relaxation, sensitivity, and knowledge of personal preferences all contribute to orgasm frequency.

When a relationship continues but does not develop interpersonally, female orgasm frequency does not increase with time (Clark and Wallin, 1965). When the quality of a relationship deteriorates over time, orgasm frequency declines (Clark and Wallin, 1965). The overriding importance of the interpersonal quality of a relationship is evident in a recent study of Swieczkowski and Walker (1978). Studying married couples, they found that the likelihood of a woman's experiencing orgasm

BOX 6-2
WHO WAS HOLDING THE STOPWATCH?

Scientists like details since they make for precision. While it may seem a little silly to ask how much time people spend in various sexual activities, these data reveal some important facts. It has frequently been argued that males do not spend enough time in certain sexual activities. Do they? The average duration of foreplay has been approximately 12 to 15 minutes for a number of years (Gebhard, 1966; Fisher, 1973; Hunt, 1974; Swieczkowski and Walker, 1978; Huey et al., 1981). The average duration of penile intromission in coitus is about 7 minutes (Gebhard, 1966; Swieczkowski and Walker, 1978; Huey et al., 1981). In Tavris and Sadd's research, 93 percent of the women said they became sexually aroused by 15 minutes or less of foreplay and 66 percent said they generally reached orgasm with 10 minutes or less of coitus. With some quick calculations, it would seem that as far as the "average" married woman is concerned, foreplay is 2 minutes too short and coitus is 3 minutes too short. Even though such a calculation may seem ridiculous, Swieczkowski and Walker (1978) actually found that college-educated married women said they would like foreplay to be 2 minutes longer and coitus to be 3 minutes longer in duration.

in coitus was related *only* to her satisfaction with the marital relationship, including satisfaction with her spouse as a person. Not surprisingly, female orgasm in coitus declines in frequency in times of interpersonal crisis and hostility (Swieczkowski and Walker, 1978).

Learning The fact that male orgasm frequency is considerably higher than that of females is of more importance than keeping score. Rather, this gender difference reflects, in considerable measure, significant differences between males and females in sexual learning. We have discussed these differences in Chapters 4 and 5 and so will only briefly refer to them here.

It is a serious misunderstanding of human sexuality to assume that "the female sexual response is much more susceptible to learning and cultural overlays than male sexuality . . ." (Tavris and Sadd, 1977:52). Males are not born "ready to go" and females are not sexually mysterious, fragile, or complex. Rather, there is a clear cultural tradition, established in early Christianity and brought to us in the Victorian period, that women are asexual. Even though recent redefinitions of womanhood have eroded this view, it has yet to result in a change in the nature of female sexual learning. Among males, sexuality is supported from the media to the peer group. As such, males explore sexuality early and with dedication. No such encouragement and support exist for female sexuality. In fact, quite the opposite has been (and still is, for adolescent females) the case. Thus, exploration of such orgasm-aiding sexual activities as masturbation remains more the territory of males than females and peer support for sexual response is seldom found in adolescent female peer discussions.

While I cannot present you with solid evidence proving that the interpersonal relationship is not so important in male as in female orgasm, this would seem to be a safe bet. I suggest that the reason for this is again found in learning. Specifically, the situation in which early sexual response and orgasm are experienced differs, on the average, for males and females. If you get to know your orgasm in

masturbation, as males generally do, the subtle learning is very different than if you get to know your orgasm response in petting behavior involving an interpersonal relationship. In the former, how you feel about your hand is of little relevance. In the latter, how you feel about your sexual partner is very important. This male-female difference is enhanced by the fact that females learn that sex should be conducted in the context of a meaningful interpersonal relationship to a much greater extent than do males.

Orgasm Goals

We began this discussion in a somewhat critical tone about the emphasis frequently placed on orgasm. This tone, quite honestly, reflects my personal and professional opinion regarding the negative results of viewing orgasm as a product. Such an approach to sexuality, in my view, often leads a person to evaluate his or her personal and sexual worth on the basis of how much and how good a product he or she produces. (Note that never having orgasm, if one is female, has been traditionally called "frigidity". The temperature label attached to the whole person is revealing). There is not a thing in the world wrong with liking and wanting orgasm experience. However, pursuit of orgasm as a goal is likely to result in placing less emphasis on those aspects of sexual interaction which really are essential for sexual satisfaction and enjoyment.

For example, many males are still trapped in the idea that it is their "responsibility" to "bring" their partner to orgasm. Women also get caught in this emphasis on orgasm as a mark of good sex and worry about "failing" to orgasm. Clifford (1978) asked a sample of women college students how they felt when they had intercourse but no orgasm. The most common response was worrying about their partner's reaction (34 percent). Another 19 percent said they felt bad about themselves.

Faking It

Given this emphasis on orgasm, combined with the raw fact that not all females always have orgasm in coitus, many women sometimes fake it to avoid any possibility of negative reactions from their partner. Among college-student females (Mahoney, 1979a) faking orgasm is rather common, but not very frequent. In my study, 62 percent of the females reported never faking orgasm, but 23 percent did so between 10 and 20 percent of the time, and another 15 percent did so 30 percent of the time or more. Males do it too. In this same study, 14 percent of the males reported that they sometimes fake having orgasm in intercourse.

Multiple Orgasm

Multiple orgasm among females is not a stable happening. Sometimes it occurs and sometimes it does not. Very few women (1 percent, in my research with college women) report always having multiple orgasm in coitus.

Unlike orgasm, multiple orgasm is not related to the number of years married or to age (Fisher, 1973). It is, however, related to a greater awareness of one's sexuality (Fisher, 1973), longer duration of penile insertion during coitus, more frequent and varied sexual activities, more spontaneous sexual activity, and greater frequency of breast and other nongenital stimulation (Swieczkowski and Walker, 1978). Multiple orgasm is also more common among women who are highly satisfied with their sexual partner, their sexual relationship, and their overall relationship with this person (Swieczkowski and Walker, 1978).

Orgasm in Coitus: Some Clarification

When we discuss orgasm in coitus we are, of course, talking about orgasm taking place sometime during sexual interaction which involves, among other things, intercourse.

In what appears to be the only investigation of its kind, Fisher (1973) really got down to the nitty-gritty. He found that married women reported the following pathways to orgasm. The majority (63 percent) usually had orgasm with clitoral stimulation followed by coitus. This dominant pattern was followed by or-

gasm through clitoral stimulation either before or after coitus (35 percent).

Actual penile insertion in the vagina plays, in fact, a somewhat minor role as far as arousal to orgasm is concerned for women. In Fisher's study, only in 57 percent of the time in which orgasm was experienced was penile insertion actually taking place.

Marriage manuals of the 1950s and early 1960s placed a great emphasis on simultaneous orgasm. This remains a marriage manual writer's ideal rather than a behavior pattern. Usually the female has orgasm before the male in coital activity (Fisher, 1973).

SEXUAL SATISFACTION AND ENJOYMENT

Scientists studying human sexuality are guilty of a serious omission in sex research. For many years, we have paid so much attention to counting who was doing what with whom how many times that we apparently forgot to ask these people if they were enjoying themselves. Yes, we have studied sexual satisfaction and enjoyment, but not nearly to the extent one would expect. Mainly, this research has been in marital sexuality. When it comes to traditionally unapproved forms of sexual interaction such as among adolescents and homosexuals, we know practically nothing in this area.

In this chapter, we discuss general patterns and factors related to sexual satisfaction in heterosexual couples. In other chapters, we will examine sexual enjoyment and satisfaction in aging, homosexuality, transsexualism, adult singlehood, divorce and widowhood, and extramarital sexuality.

How Much Satisfaction Is There?

Marital sexuality has a history of bad press as far as sexual enjoyment is concerned. The early days of marriage have been advertised as the height of sexual bliss, but popular wisdom has described sexual pleasure as being all downhill from there.

TABLE 6-7
Women's satisfaction with marital sex by number of years married.

Years Married	Those Saying Marital Sex Is:		
	Very Good or Good (%)	Fair (%)	Poor or Very Poor (%)
Less than 1 year	80	17	3
1 to 4 years	68	23	9
5 to 10 years	66	21	13
More than 10 years	65	20	15

Source: Tavris and Sadd (1977, table 7, p. 63).

In general, this dismal view of marital sexuality is not supported by research. The majority of married men and women are relatively satisfied with the sexual dimension of their marriage. Bell (1974) found that two-thirds of over 2000 married women reported the sexual aspect of their marriage as "good" or "very good." The same pattern was found for both men and women by Hunt (1974). Tavris and Sadd (1977) found that only 10 percent of the married women they studied rated marital sex as "poor."

This has not always been the case. Earlier studies found that a substantial proportion of both married men and women were less than ecstatic about the sexual dimension of their relationship. In one study (Davis, 1929), one-third of the women said that "marital relations" (a euphemism of the time) were either neutral or unpleasurable. Terman (1938) noted the same basic pattern, but found men more pleased than women.

Among adolescents and unmarried college students today, the sexual enjoyment level is very similar to that among married couples. Sorensen (1973) found that two-thirds of both males and females age 16 to 19 got "a lot of satisfaction" from their sex lives. Among adolescent males, the level of sexual satisfaction is the same regardless of age. Younger adolescent females (13 to 15), however, report less enjoyment than their older peers (16 to 19). Perhaps this finding is a reflection of less importance being attached to sex on the part of younger females and/or their struggle, beginning at this age, to reconcile sex, affection, and the "good girl–bad girl" categories which await teenage females' sexual decisions.

Factors Related to Sexual Satisfaction and Enjoyment

The length of a relationship Contrary to the traditional stereotype of the honeymoon as a period of super sex, a substantial percentage of women in the late 1950s (and probably other periods) did not find this time highly satisfying sexually (Kanin and Howard, 1958). Today, it is likely that this pattern has changed, since considerable sexual interaction is likely to have taken place with each other prior to marriage. Newlyweds, in fact, are now the most satisfied with their marital sex (Table 6-7).

Even after this period of sexual bliss, there is only a very slight decline in women's sexual satisfaction in marriage (Table 6-7). This same pattern evidently exists for males as well (Pietropinto and Simenauer, 1977). A large part of the reason for this stability in sexual satisfaction over the marital career is due to the fact that marriages low in sexual satisfaction simply do not continue (Bentler and Newcomb, 1978).

The more the merrier? The answer, as with many questions, depends. In marital sexuality today, the greater the frequency of sexual activity, the greater the sexual satisfaction on the part of women (Tavris and Sadd, 1977; Nowinski et al., 1981). It is not known, however, to what extent satisfaction is a cause or an effect of frequency; most likely, it is both.

Among young unmarried adults, quantity is more important to males than to females. Among females (but not males), greater enjoyment of the sexual component of life is related to being in a stable interpersonal relationship, the importance one's partner places on sexual activities the woman likes, the interest her partner shows in her experiencing orgasm, and the percent of her intercourse in which orgasm is experienced. For males (but not females), greater sexual enjoyment is related to a larger number of different intercourse partners, a younger age at first coitus, and a higher frequency of intercourse per month (Mahoney, 1979a). For males, the more the merrier. For females, its the quality that counts, not the quantity.

Orgasm   Numerous studies have repeatedly found that for females, greater sexual satisfaction is associated with higher frequencies of orgasm in intercourse (e.g., Terman, 1938; Bell, 1974; Clifford, 1978). However, there is not a one-to-one correspondence between orgasm frequency and sexual satisfaction. A low frequency of orgasm does not necessarily mean low sexual satisfaction (Clifford, 1978). As shown in Table 6-8, the interpersonal aspects of sexuality are more important to women than the purely physical are.

It is also not the absolute frequency of orgasm in coitus which is important to sexual satisfaction for a woman. Rather, it is whether she has orgasm as frequently as she thinks she is capable of (Swieczkowski and Walker, 1978).

Social class differences   In his now classic research, Rainwater (1965) pointed to several differences in sexual enjoyment between social classes. For both husbands and wives, the lower the social class the lower the sexual enjoyment. Further, differences between social classes were much greater for the sexual enjoyment of women than for that of men. While only 3 percent of the middle-class wives found sex to be highly unenjoyable, fully 20 percent of the lower lower-class wives felt this way. Lack of enjoyment by men was uncommon in all social classes.

TABLE 6-8
Aspects of sexual activity married women report they like the most.

Aspect of Sexual Activity	Women liking the Most (%)
Feeling closeness with my partner	40
Orgasm	23
Satisfying my partner	21
Intercourse	20
Foreplay	17
Oral sex	10
Masturbation	4
Anal sex	1
Everything	31

Source: Tavris and Sadd (1977:167).

Even more important, Rainwater found that the comparative enjoyment of a husband and wife differed by social class. In middle-class marriages, an equal level of sexual enjoyment was the rule. In lower lower-class marriages, inequality was the rule and it was typically the husband who enjoyed sex more.

While we might rightly question whether these findings apply today, the optimism that social class differences in sexual enjoyment have disappeared may be premature. Rubin (1976) found that among a sample of married couples in San Francisco, the sexual satisfaction of blue-collar women was considerably less than that among middle-class women. The reason for these apparent social class differences is found in the nature of marital relationships in different social classes in American society.

The interpersonal relationship
Since sex involves much more than "organ grinding," it is not surprising that high sexual satisfaction is not likely to be found in an otherwise unsatisfactory relationship. In one study, none of the women who rated their marital sex as "very good" rated their overall marriage as "poor," and none of the women who rated their overall marriage as "poor" rated their marital sex as "very good" (Tavris and Sadd, 1977).

One aspect of a satisfying interpersonal relationship is equity, the extent to which partners feel that there is an equality of costs and rewards between the partners. It is thus understandable that couples in equitable relationships are high in sexual satisfaction and feel more close and loving after sex than couples in inequitable relationships (Hatfield et al., 1982).

One dimension of any long-term relationship which is important in sexual satisfaction is the "togetherness" or "separateness" of the two people. In a *joint* relationship, the partners spend time together in leisure and recreation and share ideas, feelings, and emotions. In a *segregated* relationship, there is little joint activity either behaviorally or psychologically (Rainwater, 1965). The reason that social class is relevant to sexual satisfaction is that sexual satisfaction is related to the joint versus the segregated nature of the relationship. Middle-class marriages tend to be more joint, while lower-class marriages more often tend to be segregated—not all, mind you, but this is a strong tendency (Rainwater, 1965).

In any type of interaction, be it in a classroom or bedroom, being sensitive to and accurate in your perception of the other person's needs, feelings, and responses is essential to enjoyment. This sensitivity differs by the degree of segregation in a relationship. In segregated relationships (more likely to be lower in social class), Rainwater found that husbands were highly inaccurate in their estimate of their wife's level of sexual enjoyment. In joint marriages (more likely in the middle class), husbands were very accurate.

Accuracy of perception is one thing and concern about a partner's sexual enjoyment is another. Highly segregated marriages were found by Rainwater to be characterized by the husband's not only having little concern for the wife's sexual enjoyment, but also his simply being uninterested. As Rainwater (1965:105) puts it, many of these husbands simply do not ". . . accept the idea that they should be concerned or make efforts to insure that their wife find sexual relations gratifying." This attitude

was not that of the males alone. Fully 40 percent of the lower-class wives in Rainwater's study said that sex was a woman's duty, not her pleasure.

While it would be refreshing to think that greater freedom in discussing sexuality, as well as the women's movement, has changed this situation in lower socioeconomic marriages, this is perhaps not the case. Rubin (1976) found that the trend toward greater freedom of sexual discussion had actually placed lower-class women in an even more difficult position. These women see sexual attitudes, values, and behaviors as changing all around them. Their husbands often develop an interest in experimenting with some much discussed forms of sexual stimulation (such as oral-genital activity). However, the double-standard concept of "good women" and "bad women" remains right alongside greater sexual discussion. The essence of what made "good women" good was the absence of sexual feelings. "Bad women" were bad because they appeared to like, seek, and appreciate sex (Laws and Schwartz, 1977). Lower-class women, in particular, have been raised in the double standard and have learned ". . . to inhibit and repress their sexuality, (and) women can't just switch to uninhibited enjoyment as the changing culture of their husbands dictates" (Rubin, 1976:44). What these, and many other, women may find that sexual liberalization has brought them is greater social pressure ("Let's try this") and personal pressure ("I should be able to try this") to engage in sexual activities for which they have not been prepared through prior sexual learning.

The Relative and the Absolute

What is very influential in sexual satisfaction is whether one is experiencing what one thinks one should be experiencing. When reality fails to live up to expectations, sexual dissatisfaction is a likely outcome regardless of how much of any kind of interpersonal or sexual behavior is taking place (Frank et al., 1979).

One important aspect of the greater freedom of sexual discussion is that people may have their expectations raised above their reality. The media tend to suggest that wild sexual abandon is all through America. *Playboy* presents males with the image that male fantasies are actually realities. But for the average male, they are still more fantasy than anything else. *Cosmopolitan* readers continually read of the new sexual freedom and satisfaction of women. Even television gives us idealized images of the sexual success and enjoyment of its "everyday" characters. As much as I enjoy the Fonz and Hawkeye, they have sex at their fingertips by either a twist of the hips or a witty saying. While there is little doubt that, overall, greater openness regarding the topic of sex has done much to reduce (or perhaps is a result of) guilt and fears, there is probably a large segment of the population for which it has some other effect. For those vast numbers of people who do not and cannot live the *Cosmopolitan* or *Playboy* lifestyle, such images may facilitate people's thinking their sex life is pretty ho hum and somehow deficient.

Perhaps an indication of how the match between expectations and reality is related to sexual satisfaction is that greater sexual satisfaction exists among more religious married women (Tavris and Sadd, 1977). One factor here is that the position of organized religion has recently changed on the subject of sexual enjoyment. Today, the minister's message is likely to say that sexual enjoyment is a gift of God to be experienced in a personally and socially responsible manner. But perhaps an even more important factor, as suggested by Tavris and Sadd and supported by the previous research of Wallin and Clark (1964), is that religiosity serves to lower one's expectations in sexuality. Religious women, for example, are more satisfied with their frequency of coitus than are nonreligious women (the latter want more), and religious women maintain higher levels of sexual satisfaction even in light of the fact that their sexual activities are not as diverse as those of nonreligious women.

As social changes take place, we have to think twice before concluding that every day in every way the world gets better and better. What appear to be sexual benefits may have other, less desirable, outcomes.

SUMMARY

Sexual techniques are, to a considerable extent, social inventions. Whether we are discussing masturbation, coitus, or oral or anal sexuality, patterns of behavior and preferences differ from culture to culture, over time in a given culture, and among individuals within a culture.

In American society, we have seen sexual techniques change over time in diversity, frequency, and popularity. However, these changes have differed in different segments of society, and understanding this diversity is important in understanding the diversity of sexuality in American society.

Some would argue that Americans have perhaps become "technique-happy." There is certainly some truth to this assertion as reflected in the content and popularity of recent sex manuals. Technology has always, however, been central to Americans' vision of happiness. Unfortunately, technique and advanced sexual technology have almost nothing to do with sexual satisfaction and enjoyment; the basis of these are found in the nature of the interpersonal relationship which exists between sexual partners.

A NOTE OF CAUTION

In this chapter we have, by necessity, discussed sexual pleasures and techniques which may be found to prevail in middle-class, pretty much average, American, heterosexual society. It should be apparent by now that sexual pleasures are limited only by learning and that techniques depend on imagination and social approval. Almost anything can be, and is, found to be sexually pleasurable by at least a few individuals in even American society. For example, many individuals find sexual activity with strangers the most enjoyable. Many individuals obtain great sexual pleasure from being bound in leather or administering or being administered pain. The diversity of activities which people find sexually pleasurable reveals the true diversity of human beings and their almost infinite capacity for learning. Even in the light of such diversity, however, dominant patterns do appear for reasons discussed in Chapter 4.

STUDY GUIDE

TERMS TO KNOW

Cunnilingus   Fellatio   Anilingus

SELF-TEST

Part I: True-False Statements

1. Regardless of age, males are more likely than females to masturbate.
2. The frequency of masturbation among male and female college students who do masturbate is more similar than different.
3. The most common reason young adults give for masturbation is the absence of a mate.
4. Females are more likely than males to report that orgasm through masturbation is more pleasurable than orgasm through coitus.
5. Male masturbation techniques tend to be less varied than those used by females.
6. The interior of the vagina is that part of the anatomy most frequently stimulated when females masturbate.
7. Recent research indicates that the coital position most preferred by married women is male on top, face to face.
8. Females, especially college students, prefer the female-on-top coital position to the male-on-top coital position.
9. Research shows that over 90 percent of married women today have experienced oral sex.
10. Oral-genital sexual activity has become more common since Kinsey's time.
11. Males and females would rather "give" oral sex than "receive" it.
12. Black males are more enthusiastic about cunnilingus than are white males.
13. It is safe to place the penis in the vagina after anal intercourse.
14. Anal intercourse is as common today as oral-genital activity.
15. Of those women who have engaged in anal intercourse, the majority find it very enjoyable.
16. Almost one-quarter of the women in the Tavris and Sadd research had at some time used sexual aids.
17. Almost as many males as females never have orgasm in intercourse activity.
18. Mahoney, in a study of college students, found that about 14 percent of the males and 38 percent of the females had faked orgasm in intercourse.
19. Most women who have multiple orgasm do so almost all the time they have orgasm.
20. Today, the greatest sexual satisfaction among married persons is experienced by those married less than one year.
21. For women, the interpersonal aspects of a sexual relationship are more important to sexual satisfaction than the physical aspects.

Part II: Multiple-Choice Questions

Select the best of the three alternatives.

1. With regard to masturbation among married persons in the form of self-stimulation, *(a)* the majority of married persons stop masturbating once they get married; *(b)* the majority of married persons masturbate after marriage; *(c)* married males masturbate but married females do not do so.

2. Masturbation during sexual activity with one's partner (either self or other stimulation) is engaged in *(a)* rarely by married persons today; *(b)* with regularity by anywhere between one-third and two-thirds of married persons today; *(c)* only with prostitutes or extramarital partners.

3. We find less positional variation in coitus on the part of *(a)* 18-to 19-year-old college students; *(b)* young married couples; *(c)* males.

4. The research on coital position preferences on the part of women reveals that the most preferred position is *(a)* male on top, face to face; *(b)* female on top, face to face; *(c)* side by side.

5. Married women report that they enjoy *(a)* both cunnilingus and fellatio, but that they enjoy cunnilingus more; *(b)* cunnilingus but not fellatio; *(c)* fellatio a little and cunnilingus almost not at all.

6. Since the days of the Kinsey research, the percentage of coitus in which orgasm is experienced by married women has *(a)* decreased slightly; *(b)* increased rather sharply; *(c)* remained basically the same.

7. Physiological characteristics appear to be related to female orgasm in that women who are more likely to have orgasm in coitus are those who *(a)* have stronger muscles in the vagina and uterus; *(b)* have larger breasts; *(c)* have more sensitivity to touch stimulation on the breasts and thighs.

8. Research indicates that married women would prefer that *(a)* foreplay last a little longer and coitus not last as long as it does; *(b)* foreplay not last as long as it does and coitus last a little longer; *(c)* both coitus and foreplay last a little longer than they do.

9. Since the 1920s and 1930s, the proportion of married women satisfied with their sexual activity has *(a)* remained the same; *(b)* decreased; *(c)* increased.

10. Among college students, it is found that *(a)* for males, sexual quantity is more important than the interpersonal aspects of sexuality, while for females, the reverse is true; *(b)* for females, characteristics of the partner and his activities are of less importance than they are for males; *(c)* both males and females place more importance on the interpersonal aspects of the sexual activity than on the amount of sexual activity.

TOPICS FOR DISCUSSION

Sex education courses in secondary or high schools generally do not deal with sexual pleasure and technique. Do you think they should? Why? Why not? What would be the effects if they were to do so? Do you think most parents would find such coverage acceptable? Why or why not? Would you, if you are or were a parent? If sexual pleasure and technique should not be learned in a sex education course, where should one learn them?

SUGGESTED READING

Haeberle, E. J., *The Sex Atlas*. New York: Seabury Press, 1978.
   There are a variety of so-called sex manuals available on the market today, but I do not have very positive feelings about these. Most tend to be somewhat unrealistic in that they suggest and illustrate a variety of sexual techniques beyond the usual activities of most people and often are not very well informed or guided by people's preferences.

The *Sex Atlas* is not a sex manual but contains discussions in most of the chapters about various forms of sexual activity. There are also very good illustrations. This volume is unique in that it is a scholarly treatment of the specific topic as well as a discussion at times of "how to."

KEY TO SELF-TEST QUESTIONS

Part I: True-False Statements

1. T (Males are more likely to do so, and this has a number of consequences.)
2. T (Even though males are more likely to masturbate, the frequency among males and females who do masturbate is quite similar.)
3. F (The most common reason is to obtain sexual pleasure.)
4. T (This is most likely because female masturbation results in more directed stimulation of the clitoris, while for males, coitus results in more stimulation of the penis.)
5. T
6. F (This common myth perhaps facilitates males' thinking they and their parts are necessary.)
7. T (Another recent myth is that women do not like this position. Actual research on women's preferences reveals otherwise.)
8. F (They not only like this position less, but attribute negative characteristics to women pictured in this position.)
9. T (Perhaps this is the major change in sexual behavior patterns since the days of Kinsey's research.)
10. T
11. F (The research rather clearly indicates that both males and females would rather "receive" than "give" as far as oral-genital activity is concerned.)
12. F (Black males have more negative attitudes about oral-genital activity than do white males.)
13. F (Bacteria from the rectum may result in vaginal infection.)
14. F (It is still experienced by few and enjoyed by even fewer.)
15. F.
16. T
17. F
18. T
19. F
20. T (After this period there is an initial decline; however, the level of satisfaction is relatively stable over the marital career.)
21. T

Part II: Multiple-Choice Questions

1. *b* (There is a decline in frequency after marriage, but the majority continue to engage in self-stimulation.)
2. *b* (This is a common form of sexual interaction either before, during, or after coitus.)
3. *a*
4. *a* (This is contrary to recent popular arguments.)
5. *a*
6. *c*
7. *a* (The exact reasons for this are not yet clear.)
8. *c*
9. *c*
10. *a*

Chapter 7
Sexuality and Youth

Traditionally, discussion of the material that will be covered in this chapter came under the heading of premarital sexuality. There are, however, serious difficulties with the term "premarital." First, it assumes that everyone will get married—an assumption that is not precisely correct. Second, it assumes that everyone who does get married does so in her or his early twenties (premarital sex has never referred to those over age 25), an assumption that is increasingly incorrect. Still, the social definition of appropriate sexual conduct makes it clear that sexual activity on the part of adolescents and young adults (college age) who are not married is far from being totally accepted. By virtue of this social definition, the heterosexual activity of unmarried individuals at this age is a special category of sexual behavior.

Sex and youth: the worry of almost every teenager's parents and the subject of constant public attention. The sexual behavior of youth has perhaps also attracted more research attention than any other topic in sexual behavior.

All this attention originates from a variety of sources. First, in American society we associate sex with youth. We assume that young people are the most potentially sexual of any age group, adolescence often being thought of as the sudden bursting forth of sexuality. Second, marriage has traditionally been the only context in which sexual activity is totally approved. Entering marriage at a certain age was assumed to be automatic. Therefore, persons under a certain age were considered "premarital." Since premarital sex has never been approved by the majority of American society, the sexual behavior of youth was noted both closely and with alarm. Third, most people in our society (social scientists included) are convinced that we have recently experienced a sexual revolution, a set of changes in sexual attitudes and behavior which are primarily located in the teenage population.

THE STRUCTURE OF ADOLESCENT AND YOUNG ADULT SEXUALITY

A central part of the fear (or joy, depending on one's values) of a sexual revolution among youth is that adolescent and young adult sexual behavior is taking place willy-nilly and that "everyone is doing everything with everybody." This is, and always has been, far from the truth. As social scientists have noted since the 1950s, sexual behavior among youths has never been anything other than highly patterned and ordered.[1]

One of the ways in which sexual behavior in youth is patterned and ordered is in the form of a sequence of heterosexual experiences that one usually follows as one moves into and through adolescence. The first heterosexual experiences in adolescence are such activities as holding hands and kissing. While these acts are not particularly risqué from the vantage point of most 20-year-old college students, they are pretty hot stuff when they are your entry into the world of heterosexuality. Next in the *sexual behavior sequence* are behaviors rather quaintly referred to as "petting." Included here are two distinct stages. The first is *light petting,* involving manual stimulation above the waist, and the second is *heavy petting,* involving manual stimulation below the waist. Next in the sequence is *intercourse,* followed by a final series of oral-genital sexual activities (Curran et al., 1973).

Since the specific sexual activities one experiences while moving into and through adolescence are sequential (very few people have their first kiss one day and a week later engage in intercourse), we may refer to how far along the sequence one has moved as the *extensiveness* of one's sexual experience.

The extensiveness of sexual experience as an adolescent and young adult is not due to chance. Within this age group, people vary considerably in terms of this extensiveness. This variation is related to certain characteristics of individuals and the social environment in which they live.

Historical Period

One of the most important factors related to the extensiveness of sexual experience of adolescents and young adults is the historical period in which they live. Making comparisons of sexual behavior over time is a difficult matter involving some risk. Different studies have used different questions and asked the questions of different samples. It is possible, however, to piece together data from selected research and obtain a reasonably accurate picture of how the extensiveness of sexual experience has changed over time in American society.

As shown in Table 7-1, college women have changed considerably over time. Com-

TABLE 7-1

Female college students who had engaged in certain non-intercourse sexual behaviors (in percentage).

	Year		
Behavior	1951–1952	1973	1978
Deep kissing with a male	81	90	94
Manual stimulation of breasts by a male	78	76	90
Oral stimulation of breasts by a male	11	57	82
Manual stimulation of genitals by a male	33	64	83
Manual stimulation of a male's genitals	33	48	75
Oral stimulation of genitals by a male	4	34	64
Oral stimulation of a male's genitals	*	25	64

*In this study no data were obtained on this behavior.
Source: 1952–1952 from Reevy (1959); 1973 from Curran et al. (1973); 1978 from Mahoney (1979a).

[1] Only recently are popular writers beginning to discover that the sexual behavior of youth is less decadent or exciting than they had thought or hoped for.

As noted in Chapter 1, the youth movement of the 1960s often assaulted head-on the traditional adult values of sexuality. A significant part of this social revolution involved changes in the sexual values and behavior of youth.

paring 1951–1952 with 1978, the proportion of females who have engaged in each of the seven behaviors in Table 7-1 has increased, particularly in the case of the more advanced activities such as oral-genital sex. In fact, rather significant changes took place over an even shorter period of time. From 1973 to 1978, the proportion of college women having experience with each of the seven behaviors rose even more swiftly, again with the greatest increases being in oral-genital activities.[2]

[2]It is interesting to note that from 1973 to 1978 there was a dramatic change in the popularity of one behavior—mutual masturbation. With the increases over this time in the proportion of college students with coital experience, mutual masturbation, traditionally a substitute for intercourse, declined.

Age

Another obvious factor related to the extensiveness of sexual experience is age. On the average, both males and females hold hands and kiss before age 13. Necking (prolonged hugging and kissing) is reached slightly before age 14 by both males and females. Light petting is first experienced slightly before age 15 by males and slightly before age 16 by females, and heavy petting slightly before age 16 by males and slightly before age 17 by females. Moving out of adolescence and into young adulthood is accompanied by further movement along the sexual behavior sequence. For college students, the major forms of new sexual experience as they move from age 18 to 20 are intercourse and oral-genital activities (Mahoney, 1979; Vener and Stewart, 1974).

The meaning of increasing sexual experience As you have probably noticed, there are some differences between males and females in the speed with which they proceed along the sexual behavior sequence. Males and females tend first to experience kissing and necking at the same age. As soon as the first explicit sexual activity (light petting) is reached, however, males move ahead of females and remain ahead for the rest of the sequence (Curran et al., 1973).

The reason for these different rates of movement along the sexual behavior sequence is that differences in male and female sexual learning begin to be expressed in behavior (Chapter 4). The period of early to middle adolescence is one of an increasing awareness of the social-sexual dimension of life. For both males and females, heterosexuality begins to be a major aspect of life. The rating and dating

process begins. Interaction between males and females now becomes important in the dating context and begins to take on sexual meaning (Offer and Simon, 1976). Social-sexual experiences and possibilities thus start to become significant. While these emerging dimensions of life are similar for males and females, they are also notably different. Peers are now an influential reference point in one's life; they set the standards by which one judges how one is doing in the world of adolescence. As noted in our discussion of sexual learning, much male sexual activity during this period is in the context of attaining and maintaining status among one's peers. Sexual activity comes to be frequently couched in terms of "getting points" and "scoring." Much male sexual involvement in early adolescence is thus guided more by the enhancement of one's social self-image in light of peer expectations for sexual experience than by sexual or erotic desire per se (Offer and Simon, 1976).

For females, on the other hand, the prob-

The adolescent peer group has a great deal of influence on the individual.

lems are not those of losing status by not having enough sexual experience, but of losing status by having too much. While males are expected to play out the sexual "aggressor" role, females are expected to play the "gatekeeper" role. It is in these very early initial heterosexual petting experiences that males and females confront the fact of subtle, but important, male and female sexual conflict; this pattern appears to maintain itself throughout most of our adult lives.

There is a second major difference between males and females in the context of this early sexual experience. For females, the sexual must be related to the sentimental and emotional: the interpersonal relationship. Sexual involvement by females is not reinforced for its own sake, but for the extent to which it signifies or indicates romantic involvement with a male. Males, on the other hand, are simply extending their level and limits of sexual experience rather than couching increased sexual experience in greater degrees of emotional commitment and attachment (Offer and Simon, 1976). These basic differences in the meaning of sexuality for males and females make for the male's more rapid movement through the sexual behavior sequence.

The importance of petting activity

While adults tend to think of only the sexual aspects of adolescents' involvement in the early stages of the sexual behavior sequence, the nonsexual aspects are perhaps of greater significance. Petting behavior is clearly sexual activity, but it is not "real sex" in the sense of "going all the way." "Real sex" in American society is intercourse. One of the historically important characteristics of adolescent petting is that a person can engage in what is clearly sexual behavior and still remain on the accepted side of the sexual boundary by being a *"technical virgin."* Historically, petting served this function for long periods of one's youthful life, often being the only sexual activity prior to marriage. With changes in sexual attitudes over time, and the consequent increase in the proportion of adolescents with coital experience, this function of petting has diminished somewhat. Today, petting serves the same

function of being an acceptable sexual activity while avoiding intercourse, but does so for a shorter period of one's life. For many adolescents and young adults, petting is a form of sexual activity that is reasonably satisfying, but that does not involve the risk of pregnancy or the compromise of one's religious or moral standards prohibiting intercourse (Mahoney, 1980).

Petting also serves as an avenue for sexual learning. Through petting, one learns about one's own and the other sex's sexual responses and anatomy and begins to learn the subtle nuances of sexual arousal, response, and interaction between two people. An important aspect of this learning by doing in petting is that it is relatively safe in a social and psychological sense. When one has little, if any, concrete knowledge about how one goes about physical sexual interaction with a person of the other sex, jumping right into the thick of things can be pretty frightening. Petting allows slow entry into what is actually a rather complicated form of interaction between two people, and it does so in gradual steps, becoming increasingly complicated and elaborate as one moves along the sexual behavior sequence.

The Opportunity Structure

It is a general principle that the likelihood of engaging in a behavior is a function of the opportunity to engage in that behavior. This applies to how far people move for employment, how far apart people live before they get married, whether one becomes involved in delinquency, whom one selects as friends, whom one is likely to marry, and the extensiveness of sexual experience in youth.

Cross-sex interaction For both males and females, frequent and varied social and dating contact with the other sex is related to more extensive sexual experience in adolescence (Curran et al., 1973). There is, however, an important gender difference here. Social and dating contact has a greater effect upon the extensiveness of sexual experience of males than females. The reason for this is found in gender roles. Who initiates sexual activity in American society? The male. Given male initiation, opportunity in the form of frequent interaction with the other sex provides males the opportunity to seek sexual activity while providing females with the opportunity to have sexual activity only when it is sought with them. Frequent social and dating contact thus provides males with self-determined sexual opportunities while offering females opportunities determined only by others.

Dating anxiety This gender difference exists for other opportunity factors as well. For example, anxiety about dating has a greater negative impact on sexual experience for males than for females (Curran et al., 1973). Given the male initiator role, a male who is highly anxious about dating is unlikely to work up the nerve or social finesse to date, and if he does, initiating sexual interaction is likely to be even more difficult.

Physical attractiveness Physical attractiveness (as rated by either others or oneself) is also related to the extensiveness of adolescent sexual experience, but much more so for males than females (Curran et al., 1973). The male who is seen by himself or others as physically attractive uses this influential commodity in the dating marketplace to make his own opportunities for social and dating contact. The attractive female, on the other hand, does not have the initiator option and thus has to sit and wait for opportunities to come along (Reiss et al., 1980).

Freedom or expectation? This apparently greater freedom of males to initiate social, dating, and sexual interaction is simply a larger part of the definition of appropriate male and female behavior—the aggressive, assertive, take-the-bull-by-the-horns male and the passive, nonaggressive, gatekeeper female. This male freedom is more apparent than real. The other side of a freedom is an expectation. Very few males escape the social and psychological pressure to initiate sexual interaction and gain experience. One of the very real problems facing almost every male adolescent and young adult is the pressure from both self and others to conform to the male image. For example, Komarovsky (1976)

found many sexually inexperienced college males embarrassed by such a status, and Hass (1979) found that among 15- to 18-year-old males, 43 percent said they had engaged in sexual activity in a dating situation even though they personally had not really wanted to.

Religiosity

Religious institutions and beliefs in Western culture have always been the stronghold of conservative sexual values, particularly when the issue is nonmarital sexuality. This conservatism, operating at the social level, appears clearly at the individual level as well. Among both males and females, American adolescents and young adults who are more religious have less extensive sexual experience (Curran et al., 1973; Zuckerman et al., 1976; Mahoney, 1980).

This finding, however, demonstrates the close connection between religion and sex in Western culture. In tracing the history of Western culture's stance on sexuality, we have seen the basis for this relationshp. In Eastern cultures, the connection between sex and religion is much less. Among Japanese adolescents, for example, religiosity and sexual attitudes and experience are unrelated (Asayama, 1976).

Liberalism-Conservatism

Since the traditional definition of appropriate adolescent sexual activity is *"Don't,"* to engage in sexual interaction in adolescence is to move beyond the bounds set by parents, clergy, teachers, and society as a whole. That adolescents are well aware of this is demonstrated in Sorensen's (1973) study of 13- to 19-year-old students; 77 percent agreed that "the sexual behavior of most young people today would not be acceptable to society as a whole." To begin sexual activity in adolescence is thus to tread on forbidden and unsampled ground—to act contrary to traditional societal values. Having extensive sexual experience in adolescence is thus related to a wide range of nontraditional attitudes toward such things as politics, alcohol, religion, marriage, and the traditional institutions of school, police, and teachers (Curran et al., 1973; Joe and Kostyla, 1975; Joe et al., 1976; Vener and Stewart, 1974; Rorhbaugh and Jessor, 1975; Jessor and Jessor, 1975).

General conservatism may also be seen as resistance to change. Wilson (1973) has suggested that this resistance is due to fear of the uncertain. If one is afraid of the uncertain in life, one's best bet is to keep things the way they are, including one's sexual experience. Conservatism may also be related to nonextensive sexual experience in adolescence simply due to hesitation to charge headlong into the uncertain world of sexuality.

Deviance and Delinquency

Given that conservatism is a factor which is related to the extensiveness of adolescent sexual experience, it is not unexpected that engaging in generally disapproved adolescent behaviors, such as drinking, smoking, drug use, and delinquency is associated with more extensive adolescent sexual experience (Vener and Stewart, 1974).

One must be very careful, however, in making any sweeping generalization about delinquency and sexual activity. These relationships do not mean that sexual activity automatically leads to, or causes, delinquency, smoking, drinking, and drug use. What these relationships do mean is that those adolescents who have engaged in such behaviors are more likely to have extensive sexual experience than those who have not. The reason for this has nothing to do with one behavior causing another. Rather, delinquency, drug use, smoking, and drinking are nontraditional behaviors, and so is extensive sexual experience in adolescence.

This relationship between delinquency and sexual experience is limited largely to younger (high school age) adolescents. Among college students, the relationship between law violation and sexual experience does not exist (Jessor and Jessor, 1975). The explanation is that

sexual activity among older adolescents and young adults is more expected and less a violation of traditional expectations for behavior. Thus, the sexual experience of older adolescents is not associated with any general tendency toward violating traditional societal norms in the form of laws.

Personality

Even though the sequence of adolescent sexual behavior is patterned and ordered according to age and other social factors, this does not mean that when a person turns 17 or 18, he or she automatically begins engaging in a certain form of sexual behavior. Involvement in sexual activity in adolescence is to a considerable extent an individual decision-making process as well as a matter of such factors as opportunities. As such, certain personality factors influence the extensiveness of sexual experience since they influence the decision to engage in sexual activity.

Sex guilt As one would expect, given the nature of sex guilt (discussed in Chapter 4), this personality factor is related to a wide variety of sexual behaviors and responses at all ages.

High sex-guilt individuals have much less extensive sexual experience (Langston, 1975; Mosher and Cross, 1971; D'Augelli and Cross, 1975; DiVasta et al., 1981). The reason is that high sex guilt inhibits one's movement along the sexual behavior sequence because it leads to avoidance of sexual situations and possibilities.[3]

High sex guilt is also related to the form of one's sexual interactions. Some forms of sexual interaction are active or assertive, while others are passive or receptive. For example, a female's manual manipulation of the male genitals is a passive or receptive form of behavior

---

[3]It is difficult to overstate the importance of sex guilt in sexual behavior. While younger adults have more extensive sexual experience than older adults, this difference appears to be due to differences in sex guilt by generation. When you control for the influence of sex guilt on the extensiveness of sexual behavior, the differences in this extensiveness by generation disappear (DiVasta et al., 1981).

on the part of the male and an active or assertive form of behavior on the part of the female. On the other hand, manual manipulation of the female genitals by a male involves active behavior by the male and receptive behavior by the female. In traditional definitions of appropriate sexual conduct, it is the male who is assigned the active role and the female the passive role. Low sex-guilt individuals of both sexes are much more likely than their high sex-guilt peers to violate these traditional definitions of gender-appropriate behavior. Low sex-guilt females are much more likely than high sex-guilt females to engage in active or assertive forms of sexual activity, and low sex-guilt males are much more likely than high sex-guilt males to engage in passive and receptive sexual interaction (Langston, 1975).

Sex guilt is clearly an important personality characteristic which influences an *individual's* sexual experiences. Sexual interaction involves, however, two individuals. If sex guilt plays a part in the sexual behavior of a couple, whose sex guilt plays the major part? Is it the sex guilt of the male, the female, or both together which influences the extensiveness of a *couple's* sex experience? Not unexpectedly, it is the guilt of the male (D'Augelli and Cross, 1975). Couples in which the male is high on sex guilt have much less extensive sexual experience with each other than do couples where the sex guilt of the male is low. The sex guilt of the female has very little influence on *their* sexual behavior. This is a very important point in that it reveals a considerable amount about sexual decision making in adolescent couples. Specifically, it is still the male's initiating which has a primary influence, and his sex guilt thus has the greatest influence on the sexual experience that takes place in that relationship.

Sensation seeking Another important personality characteristic in the extensiveness of adolescent sexual experience is *sensation seeking* (Zuckerman et al., 1972).

Individuals differ in the amount of stimulation they prefer in their daily lives. Persons who are high on sensation seeking like to engage in activities which provide a great deal of stimulation, excitement, thrill, danger, and new experience. Skydivers, for example, are high on sensation seeking. Since sexual activity is not only highly stimulating in a sexual sense but is also traditionally taboo for adolescents, it is not surprising that both males and females who are high sensation seekers have more extensive sexual experience in adolescence than low sensation seekers (Zuckerman et al., 1972; Zuckerman et al., 1976). The fact that the forbidden nature of early adolescent sexual activity makes it more attractive to many individuals is clear in the fact that among the 13- to 19-year-olds in Sorensen's (1973) research, 40 percent of the males and 36 percent of the females agreed with the statement: "A lot of pleasure in sex would be lost if it did not seem to be such a forbidden activity." Again, the forbidden and nonconventional character of adolescent sexual activity is more attractive to younger adolescents. Both males and females age 13 to 15 were more likely to agree with this statement than those age 16 to 19.

Extraversion and self-confidence Given the initiator responsibility assigned to the male, it is not surprising that adolescent males who are more extraverted and self-confident have more extensive sexual experience than their less outgoing peers. Consistent with our previous discussion, extraversion and self-confidence have no relationship to the extensiveness of sexual experience on the part of females (Curran et al., 1973).

The Interpersonal Relationship

Social sexual activity by adolescents and young adults involves interaction between two people who exist in some form of interpersonal relationship. The nature of this relationship has a significant effect on the extensiveness of adolescent sexual behavior.

As a couple moves from casual to steady dating, the extensiveness of the sexual experience in that relationship increases (Mosher and Cross, 1971; Avery and Ridley, 1975).

There are, however, important gender differences in the necessity of affection for sexual activity to take place in a relationship. For male college students, the average extent of sexual activity in a dating relationship does not depend on the affection they have for the female (Mosher and Cross, 1971). Males tend to have as extensive sexual experience with females they do not love as with those they do love. Females, on the other hand, are much more likely to regulate the extensiveness of their sexual activity in a dating relationship by the amount of affection they feel for the male. In a 1970 study, Mosher and Cross (1971) found that for females, the average extent of sexual involvement was heavy petting with a male for whom they felt love but only kissing with a male they merely liked. The average extensiveness of a male's sexual activity in a dating relationship was heavy petting regardless of the affection he had for the female.

Affection is an important factor in sexual interaction because, historically, sex was approved only in the context of marriage. Marriage is supposed to be a relationship of affection and love. Over time, the level of affection deemed necessary for sexual interaction has declined. As we shall see, the change first went from marriage as a necessity for sexual interaction to engagement, then to "steady" dating with strong affection, and then to mere affection, and, today for many young people, to strong liking and personal attraction and respect.

The difference between males and females in the necessity of affection for sexual interaction is largely due to males' historically holding different sexual standards from those of females. For as far back as we have data, males have thought that sexual activity (at least on their part) was acceptable with lower levels of affection than have females.

Even though the degree of affection necessary for sexual interaction has declined over time, this does not mean that affection is no longer significant. The rules have not changed; they have just become less restrictive.

Affection is not the only interpersonal dimension of a dating relationship. While, historically, this may have been the interpersonal dimension which was most important, today adolescents and young adults seem to place

equal emphasis upon a relationship's being equitable and nonexploitive. Among college students, the quality of a relationship in terms of its being equitable is related to the extensiveness of sexual experiences that the couple shares, with equitable relationships progressing further sexually than inequitable relationships (Walster et al., 1978a).

Sexual bargaining does take place in dating relationships. Sorenson (1973) in his study of 13- to 19-year-olds, found that 69 percent of the males and 70 percent of the females agreed with the statement: "Some girls use sex to reward or punish their boyfriends." Further, 31 percent of the coitally experienced males and 16 percent of the coitally experienced females agreed with the statement: "On one or more occasions I've refused to ball a girl/boy unless she/he would do something that I wanted her/him to do."

INTERCOURSE

The term "sex" in American society is synonymous with coitus. While adolescent petting is just "messing around," intercourse is serious sex. This, of course, is purely a social definition since there is nothing inherent in any behavior which makes it more serious or sexual than any other behavior.

When social scientists and the public alike have talked about adolescent sexuality, they have consistently meant intercourse. One of the unfortunate outcomes of this tunnel-vision approach to sexuality is that until recently, we have almost totally ignored any of the interpersonal aspects of adolescent sexuality, such as sexual pleasure, satisfaction, and the place of sex in relationships.

Even more important, social scientists and the public (including parents) have paid the most attention to the coital behavior of females. A close review of social science research will reveal that we have spent most of our efforts charting how many adolescent and young adult *women* have ever engaged in coitus. Traditionally, with women viewed as male property, virginity was important. The term "virginity" applied, however, more to females

BOX 7-1
PREMARITAL COITUS AROUND THE WORLD

Broude and Greene (1976) examined the sexual behavior patterns in a sample of 186 different cultures around the world. As we have discussed, human diversity in premarital coitus is apparent in the percentage of cultures that exhibit the different patterns.

Male Coital Behavior	Percent of Cultures Showing the Pattern
Universal or almost so; almost all males engage in premarital coitus.	60
Not uncommon for males to engage in premarital coitus.	18
Occasional; some males engage in premarital coitus but this is not common or typical.	10
Uncommon; males rarely or never engage in premarital coitus.	12

Female Coital Behavior	
Universal or almost so; almost all females engage in premarital coitus.	49
Not uncommon for females to engage in premarital coitus.	17
Occasional; some females engage in premarital coitus but this is not typical or common.	14
Uncommon; females rarely or never engage in premarital coitus.	20

than to males. Viewed as male property, a woman who had intercourse before marriage was seen as "damaged goods." "Good" girls —the kind males wanted to marry—were supposed to be "pure" (virgins), and a girl's having "been around" resulted in her being "used property." "Good women" were not only not supposed to have an interest in sex, but they were expected to keep the "natural lust" of the male in control. The proportion of unmarried women with coital experience thus came to be taken as an indicator of the moral fiber of society (Gagnon, 1977). If all this emphasis on females sounds a little far fetched, consider that during the 1960s, when we thought a sexual revolution had hit the youth of America, it was the coital behavior of females which was counted, not that of males.

HOW MANY ADOLESCENTS HAVE INTERCOURSE EXPERIENCE?

The incidence of adolescent intercourse experience is still a major question since it does have meaning to people. Even though it is only one of the many dimensions of adolescent sexuality, it is important to obtain a clear picture not only of how many adolescents have coital experience, but also of the factors related to that experience.

Changes over Time

Most of us tend to think that the sexual past was never like the sexual present. Understanding contemporary sexual behavior patterns is simpler, however, if we view the present in the context of history.

    1650 to 1900 It is clear that intercourse before marriage is not an invention of the twentieth century. It is also clear that if we agree that sharp increases in the incidence of intercourse during the premarital years reveals a sexual revolution, there have been at least three such events in the history of American society, two of which took place before 1900. As shown in Figure 7-1, between approximate-

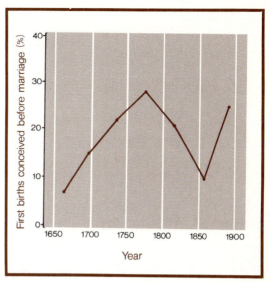

Figure 7-1 Trends in the percent of women engaging in intercourse before marriage, 1650 to 1900. This graph shows the percent of first births which were conceived prior to marriage during this period. Since it is obvious that more women engaged in intercourse before marriage than became pregnant, this graph reveals only the trend and not the actual percentages of women having premarital coitus over this period of time. The data for years prior to 1900 were obtained from church records of births, and the line shows the percent of first births taking place less than nine months after marriage. (Source: Smith and Hindus, 1975, Figure 1.)

ly 1640 and 1780, the incidence of intercourse before marriage increased considerably. Between about 1780 and 1860, the incidence declined; it then increased again from approximately 1860 through 1900 (Smith and Hindus, 1975; Smith, 1978; Gladwin, 1978).[4]

    1900 to about 1940 From approximately 1900 until the late 1920s, the incidence of intercourse before marriage continued to increase. For example, for those women who reached age 20 in 1910 or before, 13 percent had intercourse experience; for those who reached age 20 between 1920 and 1929, the proportion was 49 percent. Over this period,

[4]The reasons for these changes over time is not precisely known. For a review of the different theories, see Smith (1978), Shorter (1975) and Van Ussel (1968; 1970).

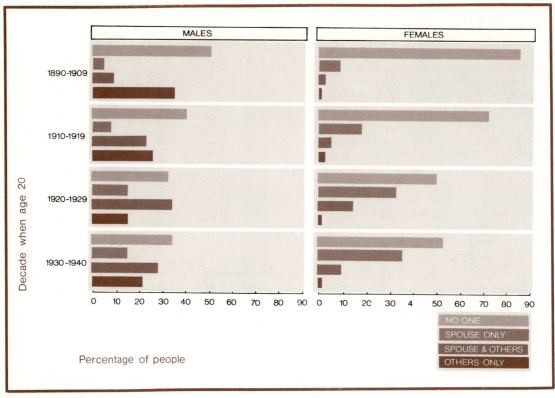

Figure 7-2 The percent of males and females who had intercourse before marriage and with whom they had intercourse. Data are for four decades in the United States. (Source: Terman [1938]; Burgess and Wallin, 1953, Tables 26 and 29.)

the rate for males had the same basic pattern, but was approximately half again as high as that among females (Terman, 1938; Burgess and Wallin, 1953).

What is more important about this period than rates are the reasons for them. The difference between males and females in the proportion with intercourse experience before marriage is a reflection of the *traditional double standard* under which sexual activity is seen as more acceptable for men than for women. The double-standard characteristic of this time period in American society is also reflected in the person with whom one had intercourse. Note in Figure 7-2 that, from 1890 through 1909, fully 36 percent of the males had intercourse *only with females other than*

their future spouse. This was the case for only 2 percent of the women in this period. Under a traditional double standard, there are two kinds of women: "bad girls" who have intercourse before marriage and "good girls" who do not. Since men wanted to marry a "good girl," they tended to have intercourse with someone other than the woman they planned to marry—a "bad girl." Thus, in the early part of the 1900s, many more males than females had intercourse before marriage and most males had their intercourse activity with women other than their future wives. Women tended not to have intercourse before marriage, and if they did, it was in the context of marriage being almost certain.

Over the period 1900 to 1940, this traditional double standard began to break down ever so slightly; this breakdown led to significant changes in the patterns of coital activity before marriage. The major change which took place during this period was not the application of the same standards of sexual conduct to males and females, but a change in the definition of when female intercourse was appropriate.

As is clear in Figure 7-2, the dominant standard for female coital behavior before marriage in the early twentieth century was abstention. Over time, this restriction changed to the acceptability of intercourse *with very strong levels of affection and commitment.* If marriage was certain, it became increasingly acceptable for a woman to engage in intercourse with her husband-to-be. This is reflected in Figure 7-2, where we see that the proportion of females who abstained from intercourse decreased over time and the proportion who had intercourse *only* with their future spouse increased. This change is, of course, evident for males as well. The proportion of males who had intercourse only with a person other than their future spouse decreased over time, and the proportion having intercourse with only their future spouse or with their spouse and others increased.

These changes, which the psychologist Terman noted in 1938, led him—as well as many others of that time—to predict that by the 1950s, there would not be a female left in the United States who had not engaged in intercourse before marriage (no predictions were made about males since their behavior was of little concern).

1940s to 1970s   Did the predictions come true? Not quite. In fact, they were not even close. Apart from having tarnish on one's crystal ball, the risky business of predicting the future is that you must assume that what happened yesterday will happen tomorrow. While not a bad bet when based on the sun coming up, social changes tend to be less cooperative.

Many social scientists argue that from the 1940s until the present, the proportion of males with intercourse experience in adolescence increased slightly while the incidence

among females continued to rise much faster. It is thought that the different rates of increasing coital experience for adolescent males and females resulted in *intersex convergence* (Christensen and Gregg, 1970) in which the proportions of males and females with coital experience before marriage became more and more similar over time. While it is true that the proportions of adolescent males and females with intercourse experience are very similar today, the reason for this similarity is not so simple as females catching up with males (Miller and Simon, 1972).

In the 1930s to 1940s, the proportion of 16- and 17-year-old males with intercourse experience was 56 percent. In 1971, this proportion was 21 percent, a rather dramatic *decrease.* In the 1930s to 1940s, the proportion of 16- and 17-year-old females with intercourse experience was approximately 8 percent, in 1971, 22 percent (Miller and Simon, 1972). Thus, *between the 1930s and 1940s to 1971, the proportion of adolescent females with intercourse experience increased while the proportion of adolescent males with intercourse experience decreased.* What happened?

From the early 1900s until the 1960s, there was a decline in the double standard. This decline, however, apparently took very different routes for males and females. Until perhaps the 1950s, both males and females tended to agree that there were "bad girls" (those who did) and "good girls" (those who did not). They also agreed that there were just plain boys (those who did if they had the chance). Males and females both expected a "good girl" to be a virgin upon marriage, but this condition was not necessary for males. Now, if males were having intercourse and females were not, who were males having it with? You bet! "Bad girls" (and their professional counterparts—prostitutes and, to a lesser extent, older married females). Who were the "bad girls"? Well, males wanted to marry a "good girl," and so the only "bad girls" were those one would not consider an eligible marriage partner. "Bad girls" were (for the mass of middle-class males) females from the lower socioeconomic segments of society. The crossing of social class lines in adolescent and young adult intercourse was thus common in male sexual activity in the 1930s, 1940s, and into the 1950s. Erhmann (1954), in a study done in the late 1940s, found, for example, that of those male college students who were dating females both in their own social class and in a social class lower than their own, 26 percent were having intercourse with females from the same social class but 64 percent were having intercourse with females lower in social class. A sizable number of lower-status females were willing to have intercourse with middle-class males in exchange for dating in which there was status to be obtained, money to be spent, and the (slim) chance of marriage. Males, however, most often had something other than marriage on their minds.

This double standard, which stated that intercourse was acceptable for males and not acceptable for ("good") females, began to change. The change for women was from abstinence to the view that intercourse was increasingly acceptable if there was strong affection and commitment. While females were coming to have this viewpoint, males were still holding on to the traditional double standard. They still felt that it was all right to have intercourse with a female you really did not care for or plan to marry (a "bad girl"). Intercourse, however, with a female you really liked and might want to marry (a "good girl") was not widely accepted. This male view is reflected in a study by Erhmann (1959) in the middle 1950s. He found that college males felt more guilty about having intercourse the more the relationship meant to them—about doing "bad" things with "good" girls. As more and more females adopted the intercourse-with-affection standard for their own behavior, males held on tight to the double standard. They thus found themselves in a sexual pickle. If they wanted to have intercourse, they had to make an affection-emotional commitment, something that was at odds with their view that "good girls" were for marriage and "bad girls" were for sex. This reluctance of males to place their intercourse in an affection-commitment context

resulted in their being increasingly denied intercourse opportunities because women from all social classes were adopting the view that intercourse was acceptable—if there was a strong level of affection.[5] As a result, the proportion of adolescent males with intercourse experience declined.

In the early 1960s, males came increasingly to accept the *intercourse-with-affection standard.* At the same time, females came to lower the level of affection necessary before they saw intercourse as acceptable or appropriate (Bell and Chaskes, 1970). Consequently, males and females came closer together in their views of when intercourse was appropriate. The result was a rather sharp increase during the 1960s in the proportion of males and females with adolescent intercourse experience, particularly in the context of lower levels of affection.

Changes in the 1970s   These changes in the 1960s continued through the 1970s. More and more adolescents came to feel that coitus was appropriate if there was affection between the partners, and the amount of affection and commitment deemed necessary declined. Today, males and females hold very similar sexual standards (Table 7-2) and the proportion of males and females with coital experience is very similar, especially among college students. Males, however, are still more liberal than females in terms of the amount of affection necessary for coitus and are more likely to have coital experience. Note in Table 7-2 the importance of love for the acceptability of intercourse. For females, the percentage saying that intercourse is acceptable goes from 42 pecent for "like each other" to 74 percent for "love." Also, however, the

[5]Another factor was at work here. During the 1950s the United States saw the rapid growth of suburbs. Prior to this time, different social classes lived in different parts of a city or town. Literally, there was "the other side of the tracks." As suburbs grew, persons from most social classes moved to them, and the ecological urban areas of different social classes dramatically declined. Such changes made it difficult for middle-class males to find lower-class females, since they did not necessarily live in any one part of the town or go to any particular high school. For college students at this time, education became increasingly available to women and to all social-class members, thus further eroding these clear social-class distinctions.

TABLE 7-2
Male and female college students approving of coitus in certain types of relationship.

Type of Relationship between the Partners	Males (%)	Females (%)
They are married to each other.	100	99
They are engaged to each other.	90	83
They are in love with each other.	85	74
They are not in love, but really like each other.	67	42
They are friends.	42	13
They are casual aquaintances.	34	9
They do not know each other.	37	7

Source: Mahoney (1979a).

difference between "like" and "love" is not nearly so great among males.

During the 1970s, the proportion of adolescents with coital experience continued to increase rapidly as the sexual attitudes of males and females came closer together and the level of affection deemed necessary for intercourse continued to lessen. In 1971, some 28 percent of all 15- to 19-year-old never-married females in the United States had at some time engaged in intercourse. In 1976, the figure was 39 percent, and in 1979, it was 46 percent (Zelnik and Kantner, 1977, 1980).

The changes that have taken place throughout the twentieth century are summarized in Figure 7-3.

Perception of sexually liberal female college students While the evaluation of a person as a desirable dating partner, marriage partner, or simply person on the basis of his or her sexual experience is not exactly the same today as it was thirty years ago, the differences are not as great as we might think. Kinsey found that 33 percent of the college-educated males studied wanted to marry a woman who had never engaged in intercourse. Another 8 percent had a slight preference for a woman with no intercourse experience, and an equal proportion said they would insist on their wife's being a virgin at marriage. This was even more true among males without a college education. Of these

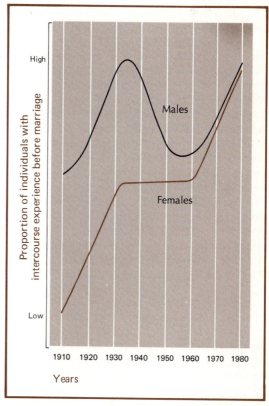

Figure 7-3 Summary of the changes in the proportion of males and females who had intercourse experience before marriage, 1900 to 1980.

men, 48 percent said their wife either *had* to be or *should* be a virgin (Gebhard and Johnson, 1979). Today, males with coital experience prefer to date females with coital experience and males without coital experience prefer to date females without coital experience. Females differ somewhat from males. Virgin females prefer also to date virgin males, but females with intercourse experience do not care about the male's intercourse experience. As far as marriage is concerned, virgin males see a nonvirgin female as an undesirable marriage partner and nonvirgin males prefer nonvirgin females as marriage partners. Females hold the same preferences for marriage partners as they do for dating partners (Istvan and Griffitt, 1980).

On a more day-to-day level, female college students who do not limit intercourse *only* to relationships involving a strong degree of affection are viewed negatively by both male and female peers. Janda et al. (1981) found that females who are sexually liberal (who have intercourse with any males they really like) are evaluated negatively by both male and female college students, especially females. The sexually liberal female college student is seen by her peers as successful in attracting men by being personable, but is not considered desirable as an acquaintance. She is seen as bad, immoral, and irresponsible, but also as warm, friendly, and likable (Janda et al., 1981). In short, the sexually liberal female today is viewed in much the same light as she was thirty years ago. Cultural traditions do not rapidly change regardless of behavior.

FACTORS RELATED TO INTERCOURSE EXPERIENCE IN ADOLESCENCE

While the proportion of adolescents with coital experience has markedly increased over time, youth has not been involved wholesale in coitus. This fact raises the question as to the factors associated with having coital experience in adolescence.

Puberty

At the onset of puberty, a number of changes take place in the reproductive system and secondary sexual characteristics. When these changes occur, we designate the person as having reached adolescence. We frequently think of changes during puberty as indicating that the person has reached a point of *sexual capacity,* or of the ability to engage in sexual behavior. These physiological changes have, however, nothing to do with sexual capacity, but the *reproductive capacity* (Gagnon, 1977:113). Males and females are physiologically capable of arousal, engaging in intercourse, and experiencing orgasm before puberty. As Gagnon points out, we confuse reproductive capacity and sexual capacity. Changes during puberty are a consequence of developing reproductive capacity. However, whether one has hair in one's public region or developed breasts has nothing to do with sexual capacity. With the confusion between reproductive and sexual capacity, these changes in reproductive potential signal that the young person will and should start to have an interest in sexuality. An important part of reaching adolescence is that one is expected to become interested in heterosexual interaction. This expectation exists, not because of the body's developing a sexual urge, but because of society's urging sexual development.

For adolescent females today, the earlier one reaches menarche the earlier one is likely to engage in intercourse (Udry, 1979). We might suggest that this fact is due to hormonal processes which spur sexual interest *or* the appearance of secondary sexual characteristics which make the maturing adolescent female more sexually attractive to males (Udry, 1979). The vast weight of evidence favors the latter. There is no direct evidence to suggest that hormonal changes in adolescence result in the onset of sexual interest or activity. Dornbusch et al., (1981) found, in fact, that sexual development had no influence on interaction with the other sex while age and peer pressure exerted a great deal of influence. Age at first dating is related to one's age at menarche (Presser, 1978), and age at first inter-

BOX 7-2

CULTURAL VARIATIONS IN ATTITUDES TOWARD FEMALE PREMARITAL INTERCOURSE

Attitude toward Female Premarital Coitus	World Cultures Having This Pattern (%)
Female premarital coitus is expected and approved, and virginity has no value.	24
Female premarital coitus is tolerated and accepted if discrete.	21
Female premarital coitus is mildly disapproved; there is pressure for virginity, but coitus is not punished and is ignored.	17
Female premarital coitus is moderately disapproved. Virginity is valued and token or slight punishment exists for coitus.	9
Female premarital coitus is allowed except with one's future spouse.	4

Source: Broude and Greene (1976).

course is related to one's age when one begins dating. Clearly, when the adolescent female reaches puberty, she begins to be treated by male and female peers, adults, and herself as a "woman" who can now do "woman things," such as date. This dating behavior increases the probability of intercourse.

Personality

While what is going on with the hormones has no direct effect on entering adolescent intercourse, what goes on in the head does. We have already seen how a number of personality factors are related to the extensiveness of adolescent sexual experience. Since coitus is merely one step in the sexual behavior sequence, these same personality factors are related to coital experience as well. Individuals who are low on sex guilt or general conservatism or high on sensation seeking or in self-

esteem are more likely to have intercourse in adolescence (Mosher and Cross, 1971; D'Augelli and Cross, 1975; Curran et al., 1973; Joe and Kostyla, 1975). This general set of personality factors simply points to the fact that being less traditional, more liberal, more adventurous, and less sexually inhibited leads to a greater likelihood of adolescent coital activity.

Liberalism

Adolescent intercourse is certainly not deviant behavior in the sense of shoplifting or auto theft, but it is also not something for which you can earn a merit badge. For an adolescent, to engage in coitus is to engage in a traditionally prohibited activity. To the extent that one is not strongly tied into the traditional values and norms of society, one is more likely to engage in coitus during adolescence. Thus, adoles-

BOX 7-3
ADOLESCENT INTERCOURSE: JAPAN, ISRAEL, COLOMBIA

Among Japanese adolescents, the proportion with intercourse experience is considerably less than in the United States. By age 18, 14 percent of the males and 7 percent of the females have engaged in coitus (Asayama, 1976). Among Israeli adolescents, coital experience among males is comparable with the figure in the United States, but the difference between males and females is much greater than in America. While Lancet et al. (1978) found that 46 percent of the 16- and 17-year-old males had engaged in coitus, only 16 percent of the females of this age had done so. This difference reflects a strong double standard prominent among many Israeli adolescents (Lancet et al., 1978). Among youth in kibbutzim, there have been, since 1970, changes in sexual attitudes and behaviors much like those which took place in the United States. As a result, kibbutz males and females have less of a double standard, more liberal sexual attitudes, and greater sexual experience than those not in kibbutzim (Kaffman, 1977; Lancet et al., 1978). Among female students at Caldas University in Manizales, Colombia, 34 percent have coital experience at an average age of 20 (Alzate, 1978). Males' average age at coitus is 17, reflecting a strong double standard. Interestingly, and for reasons which are unclear to me, the proportion of these women with anal intercourse experience seems relatively high (28 percent), as does the percentage (56) of those with oral-genital experience, given the proportion with coital experience. Obviously, Colombian women have a different sequence of sexual experiences from that of American women.

cents who have a negative attitude toward the traditional conservative institutions of society—school, police, religion—have a greater chance of engaging in coitus (Vener and Stewart, 1974). Behaviorally, drug and alcohol use are also associated with a stronger chance of coitus (Blum, 1969; Arafat and Yorburg, 1973; Vener and Stewart, 1974).

For a younger adolescent to make the move into coitus requires much more of a breaking away from the traditional attitudes and values of conventional society than is required of someone of college age. The latter is expected to be increasingly independent and to strike out on his or her own path in the sexual world. Since it is less unconventional for college-age individuals to have coitus, having a general unconventional orientation toward life is more strongly related to coital ex-

perience among young adolescents than among college students (Jessor and Jessor, 1975).

Gender
Given our previous discussions of male and female sexual learning and male and female attitudes toward coitus, it comes as no great surprise that at any age, males are more likely than females to have coital experience (Table 7-3).

Age
Sexual behavior is, as we have noted, age-graded. One is most likely to engage in certain sexual behaviors at a certain age. Intercourse is no exception. Movement into and beyond

age 16 is accompanied by a significant increase in the likelihood of engaging in coitus (Table 7-3).

Social Class

Among males and females, those who obtained higher levels of education (one of the indicators of social class) were traditionally less likely to have intercourse during adolescence. Today, this still appears to be true, at least for females. Females with lower socio-economic status—both black and white—are more likely than middle-class females to engage in coitus and do so at a younger age (Ford et al., 1981).

Religiosity: In Black and White

The transition into having coital experience is greatly slowed by religiosity—or sped up by nonreligiosity (Jessor and Jessor, 1975; Rorhbaugh and Jessor, 1975; Mahoney, 1980).

Religiosity, however, does not have the same influence on all American adolescents. While it acts as a strong personal and social control on the coital activity of white aoldescents (Herold and Goodwin, 1981), it does not do so for black adolescents. Degree of religiosity is not related to adolescent intercourse

experience for blacks, whether male or female (Christensen and Johnson, 1978).

The reason for this difference between blacks and whites is the different place of religion in the black and white cultures in American society. While the black churches in the United States adopted the religions of white Americans, they did not take on the white churches' moral stance on sexuality. Concern with the moral-sexual behavior of individuals is a relative luxury that the black church could ill afford, since dealing with the day-to-day existence of its members in a white society was problem enough (Staples, 1973).

Cultural Differences

As shown in Table 7-4, the proportion of black adolescents with intercourse experience rather dramatically exceeds the proportion of white adolescents with similar experience at the same age.

Data such as these have often been used to suggest that black adolescent females are "promiscuous" and black males are "over-sexed." Such ideas originate from the traditional sexual image of blacks in American society.

Social scientists have also attempted to explain these black and white differences through sophisticated theories of white sexuality (Christensen and Johnson, 1978). This effort has largely been fruitless (Mahoney, 1979c), since these differences can be understood only by understanding differences in sexuality in the black and white segments of American society and the factors that shape these differences.

We have already noted the difference between blacks and whites in terms of the influence of religiosity on sexuality. Also, blacks have more liberal attitudes toward premarital sex than do whites (Staples, 1978). One of the reasons is the heritage of slavery. The black woman in slavery did not have the option of virginity or nonvirginity, especially as far as white males were concerned. As Staples (1973:40) argues, "Once she accepted the fact that she did not have control over her body,

TABLE 7-3
Never-married persons in the United States with intercourse experience, 1979.

Years of Age	Males with Intercourse Experience (%)	Females with Intercourse Experience (%)
15	*	23
16	*	38
17	56	49
18	66	57
19	77	69
20	81	*

*Data were not obtained for this age group. This study focused on contraceptive behavior and females usually have their first coital experience with a male who is somewhat older.
Source: Zelnik and Kantner (1980). A National probability sample of males and females in the United States from these age groups in 1979. Tables 1 and 2, pp. 231 and 233.

TABLE 7-4
Males and females with intercourse experience, by age and ethnicity, 1979.

Years of Age	Males (%)		Females (%)	
	Black	White	Black	White
15	*	*	41	18
16	*	*	50	35
17	60	55	73	44
18	80	64	76	53
19	80	77	89	65
20	86	81	*	*

*Data were not collected for this age group.
Source: Zelnik and Kantner (1980: 231 and 233, tables 1 and 2).

BOX 7-4
BLACK MALES AND LOVE

While there has been a general tendency on the part of social scientists to ignore sexuality in different subcultures in American society, not all sexuality in America is of the white, middle-class *Playboy/Cosmopolitan* variety. Understanding black sexuality, for example, requires that one have an understanding of being black in the United States and what that means historically and in the present. I am white. I cannot pretend to fully understand being black beyond an intellectual level. I will, however, try to convey both the intellectual and "gut level" understanding we do have. In this case, it is the black male we shall discuss.

It has been repeatedly argued that the usual symbols and gestures of white male masculinity have historically been all but impossible for many black males to adopt. Traditionally, slavery emasculated the black male by stripping away all opportunities for demonstrating to himself and others that he was indeed a man. More modern conditions have aided in maintaining this condition through economic, educational, social, and political avenues. Robert Staples, a black sociologist, has argued that this situation has given rise to a black male-virility cult. One outcome is that many black males develop a dual existence with regard to women. On the one hand, they see themselves as exploiters of women because they do not want to be emotionally dependent on them. They thus behave in ways that counter any notion that they are weaklings or suckers (Staples, 1973). This, however, is mainly talk. On the behavior side, it is more often the case that black males are very supportive of black women. Nonetheless, there is peer group pressure among black males to maintain the front of virility. One of the results of this dual existence of the black male is a certain distance or aloofness emotionally and romantically. It is best described by a black male:

Black women are not made for suffering. They don't wear it well. . . . She stares, projecting her disappointment and rage on you. It always embarrasses me. I want to apologize to her simply for being a Black man, but her ears are deaf to me. She only remembers the pain and sacrifice of the importance of virginity to her was considerably reduced." This situation still remains to some significant extent for black women as part of a cultural heritage handed down from slavery.

A second major factor is that the "good woman"–"bad women" dichotomy was a white, not a black, invention. Black males never did require virginity at marriage. Additionally, many black males consider sex and dating to be one and the same. Sex is often taken as an important goal in and of itself. If the black adolescent female is going to play the dating game, she must play by the rules of the black male. He expects (perhaps even demands) sex in a dating relationship, and frequently courtship will stop if the female is not willing. If she

is not willing, others are. Black females outnumber black males, and many white females are willing to date black males while black women do not so commonly date white men. Thus, many black women are without partners (Staples, 1973).

Houston (1981), in a recent study of black and white college students, found a number of differences between black and white males. Black males were more likely to say that they are inconsiderate of their partner's sexual pleasure, that they are more interested in their own sexual satisfaction than their partner's, that sex is the most important part of a dating relationship, that they date a female for a short period of time, and that the most common reason they have for wanting intercourse is pure

a seemingly unreciprocated love. . . . Black men have a resistance to love that women have never understood. It's not a question of whether we men are using or abusing our women. We simply don't know what women are saying to us. We can easily mouth the words of love, but the underlying meaning eludes us. When the emotion manages to escape our control, our sense of helplessness is awesome. That feeling is far too alien to us so we withdraw and attempt to push it out of our minds and hearts. Our reactions are unpredictable and often cruel. We never intend to hurt, just escape. . . . If women could only fathom the anxiety of being a "man," tough and unshakable, I think they would cry for us. Living up to an image is strain enough, but love becomes a flaw in the masks we have perfected. . . . Sadly, I don't think we men can learn how to be loving from our women. The distance between us has grown too wide, the hurt has gone too deep. Men will have to learn from each other. A man must see another man in love. Men must have proof that love is not fatal, that the act of loving makes you better, not weaker. . . . At a time when many of us are better educated, earning higher salaries and looking forward to the best life has to offer, there is no one to share it with . . . our women are growing increasingly cynical to our advances, perhaps rightfully so. The same scenes have been played out so many times that even before a relationship can begin, the outcome has been decided. Men feeling that they can come and go as they please and women seeming to be grateful for any amount of attention is the rule of the day. We all call it love because we don't seem to have any other choice. . . . It took me years to be able to look into loving eyes and know what I was seeing. I'm growing and maturing because of it. I'm learning to love without putting up a smoke screen to hide the emotion. It's not easy. Moving against the patterns of a lifetime requires constant effort. . . . It frightens me a little to think that a romantic has dwelled within me for all these years, but it feels so good to finally let him free. . . . (Austin Patrick, "Men in Love," *Essence,* February 1979:57.)

physical need. On the other hand, black males in the study were less likely to say that they find kissing enjoyable in and of itself, that they have gone "steady," and that they see themselves as being romantic with their partners.

If you are now thinking that these findings and statements are racist, you have missed the entire point. Different people learn different views of sexuality (see Chapter 4). What we see here are differences in sexual learning that account for the differences between blacks and whites in coital experience in adolescence. One can compute statistics forever, but unless you understand basic cultural learning differences (even within a society), the numbers remain just numbers.

While black adolescent females are still more likely to engage in intercourse, white females are catching up. From 1971 to 1979, the proportion of 15- to 19-year-old, never-married black females with coital experience increased by 23 percent; in the same period, the proportion of white females with coital experience increased by 48 percent.

Reference Groups: Parents versus Peers

A *reference group* is that set of people an individual uses as a reference point or standard in setting and evaluating his or her own attitudes, values, and behaviors. During one's childhood and early adolescence, parents are one's primary reference group. As one moves into adolescence, however, parents begin to face competition from peers. Increasingly, particularly in sexual matters, parents lose and peers win the social tug of war. This shift from parents to peers as the primary reference group does not automatically mean that an adolescent will engage in coitus. Doing so depends on what one's peers think is appropriate and what kinds of sexual behavior patterns dominate among them. Since peers are generally more liberal in their sexual attitudes than are parents, the more one moves from parents to peers, the more likely one is to have coital experience (Walsh et al., 1976). Those adolescents who remain strongly tied to their parents

Differences in values, including sexual values, creates the generation gap. The differences between generations, however, are often much less than what the older generation imagines.

as a reference group are thus less likely to engage in coitus (Jessor and Jessor, 1975). Similarly, if one's friends are sexually conservative, the movement from peers to parents has little effect on the probability of coitus (Jessor and Jessor, 1975).

Parents are usually not in a position to compete effectively with an adolescent's peers. Not only is acceptance into one's peer group very important in adolescence, but parents generally fail to have previously established communication with their children about sexual matters.

Peers, Attitudes, Behavior

One of the single most important factors associated with beginning to engage in intercourse in adolescence is *anticipatory socialization.* Anticipatory socialization is where we become familiar with a behavior or role before we actually engage in the behavior. One anticipates the behavior and the role before the behavior occurs. This allows one to "think through" a behavior and to develop a set of behavioral standards and attitudes about the behavior before engaging in it. This process allows a person to "try it on for size" before making a behavioral commitment to the action. It is clear that an attitude toward intercourse as acceptable develops *before* one engages in intercourse (DeLamater and McCorquodale, 1979). Spanier (1976) has pointed out how developing the view that intercourse is a pleasurable activity and not disgusting is essential for movement into engaging in intercourse in adolescence.

The central importance of peers develops in this anticipatory socialization for intercourse. Adolescents develop a positive attitude toward intercourse from their peers, or more specifically, from their peers who have intercourse experience themselves and therefore serve as models. From these models one can directly have a source of information and an example for one's own anticipatory socialization into intercourse. For this reason, *the variable most strongly related to intercourse experience in adolescence is peers' experience with intercourse* (Herold and Goodwin, 1981; Delamater and McCorquodale, 1979). This is followed in importance by the variable of being in an affection relationship and then by religiosity (Herold and Goodwin, 1981).

Stages to Intercourse

While it has been traditional to talk about intercourse status in terms of virgin or nonvirgin, this is not the most accurate description of what actually takes place in adolescence. It is more accurate to think of intercourse status as involving three categories; adamant virgins, potential nonvirgins, and nonvirgins (DiAugelli and Cross, 1975; Herold and Goodwin, 1981).

Adamant virgins have not experienced intercourse and are not likely to do so until marriage. *Potential nonvirgins* have not experienced intercourse but are likely to do so before marriage, and *nonvirgins* have intercourse experience.

The most important difference between these three groups is the intercourse experience of their peer group. Further, for females, adamant virgins tend to be strongly religious and not to engage in coitus because of moral reasons. Potential nonvirgins, however, are most likely to have not engaged in intercourse because they have not met the right person. They are low in religiosity and their peers are highly accepting of intercourse.

Dating commitment is crucial in distinguishing between potential nonvirgin and nonvirgin adolescent females. Nonvirgin adolescent females have met the right person (Herold and Goodwin, 1981). There is some evidence that the reason potential nonvirgins have not yet met the right person to have intercourse with has to do with their values. Potential nonvirgin females are more career- and less marriage-oriented than nonvirgins (Herold and Goodwin, 1981). Cvetkovich et al. (1981) found that they were also the most liberal in their attitudes toward gender roles. Perhaps potential nonvirgin adolescent females do not want a steady committed relationship because it might get in the way of their careers and they may fear pregnancy which would also interfere with a career. They, however, still hold the view that coitus is acceptable only when there is affection. Not allowing this affection-commitment relationship to develop means that they have not yet engaged in intercourse (Herold and Goodwin, 1981).

INTERCOURSE AND INTERPERSONAL RELATIONSHIPS

So far, we have discussed individuals and how their characteristics are related to their having intercourse as adolescents. Intercourse takes two and is thus an *inter*personal as well as an *intra*personal behavior. In order fully to understand adolescent and young adult sexuality, we must consider that we are talking about a form of interaction taking place between two people and that the sexual component of this interaction is only one aspect of a larger interpersonal relationship.

The Place of a Relationship in Sex

Contrary to the popular notion, adolescent and young adult coitus takes place largely in the context of love or a strong liking relationship. Casual sex is not the dominant pattern among the youth of America. When I asked a sample of first- and second-year college students in 1978 what type of relationship they had with their last intercourse partner, the vast majority of both males and females indicated that it had been an interpersonal relationship which contained some strong affection (Figure 7-4).

The Place of Sex in a Relationship

The place of sex in a dating relationship is seen somewhat differently by males and females. Males are more likely to have an interest in sex as part of a dating relationship, to view sex as one of the best things about dating, and to see sex as an important goal in a dating relationship (Peplau et al., 1977; Knox and Wilson, 1981). Houston (1981) found, for example, that among college students, 55 percent of the males and only 11 percent of the females said that the most desirable thing in a date is a good sexual relationship; 79 percent of the females and only 14 percent of the males said that the most important part of a date was a good intellectual relationship.

Abstaining from Intercourse in a Dating Relationship

The fact that most adolescents, especially college students, place their intercourse in an affection context does not mean that all couples who are "going together" automatically have intercourse with each other. In a recent study of college-student couples who had been going together for an average of eight months, 18

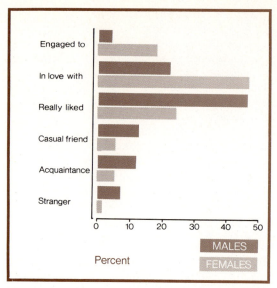

Figure 7-4 The type of relationship male and female college students had with the person with whom they most recently had intercourse. (Source: Mahoney, 1979.)

percent had abstained from intercourse in their relationship (Peplau et al., 1977).

These abstaining individuals were, not unexpectedly, more conservative in their sexual attitudes and entered the relationship with less sexual experience than nonabstainers. Even so, it is primarily the female's attitudes that are responsible for abstinence. Men in these relationships most frequently want to have intercourse (only 11 percent of the males in abstaining relationships said that their own lack of desire for intercourse was the main reason the couple abstained). The reason females in abstaining relationships give for not wanting to include coitus are most frequently moral-ethical or that it is too early in the relationship for sexual intimacy. Fear of pregnancy is also a common deterrent in the minds of both males and females (Elias and Elias, 1975).

While males and females in abstaining, but long-term dating, relationships have quite different views about the desirability of intercourse, they also have quite different reasons for never having engaged in intercourse. These reasons reflect male and female differences in sexuality with which you are now familiar. In a recent study of 18- and 19-year-old college students, I asked virgin men and women their reasons for never having engaged in coitus (the question was not quite so blunt). The most common reason given by both males (69 percent) and females (51 percent) was that intercourse before marriage was morally wrong. Males are not only less likely to have moral inhibitions, but are also less likely to have interpersonal reasons. For example, 41 percent of the females said they had not met the right person, a reason given by only 13 percent of the males. Further, only 14 percent of the females said they had not had the opportunity. Fully 38 percent of the males gave this reason. Lastly, 19 percent of the males said that the reason they had not engaged in intercourse was that their partner said no; none of the females gave this reason.

Not If, But When?
Among couples who have been going together for some time and do have coitus with each other, there is considerable variation in how long they go together before intercourse occurs. In the Peplau et al. (1977) research, 41 percent of the couples engaged in intercourse within one month of their first date and 59 percent later than one month after their first date. For purposes of comparison, these were labeled "early" and "late" sex couples. A comparison of the two categories reveals that they differ both in terms of individual characteristics and in the nature of the relationship itself.

Individuals in early sex relationships are more accepting of casual sex (with less affection and commitment required), see sex as more of a reason for dating, have more sexual experience prior to entering the relationship, and currently have intercourse with each other more often than do late sex individuals. Early sex individuals also feel less guilt about their sexual behavior, and females in early sex relationships report greater sexual satisfaction than females in late sex relationships. Early sex females (but not males) are less religious, less likely to be Catholic, less traditional in their view of the female role, and less interested in being a housewife. They are more interested in being a single career person and generally have a more positive self-image.

There are also important differences between early and late sex couples in the nature of their relationship and the place of sex in the relationship. Late sex couples are more emotionally close to each other and more likely to say that they are in love. This is a reflection, not that early sex couples have poor relationships, but that late sex couples are more likely to require love before intercourse takes place. Late sex couples, for example, have intercourse an average of six months *after* they define themselves as going together, while early sex couples have intercourse an average

Figure 7-5 The timing of the first intercourse two people have with each other in a dating relationship depending on the prior sexual experience of the male and female when they began dating each other as college students. (Source: Peplau et al., 1977.)

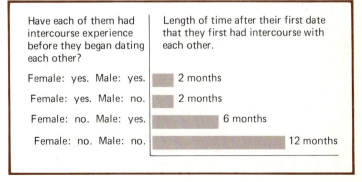

Have each of them had intercourse experience before they began dating each other?	Length of time after their first date that they first had intercourse with each other.
Female: yes. Male: yes.	2 months
Female: yes. Male: no.	2 months
Female: no. Male: yes.	6 months
Female: no. Male: no.	12 months

of one month *before* they see themselves as going together.

In the timing of intercourse in a dating relationship, males do not commonly resist the opportunity. The opportunity depends, however, on the extent to which the female acts out the traditional role of gatekeeper. As shown in Figure 7-5, if the female is coitally experienced, the couple will (on the average) engage in intercourse within two months of their first date *regardless of the male's prior intercourse experience*. If the female is not coitally experienced when the couple starts going together, intercourse enters the relationship much later, with how much later depending on the prior intercourse experience of the male (the initiator).

Too Much, Too Soon? The Effect of the Timing of Intercourse in a Dating Relationship

What effect does early versus late intercourse have on the relationship? Apart from the first-date Romeo being unlikely to be the most datable person on campus, none. Sex is only a part of the larger interpersonal relationship that is formed and bonded together by the mutual attraction of two individuals. Sex is not something which exists apart from the social and psychological dynamics of the basis of this attraction, but is merely a part of the set of characteristics of individuals that serve as the basis for the attraction in the first place. This is not to say that immediately upon being introduced, two people exchange summaries of their sexual experience, interests, and preferences. Rather, sexual behavior is shaped by a variety of individual characteristics. Attraction to another person is based largely on the degree of similarity between the two people. Thus, individuals who are attracted to each other are very likely to bring together personal characteristics which make them at least somewhat sexually compatible. Intercourse, when it becomes part of a relationship, is not a social glue that will hold an otherwise poor relationship together, nor a damnation that will split true love asunder. Rather, sex is more

likely to be affected by the relationship than the relationship by sex.

Among adolescents, however, sex for most females does imply some degree of affection and commitment. Thus, they are more likely than males to feel that coitus aids or strengthens a dating relationship (Elias and Elias, 1975).

INTERETHNIC DATING AND INTERCOURSE

Dating and sex between different ethnic groups has been, and still is, a taboo topic in American society. Sex between blacks and whites is still a subject most people would prefer that you not mention. As a consequence, social scientists have almost totally ignored the topic.

Dating and intercourse between blacks and whites (as well as between other groups which we know even less about) are common on many college campuses. The process, however, is one-sided. In the only study with college students, Sebold (1974) found that 80 percent of the black males but only 23 percent of the white males expressed an interest in interethnic dating. These desires are clearly reflected in behavior. While 90 percent of the black males had dated a white female only 12 percent of the white males had dated a black female. Further, 68 percent of the black males had dated more than five white females.

This lopsided interethnic dating pattern is also reflected in intercourse. In this same study, just under 50 percent of the white males who had dated a black female had engaged in intercourse on such a date. This was the case for 91 percent of the black males who had dated white females. Black males are also more likely to have interethnic "one-night stands." In Sebold's study, 87 percent of the black males (but only 9 percent of the white males) who had dated across ethnic lines had such intercourse experiences. Fully 40 percent of the black males had had six or more such encounters.

There are two major reasons for this skewed pattern of black-white dating and intercourse. The first has to do with the nature of college populations. The American education system gives many more educational opportunities to black males than to black females. As a consequence, black males tend to outnumber black females on college campuses, making for a scarcity of black female dating partners. The second reason is, however, far more important. A cultural tradition dating from slavery defines black women as not necessarily valued or desirable sexual partners in the eyes of white males. Beginning in colonial America and established in slavery, the black woman has been seen as a sexual object who has little or no interpersonal value and who can be freely used at will by the white male. White females, however, were traditionally viewed as desirable, yet untouchable, sexual partners for black males. Further, the black male has, since the days of slavery, been seen in the minds of whites to be a potent and feared sexual machine. The myths of racial differences in penis size are legend in this society, reflecting the attribution of sexual potency to the black male. These views are still very much with us, even among college students. Davis and Cross (1979) had a sample of college students read stories depicting sexual activity between a man and a woman. Some of the subjects read stories in which both the male and female were white, while other subjects read stories with a black male and a white female. After reading the stories, the subjects rated the characters on a number of dimensions. Not only did both male and female subjects rate the black male as more sexually potent than the white male, but when they made figure drawings of the male character, they showed a significant tendency to draw the black male (but not the white male) with a penis much larger than his body size would warrant.

The contemporary social-psychological dynamics coming out of this cultural tradition of sexual stereotypes include black male aggressiveness and white female curiosity. As Robert Staples, a black sociologist, states: "Just as these sexual stereotypes may stimulate the curiosity of the white woman, the Negro male may be equally attracted by the concept of sacred white womanhood" (Staples, 1973:48).

One of the outcomes of these patterns of interracial dating and intercourse is that black females often strongly resent black males dating white females. Such activity is a contemporary reminder of the deposits of slavery, not in the sense that black and white dating takes place, but that it is almost entirely one-sided. Not only does the black female see interethnic dating as strongly suggesting that the white female is more socially and sexually desirable, but the lack of interracial dating by white males all too clearly suggests the traditionally low status of the black woman in the eyes of a white male society.

THE FIRST INTERCOURSE EXPERIENCE

Having the first intercourse experience is a socially and psychologically meaningful event for most people. Regardless of one's petting experience, this is the big moment, this is *real sex,* the act that marks a critical transition in sexual status (virgin-nonvirgin does not apply to anything other than intercourse).

Feelings about the First Intercourse Experience

The first intercourse experience is one that is filled with an amazing mixture of different feelings. Each person generally feels good and bad, excited and anxious, curious and hesitant. Generally, however, the first coital experience is a positive experience (Christensen and Johnson, 1978). Males, however, are much more likely than females to have positive feelings following their first coital experience, with happiness, relaxation, and conquest being the most common reactions. Among negative reactions, males most frequently have a fear of the woman's pregnancy and feelings of tenseness and guilt. Even so, negative reactions are much more common among females (guilt, tenseness, fear of pregnancy, and fear of discovery) (Christensen and Johnson, 1978).

These distinctive male and female reactions to the first coital experience reflect the differences between males and females in the meaning of initial intercourse. For females, this is an experience which involves moving into a new status, the desirability of which is unclear. Apart from the underlying anxiety about pregnancy, females may fear a negative reaction from their female friends or being a less-than-desirable topic of conversation among the male partner's friends. Since it is important to females that their initial intercourse experience take place in the context of a meaningful relationship, females often feel that they were "had" because the relationship was not as meaningful as they had been led to expect. For males, on the other hand, the social and psychological risks are much less. For them, there is little at stake in the way of social standing. Having intercourse means moving into a new status which is almost certain to be positively valued by one's male peers. Males can only become "experienced," but females can become "easy lays."

The difference in the social meaning of the first coital experience is clearly demonstrated in a study by Carns (1973). Males were not only more likely than females to tell their friends about their first coital experience, but they told more friends sooner. Additionally, males were more likely to have the news received by hearty congratulations, while females were more likely to be greeted by a negative response or cold-shoulder neutrality from their female friends.

Males, however, are not entirely free from concern over their initial coital experience; the concerns are just different from those of females. The traditional male role designates the "good male" as competent, capable, knowledgeable, and skillful in all matters. Without any prior training or even a hint of practice, the young male feels the pressure of having learned what it is to be male when he encounters his first coital situation. He should know how to handle it and handle it well.

Intercourse is a unique sexual activity in American society in two ways. First, there is

seldom any coaching by parents or siblings as to what one does, and the opportunity is rare that one can learn by observing the behavior of others. Second, it cannot be done a little bit at a time. In petting, you can "go this far" one time and "this far" the next, slowly becoming versed in the complexities of sexual interaction. With intercourse, you either do or don't. The attempt by the two people cannot be easily disguised as a slip of the hand.

In the face of a lack of knowledge about what one does, the experience itself is a rather complex social and sexual situation. Even though both individuals may have considerable petting experience, even with each other, the applicability of the knowledge gained from petting is limited. One has learned anatomy, preferences, responsiveness, partial disrobing, sensitivity to the other person, the interpretation of otherwise unintelligible grunts and moans, and the sequence of erotic activities and how long to perform each. There remains much, however, which has never been rehearsed, and about which only vague and unsure images may serve as a guide. Totally undressing and being fully nude in front of the other sex, the coordination of total body movements and not just hands, knowing when one should proceed beyond the familiar petting activities, and coordinating arousal in a much different set of sexual activities all remain to be solved. Moreover, they must all be solved without asking for instructions and while maintaining a heightened level of arousal in an erotic moment (Gagnon, 1973; Simon and Gagnon, 1973). The moment itself is entwined in risk. "How does one insert a penis in a vagina?" "Will it hurt?" "Did it hurt?" "What do we do when it does not work?" "Will I stay hard?" "Am I wet enough?" "Will she enjoy it?" "It doesn't feel like I thought it would." "I hope I don't come too soon."

Age at First Intercourse

While it seems simple enough just to state the average age at first intercourse in American society today, this is not so easy. Regardless of age, not all adolescents have engaged in intercourse and we cannot say for certain when the people without experience will. If we sit around and wait until all of today's 12-year-olds reach age 30 and then ask them how old they were when they first had intercourse, we will be in the year 2000, not 1983.

We can, however, compute the average age at first intercourse for certain age groups. In 1976, the average age at first intercourse for never-married women between the ages of 15 and 19 was 18.3, a decline from 19.0 in 1971 (Zelnik et al., 1979). While we do not have outstanding data for males, it is reasonably clear that the average age for males is about one year earlier and is declining gradually as well (Vener and Stewart, 1974).

It is apparent that the average age at first intercourse has fallen significantly over time. For example, Kinsey (1953) found that for women born before 1900, only 8 percent had intercourse by age 20, and for women born between 1920 and 1929, only 21 percent had intercourse by age 20. In 1980, some 69 percent of the 19-year-old females in the United States had had intercourse (Zelnik and Kantner, 1980).

Further, Kinsey (1953) found that the age at which a female first engaged in intercourse was greatly influenced by age at marriage. Women who married younger had their first intercourse experience before marriage at a younger age; this was due to the fact that premarital coitus was usually restricted by plans for marriage. Today, plans for marriage have no influence on age at first intercourse for the majority of females (Zelnik et al., 1979).

While there are no more recent data available, a 1979 national survey indicated that the decline in females' age at first intercourse had slowed considerably (Zelnik and Kantner, 1980).

The First Intercourse Partner

Age of partner   For both males and females, the first person with whom one has intercourse is most likely to be someone older. In one study (Finkel and Finkel, 1975), 53 percent of the males of high school age had their first intercourse with someone older, 35 percent with someone their own age, and only 12

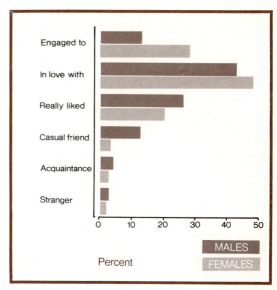

Figure 7-6 The nature of the interpersonal relationship in which male and female college students had their first intercourse experience. (Source: Mahoney, 1979.)

percent with someone younger than themselves. Being initiated into intercourse by someone older is even more common for females. For women between ages 15 and 19, the first intercourse partner is typically two to three years older (Zelnik and Kantner, 1977).

Relationship with partner   The extensiveness of the sex-with-affection standard among adolescents today is clearly evident in the person with whom one has her or his first intercourse. The majority of both males and females now, as in the past, first have intercourse in an affection-laden relationship (Sorensen, 1973; Jedlicka, 1975; Simon et al., 1972). Reflecting males' learning to view sex as valuable in its own right and females' learning to view sex as more strongly tied to affection, there are male and female differences here, as shown in Figure 7-6.

Over time, females have decreased the level of affection necessary for intercourse to take place. While engagement was almost mandatory fifty years ago, the first intercourse experience for females today typically takes place in an affectional relationship without any long-term commitment. In one very real sense, males have taken a different journey through history, having actually increased the level of affection typical in their first intercourse experience.

From the early 1900s to the middle of the century, many males had their first intercourse with a prostitute. Hohman and Shaffner (1947) found that 36 percent of the males studied in the military had their first intercourse with a prostitute. Kinsey learned that 19 percent of the college-educated males and 23 percent of those without college education had their first coital experience with a prostitute (Gebhard and Johnson, 1979). Today, this form of sexual introduction is rare. Sorensen (1973) observed that only 1 percent of the high school males studied had *ever* had intercourse with a prostitute, and Hunt (1974) found that only 8 percent of the males under age 35 had ever been to a prostitute.

One of the extremely important characteristics of adolescent and young adult male sexuality is that males move toward placing more emphasis on the interpersonal aspects of sexuality as they age. In their first intercourse experience, they are much more likely than females to have intercourse with someone for whom they have little affection or commitment. If you ask males about their most recent intercourse experience, the affection and commitment they felt for their partner are much greater than during their first such experience. Thus, as males move from their first to their most recent intercourse experience, they move closer and closer to the typical female pattern of a close relationship involving affection and commitment (Jedlicka, 1975; Mahoney, 1979). Compare Figures 7-4 and 7-6 for the clearest evidence of this.

Planned or spontaneous? The importance of one's first coital experience is clearly illustrated in the fact that approximately 40 percent of both males and females plan the event (Simon et al., 1972). The nature of this planning differs somewhat, however, for males and females. A male's plans tend to center around having sexual success, while a female's plans center around coitus taking place in a long-term relationship (Simon et al., 1972).

Future interaction For most adolescent females, intercourse signals or implies affection and commitment in her partner. This is likely to result in the female partner's feeling that her first intercourse experience strengthened the relationship between the partners. This is bolstered by the fact that she may also see intercourse as being something the male really wanted (Sorensen, 1973). Although seldom a heart-breaking event, many adolescent females report that they came to understand that their partner did not share their own feelings of affection and commitment. Many females thus see their first coital experience as a lesson in the dangers of emotional commitment with later partners (Sorensen, 1973).

Even so, the first intercourse experience is usually not the last with that person, but is repeated two or three times. The lower level of commitment and affection on the part of males is apparent here also. They are less likely than females to have repeated intercourse with their first partner (Sorenson, 1973).

The geography of first intercourse While the location of the first intercourse experience is not the type of information you are likely to find on most maps, the experience does have a geography that reflects some characteristic aspects of contemporary society. Out-of-doors, one partner's home, and a car are favored locations. The latter is, however, on the decline as the home becomes an increasingly popular location (Zelnik and Kantner, 1977). This change reflects more than an interest in comfort and a decline in the size of automobiles. Rather, more and more mothers are employed full-time—out of the home—in the labor force, making the home increasingly available. This is why teenage females whose mothers are employed are more likely to have engaged in intercourse than are those whose mothers are not employed (Hansson et al., 1981).

THE FREQUENCY OF ADOLESCENT INTERCOURSE

Lacking a clock which counts off how many times a minute adolescents somewhere in

America are having intercourse, it is a common assumption that with increased incidence has come increased frequency. The image of teenagers as rabbits reveals more about adult fears (and envy?) than reality. The most common monthly frequency of intercourse for adolescent women who have ever engaged in intercourse is zero (Figure 7-7)!

One of the important facts Kinsey brought before the world was that, regardless of what the *average* sexual anything is, there is a wealth of *individual* variation. Among college students, this is readily apparent in the frequency of intercourse. In a recent study (Mahoney, 1979a) of 18- and 19-year-old students, 39 percent of the females who were coitally experienced had had no intercourse in the last month, but 5 percent had had it twenty-one or more times. The monthly frequencies of intercourse ranged from zero to fifty-six.

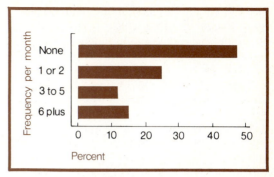

Figure 7-7 The frequency of intercourse in the last month as reported by never-married 15- to 19-year-old females in the United States who have ever engaged in intercourse. (Source: Zelnik and Kanter, 1977.)

Factors Related to Intercourse Frequency in Adolescence

While individual characteristics such as an interest in and liking of sexual activity, religiosity, ethnicity (black adolescent females have intercourse less frequently than whites), and personality all influence the frequency of intercourse, the chief factor is interpersonal opportunity. This statement does not mean the number of people of the other sex you run into in a day, but the nature of one's interpersonal relationships in a dating framework. Given the importance of the intercourse-with-affection standard, it is not surprising that the frequency of coitus increases dramatically as one moves from casual to stable interpersonal relationships. Male and female college students who are not dating anyone at all have the lowest monthly frequency of intercourse. The next lowest frequency is among those males and females who are dating several people. As we move to those students who are dating only one person, however, the frequency of intercourse more than doubles (Mahoney, 1979a). A stable relationship with one person involves not only opportunity in the form of a partner, but also the level of affection, commitment,

and silently negotiated understanding important for coital activity today. This level of interpersonal involvement is not possible when one is playing the field. By far the highest frequency of intercourse is among students who are living with someone. These high frequencies reflect not only the more liberal attitudes and behaviors of cohabiting students, but also the situation in which such essentials as privacy and continual sleeping together are routine. Such elements are not readily available in the average dormitory room no matter how much you like someone.

Interest-Activity Gaps

The human condition is often such that ideals in the mind do not match the reality of day-to-day living. In studies of the sexual activity of males, it has been noted that after age 50, males experience an increasingly wider interest-activity gap in that sexual interest exceeds activity (Pfeiffer et al., 1974).

College-age males find themselves in the same position. In one study (Mahoney, 1979a), college males said they had an ideal intercourse frequency of 6.5 times a month, but an actual frequency averaging 5 times per month. College females also have an interest-activity gap, but in the reverse direction. In this same study, the average ideal frequency among females was 5 times a month, but the average actual frequency was 6 times.

These male-female differences indicate the subtle sexual tension which develops out of gender differences in sexual learning. Ideally, males want more and females want less. What is really taking place, however, is a little give and a little take. Females engage in intercourse slightly more than they would ideally like to and males slightly less.

THE NUMBER OF DIFFERENT INTERCOURSE PARTNERS

We commonly encounter the term "promiscuity" in discussions of sexual behavior. Its usage is unfortunate for two reasons. First, the term most frequently applies to women and not men. In a society where males *get* and females *give* sex, a large number of intercourse partners is a mark of male achievement and female corruption (being easy). Second, the term is not only sexist, but also incorrect. The dictionary definition of promiscuous is *indiscriminate*. When applied to a description of one's sexual behavior, it means that one is indiscriminate in one's choice of intercourse partners. You would have to search high and low to find anyone who is indiscriminate with regard to the characteristics of his or her inter-

course partner. Some people may have less rigid selection criteria than others, but they are not indiscriminate. What promiscuous really means in descriptions of sexual behavior is that a person has "too many" different intercourse partners. Whether one has too many is a matter of personal opinion, not scientific discussion.

How Many Partners, When?

One way of looking at the question of the number of different intercourse partners is to look at the present number. How many persons is an individual currently (not at exactly the same time) having intercourse with? In this society, *serial monogamy* is the rule. At any one time, adolescent males and females tend to have only one partner (monogamous), but one relationship breaks up and another follows (serial). A recent study by Reichelt (1978) illustrates the pattern of 13- to 17-year-old females, 91 percent had only one current partner, 8 percent had two, 1 percent had three, and none had more than three.

The number-of-partners question may also apply to a given period of time, say a year. Serial monogamy and the intercourse-with-affection standard have already provided the answer. The number of partners in any period of time depends on how long one goes with a given person and how long it takes a couple to reach intimacy in their relationship, including intercourse. Reichelt (1978) found that among 13- to 17-year-old females, 53 percent had only one partner in a year, 24 percent had two partners, and only 6 percent had six or more. Owing to now familiar gender differences, males tend to have a slightly larger number of partners in any period of time (Bauman and Wilson, 1974; Mahoney, 1979a).

The third way to look at the number of coital partners is to consider the total number of different partners. Here we see some rather significant changes over time—changes which are to be expected given the development of an intercourse-with-affection standard, a decreasing level of affection necessary for intercourse, and males' and females' increasingly

TABLE 7-5
Total number of intercourse partners for unmarried females in 1953, 1974, and 1976.[*]

Number of Partners	1953	1974	1976
One	53	51	45
Two to Five	34	34	31
Six to Ten	7	9	9
Eleven or more	6	6	14

[*]The 1953 figures show Kinsey's married and unmarried women reporting on premarital experience. The 1974 data show Tavris and Sadd's married and unmarried women reporting on the same experience. The 1976 figures are for Zelnik and Kantner's never-married 18- and 19-year-old women.
Source: Tavris and Sadd (1977:48); Zelnik and Kantner (1977).

similar attitudes about the conditions under which intercourse is appropriate.

As shown in Table 7-5, these changes have been relatively recent. The pattern of the total number of intercourse partners noted by Kinsey in 1953 is almost identical to that revealed in the Tavris and Sadd research with adult females in 1974. However, in more recent national studies of the sexual experience of adolescent women 18 and 19 years of age, there is a clear movement away from only one partner (Zelnik and Kantner, 1977). This is a pattern which we should expect, given both the historical trends we have noted throughout this chapter as well as the factors that are related to adolescent sexual experience in contemporary America.

SUMMARY

In discussing contemporary patterns of sexuality among young adults and adolescents in the United States today, you are likely to note a variety of different conclusions. Some observers conclude that there have been radical changes over time, but concentrated especially in the period since the 1960s. Others argue that nothing has changed, that heterosexuality among youth is just as it was in the distant past. These contradictory conclusions center on the question of whether there has been a sexual revolution in American society in the last twenty years.

In point of fact, both conclusions are right and both are wrong. The answer is that in some ways there have been large changes, and in other ways there has not been any change. The answer to whether there has been a sexual revolution cannot be given. Any conclusion depends on what you consider "revolutionary" and what aspect of adolescent and young adult sexuality you are talking about.

It is also clear that patterns of behavior (including sexual behavior) seldom keep moving in the same direction. Going back to 1650 and coming forward to the present, it is clear that there has not been a straight progression in patterns of sexuality.

Perhaps the most accurate conclusions that can be drawn are those that have been emphasized throughout our discussion. Yes, there has been what you could call "liberalization" in both sexual attitudes and behavior among youth. This liberalization is largely a reflection of a verbal "sexual revolution" in which discussion of sexuality is more open than in the past. As such, there is less guilt associated with sexuality and more exposure to the idea of sexual activity. There has also been a decline in the level of affection deemed necessary for sexual activity to occur and greater agreement between males and females as to what this level of affection is. However, these general trends have taken place very much in the tradition of basic sexual attitudes and values which characterized American society in the beginning of the century. The nature of the interpersonal relationship is still of central importance and patterns of attitudes and behavior still follow traditional gender sexual learning, showing no radical change, simply alterations. In a very real sense, contemporary sexuality among youth is patterned by our cultural and historical heritage. Within this large pattern, however, there are individuals engaging in interaction with one another. Thus, within this cultural and historical framework are a number of individual and interaction processes which influence adolescent and young adult sexuality. So, in order to thoroughly understand heterosexuality and youth, we must consider both the social and cultural environments of the past and present as well as the individual within that environment.

STUDY GUIDE

TERMS TO KNOW

Sexual behavior sequence
Technical virgin
Sex guilt
Sensation seeking
Traditional double standard

Intersex convergence
Sexual and reproductive capacity
Reference group
Anticipatory socialization

SELF-TEST

Part I: True-False Statements

1. Religiosity influences the coital experience of white, but not black, adolescents.
2. In general, the greater the movement from parents to peers as the primary reference group in adolescence, the greater the likelihood of coital experience.
3. Nationally, the percentage of 19-year-old females with coital experience is approximately 90 percent.
4. In recent years, the proportion of white 15- to 19-year-old females with coital experience has increased more than has the proportion of black females of similar age and coital experience.
5. As males move from their first to their most recent coital experience, the amount of affection and commitment they have with their partner increases.
6. Females are more likely than males to regulate the extensiveness of their sexual activity with a person on the basis of the amount of affection they feel for that person.
7. The dominant standard for female coital behavior before marriage in the early twentieth century was coitus only when engaged to be married.
8. From the 1930s, 1940s, and 1950s until the mid- to late 1960s, the proportion of 16- and 17-year-old males with coital experience increased.
9. Today, males and females hold nearly identical attitudes about how much affection is necessary between two people before they should engage in intercourse.
10. For sexual behaviors other than coitus, the greatest changes among female college students from 1951–1952 to 1978 occurred in oral sex.
11. Sex guilt influences not only the extensiveness of sexual experience but the form of that experience as well.
12. The sex guilt of the male and that of the female are equally influential in the extensiveness of a couple's sexual activity with each other.
13. Physical attractiveness influences the extensiveness of males' more than females' sexual experience in adolescence.
14. Couples who abstain from engaging in intercourse with each other even though they have been dating for several months are characterized by both the male's and the female's desiring not to have that experience at that time.
15. Males and females are equally likely to have negative feelings following their first intercourse experience.

16. While the initial intercourse experience is often of concern to females, males do not tend to talk with their male friends about their own initial experience.

17. Contrary to what many people think, the average age at first intercourse experience has remained the same since Kinsey's time.

18. Both males and females are likely to have their first coital experience with someone who is older than themselves.

19. Females change very little in the amount of affection they had for their first intercourse partner compared with their most recent intercourse partner.

20. The most common frequency of intercourse among 15- to 19-year-old unmarried women who have ever engaged in intercourse is zero.

Part II: Multiple-Choice Questions
Select the best of the three alternatives.

1. In the interest-activity gap among college students, we find that *(a)* males would ideally like to have intercourse more frequently and females less frequently; *(b)* both males and females would ideally like to have intercourse more frequently; *(c)* both males and females would ideally like to have intercourse less frequently.

2. In patterns of intercourse between blacks and whites before marriage, we find that the dominant pattern is *(a)* a black male and a white female; *(b)* a white male and a black female; *(c)* both the above equally.

3. Generally, the first intercourse experience is *(a)* a positive experience for both males and females; *(b)* a positive experience for both males and females but more so for males; *(c)* a negative experience for females and a positive experience for males.

4. The age at first intercourse is *(a)* lower for black females than for white females but the same for black and white males; *(b)* essentially the same for both black and white males and females; *(c)* lower for both black males and females compared with white males and females, but *much* lower for black males compared with white males.

5. In the period from 1650 to the present, "sexual revolutions" in adolescent sexuality in terms of significant increases in the percentage of adolescent females having intercourse experience appear to have numbered at least *(a)* one, *(b)* three, *(c)* five.

6. The chapter discussed the changes between the 1930s and the 1960s in the proportion of males having coital experience before marriage. The major reason given for what took place was that *(a)* males changed their attitudes about when coitus was acceptable; *(b)* males held on to the traditional double standard while females came more and more to favor the idea that coitus was acceptable when affection was present; *(c)* females became more conservative and preferred to abstain from coitus.

7. Male college students in the 1940s commonly held a "good girl"–"bad girl" view of women. One of the outcomes of this view was that they had intercourse with *(a)* someone lower in social class than themselves; *(b)* a female they found acceptable as a possible marriage partner; (c) a female higher in social class than themselves.

8. The primary distinction between potential nonvirgins and nonvirgins is that potential nonvirgins *(a)* are much more religious *(b)* have not yet found the right person; *(c)* are older than nonvirgins.

9. The single most important factor influencing an adolescent to engage or not to engage in intercourse is *(a)* his or her parents' attitudes toward intercourse; *(b)* the degree to which he or she is involved in a meaningful relationship; *(c)* whether his or her peers have engaged in intercourse.

TOPICS FOR DISCUSSION

Now that you have been through the adolescent stage, place yourself in the role of a parent and describe how you would feel about your children's adolescent sexual activity. Be honest. What would seem all right for them to do? When, with whom, and at what age? Would you feel the same about a daughter and a son?

SUGGESTED READINGS

The material on heterosexuality and youth is in a rather sorry state for the student who wants to pursue the subject beyond this chapter. Books tend to be either very dated, very simple, or very biased. The really good reading is, unfortunately, found in professional journals. Before you choke, let me say that some of their articles are very much worth reading. If you are interested in a particular part of this chapter, the best thing to do is check out the references given in that discussion. Most of these are quite readable and more informative than space allows here. Each of these articles will contain references, which you can check out for focusing on a particular topic. If you really get into the thick of it, go to the *Social Sciences Citation Index* (SSCI) in your library and look in the *Subject Volume* under "Adolescent" or "Adolescence." Under that heading, look under the subheadings for sexual behavior, sexuality, intercourse, etc. This may be a very good way to become familiar with the SSCI because it is an excellent reference source when you have to write a term paper.

KEY TO SELF-TEST QUESTIONS

Part I: True-False Statements

1. T (Traditionally, black organized religion in the United States has had concerns other than personal sexual morality.)
2. T (This also depends, however, on the sexual standards held by the peers.)
3. F (What is this percentage?)
4. T (While, age for age, black females are more likely to have engaged in coitus, white females have increased more in the percentage with coital experience than have black females in recent years.)
5. T (Males come to resemble the female pattern more and more closely.)
6. T
7. F (Abstinence. This later became the standard.)
8. F (It decreased. What are the reasons for this decline?)
9. F (Males still require lower levels of affection and interpersonal involvement for coitus.)
10. T
11. T (Who is passive and active in various forms of sexual activity.)
12. F (The sex guilt of the male has the most influence because he is primarily the one who initiates sexual activity in the relationship.)
13. T (For the same reason as answer 12 above.)
14. F (In the majority of abstaining couples, the males would engage in intercourse if the female would agree.)
15. F (Females are more likely to have negative feelings.)

16. F (Yes they do.)
17. F (It has declined.)
18. T (But this appears to be more so for females than for males.)
19. T (But males change considerably. How do they change?)
20. T

Part II: Multiple-Choice Questions

1. *(a)* (This difference reflects male and female differences in sexual learning and indicates the subtle conflict and compromises made between males and females in the area of sexuality.)

2. *a* (Can you give the reasons why this is the case?)

3. *b* (Why is this so?)

4. *c* (All male and female differences in sexuality are greater among blacks than whites.)

5. *b*

6. *b* (This section, "The First Intercourse Experience," is a complex one; you should probably review it again.)

7. *a*

8. *b* (What is the primary difference between adamant virgins and potential nonvirgins? Can you mention other differences between potential nonvirgins and nonvirgins that we've discussed?)

9. *c* (Peers' sexual experience is influential because this factor allows for anticipatory —what? Why is it important? If you cannot answer these two questions, you should review this section again. This material is central to the chapter.)

Chapter 8
Traditional Marriage and Sexuality

Regardless of the sexual activities that occur, *the nature of sexuality is defined by the social context in which the behavior takes place.* Even though the same physical behaviors may be present, not all sex is the same. Marriage, and all the meanings which are attached to such a relationship, forms a special social context. As such, marital sexuality is a particular form of sexuality.

MARITAL SEXUALITY AS THE DOMINANT SEXUALITY

Despite frequent media discussions of divorce rates, marital failure, singlehood, and other alternatives to it, marriage in the United States is not a thing of the past. Marriage, in terms of the number of people, the amount of one's life spent, or purely what is most socially approved, is the dominant adult life pattern in American society, and it always has been. This means, of course, that marital sexuality is today the dominant pattern of sexuality in American society.

This dominance of marital sexuality is apparent even in sexual-social contexts which we might think do not resemble marriage. For ex-

ample, we shall see that marriagelike relationships are common among "gay" persons, and when we examine cohabitation, or "living together," on the part of single persons, we shall see that this form of relationship very closely resembles marriage.

TABLE 8-1
Males and females who are or have been married, by age.

Age	Males (%)	Females (%)
14–17	0.4	2.6
18–19	5.6	18.7
20–24	34.2	52.4
25–29	72.2	82.0
30–34	87.2	91.6
35–39	92.6	93.9
40–44	92.1	95.4
45–54	94.6	95.2
55–64	94.6	95.2
65–74	94.3	93.4
75+	95.2	94.3

Source: *Current Population Reports,* Series P-20, No. 338, May 1979. *Marital Status and Living Arrangements: March 1978,* table 1.

Numbers and Time

The vast majority of Americans do and will marry, many more than once (Table 8-1). Moreover, most people marry at a relatively young age (averaging 24.2 years for males and 21.8 years for females in 1978) and remain in a marital relationship for most of their lives. For most people, then, the great part of their sexual life and activity takes place in the context of marriage.[1]

Marital Sexuality Is Approved and Required

The dominance of marital sexuality is evident in more than raw numbers. Marriage is the only social context in which heterosexual activity in American society is totally approved. While attitudes have changed in the direction of greater acceptance of premarital sex, this approval is by no means universal and does not even begin to approach the degree of approval of marital sex. This approval is, of course, an historic outcome of traditional attitudes beginning with the ancient Hebrews (Chapter 1).

The mere fact of this widespread approval of marital sex makes it a very different sexual situation from nonmarital sex. One glaring aspect of this is that not only is marital sex approved, it is required. Sex in marriage is not an option, as it is in nonmarital relationships. For example, if one of the partners in a dating relationship desires sex and the other does not, the insistence of sexual activity by one person is considered to be at least bad manners. In marriage, however, sex is expected. The very lack of sexual activity in a marital relationship is seen by many as grounds for complaint, professional counseling, or even dissolution of the relationship.

[1]In recent years we have read discussion after discussion of how young men and women today are opting for singlehood and not getting married and perhaps never getting married. These discussions take place in the total absence of any data on what young people intend to do in this regard and in the presence of a mass of history which is very unlikely to reverse itself while you and I are alive. In 1980 a graduate student of mine, Lynn Dion, asked over 500 undergraduate males and females at Western Washington University *if* they planned to get married, and *if* things were ideal, would they get married. Over 98 percent said they planned to get married and ideally will marry.

The "Permanent" Nature of Marriage

While divorce statistics reveal that marriage in the United States is by no means a lifelong relationship, marriage is seen as properly having permanency. You are not supposed to flit in and out of a marital relationship with the same ease with which you would move in and out of a nonmarital relationship. The importance of this is that marital sexuality thus takes place in a social context in which the options for resolving sexual problems are limited. In a dating relationship, for example, an unsatisfactory sexual relationship can be resolved by dissolving the larger interpersonal relationship and seeking a more compatible partner. In marriage, this option is not nearly so acceptable. In fact, many people may believe that to dissolve a marriage for sexual reasons alone is a sign of "immaturity" or "too great" an emphasis on the physical aspects of the relationship.

ATTITUDES OF COLLEGE STUDENTS TOWARD MARRIAGE AND MARITAL SEXUALITY

The dominance of marriage as a form of adult heterosexual relationship is evident in the attitudes of college students toward marriage and marital sexuality. In 1980, Dion (1981) studied the attitudes of a large sample of male and female college students toward marriage and sexuality. While the suggestion that "things have really changed" is very popular, it is informative to note the extent to which the attitudes of the students in this study reflect quite traditional stances on the matter of marriage and marital sexuality (Table 8-2). It is worth noting that other samples of students from the same university have compared quite closely with college-student samples in other state universities across the country.

MARITAL SEXUALITY TODAY

Marital sexuality today serves a number of different needs and takes on a number of different meanings. Thus, it serves a variety of different purposes for different individuals.

TABLE 8-2
Attitudes of college students toward marriage and marital sexuality.

Statement	Percent Agreeing	
	Males	Females
A married person is usually seen by others to be more respectable than a single person.	63	45
If one is married, one does not have to feel totally on ones own.	83	83
Marriage provides a sense of security which cannot be present if you are not married.	61	41
Getting married is the natural thing to do.	48	52
In today's society, if one is not married by age 30, he or she is viewed as abnormal.	52	35
If I were 40 years old and single, I would feel guilty for not being married.	35	35
Traditional marriage no longer works in today's society.	19	16
One of the positive aspects of marriage is that it provides one with the opportunity to share one's life with another person of one's choice.	100	99
The choice to stay single receives little support in our society.	67	45
Regardless of the increasing divorce rates, I still believe that if I were to choose to get married, my marriage would be successful.	98	95
Married people are often too dependent upon each other.	65	75
A married person is usually seen by others to be more stable than a single person.	77	69
One of the positive features of marriage is that it can provide a woman with the feeling that she really does belong to a particular man.	81	63
One of the positive features of marriage is that it can provide a man with the feeling that a woman who is especially desirable really is his.	73	65
A person who is single has a greater chance of being sexually satisfied than a person who is married.	10	6
A person has a greater chance of being sexually satisfied if he or she is married rather than single.	67	54
One of the negative aspects of being single is that a sexual partner is not constantly available.	54	57
One of the positive aspects of being married is that a sexual partner is constantly available.	77	71

Source: Dion (1981), using a sample of 192 male and 314 female college students at Western Washington University.

Marital Sexuality as Sexual Experience

In the not-too-distant past, marriage was, for many men and women, the location of the first coital experience (see Chapter 7). Therefore it was in marriage that individuals experienced their greatest amount of learning by doing. Additionally, their sexual learning was limited to one person, and it was with this person that all sexual exploration, experimentation, and personal definitions of sexual preferences were established.

As sexual experience before marriage has

become more and more common, this learning function of marriage has changed. Most individuals today enter marriage with at least some sexual experience in the form of intercourse, and the marital partners have most likely had sexual experience with both each other and other persons.

We have no solid scientific data indicating the effects, if any, of these changes. We can, however, make some intelligent guesses. Quite obviously, marriage is (for the "average" person) no longer where one has one's first coital (or perhaps many another) sexual experience. At the very least, the traditional sexual trauma of the honeymoon night is much less common. Perhaps more important, the person has already experienced a considerable amount of sexual learning by sexual doing and has thus probably established some basic sexual behavior patterns and preferences. These have more than likely been communicated to one's spouse through sex prior to marriage. It is also most likely that young persons today, on the average, enter marriage with much more sexual knowledge, understanding, and calmness than was customary fifty years ago. While all these charges may have no meaning for the long-term sexual career of two people in a marriage, they have considerable impact on what their sexual interaction is like in the first few months of the relationship. The very least of these changes is that women experience more sexual satisfaction and enjoyment in the first year of marriage today than they did when Kinsey collected his data.

Marriage still remains, however, the social context in which much experimentation and sexual exploration take place. For example, Dion (1981) found that 78 percent of the males and 71 percent of the females agreed with the statement: "A person has a greater chance of developing [his or her] sexuality through a stable, long-term relationship." Even though most males and females now enter marriage with coital experience, this sexual experience tends to be neither prolonged nor diverse. Thus, marriage still serves an important role in one's sexual learning as an adult.

Also, as sexual changes take place in so-ciety, marriage is that social context in which most individuals may experiment with new forms of sexual expression and activity. This is particularly important for adults. As youth move into sexual activity in adolescence and early adulthood, they may not even notice the social changes which are occurring because they have nothing to compare the prevailing patterns with. Many older adults, however, have seen such changes develop within the span of their relationship together and have "tested" them in the context of marriage.

Sex for Procreation

One of the major differences between marital sexuality and sexual activity in other social contexts is that only in marriage is coitus resulting in reproduction approved. Traditionally, we have inherited from the ancient Hebrews the value that the supposed purpose of marital sexuality is procreation. It is also clear, however, that marital sex, for at least the last hundred years, has involved much more than procreation.

An important issue here is intention as opposed to outcome. Prior to the availability of effective contraceptives, procreation was a likely outcome of marital sex. But it was not necessarily the intention of every marital sexual episode. Since, in the absence of the widespread use of effective contraceptives, marital sexual activity contained a high risk factor, it was seen in light of its possibility of pregnancy. For the wife who did not desire another pregnancy, the options were either a low level of sexual activity or abortion (we shall discuss this in detail in Chapter 12). Thus, even when the intention of marital coitus was not procreation, this was an overriding possibility. Today, with the availability of effective contraceptives, it is much easier for married partners to both distinguish between procreation and pleasure in marital sex and not always to engage in sexual activity under the shadow of possible conception. As we shall see, this has been a much ignored aspect of marital sexuality in the past.

Sex as Recreation

One of the primary purposes of marital sexual activity today is recreation—pure and simple fun. Mancini and Orthner (1978) obtained a probability sample of 233 middle-class married couples. They gave each person a list of 96 possible leisure activities and asked them to list, in order, the 5 they enjoyed the most. Sex and affection were rated in the top five recreational favorites by 45 percent of the husbands and 26 percent of the wives.

Sex as Interpersonal and Emotional Exchange

For reasons we have previously discussed, sexuality in marriage is also a vital part of the entire emotional and interpersonal relationship between the partners. The traditional connection between love and sex, combined with the romantic love concept of marriage (remember that this was not an aspect of marriage among the Puritans), means that sexual interaction becomes a part of the larger emotional and interpersonal interaction in marriage.

As we have seen, sexual enjoyment and satisfaction are strongly tied to the overall quality of the interpersonal relationship (Chapter 6). In marriage, this is intensified, given the daily intensity of interaction with one's spouse and the relatively long-term nature of the relationship (the average marriage lasts much longer than the average dating relationship). It is no surprise that sexual activity in a marriage declines as discord increases and that marital activity ceases some time before the relationship results in divorce (Edwards and Booth, 1976a).

Sex and Personal Needs

Any sexual activity, including marital sexuality, can serve purely personal as well as interpersonal needs. Although often overlooked, sex in marriage can help to confirm masculinity or femininity and one's worth as a person; it can provide evidence of love, of control, of power, of status, or of any number of other purely personal individual needs that may appear to have little to do with sexual interaction itself.

THE FREQUENCY OF MARITAL SEXUAL ACTIVITY

While the nature of any form of sexuality should never be examined merely in terms of frequency, this factor is one sensitive indicator of the overall nature of marital sexuality.

Initiating Sexual Activity

Marital sex is seldom initiated by the same kinds of romantic preludes (acceptable seduction?) that accompany nonmarital sexual relationships. With the exception of special "dating-like" occasions such as anniversaries, the very manner in which sex in long-term relationships (such as marriage) is suggested, negotiated, and initiated is different from that in dating relationships.

The initiation of sexual activity in any type of relationship (including commercial sex) is a process of exchanging cues that communicate sexual interests. Few sexual encounters, even in a seasoned marriage, begin with blatant statements of desire and a nude leap from the dining room table with the shout of "Tally-Ho!"

In any relationship of some duration, partners come to share the sexual meaning of cues that lead to the initiation of sex without anything explicitly sexual being said. One of the important functions of such cues, it appears, is that if one person is interested and the other is not, a strong verbal or behavioral commitment need not be made or the obvious lack of consensus dealt with. In the following conversation, the communication is clear, but the risk of disagreement is minimal.

> "I think I will go take a shower before I go to bed" (meaning "I want to be clean while you and I engage in sexual interaction").
>
> "OK, I think I will go read in bed while you take a shower" (meaning "That sounds nice, I will be waiting for you.").

or

> "I think I will stay up and read a while, I really want to finish this chapter" (meaning "I am not really in the mood").

Not all marital sexual activity is, of course, initiated in the same way. As shown in Table 8-3, direct verbal communication of one's passion is common, but nonverbal communication is much more frequent.

Who initiates? The person who initiates marital sexual activity reflects traditional definitions of males as initiators and females as gatekeepers. Traditionally, females have been expected to be sexually enticing, available, and accepting and males to be sexual decision makers. Available evidence suggests that this idea is very much with us yet in that it is still the male who most often initiates (Bell, 1974; Tavris and Sadd, 1977). Among couples who do not adhere to strict traditional views of male and female behavior, there is more equality in who initiates sexual activity (Allgeier, 1981).

The frequency with which the wife initiates sexual activity may reflect more than adherence to traditional definitions of male and female sexual conduct. A wife who initiates most or all of the time may do so out of necessity rather than liberation. Married women who report that they are the prime movers also report that their husbands are somewhat less than sexual enthusiasts (Tavris and Sadd, 1977). On the other hand, a wife may not adhere at all to traditional images of male and female sexuality but never initiate simply because she is not interested in any more sexual activity. This is clear when we note that women who never initiate marital sex are also the most dissatisfied with their marital sexual life (Tavris and Sadd, 1977).

Satisfaction with Marital Sexual Frequency

Since the first research on sexual frequency, it has been a consistent finding that married men said sex did not occur often enough and married women said it occurred too often (Burgess and Wallin, 1953; Clark and Wallin, 1965; Levinger, 1966). Times appear to have changed. One change is that married women are beginning to complain not about too much, but too little, of a good thing. While the mar-

TABLE 8-3
Women's responses to "How do you let your partner know you are interested in sex?"

Responses	Percent
Caress or cuddle him	54
Touch his genitals	38
Tell him	32
Flirt	14
He just knows	18
Other	3

Source: Tavris and Sadd (1977:161–162).

ried women of yesteryear were in strong agreement that their husbands' avid sexual interest was a bit much, the married women of today tend to complain about a lack of sexual interest on the part of hubby. In Tavris and Sadd's study, for example, 58 percent of the married women said that the frequency of marital sex was "about right"; only 4 percent said it was too frequent, and fully 38 percent said it was not frequent enough. Swieczkowski and Walker (1978) found that the only complaint a sample of middle-class married women had about intercourse positions in marital sex was that intercourse itself did not occur often enough.

Marital Coital Frequency

Do you think the frequency of intercourse in marriage has increased or decreased since 1920? I bet most of you said "increased." In part this is true, but the situation is much more complex than this.

Kinsey (1953) noted that the average frequency of marital coitus had actually declined over the time covered in his research (Table 8-4). He suggested (1953:359) that this decline was due to increased consideration on the husband's part. Since married women of that era typically complained that marital coitus was too frequent, Kinsey reasoned that men were becoming more reasonable and taking their wives' feelings into account. It is also possible, however, that the increasing equality

TABLE 8-4
Average weekly frequency of marital intercourse by women's decade of birth

Decade of Birth	Average Weekly Frequency of Intercourse by Age of Women	
	21 to 25	26 to 30
Before 1900	2.8	2.5
1900–1909	2.5	2.2
1910–1919	2.5	2.1
1920–1929	2.4	2.0

Source: Kinsey et al. (1953:397, table 7).

of women in society over that period resulted in their having greater voice in both social and sexual matters. It is quite likely that they simply said "no" more often. This is even more of a possibility when we note that research through the 1960s revealed that wives still complained that their husbands wanted sex more frequently than they themselves did (Levinger, 1966). If the men had quit being so persistent, these responses would not have prevailed over time.

Between approximately the 1930s and 1960s, it is impossible to trace the frequency of marital sex year by year since there are no data of this kind. Two writers in the field of human sexuality (Hunt, 1974; Reiss, 1976) have argued that what developed over this

period was a near-historic increase in the frequency of marital intercourse. Such a conclusion appears to be more a reflection of what we think happened than a report of what actually took place. As shown in Table 8-5, the decline in marital coital frequency apparently continued until some time between 1949 and 1965. Almost certainly, 1965 is not the year in which the decrease stopped, but it is the only year for which we have reasonable data. Regardless of the exact timing, it seems that the frequency of marital coitus was still lower in 1965 than in the 1930s and 1940s.

Between 1965 and 1970, marital sex (in terms of frequency) got a second wind. As evident in Figure 8-1, there was a marked increase (14 percent) in the frequency of inter-

TABLE 8-5
Marital intercourse by average mean frequency per month, in 1938–1949 and 1965.

Kinsey, 1938–1949*		Westoff, 1965†	
Age Group	Mean Frequency per Month	Age Group	Mean Frequency per Month
16–20	14.8	Under 20	10.7
21–25	12.0	20–24	8.4
26–30	10.4	25–29	7.4
31–35	9.6	30–34	5.9
36–40	8.4	36–39	6.8
41–45	7.2	40–44	5.1

*Mean frequencies per month were calculated from the per-week data reported by Kinsey (1953:394).
†**Source:** Westoff (1974:137, table 2).

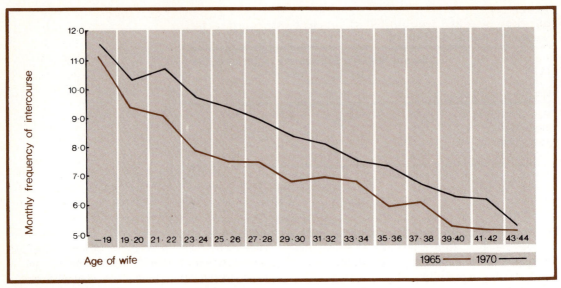

Figure 8-1 The average monthly frequency of intercourse in marriage in 1965 and 1970, when the wives are different ages. (Source: Westoff, 1974:137. Figure 2.)

course among married women age 15 to 45. In 1965, the average frequency was 6.8 times a month, and in 1970, it was 8.2 (Westoff, 1974). This increase continued through at least 1974 (we have no more recent national data), when another nationwide study reported an average monthly frequency of 9.2 times.

Why this upswing in the frequency of marital intercourse? One might reason that it was due to the youth of the sexual revolution of the 1960s entering the marriage scene. While it is true that the increases over this period were greater among younger age groups, this is not the total answer because the frequency increased among all age groups from 15 through 45 (note what we said earlier about social changes in sexual behavior being experienced in marriage). These increases in the frequency of marital coitus are probably due to a variety of factors, some of which are suggested by Westoff (1974).

Contraception Highly effective contraceptive methods increased in use by married couples over this period (1965–1970). The greater use of dependable contraception may have reduced anxiety over unwanted pregnan-

cy among married women, and therefore may have resulted in higher frequencies of intercourse.

Abortion Over this period, legal abortion also increased in availability (although not legalized in the entire United States until the Supreme Court decision of 1973; see Chapter 12). This greater availability may have also contributed somewhat to a reduction in anxiety over unwanted pregnancy since, even if contraception failed or was not effectively used, an unwanted pregnancy could be legally terminated (although with some effort).

Social changes The increased openness and discussion of sexual matters may reasonably be seen as having had some effect on marital sexuality. If one considers the amount of space that women's magazines have devoted to frank articles on sexuality in recent years, the increased openness of discussion in the popular media becomes apparent. Whether magazines and television talk shows met a need or created one is difficult to establish. At least they provided reinforcement and encouragement for greater personal attention to the sexual.

Female role changes Perhaps most important, many changes were made in definitions of the female role in general and female sexuality in particular during the 1960s and 1970s. As Westoff (1974:138) states:

> There has been a developing emphasis on the woman's right to personal fulfillment and her independence of the man. Part of this growing ideology is that the woman's traditional passive sexual role may be giving way to more assertive sexual behavior.

It is likely, however, that changes in women's roles have involved more than their simply becoming more sexually assertive. A central tenet of the women's movement is that sex is OK for women. The traditional female-role definition entailed a male-constructed definition of women as asexual. In this view, only the wanton woman has a keen interest in sex and her interests are for the purposes of men (prostitution or "easy lays"). Female sexuality in full, independent expression was thus regarded with suspicion, if not contempt. The attack made on the double standard has included an attack on the sexual double standard. As such, sex is fine for women and a female does not have to question her moral fiber to desire, seek, and enjoy it. Perhaps a major effect of the women's movement has thus been not only to make women more sexually assertive but also to influence their view of what "proper" sexuality is all about.

Westoff does in fact present some evidence in support of the idea that less traditional women are more sexually active in marriage. In the 1970 study, respondents' attitudes toward the female role were measured. Those married women with the most traditional view of the female role had a mean coital frequency of seven times per month, while those women with the least traditional view had an average frequency of nine times per month. This pattern was consistent across all degrees of traditional-nontraditional views of the female role.

Factors Related to Frequency of Marital Sex

The problem with averages is just that; they are averages. As such, a single number conceals the rich variation among individuals. A central question in understanding marital sexual behavior patterns in general and the frequency of marital sexuality in particular is that of the factors related to differences in sexual frequency in marriage.

Enjoyment of sex The more people like to do something, the more frequently they will do it. Well, almost. It is true that the greater the enjoyment of marital sex, the greater the frequency (Hunt, 1974; Tavris and Sadd, 1977). However, at least among lower social class marriages, the enjoyment of each partner does not play an equal role in influencing sexual frequency. It is the husband's enjoyment that has the most influence (Rainwater, 1965; Rubin, 1976). The reason is that the social changes over time in views of female sexuality and equality have largely been the business of the middle class. While some changes have been accepted at all levels, lower social class segments of the population remain much more strongly tied to traditional views of male and female roles. A large part of this traditional view supports male dominance in decision making, including decisions about sexual frequency.

Religiosity Since traditional Christian religious beliefs have been a conservative force in the sexual scene, it would be expected that religious individuals would have a lower frequency of sexual activity in marriage than nonreligious ones. Kinsey's research (1948; 1953) supported this assumption, but only in the case of males. Less devout married males were 20 to 30 percent higher in their frequency of marital coitus than strongly religious men. For married women, religiosity was not important. The reason for this male-female difference is most likely to be found in the traditional initiator role of the male. If it is the husband who initiates, his religiosity is important, but not that of his wife. Over time, this situation has changed. Studies in the early 1970s rather consistently found that the wife's religiosity

was related to the frequency of marital sexual activity (Hunt, 1974; Bell, 1974).

There have been even more important changes over time in the relationship between religiosity and marital sexual frequency. Contemporary religion no longer says, "Do it if you must, but don't dare enjoy it." Rather, contemporary religion advocates sexuality as a positive gift of God which can and should be enjoyed *in marriage* as a form of interpersonal sharing and recreation as well as a means to procreation. As Tavris and Sadd (1977:101) point out, the 1970s saw radical alterations of official Protestant statements on sexuality. In 1972, the Methodist church adopted the following statement which resembles many others that have appeared in recent years:

> We recognize that sexuality is a good gift of God and we believe persons may be fully human only when that gift is acknowledged and affirmed by themselves, the church and society. (Cited in Tavris and Sadd, 1977:101)

The Catholic Theological Society of America likewise now defines a moral sexual act as one which is "self-liberating, other-enriching, honest, faithful, socially responsible, life-serving and joyous" (Tavris and Sadd, 1977:101).

These changes in official religious stances on sexuality reflect the increasing emphasis of contemporary religion on individual freedom and responsibility—specifically, freedom and responsibility to establish one's own sexual-moral standards within the confines of broad guidelines.

This emphasis has not been particularly a result of sexual interests within religion. Rather, it has been an outgrowth of two characteristics of contemporary religion in America: secularization and voluntarism. Contemporary religion is voluntaristic. It is up to the individual to decide whether to be religiously involved and active. Church attendance and religious dedication are not dictated by the government or by a dominant religious order under penalty of the stockade.

Churches today exist in a marketplace in which a wide range of interesting activities and involvements compete for the individual's time and energy. Given that marital sex is one of the five favorite recreational activities of many Americans (as noted earlier), any church that condemns sexuality is not going to do well in this competition. Second, in response to this competition, contemporary religion is secular. It reflects, out of necessity, what is happening in the larger society, whether this be the issue of civil rights in the 1960s or sexuality in the 1970s. As we have discussed, one of the important recent changes in American society is that people are talking about sex and seeing sexual standards change. If religious organizations stood on the sidelines and beat the drum of abstinence, they would simply be left in the wake of it all.

These two factors, voluntarism and secularization, have thus brought about rather marked changes in organized religion's stance on sexuality. These changes are perhaps most clearly reflected in the Tavris and Sadd finding that religiosity is no longer associated with the frequency of marital coitus for women.

Age It is not the greatest scientific breakthrough to note that the frequency of sexual activity in marriage declines with age (Table 8-6). What surprises most people is that the influence of age begins to appear relatively early in life. For example, Edwards and Booth (1976a) found that among a wide range of social and marital characteristics, the age of the husband had the strongest relationship to the frequency of marital intercourse. What makes this fact important is that the sample consisted of people all under the age of 45.

It has been common to assume that the reason marital coital frequency declines with the increasing age of the husband is physiological. That is, as the male ages, he is assumed to undergo physiological changes that lower his sexual interest, ability, and activity. As we shall see when we discuss sex and aging a few pages further on, this is far too simple an explanation. Age itself is not *the* important variable. Rather, age is related to a number of other variables which may have some strong influence on marital coital frequency, and thus it appears to be important by itself.

Recent research even indicates that the age of the wife may be more strongly related to the frequency of marital intercourse than the

TABLE 8-6
Monthly frequency of marital intercourse reported by women in 1970.

Age*	Average Monthly Frequency
Under 20	11.0
20–24	10.1
25–29	9.0
30–34	8.0
35–39	6.8
40–44	5.9

*Only women up to age 44 were included since the emphasis was on contraceptive behavior.
Source: Westoff (1974:137, table 2).

age of the husband. Udry and Morris (1978) examined data from three comparable national surveys taken in 1965, 1970, and 1974. In each year, they analyzed the effect of the husband's and wife's ages on the frequency of marital sex. In 1965, the husband's age and the wife's age had an equal effect on sexual frequency. In 1970, the wife's age had slightly more effect than did the husband's, and in 1974, her age had much more influence on sexual frequency. This change is consistent with the increased influence of women in marital sexual decision making over this period.

The interpersonal relationship
Apart from age, the most important factor influencing the frequency of marital sexual activity is the nature of the marital relationship. As noted in Chapter 5, the enjoyment of sexual activity cannot be separated from satisfaction with the overall relationship in which that sexual interaction takes place. In one of the clearest studies so far, Edwards and Booth (1976a) found that social and background characteristics (other than age) had little or no significant relationship to marital sexual frequency. The factors which were found important were contextual: the nature of the marital relationship itself. It is not surprising, then, that happily married couples have intercourse six times more frequently than they argue, while unhappily married couples argue three times more often than they engage in intercourse (Edwards and Edwards, 1977).

Length of relationship   The frequency of marital intercourse declines with the length of a marital relationship (Kinsey, 1953). Over a long period, the decrease may seem to be a function of age. However, the frequency of coitus declines even in the first year of marriage, but only in marriages where neither partner has any premarital coital experience (James, 1981).

The Regularity of Marital Sexual Activity

One of the common images of marital sexual activity is that it becomes routine (every Tuesday night). This is viewed as undesirable and dissatisfying since a romantic view of sex is that it should be spontaneous and uninhibited and not seem planned.

The routinization of marital sex can, and often does, happen. For example, marital intercourse is more likely on weekends than during the week (Kunin and Ames, 1981). In any relationship where the people become very familiar with one another's preferences and responses, the day-to-day activities tend to become stabilized and patterned. This is commonly seen as less than highly desirable in a sexual relationship. In fact, Tavris and Sadd (1977) found that one of the most common dislikes married women registered about sex was that it was boring and routine. On the other hand, many people find this routine pleasing. It is stable and dependable and provides feelings of security. Sex in singlehood can be a little like mountain climbing. Each new step may be exciting because of the unknown and unexpected. For some individuals, this is a rich experience, while for others it is scary. On the other hand, walking the same path every day may be rewarding precisely for its lack of surprises or boring for the same reason.

The regularity of marital sexual activity also has another side—that of timing. Many people have an image of marriage that involves sex as regular as the finest timepiece, slowed only by marital discord and illness and stopped only by age. However, the temporary cessation of marital sexual activity is quite common. In married couples under the age of 45, approximately one-third report that they have ceased all sexual activity for some period in their marriage. The average duration of this period is two months. The most common reason for the temporary stoppage is marital discord, with illness or surgery as the second most common reason. Geographic separation, the implementation of certain birth control methods, menstruation, and psychiatric impairment are reasons cited infrequently. Exceeding all these minor reasons, however, is a decreased interest in sex, a reason cited with equal frequency by both men and women (Edwards and Booth, 1976a).

SEXUAL COMMUNICATION IN MARRIAGE

Sex is something we do, but not something we tend to talk about. Very interestingly, much less communication focuses on sex in a marriage than we would expect. In the Tavris and Sadd research, 21 percent of the women said they "always" discussed sex with their husband. Another 26 percent said they "often" did so, and while 8 percent said they never discussed sex, fully 45 percent said they discussed this topic with their spouse "occasionally." This is a low level of communication about a topic which research suggests is so central to a marital relationship.

The relative lack of open communication about sex in marriage is clearly revealed in a recent study by Schafer and Braito (1979). They found no relationship between a person's own view of him- or herself as a sexual partner and the spouse's evaluation of that person as a sexual partner. This was true for both men and women. Obviously, such discrepancies between one's own view and the spouse's view of oneself as a sexual partner can be maintained only in the comparative absence of talking about sexuality in a relationship.

As in most types of interpersonal relationships, communication leads to clarification, understanding, satisfaction, and overall, a more positive relationship. It is difficult to say whether communication about sex in a marriage leads to satisfaction or the other way around. Most likely, the two play back and forth on one another in such a way that good relationships are characterized by good communication, and good communication about sex enhances the quality of the relationship. Tavris and Sadd (1977) noted that women who frequently discussed sex with their spouses rated their marital sex as better, their marriages as more positive, and their overall marital happiness as higher than women who rarely discussed sex with their husbands. Women who do not talk about sex with their spouses evidently do not remain silent because of a state of marital perfection. A lack of open communication in marriage is simply one aspect of a generally troubled relationship that includes a troubled sexual relationship as well (Edwards and Booth, 1976a). Shaver and Freedman (1976) found that 24 percent of the males and 26 percent of the females in a nationwide sample said that a lack of communication about sexual preferences was a problem in their life.

THE IMPORTANCE OF SEX FOR THE MARITAL RELATIONSHIP

As we discussed in detail in Chapter 6, there is a clear relationship between sexual satisfaction in marriage and overall satisfaction with the marital relationship. While the chicken-or-egg question of which comes first has not yet been answered in research, Albrecht's study (1979) gives us a clue as to the importance of sex in marriage. In a sample of individuals who had been divorced and were remarried, "sexual problems" was the fifth most frequently mentioned reason why the first marriage had failed. The most frequently mentioned reason was extramarital sexual activity on the spouse's part. Shaver and Freedman (1976) found that "sex life" was one of the more important factors contributing to the general life satisfaction of married (and single) males and females. Rhyne (1981) recently found that sexual satisfaction is an important factor, if not the most important factor, in relation to overall marital satisfaction.

SEXUALITY AND AGING

In order to clearly understand any aspect of sexuality, we must consider the nature of the relationship (if any) in which it takes place. With the exception of one-person masturbation, sexual interaction occurs between two or more people who exist in some type of relationship to each other. It has commonly been assumed that physiological sexual ability all but disappears with increasing age. Thus, it has been common to talk about sex and aging as though the process of physiological aging itself were the only important fact in understanding sexual patterns among older persons. As you have probably guessed, this rather simpleminded view is just that—too simple.

Images of Sex and Aging
America is a youth-oriented society. It is also a society where sex is associated with youthful physical attractiveness. Many people thus find it difficult to put the concepts of "old" and "sex" together (Griffitt, 1980; LaTorre and Kear, 1977). As we shall see, there is also a clear double standard in the images of sex and aging. We are much more likely to see older males as sexual beings than we are to see older females as such.

Sexual Activity and Aging
We have already noted that the decreasing frequency of sexual activity in marriage is strongly related to the increasing age of the male, and that after age 35, males tend to experience somewhat of a decline in sexual interest.

A series of studies indicates, however, that stereotypical notions that older persons do not engage in intercourse are far from accurate (Pfeiffer et al., 1970; Pfeiffer and Davis, 1974; Pfeiffer et al., 1974). In this research with men age 56 to 71, only 12 percent had stopped having coitus. This was the case for 7 percent of the 56- to 60-year-olds, 20 percent of those 61 to 65, and 24 percent of those 66 to 71. The *frequency* of intercourse also declined with increasing age among these males, but not in a manner consistent with the stereotype. For example, 48 percent of the males age 66 to 71 were still engaging in intercourse on an average of once a month, and 26 percent engaged in marital coitus once a week.

The Interest-Activity Gap

One of the important characteristics of aging for men is that sexual activity apparently declines more rapidly than does sexual interest. This results in an increasingly wider gap between interest and activity with increasing age (Pfeiffer et al., 1974). We must keep in mind, however, that we also saw an interest-activity gap among college-age males (Chapter 7).

Factors Related to Sexual Activity with Aging

It has been common to assume that sexual activity and interest decline as a function of normal aging processes. As a result of this assumption, we know very little about the number and kinds of factors that account for declining sexual activity with increasing age.

Physiological factors   A number of normal changes which take place in the body with increasing age may contribute to declining sexual activity. Tactile sensitivity drops, making one less likely to respond to touch stimulation. Hormone levels fall with age, but there is no solid evidence that this accounts for declining sexual interest and activity (Voigt and Schmidt, 1977). Advancing age is also associated with a greater likelihood to develop or to have had a chronic illness. Some chronic illnesses affect the body in such a way as to affect sexual arousal and response as well as activity. Other chronic illnesses appear to be associated with declines in sexual activity and interest, but for no apparent physiological reason. (We shall discuss sexuality and chronic illnesses in detail in Chapter 17.) The fact remains, however, that no study that has examined sexuality and aging has taken into account the possible effects of chronic illness.

Normal aging is also associated with certain changes in parts of the nervous system and the vascular system that may affect arousal and response. Nervous-system response and sensitivity tend to decline with age and the elasticity of veins and arteries lessens. These changes can affect the speed and efficiency with which messages are sent through the nervous system and the process of vasocongestion. The latter commonly results in such changes as longer time to erection, smaller erection, more time to regain an erection, less vaginal lubrication, and less swelling of the orgasmic platform. The ability of the pelvic muscles to develop a high level of tension with sexual arousal may also decline, affecting the level of sexual arousal which results from myotonia.

Gender differences   When we examine the factors which are related to sexual activity in older persons, we find a very important difference between males and females. For males, the variable most strongly related to sexual activity is age. Among females, the most important variable is marital status.

The reason for this difference between males and females is that *marital status for women means the presence or absence of a socially approved sexual partner.* For women, if there is a socially approved sexual partner (called a husband), sexual activity is likely to continue. If the woman does not have a socially approved sexual partner, her sexual activity is most likely to cease. For males, the existence of a socially approved sexual partner (wife) is much less important for the continuation of sexual activity (Persson, 1980; Pfeiffer et al., 1974).

This difference is a reflection of the traditional double standard. It is no accident, you see, that we have the term "dirty old man," but without a counterpart term for women. The nature of this sexual double standard applied to older persons is clearly described by Laws and Schwartz (1977:70–71):

The older woman, more than any other, is placed in double jeopardy by the sexual script. Even if she has faithfully followed the cultural script to middle age, she has not earned any credit as a sexual person.

She can be a respectable married lady and a mother (or widow), or even a grandmother, but she is not permitted to be a sexual person. Her years of sexual experience do not, at this stage, define her sexual status. In the normal script she is considered postsexual, both because she is beyond childbearing and because no man desires her. This is bleak enough, but if she flouts the sexual script she may be exposed to ridicule or abuse. . . . While sexuality of older people is in general denied or tabooed, this is more true with respect to women than men. The double standard still persists: the older man may pursue younger women, and although his *sexual* attractiveness may not be dazzling, it is understood that other attributes—power, money, experience—can make him a viable trader in the sexual marketplace. The older woman, however, is expected to be permanently out of circulation.

These social definitions of appropriate sexuality for older men and women are especially important when we note that a married woman in the United States today can expect her husband to die approximately thirteen years before she does. Consequently, she will spend a considerable portion of her life as a nonsexually active person if she follows the traditional sexual script.

Most widows are aware of unmet sexual needs after the death of their husbands (Barrett, 1981). The socialization of female sexuality in American society tends, especially for older women, to make it very difficult for most widows to come in contact with a socially approved sexual partner. Since women learn to strongly connect sex and interpersonal relationships, and a person who has been married for forty years may find it difficult to see herself with anyone else, most widows are unlikely to seek out another socially approved sexual partner. Clayton and Bornstein (1976) studied a sample of widows with an average age of 60. They found that thirteen months after the death of the husband only 7 percent had dated and only 2 percent had engaged in inter-

course. Gebhard (1970) found that only about half as many widows had engaged in intercourse as had divorced women and that of those widows who had, the frequency was low. As Gebhard points out, in-laws and married friends of the widow are comforting but also stifling in terms of her maintaining the same patterns of behavior as when her husband was alive. A lack of sexual activity is further supported by the romantic ideal of "being loyal to the memory" of her husband (Gebhard, 1970). For males, the widower status has much less impact on sexual activity (Persson, 1980).

The male partner Even before her husband's death, the older woman is faced with a lack of sexual opportunity not of her own choosing. Research repeatedly finds that when sexual activity in marriage ceases in the later years, the cessation is due to the husband, not the wife. Pfeiffer et al. (1970) found that of the elderly married men and women who no longer engaged in intercourse, 86 percent of the women and only 42 percent of the men attributed the cessation of sex to their spouse. In another study (Pfeiffer et al., 1974), 6 percent of the men said they no longer engaged in coitus because of their wife, while 40 percent said the cessation was due to their own lack of ability.

One piece of research (Pfeiffer and Davis, 1974) has noted that there is quite a rapid decline in sexual interest on the part of older married women. The researchers argue that this is a protective mechanism. It is adaptive for a woman to lose interest in sex as she ages since the odds are that she will be without a socially approved sexual partner for a considerable period of her life. If her husband does live as long as she does, it is highly probable that their sexual activity level will drastically decline or stop altogether through no fault of hers.

Changing perception of one's partner Griffitt (1980) has suggested several factors which are important in explaining the declining sexual interest and activity of males in their later years. Many of these should be familiar, since we discussed them in Chapter 5 when we reviewed sexual learning. Our first sexual interests and arousal experiences take place in the context of youth. Sex and youthful concepts of beauty are strongly connected. As we have noted, males view sexuality more physically than do females, while females have a more interpersonal view of sexuality than do males. Griffitt suggests that as a married couple ages, the male loses sexual interest in his wife before she loses sexual interest in him. He does so because, according to youthful criteria, she becomes less physically attractive and this change is important for the male. He may remain interpersonally attractive to her (because of their long-term established relationship), however, and this is more important for her sexual interest.

Simply stated, marital partners become weaker sexual stimuli and less sexually attractive to each other as they age, particularly in the eyes of the male. Second, as we have discussed in Chapter 5, heightened sexual arousal tends to do two things with regard to the perception of a possible sexual partner. It intensifies the perception of physical and sexual attractiveness and it intensifies the perception of sexual and physical unattractiveness. Since men see aging as resulting in less physical and sexual attractiveness in women, aversion to one's aging spouse as a sexual stimulus may increase with age.

Definition of sex   Another important factor probably related to declining male sexual interest with aging is that sex is thought of as being coitus. An erect penis is necessary

for coitus. In the absence of an erect penis, or at least a rapidly erect penis, some men do not see themselves as capable of sexual interaction, which is commonly seen as physical activity involving an erect penis.

Attitudes and behavior Sexual attitude and behavior characteristics are also related to the continuation of sexual activity among the elderly. Research repeatedly reveals that for males, the amount of sexual activity in the younger years is strongly related to the amount of sexual activity in the older years. Thus, those males who begin intercourse activity relatively early and who have intercourse frequently when they are younger and in the early years of their marriage are more likely to have more frequent intercourse in their later years (Persson, 1980; Martin, 1977; Pfeiffer et al., 1974). Among older women, a generally positive attitude toward sex, a positive attitude toward sex for older persons, and a history of positive sexual experiences are related to more frequent sexual activity in the older years (Persson, 1980). For females, sexual activity in the older years is clearly related to positive sexual learning. For males, sexual activity in the older years is most likely the result of positive sexual learning as reflected in early patterns of sexual behavior. It is also possible, however, that early sexual activity on the part of males merely reflects some physiological characteristic that carries over into the older years and results in greater sexual interest and activity when one is both young and old. This physiological process is, however, yet to be demonstrated by research.

THE OTHER SIDE OF MARITAL SEXUALITY

So far, we have discussed marital sexuality as it most frequently occurs; a consensual and pleasurable activity between two people. Not all marital sexuality has this quality. Marital rape, while only recently being recognized (see Chapter 13 for a detailed discussion of rape) is very much a reality (Gelles, 1977; Groth, 1979).

Gelles (1977) correctly argues that the person most likely to force a married woman into sexual activity is her husband. The hidden nature of marital rape is partially due to the view that a wife is considered the property of her husband, and thus marital rape is not possible since a husband is supposed to have total sexual access to his wife. Closely related to this view is the confusion many marital rape victims feel about what actually has happened and their reluctance to tell anyone about their experience. Often, marital rape is seen by the victim as battering rather than sexual assault, since the two frequently go together (Groth, 1979).

Marital rape may range from forced intercourse to forcing the woman to engage in sexual acts to which she objects. Such activities range from oral or anal activity to bondage, sadism, or engaging in sex with other males for the husband's amusement and arousal.

Groth (1979) has noted that often the sexual activity itself is not the motivation for the rape. Rather, the wife's refusal to engage in the activity is seen by the husband in the larger context of his personality and the marital relationship.

Sex May Equal Power
The husband who feels that he is supposed to rule over his wife may extend this attitude to sex. When she does not answer to his demands—sexual or otherwise—he attempts to establish control by sexual domination in the form of rape.

Sex May Be Equated with Love and Affection
If a male has not learned to express love and affection in nonsexual ways, he may see the denial of sex as the denial of love. For the insecure male, this fear of loss of love can be frightening. Sex, even if brutally forced, provides a defense against this possible rejection in that is supplies him with "proof" that his wife really does love him.

Sex May Be Equated with Virility

Some men feel that *getting* sex from their wife, regardless of the method, is a sure sign of virility. Rape becomes a male's means of affirming one's manhood even in light of the wife's rejection of him as a person and a sexual partner.

Sex May Equal Punishment

In the course of an argument, the man may use forced sex as a means to degrade his wife. By raping her, he "teaches her a lesson" and at the same time expresses his anger and contempt for her. As we shall see in Chapter 13, this is a common component of many kinds of rape. The mere fact of a marital relationship does not mean that such activities cannot take place.

Sex May Be a Cure-All

Some males view sex as an indicator that everything is all right. Sex is seen as the solution for any and all interpersonal problems. Following an argument, the man may seek to reestablish the relationship by engaging in sexual activity even though the woman may resist. The nature of the sexual relationship is inconsequential to him. The only thing that is important is that sex takes place, and if that happens, it must mean that everything is OK.

Special Problems of the Marital Rape Victim

Marital rape presents special problems for the rape victim. Apart from the refusal of the public and the legal system to openly admit that marital rape is not only possible but very real, the victim is placed in a problematic position. She is living with her assailant. He not only has continual access to her, but he can continually observe her. Furthermore, the law and society grant him the right of that access and observation. Even more important, the person she would normally turn to for care, concern, and support is her assailant. She is also very likely to be confused about what is happening to her.

On the one hand, she may love her husband dearly, and on the other hand, she may hate him for what he does to her. Given the traditional, and still dominant, economic status of women, the wife may also find herself with few options other than that of tolerating her victimization (Groth, 1979).

EXTRAMARITAL SEXUALITY

Sexual activity with someone other than one's spouse while married *and* without the spouse's consent is an important aspect of marital sexuality. The reason it is important is that it takes place in the context of a marital relationship. It is *extra*marital because it is outside of the marital relationship while still being *in* a marital relationship. If one has intercourse with someone and neither person is married, the meaning of the activity is very different from its meaning when one or both of the persons having intercourse is married to someone else. In Chapter 9, we shall discuss sexual activity with other than one's spouse when both spouses agree that this is something they will do. This is not extramarital sexuality because it is *part* of the marital relationship, not something *outside* of it.

Parenthetically, it is interesting to note here that sex outside the marital relationship is not thought of as extramarital sex unless it is heterosexual sexuality. Homosexual activities are rarely, if ever, thought of as extramarital. This is most likely because the view of homosexuality is more negative than the view of extramarital sex, and the most negative view of the behavior is the name given to it. The example of Billie Jean King clearly illustrates this. When her extramarital episode became known to the media and the public, discussion focused much more on the fact that her extramarital partner was a woman than on the fact that her partner was extramarital.

Attitudes toward Extramarital Sex

Marriage has traditionally been a sacred institution in American society. Further, marriage has traditionally been seen as the only proper context for sexual activity. These two facts combined make it hardly surprising that extramarital sex finds strong disapproval. As shown in Table 8-7, this disapproval has shown no signs of diminishing in recent years.

The strong disapproval of extramarital sex is not at all unexpected, since such disapproval is a central part of the history of sexuality in Western culture and elsewhere.

At the very heart of the first civilization in the Tigris-Euphrates valley of Mesopotamia some two thousand years before Christ, adultery was strongly prohibited. A pattern which prevails throughout history is evident even here. Adultery was a trespass against a husband's property. Moreover, the double standard was strong. A husband could engage in extramarital sex but the wife could be executed for the behavior. Similar codes were present among the ancient Incas: a husband could be executed if he killed his wife—unless he found her in the act of extramarital sex. Among the Maya of Mexico, the woman, but not the man, could be executed for extramarital sex. Among the early Egyptians, male extramarital sex was permitted, but female extramarital sex was cause for divorce and the woman could be punished by being burned at the stake. Among the ancient Hebrews, Jewish law specifically stated that prohibitions against adultery ap-plied only to the wife and the offense was punishable by death. Among the early Christians, a husband had to divorce his wife if she engaged in adultery.

In more recent times, this tradition continued. On May 1, 1650, the English Parliament, under Oliver Cromwell, made adultery punishable by death, a tradition clearly evident among the Puritans of the American colonies. For example, the Puritans considered adultery one of the strongest violations against the will of God —the seventh commandment makes this explicit. The Jamestown laws of 1607 permitted the death penalty for extramarital sex, as was also the case in New England. The Puritans, however, had more than a little trouble enforcing such stringent laws. Like most death penalties for sexual offenses, execution for adultery slowly diminished. In Puritan society, it was every citizen's duty and obligation to enforce the religious-moral code, including that against extramarital sex. Thus, it was commonplace for there to be eyewitnesses, many of whom pursued their task with some enthusiasm. In 1773, Mary Angle and Abigail Galloway, walking in Boston, saw their neighbor, Adam Air, "in the Act of Copulation" with Pamela Brichford.

". . . on Seeing this We went into the House, & stood behind them as they lay

TABLE 8-7
Attitudes toward extramarital sex in the United States.
These are the responses of national samples of individuals 18 years old and older to the question: "What is your opinion about a married person having sexual relations with someone other than the marriage partner?"

Attitude about Extramarital Sex	Year			
	1973 (%)	1974 (%)	1977 (%)	1980 (%)
	(on percent)			
It is always wrong.	70	74	73	70
It is almost always wrong.	15	12	14	16
It is wrong only sometimes.	12	12	10	10
It is never wrong.	4	3	3	4

Source: Davis (1980).

out on the Floor, and after observing them some time, the said Abigail Galloway spoke, & asked him if he was not Ashamed to act so when he had a wife at home, he got up & answered, one Woman was as good to him as another he then put up his nakedness before our faces, & went away, and she on his getting off her, jumped up & ran away into another part of the House." (Quoted by Cott, 1978:22)

The apparent prevalence of extramarital sex is revealed in the petitions for divorce in Massachusetts between 1692 and 1786. In two-thirds of the 229 petitions, adultery was charged (Cott, 1978).

This long tradition of legal prohibition of extramarital sex is still with us. Thirty-eight states have laws against extramarital sex with penalties (almost never invoked) ranging from a maximum of five years in prison or a $1000 fine (Maine) to a $10 fine (Maryland). Twelve states have no laws against extramarital sex (Arkansas, California, Kentucky, Louisiana, Montana, New Mexico, North Carolina, Ohio, Oregon, Pennsylvania, Tennessee, Texas).

Types of Extramarital Sex

Given Americans' physical view of sexuality, the first thing we generally think about when we think of extramarital sex is intercourse. Extramarital sexual activity, as with all sexuality, can take a number of forms, ranging from sexual glances, comments, jokes, and flirtation to physical sexual activity. Gagnon and Greenblat (1978) describe four types of extramarital sexual activity.

Flirtation Undoubtedly the most common form of extramarital sexual activity is flirtation in the form of sexual communication through gestures and words. Flirtation, even though not involving physical sexual contact, is likely to bring the ire of one's spouse since it *implies* sexual interest outside of marriage. Since marriage is defined as sexual monogamy (a single partner, who is one's spouse), flirtation suggests sexual nonmonogamy.

Flirtation as an extramarital sexual activity can serve a number of purposes for the participants. It can be a relatively harmless fantasy activity (unless, of course, it causes marital friction) in which one engages in sexual interaction with another without engaging in physi-

BOX 8-1
EXTRAMARITAL SEX IN CULTURES AROUND THE WORLD

Broude and Green examined patterns of extramarital sex in 116 cultures around the world. The percentage of these cultures having different patterns of approval and disapproval of extramarital sex reveals the diversity from culture to culture.

Pattern	Percent
Extramarital sex is allowed for both husband and wife.	11
Extramarital sex is allowed for the husband and condemned for the wife.	43
Extramarital sex is condemned for both sexes but the wife's activities are more severely punished.	22
Extramarital sex is condemned for both sexes and punishment is equally severe for both.	23

Source: Broude and Green (1976:415–416).

cal sexual activity. It may also serve one's self-esteem needs by providing one with reinforcement that he or she is still sexually appealing to others. The central feature of flirtation is that it involves few risks characteristic of other types of extramarital sex.

Although not discussed by Gagnon and Greenblat (1978) and never examined in the research, extramarital sexuality can involve physical contacts other than intercourse. For example, Kinsey (Gebhard and Johnson, 1979) found that 9 percent of the white college-educated males and 7 percent of the white college-educated females had engaged in extramarital petting but never coitus. It is unfortunate that more recent researchers have ignored these types of extramarital sexual activities and have examined only extramarital coitus.

One-time affairs A central feature of a stable relationship with one person—as in marriage—is that free time and space tend to be limited. One's day-to-day activities and the time they take are usually well-known to the other person and structured around their coordinated activities. Extramarital sex involving intercourse requires both time and space. Thus, extramarital one-time "flings" usually take place when the married person has some "open space" in her or his life (Gagnon and Greenblat, 1978:440). Such events as out-of-town business meetings or conventions thus become prime times for the one-time, purely sexual extramarital relationship with low emotional involvement.

Casual affairs Casual affairs have longer duration than one-time flings. They involve a sexual relationship that has some interpersonal and emotional component which lasts for varying lengths of time. Such affairs are clandestine and the attempt to keep the activity secret can become a major aspect of the relationship. This secrecy and the tactical maneuvers required to keep it that way tend to add to the excitement. The very fact that one is engaging in a risky and nonapproved behavior adds a spicy bit of adventure for many people. The other side of the casual affair is that the guilt may be very high. Integrating an ex-

tramarital affair into one's life routine requires secrecy, clandestine meetings, and often lying to one's spouse. The guilt and pressure involved in an extramarital affair can become intense over time and affect both the extramarital relationship and the marriage.

Another aspect of the casual affair is that keeping it casual may be problematic. Any sexual relationship which is maintained over time tends to bring with it greater and greater interpersonal closeness and commitment between the partners. This condition may be even more intense if both persons are married. Being married means they must work together in pulling off their secret life. Discussions of how their respective spouses foul up their meetings can frequently lead to the extramarital partners coming closer together in the sense that it is "them" against "us." If one of the extramarital partners is unmarried, increasing involvement may be even more difficult to stop. When both are married, they may both have a commitment to the marital relationship. If one person is not married, that person may feel cheated and left out, particularly on special occasions when being close is a nice feeling. Many casual affairs thus become less casual and reach some crisis point in which the affair or the marriage must be broken.

The intense affair Intense affairs are of longer duration than casual affairs and take on a fundamentally different quality. They tend to be based on an established agreement between the extramarital partners as to the extent of interpersonal involvement and the future of the relationship. Such relationships may continue for years and generally fail to have a crisis point characterisitic of many casual affairs. Intense affairs commonly involve much more than sex. They are often intense interpersonal involvements in which the partners are truly in love with each other and in which they share many activities other than the sexual. Such relationships frequently develop because of a spouse's long-term illness or long absence, or a disability. In all such cases, the marital relationship remains intact but another secret relationship exists at the same time.

The Extent of Extramarital Sex

Extramarital sex is neither new nor rare in American society. Kinsey (1948; 1953) found that 26 percent of the married women had engaged in extramarital sex by age 45. By 35 years of age, 23 percent had done so, and by 25 years of age, 9 percent had had an affair. Given the traditional double standard, males were more than twice as likely as females to have such experience.

Kinsey (1953) noted gradual increases over time in the percentage of women engaging in extramarital sex. For example, only 4 percent of those women born before 1900 had done so, compared with 12 percent of those born between 1920 and 1929. Evidently, this trend has continued until the present. As shown in Table 8-8, a significantly greater proportion of women have extramarital sexual experience than noted by Kinsey.

The greatest increases over time appear to have been among younger women. While Kinsey found that 9 percent of the women studied had extramarital sexual experience by age 25, fully 20 percent of the women under 25 in Tavris and Sadd's research had such experience.[2] Similar increases have taken place among males, but males are still more likely to engage in such experience (Hunt, 1974). While one may question the Tavris and Sadd and Hunt studies on the basis of their samples, their figures on extramarital sexual involvement compare very closely with all other studies done in recent years.

Who Gets Involved and Why?

The central question in understanding extramarital sexuality is not how many people have such experience, but why. A note of caution must be offered here. We generally ask why when something is seen as "abnormal" or "deviant." For example, no one ever asks why

TABLE 8-8

Women who have ever engaged in extramarital intercourse.

Age	Percent
Under 25	20
25–29	29
30–34	30
35–39	39
40+	40

Source: Tavris and Sadd (1977).

people engage in marital sex because that is "normal" behavior.

In asking the question of why, we are not attaching any evaluation. The purpose of asking the reason for extramarital sex (I am just as interested in why people engage in marital sex) is to understand one more aspect of human sexual behavior. There is no value judgment involved and all the scientific research in the world will not provide the answer to whether extramarital sex is good or bad, right or wrong, harmful or valuable. The answers to these questions are value judgments. As such, they involve individual personal decisions.

Religiosity   Not surprisingly, given traditional religious prohibitions on sex outside marriage, religious individuals are less likely to engage in extramarital affairs (Kinsey, 1953; Tavris and Sadd, 1977).

Age   Age by itself is a variable which is related to many other variables, such as decade of birth (and thus the social-sexual values in which one was raised), length of marriage, interest in sex, etc. In general, however, younger people are more likely to engage in extramarital sex (Edwards and Booth, 1976b; Glass and Wright, 1977). This appears to be especially true for males.

The marital relationship   Age and religiosity are general social characteristics. Overall, social and background characteristics are less strongly related to extramarital sexual involvement than personal and relationship

[2]Kinsey (Gebhard and Johnson, 1979) found that 19 percent of the males and 11 percent of the females reported engaging in extramarital coitus only when their spouse or they themselves were in military service. It is again curious that these are the only data available on this form of extramarital sexual activity.

BOX 8-2
EXTENT OF EXTRAMARITAL SEX IN FIFTY-SIX CULTURES AROUND THE WORLD

Broude and Green, in their examination of sexual patterns, noted the extent of extramarital sexual activity in fifty-six different cultures. The percentage of cultures having different patterns of extensiveness reveals that, while male activity is more common, extramarital sex is not unusual for either men or women.

Frequency of Extramarital Sex	Males (%)	Females (%)
Universal or almost universal. Almost all (men/women) engage in extramarital sex.	13	13
Not uncommon for (men/women) to engage in extramarital sex.	56	45
Occasional; (men/women) sometimes engage in extramarital sex but doing so is not common.	11	16
Uncommon; (men/women) rarely or never engage in extramarital sex.	20	27

Source: Broude and Green (1976:416).

BOX 8-3
HANKY PANKY IN A DALLAS HONKY TONK

Dallas—(UPI)—A short man dressed in the fashion of the urban cowboy entered The Palms Danceland and for a good five minutes stood quietly, allowing his eyes to adjust from the early afternoon sunshine to the near-darkness of the club.

The darkness is by design. Had the cowboy's wife been sitting, dancing or hugging with another man, she would have had the chance to spot him before he spotted her, slip out the back way and head home before husband could catch her and make a scene.

He looked it over, and then eased to the bar and paid $1.05 for a can of beer, ready for another afternoon in one of the most unique spots in the country.

The Palms is a honky tonk for hanky panky, a day-time heaven for bored housewives, shift workers, off-duty policemen, truant businessmen ("Wiley—call the office," reads an inscription on the restroom wall) and anyone else looking for a good time between the hours of 9 A.M. and 3 P.M.

When co-owner Don Taylor arrives at The Palms shortly before 9 A.M. five days a week, several women are waiting already in the parking lot. By noon, the club will be filled with men and women abiding by the unwritten house rules that men buy the ladies' beer (it's free for them otherwise) and no one ever asks for a last name.

"We have all types in here," Taylor says. "Housewives, telephone operators, truck drivers, people playing hooky from their jobs. There's one Baptist preacher that comes in. I won't point him out to you, though. We've got three women that walk and hitchhike about three miles to get here.

"There's another woman who has a husband who goes fishing every Sunday. While he's gone, she jumps in the kitchen and whips up supper for the rest of the week. That way supper'll be ready every night."

Taylor says his customers have one thing in common: they're looking for a good time to break the monotony. Some do it by having a few beers, some by dancing and innocent conversation, others through adultery.

In fact adultery—or the fantasy of adultery—is The Palms strongest selling point. To accommodate, there are two day-care centers nearby (one is operated by Taylor's ex-wife) that offer discounts to Palms' customers and a motel with two-hour rates.

"What happens when they leave here is their business," Taylor says. "But for every marriage that breaks up here, I bet 10 are saved.

"Like with a husband, he'll stop at a bar on the way home from work and may not come in 'til closing time. This place kinda evens it up. As a result it makes the marriage better. It's like therapy.

"We got a lot of them that, if they couldn't come here, their marriages'd be blown.

"But don't think everybody out there's running around. Some just come to have a good time or because they like to dance or because they work at night."

Sylvia, an attractive brunette who drank only coffee on her first visit to The Palms a few weeks ago, maintains that you can go there without cheating on your mind. It's an alternative to soap operas and housework.

"I'm just here to have a good time," she says. "My husband doesn't know I'm here but he wouldn't do anything if he did. We're very liberal about it. He works at a bar during the day and he doesn't like to dance and we don't go out that much so it gives me something to do. Besides, I'd rather be home at night."

Places like The Palms formerly were known as "pressure cookers" in honor of the kitchen device that allowed the evening meal to cook while the lady of the house was out being a lady of the day.

But like everything else, the game of fooling around has been changed by attitude and technology. The pressure cooker club has been replaced by the microwave club.

Source: William C. Trott, *Seattle Post-Intelligencer*, March 27, 1979.

factors in the person's life (Edwards and Booth, 1976b). It is a repeated finding that individuals with low levels of marital satisfaction are more likely to engage in extramarital affairs (c.f., Edwards and Booth, 1976b; Glass and Wright, 1977). Such aspects of the marital relationship as feeling there is not enough love or threatening to leave home are rather strongly associated with extramarital sexual involvement (Edwards and Booth, 1976b).

One of the major components of any relationship is the extent to which the partners see the relationship as equitable—that is, when they see themselves as getting as much out of the relationship as they are putting in relative to what the other person is contributing and receiving. There is an extensive body of research on what people do when they feel there is equity or inequity in a relationship. In an inequitable marital relationship, one of the things a person does is have an extramarital affair. Both males and females who feel their marriage is inequitable for them are more likely to have an affair. They also do so sooner in the marriage and do so with more different partners than individuals who see the marriage as equitable (Walster et al., 1978b).

Length of marriage The timing of extramarital involvement relative to dissatisfaction with the marriage differs for males and females. For males, low marital satisfaction is associated with having an affair in the early and middle years of marriage. For females, it is associated with having an affair in the middle and late years of marriage (Glass and Wright, 1977). The reason for this difference is not clear. Perhaps waning male sexual interest in middle age is a factor. Perhaps males find it more difficult to leave behind the sexual freedom of singlehood, while females make more of a commitment to the marriage in the early years than do males. It is comparatively clear, however, that an unsatisfactory marriage encourages males more than females to become involved in extramarital sex, suggesting that males are more willing to "bail out" of a marriage sexually than are females (Edwards and Booth, 1976b).

Other personal factors Marital satisfaction is, however, not the only personal factor that is related to the chance of extramarital involvement. Bell et al. (1975) found that only 55 percent of those women who rated their marriage as poor had engaged in extramarital sex. An unsatisfactory relationship does not automatically mean that an affair will develop. On the other hand, 20 percent of those women who rated their marriage as good or very good had participated in an extramarital sexual af-

fair. A good marriage is not perfect assurance that extramarital sex will not take place.

Some research (for example, Bell et al., 1975) has found that in addition to marital satisfaction, the degree of sexual liberalism and general liberalism in lifestyle are important in extramarital sexual involvement on the part of women. For example, of those women in the Bell et al. (1975) research who had a low evaluation of their marriage and were liberal both sexually and in their general lifestyle, 81 percent had engaged in extramarital sexual activity. Thus, beyond the "push" factor of marital dissatisfaction, the "pull" factors of personal values are important. Regardless of one's level of marital satisfaction, one must first see extramarital sex as a possibility. Such a view is a function of certain personal values, among which are sexual and lifestyle liberalism.

One of the clearest examples that a happy and satisfactory marriage does not automatically eliminate the possibility of extramarital sex for women is what Tavris and Sadd (1977) call "the 6 percent." They found that approximately 6 percent of all married women (20 percent of those who had engaged in extramarital sex) rated their marriages as good, their marital sex as good, were totally satisfied with the frequency of marital sex, were able to discuss their sexual feelings with their spouse, took an active sexual role, enjoyed all types of sexual activity, and *had had an intense extramarital affair.* These are clearly women who were sexually and socially liberal. Their affairs were love, not just sex, affairs and had been going on for a relatively long time. These women did not flee to extramarital sex to escape a miserable marital situation. They simply had the capacity and the inclination to love two men at the same time. This is not a new phenomenon. Kinsey (1953) found that about 10 percent of the women in his study who engaged in extramarital sex had had such intense love affairs.

Extramarital Sexual Partners
Most extramarital sexual involvements are not intense affairs. Rather, they tend to be of a casual nature. Moreover, approximately half

the women who engage in extramarital sex have done so with more than one person. Tavris and Sadd (1977) found that while 50 percent of the women had only one partner, 40 percent had between two and five and 10 percent had six or more.

Extramarital sexual activity also tends not to be a one-time affair, but involves several encounters. Tavris and Sadd, reflecting the findings of other studies, found that only 18 percent of the women had sex only once with a partner. They noted that 33 percent participated two to five times with a partner and 29 percent more than six times. The casual affair is clearly the dominant pattern in extramarital sexual activity.

Prostitutes

One form of extramarital sexual relationship which receives almost no attention as extramarital sex is that with prostitutes. Clearly, this form of extramarital activity has involved, and still does involve, a significant proportion of married males. Again, the only data on this subject appear to be Kinsey's (Gebhard and Johnson, 1979). Kinsey found that 8 percent of the white college-educated males and 12 percent of the white non–college-educated males had engaged in coitus with a prostitute at least once while married. Most of these were one-time incidents.

The Sexual Activity

While a significant component of the attraction to extramarital sex may be the greener grass, this is not what actually happens for the majority of people. Extramarital sexual activities tend to be less varied than one's sexual activities with one's spouse, orgasm is less likely to be experienced in extramarital sex, and both men and women find extramarital sex less pleasurable than their marital sexual activity (Tavris and Sadd, 1977; Hunt, 1974).

The Outcomes of Extramarital Sex

The effects of extramarital sex on the participants and the marital relationship are, quite frankly, unknown. Some research has attempted to estimate the impact of extramarital sex on marriage. Kinsey (1948; 1953) asked divorced men and women whose marriages had included extramarital sex (either by the respondent or the spouse) if this activity had had anything to do with the divorce. Interestingly, 61 percent of both males and females said that *their own* extramarital affair had no effect at all on the marrige. However, 75 percent of the women and 83 percent of the men said that *their spouse's* extramarital affair had had a significant effect (note the double standard). In more recent research, Albrecht (1979) found that in a sample of remarried men and women, extramarital sex was the number one reason given for the breakup of the previous marriage.

These data, however, are to be interpreted with great caution. First, extramarital sex has historically been a valid reason for marital dissolution and thus may be commonly cited although other factors are the real "causes." Since, in most extramarital affairs, the marriage is in less than prime condition to begin with, it is highly doubtful that the affair was *the* reason for the divorce. Last, asking divorced individuals whether extramarital sex was a factor in their divorce is approaching the question backward. The real question is not how many divorces are due to extramarital sex, but how many extramarital affairs damage the marriage to the point of divorce. We simply do not know.

STUDY GUIDE

SELF-TEST

Part I: True-False Statements

1. The available evidence indicates that marriage is declining in popularity among young people in the United States.
2. In a 1980 study of college students, Dion found that the majority of respondents did not agree with the idea that traditional marriage no longer works in today's society.
3. Regardless of changes over time in the amount of sexual experience people have before marriage, marriage is still that relationship in which much experimentation and sexual learning take place.
4. Married women today most commonly complain that marital sex is somewhat too frequent, a pattern we have seen in marriage since the 1950s.
5. Kinsey found that the frequency of marital coitus declined over the period he studied.
6. From approximately the 1930s to the 1960s, the frequency of marital coitus increased.
7. Between 1965 and 1970 the frequency of marital coitus increased.
8. Between 1965 and 1970 the frequency of marital coitus increased for all age groups between 19 and 44.
9. The frequency of intercourse does not differ for happy and unhappy marriages.
10. The notion that marital coitus is more likely on weekends is a myth.
11. Approximately one-third of all married couples under the age of 45 have ceased all sexual activity for some period in their marriage.
12. All available research evidence indicates that open communication about sex is the most common sexual communication pattern.
13. By age 66 to 71, approximately 48 percent of American males are engaging in coitus once a month.
14. For males, early and frequent sexual activity is associated with more frequent sexual activity as one grows older.
15. Between 1973 and 1980, extramarital sex became more approved in American society.
16. Cross-culturally, the most frequent pattern of extramarital sex is that not uncommonly, men and women engage in extramarital sex.
17. The "6 percent" refers to the proportion of males and females who have engaged in extramarital sex today.

Part II: Multiple Choice Questions
Select the best of the three alternatives.

1. Today, marital sexual activity is most often initiated by *(a)* the man; *(b)* the women; *(c)* both equally.
2. Women who never initiate sexual activity in marriage are *(a)* the most satisfied with their marital sex; *(b)* the least satisfied with their marital sex; *(c)* the most likely not to adhere to traditional definitions of male and female behavior.
3. Between 1965 and 1970, the frequency of marital coitus *(a)* decreased for all but the youngest age groups; *(b)* increased for all age groups but increased the most for the youngest age groups; *(c)* increased for the youngest age groups but did not change for the older age groups.
4. In lower social class marriages, the frequency of marital coitus is related to *(a)* the sexual enjoyment of the wife and husband equally; *(b)* the sexual enjoyment of the wife but not the husband; *(c)* the husband's sexual enjoyment more than to the sexual enjoyment of the wife.

5. The interest-activity gap refers to the fact that among males who are older, *(a)* sexual interest declines more rapidly than does sexual activity; *(b)* sexual activity and interest decline more rapidly than does the wife's sexual interest; *(c)* sexual activity declines more rapidly than does sexual interest.

6. One of the gender differences in sexuality and aging is that *(a)* for males, sexual activity in the older years is related to the presence of a spouse, while for females, this is less important, *(b)* for females, sexual activity in the older years is related to the presence of a spouse, while for males, this is less important; *(c)* for males, physiological changes are of the greatest importance for sexual activity in the older years, while for females, physiology is of little importance.

7. The majority of adult Americans feel that extramarital sex is *(a)* always wrong; *(b)* almost always wrong; *(c)* wrong only sometimes.

8. On the basis of the data we reviewed, the percentage of married women age 40 and over in the United States who have engaged in extramarital sex is approximately *(a)* 10; *(b)* 40; *(c)* 70 percent.

9. For males and females, low marital satisfaction is associated with having an extramarital relationship in *(a)* the early and middle years of marriage for males and the middle and later years of marrige for females; *(b)* the later years of marriage for males and the early years of marriage for females; *(c)* the early and middle years of marriage for both males and females.

10. Among women who have engaged in extramarital sex, most tend to *(a)* have done so with more than six different partners; *(b)* have done so with fewer than six different partners; *(c)* have experienced more varied sexual activities in the extramarital relationship than in their marriage.

TOPICS FOR DISCUSSION

1. When a male and a female have been going together for a year and one of them has a sexual relationship with another person, is the situation the same as an extramarital relationship? Why? Why not? How? How does it affect the relationship?

2. We have discussed the concept of sexual scripts and, in this chapter, quoted an excerpt from Laws and Schwartz (1977) on the sexual script for older men and women. As a class or as a small group within your class, list what you think *should* be the sexual script for a male and a female of your grandparents' (or, if you are not in your twenties, of your parents') age. See how much you agree and disagree on various aspects of the sexual script and what these aspects are. Discuss why you agree and disagree on these aspects.

SUGGESTED READINGS

This is an unfortunate situation, but good additional readings are rare if at all in existence. This scarcity applies to all three of the major topics discussed in this chapter: marital sexuality, sexuality and aging, and extramarital sexuality. This rather dismal state of affairs reflects the lack of intellectual curiosity in these dimensions of sexuality. There are, however, many good short discussions of various topics covered in this chapter. These have been cited throughout the chapter. In our discussion, we have been able only to summarize most of these works, so if you have an interest in a particular topic, you can go to the Bibliography section in the back of this text and find those references cited for that topic you are interested in examining.

One comment is in order. Since Americans have been vitally concerned with marital relationships in the past few years, there has been a steady stream of books and popular articles telling you how to have a better marriage and how to improve your marital sexual life. You will rather consistently find that each piece is one person's opinion about what you should do and not discussion based on scientific facts. As with most cure-alls, the reading of such discussions may be good entertainment but can hardly be expected to be a sure-fire life guide.

KEY TO SELF-TEST QUESTIONS

Part I: True-False Statements

1. F (While this is often a favorite topic of those writers who tend to feel that American society is undergoing rapid social change, it is simply not true.)
2. T (Go back to Table 8-1. Marriage and marital sexuality were rated quite highly by the college students in this sample.)
3. T (The vast majority of Americans develop their sexual preferences and styles in a long-term relationship such as marriage.)
4. F (This was the pattern we saw in the first half of the twentieth-century, but more recently, married women are complaining that marital sex is not frequent enough.)
5. T (Can you explain the possible reasons for this decline?)
6. F (This is a common assumption, but the data indicate otherwise.)
7. T (During this period there was an increase. We discussed four suggested reasons for this change. What were they?)
8. T (But it increased more for the younger age groups than for the older age grous.)
9. F (How important is the nature of the relationship itself?)
10. F (Daily life for many people can simply leave them "not in the mood" at the end of the day. Weekends are a time of recreation.)
11. T (For how long, on the average?)
12. F (How is this revealed in terms of one's own and the spouse's rating of oneself as a sexual partner?)
13. T (This pattern belies the stereotype that older persons are not sexually active. For fun, go back to Chapter 7 and compare these data for older males with the data for college students.)
14. T (You cannot wear it out. Rather, if you don't use it, you apparently lose it. This saying, however, involves the assumption that early-life sexual activity is what "causes" later-life sexual activity, and this is not an established fact. There is only a relationship, but no evidence that one causes the other.)
15. F (Take a look at Table 8-7. In this period there was no change in attitudes toward extramarital sex.)
16. T (See Boxes 8-2 and 8-1.)
17. F (What does 6 percent refer to?)

Part II: Multiple-Choice Questions

1. *a* (This is because of gender roles and sexual learning.)
2. *b*
3. *b* (See Figure 8-1.)
4. *c* (More traditional gender-role definitions and behaviors are more likely in lower socioeconomic groups.)
5. *c* (Is this the only age group that experiences an interest-activity gap?)
6. *b* (Think about how this difference is related to male and female sexual learning and different sexual scripts for older males and females.)
7. *a*
8. *b* (This is not a trivia question. You should be able to tell someone the approximate percentage.)
9. *a*
10. *b* (Most have done so with fewer than six partners, and fewer times with partners with whom less pleasurable and less varied sexual activities were experienced.)

JOE MARRON/
PATRICIA DAVIS

A

Chapter 9
Heterosexual Alternatives to Traditional Marriage

As we have repeatedly seen, monogamous marriage has traditionally been the form of interpersonal relationship in which adult heterosexual sexual activity was supposed to take place in American society. Traditionally, one was expected to abstain from heterosexual activity (specifically coitus) before marriage, to get married at approximately a certain age, and thereafter to conduct all one's heterosexual sexual activity within the confines of that marital relationship and only with one's spouse.

There has never been total adherence to this sexual script in American society. Extramarital sexual activity has, as we have seen, been present and relatively common for some time. Additionally, alternatives to traditional monogamous marriage have been discussed and practiced by a few people since at least the 1800s. For example, "free love" and sexual freedom movements as well as communal marriages were widely known in the 1800s in the United States (see Murstein, 1974).

The current major alternative styles of adult heterosexual sexual relationships may be seen as taking two basic forms: alternatives *to* traditional marriage, and alternative styles of sexual relationships *within* marriage. Alternatives to marriage include singlehood and cohabitation. Alternatives within marriage principally include multilateral marriage, open marriage, and "swinging."

SINGLEHOOD

Consistent with the dominance of marriage as an adult lifestyle in American society, the term "single" has traditionally been applied to only those persons who reach the age at which most people marry but themselves do not do so. Those individuals who were once married and are now divorced and not remarried have typically been called divorced, not single. (They are often referred to as divorced even when they have remarried, suggesting the importance of the label.)

This distinction between never-married adults as "single" and once or more married adults as "divorced" is somewhat misleading. The distinction suggests two different types of people. In terms of patterns of sexual behavior and being "coupled in marriage" versus "not coupled in marriage," the distinction between the divorced and the never-married is of little use. What is more important than prior marital status is the person's age, the existence of children, past sexual and relationship experience, orientation toward marriage, and future life and relationship goals.

For these reasons we shall use the term *single* to refer to an unmarried person who is at or past the age at which most individuals do get married in American society. Within the category *single*, we may distinguish two major avenues of reaching this status for young to middle-age adults. One is never having married (never-marrieds) and the second is having been married and presently being divorced. A third possible avenue is of course, the death of a spouse, but this "single" population is small compared with the never-marrieds and the divorced and is most common among persons past middle age.

TABLE 9-1
Males and females who were never-married singles in 1978.

Age Group	Males (%)	Females (%)
14–17	99.6	97.4
18–19	94.4	81.3
20–24	65.8	47.6
25–29	27.8	18.0
30–34	12.8	8.4
35–39	7.4	6.1
40–44	7.9	4.6
45–54	6.8	4.4
55–64	5.4	4.8
65–74	5.7	6.6
75+	4.8	5.7

Source: U.S. Bureau of the Census, *Current Population Reports*, Series P-20, No. 338, table 1.

Never-Marrieds

Traditionally, never-married individuals in American society have been viewed with suspicion and even contempt (with the exception of those who are seen as being occupationally or religiously exempt from such labeling). In a society which has traditionally placed a strong emphasis on the family as the foundation of society, individuals who did not form a family unit through marriage were assigned a low status. In colonial times, men who did not marry were assessed a bachelor tax, and certain restrictions were placed on never-married women (such as not being allowed to keep certain pets). Traditional terms such as "spinster," "old maid," and "bachelor" not only suggest that the never-married person is different from the "normal" person (there are no special words for married persons), but they carry less than desirable meanings as well.[1]

Even though these images of the never-married have changed over time, there are still strong stereotypes of never-married persons. Parlee and Werner (1978) found, for example, that college students thought that persons who choose to live alone are lonelier, more withdrawn, less socially active, less physically attractive, more independent, quieter, busier, and more serious than people who live in a couple relationship. Single dwellers were also seen as less socially active, having fewer friends, being less adjusted socially, and being more organized and efficient than coupled persons. The "lonely loser" stereotype of single persons is evidently very much a part of American thinking.

Trends over time   Despite this long-standing negative image of single persons, an increasingly large proportion of adults are choosing the never-married life each year. As shown in Table 9-1, males are more likely than females to be never-married. In recent years, however, the rapid increases in the proportion of people who are never-married have been most pronounced among women. As shown in Table 9-2, the proportion of never-married women in some age groups almost doubled between 1970 and 1978. These changes in the proportion of never-married adults represent a major change in American society—a change which has affected everything from family structure to the types of residences being built.

Reasons for the changes   Several factors have probably contributed to the recent rise in the proportion of young persons selecting to be not-yet-married. Increased sexual freedom and contraceptive availability, particularly for women, have been factors. It is no

[1]These very names have strong stereotypes of sexuality attached to them. Think about the image brought forth by the term "bachelor" as compared with "spinster."

TABLE 9-2
Never-married females in 1970 and 1979, by age.

Age Group	Never-Marrieds in 1970 (%)	Never-Marrieds in 1979 (%)	% of Change
18	82.0	87.3	+ 6
19	68.8	78.9	+ 15
20	56.9	67.0	+ 18
21	43.9	56.1	+ 28
22	33.5	48.4	+ 44
23	22.4	40.8	+ 82
24	17.9	32.9	+ 84
25	14.0	26.8	+ 91
26	12.2	24.0	+ 97
27	9.1	17.5	+ 92
28	8.9	15.9	+ 79
29	8.0	12.7	+ 59
30–34	6.2	9.5	+ 53
35–39	5.4	6.6	+ 22

Source: U.S. Bureau of the Census, *Current Population Reports*, Series P-20, No. 349.
Note that the greatest change takes place between the ages of 22 and 23, jumping from a 44 percent increase for 22-year-olds to an 82 percent increase for 23-year-olds. This difference between 22- and 23-year-olds, as well as the large increases through age 27, is due to the demographic fact that the average age at marriage in the United States has long been 23. When not getting married becomes more popular, it has the greatest effect at that age at which most people have married.

longer necessary to be married in order to be a sexually active adult, and contraceptive technology has made it possible for women to control their reproductive behavior. More important for women has been the increased acceptability of the single career woman and the opportunity to be one. As educational and occupational opportunities have expanded for women, they have gained the freedom to decide what they want in terms of an adult lifestyle. Increasingly, in the United States a woman's worth as a human being is not determined solely by her marital status. She no longer has to be a Mrs. to feel fulfilled as a person and acceptable as a woman. This clear outcome of the women's movement may be one of the most pronounced effects of the changes taking place in women's roles since the greatly increasing proportion of young women who are remaining single has inititiated a major change in American family patterns. Indeed, on the individual level, higher levels of intelligence, education, and occupation are associated with single status among women (Spreitzer and Riley, 1974).

The existential movement   While the above factors have undoubtedly been important influences on the proportion of never-married young persons in this country in recent years, an even more widespread set of ideas deserves special attention.

During the 1970s and into the early 1980s, Americans saw the rising popularity of what has been called *existential thought* (Broderick, 1979). Certain aspects of existential thought have become popularly known as the *personal growth movement*. As described by Broderick, some specific aspects of existential thought have had a direct bearing on male-female relationships and the institution of marriage in American society. As Broderick points out, four basic aspects of existential thinking have been influential in this regard:

1. The individual and his or her existence and experiences are the most fundamental and important things in life. This means that the most important aspect of existence is growth and development *as a person*. Anything that stands in the way of the individual's growing and developing as a person by restricting his or her options, choices, or personal freedom should be avoided.

2. Each of us is a unique individual and therefore one person can never really come to know exactly what another person thinks or feels. Two people can share mutual love, respect, and general experiences, but they can never totally know each other.

3. Each individual is responsible for his or her own life choices. Since we are unique individuals who can never be totally known by another person and since individual growth and development are of central importance, no one can say what is right or wrong for another person or make the other's life choices. In fact, not to respect another person's right to make his or her own life choices is seen as unethical.

4. The present is the most important facet of life. The past is gone and no one knows what the future holds. Each person should therefore live life to the fullest in the present. Promises for the future do not make sense in that not only is the future unknown, but such future promises restrict one's freedom of choices. Emotional and interpersonal relationships should thus be enjoyed for the joy of their present, not the memories of the past or the promises of the future.

It is not difficult to see how these basic ideas of existential thought have probably influenced the decisions of many young adults regarding marriage. Marriage is traditionally seen as a very future-oriented bond in which two people form a single unit with the focus on the unit itself, not on the individual.

Added to these basic ideas of existential thought has also been the highly publicized divorce rate. Among many of those young people not influenced by existential views of interpersonal relationships, marriage is perhaps seen as being two people forever, and the high divorce rates in today's society make such a union seem like more of an ideal than a possibility.

The future? The extent to which the never-married status of an increased number of young persons is a permanent lifestyle or a temporary delay of marriage is yet unknown. Presently, only 6 to 7 percent of all Americans go through life without getting married. Thus, the adoption of singlehood as a permanent lifestyle by young people today would be a social change of historic proportions. In fact, the change would be in the opposite direction to what has been, and still is, a major trend in the United States. From 1960 to 1980, the marriage rate increased by 58 percent, and between 1979 and 1980, it rose by 2 percent. Currently, the marriage rate is at an all-time high in the United States in terms of its growth (*Monthly Vital Statistics Report,* September 17, 1981).

It is important to note that staying unmarried is more of an evolving choice for most people than it is of living out a firm set of beliefs (Gagnon and Greenblat, 1978). For most young, never-married people today, staying single is a year-to-year decision. The fears and concerns about traditional marriage are combined in the minds of most young adults with the long-standing tradition of marriage. The majority of college students in one study said that they planned to get married and to do so about age 25, that they were hesitant about divorce in today's marriage world, and that they were convinced that their marriage would work well (Dion, 1981). Strong (1978) asked college students how attractive various adult lifestyles were to them. Twelve adult lifestyles were rated in terms of the students' willingness to participate in each. Egalitarian marriage was by far the most popular choice among both males and females. Most important here are the ratings of traditional marrige and remaining single. Traditional marriage (traditional male and female roles) was not particularly popular among either males or females (although more so among males), but remaining single was even less favorable.

These studies, in addition to the actual rates of marriage in the United States today, suggest that the increases in the proportion of young people who are single are temporary. They only reflect a delay in marriage, not a turn away from marriage.

Informally, I have made the observation that many women today see marriage as a lifelong commitment but are afraid of the high divorce rates. The hesitation to marry stems partially from the fact that one cannot be certain that a marriage will be lifelong. Further, young women today are more likely than in the past to seek and desire an egalitarian relationship, but they are not at all certain that they can find one. Thus, singlehood is not seen as the most desirable adult lifestyle, but while one is still in one's 20s, it is all right, and marriage is still viewed at this age as having many possible emotional and interpersonal risks.

The Divorced

A second major category of single persons are those individuals who have divorced and not remarried. Since 1958, the divorce rate in the United States has steadily risen, with sharp increases taking place since 1965 (Figure 9-1). This has resulted in this nation's having the highest divorce rate of all industrial countries (Glick and Norton, 1977) and a large divorced population. Each year, there are approximately 2.2 million marriages and 1.1 million divorces in the United States, forming a pattern which results in more than 1 million persons entering single status each year. It is projected that if these divorce rates continue, almost half of all marriages occurring in the late 1980s will end in divorce.

These divorced singles are also relatively young. The average age at divorce from the first marriage in the United States today is 27 for females and 29 for males.

Remarriage Many divorced persons remarry. One of the traditionally popular characteristics of marriage in American society is that it may be *serial monogamy.* It is monogamous in that one has only one spouse at a time. It is serial in that after divorce, one marries again in a serial fashion. In 1975, some 80 percent of divorced persons remarried and did so within an average of three years following divorce

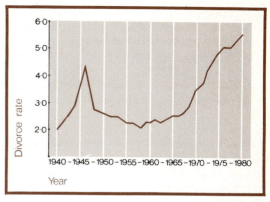

Figure 9-1 Divorce rates (divorces per 1,000 population) in the United States from 1940 to 1980.

(Glick and Norton, 1977). This means, of course, that the period of singlehood for the "average" divorced person is relatively short, but that at least a part of that period involves intimate cross-sex relationships. We shall return to a more detailed examination of dating and sexual relationships of divorced singles.

For today's college-age woman, these trends mean that for every 100 who marry, 38 will divorce; of these, 29 will remarry and 13 will divorce again (Glick and Norton, 1979).

The separated In addition to the divorced, a sizable number of people are between marriage and divorce. Individuals who are separated from their spouses constitute, at any one time, a very large population. In March 1978, the census reported 1.5 million men and 2.4 million women who were separated (*Current Population Reports,* 1979). It should be noted that these are probably underestimates in that an unknown number of persons report that an absent spouse is "visiting relatives."

The never-married, divorced, and separated in the United States thus make up a large and growing population: the single propulation. These trends in marriage and divorce have partially created a singles lifestyle in American society. We shall examine some of the major elements of this lifestyle, including the interpersonal, social, and sexual.

The Singles Business

One of the profound impacts of the growing number of singles has been economic. Commercial interests, generally wise to changing population trends, assumed that there were major differences in the social and sexual lifestyles of marrieds and singles. On the basis of this assumption, a massive "singles industry" came into being in the 1970s and continues today. A large part of this industry has been directed toward profit from bringing single men and women together in one way or another.

Singles apartments Invented in California, singles apartments became a symbol of what was assumed to be the single lifestyle. Complexes discouraging children and married couples began to offer multitudes of singles close proximity to one another.

Such residences are filled with other singles and thus are a place to conveniently and appropriately meet people. The single adult's world can easily be made up of two principle locations: work and home. Since intimate relationships with coworkers are frequently frowned upon, this leaves the home as the meeting place.

Singles complexes are seen by some as having certain drawbacks. Some complexes tend to take on the atmosphere of a sexual Olympics. Who slept with whom and how many different partners one has had in the complex sometimes become a major focus of concern. Initially, such a "swinging" environment may be exciting. However, many (or most) soon tire of a never-ending cycle of superficial and largely sexual relationships. Singles in complexes also often find the search somewhat frustrating. It is often felt that a lot of people would be very nice to know, but that finding them can be trying. "Being on the make" is a favorite activity of some, and, as the popular saying (found on many single women's walls) goes, "Before you meet Prince Charming, you have to kiss a lot of frogs." Such kissing of frogs often involves that classic male-female conflict discussed in Chapters 4 and 7. As Gagnon and Greenblat (1978) point out, it often seems as though most males in some singles complexes are looking for sex but will settle for a date, while most females are looking for a mate but will also settle for a date. Singles complexes can often provide too much interaction. One lives near, and is thus likely to run into, all those partners who did not work out. A trip to the laundry or garbage can often involve some interpersonal unpleasantness or complex avoidance strategies.

Singles bars Singles bars have largely been overplayed by the media. While they are popular, they come in a variety of forms and are not the sole meeting place of and for singles.

Many such establishments serve an important recreational function of being a place to socialize with friends and meet new people. Such establishments are often simply a place where one can count on locating one's friends after work.

Other establishments serve as meat as well as meet markets, and the sexual interests and sometimes desperate character of the clientele depresses many people. Such bars are often filled with many males and few females, and the patterns of behavior can be standardized in terms of opening lines, conversation, dress, and drink. Such an atmosphere is exciting to some and boring to others.

Advantages and Disadvantages of Singlehood

Traditionally, the single male or female was seen as a social loser, sitting lonely in his or her apartment with either cats too numerous to count or dirty dishes piled to the ceiling. Today, this image of the single person has changed somewhat. Along with the lonely loser image, the contemporary single is now often viewed as a young, swinging, upwardly mobile career person with not a worry in the world and with the sexual fantasies of society as his or her reality.

In actuality, singlehood for most people falls somewhere between these two extreme stereotypes. As in anything else, there are both desirable and undesirable aspects of singlehood. It offers independence which, regardless of the agreement married persons may

BOX 9-1

PEOPLE GET PRETTIER AT CLOSING TIME

Reasoning from a country-western song by Mickey Gilley ("Don't the Girls All Get Prettier at Closing Time"*), social psychologist James Pennebaker and his colleagues tested the hypothesis that as bars near closing time, people see one another as more and more physically attractive.

Three male-and-female pairs visited three bars near the University of Virginia campus at 9 P.M., 10:30 P.M., and midnight. They selected men and women who were not talking with a person of the other sex, were accessible, and were not obviously intoxicated. The 103 men and women who were approached were asked to rate persons of the other sex then in the bar on physical attractiveness. Both men and women saw the other-sex persons as more attractive at midnight than at either time earlier in the evening.

The researchers suggested two possible explanations for the change in perception of the attractiveness of the other sex as closing time drew near. One is that reactance may have taken place. As one's freedom to choose or act is threatened, one frequently reacts by liking the threatened choice more and more. The approach of closing time may have meant that the freedom to meet someone was threatened, and members of the other sex (the threatened choices) were therefore seen as more attractive than earlier. Another possibility is that of cognitive dissonance. If a person had come to meet someone but had not yet done so by midnight, he or she might have held two cognitions which were dissonant. "I am here to meet and leave with someone," and "I may have to do so with someone who is not physically very attractive." As closing time nears, the dissonance between these two cognitions can be reduced either by saying, "I don't care if I leave with someone" or by seeing the other-sex persons present as more attractive than they appeared to be earlier in the evening (Pennebaker et al., 1979).

Source: Copyright 1975, written by Baker Knight, Singletree Music Co., Inc.

have between them about such matters, is rarely obtained in a marital relationship. Singlehood also offers aloneness when one wants it. For a person who values privacy and time alone, singlehood cannot be beaten. Singlehood offers a person the opportunity to "find oneself", a concern of many young persons today as a result of the existential movement of the 1970s. In singlehood, a person can come to know what kind of person he or she is in the absence of a day-to-day living partner who may be the primary focus of his or her

self-definition. Singlehood also offers variety in both interpersonal and sexual relationships. One can truly experience the delightful human diversity in interpersonal-sexual relationships, an opportunity that many people find very rewarding in terms of the uniqueness of each person and each relationship.

On the other hand, many people find some real disadvantages to being single. Often, to paraphrase a lyric by Kristofferson, freedom can be another word for nothing left to do. Some people find that being single is being

The singles bar can bring out both the positive and the negative aspects of being single.

lonely rather than alone. Perhaps more important for the average single person, there are many times when the price paid for independence and time alone is the absence of anyone who is close with whom to share the day-to-day tales of life. Little things may also be problematic. Such necessary life events as errands during the day, doing laundry, washing the car, and the like are yours alone to accomplish—even when they need to be done at the most inconvenient times. There are other disadvantages, such as obtaining insurance, getting a job (being married is solidly respectable), arranging credit, and finding a residence.

Singles and Sexuality

It seems reasonable to suggest that, with the help of *Cosmopolitan* and *Playboy,* an image of singles as sexual swingers has developed.

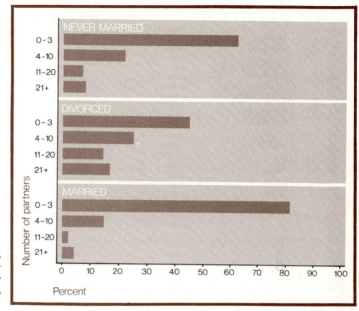

Figure 9-2 Percent of never-married, divorced, and married individuals having different total number of intercourse partners. (Source: Cargan, 1981:381, table 3.)

To what extent is this sexual image of singles accurate? The answer depends on what singles you are talking about and what you consider to be a sexual swinger.

Number of partners In regard to the total number of persons an individual has ever engaged in intercourse with, never-married men and women do not differ from married men and women (Cargan, 1981). At least on this dimension of sexual activity, the existing research suggests that never-married singles are not particularly swinging. Divorced individuals tend to fit the swinging image a bit better in that they often have had more sexual partners than either never-marrieds or marrieds (Figure 9-2). It is unclear, however, whether this greater number of partners for divorced singles comes before or after, or perhaps even during, marriage. Zeiss and Zeiss (1979) found that 50 percent of the divorced persons they studied began having intercourse within one month of their marital separation and 81 percent had done so within a year (Figure 9-3). In terms of sexual activity level, Zeiss and Zeiss found that their divorced respondents averaged intercourse every other date. This finding

cannot be taken as meaning, however, that divorced singles are frantically hopping from one bed to the next in the search for sexual ecstacy. Zeiss and Zeiss found that at any one

Figure 9-3 Percent of separated individuals who wait different lengths of time after their marital separation to have intercourse with someone other than their ex-spouse. (Source: Zeiss and Zeiss, 1979, table 1.)

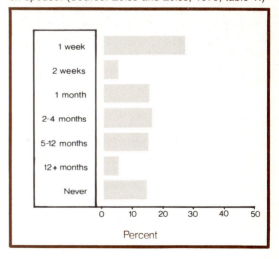

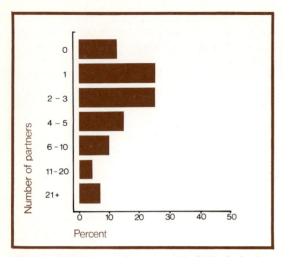

Figure 9-4 Percent of separated individuals having different total numbers of intercourse partners since their marital separation. Even though the average length of separation in this sample was nineteen months, having intercourse with a relatively small number of different people is the most common pattern. (Source: Zeiss and Zeiss, 1979, table 2.)

time, the divorced people in their sample were dating only one person and that sexual selectivity was the rule rather than the exception (Figure 9-4).

Many singles, in fact, find that sexual and dating exclusivity is a substantial problem (Stein, 1976). Even though the opportunities and attractions may be present, many single people do not feel right about being sexually active with more than one person. American society is a monogamous society.

Frequency of sexual activity With regard to sexual activity in a week's time, divorced singles are also more likely to fit the swinging image than are never-marrieds. On a weekly basis, divorced persons are more sexually active than either never-marrieds or marrieds, with never-marrieds being the least active. In Cargan's research (1981), 12 percent of the never-marrieds, 28 percent of the marrieds, and 36 percent of the divorced engaged in intercourse three or more times a week. Even among the divorced singles, however, this level of coital frequency is characteristic of

a minority. But, although divorced singles tend to have the greatest frequency of sexual activity, they still prefer more frequent sex than they actually have (Zeis and Zeis, 1979). (See Figure 9-5.)

Sexual satisfaction While there is no evidence to suggest that singles exist in sexual despair, there is also no evidence to indicate that they exist in eternal sexual bliss either. Cargan (1981) found that married individuals were the most satisfied with their sexual lives, followed by divorced persons, followed by the never-married. This same pattern is somewhat evident when individuals who are divorced compare their present sexual life with that of the period when they were married. As shown in Table 9-3, marital sex still holds a slight edge.

COHABITATION

Among unmarried individuals, living together has shown a dramatic increase in popularity in recent years. In 1960 there were 439,000 such couples in the United States. By 1970, this number had increased slightly to 523,000, but 1.56 million couples were cohabiting by 1980. This is an increase of more than 300 percent since 1960. Even though these couples make up only slightly over 2 percent of all "couples households" in the United States (far below the 12 percent figure in Sweden), this is a change of significant social importance.

TABLE 9-3
Comparison of sexual life now and when married by divorced men and women.

My Sexual Life Is/Was	Percent
Very much more satisfying while married	30
Moderately more satisfying while married	16
Slightly more satisfying while married	4
About the same now as while married	7
Slightly more satisfying now	11
Moderately more satisfying now	12
Very much more satisfying now	20

Source: Zeiss and Zeiss (1979, table 6).

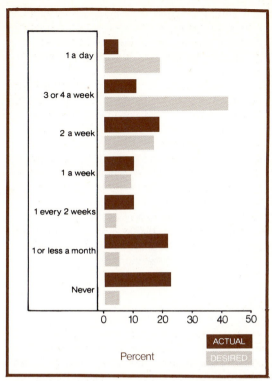

Figure 9-5 Percent of divorced individuals (male and female combined) having various actual and desired frequencies of intercourse. (Source: Zeiss and Zeiss, 1979, table 3.)

Who Lives Together?

For the country as a whole, cohabitation (no longer called "living in sin") is more likely among those under 25, blacks, residents of large cities, and the divorced. College students, however, are leading the way. In a nationwide study, Clayton and Voss (1977) found that college students were three times as likely as nonstudents to be living together.

An exact estimate of how common cohabitation is among college students is difficult to obtain. Considerable variation exists from campus to campus with the percentages of students living together running from 5 to 36 percent (Hobart, 1972; Thorman, 1973). Most recent studies agree that approximately 15 percent of all college students are currently

living together, and that approximately 25 percent have at some time been involved in such a relationship (Silverman, 1977; Bower and Christopherson, 1977). Not unexpectedly, a cohabitation relationship becomes more likely as one moves from one's first to one's last year of college.

Social Factors in Cohabitation's Increase

In recent years there has been an obvious increase in the acceptability of cohabitation relationships on the part of young people. In 1977 in the United States, 82 percent of the males and 69 percent of the females age 18 to 29 approved of cohabition (Glick and Norton, 1977).

This greater approval of living together outside of marriage has come from a variety of changes in American society. Increasingly, the traditional institution of marriage has come into doubt in the minds of many young men and women. However, the desire for close interpersonal relationships which are meaningful to the persons involved has not declined. Cohabitation has become a minimarriage in which a close day-to-day living relationship can be maintained between two people while avoiding the formal legal characteristics of marriage as a lifelong commitment, the future of which is unknown. Cohabitation is acknowledged to lack the permanency of marriage and thus to allow individuals to have the psychological freedom to pursue a career, education, or alternative affectional and emotional options should they appear. Additionally, there has been widespread acceptance and availability of effective contraceptive techniques that have made a steady, ongoing sexual relationship a possibility involving little worry about pregnancy. Colleges and universities across the country have changed their regulations requiring student on-campus residence. This change, in turn, has been accompanied by greater availability of off-campus housing in the form of apartments providing anonymity and absentee landlords who are more interested in the rent than a bed check.

Personal Motivations for Living Together

In addition to the social changes which have encouraged cohabitation, there are specific personal motives involved in wanting to live together. While economic reasons are the second most common personal motivation among both males and females (Arafat and Yorburg, 1973), they differ in the primary motive. The most common reason given by males is sex, and the most common reason given by females is possible marriage (Arafat and Yorburg, 1973). When males do give possible marriage as a reason for wanting to live together, their interests tend to be more practical than romantic in that they want to "try it out."

The importance of cohabitation as a means of either increasing overall intimacy between two persons before marriage or as a kind of trial marriage cannot be overlooked. Nationally, almost 40 percent of all cohabitation relationships result in marriage (Glick and Norton, 1978). Approximately 30 percent of the cohabiting college-student couples are living together just prior to marriage or are planning to marry (Arafat and Yorburg, 1973).

Duration

Due to either breakup or marriage, cohabitation relationships tend to be of short duration. Peterman et al. (1974) found that for 82 percent of the cohabiting males and 75 percent of the females, their relationship had lasted less than six months. Males as a whole are more likely than females to have experienced a short-term relationship, and approximately 50 percent of the males and females who have had a cohabitation relationship have had more than one (Peterman et al., 1974).

Hesitations and Concerns

There are also personal reasons for not wanting to live with someone. Many single persons face the question of exclusivity or nonexclusivity in their dating and sexual relationships (Stein, 1976). Given that cohabitation is based on the traditional monogamous marriage as a model, it means dating and sexual exclusivity.

Even though there has been a significant increase in the acceptability of living together, this is still something many young people are concerned about. Bower and Christopherson (1977) found that approximately half the cohabiting college men and women studied thought their parents did not know about their living arrangement. However, 73 percent of the males and 90 percent of the females felt that their parents would clearly disapprove if they did know.

In addition to the still somewhat "deviant" nature of living together, some recent legal incidents have made people think twice about cohabitation. Recent court cases, such as those of Lee Marvin and Michel Triola, have raised the question of responsibility and legal compensation, making cohabitation more like a traditional marital arrangement than before. Only on the surface does a cohabitation rela-

BOX 9-2
SERVICE OFFERS ALIBI FOR COED WITH LIVE-IN

Tucscon, Ariz. (AP)—"Living in sin with your boyfriend without your parent's knowledge? Use the Alibi Service."

That classified advertisement in the University of Arizona student newspaper is directed toward female college students who don't want their parents to know they have moved in with their boyfriends.

Now they can hire Lisa to act as their roommate.

Lisa, who said she was a 22-year-old student and declined to give her last name, operates the Alibi Service and makes her services available for $20 a month.

The ad first ran Thursday, and Lisa said she already has signed up two customers. She said she will accept only eight more women as clients, because keeping track of more than 10 persons could become difficult.

Lisa said her service includes taking unexpected telephone calls from her clients' parents, receiving mail for her clients and delivering messages to them. In case of calls or surprise visits, she said, she will act as the client's roommate.

For the $20 a month, her customers get the use of her name as a roommate, her telephone number and her address. In case of parental visits, the customers can pay more—at hotel room rates, Lisa said—for use of her spare bedroom to make it look as if they live there.

In addition, women who make advance arrangements to get calls from their folks can take them at Lisa's house at pre-arranged times, she said.

Lisa said she plans to meet with each of her clients for dinner, at the client's expense, to get acquainted and gather information to enable her to feign roommate status in any phone calls she receives from parents.

She said she will keep index cards listing information about her clients near the telephone so she can express some knowledge of the daughters of people who call.

Source: Associated Press News Features.

tionship appear to be more free and less formal than a traditional marital relationship.

Those Who Do and Those Who Don't

At least among college students, those who live with someone tend to be higher in social class (Clayton and Voss, 1977), far less religious (Henze and Hudson, 1974; Silverman, 1977), and generally more liberal than their peers who do not live together. This general liberalism, which involves a general movement away from traditionally accepted behavior pat-

terns, is also in evidence in the greater likelihood of cohabiting students to use drugs, to identify with a liberal lifestyle, and to consider such nontraditional relationships as contract-renewable marriage and communal living with open sexual relationships (Henze and Hudson, 1974; Bower and Christopherson, 1977).

The greater liberalism of cohabiting college students is also reflected in sexual behavior patterns. Cohabiting males and females tend to have their first intercourse experience at an earlier age, have intercourse more frequently, and be more likely to use contraception and to engage in oral-genital activity than noncohabiting unmarried couples (Catlin et al., 1976; Clayton and Vess, 1977).

While students who form cohabiting relationships differ from their noncohabiting peers in a number of ways, how do they compare with just plain married folks of their same age? In terms of past sexual experience, cohabiting males and females are considerably more liberal than their married counterparts. Compared with their married peers, cohabiting females (but not necessarily males) have intercourse at a younger age and have had intercourse with more people. Cohabiting males and females are also more likely than their married peers to have participated in activities such as group sex (30 percent of the cohabiting males, 8 percent of the married males, 12 percent of the cohabiting females, and none of the married females have done so) (Croake and Keller, 1978).

Sexual Activity in Cohabitation Relationships

The sexual histories of individuals who live together are different from those of married individuals because cohabitation reflects less commitment to and investment in traditional patterns of behavior. This greater liberalism is thus reflected in more liberal sexual behavior. Once arriving in a cohabitation relationship, however, the patterns of sexual activity take on the shape of any other living-together relationship, including marriage. The legal legitimation and public announcement of formal marriage have little to do with patterns of daily sexuality established between two people. Cohabiting and married couples therefore do not differ with respect to female orgasm in intercourse, male ejaculation problems, the frequency or incidence of oral or anal sexual activity, or overall sexual adjustment (Croake and Keller, 1978).

Levels of sexual satisfaction are generally high among cohabiting couples. In one study, 47 percent of the couples agreed that sex was "very satisfactory" and another 11 percent agreed that it was "satisfactory" (Catlin et al., 1976). When there is a difference in sexual

satisfaction between the partners, it is most frequently the woman who is the most satisfied (Catlin et al., 1976). Perhaps this is due to the fact that sexual activity is taking place in a relationship which involves some level of commitment.

ALTERNATIVE STYLES OF MARRIAGE

The existential movement of the 1970s appeared to affect not only the choice of marriage as a lifestyle but also the choice of a style of marriage. Given the dominance of marriage as an adult lifestyle in the United States, combined with the criticisms of marriage as an interpersonal institution, it was to be expected that during the 1970s we would see many suggested alternative marital styles.

Once having claimed that "the total institution of marriage in American society is gravely ill" (Roy and Roy, 1977), many set forth to prescribe a cure. These cures for the supposed ills of traditional monogamous marriage have been based on the argument that several specific things are wrong with the traditional marital institution. It is argued that all of a person's sexual, social, and personal needs cannot be met by one other person and that a monogamous, sexually exclusive marital arrangement stifles the development of the individual and results in a weakening of the original relationship (Libby and Whitehurst, 1977, McMurty, 1977). Sexual isolation in the form of monogamy is argued to result in destructive aggression against one's partner, increased apathy, unhealthy dependence, a lack of spontaneity in the relationship, sexual fantasizing, extramarital sexual affairs, and personal destruction upon the discovery of such extramarital incidents.

Given these criticisms of traditional monogamous marriage, a small number of persons have opted for experimenting with alternative marital-sexual relationships.

Open Marriage

In their best-selling book *Open Marriage,* Nena and George O'Neil introduced the concept of open marriage to Americans in 1972. As described by the O'Neils, open marriage emphasizes equality and flexibility in male and female roles in the marital relationship. The relationship is one of equal partners rather than of rigidly prescribed male-and-female and husband-and-wife activities. Perhaps more important in terms of the aspects of open marriage which have caught people's attention, open marriage emphasizes the potential for each spouse to grow as a person and to do so separately as well as with the other. This concept includes a mutual agreement not to be socially, emotionally, or sexually exclusive. One may expand one's interpersonal relationships beyond one's spouse to include social, emotional, and sexual intimacy with other persons.

It is not known exactly how many American marriages are open in both the emotional and sexual sense. Clearly, however, the concept of open marriage has had an influence on marital relationships among young persons in American society. In the absence of abundant research to support such a contention, I would suggest that many middle-class marriages today have taken on several characteristics of open marriage without the sexual and deep emotional involvement outside the marital relationship. Wachowiak and Bragg (1980) found that in a sample of marriages which had many of the other characteristics of open marriages, only 4 percent of the couples said that sex outside the marital relationship would be acceptable.

Who participates Participants in sexually open marriages may be of any age, but most are in their thirties. They tend to be urban or suburban residents and upper middle-class career persons. Whitehurst (1974) found that, in fact, many participants were influenced by the O'Neils' book.

The attractions to open marriage are rather clear cut. Most participants see it as a way to integrate opportunities for personal growth and freedom with commitment to another person and the security of a stable relationship that comes from that commitment. Participants seek variety, complexity, romance, and courtship and see an open marriage as a way of obtaining them as part of one's life. The essential characteristic of open marriage is that it is very traditional in one sense and very nontraditional in another. It combines the security and stability of traditional monogamous marriage with the variety and complexity of a nonmonogamous relationship.

There is also a strong component of gender equality among open-marriage participants; this can be expected, given the inability to maintain such a relationship under a double standard. While some might view open-marriage participants as thrill seekers or individuals who are not satisfied with their marriage, this view appears to be mistaken. Open-marriage participants are intellectually committed to open marriage and are rather idealistic about the personal and social benefits of such relationships. Not surprisingly, the participants are much less rigid in their sexual views than the general adult population (Knapp and Whitehurst, 1977).

At the personality level, there are several important differences between open-marriage participants and the general adult population. Open-marriage participants are not any more neurotic, immature, maritally maladjusted, or sexually maladjusted than the general population. If anything, they tend to be less neurotic, less anxiety-prone, less defensive, and more self-assured. Compared with the general adult population, they tend to be more individualistic, independent, willing to take risks to explore new possibilities, creative, nonconforming, indifferent to others' opinions, stimulated by complexity, unconventional, and willing to defend their personal views (Knapp and Whitehurst, 1978).

The nature of open marriages In all the open marriages included in the Whitehurst (1974) and Knapp (1974; 1975) research, the relationship was sexually open. That is, each spouse had sexual activity with persons other than his or her own spouse. In these open marriages, this emotional and sexual intimacy was based on the belief that such outside relationships are beneficial to individual growth and health in that they expand, rather than restrict, the individual's social, emotional, and sexual world. Such arrangements, however, still include the strong belief in loyalty and fidelity to one's spouse. The difference between open marriages and traditional monogamous marriages in this respect is that loyalty and fidelity become defined not in terms of exclusivity but of primacy. The spouse is not the *only* significant person in the individual's life, but is the *most* significant.

Open marriage appears to be easier for women. Both Knapp and Whitehurst report that women found it easier to make outside contacts than did men. As a result, they tended to have more outside partners than did men. In Knapp's research, women averaged almost five different partners other than the spouse and men averaged almost four partners outside the marital relationship. The women appeared not to be passive or hesitant to express their sexual ideas, interests, and needs to those men they found attractive. Males in open marriages, on the other hand, tended to be more traditional and conservative and actually had to change the most in order to adapt to a sexually open marriage (Knapp and Whitehurst, 1978).

Most relationships outside the marriage are described as involving deep friendship and affection as well as sex; approximately one-third are described as involving love and sex. The average outside relationship does not last more than two years, but it shows great variability from months to many years. The open existence of outside relationships (secret sexual relationships are no longer necessary and are strongly disapproved) often results in discussion about such relationships between spouses. It is also not unusual for a spouse and an outside partner to discuss mutual problems and make joint decisions together.

Benefits of open marriage In the existing research, the vast majority of open-marriage participants reported high levels of satisfaction and no desire to return to a traditional monogamous marriage. Most individuals saw their open marriage as providing them with both freedom and security and an increased fulfillment of personal needs of both a social and a sexual nature. Most participants reported that open marriage had actually strengthened their relationship with their spouse, bringing about increased closeness as a result of being apart (having other relationships) while being together (having the security of a primary relationship). Feelings of greater personal vitality increased self-esteem, and more freedom and development as a person are reported to lead to a greater emotional and sexual enjoyment with one's spouse. Feelings of decreased jealousy and possessiveness are also commonly reported as the relationship continues.

Knapp and Whitehurst (1978) point out, however, that not all the marriages they studied benefited from open marriage. When an open marriage was established in order to escape from the marital relationship without actually dissolving it, the result was negative (which might have been the marital outcome regardless). The reported benefits of open marriage only appear when the individuals involved have certain personal characteristics that allow them to deal with marital behavior which is clearly not traditionally approved and when a strong bond between marital partners is the basis of the mutual agreement to have an open marriage.

Women appear to benefit more from open-marriage relationships than do men. Both Whitehurst and Knapp report that their research suggests more advantages for women, such as equal social and sexual rights and a lack of a double standard; the elimination of the threat of secret affairs and what they might do to the marriage; the greater flexibility of roles within the marriage; outside relationships, allowing them to fix their own social, emotional, and sexual pace, which is often faster than that of their spouse; outside relationships, allowing them to obtain the amount of affection they feel they need and cannot obtain in a monogamous marriage; and relief that they are not the only person to satisfy all their spouse's needs.

Problems in open marriage The problems reported in sexually open marriages are not unexpected given that most Americans have learned to view sexual relationships in monogamous terms.

Whitehurst (1974) found that the biggest problem was the difficulty of open and honest discussion with friends beyond the outside relationships. A sexually open marriage in American society is not acceptable to most people. Thus, to reveal to your friends, coworkers, and relatives that this is the nature of your marital relationship is not likely to bring forth rounds of praise and applause. Knapp (1974; 1975) also found that a major problem was knowing that the very thing which was firmly believed in and enjoyed by the participants was unacceptable to the larger society, friends, and relatives.

Related to this restriction is the sometimes problematic nature of continual communication, negotiation, and honest expression of needs and feelings. In an open marriage, there is always change, and this change is unusual in the sense that it is not toward what one has learned that marriage is going to be like. For people who have been socialized in a monogamous society, the continual discussion and negotiation which must take place for openness and agreement to be maintained can be difficult.

Jealousy does appear and involves fear of losing one's spouse, feelings of possessiveness, or the desire to control one's spouse. Given that the basic tenet of open marriage is growth, development, and change, the possibility may linger in the back of one's mind that the spouse will grow in such a way that one will no longer be attractive to him or her. Even the excitement she or he may express in becoming involved in a new relationship with someone else can be more than a little disconcerting. Partners sometimes find that they do not have the same level of commitment to a sexually open marriage. This naturally leads to conflict, especially in the sharing of free time. One partner may feel lonely and left out and make demands that the other spouse spend time with her or him rather than with an outside partner. Infrequently, openness and freedom are abused; one person may have outside relationships not to expand personal growth but to escape from the spouse.

Just as open marriage appears to favor women in terms of the benefits, it also appears to disfavor women in terms of the problems. Women frequently complain that their spouse shies away from intense discussions of important issues of relationships, emotions, and needs, and that he finds refuge in sports, work, or all-male activities. Women also frequently feel that the division of labor within the household is not equal. The men are seen as lacking in the motivation to do the daily tasks of maintaining a household and as holding lower standards of neatness and cleanliness (Knapp and Whitehurst, 1978).

Multilateral Marriage

"Group marriage" is the term commonly applied to multilateral marriage. The term, however, is somewhat inaccurate since it suggests that in a group of people, each person is married to every other person. Multilateral marriage involves a group of people who have marital ties to one another in some fashion. Usually each person in the group is married to at least two others in the group. This means that your spouse would be married to one or two other people beside yourself and that you would be married to one or two people other than this one person, and so forth.

Sexually, multilateral marriages involve having sexual relations with each of one's spouses. Most frequently, this is done on some type of rotation schedule, since group sex is not common.

Advantages   Multilateral marriage is seen by its proponents as providing not only a close group experience in living, but also a broader base of intimacy, closeness, and support for an individual than is possible in a monogamous marriage. For example, it is commonly argued that multilateral marriage not only provides the individual with interpersonal variety within a close-knit group situation, but gives the individual a large number of people for support and consultation in times of crisis and stress.

Disadvantages   The problems of effectively conducting a multilateral marriage arrangement in a society where monogamy overwhelmingly dominates can be great. Not only is there a lack of support for such arrangements in the society as a whole, but most individuals have simply not learned to deal with the complex interpersonal, social, and sexual problems which can arise in multilateral marriage. In cities such as Los Angeles, such marital arrangements are reportedly more likely to succeed because there are apparently more people around who can adopt such a lifestyle.

One of the interpersonal problems commonly confronted in multilateral marriage is the demand placed on individuals. Just dealing with the interpersonal complexities of intimately relating to two or three spouses while at the same time attempting to maintain the same relationship with two or three cospouses can be difficult (Ramey, 1975). Second, such arrangements demand a degree of selflessness which most of us have not learned to offer. We all have probably at some time experienced the feelings of deprivation and emptiness when someone of the other sex whom we really cared for became socially or sexually intimately involved with another person. Jealousy thus tends to be a central problem in multilateral marriages (Ramey, 1975). Third, any time the maintenance of intimate relationships of almost any degree is attempted within a group, certain kinds of group problems emerge. It is not unexpected that multilateral marriages commonly experience problems of communication and personality conflicts within the marital group (Ramey, 1975). Even in the absence of jealousy, some multilateral marriages confront problems of coordinating a multiple number of sexual relationships. A few groups have even attempted a "sexual calendar" which notes who will be sleeping with whom on which days (Ramey, 1975).

Given that multilateral marriage is strongly at odds with traditionally accepted marriage patterns in this country, combined with the above mentioned problems, multilateral marriages tend to be rare and short-lived. Constantine (1978) was able to locate only 101 such marital arrangements in all of the United States, and by the time she could contact them, 66 of the 101 had dissolved.

Who participates On the basis of the Constantine research, the average participant in a multilateral marriage is already married to one spouse when the arrangement is established, is in his or her early thirties, and has above-average education. Participants also appear to be more sexually liberal than nonparticipants. Constantine (1978) reports that approximately half those persons studied who were involved in a multilateral marriage had previously experimented in the exchange of marital partners for the sole purpose of sexual activity.

Participants in multilateral marriage also appear to differ from the "average" monogamous marriage participant on certain personality characteristics. The Constantines (1977) found that individuals in multilateral marriages had greater heterosexual needs, a greater need for change, and less need for deference from others. Such personality characteristics partially explain the attractiveness of multilateral marriage to these individuals. Such an arrangement offers a wider range of heterosexual opportunities and many forms of change, is based on fundamental notions of equality, and certainly will not result in deference from the rest of society.

Swinging

Perhaps the sexual alternative to traditional marriage that has received the media's greatest attention relative to its actual occurrence is "swinging." A basic definition of swinging is a married couple's sharing sexual activity with another married couple or other couples. This definition is, however, somewhat too limited to encompass all the sexual arrangements that are now classified as one or another form of swinging. Today, a couple may engage in sexual activity by switching partners with another married couple, or a married couple may engage in sexual activity with a single male or female or an unmarried couple. Traditionally, however, swinging has referred to sexual partner exchange among married couples.

Types of swinging There is no single type of swinger, but rather, many different types. In general, swinging and swingers can be classified as to where they fall on a continuum depending on how the swinging is viewed by the participants. At one end of the continuum are *recreational swingers* and at the other end, *utopian swingers.*

Recreational swingers are totally, or at least primarily, interested in sexual activity and not in close friendships or intense interpersonal involvement with the people with whom they swing. In fact, such interpersonal involvements may be seen by purely recreational swingers as a threat to the marital relationship. The recently established on-premise swing clubs are the best example of pure recreational swinging. Such clubs charge a fee for "membership" and merely provide a place for a large number of strangers to engage in sexual activity with one another. One such popular establishment is Plato's Retreat in New York City (Box 9-3).

At the other end of the swinging continuum, the utopian swingers seek not only sexual activity, but a close and intense interpersonal relationship as well. They consider purely sexual or recreational swinging simply crass and undesirable. As one of the swingers in Bartell's (1971:13) research put it, "People will tell you they do all sorts of things, but when it comes right down to it they're only interested in going off to another room and screwing your wife."

A brief history Although there are no precise data to bear out this assertion, swinging was most likely not invented in twentieth-century America.

Swinging did, however, first gain public attention in the late 1950s. It was called "wife swapping," a term reflecting a male-dominated and female-property view of marriage, as well as the fact that swinging is usually initiated by males. Somewhat later, the term "spouse swapping" became popular, reflecting increasing sensitivity to egalitarianism. Most recently, the property-exchange tone has been removed through the use of the term "swinging."

Although beginning only in the 1950s, public attention to swinging focused on what was apparently not an uncommon activity. In 1955, for example, the first swingers' magazine was published. *La Plume* recorded sales of 15,000

BOX 9-3
IS THERE LIFE IN A SWINGERS' CLUB?

An orange plastic ball zips through the air, occasionally caroming off an onlooker or one of the swimmers. Two giggling women start to push a third into the water, then pull her back just in time. It is normal poolside fun, except that everyone is naked and three couples are copulating in the water.

"When you write about this," says Larry Levenson, 41, the amiable co-owner of Plato's, "don't leave out all the material that could make this place look upstanding." Levenson is harassed and sweating profusely. He has 200 couples on hand, a waiting line for lockers, and some prospective orgiasts are edgy because the bar is closed—the result of a court injunction by the state liquor authority. Without booze, he says, "it just takes everyone an hour longer to get all their clothes off."

Swinger clubs have operated furtively for years in most major cities and many small towns. Now they are going public. At least half a dozen operate openly in Manhattan. Though their legality is uncertain, revenues are high enough to justify the risk of prosecution. Open five nights a week, Plato's attracts some 6,500 fun seekers—and grosses $90,000—a month. Six-week memberships cost $5 per couple. For the $25 admission price ($10 for single women, no unattached males allowed), couples can use the disco, pool, steambath and pool table. Next to the disco is the "mat room" for orgies, and down the hall are 20 "mini-swing" rooms for one to three couples.

Levenson walks through the locker room. "This is the only place people are modest," he says. "They want to undress alone." One of the mini-swing rooms, he notes, is reserved for Plato's staff. Unlocking the door to the staff room, he finds a man and a woman inside, both naked. "Hey, that's my lady," says Levenson. "She lives with me. How are you, Mary?" Mary, a divorced mother of three, chuckles and tries to cover up until the door is relocked. "Whatever gives her pleasure gives me pleasure," Levenson says, talking loudly over the moans coming from the cubicles. "People separate when they're finished here and no phone numbers are exchanged." Exchanging phone numbers is the cardinal sin of swinging, because it can lead to emotional attachments.

A tough-looking woman stands at the liquorless bar, wearing only a flowered blouse and high heels. A bartender whispers to her. "Tell him to ask me himself," she snaps. "I don't deal through intermediaries." She has been married for 15 years and swinging for 13. Now she is jaded. She will only settle for "a man with hunger in his eyes," and no hungry-eyed man has happened by for three nights. So she strolls off to proposition a woman.

A young Israeli couple, both clothed, are sitting in voyeurs' row, just outside the orgy room. "It's a very immoral place," says the woman, giggling. Trouble is, the voyeurs' view through the narrow entrance is blocked by the "matman," a craggy fellow who stands with arms folded like Mr. Clean. Is his job to police the orgy? Matman looks incredulous. "We *never* have any trouble here. These are good people. I am more of a shepherd looking after my flock." The shepherd's main role is to see that customers join and leave the orgy in pairs. Once inside, partners do not have to stay together, but if a man leaves to go to the bathroom, he has two minutes to return, or his girlfriend will be ejected. A pudgy woman is protesting her expulsion from paradise. Matman latches on to her arm and gently guides her out. Even orgies have rules.

Matman makes a revelation: he and his wife—a hatcheck girl upstairs—are volunteers who work regularly at the club without pay. Does he at least get some free sex out of his labors? "Oh no, I never do it here," he says, staring at an enormous male derrière rising out of a sea of jiggling flesh in the mat room. "I don't want to be second, third or fourth. I do it at home where I know it's clean."

Customers try hard to brush aside fears about one possible consequence of uninhibited swinging: venereal disease. Says one: "We don't get it because swingers are just cleaner than other people." But one female newcomer, still a wallflower after two hours, admits nervously: "I'm terrified of coming down with something. How do I know who these people are and where they've been?"

Most of the patrons appear to be between 20 and 45 years old, and the staff estimates that 65% are married suburbanites, who are presumably interested in sex that does not threaten family stability. "It works," says Levenson. "You wait around until 6 A.M. when we close, and you'll see these people walking to their cars kissing and holding hands. Swinging brings them closer together, and who gets hurt by it?"

Still, there are losers even at orgies. An enormously fat woman has been sitting around in her underwear for hours, wanly looking for a man. "Swans fly with swans, ducks fly with ducks," a thin-faced young man says, glancing at her as we step around a writhing couple at the edge of the pool. Thin Face, who says he is a member of swing clubs in Chicago, San Francisco and Montreal, thinks Plato's should be more selective about people it lets in. "I mean head-wise, not bodywise," he says quickly. "Look at all those sightseers. It's not like the old days. Now it's too much of a freak show." Across the pool, the stout lady grasps the hand of a tiny Oriental man and pulls him resolutely into the mat room.

Oddly enough, there is less sexual electricity in the air than at a Rotary Club party. All the trappings of the normal sexual dance—talk, gestures and clothing—are stripped away as unessential, and emotions are under tight control. As a result, the proceedings are amiable, but flat. Like the tough-looking woman at the bar, many patrons seem bored. A pleasant young woman with a distressing overbite is standing at the bar, staring aimlessly into middle distance. "I don't know why I'm here," she says. "I'm only nude because there's nothing to do here with your clothes on."

Source: *Time*, Jan. 16, 1978, p. 53.

copies a month, revealing the fact that although swinging had not yet become cocktail conversation, it was taking place in some relatively organized fashion. In 1956, an article was published in the male-oriented *Mr.* magazine discussing the virtues and joys of swinging. This was the beginning of a long series of articles in men's magazines which would inform many American males that such an activity was a sexual possibility. In the 1960s, magazines devoted to swingers and swinging became more common. The most successful during this period, and continuing today, was *Select,* which contains some 5,000 advertisements an issue from swingers seeking contact with other swingers. During the 1960s, however, swinging was still a hidden activity. In the 1970s, it emerged from the dark recesses of American sexuality. Even though largely for titillation rather than as news coverage of the important events of the day, the mass media paid attention to swinging. *Playboy* began to give legitimacy to swinging as a sexual possibility with the appearance of swinger jokes and cartoons. Full recognition of swinging perhaps came on May 11, 1975, when the publisher of *Select* was invited to attend a conference of the Life Insurance Advertisers Association to discuss, along with representatives from such publications as *Newsweek, Penthouse, Time,* and *Sports Illustrated,* the business implication of changing lifestyles in American society. In the 1980s, swing clubs such as Plato's Retreat have been reviewed by major magazines and covered by popular television shows.

How many do it? As with any activity which is not generally accepted in the larger society, it is difficult to know exactly how many people engage in swinging. From a number of studies, we can obtain what appear to be reasonable estimates. Spanier and Cole (1975), questioning a probability sample of adults in a midwestern community, found that 1.7 percent had engaged in swinging. Hunt (1974), using a somewhat biased sample, found that 2 percent of the married males and females had participated in swinging. Tavris and Sadd (1977), in their study of female sexuality, found that 0.5 percent of the married women engaged in

swinging "often." Another 1.2 percent did so "occasionally" and another 2 percent had tried it just once. From these various studies, it appears that approximately 2 to 4 percent of the married males and females have tried swinging at least once. While this is a small proportion of all married couples, it does constitute a large number of people.

Perhaps as important as the proportion of married individuals who have engaged in swinging is the proportion who apparently have some interest in it. Tavris and Sadd (1977) found that even though 76 percent of the married women in their sample said they would never consider engaging in such behavior, 2 percent said they definitely would swing if they had the opportunity. Another 5 percent said that "perhaps" they would, and 17 percent said that they were not sure what they would do if the opportunity should arise.

Who participates? There have been many different descriptions of the kinds of individuals and couples who engage in swinging. They have characterized swingers as ranging from ultraconservative in everything except sexual behavior to ultraliberal in everything including sexual behavior. Perhaps the best single description of married couples who engage in swinging comes from the research of Gilmartin (1977), in which 100 swinging married couples were compared with 100 nonswinging married couples. It must be kept in mind, however, that swingers are like bowlers; there is no such thing as *the* bowler. Swingers represent a wide range of educational and occupational levels as well as many diverse personal characteristics.

Early learning experiences Gilmartin (1977) did find that swingers tended to have experienced less close, less controlled, and less emotionally satisfying relationships with their parents than nonswingers. This early life experience with parents is important in understanding participation in swinging for two reasons. First, it appears that this parental relationship may have had some effect on swingers' not being particularly bound by social rules—that is, on their becoming involved in an activity that does not receive social approval.

Also, this poor relationship is important for swingers' not being strongly bonded to their families as social control agents.

Second, swingers experience much earlier and more intense heterosexual involvement than nonswingers. Specifically, they tend to become romantically and emotionally involved with the other sex earlier, start dating earlier, experience more intense courtship and sexual involvement earlier, and have a larger number of sexual partners before marriage than do nonswingers. This earlier heterosexual involvement on the part of swingers is important in that in the face of a rather cold and emotionally uncharged parental relationship, swingers perhaps find social, emotional, and sexual heterosexual relations highly rewarding. These early learning experiences strongly suggest some of the factors which may underlie entry into swinging. Specifically, these factors may include not having a strong orientation toward conformity to social rules, placing a strong emphasis on individual freedom, not being constrained by the social control agents of parents, and finding sexuality and intimate interpersonal relationships in the heterosexual world highly rewarding.

Adult social participation Other characteristics of swingers in adult life further reflect this general set of core characteristics (Gilmartin, 1977). Swingers are more freedom-oriented, more liberal and humanitarian in their social values, more detached from political institutions, and much less religious than nonswingers. On this last point it is interesting to note, however, that fully 7 percent of the swinging husbands and 3 percent of the swinging wives in Gilmartin's study attended church on a weekly basis.

The general lack of connections swingers tend to have to traditional political, religious, and kinship institutions in society does not mean that they are social isolates. Gilmartin (1977) found that swingers interacted with friends (and not just swinging friends) more often than did nonswingers. Further, swingers were as involved in community clubs and organizations as were nonswingers, including the parent-teachers associations.

On one dimension, swingers are less socially active than nonswingers. This is in interaction with neighbors. Given the good chance that one's neighbors would be less than pleased to discover that a couple next door engaged in swinging, it is not uncommon for swingers to view neighbors as somewhat of a threat (Gilmartin, 1977). The friendly neighbors' dropping by for a chat or a cup of coffee at some unusual hour could result in an extremely uncomfortable and revealing situation. As a consequence, swingers tend to be less neighborly and more highly selective in their interactions with neighbors (Gilmartin, 1977).

Personal and personality characteristics Most people are probably suspicious that swingers are characterized by some set of "weird" personality characteristics. This assumption is to be expected since swinging is, from the point of view of the values of most of society, a deviant behavior. We tend to account for peoples' engaging in deviant behavior by attributing to them "deviant" personal characteristics. What little research has been done in this area using standardized personality measures suggests that this is not the case (Twichell, 1974). Gilmartin (1972; 1974) also found that swinging husbands are often less bored and suffer less anomie than nonswingers. Swinging wives tend to describe themselves as more warm and affectionate than do nonswinging wives. One fact which has been taken as a sign of psychological maladjustment on the part of swingers is their greater likelihood of having obtained psychotherapy or psychological counseling. Their doing so, however, may be due to the fact that they are more likely than nonswingers to be interested in personal growth and development. Such an interest may well lead to obtaining counseling under circumstances in which many people would generally not seek such self-exploration and introspection.

Entry into swinging Most important in the development of interest in swinging are swinging literature and the male media. Today, one is very likely to find some reference to swinging in most of the men's magazines, and even the popular media have provided coverage of the subject. The impact of written material on swinging is evidenced by the fact that in Gilmartin's research (1977), 75 percent of the swingers studied said that swinging literature was a major factor in their interest in exploring such activity.

Swingers' classifieds   There are many swingers' publications that mainly contain advertisements placed by swingers who want to get together with others. These advertisements serve two basic functions for the prospective swinger. First, they provide access to others with similar interests in a manner that is easy and involves relatively little risk. The advertisements are listed alphabetically by state for the entire nation, and people tend to be very specific about their preferences and interests. When you contact someone who has placed an ad or are contacted by someone who has seen your ad, you know that the person is at least a swinger. Thus, there is no risk of suggesting a sexual get-together with someone who will recoil in horror. Second, the advertisements themselves teach the novice about swinging. For example, there are many terms used in swinging to describe sexual activities of interest (Box 9-4). By simply reading the ads, one begins to obtain a "feel" for the nature of swinging.

- Couple, female BI, 28, 37-25-36. He, well-endowed. French, Polaroids, no rough stuff or Greek. Confidentially assured. Send SASE and full-length nude photo.
- She 5'5", blonde, 30. He 6'6", 34. Seeking attractive, versatile females and couples for mature, physical, social relationships. Sincere only. SASE, photo, phone. Discretion. All cultures in moderation.

Written instruction   Swingers' magazines such as *Select* not only provide advertisements but other means of learning about swinging. Issue 48 of *Select,* for example, states: "This literature thus provides a means of learning about an activity which you are not going to find discussed in everyday conversation or in your high school family-living class."

Socials   There are ways to enter swinging other than scanning the advertisements. Magazines such as *Select* sponsor "socials." These are large parties held in many of the major cities of the country. A hotel is reserved and interested swingers pay a membership fee of $15 to $25 a couple for a cocktail party, dancing, and the opportunity to meet other people who share an interest in swinging.

Personal reference   Once into swinging, a common way to meet others is through personal reference. Individuals who are deemed particularly desirable swingers are given the names of other people they may be interested in meeting. Through this informal personal reference system, many contacts can be made. These references are, however, reflective of an important element in swinging. Reflecting sexual standards and values in the larger society, many swingers place a great deal of emphasis on physical characteristics such as weight, breast size, and penis size. Overall physical attractiveness is also highly valued, as is youth. These characteristics determine the extent to which individuals will be referred to others, and they are rather clearly reflected in the advertisements appearing in *Select* and similar magazines. One can also make one's own personal reference system by placing a special swinger bumper sticker on one's car.

Stages in swinging   It is usually the man who initiates the idea of swinging. In Gilmartin's study (1977), none of the wives took the lead in suggesting swinging. The husband will often not come right out and mention swinging but will leave some publication or piece of pornography sitting around the house where his wife is certain to notice it. This initial suggestion leads to the first of what Gilmartin (1977) describes as five stages in moving into swinging—*revulsion* on the part of the wife. The wife's revulsion may be short-lived or permanent, depending on the strength of her learned reaction to such an idea, her ties to her family ("what would Mother think?"), how strongly she is attached to her husband, and her general level of interest in sexual exploration. In any event, Gilmartin suggests that this stage is basically one in which the husband attempts to convince the wife of the wisdom of

BOX 9-4
THE LANGUAGE OF SWINGING

Term	Meaning
AC/DC	Bisexual; swinging both ways; those who engage in both heterosexual and homosexual activities.
Animal training	Sexual activity with animals, usually dogs.
B/D or BD	Bondage and discipline.
BI	Same as AC/DC.
Discipline	Preference for disciplinary behavior in sexual activity. May involve anything from mild spankings to severe beatings that cause pain.
Dominant	The dominant person in S/M sexual activities.
English culture	Sadomasochism, using instruments for whipping (riding crops, canes).
French or french culture	Oral-genital sexual activities.
Greek or Greek culture	Anal intercourse.
Indoor sports	Swinging.
Parties	Swinging involving more than two couples.
Passive	The recipient of activities such as passive BI and passive Greek.
Polaroids, photography	Taking pictures of sexual activities.
Restraint	Mild form of bondage.
Roman or Roman culture	Group sex, parties.
Safe	Sterilized.
S/M	Sadomasochism, sexual pleasure through pain.
SASE or SSAE	Self-addressed stamped envelope.
Social	Some neutral ground (neither couple's home) on which to meet swingers without pressure or obligation.
Straight	Not interested in homosexual activities, or a term to describe a nonswinger.
Submissive	Wanting to be dominated.
TV	Transvestite interests, wearing clothes of the other sex, also called cross-dressing.
Versatile	BI, AC/DC.
Voyeurism	Observation of others engaging in sex.
Way-outs, weirdos	Generally, those who engage in B/D or S/M. Used to indicate no need to apply, e.g., "No way-outs need write."
Well-endowed	Having large penis.

exploring swinging and she reacts negatively. The result is often long and heated debates.

The second stage, *resistance,* is characterized by more of an intellectual and logical, and less of an emotional, tone. The husband is likely to attempt to convince the wife that "normal" people "just like us" engage in this kind of behavior. The resistance stage may last for several months before the *resignation* stage is reached (if it ever is). Here the wife resigns herself to try it just once. The crucial factor, of course, is whether this first experience is pleasant and rewarding. Apparently, in many cases it is not. Tavris and Sadd (1977) found that while 5 percent of the married women in their sample of *Redbook* readers had tried swinging, 2 percent had done so only once. Similar initial dropout rates have been reported for both men and women in a large sample of *Psychology Today* readers (Athanasiou, 1973).

On the basis of his research, Gilmartin (1977) argues that many people have unpleasant first swinging experiences because they violate one of the fundamental rules: They commit themselves to sexual activity without having first met the other couple (or couples) on sexually neutral ground, such as a bar, restaurant, or another couple's home. If the initial experience is not unpleasant and a few more swinging experiences are found rewarding, the fourth stage is *acceptance* on the part of the wife. Following acceptance is the final stage, *enthusiasm* in which there are no longer feelings of guilt, but a strong liking for the activity. On the basis of Tavris and Sadd's research, it would appear that fewer than 50 percent of the married couples who try swinging occasionally move into frequent swinging, or what, in Gilmartin's terms, could be called enthusiasm.

One of the interesting aspects of the movement through these stages is that they all refer to the woman's reaction. Apparently, however, many times the wife becomes enthusiastic only to find that her husband has lost his initial excitement about swinging. (Murstein, 1978b; Gilmartin, 1977). It is quite likely that the husband's enthusiasm about trying swinging is often based on a self-centered fantasy (engaging in sex with many different women). After a few initial experiences, he may encounter the reality of swinging: his wife is engaging in sex with many different men. He may find that he does hold a double standard and that this is just a bit much to take, especially if she is enthusiastic about her experiences.

The reasons for dropping out of swinging are not well researched. As shown in Table 9-4, Denfeld (1974) found that jealousy was the most common reason, followed by guilt and threat to the marriage. Henshel (1973), in a study of twenty-five swinging Toronto women, found that even though the husband tended to make the initial decision to begin swinging, dropout decisions were mainly made by the wife. Even so, 34 percent of the dropout decisions were made by the husbands and another 12 percent were joint decisions.

Open and closed swinging   As with any behavior, there are certain basic rules

TABLE 9-4
Reasons for dropping out of swinging.*

Reason	Percentage Dropping Out for This Reason
Jealousy	23
Guilt	14
Threat to marriage	14
Development of emotional attachment with other partners	11
Boredom and loss of interest	11
Disappointment	7
Divorce or separation	7
Wife's inability to "take it"	7
Fear of discovery by community or children	3
Impotence of husband	3

*These percentages of dropouts were categorized by marriage counselors who had counseled swingers. Even though these data are less than perfect, they are the only data available. The difficulties of locating a sample of ex-swingers to get their reasons for quitting are obvious.
Source: Murstein (1978b:120, table 2), adapted from Denfeld (1974).

which must be observed. One of them is adherence to either open or closed swinging behavior in any given swinging situation. Closed swinging refers to a couple's moving to a room and closing the door. Among some swingers this is acceptable, while among others it is not since it implies too much "pairing off." Open swinging involves either remaining in a room with others while engaging in sexual activity or leaving the door to a room open. This "openness" signifies to others that anyone is invited to join in the sexual activity of the couple or just to sit and watch. Open situations may frequently result in group sex in which any number of people simultaneously engage in a variety of sexual activities with one another.

Getting started   Beginning an evening's sexual activity, particularly when some or all of the people present do not know one another well, can be problematic. It is interesting that even though four couples may come to some other couple's house knowing that they all are there to engage in swinging, there appears to be a certain coyness about getting the sex started. The general social norms of not just yelling "Let's screw" apply even to situations that have been created for explicitly sexual purposes with near-strangers. Thus, pornographic movies of either commercial or homemade variety may be shown, certain sexual games may be played, or after an appropriate period and small talk, the host couple may begin to disrobe. Following traditional initiation patterns, it is generally the man who initiates sexual activity. Once the activity starts, one of the firm rules is that no one is obligated to engage in a behavior she or he does not like or to have sex with someone to whom she or he is not attracted. Of course, consistent refusal will result in not being invited back to the next get-together.

Homosexual contact   In general, male-with-male sexual contact is relatively rare and frowned upon, while female-with-female sexual contact is frequent, accepted, and even encouraged. Bartell (1971), for example, reported that in the swinging sessions he observed, 92 percent of the women engaged in sexual activity with another woman. Gilmartin

(1977) reports that male-with-male sexual contact is more common among younger than older swingers.

This difference in the incidence and acceptability of male-male versus female-female sexual contact in swinging is not particularly difficult to understand. In general, males are much more uptight about same-sex contact. Also, in the female role in American society, many forms of touching and intimacy between women are acceptable and expected in certain situations. Thus, sexual contact among women in a "hang loose" situation such as swinging is not surprising.

Murstein (1978) suggests two other reasons for the frequency of female-female sexual contact in swinging. First, most males simply cannot keep up with sexually aroused, multiorgasmic females. Thus, while the men rest, they may be restimulated by watching women make love with one another. It is also worth noting that the male encouragement of female-female sexual activity is part of a larger male definition of the erotic. Much pornography, for example, contains the mandatory sessions of female homosexual activity. Second, Murstein suggests that many women may merely be curious about what it would be like to make love with another woman. Given the nature of the swinging situation as one in which the general social norms regarding sexual activity are relaxed, as well as the male encouragement, female-female sexual activity in swinging is to be expected.

The effects of swinging on marriage   Is it true, as swingers frequently say, that the family which swings together clings together? It is certainly the case that if you ask swingers what effect swinging has had on their marriage, they provide overwhelmingly positive testimony. Such testimony, as well as any research on the question, must be considered with the fact in mind that most of the people who start swinging and drop out do so for reasons related to the marital situation and relationship. Thus, in any sample of current swingers, you are most likely talking only to those who in fact did find swinging to be of benefit, or at least of no harm, to their marriage.

From a study of swingers who volunteered to participate in research, Gilmartin (1974) found that when swingers were compared with nonswingers, there were no differences in overall marital happiness. Swinging wives, however, obtained more emotional satisfaction from sex than did nonswinging wives, and swinging husbands were more satisfied with the affection their wives showed them than were nonswinging husbands. Among swingers, both husbands and wives reported spending more time informally talking with each other than did nonswingers. In the sexual dimension, swinging couples have intercourse with each other more frequently than do nonswinging couples (Gilmartin, 1977). It has been frequently pointed out that swingers are more likely to have been divorced than nonswingers. These divorces have largely tended to occur before the present marriage and appear to be a function of quite early marriages that were not made on the most solid of attractions (Gilmartin, 1977).

These differences between swingers and nonswingers cannot be taken as suggesting some cause-and-effect relationship between swinging and a happy marriage. Rather, these differences reflect the overall characteristics of swingers we have previously discussed, the character of the marital relationship before swinging began, and the fact that when swinging results in marital problems, people tend to drop out. As with any of the alternatives to traditional monogamous marriage we have reviewed, it is not the activity itself which has any magical quality assuring individuals of personal happiness. Rather, if the individuals involved like what they do, the alternative is beneficial for the relationship. If they do not find the alternative appealing, it is likely to harm the relationship.

Pair-Oriented Existentialism

The existential movement of the 1970s did in fact have profound effects on our thinking about relationships in our society. These effects remain with us today. It is clear, however, that most Americans will not attempt to become personally involved in living out existen-

tial ideals through singlehood, multilateral marriage, or open marriage. The traditional monogamous marriage is the norm in the United States. One of the important ways, however, in which the existential movement has become integrated into the traditional monogamous marriage is through pair-oriented existentialism (Broderick, 1979:32–33). The emphasis here is on the pair, rather than the individual, as the important unit. Throughout the country, many programs and workshops have been formed to promote such changes in the traditional marital relationship. Many of these programs have been established by organized religious denominations as a way to keep in touch with the interests of the wider society while at the same time maintaining the traditional ideals of marriage as a sacred bond.

The emphasis of pair-oriented existentialism is marital enrichment through learning more positive and effective interpersonal communications and empathy with one's marital partner. This is done by practicing such activities as role reversal within the marriage where each partner learns to view the relationship from the other's point of view. Through such activities, couples work together to enrich the personal lives of both members of the pair as a couple and to provide for a more personally satisfying marital relationship that is not essentially different from the traditional monogamous marriage.

Perhaps the single greatest effect of the existential movement has been in this direction. The combination of the women's movement and existential thought has brought about considerable rethinking about the nature of male and female relationships. While we have not seen much of a turn away from the traditional monogamous marriage in this society (with the exception of singlehood, which may be very temporary), we have seen increased equality, communication, and flexibility becoming an essential part of marital and nonmarital relationships between males and females. After all the dust has cleared, I suspect that this will be the major change we shall see in the nature of male-female intimate relationships.

THE FUTURE

What does the future of adult male-female intimate relationships hold? In recent years, this question has been raised by many people and many crystal ball predictions have been made. While many of these prophecies have been scholarly and all have undoubtedly been sincere, they are nothing more than guesses. If we go back in time, we find that throughout Western culture, people have felt that male-female relationships were on the brink of crisis and that revolutionary alternatives to traditional monogamous marriage were almost certain to become popular, if not necessary. Perhaps more people feel this way today simply because of the rapidity and extensiveness with which ideas can be dispersed to millions of people. Given today's broadcasting and publishing industries, even people in the far rural reaches of American society can almost instantly be informed of the latest ideas.

Not to be outdone, I will offer my own prediction about the future of sexual alternatives to traditional monogamous marriage. Unfortunately, such observations must be made with a very small amount of data, but data which are more important than their volume would suggest.

Table 9-5 contains the data from a recent study by Strong (1978) in which a sample of college students were asked to indicate their willingness to participate in each of several adult lifestyles. The table shows the average responses for males and females. As is evident, only one adult lifestyle had an average rating as acceptable. (A score higher than 3 indicates the average response was some degree of unacceptability, a score of less than 3 indicates the average response was some degree of acceptability.) *Egalitarian marriage* was the only acceptable adult lifestyle, with long-term cohabitation coming in second (note differences between males and females) and

TABLE 9-5

The preferences of male and female college students for various lifestyles.

Lifestyle	Males*	Females*
Egalitarian marriage	2.46	1.74
Long-term cohabitation	3.25	4.19
Traditional marriage	3.38	4.36
Five-year evaluation and renewal of marriage	4.01	4.10
Rural commune with shared sex partners	4.20	4.92
Never-married	4.51	4.71
Sexually open marriage	4.91	5.40
Swinging	5.05	5.65
Group marriage	5.18	5.67
Serial monogamy	5.23	5.50

*These values are the averages for all males and all females in the study. The students indicated their willingness to participate in each of certain lifestyles on a scale ranging from 1 (very willing to participate) to 6 (not at all willing to participate).
Source: Strong (1978).

traditional marriage ranking third in acceptability. Singlehood was not acceptable for either males of females, nor were communal living, open marriage, swinging, group marriage, and serial monogamy. Perhaps most important to note here is that one of the most unacceptable lifestyle forms was serial monogamy, precisely that form of marriage that is on the increase today along with high divorce rates and high marriage rates. Combined with this is the strong preference for egalitarian marriage.

On the basis of this scant data, which I have little doubt could be replicated on almost any college campus in the country, alternatives to traditionally monogamous marriage are unlikely to take American society by storm. However, the anxiety and hesitation many young men and women feel about marriage are evident. Our current form of marriage is the least acceptable and the ideal form of marriage is the most acceptable.

STUDY GUIDE

TERMS TO KNOW

Single	Never-married
Divorced	Existential movement
Personal growth movement	Serial monogamy
Cohabitation	Open marriage
Multilateral marriage	Swinging
Open and closed swinging	Pair-oriented existentialism
Recreational swingers	Utopian swingers

SELF-TEST

Part I: True-False Statements

1. Singlehood has become so popular today that the old stereotypes of single persons do not exist.
2. In recent years, the greatest increase in the proportion of never-married people has been among females.
3. One of the basic tenets of existential thought is that two people can not only love and respect each other, but that they can also come totally to know each other as persons.
4. Many of us have probably thought that we and others change our perception of a person's physical attractiveness as the evening at the tavern winds down, but this assertion is not supported by research.
5. In terms of the total number of an individual's sexual partners, never-married people fit the stereotype of the swinging single better than do divorced individuals.
6. Nationally, only about 10 percent of all cohabitation relationships result in marriage.
7. Individuals who engage in cohabitation tend to be more sexually liberal than those who do not.
8. Women appear to benefit more from an open marriage than do men.
9. In the available research, we find that the most frequently given reason for dropping out of swinging is jealousy.
10. Female homosexual contact is common and accepted in swinging, while male homosexual contact is neither common nor accepted.

Part II: Multiple-Choice Questions
Select the best of the three alternatives.

1. Which of the following is *not* one of the four basic aspects of existential thinking? *(a)* The present is the most important facet of life. *(b)* Each individual has the

responsibility for his or her own life choices. *(c)* One's own personal growth and development are secondary in importance to those of one's family.

2. All the available evidence suggests that the recent increases in the proportion of never-married people are *(a)* a permanent change in the popularity of marriage in American society; *(b)* a temporary change in the nature of interpersonal relationships in American society and the expectation that most never-married young people will get married; *(c)* a movement away from marriage as an adult lifestyle and a movement toward cohabitation.

3. Today, out of every 100 college-age women who get married, approximately how many will divorce? *(a)* 90; *(b)* 38; *(c)* 12.

4. With reference to sexual satisfaction, *(a)* married individuals are the most satisfied; *(b)* never-married individuals are the most satisfied; *(c)* divorced singles are the most satisfied.

5. For the United States as a whole, cohabitation is most likely among *(a)* whites, those over the age of 60, residents of large cities, and those who are widowed; *(b)* blacks, those under the age of 25, residents of large cities, and the divorced; *(c)* blacks, those under the age of 40, residents of large cities, and the never-married.

6. When we examine the reasons people give for living together, we find that the most common reason given *(a)* by both males and females is sex; *(b)* by females is possible marriage and by males is sex; *(c)* by both males and females is economic benefit.

7. Comparing cohabiting and married couples on sexual behavior and activity, it is found that *(a)* married couples have higher sexual adjustment to each other and engage in more varied sexual activities; *(b)* cohabiting couples engage in more varied sexual activities, but do not differ from married couples in sexual adjustment to each other; *(c)* there are no differences between married and cohabiting couples on either sexual adjustment or activities.

8. In sexually open marriages, *(a)* the man tends to have more outside partners than does the woman; *(b)* men and women tend to have the same number of outside partners; *(c)* the woman tends to have more outside partners than does the man.

9. In research on the preferences of college students for adult lifestyles, we find that both males and female most prefer *(a)* remaining never-married; *(b)* traditional marriage; *(c)* egalitarian marriage.

TOPICS FOR DISCUSSION

1. In this chapter we have discussed the social and sexual lifestyles of single people. However, we have not discussed the various ways in which people of college age live. I have observed many different lifestyles on the part of never-married individuals in their twenties. Can you identify any additional types of never-married lifestyles? Do they tend to differ for males and females, and if so, how? Are there any other characteristics which tend to typify people who adopt one or another lifestyle? How do you think this lifestyle will be reflected when and if these people get married?

2. The United States has a high divorce rate and research shows that while the proportion of people who are never-married has been increasing, it also shows that these people plan to marry someday. As a group, discuss whether you think you will get married (or have been, or are), and why or why not.

SUGGESTED READINGS

Murstein, B. I., *Exploring Intimate Lifestyles.* New York: Springer Publishing Co., 1978.
This is a set of readings covering such topics as androgynous and contract marriage, open marriage, communes, multilateral marriage, swinging, cohabitation, and single-hood. It is good introductory work to any of these areas.

DeLora, J. R., and J. S. DeLora, *Intimate Lifestyles: Marriage and Its Alternatives* (2d ed.). Pacific Palisades, Calif.: Goodyear Publishing Co., Inc., 1975.
This set of readings covers sexuality, dating, and the family, as well as traditional marriage and its alternatives. Parts 6 and 7 are most relevant and contain good introductions to several of these topics.

KEY TO SELF-TEST QUESTIONS

Part I: True-False Statements

1. F (Research shows that even college students hold these stereotypical views of never-married persons.)
2. T (There have been major increases for both males and females, but largest among females.)
3. F (One of the basic tenets is that although two people can love and respect each other and share one another's lives, they can never truly know each other as individuals.)
4. F (Research has shown this to be true.)
5. F (Divorced people fit the stereotype better.)
6. F (About 40 percent do.)
7. T (They are also more liberal in other areas.)
8. T (Can you list some of the ways in which they benefit?)
9. T (Although the lack of jealousy is one of the basic ideas behind swinging, it is frequently not realized when the activity begins.)
10. T

Part II: Multiple-Choice Questions

1. *c* (An individual's personal growth and development are seen as being of first priority.)
2. *b* (These changes are only a delay of marriage.)
3. *b* (How many of these will remarry?)
4. *a* (They have stable, committed relationships.)

5. *b*

6. *b* (Gender differences in sexual learning visit us again.)

7. *c*

8. *c* (This is one of the indications that women benefit more and adjust better to sexually open marriage.)

9. *c*

Chapter 10
Homosexualities

Homosexuality has been called, among other things, a sin, an illness, a way of life, a normal variant of sexual behavior, a behavior disturbance, and a crime. Homosexuals are said to have been "born that way," been enticed into homosexuality by an adult, been turned to homosexuality by a lack of a strong parent, been made homosexuals by a dominating parent, been trapped in the gang stage of development, been unable to attract a person of the opposite sex, been oversexed or sexually deficient, been at a lower level of human evolution, been rebels against a bourgeois materialistic society, or been victims of various kinds of traumatic experiences. (Bullough, 1979:1)

A FRAMEWORK

Perhaps more than any other aspect of human sexuality, homosexuality has been the subject of attention from the law, religion, the public, the media, and the scientific community. The first question we must ask ourselves is, "Why all this attention?" Well, the reasons are obvious. There are so many questions to be answered. For example, "Why are people homosexual?" "What caused them to be that way?" "What do they do?" "Are they happy?" and so forth. Think about it for a minute. What other form of sexuality arouses so much curiosity? The answer is none. We do not ask, for example, why people are heterosexual or how heterosexuals "get that way." Why are such questions so commonly asked about homosexuality? The answer is that we are a heterosexual culture. Sexual interest, arousal, preference, and activity with persons of the other sex is the "right," the "normal," the "natural" way, and homosexuality of any form is viewed as "wrong," "abnormal," and "unnatural." Anything which is seen as different draws attention and requests for explanation. This is especially the case for forms of behavior that are viewed as "unnatural."

There is, however, something very special about homosexuality: People do pay an inordinate amount of attention to this form of sexuality. This very fact means that homosexuality differs from various forms of heterosexuality in an important way; it is noticed and disapproved.

The consequence of this social fact is that homosexuality takes on certain forms simply because of its status as a generally disapproved form of sexual orientation. There is therefore a second fact that must be understood in order fully to understand homosexuality. It is a socially disapproved behavior, and persons called homosexuals are thus socially oppressed persons who have formed specific patterns of adaptation to this social environment.

SOCIAL SOURCES OF OPPRESSION

As far as written history can tell us, homosexuality has always been a part of human existence. Even though the reactions to homosexuality have varied somewhat from culture to culture and time to time, the general view of homosexuality has been amazingly consistent throughout Western culture. The generally negative stance taken toward same-sex preference has not just appeared from thin air. Rather, the prevailing view of homosexuality has found active support and encouragement in the major institutions of Western culture.[1]

Religion and Homosexuality

As Bullough (1979) points out, the single most powerful force in establishing the prevailing view of homosexuality in Western culture has been religion. In both the Christian and Jewish traditions, homosexuality has been regarded as a sin.

In early Hebrew thought, homosexuality itself was not seen as an evil. Rather, it was considered an act that resulted in impurity. Semen was regarded as a contaminating substance which would make one impure. The only proper location for depositing semen was said to be the female vagina, since procreation

was the only accepted reason for sexual activity. As neither masturbation nor homosexuality involved a vagina in which to deposit semen, they were both viewed as sinful and impure acts. As Bullough (1979) suggests, this is perhaps the reason that female homosexuality is not regarded with as much disgust and hostility as male homosexuality.

The term "sodomy" is often used to refer to homosexuality, especially in a legal sense. The term, however, is basically meaningless since it is used to refer to a wide range of sexual behaviors labeled "unnatural." Depending on the particular state in which it is defined, sodomy may refer to oral or anal intercourse between two humans regardless of their sex, marital status, or agreement to engage in the behavior. Each and every year, at least one male-and-female couple is arrested somewhere in the United States for engaging in oral or anal sex with each other regardless of the fact that they did so with mutual consent. These arrests are made under the so-called sodomy laws.

The origin of the term sodomy and its association with homosexuality is important, however, because of its religious base. The term comes from the biblical story of Sodom. According to this story, God promised to destroy the wicked cities, including Sodom. Abraham argued that this act would kill the good people as well as the wicked, and so God agreed not to inflict the destruction if ten virtuous men could be found in the cities. Two angels were sent to locate these ten men, and they first went to the house of Lot and his family. While they were inside, a crowd of men gathered and told Lot to bring his guests outside so that they might "know them." Then God struck the crowd blind, turned Lot's wife into a pillar of salt, and destroyed the cities. In this Bible story, however, the sins of the city of Sodom are not actually equated with homosexuality. The Hebrew word for "to know" meant two quite different things: to get acquainted as a friend or sexual intercourse. The meaning of the term in its original context is unclear and it was only later in Jewish history, when the Hebrews were attempting to deal with the Greeks

---

[1] A complete review of homosexuality in history is beyond the space limitations of this chapter. The following discussion is greatly indebted to the outstanding scholarly work of Vern Bullough (1976; 1979). For the best treatment of the history of homosexuality, the interested reader should consult these two "must read" volumes.

BOX 10-1
ATTITUDES TOWARD HOMOSEXUALITY IN FORTY-TWO CULTURES AROUND THE WORLD

Attitude	Cultures Having This Attitude (%)
Homosexuality is accepted or ignored.	21
There is no concept of homosexuality.	12
Homosexuality is ridiculed and scorned but not punished.	14
Homosexuality is mildly disapproved and considered undesirable but not punished.	12
Homosexuality is strongly disapproved and punished.	40

Source: Broude and Green (1976:417).

It is important to note that studying homosexuality in other cultures is difficult for the simple reason that a behavior that we may call "homosexuality" might not be labeled, in another culture, as different or unusual, let alone homosexual. The question of definition is, of course, a major problem in anthropology. Does the researcher use his or her own culture's categories and means of identifying types of behavior, or does he or she adopt the categories of the culture being studied? My own view is that there is no choice but to do the latter. This approach results in not finding many prominent American behaviors in other cultures. Classic examples are the problems of anthropologists in studying religion or the family.

in Palestine, that the sin of Sodom was said to be homosexuality. It was at this point, rather than in the original biblical tale, that sodomy came to mean the sin of homosexuality (Bullough, 1979).

The sinful nature of homosexuality became, of course, a central part of Jewish and Christian religious thought, and throughout history this idea has been supported by both legal and scientific thinking. In recent years, we have seen a minor, but still historical, change in the stance of some religious groups. As the "gay liberation" movement grew and the issue of gay rights as part of human rights came to the fore, some churches took a more liberal view. This, however, has been true of only the most liberal of churches. Meanwhile, fundamentalist denominations have, if any-

thing, become more antihomosexual. Witness, for example, the Moral Majority.

Science and Homosexuality

Even though science and religion have often been in disagreement on many issues, they have not been so regarding homosexuality. While we might think that this is no longer true today, we shall see that the current scientific view of homosexuality still very much reflects the religious view that homosexuality is unnatural and a sin.

In the nineteenth century, there was an increasing attraction to science. Scientists were seen as people who could provide answers to almost any of the traditional problems society had faced. Homosexuality had a long

BOX 10-2
MODELS OF SEXUAL DEVIANCE

	Religious Model	Legal Model	Medical Model
Cause of Deviance	Demonic possession or temptation by the devil. Sinfulness	The deviant's "criminal character"	Not always known, but some natural cause (illness) assumed
Meaning of Deviant Behavior	Sin, heresy. Deviant is possessed or evil	Crime	Symptomatic of illness
Form of Intervention	Exorcism, repentance, confession	Punishment, sometimes also "rehabilitation"	Medical treatment. Drugs, electroshock, psychosurgery, etc.
Intervening Authority	Priest or other religious authority. Sometimes chosen by deviant, sometimes by society	Police, judge, correctional officer. Always chosen by society	Physician or psychiatrist. Sometimes chosen by deviant, usually by society
Rights and Duties of Deviant	Right to receive exorcism. Duty to atone for sins	Right to be presumed innocent until proven guilty. Duty to accept punishment and to "pay his debt to society"	Right to be considered sick, not evil. Duty to try to get well and to cooperate with doctors
Rights and Duties of Society	Right to condemn and isolate sinners. Duty to help them if they repent	Right to protect itself against criminals. Duty to punish them	Right to be protected from sick people who are dangerous. Duty to provide medical treatment for them
Goal of Model	To save the soul from eternal damnation	To control crime	To cure illness. To help deviant avoid blame by treating him as a medical patient

Source: From *The Sex Atlas* by Erwin J. Haeberle. Copyright © 1978 by Erwin J. Haeberle. Used by permission of the Continuum Publishing Company.

Psychoanalytic Model	Labeling Model
Individual, largely unconscious life experiences. Arrested or impaired psychosexual development	Labeling by those who cannot tolerate differences.
Symbolic acting-out of unconscious and unresolved childhood conflicts	Determined by those who label the deviant. Today mostly seen as criminal or sick
Psychoanalysis. Deviant becomes conscious of hidden conflict by means of free association, interpretation of dreams, etc.	Criminal punishment or psychiatric treatment, often involuntary
nalyst. lways chosen by deviant	Today usually a judge or psychiatrist Chosen by those who label the deviant.
ight to have his behavior terpreted as symbolic, not dged morally. uty to cooperate with nalyst	No rights. No duties
rights. uty to see deviant havior as indication of notional disturbance	Right to control socially harmful deviants. Duty to leave all other deviants alone
resolve deviant's conscious conflicts	For the intolerant: To maintain the status quo by labeling and "correcting" deviants. For the tolerant: To liberate the oppressed

history of being seen as a problem, and certain segments of the scientific community jumped headlong into investigating "the problem." Unfortunately, these were the medical segments of the scientific community.

The first physician to attempt a scientific study of homosexuality was Carl Westphal (1833–1890), a professor of psychiatry in Berlin. Westphal concluded that homosexuality was innate; a person was born with it. His conclusion was not surprising since he had a medical view of the world through what is called the *medical model*. In the medical model, an individual has some problem, affliction, illness, or disorder. The origin and the nature of the disorder are inside the individual; it is something the individual has, like cancer or the measles. To place the medical model in perspective, it should be noted that there are other world views or models (Box 10-2). From a labeling perspective or model, something is not a problem until it is identified. Cancer was not a problem until it was discovered as a physiological fact. Next, the thing which is identified must be defined as a problem. From the labeling perspective, the origin of any so-called problem, including homosexuality, is not some disorder within the individual but the labeling of a person as "different" and calling that difference a "problem." Thus, the problem is not within the individual but within society and in the things that are defined as problems.[2] Of course, one of the results of a medical view of the world is that once the problem has been identified as within the individual, the problem must be "cured." Westphal's work generated not only much medically oriented research on homosexuality but also many attempts to "cure" the "illness" and "solve" the "problem."

[2]Pollution and a concern with environmental quality are good examples. If you look at photographs of your hometown a hundred years ago, you may find that it was treeless, smoke-filled, dusty, dirty, and a general mess. The environment was, however, not a problem until it was defined as such. The same is true for the treatment of women and ethnic minorities. The discriminatory behaviors toward them have always been there, but only recently have these been defined as social and personal problems.

Also in the late 1800s, the evolutionary theories of Darwin were gaining popularity. The concepts of evolution and survival of the fittest were applied to many forms of social behavior, including the legal, economic, marital, familial, and sexual. Homosexuals (along with any others whom those in power thought were undesirable) were seen as evolutionary failures who never quite made it up the ladder of evolutionary development to the heterosexual condition. The homosexual was thus frequently seen by members of the medical community as a biological degenerate, a primitive, an animal, and a person who could never be a satisfactory member of the community.

Given the idea that one is born homosexual, there were many attempts to identify the signs of the affliction. One popular nineteenth-century view was that homosexuals masturbate. This idea fit very nicely with the fear of masturbation on the part of youth. This tendency to find the "early signs" of the "disease" in young children has not been forgotten. As this is being written, articles published in professional scientific journals discuss how you can tell if a child "has" homosexuality, and the very popular work on hormones as influencing sexual behavior amazingly argues that sexual preference is something one is born with.

Homosexuality was also frequently seen as contagious (any disease worth its salt is contagious). Given that homosexuality was both innate and contagious, the only reasonable thing to do was to place homosexuals in asylums. In this way, they could be "cared for" and perhaps even "cured." At the very least, they would not contaminate others.

Not all the nineteenth-century thinking about homosexuality was so "compassionate." Perhaps the single most important figure in the scientific view of homosexuality was Richard von Krafft-Ebing. In line with the dominant contemporary view, he saw sexual excess as certain to ruin civilization and the individual. Civilized society and individual health were possible only through "normal" sex in moderation. Normal sex was that which led to procreation and moderation was as much as it took to procreate. To his personal satisfaction, he

"demonstrated" the horrid dangers of not only sexual excess but of "perversions" (anything not normal). He described detailed case histories in which the most gruesome of sex crimes (which he described in detail) could be traced to lesser perversions and masturbation. Homosexuality was, in his view, a certain sign that the individual was well on his or her way to the commission of sex crimes.

The nineteenth century was not without individuals who had a somewhat more objective view of homosexuality. The most prominent of them was Havelock Ellis (1859–1939), who popularized the position that what is sexually "normal" varies from culture to culture. Ellis observed human behavior in many cultures and refused to cloud his observations with judgments of right and wrong, moral and immoral. In this regard, he can be valued as the forerunner of modern science and a person still actually ahead of many so-called scientists today. Ellis was not a defender of homosexuality. He simply noted that if one observes human sexual behavior, one will find that homosexuality is but one of the many forms of human diversity—nothing more, nothing less.

In more modern times, the psychiatric view of homosexuality emerged out of the medical orientation. This view was dramatically influenced by people such as Westphal. Freud is often regarded as seeing homosexuality as a "natural" form of sexual expression. However, Freud and those who followed him actually had a much less neutral view. He argued that homosexuality is a natural part of human development but that most individuals move *beyond* the homoerotic stage in adulthood. This was a fancy way of saying that homosexuals are a lesser form of human being with a distorted sexual preference due to a fault in the natural progression (evolution?) of personality *development*. To be homosexual in this view is to be a failure in personality development, just as the early thinkers saw homosexuality as a failure in biological development.

Only in the last several years has this scientific view of homosexuality begun to change. Research consistently, even today, assumes that homosexuality is not normal. Researchers look for characteristics of homosexuals which they would never look for in persons having other sexual preferences.[3] The language used by many current researchers consists largely of modern terms for nineteenth-century stereotypes. Massive research efforts are still being directed toward finding biological causes of homosexuality and ways to identify homosexuals in their childhood, if not infancy. There are repeated suggestions, and even experiments, on how to "cure" homosexuality. While masturbation has come to be viewed by most of the scientific community as not only "normal" but even beneficial, homosexuality is still seen as a problem which has its causes within the individual and which is associated with any number of other "abnormal" or "unusual" behavior patterns, all "curable" if the scientific answers can be unlocked (Smith, 1979).

Homosexuality and the Law

The vast majority of states still have sodomy laws which allow sentences of up to twenty years in jail for a conviction. Most also have public lewdness laws that carry a lesser penalty but are easier to implement against individuals suspected of homosexual activity. In addition to these explicit laws, the courts have continually ruled that individuals may be fired from jobs, not be allowed to have contact with their own or others' children, be denied insurance, be denied organizational membership, and even be denied the right to fly a private airplane solely on the basis of sexual preference. The history of homosexuality and the law is one of the true dark spots in United States jurisprudence. Even though changes are now beginning to take place, the legal status of homosexuals is still second-class and this treatment is still based on myth, stereotype, and fears based on ignorance.[4]

The nature of these laws against homosexuality is not difficult to understand. The laws reflect religious, medical, and public views of homosexuality which have come to us through a long historical tradition.[5] The basis of the harsh legal treatment of homosexuals in America today is not surprising given these antihomosexual traditions and the basis of European and American law. Modern American and European law is based on ancient Roman law, which prescribed the death penalty for anal intercourse in A.D. 390 (Bullough, 1979). In England, homosexuality was punishable by death until 1861 and by life in prison until 1967. Death sentences for homosexuality were very common in the British Royal Navy in the 1700s and early 1800s. For example, 62 percent of the death sentences in the Royal Navy in 1816 were for homosexuality (Gilbert, 1976–1977). In 1800, Virginia repealed its death penalty for homosexuality, with Thomas Jefferson suggesting that castration was the appropriate punishment for males and a ½-inch hole cut in the nose was appropriate for females (Oaks, 1979:39).

Of the nations of the modern world, it is important to note that the United States as a whole has among the most repressive laws regarding homosexuality. In the Soviet Union, homosexuality is considered a serious crime, but the maximum penalty is "only" a five-year jail sentence. In West Germany and the Scandinavian countries, there are no laws regarding homosexuality. The same is true of Japan even though the Western influence has resulted in a change of attitudes. Previously, homosexuality was not disapproved in Japan and was often esteemed.

While many changes have taken place in the laws regarding homosexuality in the United States, they have been slow and very, very piecemeal. It was not until 1979 that the Surgeon General ordered homosexuality not to be classified as a mental disease and defect, an

---

[3]A good example of this is that the public, and even research (Garner and Smith, 1976), point out that there really are gay athletes. I know of no research which has studied the masturbation frequency, oral-sex proclivities, breast shape preferences, or frequency of sex with animals among athletes compared with nonathletes.

[4]For an excellent discussion of many legal issues pertaining to homosexuality, see *Journal of Homosexuality*, vol. 5: 1 and 2, 1979–1980, *Special Issue on Homosexuality and the Law*.

[5]It is ironic that homosexuality was made a civil crime in England (in 1533) in an effort to weaken the influence and power of the church, while today's homosexuality laws are a reflection of the traditional religious views of appropriate sexuality (Oaks, 1979).

action which stopped quarantine officials from keeping people suspected of being gay out of the country.[6] Even though Governor Brown of California swore in an avowed gay male as a criminal court judge in Los Angeles, the New York City Council has six times turned down an ordinance banning sexual preference as a basis for employment, housing, hotel and motel accommodations, and credit. Oklahoma only recently passed a bill banning homosexuals from teaching and Arkansas is considering a law to prohibit homosexuals from being pediatricians (doctors specializing in the medical treatment of children).

Much of the rationale behind such legal decisions, particularly when the general public votes on gay rights, is the fear that decriminalization of homosexuality in some way will lead to increased homosexuality, homosexual activity with minors, and homosexuals using force to obtain sexual partners. Research on the incidence of such activities following decriminalization of homosexuality between consenting adults reveals that none of these dire results has taken place (Geis et al., 1976).

GAY LIBERATION AND THE GAY RIGHTS MOVEMENT

More than any other event in the history of homosexuality, the gay rights movement of the 1970s was the historic event in the status of homosexuality in American society. The movement, like many other "rights" and "liberation" movements of the decade, brought about the open discussion of homosexuality and human rights and provided the foundation for social, political, legal, and personal changes in the

view and treatment of homosexuality and homosexuals.

The Stonewall Inn Riots

Friday, June 27, 1969, is generally considered to be the birth date of the gay liberation movement in the United States. This was the day of the notorious Stonewall Inn riots. The Stonewall Inn, in New York's Greenwich Village, was a popular meeting place for gays. The establishment, like many other places where gays frequently socialized, was routinely raided and generally harassed by the police. When such raids took place, the patrons of the inn, like gays everywhere, were usually docile and resigned themselves to such treatment. On this June day, however, when the police arrived, they reacted with anger and stood their ground. The police were forced to barricade themselves inside the inn and call for reinforcements. The rioting activity continued for four more nights, and when it was all over, it was clear that the gays were no longer content to be pushed, prodded, beaten, and generally harassed by the police. The next year, the Christopher Street parade in New York, and similar parades in many other large cities through the country, drew widespread attention and support for the civil rights of homosexuals. It was clear that the reaction of homosexuals to their oppression had changed and that there was substantial support in society for this reaction.

As Bullough (1979) points out, the Stonewall Inn riots were not the beginning of the gay movement. They were simply a breaking point which crystallized a long series of events that had been building to this point for some time. The general human rights and liberation movements had been growing throughout American society all through the 1960s as people came to question traditional authority and traditional patterns of treatment of oppressed groups. The women's movement was expanding in the late 1960s, and the Watts riots in Los Angeles became an example of a minority group physically resisting oppression. Like the Watts riots in 1965, the Stonewall Inn riots in 1969 served

[6]As of this writing, however, that decision has been overturned by the U.S. Justice Department, which ruled that the Immigration and Naturalization Service must enforce the 1952 immigration law which bans homosexual foreigners from being admitted to the United States. Although I am not certain of the origin of this law, I suspect that it was in part a result of the Communist witch-hunts led by Senator Joseph McCarthy in the 1950s. McCarthy and his staff were particularly fearful that "perverts" would undermine the United States government and lead to a Communist takeover.

A candidates' night sponsored by the Harvey Milk Gay Democratic Club, San Francisco.

as a rallying point for the beginning of demands for legal and social reforms in the treatment of homosexuals in American society.

Gay Organizations

Perhaps the most significant outcome of the Stonewall Inn riots and the parades which followed was the rapid and widespread growth of gay rights organizations. By late 1973, the National Gay Task Force had been established as a viable national movement, and by 1975, gay networks and avenues of communication focused on the movement had found their way into almost every college and university, as well as many small towns, in America.

As the organizational presence of the gay rights movement made itself known, legal changes did take place as well as changes in public tolerance. However, this presence was also met with conservative political and religious backlash, much of which was centered in Dade County, Florida, the home of Anita Bryant. After her successful campaign there to rescind nondiscrimination against gays, she spread her efforts to other parts of the country.

Even though Colorado, Illinois, Kansas, Oregon, and California, as well as many cities, passed antihomosexual discrimination laws after the Dade County affair, Kansas and Oregon later rescinded their antidiscrimination laws. While antihomosexual forces have been fought off in Seattle and California as well as in other cities and states, the 1980s will probably be a period of much more conservatism in all areas of life. Gay rights—as well as those of women and other minority groups—will not fare well in this climate.

It is important to note that homosexual organizations are not totally new in American society. They go back to at least 1900 (Bullough, 1979). These early organizations were, however, not publicly visible in either title, membership, or purpose,[7] and they were in no way concerned with fighting for gay rights. It was enough, prior to 1970, simply to survive, let alone have any rights. Prior to the gay rights movement, many of the functions of

[7]It was not until the late 1960s that Bell Telephone would list any name with the word "homosexual" in its title, and only recently, have terms such as "gay" been allowed in public directories and news stories (Bullough, 1979).

BOX 10-3
NAMES AND LABELS

The term "homosexual" was coined by Karoly Maria Benkert in a pamphlet he wrote on the subject in 1869 (Bullough, 1979). With the "scientific" interest in homosexuality in the nineteenth century, there were many proposals for names of same-sex preference. *Homoerotic* (aroused by the same sex) and *homophile* (lover of the same sex—a term many homosexuals prefer since it places less emphasis on the sexual component) have been used. There has been a distinction, perhaps inevitable in a gender-conscious society, between male and female homosexuals. In the nineteenth century, cunnilingus between two women was called *sapphism* after the ancient Greek poet Sappho and *lesbianism* after the island of Lesbos where she lived. Today the term "lesbian" has become the most popular in referring to female homosexuals. There is no special term applied to male homosexuals, however. This is interesting in that it reflects the fact that female homosexuals are a double minority: they are homosexual (different) and female (different again). In recent years, people have tended to use the term "gay" rather than "homosexual" in an effort to use a term which carries less negative connotation. The application of this term to sexual preference is actually a dubious improvement. The word "gay" comes from Old German meaning sudden, hurried, impetuous, and in the Middle Ages, it took the meaning of cheerful, joyous, colorful. In the seventeenth century, it meant loose morals, and in the nineteenth, it referred to a female prostitute. The nineteenth-century Quakers used the word to describe any religious ritual they thought was meaningless (such as the Lord's Prayer and the Ten Commandments).

the homosexual organizations were limited to operating publicly under the cover of disguise. Halloween balls were a favorite organizational event for the gay community because whatever one wore could be taken as a "costume" rather than evidence of sexual orientation, and anonymity was assured.

Even after the gay movement had begun, many gay organizations had trouble in becoming established. For example, in 1976 the University of Missouri prohibited homosexual organizations on campus. The argument was that such organizations would lead to association among homosexuals and this would lead to sodomy. Since sodomy was (and still is) a crime in Missouri, the university argued that it would be supporting criminal activity. Such a stance was not uncommon. In the same year, the Supreme Court upheld the constitutionality of Virginia's law against sodomy (Haeberle, 1978).

The Case of San Francisco

The most successful example of the gay movement in the United States is San Francisco. That city has become the place to live if you are gay since it contains the largest, best organized, most accepted, and most powerful gay community in the country. Reasonable estimates suggest that as many as 175,000 people—as many as 25 percent of the adult population of the city—are gay.

The gay community is centered in Castro Street. Its core includes high-status individuals who maintain positions of prestige, power, and prominence in the legal, political, social, and financial circles of San Francisco. This gay community has rather clearly demonstrated the kind of political power that can be generated by organization and participation. Mayor Finestein attempted to court the gay vote in San Francisco by not dealing directly with gay issues, but simply by acknowledging the existence of the gay community. The mayor not only took homosexuality as a moral issue, but made comments in the *Ladies' Home Journal* which the gays considered antihomsexual. When approached by representatives of the gay community, Finestein publicly announced —in an attempt not to alienate the straight vote —that she would not pander for the gay vote in her campaign. In other words, she would make no concessions to the gay community. In doing so, she not only raised the hackles of a large segment of the gay community but drastically underestimated its political clout. When election eve arrived, the mayor was forced not only to apologize publicly, but also to promise to appoint a gay police commissioner and to give political appointments to gays in direct proportion to their numbers in the population of the city (CBS, 1980).

One of the outcomes of the growth of the gay movement in the United States has been backlash. In 1978, San Francisco Mayor George Moscone and Supervisor Harvey Milk were shot to death by the man who had lost his supervisor position to Milk. Milk was the first openly gay person elected to public office in San Francisco. Fierce rioting followed when the admitted slayer was sentenced to seven years and eight months for voluntary manslaughter. The light sentence rendered by the jury was given not solely because Milk was a homosexual. Even though this undoubtedly played a part, it was more of a case of the straight community feeling themselves oppressed and striking back (Gallagher, 1980).

CONTEMPORARY ATTITUDES

The long cultural tradition of viewing homosexuality negatively has by no means dwindled away in American society. Even though the gay movement has begun to bring about legal changes and a more open discussion of homo-

BOX 10-4
ANTIHOMOSEXUAL VIOLENCE

Part of the aftermath of the backlash against the success of the gay movement in the United States has been increased violence against gays. The incidents are largely confined to males since they are the most visible to the public. Harry (1980), in a study in Chicago, found that 24 percent of the gay men in that city had been victims of "fag-bashing," as the offenders call it; the term specifically means a group of males beating a male homosexual. It usually is a group activity in which a group of heterosexual males go into the gay community and select one or more victims at random. Other types of harassment are also common against homosexual men. Harry found that approximately 16 percent of the gay males in Chicago had been victims of extortion attempts and 35 percent of these had paid the extortionists. The law is not above involvement in all this. Of these extortion attempts, 11 percent were made by police officers. The legal system also participates in giving light or no sentences to those who harass homosexuals. For example, on February 4, 1978, a gay playwright and poet in New York supposedly made a homosexual advance. He was taken from a store by two men who beat him to death in front of several witnesses. The two men went on trial for petty larceny and third-degree assault, the combined sentences for which carry a maximum of one year in jail.

sexuality, this progress has taken place in an atmosphere of greater openness about sexuality in general, not just about homosexuality in particular. There still remains strong disapproval of homosexuality, clear stereotypes about homosexuals, and many misconceptions as to the nature of homosexuality.

As shown in Table 10-1, attitudes about homosexuality in the United States have remained relatively unchanged from the early 1970s through 1980. The vast majority of Americans say that homosexual activity is wrong, and there is by no means strong support for the civil rights of gay persons in either freedom of speech or employment.

Stereotypes of homosexuals are still prevalent today, even in the minds of college students. Every study done finds results similar to those of Elman et al. (1978). These researchers found that male homosexuals were viewed as less likable, less personally and socially adjusted, less normal, less athletic, less capable as leaders, less moral, less honest, less warm, less considerate, and less personally happy than heterosexual males. These stereotypes are indeed powerful since they override other factors found to be powerful determinants of interpersonal liking. Krulewitz and Nash (1980) found, for example, that a male was less liked by college students when it was *suggested* to them that he was gay than when it was *suggested* that he was not gay. More important, the homosexual male was seen as more dissimilar to the respondent than was a heterosexual male on several dimensions, even though the two men were actually equal in similarity to the respondent.

Is America Homophobic?

The United States has been described as a homophobic society—one in which there is widespread fear of same-sex sexuality. The research suggests, however, that negative attitudes toward same-sex sexuality involve more than phobias. These attitudes reflect a larger package of traditional and repressive attitudes in general. Specifically, negative attitudes toward homosexuality are a reflection of less tolerance of diversity and human rights (Irwin and Thompson, 1977), less tolerance of a variety of different social and interpersonal situations (Morin and Garfinkle, 1978), greater authoritarianism, greater consciousness of status, greater sexual rigidity, and greater sex guilt (Morin and Garfinkle, 1978). In addition to males being more likely to be antihomosexual than females, more positive attitudes toward homosexuality are found among the better educated, the young, people who are Jewish or not religious, and those living in the Northeast and Pacific regions of the United States (Irwin and Thompson, 1977).

Gender Attitudes

Perhaps the central feature of a negative attitude toward homosexuality is a traditional and rigid view of male and female roles (Krulewitz

and Nash, 1980; Mosher and O'Grady, 1979; Weinberger and Milham, 1979; MacDonald and Games, 1974; Morin and Garfinkle, 1978).

Research consistently points to the fact that homosexuality represents to many people a threat to strongly sex-typed views of acceptable male and female behavior. It is typically thought that homosexuals suffer from gender confusion or gender inversion. They are males or females who adopt patterns of the other sex. These are thought to include social behaviors, speech patterns, mannerisms, dress, and sexual-partner preferences. This stereotype emanates from the view that all males "naturally" want a female sexual partner and all females "naturally" want a male sexual partner. If one does not follow this pattern, one must be a feminine male or a masculine female in other ways as well. Some research even indicates that a person's personal style is more important than his or her sexual prefer-

TABLE 10-1
Attitudes of adult Americans toward homosexuality, 1973–1980.

Attitude	Percent of National Sample				
Are sexual relations between two adults of the same sex:	1973	1974	1976	1977	1980
Always wrong	74	73	70	72	73
Almost always wrong	9	5	6	6	6
Wrong only sometimes	10	8	8	8	6
Not wrong at all	15	13	16	15	15
Should an admitted homosexual male be allowed to make a speech in your community?					
Yes	63	65	64	64	68
No	37	35	36	36	32
Should an admitted homosexual man be allowed to teach in a college or university?					
Yes	49	55	54	51	59
No	51	45	46	49	41

Source: Davis (1980).

BOX 10-5

WHAT IS YOUR ATTITUDE TOWARD HOMOSEXUALS?

Below is a scale designed by Hudson and Ricketts to measure attitudes toward homosexual persons. Test your attitude by completing the questionnaire according to the instructions. After you have finished, check the instructions for scoring and interpreting your score.

Index of attitudes toward homosexuals

This questionnaire is designed to measure the way you feel about working or associating with homosexuals. It is not a test, so there are no right or wrong answers. Consider each item as carefully and accurately as you can, then place the number indicating your feeling beside each item. The numbers are: 1 = Strongly agree with this statement; 2 = agree with this statement; 3 = neither agree nor disagree with this statement; 4 = disagree with this statement; 5 = strongly disagree with this statement.

1. I would feel comfortable working closely with a male homosexual. _____
2. I would enjoy attending social functions at which homosexuals were present. _____
3. I would feel uncomfortable if I learned that my neighbor was a homosexual. _____
4. If a member of my sex made a sexual advance toward me, I would feel angry. _____
5. I would feel comfortable knowing that I was attractive to members of my sex. _____
6. I would feel uncomfortable being seen in a gay bar. _____
7. I would feel comfortable if a member of my sex made an advance toward me. _____
8. I would be comfortable if I found myself attracted to a member of my sex. _____
9. I would feel disappointed if I learned that my child was homosexual. _____
10. I would feel nervous being in a group of homosexuals. _____
11. I would feel comfortable knowing that my clergyman was a homosexual. _____
12. I would be upset if I learned that my brother or sister was homosexual. _____
13. I would feel that I had failed as a parent if I learned that my child was gay. _____
14. If I saw two men holding hands in public, I would feel disgusted. _____

15. If a member of my sex made an advance toward me, I would feel offended. _____

16. I would feel comfortable if I learned that my daughter's teacher was a lesbian. _____

17. I would feel uncomfortable if I learned that my spouse or partner was attracted to members of his or her sex. _____

18. I would feel at ease talking with a homosexual person at a party. _____

19. I would feel uncomfortable if I learned that my boss was a homosexual. _____

20. It would not bother me to walk through a predominantly gay section of town. _____

21. It would disturb me to find out that my doctor was homosexual. _____

22. I would feel comfortable if I learned that my best friend of my sex was homosexual. _____

23. If a member of my sex made an advance toward me, I would feel flattered. _____

24. I would feel uncomfortable knowing that my son's male teacher was a homosexual. _____

25. I would feel comfortable working closely with a female homosexual. _____

How to obtain your score and what IT MEANS: For the following items you must first reverse the scoring on items 3, 4, 6, 9, 10, 12, 13, 14, 15, 17, 19, 21, 24. To do so, change the number you wrote for the item as follows: Change: a 1 to a 5; a 2 to a 4; a 4 to a 2; a 5 to a 1. When you have written in these new numbers and crossed out the old numbers, add up your total number of points. From this total score subtract 25. This is your score.

The scale measures the degree to which you have dread or discomfort of being in close quarters with homosexual persons. The minimum score is 25 and represents the least amount of dread and discomfort. The maximum score is 100 and represents the greatest amount of dread and discomfort. On studies with this instrument, the average score of college students is 53. In the college students studied, 4 percent have a score of 25 or less; 7 percent have a score of 75 or more; and 55 percent have a score greater than 50. In general, a score of 0 to 25 is highly nonhomophobic; 26 to 50 is moderately nonhomophobic; 51 to 75 is moderately homophobic; and 75 to 100 is highly homophobic.

Source: Hudson and Ricketts (1980). *The Clinical Measurement Package: A Field Manual.* Copyright by Dorsey Press, 1982.

ence in terms of others' reactions. Laner and Laner (1979; 1980) found that in the case of both male and female homosexuals, their acting in a manner not consistent with traditional views of how males and females should act (personal style) was more important than sexual preference in terms of other people's reactions to gay men and women. Thus, there is considerable evidence that negative attitudes toward homosexuality are not so much a matter of same-sex versus other-sex sexual preference as they are a reflection of being uptight about male and female gender behavior.

Experimental evidence (Mosher and O'Grady, 1979) suggests that homosexuality receives a particularly negative reaction when it creates some small degree of sexual arousal in an individual who holds traditional views of proper male and female behavior. Apparently, the sex-typed person reacts to his or her own arousal with disgust and then vents this disgust toward the gay person. It is important to note here the possible connection between this process and that of reacting to sexually explicit materials. As we shall see, those individuals who react to such materials with both sexual arousal and disgust are those most likely to label these materials pornographic and to be spurred to violence by observing them. (See Chapter 14 for a complete discussion of these reactions.)

The irony of this stereotyped view of homosexuality as "out-of-gender" behavior and the subsequent dislike of homosexuals because they are a threat to how males and females "should" behave is that it is incorrect. As we shall see, in many male homosexual circles there are even more macho behavior, dress, and mannerisms than there are among heterosexuals. Among both male and female homosexuals, gay persons who act as masculine females or feminine males are viewed with some disdain. They are often seen as not being very well adjusted to homosexuality and as playing a role they think society expects them to play. Often, male homosexuals dress as females and act "swishy" to amuse and play games with the hetereosexuals who drive by to observe the gay community.

Leather clothing is an important part of the macho styles that are favored by many gay males.

THE INCIDENCE OF HOMOSEXUALITY

Any time something or someone is seen as different, especially if the difference is seen as wrong and immoral, there is great concern over "How many of them are there?" Before we can begin to address this question, we must first decide who the "them" are.

What Is Homosexuality? Who Is a Homosexual?

If homosexuality is regarded as behavior, it is easy to define. In this sense, homosexual behavior is any form of sexual activity (psychological, physical, or both) with a person of the

BOX 10-6
STEREOTYPES OF HOMOSEXUALS BY AMERICANS

The following responses of a national sample of adults in the United States were recorded in 1970 (Levitt and Klassen, 1974). Even though these data are somewhat old, there is no evidence that there has been any significant change in these views.

Stereotype	People Agreeing (%)
Homosexuals act like the opposite sex.	69
Homosexuals have unusually strong sex drives.	59
Homosexuals are afraid of the opposite sex.	56
It is easy to tell homosexuals by how they look.	39
Homosexuals are dangerous as teachers or youth leaders because they try to get sexually involved with children.	73
Homosexuals tend to corrupt their fellow workers sexually.	38
Homosexuality is a social corruption that can cause the downfall of a civilization.	49
A homosexual *should not* be allowed to work as a	
Government official	67
Medical doctor	68
Minister	77
Schoolteacher	77
Court judge	77
A homosexual *should* be allowed to work as a	
Beautician	72
Artist	85
Musician	85
Florist	87

same sex. It would seem easy, then, to define what makes one a homosexual. There are, however, many difficult and informative questions here. Is one homosexual only if one engages in sexual activity in a physical sense? What if one wishes one could or fantasizes that one does? How many times does one have to engage in homosexual activity? Is once enough? Twice? Three times? How about just plain feelings? Does a person have to think of him- or herself as homosexual? There is ample evidence that many males and fe-

males frequently engage in homosexual activity as adults and do not see themselves as gay.

All these questions appear to us to be important because we view sexual orientation as an either/or matter. We divide the world into camps, categories, and pigeon holes in terms of sexual orientation. Since sexual orientation is so important to us, we certainly should be able to place people in either one or the other category of heterosexual or homosexual. Research evidence is steadily emerging, however, which rather clearly indicates that the real world of human sexuality is not so neat that a clean division can be made between heterosexual and homosexual.

The Kinsey Rating Scale

Alfred Kinsey, in what was to be a pioneering view of sexual orientation, saw it as falling on a continuum in terms of homosexual-heterosexual (Table 10-2). Thus, rather than seeing homosexuality and heterosexuality as an all-or-nothing matter, Kinsey saw sexual orientation as a matter of degree. His continuum was supported by his research findings. He found that approximately two-thirds of all males have at least one same-sex sexual experience before age 15 and fully 37 percent of all males have at least one such experience to the point of orgasm after age 15. For females, Kinsey found that 13 percent had at least one same-sex sexual experience to orgasm after age 15. As one might expect, these data created quite a public (and professional) furor, since the either/or view of homosexuality meant that 37 percent of all males and 13 percent of all females were homosexuals.

Sexual Orientation as Two-Dimensional

The Kinsey Rating Scale views sexual orientation as being on one dimension. Sexual orientation falls on a single continuum running from

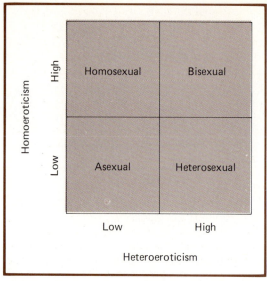

Figure 10-1 Sexual orientation as two-dimensional. (Source: Storms, 1980: 784, Figure 1.)

exclusively heterosexual to exclusively homosexual.

Much recent research quite strongly suggests, however, that sexual orientation in terms of sexual preference for the same or opposite sex is two-dimensional. Any given individual does not simply fall somewhere on the heterosexual-homosexual continuum, but may be seen as having *both* a certain degree of homosexual interest and a certain degree of heterosexual interest. As shown in Figure

TABLE 10-2
The Kinsey Rating Scale of sexual orientation.

Scale Point	Description	Males (%)*	Females (%)*
0	Exclusively heterosexual behavior	52–92	61–90
1	Incidental homosexual behavior	18–42	11–20
2	More than incidental homosexual behavior	13–38	6–14
3	Equal amount of homosexual and heterosexual behavior	9–32	4–11
4	More than incidental heterosexual behavior	7–26	3–8
5	Incidental heterosexual behavior	5–22	2–6
6	Exclusively homosexual behavior	3–16	1–3

*The range of percentages is due to such varying factors as age and marital status. The scale should be thought of as a continuum and the categories and their percentages as general locations on the continuum.
Source: Adapted from Haeberle (1978:231).

10-1, Storms (1980) suggests that the most simple description of sexual orientation consists of four possibilities. Each individual has some degree of heteroerotic interest, ranging from none to high. Each individual also has some degree of homoerotic interest, ranging from none to high. If a person is low on both homo- and heteroerotic interest, he or she may be called *asexual*. If people are high on homoerotic and low on heteroerotic interest, they may be called *homosexual*. If they are high on heteroerotic and low on homoerotic interest, they may be called *heterosexual*. If they are high on both homoerotic and heteroerotic interests, they may be called *bisexual. In all cases, it is very important to keep in mind that the boxes and labels in Figure 10-1 are matters of degree and not kind.* We are talking about two continuums, and all individuals may be seen as falling at some location on each continuum in terms of sexual interest.

Storms (1980) provided a partial test of this two-dimensional model of sexual orientation by studying the sexual fantasies of individuals who defined themselves as heterosexual, homosexual, or bisexual. His findings largely support a two-dimensional model. First, while people with different self-defined sexual orientations (heterosexual, homosexual, bisexual) differ in their erotic fantasies, heterosexuals do have fantasies about same-sex activity and homosexuals do have fantasies about other-sex activity. The difference between self-defined homosexuals and heterosexuals is a matter of degree. Homosexual males and females fantasize more about sex with the same sex than do heterosexual males and females, and heterosexual males and females fantasize more about sex with the other sex than do homosexual males and females.

The question of which people see themselves as bisexuals is important. If sexual orientation is seen as either/or, bisexual is not a possible orientation (I guess people who see sexual orientation in this way would argue that once is enough). If sexual orientation is seen as a continuum, as Kinsey did, then bisexuals should fall midway between heterosexuals and homosexuals in terms of their sexual fantasies.

That is, they should have equal amounts of same- and other-sex fantasies, same-sex fantasies more than heterosexuals but less than homosexuals, and other sex fantasies more than homosexuals but less than heterosexuals. If, however, sexual orientation is two-dimensional, as shown in Figure 10-1, then bisexuals should be high on both homosexual and heterosexual fantasies. This is, in fact, the case (Storms, 1980; Goode and Haber, 1977).

Same-sex experience of heterosexuals The two-dimensional nature of sexual orientation is revealed in the fact that a significant minority of both males and females have had at least one sexual experience with a person of the same sex. We have already noted Kinsey's findings in this regard. More recent studies provide similar results. For example, Haynes and Oziel (1976) found, in a sample of over 4,000 college students, that 12 to 17 percent of the males and 6 to 11 percent of the females had engaged in genital stimulation with a person of their own sex. Further, 6 percent of the males and 3 percent of the females were currently engaging in sexual activity with a person of the same sex. In a study of high school students, Cernkovich and Giordano (1980) found that 4 percent of the males and 3 percent of the females reported sexual activity with a person of the same sex. It is thus clear that a substantial proportion of persons who would identify themselves as heterosexual have engaged in same-sex sexual activity.

Other sex experience of homosexuals It is also clear that a substantial proportion of individuals who see themselves as homosexual have heterosexual experience. In Bell and Weinberg's (1978) large-scale study with self-identified homosexual males and females, only 74 percent of the males and 68 percent of the females currently engaged in sexual activity *only* with persons of the same sex. Further, fully 64 percent of the males and 83 percent of the females had at some time engaged in heterosexual intercourse; 14 percent of the males and 24 percent of the females had done so within the last year.

This heterosexual activity on the part of

self-identified gay persons is not merely going through the motions. Of those who had engaged in heterosexual activity at some time in their lives, only 8 percent of the males and 33 percent of the females never had orgasm in heterosexual activity. Further, 72 percent of the male and 79 percent of the female homosexuals in the Bell and Weinberg sample reported being sexually aroused by a person of the other sex at some time in their sexual history.

The two-dimensional view of sexual orientation is further supported by the observation that the frequency of homosexual activity is not related to the frequency of heterosexual activity among either college students (Haynes and Oziel, 1976) or self-identified male and female homosexuals (Bell and Weinberg, 1978). Thus, a high frequency of homosexuality does not necessarily mean no heterosexual activity. This is due to the fact that homosexuality and heterosexuality are independent sexual orientations, as shown in Figure 10-1. In a study of female college students, Goode and Haber (1977) found that those women with homosexual experience had had more heterosexual experience than women without homosexual experience. This observation is consistent with Storms's (1980) research, since in the Storms model (Figure 10-1), these women would be considered bisexual (they are high on homoerotic and heteroerotic interests).

The Question of Numbers

Now back to our original question: How many people are homosexual? As is now apparent, there is no answer to this question because there is no neat little category of "homosexuals" who are perfectly distinct in their sexual orientation from the other neat category called "heterosexuals." How much of what makes one call a person a homosexual is a matter of personal opinion, not of scientific fact. It is true that we would say that persons who are currently engaging in sexual activity only with persons of the same sex are homosexual and those engaging only with persons of the other sex are heterosexual. This definition is unsatis-

factory for a number of reasons. It does not take into account a person's past experiences, present or past interests, or present or past sexual self-view. Further, such a definition leaves out a good number of people who are not exclusively heterosexually or homosexually inclined.

Given the fact that a precise scientific definition of homosexuality is not possible because of the nature of sexual orientation, it is not possible to calculate the percentage of people who are homosexual or heterosexual. It all depends on your personal criteria and preference for placing people in sexual orientation categories.

We now have a problem. If we are to talk about homosexuality and homosexuals, we must have some means of identifying what and whom we are talking about. The definition of homosexuality we shall use throughout the remainder of this chapter is self-definition. Homosexuals will be considered those who see themselves as such. It should be kept in mind, however, that such a definition refers to a select population and in no way accurately describes the true nature of sexual orientations among humans.

THE GAY COMMUNITY

All minority groups who experience oppression as a result of their minority status tend to form a community. This community is both physical and psychological. The psychological community involves a sense of belonging, a sense of togetherness, the presence of others who offer social and psychological support, and the basis for one's self-esteem in an otherwise hostile society. The physical community may involve some identifiable physical locations, such as taverns or churches where members of the minority group often meet one another and call their own, or an entire geographical area of a city occupied by the minority group and devoted to the interests of its members.

The existence of a psychological and physical community is characteristic of most ethnic minorities in America and also of homosexuals. The complexity, intensity, or mere existence of a gay community differs from city to city, but most major cities in the United States have some form of such a community.

The Physical Community

In smaller cities, the gay community may consist of only a bar where gays gather to exchange information about social or political events and share a sense of common membership with one another. In larger cities, the physical gay community may be highly developed and may involve an entire gay culture area where the total life is the "gay life" and where anyone may enter it. Here it is readily apparent to any observer that this is a community apart from the so-called straight society. In San Francisco, for example, the gay community consists of gay bars, bookstores, restaurants, clothing stores, realtors, specialty shops, gyms, tourist bureaus, insurance companies, hotels, doctors, and dentists (one of whom teases straight society by advertising as "The Tooth Fairy"). All these establishments are gay-oriented, gay-owned, and gay-operated. Gay language is spoken here and posters, billboards, and store signs use the language of the gay world (showing that this is a community having a common sense of meanings and terms that "outsiders" do not understand). Males, in San Francisco as well as other cities, clearly dominate such areas; there is a high concentration of gay males on the streets and an almost complete absence of women and children. Social conventions clearly signify that this is the gay community. Styles of fashion (currently, one of the popular macho styles is leather) are clearly in evidence, as are the holding of hands, arms around each other, and cruising (which we will discuss). The residences of gays tend to be concentrated around such areas. However, there are usually several gay residential areas in a city rather than just one (Levine, 1979).

The gay culture regions of a large city are, like the straight world, segregated into specialized areas. For example, S/M establishments tend to be concentrated in one part of the larger gay culture area (Levine, 1979). These special areas and special establishments are important, since there is no such thing as *the* homosexual lifestyle. As we shall see, there are many different homosexual lifestyles just as there are many different heterosexual lifestyles. The difference is, however, that, unlike the heterosexual world, the homosexual community exists because of the specific sexual orientation of a large number of people. There is no such basis for the heterosexual community.

The Psychological Community

More important than the existence of a physical gay community is the existence of a psychological gay community. Of course, the existence of a clearly defined physical gay community enhances the chances that a solid psychological gay community is going to develop.

Participation in the gay community involves much more than just physically being present in a gay culture area; it involves being an active member of the community, identifying oneself as gay, and participating in the social world of the gay community. Within any gay community, people exist at all degrees of participation and commitment, from interested observer to community leader.

The gay community exists because of societal rejection. It provides a sense of identity and membership for those who are denied membership in the "straight" community. However, at the individual level, being a member requires that one be an insider, be a gay person. Being gay is not a condition but the playing of a social role. Being gay (regardless of where one falls on the two dimensions of heterosexuality and homosexuality) involves identifying oneself as gay and adopting a set of attitudes and behavior patterns appropriate to membership in the gay community.

Given societal rejection as the basis for gay communities and gay communities serving the function of providing a sense of membership and opportunities for social interaction, adopting a homosexual role is a function of association with homosexual groups. Association with homosexual groups is, in turn, a function of perceived societal rejection (Farrell and Nelson, 1976). Thus, those gay individuals most likely to participate fully in the gay community are those who most clearly feel rejection by society because of their sexual orientation. Albro and Tully (1979) found, for example, that female homosexuals tend to feel isolated from the heterosexual world and turn to the gay community for emotional support, friends, and socializing. This participation in the gay community means that one frequently associates with homosexual groups, and this association facilitates one's adopting a homosexual role and self-perception as a gay person (Farrell and Nelson, 1976).

One of the day-to-day psychological problems that any gay person may face is that of having been raised in an antihomosexual society. One must deal with the learning that "homosexuals are bad" in combination with the developing idea that "I am a homosexual." Thus, being a gay person in a heterosexual society involves certain problems of maintaining, or even developing, one's self-esteem and feelings of self-worth. The gay community serves an important function here. Ironically, the very societal rejection which creates the self-esteem problem also aids in solving it. Specifically, alienation from the general community and the openness of the gay community are the most important predictors of a gay person's self-esteem (Jacobs and Tedford, 1980). When a gay person is alienated from, and rejected by, the heterosexual society and also is attached to the gay community, he or she is likely to have high self-esteem.

The speed with which one socially and psychologically enters the gay community in large part depends on the amount of contact one has with other gay persons. In the process of fully becoming a gay person, the individual moves through a series of steps. Troiden and Goode (1980) found the following steps were experienced by males at certain ages: (1) thinking that one might be gay (16.3 years); (2) labeling one's feelings as homosexual (17.9 years); (3) labeling oneself as gay (18.9

years); associating with two or more gay people (19.4 years); and (4) having one's first homosexual love relationship (20.0 years). When one associates with others who are gay and they legitimize being gay, this process of becoming gay is sped up. When one participates in the heterosexual world, the process is slowed (Troiden and Goode, 1980).

PATTERNS OF SEXUALITY

Just as among persons with major or total heterosexual preferences and experiences, there is great diversity in the patterns of sexuality among homosexuals. Two important factors appear to shape these patterns: gender and the status of homosexuality in society. As we review the patterns, we shall see these two factors repeatedly emerge.

Cruising

Cruising is the process of going out looking for a person with whom to engage in sexual activity. While the term "cruising" has been coined to refer to homosexual behavior, it should be kept in mind that many so-called singles establishments, such as singles bars, are centers of heterosexual cruising.

As shown in Figure 10-2, cruising is predominantly a male activity. Fully 83 percent of the female homosexuals in the Bell and Weinberg study (1978) had not engaged in any cruising in the past year, while 63 percent of the males had done so more than a few times a month. It should be noted, however, that the incidence of cruising among males varies greatly. Not only are males more likely to engage in cruising than are females (a function of male and female differences in sexual learning), but males who cruise do so more frequently than females. Of the small number of female homosexuals who did engage in cruising in the past year, more than two-thirds did so once a month or less and only 12 percent cruised once a week or more. Cruising males, however, do so with some frequency. Fully 52 percent cruised more than once a week and

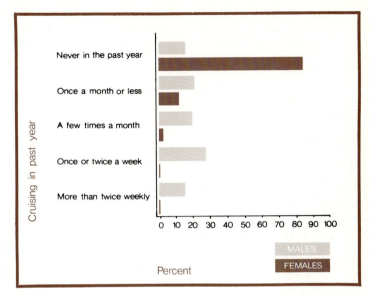

Figure 10-2 Frequency of cruising by male and female homosexuals. (Source: Bell and Weinberg, 1978: 299, table 6.)

another 25 percent did so a few times a month. Among males, cruising reveals a pattern consistent with that found among heterosexuals: Younger men cruise more frequently than older men.

Cruising Locations
Within the gay culture area, a number of locations play a part in cruising activities, and there is more diversity here than in the heterosexual world. As shown in Figure 10-3, gay bars are the most popular cruising locations for both males and females. After bars, however, cruising locations are almost totally male, with gay baths, the street, parks, beaches, tearooms, and theaters being used almost exclusively by males.

Bars Like heterosexual singles' bars, gay bars serve as important gathering places to socialize with one's friends and relatively safe places to seek and find sexual partners. Among both males and females who do cruise, the gay bar is by far the most frequently attended cruising location.

Within the gay bar, cruising activity may take many forms and styles. In general, people are looking around for potential sexual partners and the structure of the establishment may aid in viewing the possibilities, especially in male-dominated bars.

Figure 10-3 Percent of male and female homosexuals who have cruised in various locations in the past year. (Source: Bell and Weinberg, 1978: 299–300, table 6.)

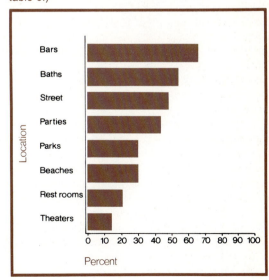

The moment I entered the bar I noticed men casually, sometimes surreptitiously, sometimes directly, looking at each other. The bar had a lighted entrance designed to allow maximum viewing by people sitting at the bar. From the moment a man enters the bar he is checked out. (Bell and Weinberg, 1978:237)

The initiator of the interaction may offer to buy a prospective partner a drink, engage him in conversation, or ask him to dance. Other methods of making contact and suggesting sexual activity are also present.

In the Purple Zebra I noticed one young man kept going into the rest room. Eventually I went in after him and noticed him exposing an erection to another at the urinal. Soon both men left, and as I looked out the front door I noticed that, as frequently happens, one was waiting in his car for the other to get his own car and follow him to their rendezvous. (Bell and Weinberg, 1978:237)

As closing time approaches, the same pattern takes shape as in singles' bars: the almost frantic search for a sexual partner.

Just before closing time everyone in the place appears as if he is looking for a lost contact lense which is somehow floating at eye level in the room. Seven people asked me if I needed a ride. (Bell and Weinberg, 1978:238)

Baths Gay baths ("tubs") are totally male. Reflecting very clear male-female differences in sexual learning, gay females simply do not go to gay baths and there are none operated for females (as far as I know). Martin Weinberg told me about a gay bath in New York that received complaints that there were no gay baths for women. In response to the complaint, the bath reserved one night a week for women only. After a few weeks of being unsuccessful in obtaining women customers, it eliminated the women-only night.

Baths are not a central part of the social life in the gay community. They are purely for

A gay bar.

sexual purposes and have as their counterpart in the heterosexual world the swingers' clubs, such as Plato's Retreat. (In fact, Plato's Retreat is located in what was a gay bath.) Gay baths, a part of the gay life in San Francisco for the past thirty years, have as their major function the provision of inexpensive places to engage in anonymous, frequent, and relatively safe sexual activity. The larger baths can accommodate some 200 people and many people may stay in the bath for many hours at a time. Inside, each person places his clothes in a locker and wraps a towel around his waist. There is usually at least one large room ("orgy room") and generally several smaller private rooms for sexual activity. One simply moves through the area engaging in sexual activities of various kinds with different people.

About seventy people were walking and creeping around the "maze" on the second floor of the bath. Some were having sex (usually mutual masturbation) standing up at various parts of the maze. In one corner was the orgy room. In the room was a large circular couch on which, for a few brief moments, were some eleven men, mostly drunk, playfully jumping on each other. Soon, three couples joined in a sex act while singing some popular song. It appeared that the sexual activity stopped short of orgasm since there was no sign of semen on the floor or couch. The atmosphere was that of a carnival or Fellini film. (Bell and Weinberg, 1978:240)

Older and less attractive men find baths one of the easier places to make sexual contacts since the dim, colored lights make it difficult to determine a person's age or physical characteristics. Still, youth and physical attractiveness remain important elements in partner selection.

There was an almost surrealistic use of lighting—multicolored, indirect, dim, and changing. People appeared to be moving

to and fro in slow motion. . . . In the (well-lit) shower room it was astonishing to see that a man who a few minutes earlier had appeared to be twenty-five was in fact forty or fifty years old. (Bell and Weinberg, 1978:240)

If one wants to keep his identity somewhat unknown, the baths are popular places. Some hustlers take their scores (clients) to baths and a few individuals ("tub freaks") have sex only at baths. Mainly, however, the patrons use the baths as alternative locations for cruising where partners are anonymous and readily available.[8]

Streets While baths are clearly locations where one comes only to engage in sex, bars are somewhat less totally sexual and streets are even less so. A person is in a gay bath for only one reason. A person may be in a bar for several reasons, and a person may be out on the street for a vast array of reasons. Given this, the streets require more discretion and subtle cues in cruising than either bars or baths.

In street cruising, a person usually positions himself or herself in some place on the sidewalk. When a prospective sexual partner is observed, one moves so as to establish some form of visual or verbal communication (glancing over, looking in the same store window, making some comment about a store display or the way one is dressed, asking for the time). If the person responds in such a manner as to indicate openness to the suggestion, a sexual activity is suggested. If this stage is passed, the two come to an agreement about what to do and they leave together. The same basic pattern of interaction prevails for other public places, such as beaches.

In some areas, heterosexual as well as homosexual men may be cruised by effeminate men ("drag queens") with the goal of finding anonymous sexual pleasure. The most common type of street cruiser is, however, simply

[8]See Weinberg and Williams (1975a) and Bell and Weinberg (1978) for excellent discussions of the social dynamics and organization of gay baths.

Gay males cruising on Christopher Street, New York City.

looking for a sexual partner with whom to spend the night or weekend.

There are also many street cruisers who are "hustlers." These are generally physically attractive men who engage in homosexual activities for profit. Many work only part-time in this occupation as a source of relatively easy money. Some are themselves gay in the sense of a self-view and are generally willing to engage in a wide range of sexual activities. Others do not see themselves as gay and engage only in receiving fellatio. The person who pays for the sex is called a "score" and the hustler may make $10 to $20 an encounter for a few minutes of sexual contact. Hustlers tend to cruise during those hours when there are nu-

merous potential customers (the noon hour, late afternoon, bar closing time). As in the world of female prostitution, the price a hustler charges often depends on his physical attractiveness and appearance (see Chapter 15).

A substantial proportion of homosexual males engage in hustling in one form or another at some point in their lives. In Bell and Weinberg's sample, 25 percent of the males had at some time been paid for sex. None of the female homosexuals had received money for sex, another reflection of male and female sexual learning in general appearing in the gay world.

A significant minority of homosexual males have also paid for sex at some time in their

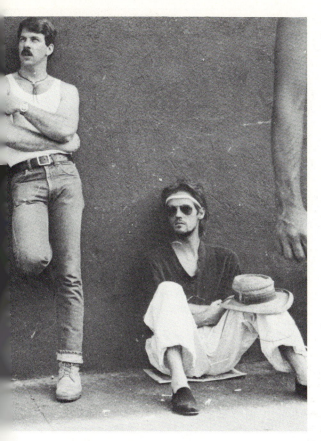

Tearooms are most frequently located in parks, travel terminals, or business buildings and are frequently near the gay culture area. They generally have certain physical characteristics such as not being highly visible to the general public, being easy to get away from in case of trouble, and having certain structural characteristics such as lockable stalls or doors which permit sexual activity privately without interference. Often a third person is used as a lookout. Individuals may cruise outside the tearoom and then go inside with a partner, or they may cruise inside.

> While I was at the urinal in a Golden Gate Park men's room, a white man in his thirties came in and stood beside me. He kept looking over and smiling at me. I noticed he was not urinating. He kept looking at the general area of my genitals. Once when he did so he said "Nice!" He turned partially to face me and I noticed he had an erection and he played with himself for a while. I told him I wasn't interested and he said, "That's a shame." (Bell and Weinberg 1978:244)

Sexual activity is usually performed in the near-privacy of a stall. Sometimes it involves people in different stalls with the wall between them having a "glory hole" through which one man can stick his penis to have fellatio performed by the person in the adjoining stall. Glory holes can be found drilled crudely through wood, metal, glass, and even marble walls.

lives (28 percent in Bell and Weinberg's sample). Involvement in prostitution is much less common among homosexual women. In this same sample, none of the females had ever paid anyone to engage in homosexual activity.

Tearooms Tearooms (in the gay vocabulary) are public restrooms which are used for cruising. Unlike other cruising locations where the expectation is for homosexual activity, tearooms are used by the general public. Therefore one runs great risk in cruising in a tearoom. There is a high probability of arrest or assault by a person who is outraged by the sexual approach. Within the gay community, tearoom cruising is viewed as disreputable.

Glory holes Given the danger of arrest or assault by an outraged "straight" person which exists in some tearooms, some establishments provide glory-hole sex. One pays about $3 to enter, and the establishment has a large number of either one- or two-person stalls which have holes cut in the walls (glory holes). Usually, each stall is connected to three others (one on each side and one in front) and a door which closes with a latch. One goes in and has glory-hole sex with as many people as he pleases through the stall

BOX 10-7
IN A GLORY-HOLE CLUB

"The dance here is simple. Walk the center aisle. Choose a booth by picking at the doors. When you find one that isn't locked, enter. You are faced almost immediately with a wall that has an oblong hole in it, pelvis high, about 4 inches long. The paint is marked and in some places peeling. . . . There are holes in each of the walls and a metal stool in the corner. There are handles screwed into the walls high above each of the holes. As I enter a booth, I see a pair of thighs through one of the holes. The person in the booth to my right is standing against one of the side holes, occasionally rubbing his groin against the wall. . . . His penis is through the hole . . . he is breathing in short takes. . . . Etiquette has it that if you are interested in the man next door, you rub your index finger along the bottom of the hole, as if you were checking for dust." (Gallagher, 1980:234)

Source: Originally appeared in *Playboy* magazine; copyright © 1979 by Playboy.

partitions. The establishments are dimly lit and thus provide anonymity, particularly for those who lead predominantly heterosexual lives. Some areas are more brightly lit, allowing exhibitionism through an open door or through a hole in the wall. Some people enter the stall and only unzip or lower their pants while others completely disrobe, depending on what turns one on. Unlike the baths, there is almost no sex at all outside the stalls. The whole idea is anonymous sex with no contact other than genital.

S/M establishments There is a side of commercial homosexuality which you will not find discussed in any text, and which is unheard of even by many gay persons. This is the S/M activity which takes place in commercial establishments. The format is much the same as the glory holes or baths in that one pays for entry to a place where certain types of activity are performed. The difference, however, is in the nature of the sexual activity. These establishments provide what is referred to as "heavy" S/M (sadomasochistic) activities. These activities commonly include bondage, discipline, dressing in uniform (Nazi storm trooper, police, biker, or other generally heavy macho style), dominations, humiliations, water sports (enemas), golden showers (urination), scatological activity (defecation and feces), and fist fucking (placing the entire clenched fist

into the rectum).[9] Within the gay community, such places, and the people who frequent them, are considered "pretty heavy" or "weird," and very few of these establishments advertise. There are establishments which fulfill milder fantasies. One such bar in San Francisco tends to attract males who like police and Nazi uniforms and advertises, "Uncut men wanted Tuesday nights."[10]

Informants tell me that there have been, and still are, places offering such activities that bolt the doors at a certain time at night so that no one can leave and that place few limits on what takes place. Reportedly, someone with some medical training is on hand to provide care until an ambulance arrives and most patrons allegedly leave on a stretcher. As might be expected, such places are not likely to be seen by the average San Francisco tourist.

[9]Fist fucking appears to be somewhat of a specialty with some people having a strong liking for the activity while most stay far away. Since the rectum has basically the consistency of a damp paper towel, serious and permanent damage is highly likely (Conchar, 1977). In 1981, the San Francisco coroner became so concerned about the number of deaths resulting from heavy S/M homosexual activity that he held private, no-expense workshops on S/M safety. These were widely criticized by some for condoning perversion.

[10]*Bay Area Reporter*, Dec. 20, 1979, p. 30. "Uncut" means not circumcised. An unknown number of gay men associate the foreskin with sexual completeness and masculinity. As a result, it is not uncommon for gay males to see a physician and to ask to have the prepuce restored (Mohl et al., 1981).

Cruising Encounters

Since most cruising takes place in locations other than where sexual activity can be engaged in (bars and the street), most partners go to one of the individuals' homes. About half the males in Bell and Weinberg's study reported that they usually go to their own home and another 29 percent said they go to their partner's home for sexual activity. Such cruising encounters are not typically "quickies." Fully 41 percent of the men reported usually spending the night with their partner and another 20 percent said they spent several hours with their partner. Only one-fifth of the males who cruised said they spent an hour or less with the other male.

Cruising Concerns

More than half the males in Bell and Weinberg's research said they worried considerably about being refused by a possible partner when they were cruising (as do heterosexual males). Somewhat fewer were frequently worried about having difficulty conversing with their sexual partner, and a substantial minority commonly worried about sexual performance, the police, being robbed, and being publicly exposed as gay (Table 10-3).

Number of Sexual Partners

Given the difference in cruising between male and female homosexuals, it is not surprising that they also differ enormously in the number of people with whom they have had sexual relations. In the Bell and Weinberg research, fully 43 percent of the males had had 500 or more partners in their homosexual career, and 28 percent had had 1,000 or more partners. Among females, the majority (57 percent) had had between 5 and 25 partners, and only 2 percent had had more than 100 different partners. With the numbers of partners for males being considerably greater, the differences between males and females reflect differences in male and female sexual learning in society as a whole.

The same pattern is found for the number of different partners in a year's time (Figure 10-4). Among males, 28 percent had had more than fifty partners in the last year, while only 6 percent of the females had had more than ten partners.

Nature of Sexual Encounters

Given the nature of cruising and the differences between males and females in cruising, the character of the relationship with different sex-

TABLE 10-3
Gay men's worries about cruising.

Worry	Men Who Frequently Worry about This Possibility (%)*
Being refused by prospective partner	58
Having difficulty conversing with partner	42
Catching a sexually transmitted disease	33**
Having partner want to do things I do not want to do	27
Being caught by the police	25
Performing inadequately sexually	24
Being robbed or rolled	19
Having one's homosexuality publicly exposed	12

*The percentages are for white males who said that they worry about each item "sometimes" or "often."
**About a third of the males often worried about getting a sexually transmitted disease. In Bell and Weinberg's study, 38 percent of the males had never contracted a sexually transmitted disease, but 34 percent had done so once or twice and 28 percent had been infected three times or more. Even so, this is an exceptionally low rate, given the number of different sexual partners gay males have had in their life. None of the females in Bell and Weinberg's research had ever contracted a sexually transmitted disease, a reflection of the male-female difference in cruising.
Source: Bell and Weinberg (1978:306–307, table 6).

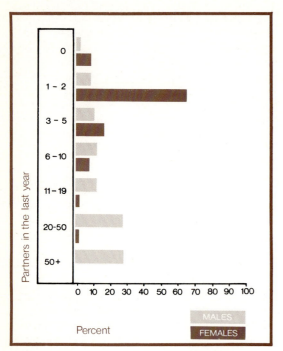

Figure 10-4 Percent of male and female homosexuals having various numbers of different sexual partners in the last year. (Source: Bell and Weinberg, 1978: 312, table 7.)

Figure 10-5 Comparison of male and female homosexuals on the percent of their sexual partners in the last year who were strangers. (Source: Bell and Weinberg, 1978: 308, table 7.)

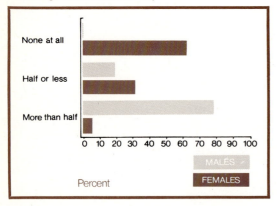

ual partners takes different forms for males and females. For males, the majority of their sexual partners are strangers, while for females, only a very small number are unknown (Figure 10-5).

Again reflecting male and female sexual learning, one-night stands are more common among gay males than among gay females (Figure 10-6). Learning differences are also reflected in social interaction with sexual partners. Gay males are much less likely than gay females to interact socially with their sexual partners after the sexual encounter.[11] Not unexpectedly, males are less likely than females to have sex with someone for whom they have affection (Figure 10-7).

Characteristics Desired in a Sexual Partner

The physical characteristics that male and female homosexuals desire in a sexual partner do not fit the common stereotypes about gay people. Among both males and females, the most frequently mentioned characteristic is body type or frame; 69 percent of the males and 68 percent of the females mention it as being important. In terms of masculine and feminine characteristics, males and females prefer persons having the dominant characteristics of the person's own sex. Males prefer a male who is masculine and females prefer a female who is feminine. Not unexpectedly, given American culture's emphasis on physical attractiveness, both males and females have a strong interest in the face, hair, and eyes of their sexual partner as well as their height. They do show significant differences, however, in their physical preferences in partners. Males

[11]By this point in the discussion, most students will have reached the conclusion that this form of sexual behavior on the part of gay males is "weird," "perverted," "extreme," etc. Now would be a good time to go back to Chapter 4 and review our discussion about the fact that we learn sexual scripts and therefore evaluate sexual behaviors on the basis of the sexual script we have learned. After reviewing that discussion, return to Chapter 1 and take another look at how sexual behavior was seen in the Victorian era or the Middle Ages. Think about your feelings.

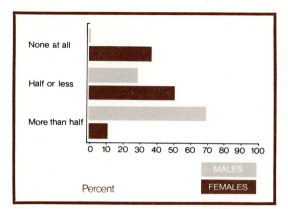

Figure 10-6 Comparison of male and female homosexuals on the percent of their sexual partners in the last year with whom they had sex only once. (Source: Bell and Weinberg, 1978: 309, table 7.)

Figure 10-7 Comparison of male and female homosexuals on the percent of their sexual partners in the last year for whom they had affection. (Source: Bell and Weinberg, 1978, table 7.)

have more interest in body hair, musculature, and genitals than do females, while females have more interest in breasts than do males.

Sexual Behaviors

Perhaps one of the greatest curiosities heterosexuals have about homosexuality is, "What do they do with each other?" As shown in Table 10-4, the favorite sexual activities of males are receiving oral-genital stimulation,

mutual oral-genital stimulation, and performing anal intercourse. Among females, the favorite activities are body rubbing, mutual masturbation, being masturbated by the partner, receiving oral-genital stimulation, and mutual oral-genital stimulation. As among heterosexuals, both males and females would rather receive than give, males are slightly more interested in oral-genital sex, and females are more interested both in less genital activities (body rubbing) and in more activities in general than are males.

TABLE 10-4
Favorite sexual activities of male and female homosexuals.

Activity	Males (%)	Females (%)
Receiving oral-genital stimulation	27	20
Performing anal intercourse	26	—
Mutual oral-genital stimulation	14	20
Being masturbated by partner	1	16
Mutual masturbation	2	13
Body rubbing	3	12
Receiving anal intercourse	5	—
Self-masturbation	5	1
Masturbating partner	0	0
Heterosexual activity	2	4
Other	13	8

Source: Bell and Weinberg (1978:330, table 9).

TABLE 10-5
The frequency of various sexual activities among male and female homosexuals.

Sexual Activity	Those Engaging in This Activity Once a Week or More	
	Males (%)	Females (%)
Body rubbing	6	19
Masturbating partner	26	40
Being masturbated by partner	26	40
Performing oral-genital stimulation	54	28
Receiving oral-genital stimulation	53	26
Performing anal intercourse	22	—
Receiving anal intercourse	19	—

Source: Bell and Weinberg (1978:328–330, table 9).

What one really prefers and what one does are not always the same. As shown in Table 10-5, both males and females masturbate their partners more frequently than their favorite activities suggest they might (sexual interaction is a process of exchange) and also perform oral-genital sex more than their favorite activities would predict. This is also the case for males in receiving anal intercourse. In terms of the frequency of sexual activity, apart from anal intercourse, females engage in more nongenital stimulation (body rubbing) and masturbation than do males, and males engage in oral-genital sex more frequently than do females.

A common myth about homosexuality is that people tend to be either active or passive in both their social and interpersonal behavior and their sexual activity. It is often assumed that some female homosexuals adopt the traditional male role and some male homosexuals adopt the traditional female role. As we have seen, this is just not so. Both males and females prefer to receive stimulation, and in the patterns of sexual behavior, exchange takes place in both giving and receiving. Among males, there is no such thing as the person who is the active insertor and the person who is the passive insertee in anal intercourse (Harry, 1976–1977; Bell and Weinberg, 1978).

Another common stereotype is that female homosexuals use penis substitutes for sexual satisfaction. About half of all female homosexuals have ever used a vibrator (most vibrators do not resemble a penis and are used for stimulation of the clitoris, not the vagina), and only about one-quarter have ever used a dildo (Califia, 1979).

It is also frequently assumed that homosexuals are "oversexed." In Bell and Weinberg's sample, 87 percent of the males and 74 percent of the females said that sex was "fairly" or "very" important to them. A summary measure of amount of sexual interest revealed that sex is no more or no less important to gays than to single and married heterosexuals (*Psychology Today,* August 1976).

AGING AND HOMOSEXUALITY

There are several very interesting aspects about questions of aging and homosexuality. First, it is noteworthy that the question "What do old homosexuals do?" is raised at all. We seem to raise this question only about categories of persons we see as deviant in the world of sex. For example, we also may inquire about what old prostitutes do but never about what "old heterosexuals" do (old people, yes, old *heterosexuals,* no). Second, we ask this question more about older gay men than about older gay women. A review of the discussion and research on aging and homosexuality reveals a clear lack of attention to elderly gay females. I suggest that this reflects the assumption that sex is more important to men than women *and* that the central feature of the gay person's life is sexual activity. While the first assumption has some merit, the second is clearly not supported. Last, the question of aging and homosexuality reflects the assumption that all male homosexuals do nothing but engage in sex, and without it they are doomed to depression and loneliness. The stereotype of the aging male homosexual is that he can no longer compete in the youth-oriented male homosexual world. He is thus no longer an attractive sexual partner and, rather than cruise for desirable and active sexual encounters, he must take a seat in a tearoom and perform oral sex on whoever comes by. He therefore becomes depressed and withdrawn and leads a life of sexual and social despair.

Such an image places far too much emphasis on sexual activity alone. It also fails to understand the nature of sexual opportunities in the gay male world which have nothing to do with one's age. We have reviewed many ways in which gay males make sexual contacts regardless of age. More important, this stereotype is not supported by the research. Weinberg and Williams (1975b), in a study of 2,500 male homosexuals in Europe and the United States, found that those males over the age of 45 attended gay bars less often, were more likely to live alone, and had less frequent sexual activity than did males under 45. These are differences we have also seen for heterosexual males.

Weinberg and Williams (1975b) failed, however, to find any difference between the older and younger homosexual males on a number of personal adjustment measures. In some respects, in fact, the older homosexual males were better personally adjusted than the younger males (they had a better self-concept and less fear of exposure as a gay person). Kelly (1977) also found no evidence for the stereotype of the poorly adjusted older male homosexual. His older respondents did not frequent tearooms to perform oral sex on whoever was willing, they did not desire children as sexual partners, and the majority reported a satisfactory sex life, with many being involved in a stable relationship with another male. Berger (1980) found that older male homosexuals were not socially isolated, depressed, anxious, dissatisfied with life, or sexually inactive.

INTERPERSONAL RELATIONSHIPS

While we have discussed in some detail the purely sexual side of gay existence, it should be made very clear that this is not all, or even most, of what homosexuality is all about. However, let there be no mistake: cruising, bars, baths, and other forms of impersonal sex are a significant part of the homosexual world. More important, however, the relative importance of impersonal sex in the world of homosexuality is dramatically different for males and females, a point to which we shall return.

While many people would like to argue that impersonal sex does not play a large part in the life of gay males (because, you see, impersonal sex is not the "best" sex in American society and people feel that it gives gay males a bad image), this assertion is not supported by the research evidence. For example, if you will go back and examine the percentage of males in Bell and Weinberg's study of homosexuals engaged in various forms of impersonal sex, you will again see that it is indeed a significant part of the gay male's sexual-interpersonal style. It is worth emphasizing the reason for this difference between gay males and females in the participation in impersonal sex. The difference reflects simply male and female sexual learning—the very same sexual learning we have seen throughout our discussion of heterosexuality.

In this regard, in the gay world we see males doing what males do and females doing what females do. More specifically, the research clearly indicates that gay males just do more male sexuality than heterosexual males

and gay females do more of what constitutes the core of female sexuality than heterosexual females. In a very real sense, what we see in homosexuality with regard to impersonal sex is males and females doing what I largely suspect many heterosexual males and females would do in a heterosexual context if they had the chance.

In a nutshell, heterosexuality involves males and females coming together. They come with quite different sexual learning, and as a consequence they have somewhat different views about what sexuality should be. Females place much greater emphasis on the emotional-interpersonal aspects while males place much more emphasis on the physical aspects. This means that heterosexuals compromise. He backs off from his physical-sexual interests a bit and she backs off from her interpersonal-emotional-sexual interests a bit. Take away this heterosexual compromise and male and female gender learning in sexuality is left to demonstrate itself almost without constraint. This is the world of homosexuality. The only other important feature to add here is that the socially disapproved status of homosexuality affects the life of the gay person.

These Gender Differences in Gay Relationships

Let's examine some of the gender differences for male and female homosexuals with regard to the nature of interpersonal relationships. Given what we have seen in the sexual behavior patterns of gay males and females, we would expect to find male and female differences in the importance of a permanent relationship with one person. This is the case. Permanent living arrangements with one person are more important to gay females than to gay males, and gay females are more likely than gay males to be in a permanent relationship (Bell and Weinberg, 1978; Harry, 1979).

These permanent relationships may acquire the status of a "marriage" in the eyes of the gay community, and often gay marriages are performed as a public commitment. While the gay community does provide some social support for marriagelike gay relationships, it is much less than the support found for marriage in the heterosexual world. This is especially so for the gay male (Harry, 1979). Reflecting differences in the heterosexual world, cruising is more commonplace for gay males, and a wide variety of sexual partners is the rule rather than the exception (Bell and Weinberg, 1978; Harry, 1979). Those males who do establish a permanent relationship with one person are most likely to be highly involved in the gay culture and community.

Many males establish an affair with one person but do not live together and do not expect each other to practice sexual exclusiveness (Harry, 1979; Bell and Weinberg, 1978; Cochran and Peplau, 1979). In general, the "average" gay male relationship is more akin to heterosexual open marriage than traditional monogamous heterosexual marriage (Harry, 1979; Cochran and Peplau, 1979). Harry (1979) found that gay females practice the greatest amount of sexual exclusivity, followed by heterosexual couples; gay males are the least exclusive. Note that gay females are at one end, gay males are at the other, and heterosexual couples are in the middle. *Heterosexuality is a clear compromise between male and female sexuality.*

Emotional Attachment

The sexually open character of gay male relationships does not mean that the individuals involved in more or less permanent relationships do not have strong emotional attachment with their partners. Cochran and Peplau (1979) compared heterosexual and homosexual couples on a number of different aspects of their relationship. They found that females—regardless of their sexual orientation—assigned more importance to emotional expressiveness and equality in the relationship than did males—regardless of their sexual orientation. They also found no difference between homosexual and heterosexual couples on romantic love, love for their current partner, feelings of closeness to their partner, satisfaction with the relationship, emotional commitment to the relationship, and frequency of seeing their partner. The only significant difference the researchers observed was that female homosexual couples practiced greater equality in their relationships than did either male homosexual couples or heterosexual couples.

Gay and nongay males and females all list honesty, affection, and intelligence as the most important characteristics in a partner. Among both homosexuals and heterosexuals, however, men place more emphasis on the physical attractiveness of their partner (Laner, 1977). This same pattern of partner preferences emerges in other research. Females, both homosexual and heterosexual, place more emphasis than do males (both homosexual and heterosexual) on emotional expressiveness and equality in a relationship with a partner (Cochran and Peplau, 1979). One other common misconception about homosexual relationships is that gay persons "reverse" gender roles. Gay males are not passive and gay females are not assertive in their intimate relationships (Falbo and Peplau, 1980).

GENDER IDENTITY AND INTERPERSONAL BEHAVIOR

Along this same line of thinking, it is commonly assumed that homosexuals "suffer" from gender identity confusion. Male homosexuals are thought to be gay because they have many psychological and behavioral characteristics typically associated with being feminine, and female homosexuals are thought to have many characteristics typically associated with being masculine. Research reveals, however, that gay persons do not suffer gender identity problems. Hassell and Smith (1975) found, for example, no evidence of gender confusion among a sample of female homosexuals. Storms (1980) compared self-identified male and female homosexuals and male and female heterosexuals and male and female bisexuals on standard measures of masculinity-femininity. There were no differences between any of the groups in masculinity-femininity.

In the most extreme statement of homosexuality and gender identity confusion, it is argued that sexual orientation is somehow determined or influenced before birth by chromosomal and hormonal characteristics of the fetus (e.g., Green, 1976; 1979). Not only does such a theory ignore the fact that male and female behavior differs greatly from one culture to the next and that, even if it did not, masculinity-femininity is not associated with homosexuality, a review of the research on hormones and sexual orientation reveals no relationship for either males (Meyer-Bahlburg, 1977) or females (Meyer-Bahlburg, 1979).

We have already examined differences in patterns of sexual behavior between male and female homosexuals and seen that, rather than there being evidence of gender confusion, males behave like males and females behave like females. This lack of gender confusion is also evident in self-perception. Homosexual males have a more masculine self-image than do male heterosexuals (Skrapec and MacKenzie, 1981).

HOMOSEXUALITIES

As the title of this chapter indicates, a single noun does not even come close to doing justice to the diversity of individuals in the gay lifestyle. There is no one kind of homosexual person any more than there is one kind of heterosexual person.

In an effort to isolate and examine various types of homosexualities, Bell and Weinberg (1978) used individuals' characteristics to identify five types.

Close-Coupled

Close-coupled individuals are in relationships in which they are closely bound together with their partner, and the relationship entails a high degree of exclusivity in terms of both sexual and interpersonal satisfactions. These gay individuals are the least likely to seek sexual partners outside the relationship; they have the fewest sexual problems, do not regret being gay, and spend more evenings at home and less leisure time alone. The males who are close-coupled seldom go to cruising locations, such as bars or baths, and do little actual cruising.

Overall, these individuals are highly adjusted. They have few problems (arrest, problems at work, assault, robbery) related to their sexual orientation. They are the least paranoid and tense and the most exuberant about life. Close-coupled women are the least likely of all female homosexuals to have sought professional help for a personal problem. Both male and female close-coupled individuals are the most self-accepting, the least depressed and lonely, and the happiest of all gay groups.

Open-Coupled

The gay people in this category live with a sexual partner, but are not happy with their situation and tend to see outside relationships. The males in open-coupled relationships do more cruising than the average gay male, and the open-coupled females do more cruising than any other gay females.

These individuals have more sexual activity than average and engage in more different sexual behaviors. They also worry more about their cruising, particularly about being arrested and publicly exposed. Even though open-coupled individuals do not differ from the average in overall adjustment, they are the least self-accepting of all gay persons.

Being open-coupled is the most common pattern for males but is relatively rare for females, who are most likely to be close-coupled.

Chapter 11
Sexual Minorities, Prohibition, and Oppression

In varying degrees, most of us have an image of what sexuality "should" be in terms of who, what, when, where, and why. The sexual script which guides our expectations and images of "good" sex is very much an ideal. While many Americans no longer believe that any sex which cannot be justified in terms of its reproductive potential should be banned, most of us do still carry an image of ideal sexuality. Gochros and Gochros (1977:xx–xxi) have described this image as the image of the sexual elite.

> The sexual elite is best exemplified by the idealized hero and heroine of the film *Love Story*. In that film the hero is a young and handsome law student and the heroine is a young and beautiful music student. They fall in love immediately, engage in premarital intercourse primarily as an expression of their love, and subsequently marry. She uses four-letter words, but, underneath it all, is a nice girl who would not dream of marital infidelity. They have a great deal of fun and never stop loving each other until she dies an elegant death. Neither seems to feel much love or affection for anyone else except her father, who is sweet but passive. One is led to

speculate that the hero is always potent, the heroine always achieves multiple sequential orgasms, and that they never need Kleenex. They seem to consider genital-to-genital intercourse in the missionary position culminating in simultaneous orgasms the logical and normal conclusion to every sexual activity that occurs 2.7 times a week immediately following Johnny Carson.

This is, of course, a bit of an overstatement about our ideal image of what sexuality should be, but it is perhaps not as exaggerated as you might first think. Not all sexualities are created equal, nor are they treated equally in any society. There are many forms of sexuality which are either disapproved, oppressed, or prohibited. In general, in American society, the further a sexuality is from this idealized image the more likely it is to encounter resistance.

There are many forms of sexuality which receive overt disapproval, prohibition, and oppression. The bases of oppression and prohibition seem to be two criteria. First, a person's sexuality may be oppressed because of the form of sexuality he or she prefers or engages in. There is a wide range of behaviors here, but many forms of sexual conduct are simply not popular in American society for a variety of historical, social, and psychological reasons. Sexual oppression here is not a matter of some logical argument. Rather, the behavior is just not acceptable, popular, or interesting to most people.

We have already discussed many forms of sexuality, including adolescent sex and homosexuality. The interesting aspect of sexual oppression on the basis of the sexual conduct performed is that the popularity of sexual expressions tends to ebb and flow over time much as fashions do. Public nudity, oral-genital activity, female sexuality, sadomasochistic activity, homosexuality, and transsexualism have all undergone rather radical changes in their popularity and relative oppression. Second, a person's sexuality may be oppressed not because of the sexual behavior engaged in but because of the person who engages in it. In this case, the physical form of the sexual activity may be perfectly acceptable and closely conform to the sexual ideal. However, because of the nonsexual characteristics of the person who engages in that behavior, his or her sexuality may be disapproved, prohibited, or oppressed. This is true for many forms of physical handicaps, certain ages, and certain marital status groups.

It must be clearly noted that whatever form of sexuality is approved or disapproved in a society at a particular time is a matter of social definition and nothing more. Approved and oppressed sexualities are matters of social convention and agreement, not higher laws of biology. What you and I approve and disapprove of sexually is due to our learning. If you are well socialized into the mainstream of a society at a particular time, there are probably certain forms of sexuality that you will strongly approve and certain ones of which you will strongly disapprove. If you had been raised in another time or place, your attitudes might be very different.

This does not mean that it is wrong to disapprove of certain forms of sexuality. Right and wrong are matters of personal moral codes and opinion. Thus, you are not less or more of a "good" person by feeling that some forms of sexuality are acceptable or that others are unacceptable except in the eyes of another person who also holds personal opinions on this issue. We all have a list of forms of sexuality we feel are disgusting, wrong, or not allowable. The important point is that this list is not based on any set of biological laws about the inherent nature of "good" or "right" sexuality. Rather, this list is an outcome of our sexual learning as members of a given society at a given time.

In this chapter we cannot even begin to discuss all the forms of sexuality which are disapproved, prohibited, or oppressed, since almost any form of sexuality you can think of probably falls on someone's list of the ill-regarded. We shall, however, discuss some of the major "unacceptable" forms of sexuality that a student in a course such as this should be familiar with or which are receiving some popular attention.

SEXUAL OPPRESSION DUE TO NONSEXUAL CHARACTERISTICS

There are many categories of individuals whose sexuality is oppressed or ignored because of purely nonsexual characteristics of those persons. In general, their sexuality is oppressed because they themselves do not fit the mold of an acceptable and appropriately sexual person. In many cases, they are denied sexuality for this reason alone. In other cases, they possess some characteristic which makes it necessary for adaptations to be made for them to be sexually active—adaptations which themselves do not fit the socially acceptable mold of ideal sexuality.

The Hearing Impaired
In 1974 a national census identified 1.8 million deaf persons in the United States (Schein and Delk, 1974). This figure includes only those individuals clinically classified as deaf. There are millions more who have varying degrees of hearing impairment short of deafness.

Even though the deaf constitute a sizable

population, it is a population whose sexuality has been virtually ignored until very recently (Fitzgerald and Fitzgerald, 1980; *Sexuality and Deafness,* 1979).

For any individual, the most important aspect of sexuality is learning. Lacking a sexual instinct which automatically directs or instigates sexuality, what one does in the realm of the sexual must be learned. The deaf person has three main avenues of learning: visual experience, direct experience, and reading. Unlike those with complete hearing, the deaf person obtains almost no sexual information through verbal communication. Even though visual sources of information are available to the deaf person, the meaning to be attached to what one sees is not automatically learned. Most visual sexual learning experiences are learning experiences only because what is seen is given some verbal interpretation—most often by one's peers.

Perhaps the most important source of sexual learning is thus missing for the congenitally deaf person or the person who becomes deaf before adolescence. Most sexual learning in adolescence takes place through verbal communication with one's peers. Moreover, this communication is subtle, fragmented, mumbled, and incomplete. Even the most skilled deaf person may be able to catch bits and pieces of this information from his or her peers, but has no chance of learning in exactly the same way exactly the same things as his or her hearing peers learn on the subject of sex.

Fitzgerald and Fitzgerald (1980) found that television and movies were the most significant sources of sexual information for deaf persons. However, what these media images communicate by visual means alone is not an accurate image of sexuality in this society. These visual images are really stereotypes of sexuality. Missing from the visual information are all the subtle verbal modifications and amendments to what appears on the screen. Consequently, this form of visual learning results in an inaccurate and incomplete view of sexuality on the part of the deaf person. Think about what kind of definition of appropriate sexuality you would come up with if you just watched television

without the sound. Of course, some forms of visual learning would provide the deaf person with a quite accurate view of sexuality. However, we do not allow people to watch others engage in sexual interaction (unless it is through the distorted image of pornography). A second major source of sexual learning for the deaf person is direct experience. Little need be said here except that (1) direct experience is a difficult means of sexual learning unless it is preceded by some significant sexual learning, and (2) direct experience is not an acceptable means of sexual learning in its entirety, although it may be an acceptable form of practice and learning under some conditions.

The deaf person is also deprived of certain forms of communication, a deprivation that affects not only learning itself, but also sexual interaction. Specifically, verbal-sound communication is lacking. For example, deaf persons, regardless of their skill with American Sign Language, are much less likely to be able to discuss with their peers such important adolescent sexual topics as love, sex and affection, sexual fantasies, masturbation, guilt, fear, and personal sexual standards.

What the deaf person can even say in matters sexual is severely limited by American Sign Language. The language, while extremely flexible, often results in rather straightforward statements from the point of view of the hearing person. For example, the statement "I like to fuck you" is unlikely to be received with much social approval from a hearing person even though the intended meaning behind the communication may be perfectly socially acceptable. This means that the deaf person may be largely confined to communicating sexually only with other deaf persons, thus largely narrowing and restricting not only his or her sexual learning possibilities but also possible sexual experiences.

Sound communication is also an important part of sexual interaction. If one or both people cannot hear, communication must be by use of the hands. It is very difficult to be passionately kissing and touching each other and doing American Sign Language at the same time. Additionally, much sexual interaction and communication are solely sound. The cues exchanged in lovemaking are often sounds in the form of moans, grunts, and sighs which communicate important feelings, preferences, and current states. Not only can the deaf person not hear these sounds but sign language does not even communicate them. The sexual world of the deaf person consists very much of the sounds of silence.

The Visually Impaired

Although the deaf and blind are frequently lumped together (as in schools for the deaf and blind), hearing- and sight-impaired persons have quite different problems (Smith, 1977).

The blind person lacks, of course, an important avenue of sexual learning—visual learning. The two major avenues of sexual learning open to the blind person are hearing and touch. Reading is a major source of sexual learning, but the information available on braille is limited and somewhat "unrealistic" when compared with the kinds of information obtained directly from peers. The written sex information translated into braille is limited in both quantity and content, and is unlikely to be *The Joy of Sex* or articles from *Cosmopolitan* or *Playboy* (although *Playboy* is available in braille).

Touch is an important means of some learning for the blind person, but not of sexual learning. American society has a strong social norm which dramatically affects the blind person: "Look, but do not touch." As a result, an adolescent who is blind may have a wealth of technical knowledge obtained from reading about sex but still be inadequately informed. For example, Hicks (1980:169) gives an example of an adolescent male who said, "I think I know *what* a girl's breasts are, but I'm not sure I know *where* they are." The blind adolescent will also not be able to see how the bodies of males and females change through adolescence or how male and female bodies differ as adults. They will not have the visual experience of how a person changes with pregnancy or with age. Without vision, an entire realm of erotic meanings is lost. How can the blind ado-

lescent learn from his or her sighted peers to differentiate visually erotic and nonerotic persons on the basis of body shape? Yet this differentiation is a central erotic stimulus in American society.

In other areas of sexual interaction the blind person also experiences a very different world from that of the sighted person. Eye contact is very important in not only initial encounters but actual sexual interaction. At social gatherings, the blind person cannot look around the room to see who might be of interest. He or she must be told by a third person, wait for someone to encounter him or her, or interact with the nearest person (Hicks, 1980). This is particularly difficult for males. In our society, they are expected to take the initiative in cross-sex encounters. Taking the initiative when you are blind is very, very difficult. The opposite problem confronts the blind female. When encountered by a male, she has only nonvisual information to process who and what this person is. Visually impaired persons also have mobility problems. Even if a male is told that there is a woman across the room whom he might like to meet, getting there is a problem. And the woman can often be physically trapped simply because mobility in "escape" is difficult.

The blind person may also have some difficulty in such routine activities as knowing how to dress and monitor appearance. It is very hard to engage in a certain sexual self-presentation by appearance (very important in our society) when one cannot see how either another or oneself looks. Certain mannerisms may also inhibit the blind person's social acceptability. He or she may give certain inappropriate or antisocial signals to others. For example, the congenitally blind develop certain mannerisms, called "blindisms," that consist of such behaviors as rocking back and forth, eye poking, and twiddling fingers (Hicks, 1980). Such activities are not likely to aid one in social interaction even though they are quite expected in a blind person.

Even in the absence of the above problems, the blind person, like people with various types of physical disability, is relatively immobile. The difficulties of mere transportation and physically moving from one place to another dramatically limit one's opportunities for social and sexual interaction.

The Developmentally Disabled

The developmentally disabled (mentally retarded) person suffers from problems not only of inadequate sexual learning, but also of social stigma. There has been an historic fear of the sexuality of retarded persons. One form of this fear was that if the sexuality of retarded persons was not controlled, they would reproduce and overpopulate the earth. A study was done at the turn of the century in the United States which reported on how many IQ points the intelligence of the country would drop if the mentally retarded were allowed to procreate at the same rate as the rest of the adult population. One of the responses to this fear has been the sterilization of retarded persons. This fear has also been accompanied by the myth that retarded persons are more sexual than other people. This is a myth much like that of black sexuality. It is assumed that the retarded person is somehow more "primitive" and thus "animallike." Since it is widely assumed that sex is some natural biological urge and thus a characteristic we humans share with our animal ancestors, it is thought that the "more primitive" retarded person is also sexually primitive. (See Evans and Skeen, 1981, for a discussion of sexual stereotypes of the mentally retarded as held by parents and professionals.)

People, including parents, often feel that the developmentally disabled person cannot properly deal with sexual feelings. This is often true because of a lack of sexual learning opportunities for the retarded person. Many parents feel that they should keep sexual information from developmentally disabled children. As a consequence, the child obtains only fragmented and unclear images of the sexual and thus often behaves in a socially unacceptable manner because of this inadequate learning.

Myerwitz (1971) found that one-third of the crimes committed by retarded persons were sex-related. However, rather than being acts of unbridled passion or violence, such sex-related crimes are acts which are the result of ignorance due to a lack of sexual learning in tune with the rest of society. Urinating on the sidewalk because one does not know how to locate a restroom and is unaware of exhibitionism, not having one's pants properly zipped, and "making a pass" without the expected level of social grace and finesse are the results of deficiencies in social learning. Gebhard et al. (1965) found, for example, that one of the three major categories of males arrested for exhibitionism were the retarded who did not know better. Also, no small amount of discrimination against the developmentally disabled person who engages in a socially inappropriate sexual act is owed to the image of the developmentally disabled individual as "oversexed." For example, a young, well-dressed, handsome executive male who pats a woman on the buttocks is most likely to be treated very differently from a retarded male who does the same thing.

Most retarded persons experience an oppression of their sexuality by others. Parents of developmentally disabled children not only tend to keep sexual information from the child, but act in a sexually protective manner as well. Parents of developmentally disabled females, for example, often keep them from contact with males in fear that they will be taken advantage of sexually. This isolation from "normal" society because of fears of sexual activity has also taken formal channels. Kempton (1977) recalls working in an institution for the developmentally disabled called the Institution for Childbearing Women. This was a facility for developmentally disabled women of childbearing age who were never permitted to be in the company of any male except a close relative, and thus did not experience exactly the type of social environment that facilitates sexual or social interaction learning.

The actual learning disability of the retarded person also places restrictions on his or her sexuality. Many developmentally disabled persons are not capable of learning to have a successful heterosexual-partner relationship

(Kempton, 1977). For these people, their only form of sexual activity may be masturbation. This is, however, not a form of overt adult sexuality which receives much outright approval in this society. Moreover, engaging in masturbation on the part of the developmentally disabled person may be taken as proof positive of the person's "abnormal" sexuality; we must remember that not too many years ago, many Americans were convinced that masturbation caused mental disturbances.

Even those developmentally disabled persons who are capable of having a happy interpersonal-sexual relationship with another person are likely to be ill-equipped as far as sexual learning is concerned. It is not at all uncommon for such persons to have no concept of the sexual processes they are perfectly capable of participating in and fully enjoying. A psychologist (cited in Kempton, 1977:244) told of a developmentally disabled couple whose experience sadly makes the point. The retarded man and woman had been married for two years and lived in the home of the woman's mother. In this two-year period, they had never engaged in intercourse because they had no concept of how a penis and a vagina could be used for sexual interaction between a man and a woman. Their view of making love for these two years had been to lie together in bed and affectionately rub each other's bodies.

The Institutionalized Mentally Ill

We place people in institutions for many reasons, not the least of which is that we don't much care to observe on a daily basis what we consider society's "rejects." Some persons come to be categorized as rejects on the basis of law violations; others are so placed on the basis of age (nursing home residents) or what we call mental illness. Regardless, all these institutionalized persons tend to be located in what are called total institutions—total because the life of the institution encompasses and controls one's entire life. In such an environment, individuality (except as an expression of some acceptable form of "weirdness") is a rarity, including sexuality (Ginsberg, 1977).

Many people feel that if a person is mentally ill, he or she has no sexual interest. This, however, is rarely the case. Wasow (1980) found that among a relatively small sample of mental patients, only 11 percent said they currently had no sexual problems. One must have sexual interest to have sexual problems.

The very structure of most mental hospitals is such as to ensure the repression of patients' sexuality. Not unexpectedly, Wasow (1980) found that the most common sexual problem mentioned by mental patients was "no partner." In the absence of a heterosexual partner, one is left with either homosexual activity or masturbation; neither option is likely to evoke much support from the hospital staff. Such behaviors may, in fact, be used as evidence of the person's mental illness. In a severely total institution, the very structure of the person's life may require what is considered socially unacceptable sexual activity. For example, public masturbation is not acceptable even though one's days may be such that if one is going to masturbate, one will have to do so in public.

Nursing Home Residents

While some research suggests that neither college students nor nursing home staff have a negative attitude toward sex among the elderly (LaTorre and Kear, 1977), research within nursing homes suggests otherwise. Kaas (1978) found that nursing home staff members were not particularly negative in their attitudes about sexuality on the part of the residents, but their actions were less than encouraging. Wasow and Loeb (1979) found not only negative attitudes by the nursing home personnel, but outright resistance to sexuality among the residents.

Sexual oppression by staff in nursing homes is not unexpected. Not only is there a long tradition stating that sex should cease after a certain age, but sex is also supposed to be private. Except in the arena of commercial sex, most of us do not really care to know that two people are engaging in sexual activity just down the hall. Given the nature of most nursing home facilities, the staff cannot avoid such knowledge and they are quite likely to find it uncomfortable.

A considerable amount of the sexual oppression in nursing homes comes from the residents themselves. Many residents feel that sexual activity is acceptable for other residents, but not for themselves (Wasow and Loeb, 1979). One of the major reasons for this self-imposed restriction on sexuality is that many residents of nursing homes feel they are not sexually attractive (Kaas, 1978). Even if residents do see themselves as fitting the cultural mold of an acceptable sexual person, they themselves need a degree of privacy for sexual interaction, which is not often available (Kaas, 1978). White (1982) also found that in a sample of nursing home residents 91 percent had no sexual activity at all in the previous month, but 17 percent said they would like to if they had a partner and privacy.

The Physically Disabled

There are many different kinds of physical disability ranging from those existing at birth to those acquired during or after adolescence. These disabilities may encompass such factors related to one's sexual activity as impaired motor control, impaired physical movement, a lack of physical sensation in certain "sexual" areas of the body, physical deformities affecting attractiveness, or altered physiological functioning due to amputation or alteration of bowels or bladder (see Chapter 17 for more detailed discussions).

Perhaps more than any other category of the sexually oppressed, the sexuality of the physically disabled has received considerable attention in recent years. This attention has resulted in many members of the public, health care professionals, and the disabled themselves seeing sexuality as a vital, possible, and enjoyable part of the life of the disabled person. In recent years, many booklets have been published informing the physically disabled and their partners how to adjust their sexuality to their particular disability. (See, for example, Shaul et al., 1978, *Toward Intimacy: Family Planning and Sexuality Concerns of Physically Disabled Women.*)

While we cannot discuss in detail all the facets of sexuality for all types of physical disability, it is important to examine some of the major attitudes, characteristics, and adjustment methods for some types of disability. By the very nature of the stigma attached to physical disabilities and the disabled in American society, this is a subject in human sexuality with which most people are unlikely to have any experience or about which they have any knowledge.

Many physically disabled people will tell you that the sexual activity itself is not the hard part. Rather, the difficulty is one's being seen by others as a potential sexual partner. This view of the disabled person as not being an acceptable sexual partner may develop if a person is married and suffers the disability after marriage. But it is perhaps even more severe for the person who is single and physically disabled.

Negative attitudes toward the sexuality of the physically disabled are quite common (as shown in Table 11-1). Haring and Meyerson (1979) asked 110 college students to complete sentences regarding the sexuality of the handicapped. (They were referred to as "crippled" so that attention was focused on motor impairments of the limbs.) Each completed sentence was then viewed as indicating the student's attitude toward that specific behavior and coded as either a positive or negative statement. The percentages of students with negative attitudes toward various aspects of the sexuality of the handicapped are shown in Table 11-1.

These attitudes exist not only with others but also frequently with oneself. For a variety of reasons, disabled persons may see themselves as no longer either sexual persons or unacceptable sexual persons. For example, the male who has been socialized into a society in which an erect penis is a central sign of masculinity may well have some serious sexual self-image problems resulting from a spinal cord injury which makes erection difficult or impossible.

The physically disabled woman in particular may confront the problem of being an attractive sexual "object" only because of her disability. There are males who have fetishes for certain kinds of disabilities such as ampu-

TABLE 11-1
Attitudes toward the sexuality of the handicapped.

Dimension of Sexuality	Students Reporting Negative Reaction	
	Females (%)	Males (%)
A crippled young woman naked	100	90
A crippled young woman masturbating	54	54
A crippled young woman buying contraceptives	43	50
Sexual intercourse between a crippled young woman and a noncrippled male	8	8
The adequacy of sexual functioning on the part of a crippled woman	48	70
The enjoyment of sex by a crippled woman	50	51
A crippled woman being sexually active	48	51
The sex needs of a crippled woman	40	47
Two crippled people needing a third person to arrange their bodies for sex play	56	38
The amount of sex knowledge possessed by a crippled woman	28	36

tation. As one female amputee said, "This 'sicky' thought I'd be a kinky trip" (Shaul et al., 1978:15).

Some males either want to be nurturant or they have severe feelings of inadequacy such that they cannot become sexually aroused unless their partner is physically disabled in some way. Two disabled women recalled sexual relationships: "He wanted someone to nurse" (Shaul et al., 1978:15); "He didn't think he could 'make it' with a nondisabled woman" (Shaul et al., 1978:15).

Regardless of the nature of the physical disability, it is clear that a person and his or her partner can make adaptations in their sexuality to provide for an emotionally, physically, and psychologically satisfying sexual existence. In many cases, the person's disability may be such that a redefinition of sexuality is necessary. As we have repeatedly discussed, Americans tend to have a very genital, physical view of sexuality. Most of us tend to discover at some time in our life, however, that intimacy is what is important and that the delight in sex is the degree of interpersonal emotional, psychological, and physical intimacy. Thus, persons with severe paralytic disabili-

ties, arthritis, or other dysfunctions may have to change their definition of "good" sex from erections, vaginal lubrication, and orgasms to touching, caressing, holding, or other forms of sexual intimacy and physical activity.

"We don't do much 'hard core sex,' but find our greatest fulfillment in slow, deep touching and holding. We can't seem to get enough cuddling. It's different I guess . . . 'cause we can't do much moving, but that doesn't seem to detract from our pleasure." (Comment of a woman with severe rheumatoid arthritis, quoted in Shaul et al., 1978:19)

Other forms of adaptation to a disability may require only placing more emphasis on common sexual activities. Consider the remarks of two paraplegic women with spinal cord injuries:

"If there were an oral sex fan club, I'd be president."
"I really like going down on my partner 'cause I can totally control what's going on and I experience so much sensation in my mouth . . . whereas, I can't control my

vagina at all or feel anything there. . . ."
(Quoted in Shaul et al., 1978:19)

Other forms of adaptation may involve experimentation with different intercourse positions that are comfortable and possible. For many physical disabilities, the clearly standard American missionary position is problematic. For males with multiple sclerosis or muscular dystrophy, the self-support in this position is very difficult. For males and females with severe arthritis, the missionary position is problematic, and for women with extreme bowel or bladder surgery requiring a catheter or ileostomy, it is uncomfortable and difficult.

All these adaptations require communication beyond that which most people practice

and levels of patience with one's physical status which may be demanding. For example, adapting to the existence of a catheter can be very problematic for a woman if she cannot face her sexuality and her disability with total openness and honesty. Furthermore, these adaptations are not always easy in a society which has inherited a set of sexual values and traditions that encourage us not to talk about sex and to ignore physical disabilities. Even though many people regard sex as a basic human need right along with eating, not many people would be willing to assist a severely disabled man and a woman into a position where they could engage in sexual activity even though the same people would gladly help them reach the dinner table (Heslinga,

In recent years there has been a greater emphasis on the abilities of disabled persons. This is reflected in more attention being given to sexuality and the disabled. This photo was taken during an archery match at the Twenty-first International Stoke Mandeville Games for the Paraplegics, Aylesbury, England.

1977). For some disabled couples, the assistance of an attendant is necessary. These adaptations to physical disability are very informative, since some consideration of them reveals how narrowly any society defines what "normal" sexuality consists of.

SEXUAL OPPRESSION DUE TO SEXUAL CHARACTERISTICS

By far the best-known forms of sexual oppression take place on the basis of the sexual preferences of individuals. (For example, dressing in clothes of the opposite sex, voyeurism, sex with animals, being aroused by pain, or being tied-up.) Some writers have referred to these sexualities as "specialized" sexual interests. This term is, however, quite inaccurate. Sexual preferences that are oppressed are no more specialized than sexual preferences that are not oppressed. For example, a person who prefers to be sexually aroused by pain has no more of a specialized sexual interest than the person who prefers to be sexually aroused by a large penis or large breasts or oral-genital sex.

These various sexualities are simply those which are preferred and adopted by a minority of individuals—those who are not in a position of influence and power sufficient to change social definitions of acceptable sexuality.

We tend to have a very different orientation toward sexual oppression which occurs because of a person's nonsexual characteristics and that which takes place because of a person's sexual characteristics. While most of you probably read the preceding section with a sympathetic feeling, and perhaps even a feeling that something should be done to enhance the sexual opportunities for those individuals discussed, you will probably not have the same reaction to individuals described in this section. The fact of sexual oppression is the same, but individuals whose sexuality is oppressed because of their sexual preferences experience this oppression simply because we do not approve of their sexuality.

Again, those forms of sexuality which are disapproved are in that category because of

agreed-upon social definitions. There are no "natural" laws of proper sexuality. There are, however, social and personal values about sexuality, and these are frequently transformed into legal statements.

The existence of sexual oppression does not mean that these various forms of sexuality should be liberated from oppression and treated as normal, natural, or good. What is normal, natural, and good or abnormal, unnatural, and bad is a matter of social definition. If and when the social definitions of these sexual preferences change, public sentiment will reflect this change and call for less oppression. Such changes are not uncommon. For example, the status of homosexuality, masturbation, and transsexualism has changed considerably over time.

Transsexualism
Transsexualism, or in the more modern terminology—the *gender dysphoria syndrome* —is said to exist in a person who feels that he or she is really a member of one gender trapped inside a body having the sexual characteristics associated with a person of the other gender. Thus, a male transsexual is a person who has male genitals, hormones, chromosomes, and secondary sexual characteristics but who feels like a female.

Transsexuals have been known throughout history (Bullough, 1975; 1976). The first truly well-known case was that of Christine Jorgensen, who obtained a sex reassignment operation from male to female in 1952. More recently, the case of Dr. Rene Richards, the professional tennis player, received widespread notoriety and acceptance in American society. The term "transsexual" was coined by Dr. Harry Benjamin in 1966. Benjamin (1978) recalls that the first case he personally knew of was referred to him by Alfred Kinsey. At that time, there was no identification of, or label for, the desire to be a person of the other gender; this fact, we shall see, has come to be of some importance recently.

Over time, there has been increasing acceptance of transsexuals and their feelings. Even though the first human experiments on

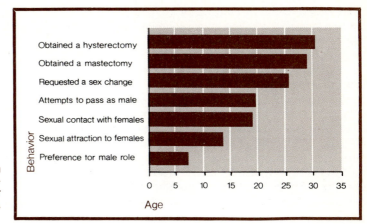

Figure 11-1 Average age at which female-to-male transsexuals experience the sequence of events in their transition from female to male. (Source: Pauly, 1974:500, Figure 2.)

sex reassignment surgery were conducted in the late 1920s, the procedures for removing and reconstructing sexual organs did not become somewhat refined until the middle 1950s. During the 1960s and 1970s, such surgical procedures continued to be developed and are still being explored today as several "gender service," "gender identity," and "sex reassignment" centers have emerged in the United States.

Patterns of behavior Transsexuals are not homosexual in terms of self-perception. While they are sexually attracted to and have experience with, persons of their own sex, they do not see these factors as homosexuality since they see themselves as a person of the other sex. In a review of research on female-to-male transsexuals, Pauly (1974) found that 100 percent of the persons studied had a sexual attraction for females, 86 percent had sexual contact with females, and 76 percent had a stable relationship with a female. However, none of these women saw their relationships as homosexual. A substantial proportion of transsexuals make an attempt to live as the gender to which they are designated by virtue of their genitals. Pauly found that of female-to-male transsexuals, 57 percent had dated men, 48 percent had engaged in intercourse with men, 19 percent had been married to a man, and 16 percent had children.

As part of the pattern of attempting to be the gender they feel, transsexuals most fre-

quently engage in cross-dressing—wearing the clothes of the gender they want to be. Pauly found that only 10 percent of the female-to-male transsexuals studied never cross-dressed before puberty, and after puberty, fully 93 percent cross-dressed either consistently or as often as possible. Cross-dressing behavior is an early behavioral process in the sequence of life events for the transsexual person (Figure 11-1).

Sex reassignment surgery Sex reassignment surgery involves the removal of the genitals and their replacement with structures which resemble the genital structure of the other sex. These procedures are far from perfected and require rather elaborate modification and reconstruction of tissue. In general, changing one's genital appearance from male to female is easier and more successful than changing from female to male. It is surgically simpler to construct an artificial vagina than it is to construct an artificial penis. In penis construction surgery, it is very difficult to make the penislike structure rigid enough to be functional in vagina-penis intercourse.[1] Even in the construction of a vagina, many difficulties and problems are confronted. For example, after a vagina has been constructed, the individual

[1]Methods of surgically reconstructing a penis began in 1936 in Russia and were later refined in Russia in 1944 and London in 1948 (Noe et al., 1978). Evidently Russian and Western European acknowledgment of female-to-male transsexualism preceded its formal naming by a number of years.

must wear a dilator to keep tissue from growing and closing the orifice. Internal growth of hair and overall infection are continual problems.

Sex reassignment is a long and difficult process and surgery is the final stage in the transformation of gender. The process begins with the person's application for sex reassignment. The application is followed by a battery of tests and a period of preparation for surgery. This preparation period differs from institution to institution, but generally involves the person's living as the gender he or she wants to become, hormone treatment to bring about certain physiological changes, electrolysis to remove hair in the male-to-female case, and perhaps even voice training and behavior training to adopt the characteristics of the other gender. Following surgery, hormone treatments must continue, and there is a rather long period of both physical and psychological adjustment. The entire procedure of sex reassignment can be very expensive, costing as much as $14,000 or more.

The current debate There is currently a great debate taking place within the medical profession regarding the wisdom of sex reassignment surgery. During the 1960s, the questions focused on whether such surgery should actually be performed. These questions were rather quickly resolved with numerous sex-change operations (there have been some 4,000 plus in the United States to date) and the establishment of sex reassignment centers in many hospitals.

In the 1970s, the questions about sex-change operations changed to focus on who should obtain the surgery as a concern developed over applicant screening procedures. At any given time, there are some 40,000 to 50,000 applicants for sex reassignment surgery in the United States. As a consequence of the concern over screening, several criteria were developed to determine whether a person was suitable for the operation. These criteria, however, were never agreed upon by medical personnel and they were never based on any solid data regarding the outcome of sex reassignment surgery. In the early 1980s, we see

With the increasing prevalence of sex-reassignment surgery, an increasing number of transsexual individuals marry a person of their former sex following sex-reassignment surgery. Here prison inmate Robert Barnes, 29, and his transsexual bride Kate Bies, 50, pose for their wedding picture in 1977. Prison officiais at the California Medical Facility in Vacaville say she is the first transsexual to marry a California prison inmate.

attention again being directed to the question of whether sex-change operations should be performed. Presently, the medical profession is split on the issue. Some argue that such surgery is necessary for the individual to have any semblance of life adjustment and that there are sufficient data showing such adjustment. Others contend that sex reassignment surgery does not solve the problems faced by transsexuals, that the data indicate that surgery does not assure adjustment in life, and that there may not even be a need for such surgery.

The outcome of sex reassignment surgery   One of the severe problems in this area is, as in the case of sexual therapy, the inadequacy of research on the social and psychological outcomes of surgery. Apparently, serious questions should be raised regarding whether sex reassignment surgery actually contributes to the transsexual's life adjustment. It is very clear that such surgery has been viewed by many in the medical profession as a medical and surgical challenge. This enthusiasm over a challenging restructuring of tissue has not been balanced with the collection of data testing the assumption that surgically changing one's genitals can improve one's social and psychological existence.

A recent study at one of the major sex reassignment centers in the country has called the entire issue of this surgery into question, and the result has been a severe curtailment of the procedure throughout several areas of the United States. The Meyer study at Johns Hopkins University (Meyer and Reter, 1979) found that transsexuals tend to have severe psychological problems and that surgery does nothing to cure these problems. Comparing a group of transsexuals who had sex reassignment surgery with a group who had not, Meyer found no significant difference in the life adjustment of the two groups. An even more recent study (Lothstein, 1980) reported, however, that social and psychological adjustment following sex reassignment surgery was relatively high. Lothstein measured the life adjustment of a group of both male-to-female and female-to-male transsexuals over a three-year period following surgery. He reported that 65 percent of both male-to-female and female-to-male patients were aided in their social and sexual life adjustment by the surgical procedure. Even considering the anatomical and physical problems involved in such surgery, Lothstein found that 67 percent of both groups said that their sex life improved following the

surgery. As he points out, universal success or difficulty in adjusting following, or as a consequence of, sex reassignment surgery is not to be expected. Many factors determine the extent to which such surgery will benefit the individual, not the least of which is the individual's psychological status prior to surgery.

While sex reassignment surgery is given great importance by most persons requesting such treatment, a change in genital structure does not remove all reminders of one's past sex and replace them with anatomical symbols of the other sex. For example, Lothstein found that 50 percent of the male-to-female transsexuals reported the sensation of a "phantom" penis up to two years after surgery, and that some persons reported ejaculation sensations upon orgasm. Even if these reminders do not take place, the continual need to take hormones and, in the case of male-to-female transsexuals, the clear fact that one cannot become pregnant serve as reminders of one's past.

The nature of transsexualism   For many years, the desire to be a person of another gender was taken at face value by professionals in the field. If someone said he or she really wanted to be a male or female, the statement was accepted as a valid summary of the person's psychological position. Recently, however, the whole concept of transsexualism has come under scrutiny, and simultaneously has come criticism of sex reassignment surgery.

Prince (1978) argues that the popularity of transsexual surgery has merely supplied many people with a label to attach to themselves. One of the consistent reports from professionals in this area is that persons applying for sex reassignment surgery are frequently "ideal" cases according to the diagnostic criteria. There is clearly a large underground of communication among transsexuals, such that those who are interested come to know the behaviors and verbalizations which will result in approval of an application. The mere existence of a category called "transsexual" provides an individual who is having problems of living with a diagnosis as to the cause of these problems. Sex reassignment surgery provides the individual with a solution to these problems once the diagnosis of their basis has been made.

In this vein, Morgan (1978) argues that many of the persons who apply for sex reassignment surgery are not transsexual. From his own clinical work, he suggests that 10 percent of the applicants for male-to-female surgery are suffering from severe mental illness. These are individuals whose schizophrenia centers on the subject of gender and whose paranoia focuses on their present gender assignment. The request for sex change in these cases has nothing to do with transsexualism. Morgan argues that another 30 percent are homophobic homosexuals. These are men who prefer sexual activity with males, but at the same time see homosexuals as sick and disgusting. They simply cannot deal with their sexual preference and request a sex change to solve the dilemma: If they become female, they can have sex with males and will not have to see their behavior as homosexuality. Another 20 to 25 percent, argues Morgan, are sexually ambiguous and have an "inadequate" personality. These are individuals who are not sex-typed as either male or female. They are androgynous persons who cannot deal with their lack of stereotypical gender identification.

It is commonly assumed, as reflected in the very definition, that transsexuals reject the gender associated with the genitals they possess. Some recent research, however, calls this assumption into question. Fleming et al. (1980) studied 55 male-to-female and 17 female-to-male transsexuals. Both groups were found to have a strong identification with the other gender, but this feeling was by no means universal and not as strong as would be suggested by a reading of the case study literature on transsexualism from the medical profession. There were also important differences between the two groups. Using a standard measure of gender identity, it was found that female-to-male transsexuals were equally accepting of the male and female aspects of their personalities. They did not reject the feminine aspects of their personalities and were not particularly

exaggerated in gender behavior. They were closer to being androgynous (having both male and female personality characteristics rather than being strongly sex-typed in either traditional male or female personality characteristics). Male-to-female transsexuals were more rejecting of their masculinity than females-to-males were of their femininity.

In general, the research of Fleming et al. (1980) suggests that strong sex-typing toward the gender of preference is not the rule among transsexuals applying for sex reassignment surgery. Rather, they are closer to being androgynous, as many actually are. These androgynous transsexuals are not, as has been argued, seeking sex reassignment in order to gain access to a gender they feel is more appropriate for them or to flee from a gender they feel is incorrect for them. Rather, they are flexible in gender orientation and can deal with either the male or female gender. This, of course, raises serious questions about the necessity and value of sex reassignment surgery. Many professionals suggest that the intense desire for surgery is a phase which most transsexuals go through and that it does not last. Many argue that psychological counseling and other behavior adaptations should be used in place of surgery and that these alternatives would provide the individual with the opportunity to live as a member of the other gender without the expense, psychological stress, and physical trauma of a sex-change operation. Prince (1978) points out that it is perfectly possible to change one's name, legal identification, passport, bank accounts, credit cards, etc., and thus be a member of the other gender regardless of the character of one's genitals.

Prince (1978) also raises what, in light of the research cited, is perhaps the most profound criticism of transsexual surgery. Prince quite correctly points out that *the concept of sex reassignment surgery is based on the mistaken assumption that genitals equal gender.* In a society in which a penis is the ultimate symbol of "manhood" and a vagina (and breasts) are the ultimate symbol of "womanhood," it is reasonable to expect people to think that anatomy equals gender. In actuality, anatomy has nothing to do with gender. "Womanhood" and "manhood" are social definitions of appropriate masculine and feminine behavior involving literally thousands of behaviors having nothing to do with a penis or vagina. The mere presence of certain genitals is no assurance that the person behind the genitals will become a person of male or female gender. Transsexuals, however, believe that genitals are important for gender. In male-to-female operations, for example, the patient's single biggest concern is whether the vagina will function for intercourse. Hastings and Markland (1978) also report that breast size is very important to these transsexuals as well.

The view that genitals determine gender is thus a distorted and strongly genital-focused view of maleness and femaleness and one that reveals a lack of understanding of the nature of gender in social and personal life. It is very interesting to note that many of the professionals who have been active in promoting sex reassignment surgery argue that gender behaviors are biologically determined. Many of these professionals apparently really do believe that genitals equal gender, and thus, if you change a person's genital structure, that person will, by some magic process, become a person of the gender associated with that new genital structure. Such a view is far too simplistic a definition of what makes up gender in any society.

Transvestism

As with many variations in human sexuality, we confront a definition problem when discussing transvestism. In a very general sense, transvestites are individuals who wear the clothing of the other sex; they engage in what is called *cross-dressing*. This definition, however, seems to be too broad since many different individuals wear clothing generally thought appropriate for only the other sex. Female impersonators in stage shows, male homosexuals who like to cross-dress (called "queens" in the gay community), some transsexuals, and many persons adopting current fashions all

may wear clothing associated with the other sex.

Originally, Magnus Hirshfield coined the term "transvestite" to apply to heterosexuals who compulsively cross-dressed for reasons other than fashion conformity or to make money. Recent writers in the field have not followed Hirshfield's initial use of the term and have applied the term to both heterosexual and homosexual cross-dressing. As we shall see, this usage is in error.

Types of transvestites Rather than attempt to label all or any one form of cross-dressing as transvestism, it makes considerably more sense to note that there are different kinds of transvestite activity and thus different kinds of transvestism. Benjamin (1966) distinguished three types of transvestites. These are useful in understanding the range of transvestite types. The *pseudotransvestite* tries cross-dressing for exploratory reasons. The activity is done for kicks and not to fill a need or desire to dress in female clothing. This man feels masculine and has a conventional pattern of male sexual behavior. The *fetishistic transvestite* dresses periodically in female clothes because they are fetish objects for him. They bring about sexual arousal. He does not necessarily identify with being a female. He feels masculine and rejects any idea of changing his sex. The *true transvestite* sees himself as a male but is not entirely convinced of this self-image. He may frequently cross-dress and practice female behaviors such as using makeup. The cross-dressing is not intended for sexual arousal, but to relax. The relaxation comes from relief from his discomfort with his gender. The tension he feels comes from his being in between male and female in his own feelings. This person is heterosexual in his orientation, but when he cross-dresses, he may feel an attraction to males. He is, however, not homosexual in his sexual preference and he is not a transsexual since he rejects the idea of a sex change.

Transvestite sexual orientation There is very little adequate research on the characteristics and behavior patterns associated with cross-dressing. Most research in this

Some men who cross-dress do so in a very convincing manner, others are less convincing.

area either suffers from confusion over exactly what is being studied (the definition of transvestism) or uses a sample of people seeking psychological or psychiatric counseling. There are, however, two notable exceptions; the studies of Prince and Bentler (1972) and Gosselin and Wilson (1980). The Prince and Bentler study used a sample of 504 males who engaged in cross-dressing and whose names were obtained from *Transvestia,* a magazine for cross-dressers. The Gosselin and Wilson study consisted of 269 male cross-dressers in England who were contacted by means of the Beaumont Society, an organization "dedicated to providing transvestites with a means of self-acceptance, peace of mind and understanding, in place of loneliness, fear and self-condemnation" (quoted in Gosselin and Wilson, 1980:33). From these two studies we can obtain the most currently accurate description of cross-dressing in terms of sexual behavior patterns.

Cross-dressers are predominantly heterosexual in their self-defined sexual preference.[2] Prince and Bentler (1972) found that 89 percent of the males in their sample said they were heterosexual. Nine percent said they were bisexual and only one percent said they were homosexual. Even though 28 percent of the males in this study had had at least one same-sex sexual experience in their lives, this figure is lower than that among males who do not cross-dress (see Kinsey, 1948, for an example). Further, these men said that their sexual interest in women was "average" (64 per-

[2]Transvestism is the term almost universally applied to males dressing as females. This fact has two interesting aspects. First, much more latitude is given to women than to men regarding gender-appropriate dress. Women can easily wear male clothing while the reverse is not the case. Second, during the frontier period, many women wore male clothes to disguise their gender and to live as males, and they were not labeled transvestites (Bullough, 1976). Throughout history, however, males who have cross-dressed have been considered deviant.

cent), "above average" (24 percent), and "below average" (14 percent). Clearly, transvestism in the majority of cases is characterized by liking to dress in a certain way and not by a same- or other-sex sexual preference.[3]

Dressing behavior For most of the men in the Prince and Bentler study, cross-dressing had been a pattern for some time. Fully 54 percent said they were cross-dressing before the age of 10. In general dressing preferences, the most favored articles of clothing were lingerie. The vast majority (85 percent) of the men in this sample preferred, however, to dress in the full female costume rather than in just single pieces of clothing. Much cross-dressing is completely private. It is, in fact, the most common pattern. Only 34 percent of the males in this study had ever done any cross-dressing in public.

Dressing and sexual activity One of the more important aspects of cross-dressing is wearing certain preferred articles of clothing during sexual activity. In the Prince and Bentler sample, the single most popular piece of clothing to be worn during heterosexual intercourse was a nightgown (27 percent of the men). Panties (preferred by 20 percent), padded bras (18 percent), stockings (17 percent), and high heels (11 percent) were also frequently preferred during coitus.

Here we see one of the problems with defining transvestite activity as always being a fetish. Wearing certain articles of female clothing during coitus is relatively common, but cross-dressing is also done at times other than during sexual activity. This fact makes it difficult to see transvestism as *only* a fetish activity in which some object (clothing) is needed in order to experience sexual arousal. For example, in the Prince and Bentler study, 11 percent of the men had ridden on a bus or subway, 13 percent had gone to a restaurant, 13 percent had purchased cosmetics, and 13 percent had gone to a play or other entertainment while cross-dressed. Clearly, cross-dressing may be fetishistic for some and a psychological relaxation for others (Benjamin, 1966).[4]

Marital status and life In the Prince and Bentler study (1972), 64 percent of the cross-dressers were currently married, and in the Gosselin and Wilson (1980) research, 65 percent of the men had steady female sexual partners. Another 14 percent of the Prince and Bentler sample had been married at some time. Not unexpectedly, married transvestite males frequently find that their partner is somewhat to highly displeased with their behavior (Gosselin and Wilson, 1980). Of those males in the Prince and Bentler research who were divorced, 34 percent said the divorce was directly attributable to their cross-dressing. Of those who were presently married, most (80 percent) said their wife was aware of their cross-dressing. Of these men, 20 percent said their wife was completely antagonistic to their cross-dressing. However, 21 percent of the wives allowed their husbands to cross-dress only at home but not in her presence, 12 percent allowed him to cross-dress only at home and in her presence, and 23 percent of the wives were totally accepting and cooperative in his cross-dressing.

Sexual satisfaction Even given these somewhat common problems of partner acceptance, Gosselin and Wilson (1980) found that transvestite males were not significantly less sexually satisfied with their partners than were a control group of heterosexual males who did not cross-dress. This may be partially due to the fact that cross-dressing does not always require a partner for satisfaction (the true transvestite) (Gosselin and Wilson, 1980). In terms of overall sexual satisfaction, however, transvestite males appear to be less satisfied than heterosexual males who do not cross-dress (Gosselin and Wilson, 1980).

Voyeurism

Voyeurism or peeping Tomism is a crime in all states and is regarded by most people as devi-

---

[3]The idea that homosexual males who cross-dress are transvestites is somewhat humorous. Homosexual "queens" frequently dress in female clothing as a put-on for tourists (San Francisco is famous for this), and those who cross-dress seriously are often seen with amusement by the gay community.

[4]Some women's department stores in major cities have a person who more or less specializes in helping male cross-dressers find clothing, shoes, cosmetics, etc.

ant behavior. The voyeur obtains sexual pleasure in some degree from observing others' bodies, "sexual" anatomy, or sexual acts. In a very real sense, we again have problems of definition. Some have suggested that the distinguishing feature of voyeurism is that the watching takes place without the observed person's consent. Defining voyeurism this way would certainly draw a distinction between paying to see a woman undress when she knows she is being observed and watching a woman undress in her home when she does not know she is being observed (the vast majority of voyeurs are men who observe women). What, however, is the difference between the man who likes to look at photographs of nude women who pose for "skin" magazines and the same man who likes to look at nude photographs of celebrities taken without their knowledge (a recent popular feature in some skin magazines)? This man is the same person. Is he a voyeur in one case and not a voyeur in the other?

Gagnon (1977) has suggested that a great many people are voyeurs in that they will look when the opportunity arises, but few are peeping Toms who will walk up to a window, climb over a fence, or sit and wait in order to watch. Here again there are problems. The field research of Feigelman (1977) reveals that in some occupations, going out of one's way to observe a woman undressing while she is in her home is accepted and even expected behavior. Feigelman studied high-rise construction workers on the job and found that they quite commonly observe women in nearby apartment buildings. The watching is not only considered acceptable by many of these men, but is seen as one of the fringe benefits of the job. There are often a set of clear rules about the behavior. Not only are elaborate structures often erected to make their watching go unnoticed by the woman, but when one sees something "good," one is expected to tell others, and not do anything to alert the woman to their observing.

Discreet peeping entails being absolutely quiet while at the windows. I overheard a conversation between an electrician and a lather which points this up rather vividly. The lather was complaining that peeping was no longer as good as it used to be during the early stages of the construction job. The electrician offered an explanation. "Well, you know why it is—it's because of the plasterers. It's because they've come on the job. They are crude sons of bitches. They yell at the woman and before you know it, all the blinds are drawn and there is nothing left for us anymore. They don't know how to watch." (Feigelman, 1977:38)

It seems safe to assume that these construction workers are not arrested for their peeping, and that if the police were notified, nothing more than a "knock it off" would be said. Further, as we read about this type of peeping, we might think it crude and unfair to the women, but I doubt that most people would consider these men to be real peeping Toms.

What appears to distinguish real peeping Toms from men who simply look if there is a chance is the compulsive nature of the act. The person most likely to be socially and legally considered a peeping Tom is the one who makes the peeping not just a part of his walk to the store or his job or his magazine reading, but a part of his life. The peeping takes on a compulsive nature as a source of sexual gratification. The peeper almost never watches a woman he knows, preferring, instead, the novelty of a stranger (Gebhard et al., 1965). Frequently, masturbation accompanies the peeping to the point of orgasm, and it is not uncommon for an exhibitionist also to engage in peeping. In the majority of cases, the peeper is harmless, not particularly desiring contact with the woman he is watching. This, however, is not always the case. Some peepers watch first and then attempt to rape their victim; this is especially true of those peepers who enter a residence to peep or who attempt to attract the attention of the woman they are observing (Gebhard et al., 1965).

Voyeurism may also be associated with certain fetishes. For example, the person may have a urination or defecation fetish and combine it with voyeurism by watching other people performing such acts. It is reported that Hitler obtained sexual arousal by closely observing women urinate and defecate (Lancer, 1972).

Peeping most often involves watching a woman who is nude or partially nude. Some individuals, however, obtain considerable sexual gratification from observing others engage in sexual activity in their presence *(triolism)*. A common form of triolism is in swinging, where a couple like to engage in sexual activity with each other while watching others do the same. The following advertisement by a swinging couple concerns triolism.

Married couple enjoy watching and being watched. We do not swing. Enjoy good friends and photography. Photo please.

Triolism often takes other forms as well. In some cases, a husband may watch his wife engaging in sexual activity with other males either while he is present or while he is hiding and cannot be seen.

Hirschfield (1948) reports a case in which cooperation of the wife was obtained through coercion. This man would invite a foreign business connection over for dinner. Then he would conceal himself in another room and watch while his seductively dressed wife met the guest and claimed her husband had been called away on urgent business. She was then, according to her husband's demands, to wine and dine the guest, following which she was to seduce him. This seduction was to culminate in sexual intercourse on the divan, which was within unobstructed view of the husband's hiding place. The wife would then quickly dismiss the guest and the husband "rushed forth from his hiding place and carried out the sexual act with his wife with passionate ardor." (Smith, 1976:586)

Exhibitionism

The exhibitionist obtains sexual pleasure from others seeing parts of his or her body which have sexual meaning. Again, we must consider some definitional issues in terms of what is and what is not exhibitionism.

Exhibitionism is sometimes defined as the act of exposure without the consent of the observer. This is not necessarily accurate. The person may not consent to the exposure before it happens but also may not disapprove of it either. It is also difficult to base the definition of an act performed by one person on how the other person reacts. Specifically, a man may try to expose himself, but if everyone he confronts likes his act, he cannot, according to this definition, be an exhibitionist no matter how hard he tries.

People who dress in ways which expose (in varying degrees) their "sexual" anatomy are commonly referred to in everyday discussion as "exhibitionists." Some professionals have attempted to argue that this is not really exhibitionism because these people expose themselves to arouse others sexually and gain their attention rather than to arouse themselves sexually. This distinction between the person who wears daring clothing and the person who flashes his raincoat open is dubious. The person in daring clothing may very well obtain sexual pleasure from revealing him- or herself, and the majority of males arrested for exposing their penis to an unsuspecting woman in public hope that she will be impressed by the size of their penis and will enjoy seeing it (Langevin et al., 1979).

Even the activity of exposing oneself in a rather compulsive manner does not appear to be a distinguishing characteristic of those arrested for exhibitionism. While the male who repeatedly exposes his genitals to unsuspecting women may well be compulsive, so may the person who dresses so as to expose parts of the body having sexual meaning.

The essential characteristic of what we clinically refer to as exhibitionism and not just "sexy" behavior is that the exhibitionist engages in the act in such a manner, in such a place, and in others' presence so that the behavior is socially unacceptable. For example, the young woman who takes off all her clothes while standing on a balcony overlooking a street during Mardi Gras is engaging in socially acceptable behavior in that particular situation. (She will likely get police attention, but will not be labeled an "exhibitionist".) The couple who two years ago engaged in intercourse in the same place on the same occasion will probably be classified in the same way. High school age males who place their bare buttocks against the back window of a car on Main Street are engaging in "mooning," not exhibitionism. However, the male who drives slowly down the street and exposes his erect penis to a woman walking on the sidewalk is not engaging in acceptable behavior in that situation. This is exhibitionism.

Exhibitionism is a relatively common offense. Allen (1969) reported that over one-third of all sex offenses acted on by the police were cases of exhibitionism. Additionally, there are many cases which are never reported to the police. There are also males who are arrested for exposure who cannot really be considered exhibitionists. The retarded male, for example, may expose his penis in a public place because of inadequate social learning rather than because of a desire to obtain sexual gratification; many arrests for exposure also are made as the result of inappropriate acts while drunk (Gebhard et al., 1965).

The largest single category of men (women exhibitionists are practically unknown) arrested for exposure consists, however, of those who planned the act for the purpose of obtaining sexual gratification and have repeatedly engaged in exposure using a fairly standard set of activities (Gebhard et al., 1965). The relatively standard pattern of exposure is for the man to approach a woman quite closely and expose ("flash") his often erect penis (frequently while masturbating). The woman responds with shock and the man quickly leaves the scene (Gebhard et al., 1965).

The exhibitionist generally seeks women who are strangers (Gebhard et al., 1965; Macdonald, 1973) and avoids further contact with the woman once he has exposed himself to

her (Mohr et al., 1964). The exhibitionist also tends to avoid exposing himself to females who might cooperate sexually or might not be shocked by the exposure (Gebhard et al., 1965; Langevin et al., 1979). Shock is not, however, the only reaction the exhibitionist is seeking. Langevin et al. (1979) found that approximately half the exhibitionists studied hoped that the woman would enjoy seeing the male's genitals and that she would be impressed by the size of his penis (which is not known to be any larger for exhibitionists than nonexhibitionists, but no precise measurements have been taken). Almost half the exhibitionists in this study also desired to have sexual relations with the woman to whom they exposed themselves. About half these men said that if the woman were receptive, they would have sex with her while exposing themselves, and half said that they had tried to engage in sex with a woman while exposing themselves.

There appears to be a rather strong connection between exhibitionism and voyeurism. Many exhibitionists also engage in voyeurism and masturbate to orgasm while peeping (Langevin et al., 1979). The connection here appears to be that voyeurism is safer than flashing and one has longer to experience sexual arousal and stimulation to the point of orgasm than one has when flashing and running.

The social and psychological experiences and patterns associated with exhibitionism remain largely unknown. While a number of theories have been offered suggesting that the exhibitionist is retarded in the social-sexual area, these are not yet supported by research.

After a rather in-depth analysis of groups of male exhibitionists, Langevin et al. (1979) concluded that exhibitionists had more in common with nonexhibitionists than has been thought. It has been generally assumed that men who repeatedly expose themselves have some notable social, psychological, or sexual characteristic. Research fails to support this. As Langevin et al. found, it is difficult to isolate any set of characteristics which typify males arrested for exhibitionism.

One of the more prominent theories on the

cause of exhibitionism is that exhibitionists are sexually inhibited by normal female courtship and seductive behavior. Since the exhibitionist most often attempts to avoid females who he thinks might cooperate sexually, it is thought that he acts at a distance and with haste so as to avoid any possibility of female cooperation or seduction. Kolarsky et al. (1978) tested this idea by comparing males who were and those who were not legally labeled exhibitionists. They compared these two groups in their sexual arousal to films of female seductive behavior and found no significant differences between them. Of course, one of the reasons they found no difference may have been, not that the theory is incorrect, but that there are different types of exhibitionists. Recall that a substantial proportion of the men studied by Langevin et al. (1979) did want sexual activity with the woman to whom they exposed themselves if she would cooperate.

Two notable facts about exhibitionism are in serious need of consideration. The first is that it is not universal. Exhibitionism is apparently much more common in Western than non-Western cultures. For example, it is very rare in Africa and virtually unknown in Japan (Roothe, 1973). The second fact is that, like most sex offenses against others, it is almost totally a male activity.

Exhibitionism also frequently takes on forms other than the male exposing himself in public to a female stranger. Exhibitionism may consist of an erotic activity in which the other person is a willing observer. While the former type of exhibitionism is almost totally a male activity (reflecting forced observing?), the latter is often engaged in by females, as the following advertisements illustrate.

Oversexed female masturbator gets off violently by exposing herself, any position, anywhere. Send phone.

Young couple. We do not swing but like to watch and be watched. Send photo and phone for quick reply.

Fetishes

As Gebhard (1977a) has pointed out, the question of definitions is often a stumbling block for sex research. Since a long tradition of everyday use of many sexual terms frequently exists before scientific research is done on a subject, the scientist often works in the middle of many different definitions of the same sexual term. The subject of fetishes is a good example of this problem of definition. A review of the literature in the subject of fetishes quickly reveals little precise agreement as to exactly what constitutes a fetish.

Of course, every writer or researcher tends to feel that his or her definition is somehow better than anyone else's, and I am no exception. The definition we will follow is based mainly on the work of Gebhard (1977a) with some minor modifications. *A fetish is some degree of sexual preference for inanimate objects.* The preference for inanimate objects is focused on how one becomes sexually aroused. The most important feature of a fetish is that *it is a matter of degree.* The person's sexual preference for inanimate objects may be anywhere on a continuum from an aid to becoming sexually aroused to a total dependence on only that object for sexual arousal. In terms of one's sexual partner, the fetish may simply take the form of consensual sex play or it may be at the other end of the continuum where a person-partner is totally displaced or substituted by the inanimate object.

Following Gebhard (1977a), fetishes can be classified in terms of four degrees of sexual preference for an inanimate object:

- A *slight preference* for the presence of an inanimate object during sexual activity with one's partner may exist. Being more sexually aroused by such things as silk sheets rather than cotton ones on the bed is an example of a slight preference degree of fetish.

- A *strong preference* for the presence of an inanimate object may appear when the person does not find silk sheets just somewhat of a turn-on, but will go out of his or her way to have silk sheets on the bed during sexual activity.

- A *necessity* for the presence of an inanimate object occurs when the person cannot become sexually aroused unless the inanimate object is present.
- The *actual substitution* of a person as a sexual partner by the inanimate object is the most extreme degree of fetishism.

Where on this continuum of degree of dependence on an inanimate object for sexual arousal the activity is called "deviant" is a matter of personal opinion. What little research exists (Gosselin and Wilson, 1980) suggests that in everyday heterosexual activity, many males with a strong preference for an inanimate object have a wife or other steady female partner who participates. (Fetishes are reported to be almost nonexistent among women.)

> "When my husband first told me about his preference, I must admit that I was puzzled, slightly frightened and somewhat resentful. In the end, however, it turned out to be making a bit of a mountain out of a molehill about it. Nowadays I occasionally wear the sort of things he likes me to wear, and, although it makes me look a bit stark, it makes him so happy that I haven't the heart to stop it altogether. I mean, it's not as if it was grotesque." (Quoted by Gosselin and Wilson, 1980:48)

If, however, the fetish is of a necessity degree, it is less likely that the fetishist will be involved with a partner because the behavior is obnoxious rather than fun or tolerable (Money, 1977; Gosselin and Wilson, 1980). Therefore, married males who have a fetish that is a necessity are unlikely to have their wives as participants (Gosselin and Wilson, 1980). If the fetish involves actual substitution, the inanimate object becomes the sexual goal and a person-partner is irrelevant. At this degree of fetish, the person is likely to have even more association with the object than just during sexual arousal. He may have collections of the object in the form of either photographs or real objects of that type. Most often, the person lives alone and thus has the privacy to indulge as much as he wants in his particular fetish (Gosselin and Wilson, 1980). For those men who have a strong preference or a necessity degree of fetish and a partner who is unwilling to cooperate, there are numerous prostitutes who specialize in fetishes.

Gebhard (1977) has further distinguished between two major types of fetishes; *media* fetishes and *form* fetishes. In a media fetish, the interest is in the material making up the inanimate object and not in its form. A leather or rubber fetish is an example of a media fetish. The person with a rubber fetish, for example, is not so particular about what the object is as long as it is rubber. In a form fetish, the object itself is of more interest than the material of which it is made. Form fetishes are almost innumerable, but some objects are more popular than others. High heels and nylons are often the objects of form fetishes.

> High heels and nylon lover. I will try anything with anyone if we both wear high heels and nylons. (Advertisement placed in sex newspaper)

Interestingly, some objects which we might think would be involved in form fetishes are not popular. As Gebhard (1977) points out, bra fetishes are rare while underpant fetishes are relatively common.

> Sexy soiled panties for sale. Buy worn panties, girdles, nylons. (Advertisement placed in sex newspaper)

Form fetishes also rise and fall in their popularity. For example, a corset fetish was quite common a number of years ago (to the extent that some corset shops provided peep holes in dressing rooms that men with a corset fetish could rent). Today, corset fetishes are rare. Gebhard (1977) suggests that this change had something to do with the change in women's styles. A corset went from being associated with a "sexy" female figure to being seen as a piece of "matronly" attire.

The development of a fetish   It has been assumed that fetishes are learned by some object's being intimately associated with sexual arousal and thus itself taking on sexual meaning. The classic experiment of Rachman (1966) in which males were conditioned to experience sexual arousal when viewing pictures of shoes is perhaps a clear experimental example of how a fetish can develop from a process of classical conditioning. It may well be the case that such conditioning, where an object which generally has no sexual meaning acquires sexual meaning by being paired with an object which does create sexual arousal, can take place in one trial. That is, fetishes may well be developed through one meaningful incident which has a significant impact on the person.

Recent research indicates that fetishes can also develop when one cannot tolerate one's own fear of being rejected by a woman. When one cannot tolerate this fear of rejection by a particular woman, one may isolate some aspect of the person on which to focus his sexual arousal. LaTorre (1980) demonstrated how a fetish may be developed in this way. He experimentally manipulated males being rejected for a date by a woman who had supposedly written a short autobiography that the males read. After two supposed rejections by the woman, the males rated the woman's clothing and body parts more favorably than they rated the woman herself. The males who were not rejected, on the other hand, rated the woman herself more favorably than they did her clothes or body parts. This suggests that fetishes for certain articles of clothing may often be developed as an attempt to "hold on" to a sexually desired female. This research also has some bearing on a behavior closely related to fetishism—that of partialism (which is discussed in the next section).

While there is almost no solid research on the patterns of behavior on the part of fetishists, Gosselin and Wilson (1980) found that men with a fetish were more introverted (less outgoing, more withdrawn) than a control group of heterosexuals. Also, men are much more likely than women to have a fetish, especially in the more extreme degree. Gosselin and Wilson suggest that one reason may be that men are more sensitive to visual stimuli than are women and are thus more likely to associate sexual arousal with the sight of an inanimate object. A second factor possibly accounting for the greater frequency of fetishes among men is biofeedback (Gosselin and Wilson, 1980). As we saw in Chapter 5, men are' more sensitive to the physiological cues indicating their sexual arousal than are women. It is quite possible that many men develop a fetish by noticing that sexual arousal took place in the presence of a certain object and then developing a perference for this object. Not to be forgotten in thinking about the greater frequency of fetishes among males is that males are much more likely than females to learn that sex can be separated from the interpersonal, a fact that at least makes the development of a strong fetish possible.

Sexual satisfaction   We have an image of the fetishist as a person with a low level of sexual satisfaction. The research of Gosselin and Wilson (1980) suggests this is not necessarily the case. In a study of rubber and leather fetishists, they found almost no difference between those heterosexual males with and without a fetish in terms of overall sexual satisfaction. One of the significant differences between those heterosexual males was that the fetishists engaged in the sexual activities they fantasized about more frequently than they actually had the fantasies, while the nonfetishists fantasized about sexual activities more frequently than they actually engaged in them.

Partialism

Caprio (1961), and more recently Gagnon (1977), have appropriately distinguished between fetishism and partialism. While a fetish is having one's sexual arousal dependent (in varying degrees) on an inanimate object, a *partialism* is having one's sexual arousal dependent (in varying degrees) on some particular part of the anatomy.

Most people engage in some mild forms of partialism in that they find some parts of the human body more sexually arousing than others. In fact, as we noted in Chapter 5, having the partialisms your culture defines as appropriate is a large part of being an accepted member of a society.

A major difference between partialism and fetishism is that some degree of partialism is probably characteristic of almost everyone and the extent of partialism is limited. While a fetish can take the form of the person's substituting the object for a live partner, this degree of dependence is not possible in partialism unless necrophilia (sexual activity with a corpse) is practiced.

Partialisms also differ in their popularity. It seems reasonably safe to suggest that breast partialism is common in American society. (This is perhaps the reason bra fetishes are uncommon; we find breast partialisms and underpants fetishes common and bra fetishes and female genital partialisms uncommon. This is to be expected if fetishes and partialisms originate in the manner suggested by LaTorre [1980].) In general, it appears that partialisms are more acceptable than fetishes. It is reasonably acceptable to be a "breast man" or a "leg man" even to the point of being rather dependent upon these body parts for sexual arousal. A partialism is labeled as deviant when the body part which is the focus of attention does not fall in the range of accepted sexually arousing body parts.

> Young White Male seeks cute females 18–30 with extremely long hair. Hair worshipped. (Advertisement placed in a sex newspaper)

As we have noted, much of the sex magazine business is focused on the existence of partialisms, with a strong tendency for magazines to specialize. (*BUF: The Big Up Front Swinger, Gent: Home of the D Cups, Boobs and Buns* are but a few of the titles of magazines published monthly.)

Sadomasochism

Sadomasochism refers to two forms of sexual preference which complement each other. *Sadism* is obtaining sexual pleasure from inflicting pain on another person. *Masochism* is obtaining sexual pleasure by having pain inflicted on oneself.

Sadomasochism (S/M) often takes the form of a partnership in which one person prefers to receive and the other to administer pain. It is, however, a myth that pain is the important element in S/M activity. For the majority of people who like such activity, the sexual pleasure comes not from actually inflicting or receiving pain, but from the fantasy of doing so while engaging in S/M activity (Gosselin and Wilson, 1980). A large part of the activity involves acting out an S/M script in one's sexual activity rather than finding sexual arousal in giving and receiving pain. There is usually a distinct set of roles to be played, and most participants assume that each partner will understand and agree to a certain degree of playing out sadism and masochism. Most masochists do not want a partner who is genuinely sadistic, but a person who will play the role of administering pain within acceptable limits. The same applies to most sadists in S/M activity. Most often, the activity takes the form of mock violence and most people who engage in S/M prefer "light" or low pain (Gosselin and Wilson, 1980; Spengler, 1977; Lee, 1979).

> "My wife and I do play dominance and submission games, and maybe we have the marks to prove it on occasion. But the one playing top dog watches like a hawk to make sure we stop when the other one doesn't like it anymore." (Quoted by Gosselin and Wilson, 1980:54)

Most people who engage in S/M activity do not have all their sexual arousal dependent on the sadistic and masochistic behaviors. Rather, they use S/M as an arousing addition to other sexual activities, be they heterosexual or homosexual in form. In Spengler's study of S/M men in West Germany, only a minority preferred exclusive S/M sexual activity and only a small proportion could reach orgasm by S/M activity alone. Almost half this sample of S/M active males generally had orgasm without any S/M activities.

S/M activities are often associated with

bondage and discipline (B/D) in which one person obtains sexual pleasure from being tied up or bound in some way and another obtains pleasure from doing the binding and perhaps pretending to administer stern discipline or even forms of humiliation and degradation. The more extreme forms of B/D, degradation, and humiliation S/M activities take place, however, with a low frequency. The most common ones tend to involve light flagellation (spanking or whipping) and mild bondage (Spengler, 1977).

Fetish fantasies are often a significant part of S/M activity. Given the emphasis on bondage and dominance of mild forms, certain form and media fetishes frequently play a part in S/M sexuality. These tend to be materials and forms which convey the meaning of dominance and discipline, such as leather clothing and boots (Spengler, 1977).

Obtaining willing partners for S/M activities can be difficult since sadism and masochism are generally socially disapproved forms of sexual behavior. Gosselin and Wilson (1980) found, for example, that only 17 percent of the S/M males they studied engaged in their S/M activity at home. Spengler (1977), in his study of S/M males in West Germany, found that 41 percent of the married males had kept their S/M activity secret from their wives. This problem of finding willing partners is magnified by the fact that masochists are more common than sadists (Gosselin and Wilson, 1980).

One outcome of this difficulty in finding a willing partner for a sexual activity which demands a partner (unlike more extreme forms of fetishes) is that many males (females have not been completely studied) go to prostitutes specializing in S/M sexual services. There are also S/M clubs for both heterosexual and homosexual populations. The clubs offer any range of activities, some being equipped with elaborate props, equipment, and even torture chambers and offering very specialized behavior. There are also S/M magazines directed toward either heterosexual or homosexual interests, as well as films and social-sexual organizations throughout the world dedicated to S/M sexuality. Another way of obtaining partners among gay men is by cruising and picking up a complementary partner. One of the very real dangers for the masochist in this type of activity is encountering a person who not only is willing to play the sadist role but who really wants to inflict extremely severe pain.

The contacts S/M males make with others of like interest tend to be one-time affairs. In the Spengler study, the typical pattern was a low frequency of S/M activity with a relatively large number of partners (five experiences in a year with five different partners).

One way in which to contact partners and to conduct this socially disapproved sexual interest is by participation in the S/M subculture. In any major (and even many minor) cities, one can find an S/M subculture composed of a set of people who float in and out of contact with one another and are sexually isolated from the rest of society. Sometimes this subcultural activity may be rather organized in the form of social-sexual organizations and activities. One of the features of such meetings is secrecy as to who attended. Anonymity is a special rule of S/M subcultural participation (Spengler, 1977) because of the difficulty in finding partners and the disapproval of the behavior by the larger society. One of the very real social-psychological functions of participation in an S/M subculture is self-acceptance, according to Spengler. Given the disapproval of the behavior, the tendency for partners to be known only sexually, and the secrecy of one's sexual interests, social interaction with others who share this sexual preference is important for accepting oneself as a person (Spengler, 1977).[5]

---

[5]In England, there is an interesting stereotype about S/M sexual preference and social class. It is nicely summarized by Gosselin and Wilson (1980:130):

> A . . . view promulgated particularly by tabloid newspapers is that of a corrupt aristocracy practicing all kinds of kinky sex in response to either boredom or boarding school discipline, because they have the power, money, and leisure to indulge themselves. . . . The attitude of the general public toward this imagined perversion of the nobility is somewhere between disdain for an upper class that has lost its way and fallen into decadence, and envy for a group who are suspected to be connoisseurs of sexuality as much as food and wine.

Gosselin and Wilson, however, found no relationship between social class and S/M activity.

It is virtually impossible to draw a distinct line and say that all *these* people are sadomasochists and all *those* people are not. As we have noted, only a small minority of people who engage in what we would clearly call sadomasochistic activity use S/M alone for sexual arousal. This becomes very clear in an examination of advertisements placed by individuals seeking S/M as part of their sexual activity.

> Couple w/ dominant female. Good looking 32 year old White male would like to be your slave. Discreet.

> Tender young novice, 23, hubby watches or participates. Enjoy mild spanking and restraint. Send spicy letter, phone, photo.

It is also true that many sexually stimulating behaviors are engaged in which we would not identify as the practice of sadomasochism, but which certainly involve the essence of the behavior. There is a continuum in the extent and degree to which people use S/M for sexual stimulation ranging from not at all to totally. Kinsey (Gebhard and Johnson, 1979) found, for example, that 25 percent of both the males and females studied experienced sexual arousal from mild biting and pinching, and 4 percent enjoyed other forms of mild pain while having sex. In more recent research, Hunt (1974) found that 6 percent of the males and 3 percent of the females under age 35 had obtained sexual pleasure from inflicting pain on another person, and 4 percent of the males and 6 percent of the females had received sexual pleasure from having pain inflicted upon them. We have continually noted the way in which patterns of sexuality conform to traditional definitions of males and females in American society. It is interesting here to note that males are more likely to take the active (sadistic) role and females the passive (masochistic) role, another appearance of traditional gender role learning.

Bestiality

Bestiality or *zoophilia* refers to sexual activity with animals. As we have noted, this activity was apparently rather common in the American colonies and met with harsh punishment. Today, most states define sexual activity with animals as a crime of perversion carrying strong penalties.

While there is little research on the subject, bestiality is more common than most people probably realize. Kinsey (1948) found that 17 percent of the males who, as adolescents, had lived on farms had had sexual contact with an animal to orgasm and probably many more had had sexual contact short of orgasm. These incidents were usually in adolescence and involved intercourse, or the animals' licking or sucking the male's genitals, or masturbation of the animal. Urban youth have much less sexual contact with animals than rural youth and what activity they do have tends to be with dogs and cats (Kinsey, 1948). Although females are much less likely than males to have sexual contact with animals, it is not unheard of. In Kinsey's research, 4 percent of the females had had such a sexual experience at some time in their lives—most often in adolescence with a dog or cat. The activity usually involved the animal's licking their genitals, masturbating the animal, or having intercourse with the animal.

Sex with animals on the part of adults is usually regarded as a very unusual sexual activity. It is, however, of interest to an unknown number of people. Not only will most long-time rural residents be able to tell you of some incident they know about, but pornographic materials showing women engaging in sexual activity with animals are readily available in the United States. Persons advertising for bestiality can also be found in the sexual classifieds of magazines and sexual newspapers.

> White couple 37 and 38 seeks couples or singles. We love all cultures except pain. Pet training welcome. Send photo. Will answer all. Lets go.

> Hot and horny gal. Very attractive and sexy. Loves french, greek, animal (dog) training.

Necrophilia

Necrophilia is having an erotic interest in dead persons. This is apparently an extremely rare sexual interest and one that is not well studied. This particular sexual preference is apparently often associated with serious psychological disturbance, not an unexpected evaluation given the degree to which this sexual interest deviates from what is acceptable in society (Templer and Eberhardt, 1980).

Necrophilia also takes the form of prostitution. In some of the larger cities, prostitutes provide services to necrophiliacs by using makeup so as to resemble a dead person.

Coprolalia

Coprolalia is the obtaining of sexual pleasure by using or hearing certain "dirty" words. Again, it is unclear where to draw the line between what are considered acceptable and unacceptable sexual behaviors. Many people enjoy saying certain generally forbidden words, or hearing them said, while engaging in sexual activity. For these people, however, this activity adds to their arousal but is not absolutely necessary. Unacceptable behavior is generally identified when the person depends on such stimulation for arousal to take place or violates the sexual script and engages in such behavior in an inappropriate situation with an inappropriate person.

One form of coprolalia is the obscene telephone caller. This is most often a male who gets sexual pleasure by calling a woman and saying sexually related and prohibited things to her, frequently while masturbating. Recently, this particular sexual interest has taken on a new business twist. Many male-oriented skin magazines list advertisements for "telephone sex" in which you can call a number and a woman on the other end of the line will "talk dirty" to you. Males who engage in telephone coprolalia can often not only greatly disturb women by making obscene telephone calls to their homes but can create real problems for social service agencies having "hot-lines" or "crisis-lines" where women are likely to answer the phone. (See Lester, 1977: "Telephone Counselling and the Masturbator.")

Klismaphilia

As we have noted, erotic activity involving the anal region has become somewhat more popular among heterosexual individuals in recent years, but it still remains one of the least popular and least common of heterosexual activities.

Some individuals derive erotic pleasure from being administered and administering enemas; this preference is called *klismaphilia.* Such erotic activities are thought to become attractive because of a person's having been given enemas in childhood and having had the experience associated with some tactile or erotic pleasure. Since many of the nerves to the genitals also supply the anal region, this association is physiologically not difficult.

Such activities are sought through prostitution and advertising for sexual partners and are referred to as "water sports."

Coprophilia

Coprophilia is having an erotic interest in feces. This is a rare erotic preference. However, a close reading of classified advertisements in sexual newspapers reveals infrequent requests of this nature. Some prostitution meets this need where men pay to observe a woman defecate. This was apparently one of Hitler's erotic inclinations.

Urophilia

Urophilia or urolagnia is an erotic interest in urination or urine. This interest may take the form of a range of activities from enjoying watching others urniate to being urinated on (called "golden showers") to drinking urine. This is a sexual interest most likely to be found among those heavily involved in S/M activity where the urination represents a form of being dominated.

Urethralism

Urethralism is an erotic interest in inserting objects into one's own urethra. While this occurrence is unknown among adults, it is a relatively common activity of experimentation among children. With them, however, it is not an erotic interest, but a matter of curiosity.

Amputism

Amputism, or *apotemnophia,* is an erotic interest in amputation. As with many rare sexual interests which deviate strongly from the acceptable, there is little known about amputism. One report suggests that there are two forms of amputism: partner and self. Partner amputism involves a strong desire for sexual activity with an amputated partner. Self-amputism involves the sexually-related wish of amputation of one's own limbs. Self-amputism is frequently associated with self-bondage and fantasies about being amputated. For both types of amputism, actually engaging in the activity is rare. Most often, amputism takes the form of fantasies. These fantasies are often supported by what Wenig (1980) calls the "sexual underground business" of partially fabricated letters columns in male skin magazines. As we noted earlier, a female amputee may often face the problem of attracting a male with a partner amputism.

STUDY GUIDE

TERMS TO KNOW

Transsexualism	Transvestism
Gender dysphoria syndrome	Cross-dressing
Pseudotransvestite	Fetishistic transvestite
True transvestite	Voyeurism
Exhibitionism	Fetish
Media fetish	Form fetish
Partialism	Sadomasochism
Bestiality	Necrophilia
Coprolalia	Klismaphilia
Coprophilia	Amputism
Triolism	

SELF-TEST

Part I: True-False Statements

1. Transsexual individuals see themselves as homosexual.
2. Sex-reassignment surgery is the first stage in the transformation of gender in a transsexual individual.
3. In general, the research on the gender identity of transsexuals indicates that they tend to be strongly sex-typed toward the gender of their preference.
4. Sex-reassignment surgery is based on the mistaken notion that genitals equal gender.

5. Persons who feel that they are a person of one gender trapped inside the body of the other gender are called transvestites.
6. Cross-dressers are predominantly homosexual.
7. The majority of cross-dressers either are married or have a steady female partner.
8. The exhibitionist generally seeks women who are strangers.
9. Exhibitionism is found in all cultures.
10. A fetish is not being able to become sexually aroused unless some inanimate object is present.

Part II: Multiple-Choice Questions
Select the best of the three alternatives.

1. Those individuals who feel that they are a member of one gender trapped in the body of the other gender are *(a)* cross-dressers; *(b)* transvestites; *(c)* transsexuals.
2. In terms of actually measured gender identity, *(a)* male-to-female transsexuals are more rejecting of their masculinity than female-to-male transsexuals are of their femininity; *(b)* both male-to-female and female-to-male transsexuals are equally rejecting of a masculine identity; *(c)* both male-to-female and female-to-male transsexuals are equally rejecting of a feminine gender identity.
3. In examining the research on the social, psychological, and sexual characteristics of men who repeatedly expose themselves, it is found that *(a)* exhibitionists have a much stronger sex-drive than nonexhibitionists; *(b)* exhibitionists tend to be introverted more than nonexhibitionists; *(c)* no differences apparently set exhibitionists apart from nonexhibitionists.
4. A rubber fetish is an example of *(a)* form fetish; *(b)* media fetish; *(c)* klismaphilia.
5. If an individual's sexual arousal depends (in varying degrees in different individuals) on some part of the human body, the person has *(a)* partialism; *(b)* media fetish; *(c)* form fetish.
6. Most masochists desire a sexual partner who will *(a)* administer severe pain as part of the sexual activity; *(b)* be a true sadist; *(c)* play the role of administering pain within acceptable limits.

TOPICS FOR DISCUSSION

Consider that you have either severe visual or hearing impairment. Make a list of how this condition would affect your sexual behavior and why. Do not consider just physical sexual activities, but interpersonal aspects as well, such as first interaction with a person, developing it to the point of a sexual relationship, and knowing your partner. Discuss your descriptions in class in terms of how the dominant sexual script and patterns of acceptable sexual behavior in American society make for sexual oppression for those with these impairments.

    We have discussed some of the problems in distinguishing patterns of behavior considered acceptable from those labeled exhibitionism, voyeurism, etc. Take any one of these behaviors and see whether your class or discussion group can agree on what it is that makes one behavior (e.g. watching men or women in bathing suits on a beach) acceptable in this society while other similar behaviors are not acceptable.

SUGGESTED READINGS

Gosselin, C. and **G. Wilson,** *Sexual Variations: Fetishism, Sadomasochism, and Transvestism.* New York: Simon & Schuster, 1980.
This is an excellent study of these behaviors and a good source of more in-depth material than covered in this chapter.

Archives of Sexual Behavior. 1978, vol. 7.
The entire issue is devoted to the debate on transsexualism.

Newton, E., *Mother Camp: Female Impersonators in America.* Englewood Cliffs, N.J.: Prentice-Hall, 1972.

Ackroyd, P., *Dressing Up: Transvestism and Drag: The History of an Obsession.* New York: Simon and Schuster, 1979.
This is a brief history containing many photographs of classic and not so classic cross-dressers and transvestites through history.

KEY TO SELF-TEST

Part I: True-False Statements

1. F (They desire sexual activity with a person of their own sex but see themselves as a person of the other sex.)
2. F (It is one of the final steps.)
3. F (They tend to be androgynous.)
4. T (Of the many ways by which one can change one's gender identity, changing one's genitals is one of the least effective.)
5. F (What are they called?)
6. F
7. T
8. T
9. F
10. F (This is only one form of a preference for inanimate objects.)

Part II: Multiple-Choice Questions

1. *c*
2. *c*
3. *a*
4. *c*
5. *b*
6. *a*
7. *c*

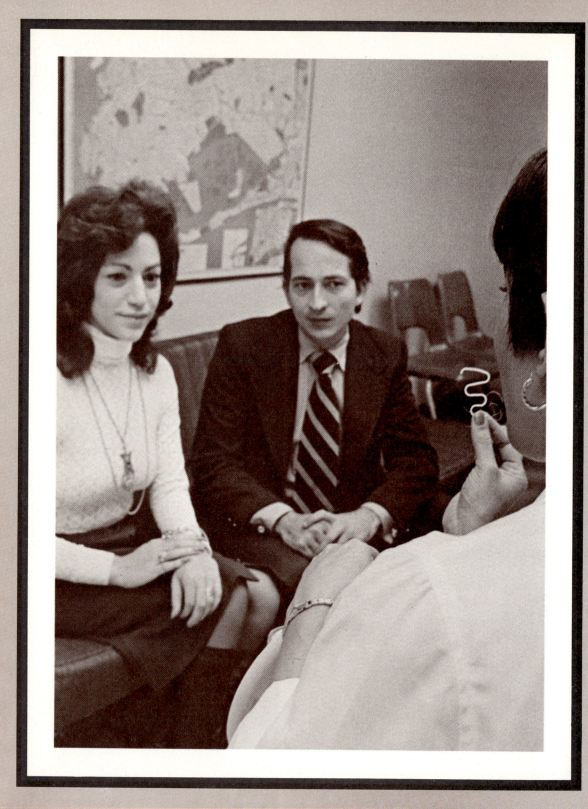

Chapter 12
Contraception and Abortion

The traditional religious view that sex is for the purpose of procreation has never been the sole, or even most common, motivation for engaging in sexual activity in the form of coitus. Thus, throughout time and in many cultures, there has been a concern about how to engage in recreational intercourse without conception or birth. Consistently, people have made concerted attempts either to lessen the chance of conception in intercourse (contraception) or to avoid birth once conception has taken place (abortion).

METHODS OF CONTRACEPTION

Contraception includes behaviors and devices which interrupt the process of conception by either preventing fertilization of an egg or by preventing a fertilized egg from being implanted in the uterus. Contraceptive methods vary greatly in terms of the processes used to accomplish one or both of these ends, the effectiveness of the method, the side-effects of the method, and the patterns of actual use.

Coitus Interruptus

Coitus interruptus or withdrawal is preventing conception by withdrawal of the penis from the vagina prior to ejaculation (interrupting coitus), thus preventing conception. This method has the advantage of being inexpensive, requiring no supplies and no assistance from medical professionals. On the other hand, it requires a great deal of self-control by the male, a high level of motivation, and considerable practice, during which pregnancy is a likely result. In order to be effective, the penis must be withdrawn from the vagina before the male feels that ejaculation is inevitable, since semen can flow into the penis before the actual sensation of ejaculation itself is felt.

Given these factors, withdrawal is among the least effective methods. Other drawbacks involve how withdrawal may affect sexuality. Most people find the sudden stopping of intercourse at the height of passion to be somewhat less than a satisfying experience.

Condom

A condom is a cylindrical sheath made of rubber or animal skin (the latter is rare today) which fits over the erect penis and traps the ejaculate in the tip.

To be effective, a condom must either have a built-in reservoir in the tip or a ½-inch space between the tip of the penis and the end of the condom in which to collect the ejaculate.

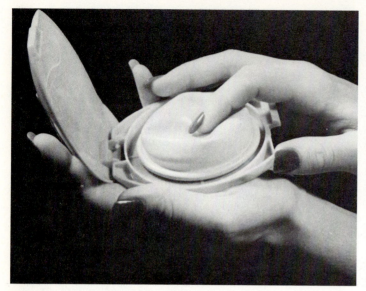

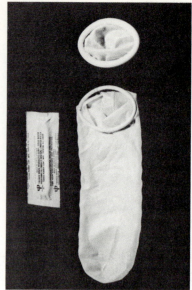

Birth-control devices: (a) diaphragm
and (b) condom, rolled (top)
and unrolled (bottom).

BOX 12-1

ORIGIN OF THE CONDOM

It is commonly rumored that the condom was invented by a Dr. Condom, a physician in the court of Charles II (1650–1685). Himes (1936), in an exhaustive attempt to verify this, concludes that the story is most likely a myth. The exact origin of the word "condom" remains unknown. The first published report of the condom was in a work of the Italian anatomist Fallopius (for whom the fallopian tubes are named) in 1564. He refers to a linen sheath fitted over the glans of the penis with the foreskin drawn over the top to hold it on. The purpose of this device was prevention of venereal disease, not contraception. A forerunner of those who complain about intercourse with a condom providing less sensation was Mme. de Sévigné who, in letters to her daughter in 1671, warned that such devices were "armor against enjoyment, and a spider web against danger" (Himes, 1936).

The precise time when the condom came to be regarded as a contraceptive device is unknown. However, Casanova (1725–1798) made it clear in his memoirs that he used condoms for this purpose and that they consisted of full tubes made from animal intestines. Part of the scant knowledge about the origin of the condom has to do with the fact that no one would claim the honor of the invention. The French referred to the condom as the "English Cape" and the English returned the compliment by calling it the "French Letter" (Himes, 1936).

After ejaculation, the condom must be held around the base and against the penis to prevent ejaculate from escaping. The penis must also be removed from the vagina before erection declines or semen may escape, or worse yet, the condom may be left behind upon withdrawing the penis. Even though a condom should always be checked for punctures before use (manufacturing standards are high but not perfect), this often is difficult. The powder used on many condoms as a lubricant can seal any holes when mixed with the water vapor from one's breath.

Contraceptive failure with the condom is reasonably high, with 10 percent of all users having a failure in the first year of use (*Population Reports,* September 1979). Most of these failures are due to the users, not to the product. Under ideal conditions—which never exist, since any contraceptive involves how people use it—the failure rate is much lower.[1]

Advantages The condom has several advantages. It is inexpensive, available without a physical examination or prescription, and protective against sexually transmitted disease.

Disadvantages The disadvantages of the condom include the care in user behavior required to make it effective, its often being associated with prostitution (mainly in countries other than the United States), and its often being seen as dulling sensation in the penis ("taking a shower with a raincoat on").[2]

---

[1]The failure rates reported throughout this chapter are *overall* failure rates for contraceptives. There are really two types of contraceptive failures and thus two different failure rates. *Delay* failure refers to a contraceptive failure when the user wants to delay a pregnancy. *Avoid* failure refers to failure to avoid a pregnancy entirely, rather than merely delay when it occurs. Delay failures are generally twice those of avoid failures regardless of the contraceptive method used, thus emphasizing the importance of user behavior in contraception (*Population Reports,* September 1979).

[2]In recent years, there have been attempts to overcome some of these complaints by manufacturing condoms in different colors, using thinner material, and making condoms with ridges and bumps for extra female stimulation. It should be noted that bumps and ridges generally do not provide any extra stimulation for the female. They do not make contact with the clitoris, which is most often stimulated by movement of the clitoral hood and not direct contact with the penis, and the inside of the vagina is stimulated by pressure and a feeling of fullness rather than little bumps and doodads. Flashy appearance is not really new. Condom boxes in the 1920s and 1930s were made of tin and elaborately decorated. Today they are collector's items.

Other disadvantages include the requirement of proper storage (not in a wallet) and the risk of reaction in a small proportion of people who are allergic to the commonly used rubber material.

Some people also object to the fact that the stream of sexual arousal can be interrupted with condom use since one first has to have an erection before it can be placed on the penis. Some see the stopping to put the condom on as a distraction, but it can just as easily be seen as a part of sexual interaction. Last, there is the fact that the penis cannot remain in the vagina after ejaculation, thus effectively stopping intercourse at this point. There is also the possiblity that condom use may be associated with breast cancer, although this connection has by no means been established. Gjorgon (1980) found that the predominant method used by women who had breast cancer was the condom. The reason he suggested for this finding is that the prostoglandins in semen may act as a protection against some forms of cancer; with a condom, semen is never deposited in the vagina and thus cannot be absorbed into the bloodstream through the vaginal walls.

Spermicides

Spermicides are chemical substances that kill sperm cells. They are available in many forms, including jels and creams inserted into the vagina with a syringe or applicator, aerosols, suppositories inserted manually or with an applicator, and foaming tablets. All spermicides must be inserted in the vagina before intercourse.

The failure rate for spermicide contraception alone is 15 percent in the first year of use (*Population Reports,* September 1979). This low effectiveness is most often due to user behavior.

In order for a spermicide to be effective, two processes must take place. The substance must first block the entrance from the vagina to the cervix so that sperm cells cannot get past. Second, it must kill the sperm cells. Low effectiveness usually results from not using enough spermicide, not waiting long enough after application before having intercourse (check the instructions), and having intercourse a second time without another application of the spermicide. Poor quality of the spermicide does not result from its lack of effectiveness per se. Rather, sperm cells may lodge in the tissue folds of the vagina and live longer than the spermicide remains effective. When no one is looking, they then hightail it up the cervix.[3]

Advantages Spermicides do not require a physical examination or prescription (although they did require the latter in the past). They can be used with little preparation or planning for coitus (unlike the pill or the intrauterine device), and they do not involve the harmful effects of hormones.

Disadvantages Spermicides are often messy because of leakage from the vagina. Also, there is a need with some brands to wait a certain period of time before engaging in coitus; the spermicide must be reapplied for each intercourse session regardless of how close together they are; and some people feel a warm or tingling sensation from the chemical. Spermicides also inhibit cunnilingus and application requires an interruption in the flow of sexual events (unless one knows "for sure").

Health effects The single biggest disadvantage of spermicides is that they are implicated in severe birth defects. For example, in one study infants born to mothers who had been using a spermicide in the ten months prior to conception had slightly more than twice the rate of congenital birth defects as infants born to mothers who had not used spermicides (Jick et al., 1981). The birth defects were limb deformities, cancer, and Down's syndrome. A number of other studies

have also found spermicide use associated with limb deformities in newborns (Smith et al., 1977; Strobino et al., 1980; Warburton et al., 1980). Spermicide use is also associated with a greater risk of spontaneous abortion (an abortion of the fetus that is not induced). Jick et al. (1981) found, for example, that spontaneous abortion was almost twice as likely for women who had used spermicides as for women who had not.

It is not clear why spermicides may cause birth defects. The sperm cell could be damaged by the chemical but not killed, the chemical could move into the female reproductive tract and damage the egg cell, or the chemical could be absorbed through the bloodstream and move into any number of body tissues, including those involved in reproduction.

Douche

The long-used method of douching or flushing the vagina with either water or a spermicidal agent after intercourse is the least effective of all contraceptive methods. Thinking that douche is a contraceptive method is, in fact, based on a serious misunderstanding of anatomy and the speed of sperm. From the time of ejaculation it takes sperm less than 90 seconds to enter the cervix. It is virtually impossible, as well as not very romantic, to leap up immediately after ejaculation, run to the bathroom, and thus complete a douching procedure before sperm cells enter the cervix.

Diaphragm

The diaphragm is a mechanical means of blocking sperm from entering the cervical opening. It consists of rubber in the shape of a saucer. A circular ring of flexible metal is covered with rubber and inside this ring is a thin piece of dome-shaped rubber. The diaphragm is manually inserted into the vagina and fits over the cervix (Figure 12-1). Proper and effective use requires a physician's taking measurements of the cervix for proper fit, the use of a contraceptive cream or jelly on the diaphragm before insertion in the vagina, and

---

[3]With increasing concern over the health hazards of the pill, some manufacturers of spermicides launched a heavy advertising campaign to take advantage of many women's search for another contraceptive method. The advertisements strongly suggested that the spermicides were as effective as the pill or the intrauterine device, which they are not. On Feb. 18, 1980, the Federal Trade Commission reached agreements with several major manufacturers in which they ceased such claims and had to indicate, among other things, that users must wait a certain period of time after application for the product to be effective.

leaving the diaphragm in place after inter-course until there is little chance of live sperm being in the vagina (six to eight hours).

Advantages The diaphragm does not interrupt the flow of sexual events leading to intercourse, since it may be inserted up to six hours before coitus actually takes place (but most spermicides do not last this long). The diaphragm is effective when used properly, it is inexpensive after the initial cost of purchase, and it itself has no chemical or mechanical effect on normal bodily processes, as does the pill or the intrauterine device (IUD).

Disadvantages The diaphragm must initially be fitted by a physician. This involves more expense than other contraceptive meth-ods and it requires that the woman see a medi-cal professional (which makes it unpopular among teenagers). Some people are allergic to the rubber material, and user failure tends to lessen its effectiveness. The failure rate is 13 percent in the first year of use (*Population Reports,* September 1979), principally because of lack of proper spermicide use in conjunction with the diaphragm. Also, considerable weight loss in the woman may alter the fit so as to reduce effectiveness. The diaphragm may also be dislodged by contact with the penis in the woman-on-top position (Mims and Swenson, 1980).

Cervical Cap

The cervical cap is moderately popular in Eu-rope, but has never found much acceptance in the United States. This device is roughly the shape and size of a large thimble and fits over the end of the cervix.

Advantages The cervical cap does not have to be inserted and removed with each act of coitus and it does not involve chemicals. It is inexpensive once the initial cost is covered and it does not interfere with the flow of sexual events in coitus.

Disadvantages The disadvantages currently outweigh the advantages. In recent studies with women selecting the cervical cap (*Family Planning Perspectives,* January–February 1981), there has been a failure rate

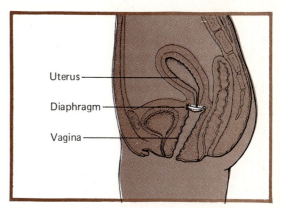

Figure 12-1 The proper placement of a diaphragm.

of 8 percent. More important, 39 percent of these women stopped using the cap shortly after starting. The most common reasons for discontinuation were distrust of the cap's effec-tiveness, pain or discomfort in one or both partners (the penis can make contact with the cap with deep penetration), and problems in inserting and removing the cap (it must be re-moved once a month for menstrual flow to pass from the uterus into the vagina).

New developments Recent develop-ments appear to hold some promise for the cervical cap as far as some of these com-plaints are concerned. A new cap is made from an impression of the woman's cervix (a tech-nique used in dentistry), thus providing a very accurate fit. The new cap also contains a one-way valve which allows menstrual flow out but keeps sperm from getting in. Thus, it does not have to be removed each month. In test cases, the new cap has proven highly effective and has been worn by some women for as long as twenty-two months without removal (*Intercom,* 1979).

Pills

There are several forms of birth control pills, but the most commonly used is the *combina-tion pill,* so-called because it contains a combi-nation of two synthetic hormones.

The primary hormone of the combination pill is an estrogen. Orally ingesting synthetic estrogen artificially raises the estrogen level in the body. Since a lowering of the estrogen level during a normal menstrual cycle is what stimulates ovulation, the artificial estrogen acts to suppress ovulation. (Therefore the pill is called an ovulation suppression method.) If there is no ovulation, there is no egg to be fertilized and conception cannot take place.

The second hormone in the combination pill is a progestin. A higher level of progesterone (progestin is synthetic progesterone) in the body aids in suppressing ovulation, thickens the cervical mucus, and changes the lining of the uterus. The thicker cervical mucus makes sperm travel through the cervix difficult, and the change in the lining of the uterus makes implantation of a fertilized egg much less likely.

Use Pills generally come in packages of 21 or 28. If it is a 21-pill package, they are taken for 21 consecutive days starting on the fifth day of the menstrual cycle. If it is a 28-day package, they are taken daily and 21 of the pills are active and 7 are inert. For the 21 days during which the pills are taken, ovulation is suppressed because of the higher levels of hormones. After the last pill is taken (or the last noninert in a 28-pill package), these hormone levels drop to normal and *withdrawal bleeding* in the form of menstrual flow takes place. This is called withdrawal bleeding because the lining of the uterus sheds owing to withdrawal from the high hormone levels and not because ovulation has taken place without the egg's being fertilized (as would be the case if the pill were not used). No egg cell ever matures while a woman is using the pill because, with the high estrogen level, the body chemistry system "thinks" that an egg is maturing when it really is not.

Advantages: Contraceptive, cosmetic, comfort One of the major advantages of the pill is, of course, its effectiveness. Theoretically, the pill should have a 1 percent failure rate. In actual use, the failure rate is 2 percent in the first year of use. The difference between the theoretical and actual failure rate is due to the user's forgetting to take the pill every day. Another major contraceptive advantage of the pill is its convenience. It is a form of contraception which does not interfere with any given act of intercourse and thus allows spontaneity and freedom from planning for coitus to occur. The pill also has comfort and cosmetic advantages. The elevated hormone levels are associated with the clearing of acne and the reduction of menstrual cramps and tension and menstrual flow.

Advantages: Less risk of certain diseases There is evidence that pill use is associated with less chance of rheumatoid arthritis and ovarian cysts (Ory et al., 1980), benign breast diseases such as fibroadenoma, chronic cystic disease, and breast lumps (Ory et al., 1976; Brinton et al., 1981; Ramcharau et al., 1981). There is also some suggestion that pill use may protect against cancer of the uterus. This, however, remains to be demonstrated (Ory et al., 1980; Ramcharau et al., 1981). Hulka et al. (1982) recently found that in combination pills progestin protects against uterine cancer while estrogen by itself appears to increase cancer risk. A major health advantage of the pill is that its use is associated with a decreased risk of the serious sexually transmitted disease, salpingitis. In Chapter 16 we will discuss salpingitis in detail, but for now we need only note that it is implicated in a wide range of serious health problems for women. The actual risk of salpingitis among pill users is about half of what it is among women who do not use the pill (Senanayake and Kramer, 1981). This is a powerful effect, given that salpingitis risk is greater with greater sexual activity and greater sexual activity is associated with pill use. The mechanism by which this protection against salpingitis through pill use works is unknown. Senanayake and Kramer (1981) suggest three possible factors: (1) the progesterone in the pill increases the density of the cervical mucus and thus might inhibit bacteria from entering the cervix and uterus and causing salpingitis; (2) the decreased menstrual bleeding associated with pill use may reduce the amount of culture medium for the salpingitis bacteria to grow; and (3) the relative inactivity of the uterine muscle caused by the pill may decrease the chance of bacteria being propelled upward into the uterus.

Disadvantages Medical research continues to investigate the exact nature and seriousness of the negative side-effects of pill use. These we shall discuss in detail as serious health risks. There are, however, several well-known side-effects of the pill that, although not generally considered serious health risks, are often definite disadvantages from the perspective of the user. Since high hormone levels introduced by the pill imitate pregnancy, there are often side-effects similar to pregnancy: water retention by the body, weight increase, breast enlargement and tenderness. There may be spotting (a small amount of menstrual bleeding between periods) and increased vaginal discharge. While these side-effects are generally thought of as medically minor, they are often serious enough from the user's point of view that 25 to 50 percent of the women who try the pill discontinue its use within one year (Hatcher et al., 1978).

Health risks: Circulatory disease
Several studies from the noted Royal College of General Practicioner's Oral Contraceptive Study in England have clearly established a relationship between taking oral contraceptives and circulatory and heart disease. In this study, women who used the pill were found to have a 40 percent higher death rate than women who never used the pill (Layde et al., 1981). These higher death rates for pill users are mainly due to more risk of death from circulatory and heart disease (Vessey et al., 1981; Layde et al., 1981). Several studies also reveal that pill use increases the risk of developing high blood pressure, stroke, cerebral hemorrhage, and blood clots (Fisch and Frank, 1972; Weir et al., 1974; 1975; Ostrander et al., 1980; Lowe et al., 1980; Sartell et al., 1969; Royal College of General Practicioners, 1977). The risk of increased blood pressure with pill use only applies, however, to Caucasian and not black women (Blumenstein et al., 1980).

The exact reasons for all these increased death risks associated with pill use are not yet clearly understood. However, pill use is associated with higher serum cholesterol levels in the blood and cholesterol is a causal factor in heart attack (Ostrander et al., 1980). Lowe et al. (1980) found that the blood of women who use the pill is thicker than that of women who do not use the pill. One of the reasons that men have much higher heart-disease rates than women may be blood thickness, since women who menstruate have thinner blood than men. Pill use may counteract this sex difference in heart-disease risk.

Risk of death with pill use is three to four times greater among women who smoke, regardless of their age (Layde et al., 1981). Also, the negative health effects of smoking are intensified by pill use (Ramcharau et al., 1981). It is difficult to overemphasize the accumulated risks of heart disease and death associated with the combination of pill use and smoking. Rosenberg et al. (1980) found that pill use has an effect on the chances of heart attack independent of other known heart-attack risk factors and that when smoking and pill use are combined, the risk of heart attack is greater than the sum of these two risk factors together. (See Figure 12-2.)

Age is also a factor in pill use risk since, for women 35 to 44, the overall risk of death is 3.5 times higher among pill users than among women who have never used the pill.

Health risks: Cancer of the cervix
As late as 1977, the relationship between pill use and cervical cancer was unclear (Knab, 1977). But more recent research has begun to find an association, although it is not clear why such an association exists. Several studies have reported that long-term pill use is associated with a greater incidence of cervical cancer (Harris et al., 1980; Swan and Brown, 1980; Peritz et al., 1981). However, there is a clear relationship between risk of cervical cancer and the frequency of coitus, age at first coitus, and number of partners (Rotkin, 1973; Swan and Brown, 1981). Since selecting the pill as a contraceptive is associated with more frequent coitus, perhaps an earlier age at starting regular coitus, and perhaps a larger number of coital partners, it is entirely possible that the relationship which has been observed between pill use and cervical cancer is due to

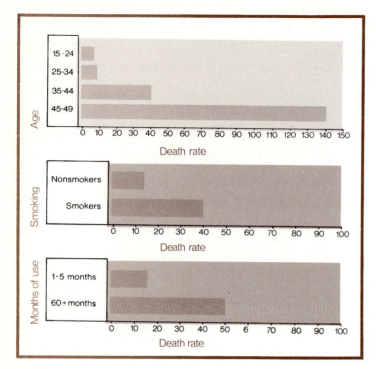

Figure 12-2 Typical patterns of death rates (number of deaths per 100,000 women) among pill users by age, smoking or nonsmoking behavior, and months of pill use. (Source: *Population Reports,* series A, number 5, January 1979, "Oral Contraceptives.")

the greater sexual activity of pill users and not to the hormonal effects of the pill itself. Swan and Brown (1981) found support for this hypothesis. When they controlled for these sexual activity facors, they found no relationship between pill use and cervical cancer. The tentative conclusion would have to be that the pill itself is not a factor in the risk of cervical cancer. However, many researchers believe that cervical dysplasia (abnormality) progresses to cervical cancer in some women and there is evidence that oral contraceptive use can hasten this progression (Check, 1980). On the other hand, Hulka et al. (1982) suggest that if the oral contraceptive contains only estrogen the risk of uterine cancer is increased.

Health risks: Breast cancer There is good theoretical reason to suspect that pill use may be implicated in the development of breast cancer in women. One of the factors that appears to be associated with an increased risk of breast cancer is endogenous estrogen production (estrogen produced by the body itself). The longer one's body produces the normally high levels of estrogen associated with the reproductive years, the greater one's risk of breast cancer (Carlile, 1981; Miller, 1981; Paffenbarger et al., 1980). Thus, having early menarche and/or late menopause is associated with an increased risk of breast cancer, while having an oophorectomy (surgical removal of an ovary) before menopause is related to a decreased risk of breast cancer (Miller, 1981).

These facts prompted researchers to suspect that estrogen increases due to pill use might increase the risk of breast cancer. While some studies have suggested a relationship between pill use and breast cancer, they have been criticized for the research methods used (Jick 1980a; 1980b). Larger studies which appear to be relatively free of these research problems have failed to find a relationship between pill use and breast cancer (Vessey et al., 1979; Vessey et al., 1981; Kay, 1981). Gjorgon (1980) even found that pill use may inadvertently "protect" against breast cancer. He observed that women using any contraceptive method which exposed the vagina to semen (called nonbarrier methods because they do not provide a barrier against semen contacting the vagina) had significantly lower rates of breast cancer than women who used barrier methods. Gjorgon suggested that this may be due to the fact that semen is rapidly absorbed by the vagina and enters the blood stream and that the prostoglandins in semen may act as a protection against breast cancer.

Other health effects   While issues other than cancer and heart and circulatory disease have not received a great deal of attention with regard to pill use, women currently using the pill have higher levels of glucose and insulin (factors in diabetes) than women who have never used the pill (Ostrander et al., 1980).

Postcoital Pill

The postcoital pill (taken after coitus) has not been approved for sale in the United States but continues to be tested and to gain public attention. Postcoital pills come in two types: a natural and a synthetic estrogen. Testing indicates that while highly effective, the postcoital pill is not as effective as the regular pill, and the intake of synthetic estrogen in this form is accompanied by nausea and vomiting (Dixon et al., 1980).

Mini Pill

The mini pill most often contains only progestin, which acts to thicken the cervical mucous and alter the lining of the uterus. While the theoretical failure rate of the mini pill is 1 to 1.5 percent, the actual failure rate in use is 5 to 10 percent (Hatcher et al., 1978).

Depo Provera

Depo Provera is the trade name for progestin which is injected once every three months.

While the "shot" is used in more than eighty countries, including ten in Western Europe, it is still banned in the United States. (See Gold and Wilson, 1981, for a review of the debate between opponents and proponents of Depo Provera.) The obvious advantage of the shot is that it avoids continual administration of the pill and thus user failure is less likely. However, the extent and seriousness of side-effects remain unclear enough that the drug has not been approved for use in this country.

Natural Methods

The commonly called "rhythm" methods of avoiding conception are the only "natural" forms of contraception, since they involve abstaining from coitus during that part of the menstrual cycle when conception is most likely. Given that nothing except abstinence interferes with the act of conception, this is the only form of birth control formally approved by the Roman Catholic Church.

The key to natural birth control is being able to determine when one is most likely to conceive. There are various methods for making this determination.

Calendar method   The traditional natural method involves counting the days to determine the period of greatest risk of conception. Assuming a perfect twenty-eight-day menstrual cycle, the woman ovulates on the fourteenth day before menstrual flow begins. Add one day before the fourteenth and one day after for a safety band, and this is the time when conception is most likely. However, three days are added to the front of this period to guard against sperm remaining in the vagina and cervix and two days are added to the end to allow for eggs which may last longer than normal. This makes an eight-day period when intercourse should not take place if conception is not wanted.

The principle problem with the calendar method is that few women have regular menstrual cycles. Thus, with an irregular cycle you do not know for sure when ovulation will take place until it actually occurs. To safeguard against an irregular menstrual cycle, one can abstain for a longer period, thus covering all eight-day segments around one's different ovulation dates. This, however, could be more than two weeks in some cases. The 19 percent failure rate for the calendar method is not unexpected (*Population Reports,* September 1979). Of course, the calendar method can be combined with another method such as the condom, using the additional method during the period of assumed risk.

Basal body temperature   A somewhat more sophisticated method of determining the period of conception risk is by body temperature. Just before ovulation, body temperature drops about 0.2°F. Approximately twenty-four to seventy-two hours later, temperature increases significantly at the time of ovulation. Basal body temperature must be taken, however, each morning immediately when waking before *any* activity takes place, and many other factors can influence an accurate reading of temperature.

Cervical mucous   The cervical mucus changes systematically during the menstrual cycle. The first few days after menstruation, no mucus is produced and the vagina feels dry. Then the mucus becomes white and cloudy and continues to increase in amount. Then for a period of about two days, the mucus becomes slippery and stringy and much like raw egg white. One may have the sensation of vaginal lubrication during these two days. Ovulation takes place within twenty-four hours of the second day of this change in the cervical mucus. This mucus can be checked when one urinates by using paper to wipe the vagina opening.

Sympotothermal method   Perhaps the most accurate and safe natural method is that which uses a combination of other methods to determine when conception is most likely. One such method is the *Thyma's Double Check* which involves taking basal temperature, checking cervical mucus, plotting the duration of the six previous menstrual cycles, and monitoring certain menstrual symptoms such as breast tenderness and lower abdominal pain (Wade et al., 1979). A recent test of the cervical mucus method alone in comparison to

the Thyma's Double Check indicates that, while neither method is popular or very effective, the Double Check is more effective. Wade et al. found that 74 percent of the women using the cervical mucus method and 64 percent of the women using the Double Check stopped using it in a short time, and 22 percent of the women using cervical mucus and 11 percent of the women using the Double Check became pregnant.

The Intrauterine Device (IUD)

The intrauterine device (IUD) is a small plastic device which is inserted into the uterus by a physician (Figure 12-3). Similar devices have been known for centuries. Arab camel drivers have long inserted pebbles into the uteri of their camels to prevent conception on desert trips and intrauterine contraception was mentioned by the early Greeks (Himes, 1936). It was not until 1957, however, that clinical reports on the IUD were available from Japan and Israel, and the IUD was not introduced to the American public until 1960 with the approval and sale of the Lippes loop.

Exactly how the IUD works to prevent conception is not known. The majority opinion is that it irritates the lining of the uterus, making implantation highly unlikely. It has been suggested that the use of antibiotics, or even aspirin, can reduce the effectiveness of the IUD by reducing inflammation in the uterus (Boston Women's Health Book Collective, 1976).

IUDs come in two forms, medicated and nonmedicated. Medicated devices, such as Copper 7 and Progestasert T, have an additional contraceptive method. The Copper 7 is wrapped with copper wire, which affects the enzymes involved in the implantation process. The Progestasert T slowly releases progestins which affect the uterine lining and the mucous of the cervix.

Advantages   The major advantages of the IUD are effectiveness and convenience. Once it is inserted, no other contraceptive preparation prior to or after coitus is necessary. Another characteristic which many women today see as an advantage is that the

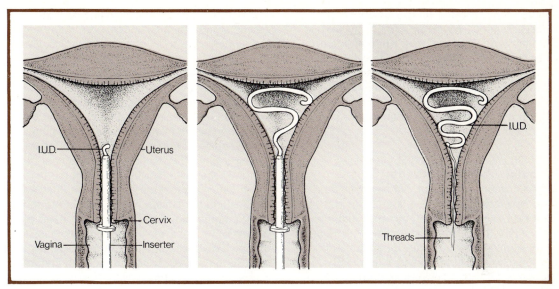

Figure 12-3 The insertion of an intrauterine device (IUD). The inserting instrument is placed into the cervical canal through the cervical opening. The IUD is then pushed out of the inserter and placed in the uterine cavity. After the inserter is removed, the small threads from the IUD protrude into the vagina so that the user can check from time to time to see if the IUD is still in place. Yes, the string can irritate the glans of the penis during intercourse, but this is almost never noticeable to the male. Ideally, the IUD should be inserted during the menstrual flow when the cervical opening is most relaxed. The menstrual flow also hides any small amount of normal bleeding that may occur after inserting the IUD, and the physician can be certain that the woman is not pregnant. (Mims and Swenson, 1980.)

IUD is nonhormonal and thus is an effective and safe alternative to the pill. A third advantage of the IUD is its effectiveness. While the theoretical failure rate is 1 to 3 percent, the actual failure rate is 4.2 percent in the first year of use (*Population Reports,* September 1979).

Disadvantages   There are, however, certain "minor" disadvantages to the IUD. Between 5 and 10 percent of all women, in their first year of use, experience heavy menstrual bleeding, cramps, spotting, or spontaneous expulsion of the IUD. These side-effects result in 8 to 10 percent of the women who have had an IUD inserted having it removed within the first year (Stewart et al., 1979). Placement of the device can also be a common problem, since many women experience considerable discom-

fort during and immediately after insertion of the device. Much more serious, but much less common problems involve infection after placement and perforation of the uterus during or after placement.

Health effects   For some time there has been concern that the IUD may be associated with a greater chance of ectopic pregnancy. Recent research indicates that this is not so. In fact, a woman who has never used any contraceptive method has a greater risk of an ectopic pregnancy than does a woman who has used an IUD (Ory, 1981). Also, the risk of an ectopic pregnancy is no different for the medicated and nonmedicated IUDs (Ory, 1981). Concern has also existed over the years about IUD use being associated with a greater chance of birth defects. This also appears not to be the case (Savolainen et al., 1981). There is, however, a relatively serious health risk: IUD users have 1.5 to 4 times greater risk of salpingitis than do women who do not use the device (Senanayake and Kramer, 1981). This risk is possibly due to the IUD itself causing inflammation of the uterus, thus providing a more hospitable environment for infection.

Possible Future Methods

There has been considerable research recently into new contraceptive methods in an effort to find safe, convenient, and effective alternatives to the pill. "Considerable," however, is relative to how much research was conducted in the 1970s. It must be remembered that ½ of 1 percent of all the money spent on medical research goes into contraceptive research. While the Carter administration founded the Contraceptive Branch of the National Institute of Child Health and Human Development to aid in the production of new contraceptive methods, the future of contraceptive research under a more conservative administration remains in serious doubt.

Male methods   While we have often heard much talk about a male pill, this remains largely talk. In a number of countries, for many years attempts have been made to develop a substance which would inhibit the production of sperm, inhibit sperm movement, inhibit sperm maturation, and/or inhibit the ability of the acrosome to produce enzymes for penetrating the egg cell. These attempts have been directed toward altering the seminiferous tubules or by hormonal control of the male reproductive system. These efforts have almost universally resulted in ineffective methods or methods which produced disagreeable side-effects ranging from loss of erection ability to purple eyes when consuming alcohol (actually not such a bad idea—you would know if he is telling the truth about being on the pill). Currently, there is some discussion of moving from a way of affecting the male reproductive system itself to an immunilogically based pill that would activate the body's immune system to kill sperm cells.

Another male possiblity which has received some attention is *gossypol*. A derivative of cottonseed oil, gossypol was accidently discovered by the Chinese in the 1950s when investigation was made of a geographical area in China with a very low birth rate. It turned out that the people in this area used nothing but crude cottonseed oil for cooking, and since 1972 the Chinese have been testing it as a contraceptive (Maugh, 1981). Gossypol suppresses sperm production and movement of sperm in the epididymis. Apart from the perhaps disturbing fact that gossypol is used as a pesticide in the United States, it appears to have a number of side-effects which need examination. It apparently causes weakness, stomach distress, nausea, and reduced appetite (Benditt, 1980) as well as a reduction of potassium in the body which, in turn, results in a form of paralysis (Quian et al., 1979; 1980). This potassium problem appears, however, to be avoided by increasing potassium intake (Quian et al., 1980).

Female methods   Much more attention is being given to new female contraceptive methods, and it appears that these methods generally hold more promise than those for males.

One such method is the *ICD* (intracervical device). This is a hollow cylinder containing progestin and fitting in the cervical canal. It releases steroids which thicken the cervical mucus and this, in turn, stops the passage of sperm cells into the uterus and oviducts (Benditt, 1980).

Another promising method is an *elastic plug* inserted by a physician into the oviducts. The plug jells and forms a tight seal, thus blocking the passage of both egg and sperm. A loop is attached to the plug and extends into the uterus for removal. Preliminary reports indicate that the device has no apparent side-effects, is less uncomfortable than having an IUD inserted, requires no operative procedure, and has no effect (at least on rabbits) on conception after removal.

Cervical sponges containing a spermicidal agent and inserted into the cervix as much as two days prior to coitus are also being tested. The sponges are disposable and are expected to cost between 75 cents and $1.25 each.

   Subdermal implants are also receiving attention. These are small capsules which are implanted just under the skin and slowly release a contraceptive agent. Two types are being tested. One of them contains natural estrogen and is implanted under the skin of the abdomen. Tests indicate that this estrogen method does not have the negative side-effects commonly associated with the pill, but the long-term health effects and effectiveness of this method remain to be studied (Nezhat et al., 1980). A second subdermal implant contains progestin-based steroids and is placed in the skin of the arm. Some volunteers have had these devices for up to ten years, and testing indicates that retention is high overall. Of these women in the testing, 40 percent still had the implants after five years. Other than 20 percent of the users having irregular menstrual bleeding, the side-effects are not yet fully known (King, 1981). Besides convenience, the major advantage of subdermal implants may prove to be high effectiveness with lower (and thus possibly safer) hormonal doses than required with the pill (Beck et al., 1981).

Surgical Sterilization—Males

Surgical sterilization involves any of a number of procedures in which the individual in rendered incapable of reproduction. In males, the common procedure is *vasectomy*.

   The surgical procedure   Vasectomy is so called because it involves the cutting and typing of the vas deferentia. This minor operation involves a small incision made in each scrotal sac. The vas deferens is cut in half and tied off at the two ends (Figure 12-4). The operation is usually done in a physician's office under local anesthetic and takes about twenty minutes to complete. For a couple of days, there is some local discomfort, and strenuous activity (that might tear the incision) is not a good idea. Usually, the patient may return to intercourse activity within a week. However, he is still not sterile at this time and other contraceptive means must be used if the risk of pregnancy is to be avoided. Within two to three

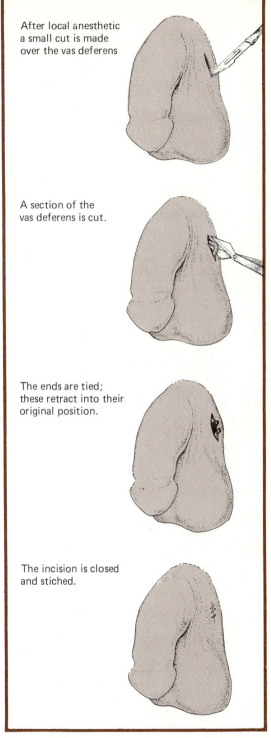

After local anesthetic a small cut is made over the vas deferens

A section of the vas deferens is cut.

The ends are tied; these retract into their original position.

The incision is closed and stiched.

Figure 12-4 Surgical procedures in performing a vasectomy.

months, all the sperm cells between the point of the vasectomy and the penis should be gone. At this time, sterility is confirmed by a semen analysis performed by a medical laboratory (many males find that the worst part of the whole procedure is going into the little room and providing a fresh semen specimen).

Effects on health   The result of a vasectomy is that the ejaculate does not contain sperm cells since they can no longer get by the point in the vas where the incision and tying-off were made. The operation has no physiological effect on any aspect of sexual functioning, including the volume of ejaculate. Most of the ejaculate, you will recall, comes from the prostate gland and not sperm cells. Sperm cell reproduction remains the same as before the procedure and the sperm are simply absorbed by the body. Here is where there has been some concern about the health effects of vasectomy. To the immune system of the body, sperm cells are foreign. The reason is that the immune system develops early in life but sperm cells are not produced until puberty. It is thought that when the sperm are trapped in the body as a result of a vasectomy, the body produces antibodies to fight the foreign sperm cells. The antibodies, in turn, may lead to a hardening and thickening of the walls of the arteries, a condition which is a major contributor to heart disease.

Although there have been studies on rhesus monkeys which confirm this process (e.g., Clarkson and Alexander, 1980), it is not perfectly accurate to generalize these findings to humans. As of this writing, a number of human studies are under way to test this process. In one human study which has been completed with over 4,000 vasectomized males, there was no association between vasectomy and nonfatal heart attack (myocardial infarction) (Walker et al., 1981a). Other evidence for the lack of serious health risks in vasectomy comes from a study of over 6,000 males with vasectomies (Walker et al., 1981b). Here it was found that men with vasectomies had higher rates of hospitalization for a variety of genitourinary diseases in the brief period following vasectomy, but that there were no other differences between men who did have and those who did not have a vasectomy.

Reversal   The contraceptive advantage of male sterilization is that it relieves the woman of the burden of contraception and it is virtually 100 percent effective. The major disadvantage, apart from some males mistakenly equating vasectomy with castration or feeling that their "manhood" has something to do with the ability to impregnate a female, has been that it is irreversible. Since sterilization operations were first done, there has been research on retying the vas and thus returning the flow of sperm cells. Until quite recently, the most commonly quoted rate of success in reversal operations was 5 percent (success is the female partner's pregnancy). With the development of microsurgery techniques (surgery performed at the microscopic level), vasectomy reversal may become highly successful. Dr. Sherman J. Silber of St. Louis reports that in more than 1,200 vasectomy reversal operations he has performed with microsurgery, 71 percent have been successful owing to the delicate surgical procedures (*Sexuality Today,* October 6, 1980).

The verification and further development of reversal surgery appear to be in increasing demand in the United States as males in their thirties who either delayed marriage or remarried now want to reverse a prior vasectomy. If such reversal procedures become highly successful, sterilization could become an even more popular method of contraception than it is today.

Surgical Sterilization—Female

The most common form of female surgical sterilization consists of blocking the oviducts so that an egg cell cannot pass toward the uterus and a sperm cell cannot make contact with an egg cell. This is commonly called *tubal sterilization* since the procedure is performed on the fallopian tubes, or oviducts. The various tubal sterilization procedures differ on the basis of two major characteristics: the surgical means of approach to the oviducts and the means by which they are blocked.

Methods of approach   The most common technique is a *laparoscopy,* a procedure made possible by the development of optical tools in the form of very small fibers (fiberoptics).[4] In laparoscopy, a very small incision, or even a puncture, is made in the lower abdominal area. A laparoscope is inserted into the abdominal cavity through the puncture, allowing the surgeon to view the internal organs, including the uterus and oviducts. The abdominal cavity is partially filled with gas. This allows the intestines and bowel to fall away from the oviducts. An instrument (uterine elevator) is inserted into the vagina and is used to elevate the uterus and rotate it so that the oviducts become accessible to the laparoscope. Using surgical instruments attached to the laparoscope, the oviducts can then be blocked. In a *minilaparotomy,* a somewhat larger incision is made immediately above the pubic hair line and no gas is used in the abdominal cavity. Instead, the uterine elevator brings each oviduct into view of the laparoscope, which has been inserted through the incision.

A much less common approach is a *culpotomy* in which an incision is made in the upper end of the vagina. While laparoscopy is the predominant method utilized today, *tubal ligation* was the dominant method prior to the advent of the laparoscope. This procedure involves a much larger incision in the abdominal area and a standard surgical approach to the oviducts (Figure 12-5). Tubal ligation was often performed immediately after childbirth.

Methods of blocking A number of procedures may be utilized for blocking the oviducts. They include, among others, cutting and tying the oviducts, the use of clips to seal the passage, and cauterization (an electrical burning procedure) in which the oviducts are cut and sealed in one procedure. Cauterization is being used more and more with the increasing popularity of sterilization operations, and some physician-surgeons argue that it is pref-

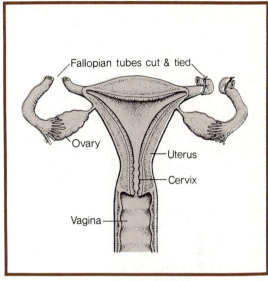

Figure 12-5 The basic procedure in a tubal sterilization. This illustration shows the cutting and tying of the fallopian tubes (oviducts).

erable to laparoscopy using bands or clips. The cauterization procedure is seen as being safe and effective, presenting little postoperative pain, and maintaining the possibility of reversal (which we shall discuss) (Seiler et al., 1981).

Although tubal sterilization may be performed in a doctor's office, it normally requires a short hospital stay. In 1981 the average stay was three days (Center for Disease Control, 1981). This is a considerable improvement over the average of one week in 1970, and the shorter period is due to the laparoscope (Layde et al., 1981).

Reversal When tubal ligation was the dominant procedure, tubal sterilization was considered irreversible because of the damage done to the oviducts in the cutting and tying. With the increased use of the laparoscope, a large percentage of tubal sterilizations are now successfully reversible (successful again meaning conception). A recent survey of different reversal procedures reveals that the pregnancy rate after reversal has ranged between 60 and 80 percent since 1976 (Henderson, 1981). There is still considerable debate, how-

---

[4]Female sterilization can also be accomplished by removal of the ovaries or the uterus. These major surgical procedures result in sterilization but are not performed for that purpose. There is also a surgical sterilization procedure called a fimbriectomy, which involves the removal of fimbrae and the closing of the end of the oviducts. Rarely performed, this remains a controversial method (Kroener, 1969).

ever, about what type of sterilization procedure and reversal technique results in the highest rate of reversal. Wulf (1981) contends that reversal is most likely to be effective when the original surgery was performed on the straight, narrow section of the oviduct near the uterus and least likely to be effective when it was performed on that part of the oviduct where fertilization normally takes place. Others argue that with microsurgical techniques, the location of the original oviduct blocking makes no difference in success (Grunert et al., 1981). There is also debate over the value of using microscopes in the reversal procedure. While some (e.g., Grunert et al., 1981) argue that microsurgery is what makes for high reversal rates, others contend that microsurgery is not a factor (Henderson, 1981) and that the important factors are where the oviduct was originally cut, how it was blocked, and the length of the oviduct after sterilization surgery (Henderson, 1981). Clearly, as reversal operations become more common, precise clinical studies will establish the factors associated with high reversal rates.

While we lack good data on the characteristics of men who want their vasectomy reversed, some research has been done on the characteristics of women requesting reversal of tubal sterilization. A consistent pattern emerges which reflects the high divorce rates today: The vast majority of women seeking reversal do so because they have divorced and remarried, and they want children in their present marriage (Grunert et al., 1981; Thompson and Templetin, 1978). Other major, but much less frequent, reasons include the death of a child and the desire for more children by the same partner (Grunert et al., 1981).

THE DEVELOPMENT OF BIRTH CONTROL IN THE UNITED STATES

While contraception is openly discussed and readily available in most of American society today, this has only recently been the case. The current status of contraception is the result of a long-term birth control movement.

While today is not the final chapter in this story, we cannot understand the current status of contraception in the United States without having some overview of how we got to where we are today.

The Beginning of the Movement

Compared with most of Europe and Scandinavia, the United States was in the dark ages of birth control until at least the 1940s. In 1831, Robert Dale Owen wrote the first American discussion of birth control, entitled *Moral Physiology, or A Brief and Plain Treatise on the Population Question.* This work marked the beginning of a national debate on contraception (Reid, 1978).[5] Contraceptive methods at this time were not sophisticated. Owen recommended withdrawal as the best method, and writers who followed him suggested douche and rhythm.

America, however, was becoming an industrial society and people were beginning to take a more manipulative view of their world. Americans were growing concerned with convenience and material well-being, and these were things that were seen as obtainable if you pulled yourself up by your bootstraps and took control of what happened to you. During this period, discussions of family limitation became popular with many Americans since the major drain on economic well-being was a large family.

In 1837 Charles Goodyear—whose father had earlier invented the spring-steel hay-and-manure fork—vulcanized rubber. In 1846 Alexander Parkes, a British chemist, obtained a British patent to improve vulcanization by a method called the "cold cure." This cold cure of rubber made it possible to produce delicate rubber items. In 1848 Goodyear obtained U.S. Patent 5536 to manufacture "hollow rubber articles" in the United States. This development

---

[5]The major part of this discussion is greatly indebted to Reid's work (1978). For a complete and detailed history of the birth control movement in the United States, this work should be consulted, as well as Himes (1936). For more modern times, the work of Djerassi (1979) is very important.

opened the way for the manufacture of condoms (and rubber gloves) on a mass scale (Bullough, 1980).

All through the 1800s, however, knowledge about, and devices for, contraception were not widespread in America. While condoms, diaphragms, and pessaries were in use, they were limited.[6] For example, it was not until 1876, at the World Exposition in Philadelphia, that condoms were officially introduced to this country—an event for which, by the way, there was no centennial commemoration in 1976 (Bullough, 1980).

Suppression

Moralistic suppression of the growing birth control movement gained solid footing in the 1870s. Following the Civil War, a strong "purity movement" appeared in the United States. This movement was directed toward the abolition of slavery and also of all vices, among which was contraception.

Under pressure from the lifetime president of the New York Society for the Suppression of Vice, Anthony Comstock, Congress passed the so-called Comstock Act in 1873. This legislation prohibited the mailing of obscene material and specifically mentioned contraception as a target.

Anthony Comstock started his career fighting "demon alcohol," but later devoted his life to stopping the flow of all sexual knowledge, information, and discussion—including contraception. After the passage of the Comstock Act, he personally conducted a reign of moral terror in the United States for some forty years. He was appointed a special agent for the U.S. Post Office and given the right not only to open any mail for inspection, but also personally to decide what was obscene. Since he was not exactly a sexual liberal, his efforts

resulted in many arrests and convictions. Entrapment was one of his favorite methods, and he evidently took personal pleasure in the grief he created. Those who knew him said he prided himself on having been personally responsible for at least sixteen suicides (Reid, 1978). Needless to say, Comstock played a central role in suppressing the birth control movement in the United States for many years.

The Fight against Suppression

Many individuals who advocated the use of contraception prior to World War I were considered radicals in many ways other than their ideas about birth control. Emma Goldman, for example, was a vocal advocate of contraception. She was also considered radical in her views on male-and-female relationships, sexuality, and marriage. Being generally regarded as antimarriage and antichildren was not conducive to wide acceptance of her views on contraception.

Without a doubt, the single most important figure in the birth control movement in the United States was Margaret Sanger (Sept. 14, 1879–Sept. 6, 1966). From 1914 on, she led a successful battle against Comstockery, the connection between obscenity and contraception, the apathy of the medical profession on the issue of birth control, and the unavailability of contraceptive methods and information. She was not only the head of the birth control movement. She organized research on contraception, obtained manufactures of contraceptives, fought court battles, and played a key role in the planned parenthood movement, the development of the birth control pill, and the spread of contraceptives in Asia.

Sanger argued that men had to realize that women had a right to control their own bodies. She was horrified at the burden women were under with the continual risk of pregnancy and the methods of abortion they resorted to in order to avoid unwanted births. Sanger saw no reason why a woman should have to sacrifice sexual activity in order to avoid unwanted pregnancy. She was clearly a radical in her time, and in many segments of American soci-

[6]Pessaries are devices inserted in the vagina which often contained a supposed spermicide. They are the oldest known contraceptive method, records of which go back to ancient times. The earliest pessaries involved a spongelike material soaked in crocodile dung. The effectiveness of this method is debated, but it was apparently low and dependent on the crocodile's diet (Himes, 1936).

Margaret Sanger before a Senate sub-committee in 1932 testifying in support of a bill to permit the transportation and distribution of birth-control information and materials by properly licensed physicians.

ety today she would be viewed the same way. However, unlike many of her colleagues, she did not alienate her opponents and the general public. She was personally and politically effective in winning support for her ideas, and this was the key to much of the birth control movement's success.

In 1912 and 1913, Sanger became involved with textile workers' strikes for higher wages and better working conditions. She soon realized that more money was not the answer to these women's life problems since higher wages did nothing to deal with their continually pregnant status. In 1912 and 1913 she wrote several articles for a socialist newspaper on female sexuality, and on February 19, 1913, she had her first legal encounter with the Comstock Act. The United States Post Office decided that an article of hers on syphilis was obscene.

In March of 1914, Sanger published the first issue of *The Woman Rebel,* which the Post Office also declared in violation of the Com-

stock Act for its discussion of contraception. In this issue, she declared that the newsletter would advocate the prevention of conception. Issues which followed were also prohibited by the Post Office and the only issue that escaped censorship was that of June 1914, in which she coined the term "birth control" in place of contraception.

Faced with nine counts of mailing obscene material and a possible forty-five years in jail, Sanger left the United States for Europe in October 1914. Previously, she had also published a secret pamphlet called *Family Limitation,* which gave women specific contraceptive information. During her voyage to Europe, she continued to publish this booklet, which eventually was translated into thirteen languages and had a total circulation of over 10 million (Clinch, 1980).

In Europe, Sanger met a number of influential people, perhaps the most important of whom was Havelock Ellis. She greatly admired Ellis and he strongly influenced her in the tactics she used in her later work.[7] She also learned that the proper use of a diaphragm required careful measurement by a physician. Prior to gaining this information, she had advocated that women teach each other to use the device—a good indicator of the state of contraceptive knowledge in the United States at that time.

While she was in Europe, Comstock posed as a desperate husband seeking contraceptive advice and information. He convinced Sanger's husband William to provide him with a copy of *Family Limitation* and then promptly had him arrested. Comstock thought he could convince Sanger to trade his jail sentence for knowledge of Margaret's whereabouts. This was a serious miscalculation of both William Sanger and the public. The Sangers became martyrs and gained moral and financial support from many wealthy individuals (especially women). The trial of William Sanger was a circus, with some twenty people arrested for demonstrating and distributing contraception literature. During the trial, Comstock "caught a chill," and he died a short time later. William Sanger received a thirty-day jail sentence and the birth control movement made a giant step forward.

When Margaret Sanger returned to the United States in 1916, her case was well-known. The judge, the district attorney, and even President Woodrow Wilson received numerous letters in her support. The government decided not to prosecute.

On October 16, 1916, Margaret Sanger and her sister, Ethel Byrne, opened the first birth control clinic in the United States at 46 Ambroy Street in the poor and overcrowded section of Brooklyn, New York. At 7 in the morning of the opening day, a line of women stretched around the block. The clinic saw 140 women that first day and 488 women in the next ten days. Then the police arrested Sanger and Byrne for "maintaining a public nuisance" and closed the clinic. The two women each received thirty days in jail. Again, the attempt at legal suppression aided the cause. Sanger

spent most of her thirty-day sentence teaching the other women inmates about contraception and making numerous statements to the news-hungry press about prision conditions. Byrne went on a hunger strike and the newspaper accounts of her forced feeding through a tube inserted in her esophagus made the headlines (Clinch, 1980). The upshot of all this was that in her appeal to the New York State Supreme Court (where her conviction was upheld), the judge decided to allow physicians to prescribe contraceptives to married persons in New York for health reasons other than the prevention of venereal disease; this had been the only legal reason for either contraceptive advice or prescription before this time.

This decision marked the way for the slow erosion of laws and attitudes which prohibited contraceptives and their availability. In 1942 the Sanger-organized and founded Birth Control Federation of American changed its name to Planned Parenthood Federation. This organization continues Sanger's work even though she herself despised the name change.

The Medical Profession

In the 1920s and 1930s, contraception was under the strict control of the medical profession. Contraceptives could be bought only with a prescription, and then condoms were generally sold only for "prevention of disease" and douches for "feminine hygiene." The medical profession as a whole made no attempt to change these laws even though many doctors apparently prescribed contraceptives for birth control purposes.

Given this legal situation, very few legitimate businesses were willing to take the risk of selling contraceptives without prescriptions. Given the public demand for contraception, much contraceptive material was sold under the counter. Even though diaphragms were valued, they were difficult to obtain. Most were shipped from Europe and frequently confiscated by customs.

Not only did the medical profession stand by in apathy regarding the legal situation, but it steadfastly refused to deal with scientific re-

[7]For an excellent discussion of this relationship and this part of Ellis's life, see Grosskurth (1980).

search in contraception. An influential person here was George Kosmak (1873–1954), not only a strong opponent of birth control but also editor of the *American Journal of Obstetrics and Gynecology.* He consistently argued that women were shirking their natural duty to bear children if they practiced birth control. Contraception, he contended, was not needed, since abstaining from sex was a perfectly adequate method. Males, of course, had the widespread availability and popularity of prostitution, perhaps one of the reasons that condoms could be prescribed for the prevention of disease.

All during the 1920s, the American Medical Association (AMA) avoided the question of clinical studies of contraceptives. Such studies were essential for medical support of contraception. In 1925, R. L. Dickinson finally convinced his colleagues in AMA's Section on Obstetrics, Gynecology, and Abdominal Surgery to pass a resolution recommending the "alteration of laws wherever necessary, so that physicians may legally give contraceptive information to their patients in the regular course of their practice." The resolution, once passed, was ignored by the AMA until 1935. By this time, a very large business in "feminine hygiene" had grown up, complete with false advertising and useless products. Without medical standards and control, contraceptive quackery and bogus formulas had become big business. In 1937, the AMA finally recognized birth control as part of medical service.

After 1937, the medical profession's reluctance to become involved in contraception declined, but not very rapidly. For example, Ernst Grafenberg, a German gynecologist, began experimenting with intrauterine devices in 1909. In 1930 he reported on the IUD's high effectiveness. While a few physicians in the United States (including Margaret Sanger's personal physician) secretly fitted IUDs, the medical profession refused even to consider the device. In 1947, the *American Journal of Obstetrics and Gynecology*—the major source of contraceptive information for physicians at that time—refused to publish a paper on the IUD. Even though 1959 saw the public beginning of the modern contraceptive revolution with the

approval of the birth control pill by the Food and Drug Administration (FDA) for the treatment of menstrual disorders, this point was reached by prodding the medical profession into clinical testing. In June 1960, Enovid 10, the first United States birth control pill, was approved by the FDA and put on the market by G. D. Searle and Company. In the same year, the IUD was marketed in the form of the Lippes loop. From this point on, contraceptive patterns were to change in revolutionary fashion in the United States, but in spite of, rather than owing to, the medical profession.

It was not only the medical profession which inhibited the development of contraception and contraceptives in the United States. The legal system continued to play a significant role in suppression even after the 1937 move by the AMA. In the same year, *Consumer Reports* provided information on contraceptives to subscribers who signed a document stating that they were married and had been advised by a physician to use contraception. In 1941 the post office decided not to allow the publication to go through the mail to American families.[8] In 1977, two drug stores in Beverley, Massachusetts, were charged with publicly displaying condoms and selling them without a prescription; both acts are violations of the Massachusetts Crimes against Chastity Law.

PATTERNS OF CONTRACEPTIVE USE

With time, the patterns of contraceptive use in the United States have changed dramatically and are still changing. Overall, the general trend has been for more frequent, widespread, and effective contraceptive behavior.

Early Use of Contraceptives
The suppression efforts by moralists, the medical profession, and the federal and state governments led to not only the slow development

---

[8]This was done despite the fact that more than 2 million people observed a 1939 World's Fair display where R. L. Dickinson showed sculptures of fetal growth, conception, and birth.

TABLE 12-1
The proportion of contraceptive uses according to contraceptive method, 1934.

Contraceptive Method	Use of This Method as Percentage of All Uses
Withdrawal	30
Condom	25
Douche	21
Jelly or suppository	9
Lactation	5
Pessary	4
Sponge	2
Rhythm	2
Abstinence	1
Other	2

Source: Himes (1936:337, table 1), based on research by Kopp (1934).

of contraception in American society, but a profitable illegal industry as well. Contraceptives were in high demand in the 1930s. Since they were illegal, there was a large profit to be made. This profit was not, however, confined to under-the-counter sales. In 1936 (Himes 1936), 144 condoms cost $4.80 to manufacture, were sold to druggists or other retailers for $6, and sold to the public for $24, a 400 percent markup. Additionally, the testing of condoms was expensive and ill-perfected. Thus, there were numerous failures during use. In 1936 Himes examined the sale of condoms in the United States. In that year, there were approximately 1.8 million sold by druggists and another 2.6 million by "other outlets." In this same period, Americans annually spent over $200 million on "feminine hygiene" (contraceptive douches) (Reid, 1978).

If all these sales were taking place in light of the legal restrictions on contraceptives, Americans were either among the most diseased population in the world or they were actively attempting to practice contraception as best they knew how and were able. This was indeed the case. Various studies in the 1930s reveal that somewhere between 60 and 90 percent of the married women were practicing contraception of some form (Davis, 1929; Blair, 1933; Hamilton, 1929; Stone, 1933; Kopp, 1934; Pearl, 1934). The frequency with which

various contraceptives were used reflects the fact that the overall effectiveness of birth control was low (Table 12-1).[9]

These figures of use rates reflect women from higher social classes in American society and/or women who were attending birth control clinics. At this time, contraceptive use differed widely by social class, and thus these studies of middle-class women fail to reflect contraceptive behavior in all segments of society. In a much more representative sample of married women, Pearl (1934) found that only 42 percent had used contraception at some time. However, as shown in Table 12-2, fully 67 percent of the "very poor" and 61 percent of the "poor" married women *never used contraception of any kind,* compared with 22 percent of the well-to-do. Similar patterns by social class were found by Kinsey (Gebhard and Johnson, 1979).

1940 to the Present

From the 1930s to the present, the types of contraceptives used and the proportion of

[9]Dawson et al. (1980) have recently reported research findings which suggest that the overall contraceptive effectiveness for women at this time was relatively high. Unfortunately, this is a serious error based on the fact that Dawson et al. lumped women from before 1940 and after 1940 together. As we shall see, patterns of use changed greatly in the 1940s.

TABLE 12-2
Incidence of married women's contraceptive use by social class, 1934 (by percentage of group).

Incidence of Contraceptive Use	Income Category				
	Very Poor (%)	Poor (%)	Moderate Circumstances (%)	Well-to-Do Rich (%)	Total (%)
No contraception used	67	61	49	22	55
Regular and steady practice of contraception	12	17	20	22	18
Contraception practice intermittent; mainly for planned children	13	13	24	48	20
Contraception practice intermittent for reasons other than planning	8	9	6	9	8

Source: Pearl (1934), from Himes (1936:340, table 2).

women using them have changed considerably. In 1940, the douche was still among the most popular contraceptives, along with spermicidal jelly, the diaphragm, and the condom. By 1965, the pill had been on the market for five years and already was being used among 28 percent of the married women in the United States. From 1965 to 1974, diaphragm use continued to deline, as did use of the condom and rhythm. Over the ten-year period from 1965 to 1975, the modern contraceptive revolution was evident. By 1975, 34 percent of all married couples were using the pill and another 31 percent were sterilized (both male and female) (Westoff and Jones, 1977).[10]

Current Trends

Since at least 1940, the general trend has been toward more effective contraceptive use. This is most clearly evident in the widespread

[10]It should be noted that publicity about the pill's having certain health risks apparently resulted in considerable discontinuation of pill use during this period. Between 1970 and 1975, media coverage of these effects was directly related to discontinuation of pill and IUD use (Jones et al., 1980). Between 1974 and 1976, for example, there was a 66 percent increase in the proportion of women under 30 who thought that the pill was "not safe" (Blake, 1977).

use of the pill after 1965. More recently, this trend has continued with the rise in sterilization as a form of contraception. Between 1970 and the present, sterilization challenged the pill as the leading form of contraception. In 1970, there were 4.7 tubal sterilizations per 1,000 women age 15 to 44. In 1977, the figure was 14.7 per 1,000 women of this age group (Peterson et al., 1981). Today, tubal sterilization is the third most frequently performed female surgical procedure in the United States, following abortion and abortionlike diagnosis procedures. In 1970, one partner was sterilized in 16 percent of all marriages. By 1979, this had increased to 35 percent of all marriages (Westoff, 1976; Westoff and McCarthy, 1979). During the 1970s, sterilization operations also changed from frequently being done after the birth of a child to also being performed before having children (Peterson et al., 1981). Even though there were 702,000 tubal sterilizations performed in 1977, their popularity may have peaked in that year. In 1978, this number dropped to 653,000, showing a decline in the proportion of women of childbearing age having sterilizations (Peterson et al., 1981; Center For Disease Control, 1981).

Among white married couples, males and females are equally likely to be sterilized.

Among black married couples, however, nine out of ten sterilizations are female (Westoff, 1976). Over time, white couples have also changed their sterilization pattern. In 1971, 70 percent of all sterilizations in white marriages were male. Since then, male sterilizations have decreased and female sterilizations have increased.

Sterilization is most common when two partners decide they do not want another child. Sterilization is also more common among those couples who have had an unwanted pregnancy and those who have a relatively large number of children (Westoff and McCarthy, 1979). Most married couples who select sterilization do so when the wife is 25 to 34 years of age, and only 25 percent of the married-couple sterilizations are done when the wife is under age 25 (Westoff and McCarthy, 1979). Sterilization on the part of never-married women is rare, amounting to only 5 percent of all tubal sterilizations (*Family Planning Perspectives,* July–August 1979).

Even though the formal position of the Catholic Church forbids sterilization, the actual differences between Protestants and Catholics are small. Among married couples who do not intend to have any more children, 30 percent of the Catholics and 39 percent of the Protestants are sterilized (Westoff and McCarthy, 1979).

These patterns of sterilization in the United States reflect more favorable attitudes toward the procedure. A March 1979 Gallup poll reported that 64 percent of adult Americans approved of contraceptive sterilization. Those least likely to approve are persons over 50, nonwhites, and Catholics. The lowest level of approval (9 percent approving) is on the part of nonwhite males (*Family Planning Perspectives,* September–October 1979). In this same Gallup poll, 18 percent thought that sterilization would have no effect on their sex life. Another 61 percent said they would probably worry less about pregnancy, 37 percent said they would probably enjoy sex more if sterilized, and 25 percent said they would probably have intercourse more often if sterilized.

WORLD CONTRACEPTION PATTERNS

It took the human population of the world between 2 and 5 million years to reach one-half billion people (about 1650). By 1930, the world population had risen to 2 billion and by 1975 had doubled to 4 billion. In the year 2000, the world population is projected to be between 8 and 11 billion people (Figure 12-6).

A concerted effort has been made in recent years to provide worldwide contraceptive information, education, availability, and use. As shown in Figure 12-7, actual use varies greatly from one country to the next. While 70 percent of the married female population of childbearing age in the United States uses some form of contraception, only 2 percent of similar women in Ghana do so. In many countries, contraception is still illegal.

Even when there is no ban on contraceptives, the introduction of such devices, methods, and behavior patterns into a culture in which they are foreign is often difficult. For example, an attempt was made in one village to have women use the rhythm method by having them wear a bead necklace with two colors of beads. On each day they were to move a bead, and when they came to the red beads, they were to abstain from intercourse. Apart from forgetting to move the beads or moving more than one a day, researchers found many of the villagers had placed the necklace around the neck of their goat since they thought that it would make the animal pregnant. In another case, a team of researchers went into a village and carefully demonstrated how to use a condom by placing the device over the end of a bamboo pole, and left a supply of condoms with the villagers. When they returned some months later, many of the women were pregnant. Upon being asked what had happened, the villagers replied that the condoms did not work—pointing to bamboo poles with condoms on the ends. In most of these cases, the problem in use is that the agencies supplying the information and contraceptives are not familiar with the culture. Often, instructions for use are given in technical language ("Insert the suppository near the

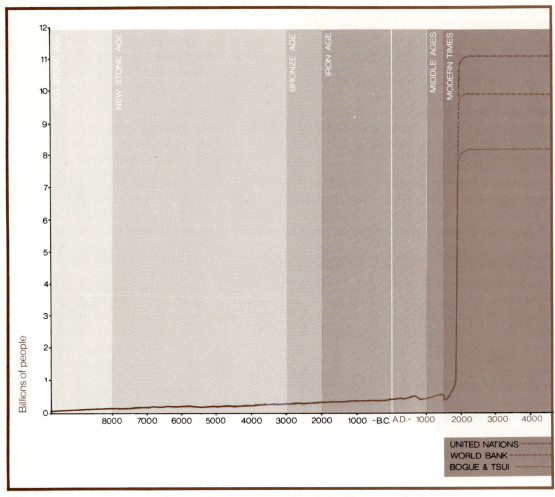

Figure 12-6 World population growth. It took between 2 and 5 million years for the population of the world to reach half a billion in about 1650. By 1930 the population reached 2 billion and had doubled to 4 billion by 1975. Future projections for population growth vary. The dotted lines show three different future population estimates: the United Nations estimate is 11 billion about the year 2125; the World Bank estimate is 10 billion about the year 2090; University of Chicago demographers Donald Bogue and Amy Ong Tsui estimate 8 billion about the year 2050. Although all three estimates project a stabilization of the world's population, there is some doubt about the actual number of people at the point of stabilization. (Source: *Intercom,* volume 7, numbers 11–12, 1979, page 4.)

posterior fornix of the vagina") or through illustrations that are unclear or incorrect. (One set of instructions for suppositories showed the vagina in the position of the anus.)

It is also common for people in less developed countries not to want to limit the number of children they have. Their values often re-gard children as a farm labor force, and to be without many children is to be without enough help.

There is also another aspect to worldwide contraceptive use patterns. This is the practice of "dumping" contraceptives (and many other items, such as drugs) which have been banned from use in the United States. In two particularly well publicized such occurrences, serious ethical questions were raised. The IUD Dalkon Shield went on the market in the United States in 1971. After only a few months, reports began to appear concerning dangerous side-effects from its use, such as infection of the uterus, blood poisoning, spontaneous abortions, ectopic (tubal) pregnancies, perforation of the uterus, and vaginal infection. By 1974, seventeen deaths were attributed to the product (Ehrenreich et al., 1979). After finally being taken off the market, the product was dumped into other countries having less stringent criteria for approval of such devices and was readily supplied to unsuspecting women. Depo Pro-

vera, a contraceptive drug administered by injection, has never been approved for use in the United States because it apparently causes cancer, menstrual disorders, breast nodules, sterility, and birth defects. This drug has been dumped and used in several other countries.

There are many ways in which the dumping takes place. The name of the product is changed, and its side-effects are not revealed or are even hidden. Formulas for a drug can be changed slightly to obtain approval in another country, or the product may be approved in a country with very lax regulations and then marketed in a country which will accept the first country's approval. The end result in any case is that a potentially, and often actually,

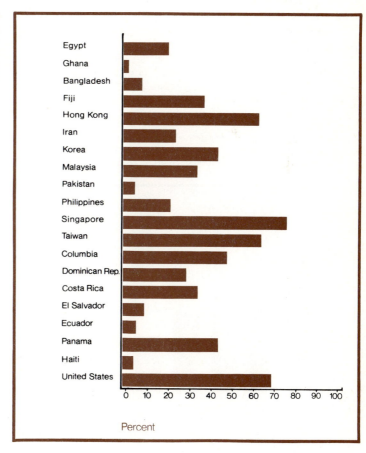

Figure 12-7 Percent of married women of reproductive age using any type of contraceptive in selected countries. (Source: *Population Reports,* series A, number 5, January 1979, "Oral Contraceptives," table 6.)

dangerous contraceptive is made available and used by unsuspecting women to the profit of corporations and private individuals (Dowie, 1979).

ADOLESCENT CONTRACEPTIVE BEHAVIOR

In our previous examination of adolescent sexual behavior (Chapter 7), it was made clear that intercourse on the part of adolescents is not rare. It is also true, however, that intercourse activity exceeds contraceptive use.

The Frequency of Use

The principal characteristic of adolescent contraceptive use is that it is either not used or used inconsistently. Among coitally active 15- to 19-year-old, never-married females in the United States, only 34 percent *always* use contraception when they have intercourse. Another 39 percent *sometimes* use contraception, and fully 27 percent *never* use it (Figure 12-8) (Zelnik and Kantner, 1980).

Figure 12-8 Percent of coitally active American adolescent females at various ages who never use contraception when they have intercourse. (Source: Zelnick and Kanter, 1977, table 9.)

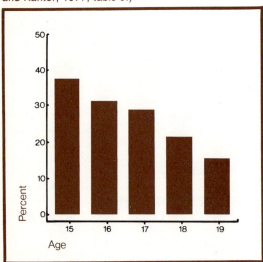

Among college students, the frequency of contraceptive use is also low. In a major study, only 50 percent of the male and 44 percent of the female college students reported always using contraception when they engaged in coitus (Delamater and McCourquodale, 1979). Among males, but not females, being a college student means that one is more likely to use contraception. While 50 percent of the college-student males always used contraception, it was used by only 28 percent of the nonstudent males of the same age living in the same city. Among females, there was no difference in contraceptive use between students and nonstudents.

Types of Contraception Used

Not only is contraception infrequently used by adolescents when they engage in intercourse, but the type of contraception used is often not very effective. As shown in Table 12-3, the pill is the most commonly used method, followed by the condom. However, the last time they had intercourse, fully 19 percent of the 15- to 19-year-old females in the United States used withdrawal and another 2 percent used douche. When we add these ineffective contraceptive methods to the percentage of 15- to 19-year-old females who used no contraception, approximately 50 percent were unprotected from pregnancy the last time they had intercourse.

Contraceptive methods are more effective, however, in the most recent intercourse than in the first intercourse. Zelnik and Kantner (1980) found that fully 36 percent of the 15- to 19-year-old females in the United States used withdrawal in their first intercourse experience and only 19 percent used the pill.

The adverse publicity on the pill and IUD in the 1970s has affected the popularity of these methods among married women and teenagers. From 1971 to 1979, pill and IUD use declined among unmarried 15- to 19-year-old females, and diaphragm and rhythm use increased (Zelnik and Kantner, 1980). There is some evidence that diaphragm use has risen considerably among female college students in

TABLE 12-3
Contraception method used in most recent intercourse by 15- to 19-year-old unmarried females in the United States, 1979. *

Type of Contraception	Females Using in Most Recent Intercourse (%)
Pill	40.9
Condom	23.3
Withdrawal	18.8
Rhythm	5.8
Foam	3.9
Diaphragm	3.5
Douche	2.1
IUD	2.0

*The figures are for females using contraception at their last intercourse.
Source: Zelnik and Kantner (1980:237, table 10).

particular. Harvey (1980) found that from 1974 to 1978, the proportion of women contraceptive users using the diaphragm went from 6 to 34 percent. Diaphragm use also appears to increase with age among female college students, while pill and IUD use declines with age.

While we might think that these changes reflect more responsible contraceptive behavior, this is not always the case. Among 15- to 19-year-old females, declining pill and IUD use has been accompanied by a greater use of withdrawal (Zelnik and Kanter, 1980).

Factors Related to Adolescent Contraceptive Use

Research consistently points to a single most important factor related to adolescent contraceptive use: whether one views oneself as a sexually active person (Bardwick, 1973; Cvetkovich et al., 1975; Goldsmith et al., 1972; Reiss et al., 1975).

Given the traditional prohibitions against intercourse on the part of unmarried teenagers, many sexually active teens do not have this self-view. It is entirely possible for one to engage in intercourse and not say, "I am a person who has intercourse." Many adolescent females struggle with putting together the view "I am a good person" with the view "Inter-

course is bad." Unless one develops this self-view as a sexually active person, contraceptive use is unlikely and effective contraceptive use is very unlikely. Most effective contraceptive methods involve going to someone and making the announcement, "I am a person who engages in intercourse." The person who has not come to grips with his or her coital behavior is very unlikely to do this. It is thus not surprising that among adolescents engaging in intercourse, high sex guilt is related to being more embarrassed about obtaining contraceptives, thinking that contraceptives are difficult to obtain, having a large number of rationalizations for not using contraception, and using less effective contraceptive methods (Upchurch, 1978; Herold, 1981).

What must be kept in mind here is that the intercourse behavior of adolescents is not necessarily the result of a rational, logical, long-deliberated discussion with their partner. As we have seen, all kinds of factors influence whether one engages in intercourse in adolescence, and these factors may have no bearing on contraceptive use in that intercourse. For example, 82 percent of all 15- to 19-year-old females who become pregnant do not want the pregnancy, but only 31 percent of them use any contraception to prevent it (Zelnik and Kantner, 1980).

Many adolescents operate on a daily basis

without a great deal of future orientation, especially when it comes to sex. This approach is not likely to facilitate one's planning or being prepared for intercourse at some future time (Cvetkovich et al., 1981). It is not uncommon to hear adolescents complain that contraception makes sex seemed planned and not spontaneous.

Many adolescents also live with what Cvetkovich calls "fables" in order to discount the fact that they might become pregnant. One of these is the *sterility fable* in which teens of high school age will tell you that they are too young to become pregnant or that they do not have intercourse at the right time of the month (although most do not actually know the safe period in the menstrual cycle) (Zelnik and Kanter, 1979).

The resistance to seeing oneself as a sexually active person who could thus be involved in a pregnancy is related to certain individual and personality characteristics. Adolescents who hold traditional values are less likely to be contraceptive users even if they are sexually active (Joe et al., 1979). High sex guilt should also be an important factor in contraceptive use, since using contraception forces one to admit that one is engaging in intercourse, something the high sex-guilt person is unwilling to do. This is the case. High sex guilt is related to the nonuse of contraception (Bardwick, 1973; Gerrard, 1974; Upchurch, 1978; Herold and Goodwin, 1981), use of less effective contraceptives when using them at all (Herold and Goodwin, 1981), greater embarrassment about obtaining contraception, and having rationalizations for not using contraception when having coitus (Herold and Goodwin, 1981).

Certain other factors are also related to using contraception. Being involved in a serious relationship in which there is communication about contraception (Fisher et al., 1979; Thompson and Spanier, 1978), having liberal gender-role attitudes (Fisher et al., 1979), having peer-group support for contraceptive use (Thompson and Spanier, 1978), and having the view that you are in control of what happens to you (Fox, 1977) are all related to more consis-

tent contraceptive use in intercourse by adolescents.

Available Contraception and Adolescent Intercourse

One of the popular arguments used by those who oppose the availability of contraception to teenagers is that greater availability causes increased sexual activity. There is no evidence to indicate that adolescents begin having intercourse because contraception is available. In fact, the evidence is that the majority of adolescents engage in intercourse *before* they begin to use contraception (Zelnik and Kantner, 1980). The research does indicate that adolescent females who obtain the pill are already engaging in intercourse when they do so, and that they tend to increase the frequency of their intercourse after beginning pill use (Reichelt, 1978; Garris et al., 1976; Zabin and Clark, 1981). This increase appears to be due to actual intercourse frequency being brought into greater agreement with ideal frequency (Garris et al., 1976). Contraceptive use is not associated with an increase in the number of intercourse partners (Reichelt, 1978), but rather, with being involved in a somewhat committed relationship with one person (Fisher et al., 1979).

The fact remains that contraception plays a very small role in adolescent intercourse decisions. If the availability of contraception were a necessity for teenagers to engage in intercourse, there would be far fewer unmarried teenage pregnancies each year.

ADOLESCENT PREGNANCY

Given the relatively low and ineffective use of contraception among sexually active adolescents, a quite common outcome is pregnancy.

How Many Teenage Women Become Pregnant?

As shown in Table 12-4, 1.5 percent of *all* 15-year-old females in the United States have had

TABLE 12-4
Teenage women who have had a premarital pregnancy, by age and ethnicity.

Age	All Females (%)	White Females (%)	Black Females (%)
12	0.0	0.0	0.0
13	0.0	0.0	0.0
14	0.1	0.0	0.6
15	1.5	0.8	5.7
16	4.2	2.8	13.2
17	8.5	6.2	23.1
18	11.9	8.3	33.7
19	20.6	17.1	42.8

Source: Zelnik et al. (1979: table 5).

an unmarried pregnancy. This proportion increases with age, with 21 percent of *all* 19-year-old females having been pregnant without being married.

Not all unmarried teenage women have engaged in intercourse. Therefore, these percentages do not reflect the true pregnancy risk among adolescent women. As Table 12-5 shows, 16 percent of coitally experienced 15-year-olds have been pregnant at least once, and this proportion increases to 35 percent of all coitally experienced 19-year-olds. As is also clear in Table 12-5, the chance of pregnancy is much greater for black than for white adolescent females.

Given the fact that 49 percent of the 15- to 19-year-old females in the United States did not use any contraception the first time they

had intercourse, and of those who did, 47 percent used an ineffective method, it is not surprising that the risk of becoming pregnant within a short time after one's first intercourse is high. Among adolescents, 7 percent of the white and 13 percent of the black females in the United States become pregnant within one month of their first intercourse experience, and 38 percent of the white and 43 percent of the black 18- and 19-year-old females in the United States get pregnant within two years of their first coital experience (Zelnick and Kantner, 1979).

How Adolescent Pregnancies Are Resolved
What do unmarried teenage women do when

TABLE 12-5
Sexually active teenage women in the United States who have had a premarital pregnancy, by age and ethnicity.

Age	All Females (%)	White Females (%)	Black Females (%)
15	16.0	11.2	25.2
16	21.6	16.9	33.9
17	25.8	21.3	39.9
18	31.0	27.1	45.3
19	34.7	30.7	52.8

Source: Zelnik et al. (1979: table 6).

TABLE 12-6
Outcomes of pregnancies to 15- to 19-year-old unmarried females in the United States, 1979.

Outcome of Pregnancy	All Females (%)	White Females (%)	Black Females (%)
Live birth	49	39	71
Abortion	37	45	20
Miscarriage and stillbirth	14	16	9

Source: Zelnik and Kantner (1980:234).

they become pregnant? One of the ways to examine this question is to see how first pregnancies are resolved, since they constitute the majority of all teenage pregnancies (see Table 12-5).

One of the ways to resolve the pregnancy is to get married either shortly before or shortly after the outcome of pregnancy. This, however, is not a common choice. While 15.5 percent of the pregnant 15- to 19-year-old females marry before the outcome of the pregnancy and 14 percent marry after the outcome, 70 percent do not marry before or after. Nonmarriage is more common for blacks (88 percent) than for whites (63 percent). However, fewer

and fewer white adolescent females are selecting marriage as an option each year (Zelnik and Kantner, 1980).

Of teenage women who do not marry either before or after the outcome of the pregnancy, there are a number of different pregnancy results. As shown in Table 12-6, the most common outcome of the unmarried teenage pregnancies is live birth (49 percent); the second is abortion (37 percent). Here again, there are differences between black and white adolescents, with black females much more likely to have a live birth and white females much more likely to have an abortion. During the 1970s, live birth became a less common

Given the great number of teenagers who engage in sexual intercourse, which cannot be governed by federal legislation, the price which has to be paid for not making contraceptives legally available to teenagers is very high.

choice and abortion a more common one. In 1971, of all unmarried pregnant adolescent females, 23 percent had an abortion and 67 percent had a live birth. In 1979, abortion was the choice of 37 percent and live birth was the choice of 49 percent. Fewer than 1 percent of all live births to these women result in the child's being placed for adoption.

Intended Teenage Pregnancy

Not all teenage pregnancies are accidents. In 1979, approximately 18 percent of all first teenage pregnancies were intended (Zelnik and Kantner, 1980).

The reasons why unmarried teenage women intend to become pregnant have not been well researched. Some factors appear to be an attempt to escape from an undesirable home environment, a wish to become independent, and the traditional view that it would just be "nice" to have a baby, and that this would make one feel more like a woman.

Whether a teenage pregnancy is intended or not makes a difference in the outcome of the pregnancy. Intended pregnancies are much more likely to result in a live birth and much less likely to result in an abortion (Zelnik and Kantner, 1979). Miscarriage is also more common in the case of an unintended pregnancy, suggesting that attempting to miscarry is a somewhat common result of an accidental teenage conception.

Effects of Unmarried Teenage Births

There are two major consequences of unmarried teenage births: biological advantages and social disadvantages (Morris, 1981). In terms of biological advantages, teenage mothers and their children fare better biologically and physically than do non-teenage mothers and their children (Rothenberg and Varga, 1981). It is a myth that teenage mothers and their children risk all kinds of physiological hazards—a myth probably built around the social disapproval of teenage motherhood. In the social arena there are, however, a number of negative outcomes related to teenage parenthood.

In an unmarried teenage birth, adoption is

rare. The dominant pattern is that the child resides with the mother. This means that each year a large number of single-parent families are created by teenage births.

Teenage parenthood, whether marriage takes place as a means of avoiding an illegitimate birth or not, is related to less lifetime formal education, lower income, increased poverty and dependence, and higher levels of childbearing for the mother (Trussell, 1976). In general, a severely diminished quality of life is a consequence of teenage childbearing, and it is independent of the personal characteristics of the teenage parents themselves.

When teenagers do marry either before or immediately after the birth of the child, there are other negative outcomes. The marriage is less stable, owing to a sharp disruption of the usual adolescent and young adult courtship process and the limited life chances and economic resources of the couple (Furstenberg, 1976). Even among white middle-class married couples whose marriage is stable, a premarital pregnancy is associated with a lower economic status in terms of financial assets and a larger number of children (Freedman and Thornton, 1979).

Clearly, the improved use of effective contraception by unmarried teenagers has many positive effects for both the individual and society.

ABORTION

The medical definition of abortion is: "The termination of a pregnancy after the implantation of the blastocyst in the endometrium but before the fetus has attained viability" [the ability to survive outside the uterus] (Tietze, 1979:1). While this definition may be rather boring, the topic is one of the most hotly debated social issues in the United States today. The complexity of the abortion issue is in large part due to the fact that abortion is a moral and ideological issue and is connected to both political battles and personal concerns other than the termination of a pregnancy. This complexity is not new. The questions we are dealing with today on the abortion issue have appeared many times before in the stormy history of abortion in this country, and they will (barring some innovation such as fetal transplants from one woman to another) remain with us for some time.

Abortion around the World

In order to place the abortion issue in some perspective, it is useful to compare the legal status and incidence of abortion in the United States with the rest of the world.

The legal status of abortion varies greatly from one country to the next. Basically, there are five conditions under which it is legally allowed throughout the world.

Abortion is prohibited with no exceptions. Nine percent of the world's population lives in countries which do not allow abortion for any reason (many South American and Moslem countries, Taiwan, and Zaire).

Abortion is permitted only to save the life of the mother. Eleven percent of the world's population resides in countries where abortion is allowed for this reason only. Examples are Algeria, Iraq, and Guatemala.

Abortion is permitted if the woman's health is in danger. Fourteen percent of the world's population resides in such countries. Some countries allow abortion only for danger to the mother's physical health (e.g., Cuba, East Germany, New Zealand), while others include both physical and mental health (e.g., Japan, Peru, Switzerland).

Abortion is permitted if certain social factors exist. These factors include poverty, poor housing, and nonmarried status. Twenty-five percent of the world's population lives in such countries (e.g., Romania, Zambia, Uruguay).

Abortion is granted upon request without any necessary reason. Worldwide, this is the single most common stance on abortion, involving 39 percent of the world's population in such countries as Norway, Sweden, Israel, and the United States (Tietze, 1979).

As a consequence of these different legal conditions, abortion rates vary greatly from country to country (Figure 12-9).

Abortion in the United States: The Past

In 1800 there were no laws in the United States regarding abortion. The legality of what is today called abortion was defined by English common law. That law did not recognize the existence of a fetus until "quickening" took place. After quickening, English common law stipulated that expulsion of a fetus was a crime because the fetus had taken on a separate existence.

Quickening refers to the perceptible movement of the fetus, usually in about the fourth or fifth month of pregnancy. The importance of the concept of quickening—which had existed for centuries—is that there were no medical tests for pregnancy. The mere absence of menstrual flow could be, and was, considered due to some "obstruction." It was perfectly legal and appropriate to perform procedures to "remove an obstruction." These procedures were, of course, means of abortion but they were not called that by name.

Thus, in 1800, women were free to terminate a pregnancy (remove an obstruction to menses) up until the time of quickening. After this point, doing something to abort the fetus constituted the crime of homicide (Mohr, 1977).

Early Popularity of Abortion

In the early 1800s, abortion was practiced as a home remedy. With very few physicians and a largely rural population, most American homes had a do-it-yourself medical book containing supposed cures for a wide range of common ailments. Among those usually listed in such books was "Obstructed Menses." Suggested remedies for obstructed menses included bloodletting, bathing, quinine drinks, black hellebore (a plant which causes violent diarrhea), vomiting, lifting heavy weights, reaching too high, jumping from high places, and strong blows to the stomach (Mohr, 1977). "Taking a cold" was a popular euphemism for missing a menstrual period and one medical procedure suggested to cure this condition was the pulling of a tooth. John Burns, a Scottish medical

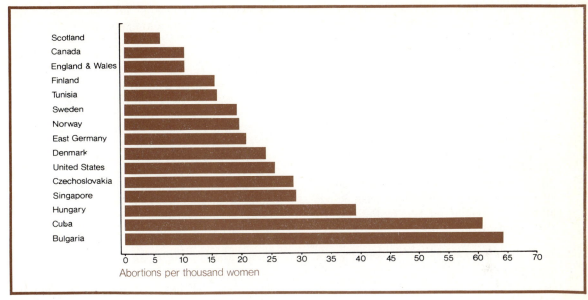

Figure 12-9 Abortion rate in selected countries of the world. (Source: Data from Tietze, 1979, table 2.)

professor, noted that pulling a tooth when the woman was pregnant often brought about a sudden expulsion of the fetus. The abortion was due, of course, to pain and shock from having a tooth extracted without anesthesia (Mohr, 1977).

The First Laws

The first abortion laws in the United States went into effect between 1821 and 1841. These laws, however, were mainly attempts to deal with common medical practices of the time and were not specifically aimed at regulating abortion itself.

In May of 1821, Connecticut passed the first law—a statute making it illegal to administer, but not to take, an abortifacient (anything which induces abortion). In 1834, Ohio made it illegal to attempt abortion either before or after quickening. The fact that these laws were more concerned with regulating medical practice than limiting abortion is reflected in the fact that this 1834 Ohio law also stated that a

doctor could not prescribe medication while drunk (Mohr, 1977). Several states followed the lead of Connecticut and Ohio, and by 1840, twenty-six states had some type of abortion law. Abortion, however, was not a political issue and there was no public outcry for or against it at that time.

The Medical Profession

In the mid-1800s, abortion was not only publicly known but was a big business, given the nature of contraceptive technology and use. A major part of the abortion business was the sale of abortifacients. In one week in 1845, the following remedies were advertised in the *Boston Daily Times* (Mohr, 1977):

Madame Restell's Female Pills
Madam Drunnette's Lunar Pills
Dr. Peters' French Renovating Pills
Dr. Monroe's French Periodical Pills

The profit from abortifacient pills was large.

They sold wholesale for $7.50 for 600 and retailed to the customer for 50 cents each.

Many establishments run by nonmedical personnel performed abortions. In major cities such establishments were well-known and apparently profitable. The magnitude of this aspect of the abortion business is perhaps best revealed by the fact that in 1871, one popular abortionist spent $60,000 on advertising alone (Mohr, 1977).

In the latter part of the 1800s, the abortion business also included selling tools for at-home abortions. One of the less offensive of such devices was a syringe for injecting substances into the uterus, sold by Parke-Davis and Company (Mohr, 1977).

From 1859 to 1900, the American Medical Association became firmly committed to outlawing abortion. Even though some physicians had serious moral reservations about abortion, the major reason for this massive effort by the AMA was professionalism (Mohr, 1977). The AMA wanted to establish itself as a professional organization which would form a closed guild regulating who could and who could not practice medicine. In order to do this, there had to be laws to enforce a set of professional standards and qualifications for carrying out medical procedures. Outlawing abortion was an important step in outlawing individuals who engaged in medical practice without medical training. It was also true that many leaders in the AMA thought that it was a woman's duty to bear children (Mohr, 1977).

This effort by the AMA to have antiabortion laws established was strongly aided by the "purity" movement of the late 1800s. The Comstock Act of 1873 was of no small value, and the press cooperated by frequently publishing horror tales of abortions. After 1873 (the passage of the Comstock Act) the public visibility of abortion rapidly declined. Between 1860 and 1880 at least forty antiabortion laws of various kinds were placed on the books of states and territories. Thirteen jurisdictions which had no abortion laws made some up and twenty-one jurisdictions made existing laws more strict (Mohr, 1977). The outcome of these laws was that a woman could obtain a legal abortion only if her life was in danger, with a few states allowing abortion if there was a serious threat to her health (Mohr, 1977).

The Twentieth Century

These abortion laws of the late 1800s defined the legal and social status of abortion in the United States until the 1970s, when contemporary changes began. These changes were preceded, however, by a series of influential events.

In 1955 a Planned Parenthood conference on abortion was held. Although this conference brought about no legal changes, it did stimulate discussion about the abortion issue.

In 1962 the American Law Institute drew up the Model Penal Code. Part of the code recommended more liberal abortion laws. It was specifically recommended that abortion be allowed if the physical or mental health of the mother was in danger, if the child would be born with grave physical or mental defect, or if the pregnancy was the result of rape or incest (Tietze, 1979).

In 1962, another important social event took place. Sherri Finkbine attempted to obtain an abortion when it was discovered that she had taken the fertility drug Thalidomide, a drug implicated in serious birth defects. Ms. Finkbine was scheduled for the abortion in a local hospital when the news was leaked to the media (by a friend). The media promptly covered the story and the physician and the hospital swiftly decided against the abortion. Sherri Finkbine found herself unable to obtain an abortion in the United States (abortions, even though against the law, were always available to those who could pay for them). She and her husband flew to Sweden where she obtained the abortion of a severely deformed fetus. The Finkbine case was national news and it raised a public furor over the question of abortion and a woman's right to have control over her pregnancy and body. America was becoming aware of a budding twentieth-century abortion controversy.

In 1967, abortion reform began with Colorado enacting new abortion laws based on the

Model Penal Code. In 1970, Hawaii, Alaska, and New York (and Washington State by popular vote) enacted laws which did not specify the conditions under which an abortion could be obtained, thus making it available upon request.

The 1973 Supreme Court Decision

In 1973, the United States Supreme Court gave its ruling on the case of *Roe v. Wade.* Roe was a Texas resident who was denied an abortion under the 1850 Texas abortion law and Wade was the Texas attorney general. In this ruling, the Court not only struck down the 1850 Texas abortion law, but all other such laws in the United States which had been established in the 1800s.

In this decision, the Court spelled out three central concerns in the issue of abortion:

1. The constitutional right of all citizens to privacy
2. The right of the state to protect maternal health
3. The right of the state to protect developing life

In an attempt to reconcile these three issues, the Court basically (although not explicitly) divided human gestation into three equal periods or trimesters. Each of these trimesters was governed by a different legal concern with regard to the issue of abortion.

First Trimester. The Court ruled that in the first three months of pregnancy, the woman's right to privacy prevailed. It was her right, ruled the Court, to decide her future privately without interference from the state. This gave a woman the right to obtain an abortion and struck down all existing laws against abortion in the first three months of pregnancy.

Second Trimester. In the second three months of pregnancy, the Court ruled, the right of the state to protect maternal health prevailed. The Court thus ruled that a state could insist that certain standards of medical procedure were practiced in abortions during this period of pregnancy. This gave states considerable latitude to regulate the conditions under which an abortion could be obtained in the second trimester.

Third Trimester. The Court finally ruled that in the third three months of pregnancy, the state's right to protect developing life prevailed. It was thus ruled that a state could prohibit abortion during this period except when necessary to protect the life of the mother.

This 1973 Supreme Court ruling governs the issue and status of abortion today. No state may outlaw abortion in the first three months of pregnancy. In the second three months, a state can basically set the conditions under which an abortion can be obtained. In the final three months, a state may totally prohibit abortion unless there is danger to the mother's life.

Of course the outcome of this decision has been great state-to-state variation in the conditions under which second-trimester abortions can be obtained and a great deal of legal jockeying by many states in an attempt to find a loophole in the decision on first-trimester abortions.

Recent Legal Debates

Since the 1973 decision, there have been many attempts to find a way around the Supreme Court decision, and the Court itself has passed down several other decisions regarding abortion.

Among the more important battles has been the right of women under the age of 18 to obtain abortions. In 1976, the Court ruled that a woman does not have to obtain permission from her husband or parents to obtain an abortion. In 1979, the Court further ruled that a "mature" woman under age 18 does not need her parents' consent for an abortion. In 1981, the Court ruled that only under certain conditions can a state require a physician to notify a minor woman's parents before she has an abortion. The parental consent for minors is, as of this writing, still being fought in the courts. As of 1982, 38 percent of all hospitals and 19 percent of all abortion clinics required either parental consent or notification for minors under 18 years of age (Henshaw et al., 1982).

There have also been many attempts to curtail abortions, including the 1981 Utah law requiring physicians to show abortion-seeking patients a booklet containing color photographs of a fetus at least 24 hours before they perform an abortion.

Up until the present, the most noted issue in abortion is the controversial Hyde Amendment. This legislation, partially enacted in 1976, basically says that states are not required to pay for abortions under the Medicaid program if the abortion is not ruled as medically necessary and that public hospitals do not have to provide abortion services.

The Outcome of the Hyde Amendment

When the Hyde Amendment was passed, and still today with states following the lead and stopping state funding of abortion, pro-life and pro-choice advocates predicted that certain things would happen. Pro-life advocates hoped that the discontinuation of government funding for abortions would stop low-income women from having abortions. Pro-choice advocates argued that low-income women would still have abortions, but that they would resort to illegal, and thus less safe, abortions.

Both sides were wrong. Of all the women who were possibly affected by the Hyde Amendment, 85 percent lived in states which continued abortion funding, and only 15 percent lived in states which stopped abortion funding. Of those women residing in the latter states, 76 percent of those seeking an abortion had them paid for by personal, private or other public sources. Another 20 percent of these women carried their pregnancy to full term and 4 percent obtained an illegal abortion (Cates, 1981). These patterns appear to differ by state. In some states, it is estimated that as many as 35 percent of the women who could not obtain state funds for an abortion carried the pregnancy to term. In any event, the incidence of illegal abortion has been less than

expected and the curtailment of government funds has not universally stopped abortion on the part of low-income women (Cates, 1981). This is a pattern which is likely to prevail throughout the more conservative 1980s, in which more and more states will debate the funding of abortion under political pressure from both sides of the abortion controversy.

Children of Unwanted Births

A recent study in Czechoslovakia raises some serious questions about the life chances of children born to women who wanted, but were denied, an abortion. This study matched 110 children born to women who were denied an abortion with 100 children born to women who did not request an abortion. These 220 children were then tracked in adolescence and a number of measurements were taken periodically.

While it may be problematic to generalize the findings from a Czechoslovakian study to children in the United States, the results of this research deserve some thought. It was found that the children born to mothers who were denied abortion had less satisfactory school, social, and family lives than the control children. This was observed especially for males and only children. Not only did the children of mothers denied abortion have lower school grades, worse integration with their peers, and a higher incidence of serious behavior disorders requiring therapy, but a higher incidence of illness as well (Matejcek et al., 1978; 1979; 1980. See David and Matejcek, 1981, for a review and summary).

The researchers suggest that the children born to mothers who were denied abortion fared less well in life because they were subtly unwanted children. They were thus subjected to a family environment that was less accepting and generally inferior. Such an interpretation is supported by the descriptions these children gave of their parents and home environment.

It may well be the case that the abortion issue involves more than pro-life versus pro-choice.

The Abortion Activists

Today abortion is a hotly contested political issue focused by two dominant political-action organizations: the National Abortion Rights Action League (NARAL) and the National Right To Life Committee (NRLC). As we might expect, the composition of the membership of these two organizations differs dramatically in ways which reflect the NARAL's being pro-choice (supporting abortion availability for those who choose it) and the NRLC's being pro-life (not supporting the availability of abortion but arguing for protecting the fetus as developing life).

NRLC members, compared with NARAL members, are:

- More likely to have been reared in large families, prefer large families, and have large families
- More likely to be Roman Catholic (70 percent of NRLC members, compared with 4 percent of NARAL members) and less likely to be Jewish
- More likely to report that religion plays an important part in their life
- More likely to have had a problem becoming pregnant
- More likely to have had a miscarriage
- More likely to have had an unplanned pregnancy
- Less likely to use the pill or sterilization
- More likely to oppose sex education in the schools
- More likely to oppose birth control information for teenagers
- More likely to feel that premarital, extramarital, and homosexual relations are wrong
- More likely to take a conservative stance on the rights of women
- More likely to oppose the Equal Rights Amendment
- More likely to be Republican (Granberg, 1981a)

The abortion controversy has been, and continues to be, part of the American political scene.

In the 1980s, political block voting on the issue of abortion has come to the front. While it is realized that the abortion issue played a significant part in many 1980 elections, it is clear that the NRLC holds the upper hand here because its members are more likely than NARAL members to be single-issue voters. That is, they are more likely to vote against a political candidate because of his or her stance on abortion regardless of where the candidate stands on other issues (Granberg, 1981a).

It is also important to note that neither NARAL nor NRLC members are unyielding in their respective abortion stances. Of the NRLC members in Granberg's research (1981a), 70 percent said they favored abortion if the woman's life was in danger and 40 percent of the NARAL members said they opposed abortion for the reason that the child was not expected to be of the desired sex.

Attitudes of the General Public

Traditionally, attitudes toward abortion on the part of the general public have differed depending on the reason for the abortion. This is still the case today. As shown in Table 12-7, the majority of Americans approve of legal abortion for what are called the "hard" reasons (danger to the woman's health, rape, defect in the child). A much larger proportion disapproves of abortion, however, for the "soft" reasons (poverty, being unmarried, not wanting any more children).

Pro-Life versus Pro-Choice—or Something Else?

It is argued by pro-life advocates that their position on abortion reflects a general set of values regarding the value of all human life. Pro-choice advocates contend that their stance on abortion reflects a general set of values supporting civil rights. Are these contentions really the case?

Granberg (1981b) compared pro-life and pro-choice individuals in a national sample. He found that pro-life advocates were not pro-life in terms of their stance on gun control, capital punishment, military spending, or spending on health care. Pro-choice advocates appeared to be much more consistent, being generally in favor of civil rights across a wide range of issues.

Correlates of Abortion Attitudes

If the issue, at least for pro-life advocates, does not appear to be pro-life on issues other

Table 12-7
Attitudes of adult Americans toward abortion.

Do you think a pregnant woman should be able to obtain a legal abortion if:	Yes (%)	No (%)	Don't Know (%)
The woman's health is seriously endangered by the pregnancy?	88	10	2
She has become pregnant as a result of rape?	80	16	4
There is a strong chance of serious defect in the baby?	80	16	3
The family has a very low income and cannot afford any more children?	50	46	4
She is not married and does not want to marry the man?	46	49	4
She is married and does not want any more children?	45	51	4

Source: Davis (1980). Data are from a national probability sample of persons 18 years old and over in the United States in the spring of 1980.

than abortion, what are the correlates of attitude toward abortion?

While many of you are not going to like this, the research findings present a relatively clear and consistent picture of the correlates of a pro-life abortion position. This attitude is usually associated with a punitive attitude in general and toward sexuality in particular. Prescott and Wallace (1978) found that those individuals strongly opposed to abortion were characterized by a set of values which favored repression and punishment of sexuality. This attitude is perhaps the reason that individuals who are overall opposed to abortion tend to see it as an appropriate reward for an unintended pregnancy taking place in an approved relationship with the use of contraception, and the denial of abortion as punishment for pregnancy in a disapproved relationship with ineffective contraception (Allgeier et al., 1979). This punitiveness is also the reason that high sex guilt is related to disapproval of abortion (Allgeier et al., 1981).

It must be kept in mind that these attitudes and their correlates are not restricted only to the general public. Prescott and Wallace (1978) found that those legislators who voted for antiabortion laws also tended to vote for sexual repression in the form of other laws against premarital sex, homosexuality, and extramarital sex.

The Incidence of Abortion in the United States

The number of legal abortions performed annually in the United States has increased from 23,000 in 1969 to 1.5 million in 1980. This increase means that the number of abortions relative to the number of live births has risen also. In 1973, there were 239 abortions for every 1,000 live births. In 1978, there were 406 abortions for every 1,000 live births (Forrest et al., 1979).

It must be noted, however, that while the raw number of abortions has increased each year, the rate of increase has actually been declining. For example, from 1973 to 1974 there was a 21 percent increase in the number

of abortions in this country. From 1979 to 1980, the number increased only 9 percent (Forrest et al., 1979; Henshaw et al., 1981; 1982).

The popularity of abortion has resulted in a significant minority of women terminating pregnancy through abortion. In 1980, the pregnancy of 25 percent of all pregnant women was terminated by abortion (Henshaw et al., 1982). Obviously, a significant proportion of women in the United States thus have experience with abortion. In 1980 in the United States, 3 percent of all women between the ages of 15 and 44 had an abortion; from 1967 through 1978, more than 14 million women obtained an abortion. Thus, roughly one out of eight women in this age group has had an abortion (Forrest et al., 1979; Henshaw et al., 1982).

Abortion Needs and Services

Even given what many people consider to be very high rates of abortion, there are many women each year who want an abortion but cannot obtain one because the services are not available (Figure 12-10). In 1979, for example, 29 percent of the women seeking abortions were unable to obtain them (Henshaw et al., 1981).

Opponents of abortion have long realized that one of the ways to limit the procedure despite Supreme Court decisions to the contrary was to limit abortion services. This was the rationale behind the Hyde Amendment. States thus differ dramatically in the extent to which abortion services are available; this fact makes the availability the single best predictor of state abortion rates (Borders and Cutright, 1979).

Given the differential availability of abortion from state to state, many women travel out of their home state for an abortion. In 1979, for example, 69 percent of the women residing in West Virginia who had an abortion went to another state for the service. Only 1 percent of the women who lived in California and had an abortion had it done in another state (Forrest et al., 1979).

Very clear health risks are associated with travel to obtain an abortion. Those women who travel tend to have the abortion later in the pregnancy, and the later the abortion is performed, the greater the risk. Also, distance makes diagnosis and treatment of complications from abortion more difficult and thus riskier (Forrest et al., 1979).

Even when abortion services are available, some women delay the procedure until late in the pregnancy. When access to abortion is limited by a lack of abortion services, the delay in having it is related to social and demographic characteristics of the women (young, black, and lower socioeconomic status women tend to delay). When abortion services are available, the delaying of abortion is related to the individual characteristics of low education and having irregular menstrual cycles (Burr and Schulz, 1980).

Who Obtains Abortions?

As has been found in every year from 1973 to 1978, the women who obtain abortions are predominantly white, young, childless, and unmarried. As shown in Figure 12-11, the abortion rate is highest for 18- and 19 and 20- to 24-year-old women. In 1977, 68 percent of all abortions were performed on white females

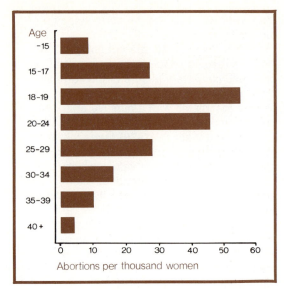

Figure 12-11 Abortion rates in the United States for various age groups. (Source: Forrest et al., 1979, table 5.)

Figure 12-10 Percent of abortion needs met in the United States from 1973 to 1978. (Source: Forrest et al., 1979, table 1.)

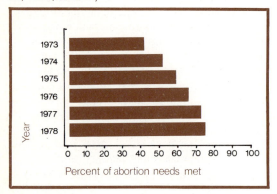

and 77 percent of all abortions were performed on unmarried women (Forrest et al., 1979).

Abortion and Contraception

As Westoff et al. (1981) point out, it is difficult for many people to understand why the abortion rate in the United States is as high as it is, given the widespread use of effective contraception. However, if you think back about (1) the women who have most of the abortions and (2) the nature of the contraceptive behavior of unmarried people, this is not so hard to understand.

In a study in Illinois, Westoff et al. (1981) found that half the abortion patients used no contraceptive method at the time they became pregnant. He and his associates estimate that approximately 70 percent of all abortions could be averted if all women at risk of an unintended pregnancy used the pill or IUD. These contraceptives, however, are not particularly desirable since they are associated with known health risks. If more women move away from using the pill and IUD because of the noted health risks, abortion patients will continue to increase in numbers. Even when low health-risk contraceptives are used, pregnancy can occur. Westoff et al. (1981) found that almost 50 percent of the women over 20 who had an abortion were using contraception when they became pregnant.

It must be kept in mind that 55 percent of all pregnancies in the United States are unintended and that almost half of these pregnancies are terminated by abortion (Henshaw et al., 1982). Thus, total contraceptive effectiveness and use would drastically lower the number of abortions performed each year.

While it is popular in some circles to argue that many women use abortion rather than contraception, this is simply not so. Conscientious contraceptive users are more likely to have an abortion for an unwanted pregnancy than nonconscientious users (Westoff et al., 1981; Rosen et al., 1979). After an abortion, the use of contraception also increases from what it was before abortion (Evans et al., 1976).

It is clear that abortion does not reflect contraceptive irresponsibility. Rather, it largely reflects a contraceptive bind in which American society has placed women. The most effective contraceptive methods today are either permanent (sterilization is hardly viable for a 19-year-old single person) or known to have serious health risks. Safe methods tend to be less than reliable. In a very real sense, the answer that many people seek is to be found in the development and availability of safe, effective contraception (note that pro-life advocates of the NRLC are also strongly against contraceptive availability to those women who are most likely to have an abortion).

Repeat Abortions

Another common view is that many women have abortions repeatedly as a means of avoiding unwanted births. While this is not quite the case, repeat abortions are more frequent than we might think. In 1979, for example, 73 percent of all women who had an abortion had their first, 20 percent had their

second, 4 percent had their third, and 2 percent had their fourth (Forrest et al., 1979).

The Psychological Outcomes of Abortion

There are two different sets of psychological outcomes from having an abortion: *subjective feelings* and *objective changes* in psychological status. These two sets of psychological outcomes are not necessarily related to each other (Robbins, 1979).

Research reveals that at least some women feel regret following an abortion (Lask, 1975). Evans et al. (1976) found that among a sample of adolescent women who had had an abortion, 20 percent said, six months after the procedure, that they wished they had not had it. The women who regret having an abortion tend to be younger and ambivalent about the abortion in the first place (Evans et al., 1976). In their review of research on the psychological effects of abortion, Doane and Quigley (1981) point out that guilt, grief, and crying account for over 50 percent of the negative postabortion feelings and that these reactions most often last a short time. Some studies have even found that these negative subjective feelings are more common for live births than with abortions (Doane and Quigley, 1981).

With regard to objectively measured psychological status following an abortion, the long-term outcomes are most often positive, if any change takes place at all (Payne et al., 1976). An important consideration here is our prior discussion of the long-term effects of illegitimate births. It may well be the case that if research were to compare the psychological effects of an abortion with the psychological effects of illegitimate birth and its socioeconomic consequences, the former would be more positive.

Illegal Abortion

There are no solid data on the exact number of illegal abortions that have been, or are being, performed in the United States. Estimates for the 1950s range from 200,000 to 1.2 million a year, but there is no really sound basis for any of these figures (Tietze, 1979). During the 1960s it was popular to quote the figure of 1 million illegal abortions annually. Glick and Norton (1977) estimated that in 1970 there were 530,000 illegal abortions in the United States; with the Supreme Court decisions, the number had declined to 10,000 by 1975. Regardless of the varying numbers, it is clear that the incidence of illegal abortions has declined considerably since at least 1973.

While it is commonly thought that all illegal abortions are butcher jobs done by some hack in a back alley, this was not always the case. During the 1950s and 1960s, many abortions were performed in first-class hospitals by first-class physicians giving first-class medical care. However, it is also true that on the average, illegal abortions are much more likely to be performed in a less-than-safe setting by a less-than-competent individual. For example, in the southwestern part of the United States, medical and death records show that 50 percent of all known illegal abortions in the nation occur along the Mexican border (Moore, 1980).

As we noted earlier, many people argued that one effect of the Hyde Amendment's cutting off federal abortion funds for low-income women would be a significant increase in illegal abortion. This has not been the case. Cates (1981) found that only 1 percent of the 395,000 women who were eligible for Medicaid and who needed an abortion in 1978 had an illegal abortion. This 1 percent was, however, 2,000 women.

Abortion Procedures

There are three main methods of performing abortions: vaginal evacuation, stimulation of uterine contractions, and major surgery.

Vaginal evacuation methods The traditionally standard abortion procedure is dilation and curettage (referred to as D&C). This method is more accurately described as *surgical curettage* (Tietze, 1979). *Dilation* refers to the stretching of the cervical canal by inserting a series of metal dilators, each one slightly larger than the one before. When the cervical canal is open wide enough to allow passage of the appropriate instruments into the uterine cavity, the contents of the uterus are removed with forceps and all remaining tissue is scraped from the uterus with a metal instrument called a curette. In early pregnancy, the use of forceps may not be necessary. Of all abortions performed in the United States, 9.4 percent are done by surgical curettage. (Tietze, 1979).

In recent years, surgical curettage (or D&C) has been replaced with a second type of vaginal evacuation procedure called *suction curettage* or *uterine aspiration.* This method was developed in China in 1958 and introduced into the United States in 1966 (Tietze, 1979). With this method, the uterine canal is first dilated as just described and a tube is inserted into the uterine cavity. The tissue within the uterus is removed through a vacuum method rather than with a curette. A recent modification of this procedure involves a flexible tube with an opening on each side. This allows the tube to be placed against the uterine wall without risking perforation. The average time required to perform suction curettage is less than five minutes. Today, 84 percent of all abortions in the United States are done by suction curettage (Tietze, 1979).

A variation of suction curettage is "menstrual regulation." This is simply a modern form of dealing with "obstructed menses." Suction curettage is performed in the first two weeks after a missed period, a time when pregnancy cannot be accurately determined. The procedure usually requires neither anesthesia nor dilation. Being very popular in less developed countries, the procedure is controversial since it is assumed to be frequently performed when no pregnancy exists (Tietze, 1979).

The dilation process used in abortion may also be accomplished with the use of a marine plant called laminaria. When the stems of this plant are dried, they expand greatly in moisture. Having this characteristic, they may be used to dilate the cervix. Laminaria is often used in the second three months of pregnancy. The dilation process is much slower and thus reduces the possibility of injury from too rapid cervical dilation by mechanical means (Tietze, 1979).

Stimulation of uterine contractions

In the second three months of pregnancy, abortion may be induced by the stimulation of contractions of the uterus. In the United States, the most common method of inducing abortion in this manner is by replacing a small amount of the ambiotic fluid with a saline (salt) solution. The uterus is tapped through the wall of the abdomen by means of a needle. Through this needle, approximately 200 milliliters of ambiotic fluid is extracted and replaced with saline. The fetal heartbeat usually stops within one-and-a-half hours and labor begins within twenty-four hours, with the expulsion of the fetus and placenta a few hours later. Other substances may also be used to stimulate uterine contractions, the most recent being prostaglandins. Currently, in the United States 6 percent of all abortions are by means of stimulation of uterine contractions (Tietze, 1979).

A newly developed method of inducing abortion by means of stimulating uterine contractions is perhaps somewhat less violent. A vaginal suppository containing prostaglandins is inserted in the vagina and then, twenty-four hours later, an intramuscular injection of prostaglandin is given if necessary. Two-thirds of the patients abort with only the suppository in an average of fifteen hours after insertion (Lauersen et al., 1981).

Major surgical procedures

There are two major surgical methods which are used in the termination of a pregnancy: hysterotomy and hysterectomy. *Hysterotomy* is a cesarean section performed before the fetus is viable (able to survive on its own). An incision is made through the wall of the uterus and the fetal material removed. This procedure is used only rarely and in cases where the woman's health would be in danger if other methods were used. The same surgical procedure is also used to deliver a viable fetus in cases where passage of the birth through the birth canal is not feasible. *Hysterectomy* as an abortion procedure involves the removal of the

uterus and cervix, but not the ovaries. This method of abortion is also used only rarely. Both these surgical methods combined account for only 0.2 percent of all abortions in the United States (Tietze, 1979).

Complications in Abortion

The amount of risk involved in abortion depends on a number of factors, the most important of which are the medical conditions in which the procedure is performed.

Serious complications

Serious medical complications during the abortion procedure itself are rare if the procedure is done in a qualified medical setting. Such complications include perforation of the uterus by one of the curettage or suction instruments, injury to the intestines or other organs by perforation of the uterus, major hemorrhage, laceration of the cervix, disturbances of blood coagulation ability due to saline injection, and the effects of anesthesia. The most frequent complications following abortion involve fragments of the placenta being left in the uterus, which results in bleeding, infection, and blood clots (Tietze, 1979). As shown in Figure 12-12, both minor and major complications are much more likely the later in pregnancy the abortion is performed.

Mortality in abortion

The later in pregnancy an abortion takes place, the greater the risk of death, particularly after fifteen weeks (Figure 12-13). In the United States, from 1972 through 1975 the major causes of death due to legal abortions were infection (27 percent of all abortion-related deaths), severe blood clotting (26 percent), anesthesia complications (15 percent), and hemmorrhage (10 percent).

The risk of death also varies by the type of abortion procedure. In this country, the death rate for suction curettage is 1.4 deaths per 100,000 abortions. For surgical curettage (D&C), the rate is 6.6 per 100,000 abortions. Saline abortions have a death rate of 14 per 100,000 and hysterectomies a rate of 42 per 100,000.

Overall, the risk of death from abortion is

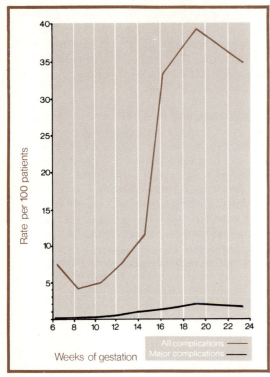

Figure 12-12 Number of women per 100 abortions who have minor and major complications from the abortion by weeks of gestation (pregnancy) before the abortion is performed. (Source: Tietze, 1979:83, figure 8.)

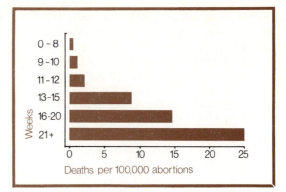

Figure 12-13 Number of patient deaths per 100,000 abortions in the United States from 1972 to 1976 by the week of gestation (pregnancy) in which the abortion was performed. (Source: Tietze, 1979:83, figure 9.)

Abortion has not always been a relatively safe procedure. While it is difficult to obtain good data on abortion-related deaths from the past, limited data indicate it was very high. From 1943 to 1947, the death rate from abortion in New York City was 400 deaths for every 100,000 abortions, and in the United States as a whole between 1963 and 1968, the rate was 72 per 100,000 abortions (Tietze, 1979).

Abortion and Future Pregnancy Outcomes

In our discussion of contraception, it was perhaps clear that research on the possible negative effects of various methods comes long after the widespread use of the method. This has especially been so for the pill, the IUD, and spermicides. This is also true for abortion. As we have seen, abortion is a common procedure. However, research on its effects on future pregnancy outcomes is relatively rare by comparison. Today, there are still many more questions than there are answers.

Prior abortions and fetal and neonatal death A number of studies have found that fetal death (death of the fetus before birth) and neonatal death (death of the newborn) are more likely for women who have had a prior abortion than for those who have not (Harlap and Davies, 1975; Richardson and Dixon, 1976; Madore et al., 1981). Another re-

very small. In 1978, there were 1.5 million abortions performed in the United States, with 9 abortion-related deaths. This rate is even smaller today. A good part of this decline in the risk of abortion death has been due to the greater availability of abortion services. Their availability means earlier abortions and, from 1973 to the present, the average abortion has taken place earlier in the pregnancy than in the past (Forrest et al., 1979).

Today, the risk of death from an abortion is much less than the risk of death due to pregnancy and childbearing. For example, for 25- to 29-year-old females, the death rate due to pregnancy and childbearing is 12.5 per 100,000; for women 30 to 34 years of age, it is 24.9 per 100,000 (Moore, 1980).

cent study found that miscarriage was not related to having had only one prior abortion, but women who had had two prior abortions had 2.2 times the risk of miscarriage and women with three or more prior abortions had 8.1 times the risk of miscarriage of those women with no or one prior abortion (Levin et al., 1980). However, Madore et al. (1981) examined the effect of several different variables on fetal and neonatal deaths and found that prior induced abortion had a significant, but small effect.

Other pregnancy outcomes The findings are less clear for the effects of abortion on other adverse pregnancy outcomes. Some studies have found no relationship between prior induced abortion and spontaneous abortion (Harlap and Davies, 1975; Roth and Aoyama, 1974; Madore et al., 1981). A recent study suggests, however, that other negative pregnancy outcomes are more likely for women who have had a prior abortion (New York State, 1980). In this research, a large sample of women who had had prior abortions were compared with a control group of women who had never had an abortion. It was found that the women with a prior abortion were more likely to have adverse pregnancy outcomes in the form of low birth weight, premature birth, labor complications, and miscarriage.

While the present research does not exactly pinpoint the effects of abortion on all characteristics of future pregnancy, it is reasonably clear that prior abortion is associated with greater future pregnancy risks.

STUDY GUIDE

TERMS TO KNOW ·

Hysterotomy

Hysterectomy

Laminaria

Obstructed menses

Surgical curettage

Suction curettage

Pro-life and pro-choice

Hyde Amendment

1973 Supreme Court decision

Condom

Avoid failure

Margaret Sanger

IUD

Mini pill

Postcoital pill

Gossypol

Vasectomy

Anthony Comstock

Charles Goodyear

Laparoscope

Spermicides

Coitus interruptus

Lippes loop

Subdermal implants

Thyma's Double Check

Basal body temperature

Natural methods

Combination pill

Cervical cap

Diaphragm

Douche

Delay failure

SELF-TEST TRUE-FALSE

Part I: True-False Statements

1. If the male withdraws his penis from the vagina when he feels that he is about to ejaculate, withdrawal can be an effective contraceptive method.
2. With the condom, the penis should not remain in the vagina after ejaculation.
3. The condom was invented by Dr. Condom in 1660.
4. One of the major disadvantages of spermicides is that they are implicated in serious birth defects when a pregnancy occurs.
5. It is not possible for douching to be an effective contraceptive method.
6. The diaphragm can be an effective contraceptive method when used alone.
7. The risk of death has been shown to be greater among pill users than among women not using the pill.
8. While the calendar method of natural birth control is not very effective, the Thyma's Double Check method is equal in effectiveness to the IUD.
9. Women who have used an IUD have a greater chance of an ectopic pregnancy than women who have never used this device.
10. One of the disadvantages of vasectomy is that it noticeably lowers the volume of ejaculation.
11. In a laparoscopy, the oviducts (fallopian tubes) are not blocked as in a tubal ligation.
12. Even with recent advances in surgical techniques, both male and female sterilization methods remain irreversible 90 percent of the time.
13. In the development of widespread use of contraception in the United States, the medical profession fought against the attempts at suppression.
14. In the 1930s the use of contraception differed greatly by social class.
15. The most common contraceptive method employed by 15- to 19-year-old never-married females is the condom.
16. Black adolescent females are no more likely than white adolescent females to have an unmarried pregnancy.
17. Prior to 1821 in the United States, there were no laws dealing with abortion.
18. The 1973 Supreme Court decision on abortion ruled on the legality of abortion by stating three constitutional issues of relevance: privacy, states' rights to protect maternal health, and states' rights to protect developing life.
19. The major result of the Hyde Amendment was that most low-income women who would have had a government-funded abortion carried their pregnancy to term.
20. The chance of serious complications in an abortion increases the later the abortion is performed in the pregnancy.

Part II: Multiple-Choice Questions
Select the best of the three alternatives.

1. That contraceptive method which has been implicated in serious birth defects is (a) the pill; (b) the IUD; (c) spermicides.
2. Which of the following major health effects is associated with pill use? (a) heart and circulatory disease; (b) breast cancer; (c) birth defects.
3. A vasectomy involves (a) implanting a hormonal contraceptive just under the surface of the skin; (b) blocking the vas deferentia; (c) stopping the testes from producing sperm cells.

4. In the 1970s, the most popular and most frequently used form of contraception was the *(a)* condom; *(b)* IUD; *(c)* pill.

5. Which of the following is the most accurate statement concerning American contraceptive use in the 1930s? *(a)* A majority of married American women practiced contraception of some kind, but the type of contraception used was frequently not very effective. *(b)* A majority of American women used some form of contraception but that use differed by social class. *(c)* A majority of American women used some form of contraception that was frequently ineffective, and use was highest in the highest social classes.

6. "Dumping" contraceptives refers to the practice of *(a)* selling faulty and dangerous contraceptives in other countries; *(b)* selling contraceptives under the counter in the United States in the 1930s because they were largely illegal; *(c)* the U.S. Post Office's way of dealing with contraception in accordance with the 1873 Comstock Act.

7. The factor most strongly related to adolescents' using contraception when they have intercourse is *(a)* the frequency of intercourse; *(b)* their self-perception as a sexually active person; *(c)* the availability of contraception of some form.

8. Approximately what percent of all 19-year-old never-married women in the United States have been pregnant? *(a)* 10 percent; *(b)* 20 percent; *(c)* 40 percent.

9. Among all 15- to 19-year-old females in the United States who have an unmarried pregnancy and do not get married, the most common outcome of the pregnancy is *(a)* live birth; *(b)* abortion; *(c)* miscarriage or stillbirth.

10. Prior to 1800 in America, *(a)* there were no laws dealing with abortion itself; *(b)* abortion was illegal after the second month of pregnancy; *(c)* most jurisdictions had laws regulating abortion, the regulation depending on the trimester in which the abortion took place.

11. Evidence from the Czechoslovakia study indicates that children born to women who wanted the pregnancy terminated by abortion *(a)* fare as well as children of wanted births; *(b)* fare significantly less well than children of wanted births; *(c)* were more likely to be male than children of wanted births.

12. In examining whether pro-choice advocates uphold a set of beliefs favoring civil rights in areas other than abortion and whether pro-life advocates uphold a set of beliefs upholding the value of all human life, research reveals that *(a)* pro-choice advocates tend to be generally in favor of civil rights and pro-life advocates tend to value all human life; *(b)* pro-life advocates tend to value all human life, but pro-choice advocates do not favor civil rights except in the area of abortion; *(c)* pro-choice advocates favor civil rights in general, but pro-life advocates appear to be pro-life only on the issue of abortion.

13. The women in the United States who obtain abortions are typically *(a)* white, young, married, childless; *(b)* black, young, childless, unmarried; *(c)* white, unmarried, young, childless.

14. The death rate for mothers due to abortion is *(a)* lower than that for pregnancy and childbirth; *(b)* higher than that for pregnancy and childbirth; *(c)* the same as that for pregnancy and childbirth.

TOPICS FOR DISCUSSION

1. If you were responsible for the availability of contraceptives to teenagers in the United States, what would you do? How available would you make them? Why? What effect would this probably have? How would you make—or not make— contraception available? Why would your methods be effective or ineffective in limiting or increasing the availability of contraception?

2. Should abortion be legal in the United States? Under what conditions, if any, do you think it should be available? To whom should it be available? Should abortions be funded by state or federal government funds? Why should abortion under different conditions be, or not be, available?

SUGGESTED READINGS

By the time you read this text, there will probably have been much legal and social debate on the issue of abortion. The best single source of materials on this topic is the journal *Family Planning Perspectives.* Any college library should have it.

There are two exceptional books on the politics and history of contraception in the United States. Both are strongly recommended.

Mohr, James C., *Abortion in America: The Origins and Evolution of National Policy, 1800–1900.* New York: Oxford University Press, 1978.

Djerassi, Carl, *The Politics of Contraception.* New York: W. W. Norton, 1979.

For an exceptional book on the history of abortion in America, see

Reid, J., *From Private Vice to Public Virtue: The Birth Control Movement in American Society Since 1830.* New York: Basic Books, Inc., 1978.

KEY TO SELF-TEST

Part I: True-False Statements

1. F (Ejaculate may actually exit the penis before one has this feeling.)
2. T (Some or all of the erection of the penis declines immediately after ejaculation, making the condom less tight and making it possible for ejaculate to escape into the vagina.)
3. F (Who did invent it?)
4. T (For several extra points, name the possible ways in which spermicides may relate to birth defects.)
5. F (Perhaps anything is possible, but it is extremely improbable. Why?)
6. F (It must be used with a spermicide.)
7. T (What difference does smoking make? What kinds of diseases are more likely among pill users?)
8. F (None of the natural birth control methods can be considered highly effective.)
9. F (This was thought to be the case, but recent research reveals otherwise.)
10. F (Why is this false?)
11. F (Laparoscopy is merely a surgical means of access.)
12. F (What are the current reversal rates for males and for females?)
13. F (What was the medical profession's role?)
14. T (Which social-class group had the most and which the least use?)
15. F (Which one is it?)
16. F
17. T (Except those which applied to homicide after quickening took place. Can you explain why the concept of quickening was important?)

18. T (Can you describe how these three were reflected in the Supreme Court's decision about abortion?)

19. F (What did most do?)

20. T

Part II: Multiple-Choice Questions

1. *c*

2. *a*

3. *b* (What happens to the sperm cells that are produced?)

4. *c* (What method was a close rival in the 1970s?)

5. *c*

6. *a*

7. *b*

8. *b* (Actually, it is 21 percent.)

9. a

10. *a* (Abortion was not even recognized. Recall the terms "quickening" and "obstructed menses.")

11. *b*

12. *c*

13. *c*

14. *a*

Chapter 13
Sexual Coercion

Human sexuality takes on a wide range of uses, motivations, and outcomes. Sex can range from delightful joy and intimacy shared with another person to force, manipulation, rage, brutality, and fear.

There is nothing that is fun or funny about the aspects of human sexuality that we will discuss in this chapter, but they exist. Many people would prefer not to know about this dark side of human sexuality, but knowledge is the first step in change.

There are many different forms of sexual coercion which involve a wide range of specific sexual and coercive behaviors. The central feature of all forms of sexual coercion is, however, that sexual activity of some form is sought from a person when that person is an unwilling participant.

RAPE

The word "rape" immediately calls forth a mental image and perhaps some gut-level feelings, but a precise definition of the term is difficult. The legal definition of rape across the various states has some common elements, but in exact terms there is great variation in what legally constitutes rape. These legal definitions have also changed over time. In the last few years, many states have established degrees of rape so as to facilitate prosecution in sexual assault cases.

In general, the legal definition of rape involves sexual intercourse (vaginal, anal, or oral) through one person's use of force without the consent of the other person. This definition tends to focus on *penetration* of some orifice by a penis or some other object. Penetration, however, is not the central element in rape. Behaviorally, we are talking about forced sexual activity. It is difficult to see why forcing a woman to masturbate a man is any different from forcing her to fellate or have intercourse with him.

Attempted Rape

There is also often a distinction made in legal circles between attempted rape and completed rape. In our discussion of rape, we are referring to both attempted and completed rape, since the only thing which behaviorally distinguishes the two is the "success" of the assailant. Rape for our purposes refers to any form of forced physical sexual activity. In most cases we will be talking about forced vaginal-penile intercourse. When other behaviors are involved in rape, they will be noted.

Statutory Rape

Statutory rape is generally defined as intercourse with an "underage" *female* whatever the age of the male and regardless of whether the woman consents to the intercourse. The age at which one is "underage" varies from 13 to 21 in different states (Sherwin, 1977). While there is a wide range of opinion regarding statutory rape laws, it is clear that they can be misused and dangerous to males. For example, if a male and a female of the same age decide that they would like to have intercourse with each other and she is under the legal age of consent, he can be charged with statutory rape without the female's ever filing a complaint. In March 1981, the United States Supreme Court handed down a final ruling in a statutory rape case in California. A teenage male was charged with statutory rape for having intercourse by mutual consent with a teenage female friend. He argued that the law is discriminatory since only males can be charged with statutory rape. The Supreme Court ruled that there is nothing unconstitutional about the law and that the reason for its existence is, in part, that it acts as a deterrent against premarital pregnancy.

How Many Rapes Take Place?

This is an important question in understanding not only the extent, but also the social bases, of rape in American society. Unfortunately, we do not have a precise answer. There is simply no way to know the exact number of rapes that take place each year in this country. Although a variety of methods are now used to estimate the annual number of rapes, all these methods have severe shortcomings which result in a massive underestimation of the extent of rape.

Police statistics   Police statistics, which are passed on to the Federal Bureau of Investigation to be included in the FBI statistics, are known to drastically underestimate the occurrence of rape. It is commonly assumed that the FBI knows of only about 50 percent of all rapes (Amir, 1971; McDermott, 1979). As we shall see, however, the proportion of rapes known to the FBI is much lower than 50 percent. One reason is that some rapes are reported to the police and not classified by them as a rape. A more important reason is that many rapes are never reported to the police (Box 13-1).

Victimization surveys   Each year since 1972 the Law Enforcement Assistance Administration (LEAA) has conducted national victimization surveys. These involve national samples in which individuals are asked if they have been a victim of a crime in the last year. If they say yes to any of the crimes listed, they are asked questions about the nature of the incident.

While victimization surveys are more accurate than police statistics in estimating the number of rapes, they still have problems which make them less than accurate. First, respondents are not asked directly if they have been the victim of a rape, but if they have been the victim of an assault. If the respondent says yes to the assault question, he or she is questioned to determine whether the incident can be classified as a rape. Second, many rape victims will not tell the interviewer that they have been raped. These reporting factors lead to approximately one-third of all rapes not being classified as such in victimization surveys (McDermott, 1979). Third, many women are victims of what is actually a rape but they either do not see it as such or are confused enough about the incident that they do not define it as a rape. These are the so-called date rapes (an unfortunate term, for reasons we shall discuss), but they are real rapes.

Other data estimates   The LEAA 1978 victimization survey estimated a total of 171,000 rapes in the United States each year. If we add to this the number of rapes which the survey did not tap because of the assault question and because respondents did not want to tell the interviewer they had been raped, this number increases to 227,400 rapes per year. But this number is not even close.

BOX 13-1

REASONS WHY RAPES ARE NOT REPORTED TO THE POLICE

Reason for Not Reporting	Persons Giving This Reason	
	In Attempted Rape (%)	In Completed Rape (%)
Nothing could be done	49	23
Not important enough	15	4
Police would not want to be bothered	7	14
Didn't want to take time; inconvenient	4	1
It was a private or personal matter	19	53
Didn't want to get involved	6	14
Fear of offender retaliation	10	19
Reported it to someone else	12	7
Other reasons	14	11

Source: McDermott (1979, table 35).

A number of studies have asked female college students if they have been a victim of physically forced sexual intercourse against their consent. If we compute the percentage of women who generally say yes to determine how many women this is, we have another 880,750 rapes per year. We now have a total of 1,108,180 rapes annually. Even this figure is too low. If we assume that date rape is as common among older high school females and college-age females who are not college students as it is among female college students (evidence suggests it is probably higher), we arrive at a figure of about *3.5 million rapes a year in the United States.* Compare this with the 500,000-a-year figure that many experts think is too alarmist, and you can see that we have not even begun to realize how common rape is in American society.

Stranger-Stranger Rape

The common stereotype of rape is that of a female raped by a male who is a total stranger. This is the classic rape described in the media, and while it gains the morbid attention of re-

porters and is perhaps the most feared form of sexual coercion, it is not the most common form of rape.

There exists a vast unknown about the rapes in which the victim and the assailant know each other. There have been numerous estimates of what proportion of all rapes involve nonstrangers. Social scientists have consistently argued that about half of all rapes are of this pattern (Amir, 1971). On the other hand, recent victimization surveys (cf., McDermott, 1979) suggest that approximately 74 percent of all rapes are stranger-to-stranger. In actuality, both figures are incorrect. We have already seen that probably about 880,000 female college students experience forced intercourse each year. A vast proportion of these experiences involve a victim and an offender who know each other. Taking these rapes into account, it is conservative to estimate that about 4 to 5 times as many rapes involve a known assailant as involve a stranger. These are rapes, however, that receive almost no attention and about which we know almost nothing.

What we do know something about are stranger-to-stranger rapes. While the characteristics of these rapes obviously do not provide much of an overall profile of rape in American society, it is important to review the characteristics of rape as we know it—stranger-to-stranger rape (S-S).

Geography　Rape rates (the number of rapes per 100,000 inhabitants) are higher in large cities than in small towns and rural areas. Regionally, rape is most common in the Western states and least common in the Northeast. Within large cities, rape is more common in areas having low average incomes, low average education, high rates of unemployment, a high proportion of young people, and a high proportion of blacks (Rabkin, 1979).

Time　Rape varies by the season of the year, time of day, and day of the week. Rapes are most frequent in the summer, tending to

peak in August (Rabkin, 1979). They are more common on weekends and between midnight and 6 A.M. (McDermott, 1979).

Age　Females of any age are potential rape victims. Actual known rape victims range from under 4 to over 80 years of age. The rape rate is the highest, however, for females age 16 to 19 and 20 to 24 (Figure 13-1).

Social class and ethnicity　Black women are almost twice as likely as white women to be victims of a stranger rape (McDermott, 1979). Moreover, among both black and white women, the S-S rape rate for those with little education and income is more than twice that of middle and high socioeconomic females (McDermott, 1979).

Number of victims and assailants　While the most common S-S rape situation involves one assailant and one victim, it is not always the case. In approximately 23 percent of all S-S rapes, there is more than one assailant. Multiple-assailant rapes are more likely to involve both younger victims and assailants. Multiple-victim rapes also take place, although they are relatively rare. Approximately 91 percent of all S-S rapes involve only one victim, 7 percent two victims, and 2 percent three or more victims (McDermott, 1979).

Location　As shown in Table 13-1, the most common location for S-S rapes involves public places—streets, parks, playgrounds, etc. In and around the victim's home is the second most usual location, a fact reflecting the often planned nature of S-S rapes.

Weapons　Whether or not the assailant in an S-S rape will use a weapon to force the victim to submit is equally likely. In approximately 40 percent of these rapes, a weapon is used, and in 46 percent, no weapon is present. In the remaining 14 percent, the victim is unsure about the presence of a weapon. The most common weapon is a knife (noted in 60 percent of all S-S rapes involving a weapon). The next most common is a gun (30 percent). The younger the victim in an S-S rape, the less likely is the presence of a weapon; and the presence of a weapon increases the chance that an attempted rape will result in a completed rape (McDermott, 1979).

Figure 13-1 Attempted and completed rape rates in the United States. Note that the completion ratio (the number of rapes relative to the number of attempted rapes) is much higher for older females than for younger females. (Source: McDermott, 1979:5, figure 1.)

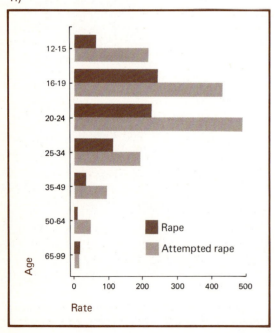

TABLE 13-1
Where stranger-stranger rapes take place.

Location	Percentage of Stranger-Stranger Rapes
On street, in park, playground, etc.	47
At or in the victim's home	18
Near the victim's home	14
Inside a commercial building	9
Inside an office or factory	1
In a vacation home, hotel, or motel	1
In a school	1
Other places	9

Source: McDermott (1979:19, table 10).

The most common location of stranger-stranger rapes are areas where there are many strangers—public areas. The second most common locations are in or near the victim's home, which may reflect an element of planning which we will discuss later in describing different types of rapes and rapists.

Self-defensive action by victim   In the majority (72 percent) of S-S rapes, the victim responds to the assault with some overt self-protective action. The most usual response is to attempt to attract attention or get help (48 percent). In another 45 percent, the victim attempts to use physical force. In 29 percent of these rapes, the victim resists without strong physical force, and in 22 percent, the victim attempts to argue, threaten, or reason with the assailant (McDermott, 1979).

Injury   Rape almost always involves some form of physical injury to the victim. The very act of forced vaginal penetration can involve extensive pain. S-S rapes most frequently involve additional injury as well. In 92 percent of the completed and 62 percent of the attempted rapes studied by McDermott in twenty-six American cities, the victim received additional injuries. The most frequent were cuts, bruises, black eyes, and scratches. Internal injuries or broken bones or teeth each occur in approximately 6 to 7 percent of S-S rapes, and knife or gunshot wounds in 2 to 3 percent. Additional physical injury in S-S rape is less likely when the victim is younger, since the assault itself is more intimidating.

Self-protective action taken by the victim during an S-S rape is also associated with additional physical injury. Women are generally advised to take some strong form of self-protective action when attacked. However, in S-S rapes, women who do so increase their risk of physical harm. Given the type of injuries which victims do receive and the fact that overt action by the victim does frequently stop the rape or some specific sexual activity in the rape situation, women are often advised to resist by using physical violence. Violent physical resistance works, however, only for some types of rape situations. As we shall see, there is also a very real and unknown danger in taking overt self-protective action. In some kinds of rape, the assailant is willing to use whatever force is needed to subdue the victim, including physical violence. In other types of rape, the assailant reacts to the victim's action by increased rage, anger, and violence. Chappell and James (1976) asked convicted rapists what would push them to injure a victim. In response, 46 percent said "struggling" and 44 percent said "screaming." But the victim in an S-S rape (and even some nonstranger rapes) has no way of knowing what the assailant's reaction will be. While the chances of being crippled or experiencing life-threatening violence are actually low in S-S rapes, the danger is still present.[1]

[1]A very, very small proportion of all rapes are murder rapes even though these cases receive the most media coverage.

Victim-offender similarity In stranger-to-stranger rapes, the victim and the offender tend to have similar demographic backgrounds and characteristics. Both victims and offenders are likely to be from low socio-economic categories and to be young and black. Predominantly, rapes do not take place across age, social class, or ethnic lines (McDermott, 1979).

The Social Bases of Rape

"Why?" has been a continuing question in the study of rape. Unfortunately, finding an accurate answer to this question has been hindered by inadequate research methods and a limited view of rape. In attempting to answer the question, the research emphasis has been placed on the individual rapist. However, a very select population—convicted rapists—has been studied. We know that these rapists represent less than 1 percent of all males who have raped. Additionally, convicted rapists appear to be more crime-prone, less educated, and generally less tied into the mainstream of American society than are the rapists who remain unknown (Smithyman, 1979). Perhaps most important, the convicted rapist is more violent and represents a special type of rapist. For years we have known that there are many types of rapes and that many (if not most) of them do not fit the "classic" violent-stranger rape. However, researchers have, with few exceptions (Kanin, 1967; Smithyman, 1979), ignored rapists other than those who are convicted. Research is now slowly revealing that rape is more accurately viewed as an outcome of the "normal" fabric of society rather than the "abnormal" emotional structure or personality of individual rapists.

Seeing victims and assailants The first social basis of rape is that an individual must have the idea that rape of another person is a possibility. While there are both males who never even dream that they could rape a woman and females who actually do rape men and other women, the great majority of persons who rape are males and by far the largest group of persons raped are females. The essential element here is that in gender and sexual learning, males learn ever so faintly that they *can* be a person who *forces* a woman to have intercourse.

Consider for a moment that female sexual aggression against males is very, very rare in our society. The reason for this is obvious. A male must have an erection and males are generally heavier and stronger. However, the reason for less female sexual aggression against males is not so obvious. First, we are not talking just about intercourse, but about any form of sexual aggression. Females simply do not tend to engage in sexually aggressive behavior whether it involves forced intercourse or forcing a hand inside a male's pants. Here, the difference between male and female is not a matter of erections and muscles. It is a matter of social learning. Males learn that they can be sexual aggressors against women. Females do not learn that they can be sexual aggressors against males. In fact, females learn that they can be sexual victims (Burt and Estep, 1981).

Evidence that these facts are the result of social learning and not some inherent characteristics of male and female members of the human species comes from cross-cultural research. Among the Arapesh of New Guinea, males do not rape females; females rape males. The Arapesh male has great fear of being sexually assaulted by a group of females who, in the completion of penis-vagina intercourse to the point of male ejaculation, are seen as stealing his semen for evil doings (Mead, 1935). These rapes are not, as many males have commented, fun. The assault frequently involves physical brutality against the victim and the women urinating and defecating in his face.

Gender These social bases on which are established the definitions of possible victims and offenders are focused on definitions of male and female sexuality. Other aspects of male and female gender learning are important social bases of rape. Males learn that they *should* seek sex; it is part of being male. Many (if not all) rapes are in part an extreme form of this male gender learning. Males also learn

that power, aggressiveness, and obtaining what one wants are major aspects of being male.[2] Carrying these views into sex is not such an extreme acting out of these aspects of the male role. In fact, the connection between male power, aggression, and taking by force is rather frequent in movies, advertisements, and "humor."

Gender learning by females has much less to do with rape. While many writers have suggested that certain aspects of the traditional female gender role make rape more likely, this is a serious misunderstanding of the nature of rape. Perhaps many attempted rapes would not be completed if females saw themselves as more assertive, physically strong, and less "ladylike" (it is not ladylike to punch, yell,

vomit, etc.). However, the fact is that rape would still be attempted. You can change female gender learning all you want and you will still have rape because of the simple fact that rapes are committed by males. Suggesting that women can decrease rape by changing what they learn as proper female behavior may aid some individuals in avoiding rape. While it is true that this is in many cases important, it is equally true that this learning is not a solution to the problem, but a reaction to its presence. Thinking that changes in the female role or female behavior will have any effect on the *existence* of rape is similar to suggesting that you can stop the rain by buying a bigger umbrella. Rape will decline in American society when certain components of the male role change.

Rape is a very serious social and psychological problem—a problem which should be embarrassing to any American citizen. It is

[2]Kanin (1969) found that many males attempted forced sexual activity of some type with a female on a date because of male peer pressure to acquire sexual experience.

BOX 13-2
MALE RAPE VICTIMS

The rape of males does take place. Most often it involves males raping other males and it frequently occurs in prisons. While some prison officials have denied that such rape is common, others familiar with the workings of such institutions argue that it is quite usual. Dr. Anthony Scacco estimates that a male prisoner is raped every fifteen minutes in the United States (*Sexuality Today*, September 29, 1980). The extent of such rapes is perhaps best illustrated by Judge Stanley Gartenstein's refusal, in 1980, to send a 23-year-old male to prison because he felt that the defendant would certainly be raped shortly after his being admitted. Male rape in prison underscores many of the aspects of rape we have discussed. The male victims are usually slight of build and generally have what would be stereotyped as "feminine" body build and features. These are not homosexual rapes and they are not purely for sex. Rather, the rape represents power and dominance in the prison subculture.

Not all male rapes take place in prison. Since rape crisis centers have become aware of the problem of male rape, there seems to be a general trend across the country for an increase in the reporting of male rape.

also a problem which receives the attention and concern largely of only women. In professional and volunteer activities dealing with rape counseling and prevention, I find very few males concerned or even present. As a consequence, it is women who most frequently suggest that women should do certain things to solve the problem.

I have very strong feelings about this. Rape is a problem for women that is generated and continued by men. It is up to men to solve the problem, not women. There are many ways in which men can personally have some effect on the general attitudes of males toward women and rape. Those of you who are men can refuse to be party to the rape and sexual abuse jokes so common in many male circles. You can tell your male peers the truth about the myths of rape. You can, in general, administer punishment rather than positive reinforcement for discussions which encourage a rape attitude toward women. This may not make you especially popular among some of your male friends, but I think it is the moral responsibility of all men to do what we can to stop the sexual abuse and assault of women where the

problem begins—in the minds, talk, and actions of us men. This responsibility of males is supported by research. Malamuth et al. (1980a) found that in a sample of male college students, the single most important factor predicting their saying that they themselves would be likely to rape a woman was their thinking that other males would do the same thing. This is perceived male peer-group approval (or at least acceptance) of rape. We have seen the importance of this peer-group influence in many aspects of male sexuality, and it is no different in the case of rape. This peer influence can be changed when enough males make it clear that rape is not acceptable.

Forced Sex Is Not Unusual
In order fully to understand the social bases of rape, we must stand back and take a serious look at the frequency of forced sexual activity. Almost universally, scientists and the public have adopted a tunnel-vision view of rape. It is typically thought of as the "classic" rape situation which involves a victim and an offender who are strangers, an attack involving violence

(beyond that of the attack itself), strong resistance on the victim's part, and a victim complaint. Rape, however, is any forced sexual activity against one's consent, and, while the legal system frequently disagrees, it may involve other than penetration of the vagina, mouth, or anus.

If we look around, we find that forced sexual activity against the will of the female is quite common. Kanin (1957) found that 62 percent of the females studied had been victims of a sexually aggressive offensive physical action by a male during their last year in high school. The males who engaged in these behaviors were not emotionally disturbed strangers jumping out of the bushes in the night. In 44 percent of the cases, the male was a steady boyfriend or fiancé. This forced sexual activity did not involve just feels and grabs. Of the females, 21 percent had experienced attempted or completed forced intercourse in this one-year period and 9 percent had experienced forced intercourse involving additional physical violence. The intercourse incidents were not simply with a blind-date sex maniac. Of these intercourse events, 14 percent were on a blind date, 26 percent were with a male the woman had dated occasionally, and 60 percent were with a steady boyfriend or fiancé.

In 1967, Kanin studied male college students. Twenty-five percent of them reported at least one attempt at physically forcing a female into intercourse against her will where the result was her either fighting or crying. The 87 males who reported such behavior told of engaging in a total of 181 such acts involving 142 females. In more recent studies, we find the same pattern (Herold et al., 1979a). For example, in a follow-up study, Kanin and Parcell (1977) found that among a sample of college females, 83 percent had been sexually offended by some overt male physical activity and 69 percent had had such experience since starting college. Of these cases, 24 percent involved forced intercourse and 3 percent intercourse with additional physical violence.

These high rates of forced sexual activity are not isolated just among high school and college students. Burt (1980) obtained a probability sample of adults in Minnesota. She found that 27 percent of the women had been the victims of an attempted but unsuccessful incident of forced sexual activity against their will. Fully 8.4 percent of the adult women said yes to the question, "Have you ever had anyone force sex on you against your will?" and 9.6 percent had engaged in sexual activity with a male because they were afraid that he would use physical force if they did not comply.

All these reports mean that males' physically forcing females into sexual activity is not rare. It happens—it happens in usual situations, and if we look at forced sexual activity in general and not just at intercourse, it happens to most females.

The Approval of Forced Sex

While there is no question that the classic violent-stranger rape is strongly disapproved in American society, forced sex does find approval in varying degrees. A substantial proportion of both males and females feel that forced intercourse is acceptable under certain conditions. In other words, there are conditions under which a proportion of both males and females approve of rape. This approval, furthermore, exists to such an extent that it is not even thought of as rape.

Giarrusso et al. (1979) presented 14- to 18-year-old males and females with a list of situations and asked them to check yes or no to the query of whether it was acceptable in each condition for a male to hold a female down and physically force her to engage in intercourse. Only 44 percent of the females and 24 percent of the males said that none of the conditions made this acceptable. As shown in Table 13-2, a substantial proportion of both the males and females said that in certain conditions rape is acceptable.

Male Sexual Access Rights

What is the basis of the attitude that it is acceptable for a male to physically force a female to engage in intercourse under certain conditions? While we are only now beginning

TABLE 13-2
Percent of high school and college students saying it is acceptable for a male to hold a female down and physically force her to engage in intercourse in different conditions.

Condition	High School Students*		College Students†	
	Males	Females	Males	Females
He spends a lot of money on her	39	12	13	8
He is so turned on he cannot stop	36	21	15	9
She has had sexual intercourse with other males	39	18	25	7
She is stoned or drunk	39	18	21	6
She lets him touch her above the waist	39	28	36	12
She is going to have sex with him and changes her mind	54	31	40	22
They have dated for a long time	43	32	42	17
She has led him on	54	26	42	28
She gets him sexually excited	51	42	45	25

*High school students data are from Giarrusso et al. (1979).
†College-student data are from my own research with college students in 1979–1980.

to acknowledge that such attitudes do in fact exist, I suggest that these attitudes are due to a long-standing concept of *male sexual access rights* in Western (and other) cultures. This is the view that males have a right of sexual access to females under certain conditions. When these conditions are met, forced sexual activity (within limits of force) is seen as acceptable. When these conditions are not met, forced sexual activity is seen as unacceptable.

Male property Historically, the idea of male sexual access rights is based on the view that females are male property. The female body—and the ability to control access to it—is now owned by her, but by a male such as her father or husband. Throughout history, rape has been seen as an offense against the male who owns her, not against the woman herself. The offense itself has historically had little to do with the physical and emotional damage to the woman. Rather, her being raped made her "used property" or "damaged goods" and less valuable to her owner.

One has always been seen, in Western culture, as having the right to do what one wants with one's own property. When applied to females, this view made rape of one's property common, but not defined as a violation of either social or personal rules. For example, a feudal lord during the Middle Ages in England had free sexual access rights to his new serf's bride, since the serf and all he owned was the property of the lord (Frumkin, 1961). In colonial America, this same view was apparent in the common rape of Indians and blacks (Bullough, 1976). This property concept during colonial and slavery days had other effects—namely, the execution and castration of black males who raped or attempted to rape a white female (Frumkin, 1961).

BOX 13-3

MARRIAGE AND MALE SEXUAL PROPERTY

In 1979–1980 I asked a sample of first- and second-year college students in introductory sociology courses a number of questions about forced intercourse activity between a male and a female. One of the questions included in the questionnaires was whether it was acceptable for a male to hold a female down and physically force her to engage in intercourse if (1) the man and woman are currently married to each other, (2) if the man and woman are currently married to each other but are separated at the time, and (3) if the man and woman were married to each other but are now divorced. The responses are shown below.

Marital Status of Man and Woman	Persons Saying Rape is Acceptable	
	Males (%)	Females (%)
If they are married to each other	42	16
If they are separated from each other	21	5
If they are divorced	6	0

Attempted rapelike behavior in some cultures is also a means of acquiring females as property. Among some Mexican, Central American, and South American groups, rape is part of the courtship process (Beals, 1961). Near a river, the young male ambushes the female, smashes a water jar on her head, and attempts to tear off her clothes. Her companions come to her aid and a fight takes place. If the male is driven off, he is rejected for marriage. If he succeeds in stealing her clothes, he is on his way to shortly being accepted as a marriage partner.

Today, the attitude that a wife is a husband's sexual property still exists (see Box 13-3). In such a view, it is not possible in the eyes of the law (and much of society) for marital rape to take place since the husband is seen as having sexual access to his wife.[3]

[3]It is commonly thought that the laws which state that a husband cannot possibly rape his wife because he has total sexual access to her came from English common law. This is not the case. These laws came from a decision by a judge in the United States in the 1800s, and after that decision, England changed its marital rape law to make marital rape not possible.

It was not until 1977 that any state had a law making marital rape a legal possibility. Most states today specifically exclude husband-wife rape in their rape laws.

The property notion of male sexual access rights also finds its way into dating relationships. Note in Table 13-2 that 43 percent of the males and 32 percent of the females said rape is acceptable if the male and female have been dating a long time.

Male arousal and release   Perhaps based on the view that males have "natural sexual urges" which are simply part of being male (Chapter 1), the male is considered to have sexual access rights if "he is so turned on he cannot stop" (Table 13-2). The approval of rape (Table 13-2) is even greater if the male's sexual arousal is brought about by the female—"she has led him on," "she gets him sexually excited." As we shall see, this aspect of male sexual access rights is reflected in other ways as well. Males are judged to have these rights if the female behaves in a "sexy" manner or dresses in what is considered a sexually arousing fashion. The use of such an argument by defense attorneys in rape cases is well known.

Even judges employ this aspect of male sexual access rights. In 1977, Judge Archie Simpson acquitted a 15-year-old male who had raped a high school female because he thought her dress was so short that she had excited the young man's passions beyond what he could reasonably be expected to resist.

Any sex equals all sex   It is also assumed that a male has sexual access rights if a female grants access to some parts of her body—even visually. Sometimes females are assumed to be asking for sex if they dress in revealing clothes. It is clear, however, that sexual access rights are assumed to be granted if some overt sexual activity occurs. For example, a sizeable proportion of the males and females in Table 13-2 said it was acceptable for a male to force a female to have intercourse if "she lets him touch her above the waist."

Prior sexual experience   Male sexual access rights are assumed to be granted if the female has prior sexual experience. If she has engaged in intercourse with other males, a minority of the females and a substantial proportion of the males find rape to be acceptable.

Purchasing sex   The purchase of sexual access to females by males has a long history in Western culture in the form of prostitution. Today we find the same concept in the idea that males can purchase sexual access rights by spending money on a date.

Attributing Responsibility to Rape Victims

Rape victims are often seen as responsible for being raped. This view is closely related to the concept of male sexual access rights. Research reveals that the extent to which a woman is seen as responsible for the rape varies by certain characteristics. These characteristics are interpreted by the observer as suggesting that the male has sexual access rights to that woman.

A divorced victim is seen as more responsible than a married victim (Feldman-Summers and Lidner, 1976). A victim wearing "sexy" clothing is held to be more responsible than a victim dressed in "bulky" clothes (Selby et al., 1977). A physically unattractive victim is considered more responsible than a physically attractive victim (Seligman et al., 1977; Calhoun et al., 1978). A Catholic nun is seen as less responsible for her rape than a social worker, who, in turn, is believed less responsible than a topless dancer (Smith et al., 1976; Luginbuhl and Mullin, 1981). A woman who has previously been a rape victim is judged to be more responsible than a woman who is raped for the first time (Calhoun et al., 1976). All these characteristics relate to the male's being granted sexual access rights in the minds of observers. Divorced women are assumed to "mess around"; wearing "sexy" clothing means advertising sexual availability; the topless dancer has already allowed visual sexual access; previous rape experience is merely repeating what was done the first time; and the physically unattractive female *must* have done something to lead the male on because it is assumed that he would be more likely to rape physically attractive females (DeJong and Anabile, 1979).

The view that rape victims are responsible for rape to the extent that they activate male sexual access rights is not unique to American society. While cross-cultural research has been sparse, Kanekar and Kolswalla (1981) found that in India a rape victim was believed more responsible for the rape when she was dressed in a "provocative" manner and when she was divorced rather than married.

One major outcome of this attribution of responsibility to victims is that the more responsible the victim is seen to be, the less responsibility is assigned to the assailant. Characteristics of the assailant also play a part here. A male who is in a high-status occupation (a scientist, for example) is seen as less likely to be guilty of a rape than a male in a low-status occupation (say, a janitor) (Deitz and Byrnes, 1981).

Male-Female Differences in Reaction to the Victim

Males and females see rape and rape victims very differently. Males attribute greater responsibility to the victim than do females (Krulewitz and Johnson-Payne, 1978; Krulewitz and Nash, 1979; Selby et al., 1977; Deitz and Byrnes, 1981). Males are more likely than females to think that the victim's personality contributed to her assault, and that the victim's behavior prior to the rape was a contributing factor (Selby et al., 1977). Males place more emphasis on the victim's dress and appearance as provoking a rape and are more likely to say that the victim was initially seductive and then changed her mind (Selby et al., 1977). Males are more likely to say that the victim enjoyed being raped and are less prone to see the victim as experiencing pain and trauma (Malamuth et al., 1980a). Males are more likely than females to see the victim as resisting the rapist and to consider the rapist as justified in his behavior (Malamuth et al., 1980a).

All these differences between males and females in the perception of the rape situation point to the fact that *females are much more likely than males to see rape as rape, while males are more likely to see it as a situation in which other social and sexual factors are important.* This was quite clear in a recent study which examined college students' views of the victim and assailant in rapes involving individuals of the same and of different ethnicity (Coffman and Mahoney, 1981). In this study, a rape was described and the victim and the assailant were each mentioned as being either black or white. Whether the victim or the offender was black or white was much more significant to males than females (especially in the case of a black male raping a white female compared with a white male raping a white female). For females, a rape was a rape. For males, their perception of the rape situation differed greatly depending on the ethnicity of the victim and the offender.

While these gender differences exist, it must be kept in mind that these rape myths

are learned. The research cited above reveals that they are more likely to be learned by males than females. However, females are not immune from such learning. Malamuth et al. (1980a) found that the female college students in one study thought that over 25 percent of all females would derive some pleasure from being raped.

Proclivity to Rape

From our earlier discussion in which it was shown that males' physically forcing females to engage in sexual activity is rather common, one would suspect that perhaps many males have at least entertained the idea of rape.

Evidence for a rather widespread proclivity to rape on the part of males comes from a series of studies by Malamuth (Malamuth and Check, 1980; Malamuth et al., 1980a; Malamuth et al., 1980b). In one study (1980a), males heard a taped description of a rape and then responded to a series of questions regarding how they would have acted. When asked if they would be likely to act as the rapist in the recording did, 17 percent said they would be at least somewhat likely to do so. When asked the same question with the assurance of not being punished, 69 percent said they would be at least somewhat likely to do what the rapist did and 37 percent said they would be likely to rape a woman.

Evidence for at least thoughts of rape comes from studies of sexual fantasies. Crepault and Couture (1980) found that 33 percent of the males they sampled had fantasized about raping a woman while they were having intercourse with their regular partner; that 11 percent had accompanied their intercourse with the fantasy of beating up a woman; and that 15 percent had fantasized about humiliating a woman in some way.

Correlates of Proclivity to Rape

Given the fact that most research on rapists has been guided by the mistaken assumption that the rapist is a mentally deranged, abnormal creature emerging from the bushes, there has been very little research on the correlates of rape proclivity.

Not all males have a proclivity to rape and not all males have it to the same degree. Malamuth and Check (1980) found that college-student males with this proclivity tended to have a callous attitude toward women and to be sexually aroused by depictions of sexual violence against women.

Inhibiting Rape

The common view of the rapist is some violence-prone, emotionally disturbed stranger who uses rape as a vehicle to degrade and humiliate women in a violent manner. While we shall see that this is true in some types of rape, it is not an accurate view of the total rape picture. Rather than think that rape comes about when a male is *driven* by some abnormal forces, it is perhaps more accurate to think of rape as the *outcome* of such "impulses" in some types of rapes and the *reduction of inhibitions* against rape in other types.

We have already seen that the social bases of rape are solid and widespread. We have already observed that forced sexual activity is a relatively common occurrence. We have also seen that a substantial proportion of males evidently do not totally discount the idea of rape. A central question is this: What are the factors which inhibit rape, rather than the factors which drive males to rape?

Social stigma Even in the most violent rapes, the assailant knows that his behavior is extremely deviant. Given the evidence we have examined, it seems a safe bet that the social stigma attached to rape often acts as a deterrent. Malamuth et al. (1980a) found, for example, that a much greater proportion of college males were willing to consider the possibility of rape if they could be assured that their actions would not be known to anyone except the victim.

Violence Some types of rape take place precisely because of the violence involved. For some rapists, combining violence with sex is sexually attractive and exciting. For most males, however, sex and violence do not go together, and thus the connection between violence and sexual activity is not at all attractive. Rape may often be inhibited precisely because of the physical violence necessary in such behavior. Barbaree et al. (1979) found that when a group of convicted rapists were compared with a group of nonrapists, violence mixed with sex did not create more sexual arousal in the rapists, but that the violence failed to inhibit their arousal as it inhibited the nonrapists. A series of studies (Malamuth and Check, 1980; Malamuth et al., 1980a; Malamuth et al., 1980b) has consistently found that depictions of forced sex create less sexual arousal than depictions of mutually consenting sexual activity.

Reaction of the victim Still, it must be kept in mind that in the series of studies done by Malamuth and associates on reactions to rape depictions among college students, many males and females (but significantly more males) are sexually aroused by rape depictions.

A key factor, however, which influenced the amount of this arousal created by a rape depiction was the reaction of the victim. Specifically, when the rape victim is described as experiencing involuntary sexual pleasure and/or orgasm during the rape, subjects are more sexually aroused by the rape depiction (Malamuth and Check, 1980; Malamuth et al., 1980b). This is the case for both males and females, but much more so for males (Malamuth et al., 1980b). In fact, when the rape victim is described as having an involuntary orgasm during the rape, male college students are apparently as sexually aroused as are convicted rapists when they are exposed to depictions of a violent rape (Malamuth et al., 1980b).

There is, however, a very significant difference between males and females in their sexual arousal while being exposed to a depiction of a rape. *Females* tend to be aroused by the rape depiction when the victim is described as experiencing an involuntary orgasm and no pain. *Males* tend to be sexually aroused by the rape depiction when the victim is described as experiencing an involuntary orgasm and pain (Malamuth et al., 1980b).

Before jumping to the conclusion that males are sexually aroused by females experiencing pain in a violent rape, we must note that there is no evidence for this interpretation. While this male reaction is not yet understood, Malamuth and Check (1980) and Malamuth et al. (1980b) have suggested much more reasonable answers—answers which take us back to our consistent discussion of differences in male and female sexuality as the result of sexual learning and sexual scripts. A significant part of male sexuality is embodied with the whole idea of power (potent?), getting sex, and "scoring." Rape as forced sex is not very far removed from the traditionally acceptable sexual script of the strong, virile male sweeping a female off her feet and carrying her to bed. The traditional sexual script also says that females are to be gatekeepers, and thus the proper female shows a little resistance to male sexual advances (females who are sexually aggressive and show a high interest in sex are moved toward the whore end of the wife-mother-whore continuum).

Further, it is a central part of the traditional sexual script that females show their *real* sexual feelings while *in* sexual activity, *not before* it. The traditional script says females are to be modest while working up to sex, to be responsive and to show pleasure during sex, and to be modest after sex. It does not take very much of a mental twisting of the traditional sexual script to think that if the woman experiences orgasm (even involuntary) during a rape, she is doing what the sexual script says she is supposed to do. This may create the sexual arousal to rape depictions when the victim is seen as experiencing involuntary orgasm. What about the males' reaction to pain on the part of the victim? It may well be that female subjects identify with the victim, and thus, when she is described as being in pain, they are not sexually aroused by the rape depiction even when she does experience involuntary orgasm. Males, on the other hand, may not identify with the rape victim but, instead, may be aroused by the fact that the

victim was described as experiencing an involuntary orgasm *despite* being in pain (Malamuth et al., 1980b).

Alcohol It is a common finding that alcohol is often involved in sexual assaults. In Chapter 5, we noted that thinking you have consumed alcohol increases your sexual arousal regardless of your actual alcohol consumption. It was pointed out that this is due to the drinking role. When one drinks, one is supposed to "get loose" and lose one's inhibitions. In the case of rape, alcohol lessens inhibitions in the same manner. Male college students in one study were highly aroused sexually (measured by actual erection) by a film showing a rape when they thought they had consumed alcohol regardless of what they had actually drunk. When they believed they had not consumed alcohol, they were significantly less aroused by the rape film regardless of their actual consumption. Further, those males who thought they had drunk alcohol experienced the same level of sexual arousal while watching the rape film as they did while watching a film of mutually consenting heterosexual intercourse (Briddell et al., 1978).

These research findings, combined with those discussed above, suggest that alcohol may play a significant role in lessening some males' inhibitions about rape. In other words, alcohol makes the normally present inhibitions against rape less powerful, and sexual learning in terms of male sexuality, the male gender role, and male sexual access rights comes to take the form of actual behavior.

Absence of social controls When normal social controls are absent, rape is more likely. Often such controls are lacking when an individual is placed in an unusual situation. Rape of villagers by American soldiers in Vietnam was very common (Brownmiller, 1975). In situations such as war, the social situation is obviously not normal. The rapes that occur in such situations are not due to males going berserk, but to males finding themselves in a spot where the usual social constraints against such behavior are absent.

Absence of personal controls In most rapes, the rapist is well aware that rape is an extremely deviant behavior. However, the individual may have personality characteristics that negate this learned definition of rape or may actually turn it into an inviting activity. If rape is defined as an abhorrent act, then it is possible to vent one's hostility toward women by subjecting them to such an act. Personal controls may also be absent because of situational reductions in personal inhibitions. As we shall discuss next, some kinds of rapists have a strong need to demonstrate that as males, they are superior to women. This feeling may be aggravated by a conflict with a female (mother, wife, sister, boss) to the point where they seek out a rape victim. Most of the time, they are able to control their prior learning, but certain situations become so ego-damaging that their personal controls disappear.

Types of Rapes and Rapists

There is no such thing as a typical rape or rapist. There are, however, different types of rapes, and these types correspond to the nature of the rapist in terms of the motivation behind his behavior. These individual motivations result in different forms of behavior in the rape situation.

The different types of rape and rapists do not fit into neat categories having precise characteristics. Rather, they fall on a continuum. This continuum involves the extent to which the goal of the rapist is sexual gratification alone or power and anger alone (Table 13-3). Along this continuum, we can describe various types of rapes and rapists according to domi-

nant characteristics, but there are no absolutely clear dividing lines making for distinct categories (Groth et al., 1977).

The different types of rape shown in Table 13-3 are distinguished by the degree to which (1) sexual activity is a means to a goal or a goal itself, and (2) violence and force are themselves a means to a goal or goals. At the far left of the continuum, the primary goal of the rapist is sexual gratification, and physical force or violence is a means to obtain that goal. At the far right of the continuum, violence and force are the rapist's goals, and sexual behaviors are merely a means to his acting out that goal.

Sexual gratification rape While some social scientists refer to something called "date rape," there is a real danger in the use of such a term. The use of the modifier "date" suggests that this is a special kind of rape or an activity which should be considered to be different from other rape situations. While sexual gratification rape in a dating situation may be viewed by the victim and the offender as far different from a violent attack by a total stranger, the difference is a matter of degree, not of kind.

In sexual gratification rape, sexual gratification is the assailant's primary goal and the demonstration of power, violence, or force is of little importance to him. Sexual gratification is the goal and he will use only the amount of force necessary to accomplish this goal. At the far left-hand side of Table 13-3, the sexual goal may be abandoned if more than slight physical force is necessary. As we move to the

TABLE 13-3
The continuum of different types of rape.

Sexual Gratification Rape	Power Rape	Anger Rape
Sexual gratification as the goal, force as the means	Mixture of sexual gratification and demonstration of power and control as goal and means	Violence, degradation, and humiliation as the goals, sex as the means

This conceptualization is based, in part, on the work of Groth et al. (1977).

Rape crisis clinics have brought about massive social change in terms of helping rape victims cope and recover. Given the case loads that centers like this throughout the country carry, it is a sobering thought to consider that such efforts have existed for only a few years while rape has been occurring since the beginning of American society.

right of the table, the use of power to accomplish the goal of sex becomes more important to the rapist. As we move to the right, the rapist is more likely to assault a stranger and to use more physical force than is necessary to obtain sexual submission. In general, sexual gratification rape is characterized by the rapist's wanting sex and using varying degrees of physical force to obtain it. Most commonly, the amount of physical force and violence is minimal. Often this type of rape is impulsive rather than planned. For example, the rapist may be engaged in a robbery and find a woman alone. He then seizes the opportunity for sexual activity and uses force to obtain it.

The use of force in sexual gratification rape does not necessarily mean that the rapist has some form of psychological or emotional disturbance. Rather, it may indicate that the rapist has clearly learned some major themes and images common in American society. The use of "masculine" force to sweep a woman away is not only a popular macho image (take a look at the scene in *Gone with the Wind* sometime), but images such as the caveman dragging a woman off by the hair for sexual purposes are common in male "humor." Sexually violent depictions are, in fact, rather common in male-oriented media. Malamuth and Spinner (1980) found that in *Playboy* and *Penthouse,* the prevalence of sexually violent

material increased from 1973 to 1977, with *Penthouse* having approximately twice as much of such material as *Playboy.* Worth more than a casual mention is the fact that when the much more violent *Penthouse* hit the newsstands, it made a severe dent in less-violent *Playboy's* sales.

Power rape   Until recently, rape was considered a sexual act in terms of the rapists' motives. While a great many rapes are for sexual gratification, we now know that certain types of rape are not sexually motivated. Rape, while always an act involving violence in some form (even if only implied), may be an act in which sex is the goal and violence is the means or violence is the goal and sex is the means. Power rape is an act in which the goal of the rapist is to obtain power and control over a female. He wants the woman to submit to him and engage in sexual activity as proof of his power and control over her. Sexual gratification is a part of power rape, but the rapist's primary interest is to demonstrate to himself and the woman that he has more power than she has and that she is in his control. The sexual activities are merely a means (a very important means in our society) by which this can be demonstrated. The rapist does have a strong interest in sexual activity, but this interest is closely connected to his use of force to dominate and control his victim. He may even be unable to become aroused unless the woman resists, so that he can use force to demonstrate that he can make her submit to something she does not want to do. He may even plan the rape carefully and, with great sexual arousal and anxiety, fantasize about the details of what he will do when he attacks the victim.

In repeated studies of *convicted* rapists, power rape is the most common form. Groth and Burgess (1977) found in one study that 65 percent of the convicted rapists were power rapists. Of all rapes, however, power rape is a small minority. (Less than 0.1 percent of all rapes result in any conviction.)

The power rapist has a stereotyped view of maleness. In many ways, he has over-learned the traditional male role. In his view, males are superior, powerful, and should be in control of women, and they can demonstrate this aspect of their maleness by forcing sexual activity on a woman (Groth et al., 1977). Keep in mind the study discussed previously where one-third of the males sampled had, while having coitus with their regular partner, fantasized about raping a woman.

Anger rape   Anger rape is the nonsexual use of behaviors having sexual meaning. In anger rape, the assailant is not motivated to obtain sexual gratification but to vent his anger, rage, contempt, and hatred on the victim. Sexual actions are a means to do this because it is possible to humiliate and degrade a woman in this manner. This type of rape most frequently involves violent physical assault in which much more force is used than is necessary to obtain sexual submission of the victim. Physical violence is important to the rapist for its own sake, not as a means to obtain a sexual goal. The goal is violence and hatred, and sexual activity is only an avenue of degradation and humiliation (Groth et al., 1977).

Generally, the anger rape is an act of revenge for what the assailant sees as rejection and hurt he has suffered at the hands of women. The purpose of the rape is to get even through humiliation, abuse, violence, and degradation. The victim is usually a total stranger and the rape is usually not planned. The attack is much more likely than other types of rape to be focused on acts which the assailant thinks are degrading for the woman. Oral and anal intercourse are common. Damage to the victim's breasts and genitals, the use of foreign objects for vaginal penetration, or even urination on the victim or her clothes may be inflicted for purposes of degradation.

Groth and Burgess (1977) estimated that 35 percent of the convicted rapists studied were anger rapists. Frequently, anger rapes may be precipitated by a conflict with a female, but there is a tendency for a lifelong pattern of hostility toward women. It is in anger rapes that the victim's life is in the greatest danger. Anger rapists often do not appear dangerous and may frequently be quite attractive and skilled in interpersonal dealings with women. These skills may be used (as they have been in some infamous recent rape-murder cases) to entice the victim into accompanying the assailant.

Group rape   Group rape may take many forms.[4] It may be primarily sexual gratification rape or it may take the form of power or anger rape. Group rape is, however, fundamentally different from lone assailant rape in some important aspects (Holmstrom and Burgess, 1980).

Group rapes are characterized by male camaraderie and performance with and for one's peers. Often the leader of a group rape is sexually stimulated by the presence of other males to observe his "performance." To a considerable extent, group rape is as much an interaction between the assailants as it is interaction between any one assailant and the victim or victims. As Geis (1971: 101, 113) has pointed out, the males in a group rape respond not only to their own personal motives and the sexual interaction with the victim, but also to how they think they must act in the presence of other males.

---

[4]Group rape may also be for different purposes in different cultures. Among some Plains Indians, a wife who had engaged in extramarital sex would be turned over by her husband to as many as twenty males for organized group rape punishment (Voget, 1961).

Group rape may also involve participation by females other than the victim. Female accomplices of the male assailants may entrap the victim (or victims) and may willingly participate in intercourse with the males as part of the situation (Holmstrom and Burgess, 1980).

We have noted repeatedly how the basic foundations of various forms of rape can be found in the very structure of our society. This is also true for group rape, which might be considered an extreme acting out of male sexual learning. We have seen how, during adolescence, the male peer group becomes important as a reference point for the male and his sexual behavior. Much male adolescent sexual activity takes place not just for his own personal gratification, but for status among his peers. Group rape shares this characteristic with adolescent male sexual activity. This has been a central part of other aspects of adult male sexuality in American society. Prostitution in the past often involved much male camaraderie. Males would frequently go out for a "night with the boys" which would include engaging (privately, but in the context of a group excursion) in sex with a prostitute. The sexual experience here was something shared in a social and psychological sense with one's peers and involved a demonstration of male camaraderie and adherence to male standards of sexual performance. The hiring of prostitutes for bachelor parties and the males' taking turns at intercourse (not uncommonly in the visual presence of the other males) has many of the components of group rape.

The Effects of Rape on the Victim

Just as most research has concentrated on a very small and unrepresentative proportion of rapists and rapes, the same has been true of studies of victims and their reactions to rape. In general, studies of the effects of rape on victims have been limited to victims of power and anger rapes. This approach does not mean these studies are not valuable; they are of extreme value in understanding what can be done to help the rape victim cope with the effects of rape. It does mean that we know

almost nothing about the reactions of victims to so-called date rape. There are important questions about the effects of such assaults which remain to be answered.

Some perspective: the rape itself

The rape situation itself involves severe psychological and physiological reactions on the part of the victim—reactions which reveal the shock and trauma of the event. Psychologically, the victim experiences feelings of anger, terror, exhaustion, racing thoughts, worry, shame, humiliation, helplessness, and fear. Physiologically, victims experience common fear reactions: racing heartbeat, rapid breathing, shaking and trembling, as well as pain (Veronen et al., 1979).

Very, very few males will ever personally understand what this situation is like. It is simply not a part of the male experience. One way, however, for a male to get some gut-level feeling for what it is like to be a rape victim is to imagine oneself in a situation which happens every day in this society. You are sent to prison. As soon as you arrive in your cell, you are approached by several inmates. You are first beaten up a little just to let you know that you are powerless. This, if you are lucky and don't resist too much, will result only in some broken teeth or a broken nose or jaw as well as a few kicks in the stomach, the crotch, or both. Your pants will be pulled to your ankles, you will be bent over forward and men will take turns ramming their penises up your anus until they ejaculate. At the same time, it is quite likely that you will have your head grabbed and your mouth forced over another male's erect penis. You will be told to suck it or you will have your face completely broken. You do what they say until he, and whoever else wants to, ejaculates in your mouth. This is not the last time this will happen. You are in a situation where it is very easy to kill a person and you will have two choices—be raped or die.

If this description makes you a little sick to your stomach, you are beginning to have some slight (but not totally realistic because you know your chances of going to prison are very slight) understanding of rape.

TABLE 13-4
Psychological and physiological reactions during and after rape, in percent of victims reporting.

	During Rape	2 to 3 Hours after Rape
Psychological Reactions		
Anger	80	80
Ashamed	72	80
Confused	92	80
Depressed	48	84
Exhausted	52	96
Feelings of unreality	64	60
Guilty	48	52
Helplessness	88	76
Jumpiness, restlessness	—	88
Racing thoughts	80	80
Scared	96	88
Terrified	92	80
Withdrawn	24	76
Worried	96	96
Physiological Reactions		
Dry mouth	44	52
Physically relaxed	4	12
Headache	16	60
Racing heart	84	48
Numbness	60	48
Pain	72	68
Rapid breathing	64	44
Shaking or trembling	96	96
Tight muscles	68	68

Source: Veronen et al. (1979, table 1).

After rape: Rape trauma Most power-oriented, and perhaps all anger rapes result in extreme trauma for the victim. On the basis of their research with rape victims, Burgess and Holmstrom (1974) have described the nature of *rape trauma.* The trauma of rape involves two basic stages related to the time which has passed since the assault.

The *acute phase* is a severe disorganization of one's life accompanied by strong psychological and physiological reactions. In the immediate hours after the attack, the victim experiences a variety of emotions, including shock, disbelief, fear, anger, and extreme anxiety (Table 13-4). Even though these inward reactions tend to be the same for almost all victims, the outward behavior may be either *expressive* (releasing feelings through crying, sobbing, smiling, restlessness, or tenseness) or *controlled* (the inward feelings are bottled up inside). Physiological reactions in the acute phase include the physical trauma of being beaten and general soreness from the attack, muscle tension involving headaches, fatigue, and severe sleep disturbance. Gastrointestinal problems are common in the form of stomach pains, loss of appetite, nausea from antipregnancy medication, and nausea from the attack itself. Genitourinary problems also frequently result, including vaginal discharge, itching, burning sensations during urination, and general vaginal pain.

The acute phase continues for several weeks after the attack, and feelings of humiliation, fear, embarrassment, anger, revenge, self-blame, and concern about future physical violence are common. The fear reactions of victims are a central part of the rape trauma. Even though these reactions diminish greatly after about three months, there still remains a core of fear and anxiety concerning many previously routine aspects of social life (Table 13-5) (Kilpatrick et al., 1979; Veronen et al., 1979).

The *reorganization phase* of rape trauma diminishes severe reactions on the victim's part, but the problems of getting one's life back to what it was before the rape remain. How quickly and completely the victim reorganizes depends on several factors, including her personal psychological characteristics, the social support networks in the form of friends,

relatives, spouses, and rape counselors, and the manner in which she is treated as a victim (Burgess and Holmstrom, 1978; Atkeson et al., 1982).[5]

Even though the extreme fear and anxiety reactions of the acute phase diminish three to six months after the attack, they are still very much present. Nightmares are common and fear of places and situations suggestive of the rape are frequent (Kilpatrick et al., 1979; Veronen et al., 1979). The reason for these fears is that *a very crucial learning process takes place during the rape.* Through classical conditioning (Chapter 4), characteristics of the rape situation (activities, body parts, the per-

[5]Recalling our earlier discussion of how victim and assailant characteristics influence people's perception of the rape victim, Deitz and Byrnes (1981) found that observers thought that the psychological impact of rape on the victim is less when the rapist is physically attractive.

TABLE 13-5
Fears of rape victims at four periods following the rape, listed in order from most (1) to least (10) severe.

6–10 Days after Rape	1 Month after Rape
1. Being alone	1. Darkness
2. People behind you	2. Being alone
3. Man's penis	3. Strangers
4. Venereal disease	4. People behind you
5. Testifying in court	5. Testifying in court
6. Being in a strange place	6. Walking on a dimly lit-street
7. Crowds	7. Door slamming
8. Anal intercourse	8. Being in a strange place
9. Darkness	9. Venereal disease
10. Blind dates	10. Being awakened at night

3 Months after Rape	6 Months after Rape
1. Being alone	1. Being alone
2. Strangers	2. Talking to police
3. People talking about you	3. Crowds
4. Being watched while working	4. Strangers
5. Going out with new people	5. Being awakened at night
6. Angry people	6. Blind dates
7. Sudden noises	7. Insane people
8. Being criticized	8. Going out with new people
9. Insane people	9. Sudden noises
10. Speaking in public	10. People behind you

Source: Veronen et al. (1979).

One political outcome of rape is that it increases the tension between males and females.

son, the place) become associated with the fear and violence which were experienced. After the rape, similar places, situations, noises, people, and other reminders evoke the same fear and anxiety responses the victim experienced during the rape. One of the very real problems in dealing with rape is that these responses must be unlearned and removed from the individual's life.[6]

Effects of Rape on Sexual Behavior
Given the sexual focus of the personal violence and fear in rape, most victims find themselves conditioned by the rape to have certain responses to sexual activity.

Burgess and Holmstrom (1979) found that the most common reaction of rape victims with regard to sexual activity was a sharp decrease. Of the victims studied who had been sexually active before the rape, 71 percent decreased sexual activity. This figure included 38 percent who gave up sex entirely for at least

[6]The more sudden and violent the rape, the greater are the long-term effects on the victim because of the severity of the rape trauma and the power of that classical conditioning in the form of high intensity (Ellis et al., 1981).

three months following the rape. Only a minority of the rape victims studied by Burgess and Holmstrom—19 percent—reported no change in sexual activity. Among these women, however, 50 percent reported changes in their responses to sex, including flashbacks, worrying about their partner's reaction, aversion to certain sexual activities, discomfort and pain, difficulty with sexual feelings in general, and lack of orgasm response. A minority (9 percent) of the victims in Burgess and Holmstrom's research increased their sexual activity following rape. Sometimes this increase was an attempt to counter the negative rape experience by positive sexual interaction. In other cases, however, the increase reflected a change in sexual self-concept along the lines of abandoning previous sexual values. Burgess and Holmstrom (1979) reported that some women engaged in coitus with almost any available male and some began prostitution. The extent of these reactions is not known exactly, but can be assumed to be relatively rare.

It is a common view that females with little sexual experience before the rape will be more adversely affected than females with more sexual experience. The level of sexual experience before the rape is irrelevant, however, for recovery after the rape, even when the rape is the female's first intercourse experience (Burgess and Holmstrom, 1979). This is because the rape is primarily a fear and violence experience for the victim and not a sexual experience. Additionally, the magnitude of the classical conditioning which takes place in the rape is so great that prior sexual experience simply becomes meaningless for recovery. As mentioned earlier, this may be quite different in sexual gratification rapes involving little violence. Such an experience may well have a dramatic influence on the female's view of heterosexual activity if it is an early or a first sexual experience.

The rape experience affects not only sexual activity, but sexual satisfaction as well. Feldman-Summers et al. (1979) measured the self-reported sexual satisfaction of rape victims one week before the attack (retrospectively), one week after the rape, and two months after the rape. They found that for several dimensions of sexuality, sexual satisfaction dropped significantly one week after the attack and then increased slightly in the following two-month period. The level of sexual satisfaction two months after the rape was still significantly less than before the rape experience. Very importantly, those dimensions of sexuality which are apparently not affected by the rape experience involve activities completely absent from the rape situation—orgasm by self-manipulation, orgasm by fantasy, holding hands with one's partner, hugging the partner, talking with the partner, and being held by the partner. This is to be expected, since the conditioning which takes place in the rape situation is specific to those sexual activities involved in the rape. Tenderness and interpersonal communication are not part of rape.

These findings have important implications for helping rape victims recover and regain their previous sexuality. Reentry into sexual interaction is best accomplished gradually by means of those activities which are not fear-conditioned by rape. This approach allows for positive feelings to be associated with sexual interaction and opens the way for communication with one's partner and talking about the fears and anxieties the victim has about her life in general and sex in particular.

This reentry into sexuality can be a complex and difficult process. Apart from making the decision to resume sexual activity and dealing with her own emotional and physiological responses to sex, the victim is often concerned about the reactions of her partner (Burgess and Holmstrom, 1979). Common concerns include how her partner feels about the rape itself: Does he think it was her fault? Does he believe her? Does he think she enjoyed it? Does he think that she really wanted to be raped? She is also anxious about how her partner feels about her: Does he see her as spoiled and undesirable? Does he see her as different? How does he feel about her being "sexually known" by another male? These are all concerns which are frequently difficult for the victim to discuss with her partner, but which may be confronted in the context of understanding and communication.

The Effects of Rape on Society

The presence of rape has a significant impact on relationships between males and females. As long as rape is a reality, many women will view many males with suspicion. In recent years, rape has become a political issue in the women's movement. A significant proportion of the women's movement already involves a subtle, but present, tension between males and females, augmented by recent public discussions of rape.

The presence of rape also affects males and females in more personal ways. Herold et al. (1979a), in a study of female college students, found that only 18 percent said they never worried about sexual offenses or assaults and fully 36 percent said they were generally moderately to very worried about such incidents. In a more recent study of male and female college students, Burt and Estep (1981) found that 67 percent of the females but only 7 percent of the males said they worried about sexual assault.

Burt and Estep (1981) have further demonstrated that a very significant part of female sexual learning in adolescence and young adulthood is learning sexual fear, vulnerability, and danger. Adult males do not learn to view the world as sexually dangerous, while adult females have been, and are, learning this view from friends and family in the form of warnings and cautions (Burt and Estep, 1981). It is difficult to understand how even the most insensitive person would not be outraged that, in a supposedly free society, real day-to-day freedom from sexual fear exists only for males.

Again, the solution is not to be found in obtaining a black belt in karate or arming oneself with a can of mace. Accepting such solutions to the problem is implicitly to say that its existence is acceptable. This is like dealing with the problem of cancer by telling people how they can adjust only when they become cancer victims. As an important aside, women should note that the "solutions" to the problem of rape often increase one's danger. For example, the macelike sprays are good only if the wind is not blowing in the woman's face, if the chemical totally repels the assailant, and if he does not use the spray to immobilize her.

SEXUAL COERCION OF CHILDREN

Children may be victims of sexual coercion in many ways. While we typically think of the child victim as involved in an adult-child sexual contact, this picture is not exactly accurate. As we shall see, the sexual contacts of children involve both strangers and family members, and these family members include both siblings and other relatives. Further, these sexual contacts differ greatly in the degree and nature of the coercion involved.

A common term used when discussing the sexual coercion of children is *sexual molestation.* This generally refers to any form of sexual activity taking place between an adult and a child. This term has limited usefulness since, as we shall see, a considerable amount of the sexual coercion of children is by siblings who are not adults. *Incest* is another term of little use in this discussion. Incest refers to sexual activity between family members who are not defined as appropriate sexual partners. Not only does the definition of an appropriate sexual partner differ greatly from culture to culture, but from state to state as well. Further, incest is not necessarily sexual coercion. While the young child does not have the legal or social capacity to consent to sexual activity, incest may be between two adolescents, an adult and an adolescent, or two adults, and it may not only have the possibility of being mutually consenting, but it may actually be so. In a more clinical sense, the term "pedophilia" (from the Greek *pais,* meaning boy or child, and *philein,* meaning to love) is often used. A *pedophile* is one who has a sexual preference for children. As we shall see, this term is also imprecise. Most of the adults who sexually coerce children do not do so because they prefer children as sexual partners. Rather, they find children acceptable sexual partners (Gebhard et al., 1965).

Incidence of Sexual Coercion of Children

Official police statistics on the sexual coercion of children are woefully inaccurate. Sarafino (1979) estimated that, on the basis of police records, some 336,000 children are victims of sexual offenses by adults in any given year. Herold et al. (1979a) found that 9 percent of the college females studied had experienced an attempted or completed sexual assault before the age of 14. In a more comprehensive study, Finkelhor (1979) found that among 796 college students in New England universities, 19 percent of the females and 9 percent of the males had been sexually victimized as children.

There is also that vast area of unknown sexual exploitation of children which has no chance of being detected by the family or police or of being reported by the child. It is clear that there are between one-half and one-and-a-half million persons under the age of 16 involved in prostitution in the United States—and thousands more involved in pornography.

TABLE 13-6
Relationship between the child and the offender in incidents of child sexual coercion.

Relationship of Offender to the Child	Male Victims (%)	Female Victims (%)
Family member	17	43
Acquaintance	53	33
Stranger	30	24

Source: Finkelhor (1979, p. 58, table 4-3).

The Nature of Coercion

Groth and Burgess (1977) distinguish between *sexual pressure* and *sexual force* in the sexual coercion of children by adults. Sexual pressure involves two types of activity. The child may be *enticed* or persuaded to engage in sexual activity, or the child is *entrapped* into feeling obligated to be a sexual partner. Sexual force may also take two different forms. The force may be *exploitive* in that the adult uses threat or physical force, or the force may be *sadistic* in that the physical violence of the assault is itself an erotic activity in the offender's mind.

The most common form of coercion in reported sexual assaults of children is exploitive (Groth and Birnbaum, 1978). This quality also appears to be most frequent in incidents not reported to the police. Finkelhor (1979) found that 55 percent of both the male and female child sex victims said that exploitive force was used to gain their sexual cooperation. The second most common type of force appears to be sexual pressure of some form; in a substantial majority of cases known to the police (20 percent), sadistic force is involved (Groth and Birnbaum, 1978).

The type of force involved in the sexual coercion of children depends on a number of factors, such as the age of the child, the type of sexual activity, the characteristics of the offender, and the relationship between the offender and the victim. As Gebhard et al. (1965) pointed out, the issues of the kind and the degree of force may simply be irrelevant except in the case of sadistic force. For example, the power of a loved father over a child is very, very great. To say that using this love to obtain sexual activity is more or less coercive than a verbal threat of physical harm by a stranger is to seriously misunderstand the dynamics of this situation for the child.

The Nature of the Incidents

Perhaps the most accurate overview of coercive sexual experiences of children comes from a recent study by Finkelhor (1979) involving several hundred college students who reported being victims through an anonymous questionnaire.

The offender As shown in Table 13-6, the relationship of the child with the offender differs for males and females. In either case, strangers make up a small number of the offenders, and for males, the offender is considerably more likely to be an acquaintance than in the case of females. The offenders of males also tend to be slightly younger than the offenders of females (average ages of 32 and 27, respectively) (Finkelhor, 1979), and in a substantial minority of the cases, the offender is an adolescent—often a cousin or sibling.

Age of the child For males, the average age of sexual victimization is 10.2 years, and for females, 11.2 years. However, fully 14 percent of the female victims and 18 percent of the male victims had an experience between the ages of 4 and 6 (Finkelhor, 1979). Females are twice as likely as males to be victimized between the ages of 7 and 9, and males are twice as likely as females to be victims between the ages of 13 and 16.

The sexual activity Coercive sexual activity with children when the force is not sadistic is most often that of genital fondling and touching. This, however, is more common for male than female victims (18 percent of the females' experiences and 55 percent of the males') (Finkelhor, 1979). Coitus is relatively rare for female children (4 percent having this type of experience), and exhibitionism by the offender is relatively common (20 percent of the cases). While most people probably think of heterosexual activity when they think of the sexual coercion of children, this is not always the situation. In 84 percent of the cases involving male children, the sexual activity was homosexual, and in 94 percent of the cases involving female children, the sexual activity was heterosexual. This underscores the fact, of course, that a very large majority of the offenders are males. When the offender is a female, she is younger than when the offender is a male, and she is much more likely to make a homosexual advance than is a male offender. For example, in the Finkelhor study, 67 percent of the sexual advances made by women were homosexual, while only 14 percent of the sexual advances made by men were homosexual. While most of those who sexually coerce children are males, it should not be assumed that this coercion is only a male activity. In a recent study with over 900 college students, Fritz et al. (1980) found that 60 percent of the males victimized as children had been victimized by a female.

Reaction of the victim In the majority of child sexual coercion incidents which do not involve sadistic force, the female child views the incident as a negative experience. However, while 66 percent of the females said their child victimization experience was negative, 7 percent said it was positive (Finkelhor, 1979). Males are much less likely to view these childhood coercive experiences as negative. In the Finkelhor study, 38 percent of the victimized males viewed their experience as undesirable (compared with 66 percent of the females). The most important factor in how traumatic the experience is for the child is the amount of force used (Finkelhor, 1979). The second most relevant factor related to the child's trauma is the age of the offender. The

older the offender, the greater the trauma. It must be kept in mind here that we are talking about offenders who range in age from 10 to late adulthood. Some factors which have been thought to be important in the trauma the child suffers do not appear to be related to trauma. For example, the sex of the offender, the duration of the coercion, the child's age, whether anyone was told of the incident, the relationship between the victim and offender, and whether or not intercourse was involved are all unrelated to the victim's trauma.

The long-term effects of childhood sexual coercion is an issue which has been debated for some time. It appears that not all children who are victims of sexual coercion are affected by the experience (Bender amd Blau, 1937; Gagnon, 1965). For example, Fritz et al. (1981) found that 23 percent of the female and 10 percent of the male victims of childhood sexual coercion had problems in their adult sexual adjustment; it is unknown how many of these problems would have been present without the childhood experience of sexual coercion.

Sexual Coercion by Brothers and Sisters

Sexual activity taking place between siblings is a subject which has received almost no research attention. In one study, Finkelhor (1980) found, however, that such activity is far from rare. Surveying 796 male and female college students from six New England colleges in 1977–1978, he found that 13 percent reported a sexual experience with a sibling. This was the case for 15 percent of the females and 10 percent of the males. These sibling sexual activities are primarily heterosexual. Of all the incidents reported by these college students, 74 percent were heterosexual and 26 percent were homosexual (16 percent sexual activities between brothers and 10 percent sexual activities between sisters).

While the students in this sample reported having had these sexual experiences anywhere between ages 3 and 19 or more, the most common was after age 8. Forty percent reported that the sibling sexual activity had taken place before they were 8 years old.

The kinds of sexual experiences range from exhibiting genitals to intercourse and attempted intercourse. While the fondling of genitals is the most common sexual activity experienced by those under age 8 (Table 13-7), this age group also has a slight chance of attempted or actual coitus.

Most of these sibling sexual experiences are not a one-time only affair, and a substantial number continue for some time. For example, while 33 percent of the incidents happened only once, fully 27 percent continued longer than one year.

It cannot be automatically assumed that all sibling sexual experiences involve coercion. In the Finkelhor study, however, 25 percent of the incidents involved some kind of force. Not unexpectedly, females are much more likely than males to be the victims of sexual coercion by a sibling. In 82 percent of the coercive incidents in this sample, the female was the victim. The female sibling is also most likely to be younger than her brother when they engage in sexual activity. In 70 percent of those cases where the siblings differed more than 5 years in age, the female was the younger. While it is rare that children who have sexual experiences with their siblings ever tell anyone (only 12 percent do so), this secrecy is much more common when force is involved. This means, of course, that, much as in the case of parent-child sexual activity, many children are left holding inside a painful secret in many cases.

It should also not be assumed, however, that all sibling sex is a negative experience for those involved. In this study, 30 percent of those who had sex with a sibling said it was a positive experience, 30 percent said it was negative (the more frequent reaction of those who were coerced), and 40 percent said they had no strong feelings in either a positive or negative direction. These negative effects, however, are almost all reported by females rather than males. This is a not unexpected difference given the fact that females are more likely to be the victims of sibling sexual coercion. The most important factor Finkelhor

TABLE 13-7

Types of sibling sexual activity by age of person at time of experience.

Type of Sexual Activity	Age at Time of Experience (% of Age Group)		
	0–8	9–12	13+
Exhibiting genitals	40	24	5
Fondling and touching genitals	53	60	64
Intercourse and attempted intercourse	5	15	18
Other activities	0	2	13

Percentages do not always total to 100 for an age group owing to rounding.
Source: Finkelhor (1980, 176, table 2).

found related to negative experiences in sibling sex was the amount of age difference. The type of sexual activity and the person's actual age were not factors in reaction to the experience. Most likely, age difference is the most important because a wide age difference involves coercion rather than sibling sex play and exploration.

A significant portion of incest incidents in American society are sibling-sibling sexual activity. Finkelhor (1979) found that 39 percent of the incest reported by females and 21 percent reported by males involved siblings, and only 4 percent of the reported incest cases for females involved the father.

Cousins are also common sexual partners. In fact, for males, a female cousin is the most likely blood-related sexual partner, followed by a brother or sister. For females, a brother is the most likely related partner, followed by a male cousin (Finkelhor, 1979).

Father-Daughter Sexual Activity

The best single source of detailed information on the nature of father-daughter sexual contact comes from the now classic research of Gebhard et al. (1965). While this research is somewhat dated, there is no evidence that it does not apply today.

Gebhard et al. found that the nature of

father-daughter sexual contact differed significantly by the age of the daughter.

Daughter under age 12 The average age of the father in these cases was 34, and in two-thirds of the cases, this was his first offense. The average age of the child was 9 and was rather consistently the oldest daughter if there were two or more female children in the family. These incidents typically do not involve force or the threat of force, even though a large minority involve drunkenness at the time of the offense.

Such incidents occur repeatedly. While 30 percent of the fathers had been engaging in sexual activity with their daughters for one month or less, 18 percent had been doing so for one to two years and 19 percent for three or more years.

When the child is under 12, such father-daughter incidents seldom involve coitus (9 percent coitus, 9 percent attempted coitus). Genital manipulation (42 percent of the cases) and oral-genital activities (39 percent) are the most common forms of sexual contact.

Daughter age 12 to 15 These situations are similar to those involving younger children, but owing to the age of the child, the sexual conduct varies. The average age of the father is somewhat older (39) since the child is older (average age 14). Alcohol is commonly involved and the greatest number of the incidents are premeditated (84 percent). Sexual activities generally involve intercourse (72 percent) and nongenital petting is rare. These situations also seldom involve direct physical force or threat of force, but in 6 percent of the cases, the mother was an accomplice through knowing about the activity and either doing nothing or encouraging the daughter to cooperate.

Daughter over age 15 Gebhard et al. (1965) found that in almost two-thirds of these incidents, the female was between 16 and 17 years of age. In 20 percent, she was 18, or 19, and in another 20 percent 20 to 25. Among older daughters, most had begun sexual activity with their father before the age of 16. With this age group, the general nature of the sexual activity involved becomes more adult; alcohol tends not to be a factor, fewer incidents

are planned before the event, and almost all involve intercourse.

Child Sex Initiation Rings

It is not uncommon for adult-child sexual coercion to take place in the form of a "ring." This consists of the "simultaneous involvement of a number of children in sexual activities with an adult who capitalizes on his legitimate role in the lives of [the children] to recruit them into his illegal behavior" (Burgess et al., 1981:112). The adult-child sex ring is thus characterized by two major factors. First, the adult who initiates the children into sexual activity with him has a position of authority and familiarity to the children so that he has some power over them and is not a stranger. Second, the children in the ring know one another and are aware of each other's sexual activity with this adult (Burgess et al., 1981).

There appear to be specific ways in which such child sex rings operate (Burgess et al., 1981). The children are rather quickly made aware of the fact that sexual activity is one of the requirements for membership in the group and that the other children in the group abide by this requirement. The initiation of the children into sexual activity usually begins indirectly (for example, showing the children pornographic photos), with some pressure on the children to exhibit themselves, the adult's own exhibitionism, and his fondling of the children. The initial sexual activities involve fondling and often oral sex performed by the adult upon the child. Aggressive vaginal and anal intercourse usually takes place after the children are committed to membership in the group.

Continuation of the child sex ring depends on secrecy. The childrens' secrecy is usually maintained by one or more of three methods. The adult in most situations will use *threat of retaliation* in the form of physical assault. A common ploy is also *blackmail*. The adult will often give children cigarettes, drugs, or alcohol to get them to participate and then threaten to tell the child's parents about their acceptance of such gifts if the child does not keep the sexual activities a secret. The inability of the child to understand the relative seriousness of various offenses (parents' knowing about the child's smoking versus the child's being involved in coercive sex) clearly indicates why adult-child sex is almost always coercive by definition. The adult may also use peer pressure to maintain the secret by telling the child that he or she will miss out on all the fun things the group does (go to the zoo, ride in cars, etc.) or reminding the child of what the other children in the group will think if secrecy is not kept. Cohesiveness does develop among the children in the group, and this peer pressure can be an important factor in keeping the children in the group: "I didn't want them to think I couldn't do it"; "Everyone else was doing it" (quotes from children in Burgess et al., 1981:113). Children in the group may also be very competitive in attempting to gain and keep the attention of the adult, and the adult may use this tendency to maintain continued cooperation in sexual activities.

Such child sex rings, the frequency of which is unknown, eventually break down with the aging of the children, their inadvertent disclosure of the activity, and the parents' suspicion. Such disclosure most commonly results in the arrest of the offender, but both the parents and the child must still face the difficulty of dealing with the incident.

Legal Obstacles and Changes

There have been many legal obstacles to the effective prosecution of offenders in child sexual abuse cases. First, the victim may not report the abuse to anyone until after the statute of limitations has run out. Thus, by the time the child is old enough to tell someone, so much time has passed that nothing can be done through the legal system. Second, most parents and prosecutors refuse to let a young child be subjected to the frightening experience of a trial and the subsequent trauma of a cross-examination by the defense attorney. Since most states do not allow hearsay evidence to be presented, courts do not allow the testimony of a child which has been given to another person outside the court to be presented as evidence. In 1982, Washington state was the first state to revise these laws. The

statute of limitations was extended from three to five years, and hearsay evidence was allowed in child sexual abuse cases if there was collaborating testimony or evidence. If adopted by other states, these changes will dramatically increase effective prosecution in child sexual abuse cases.

SEXUAL HARASSMENT

Sexual harassment is legally defined as "unwelcome sexual advances, requests for sexual favors, and other verbal or physical conduct of a sexual nature" (Hamer, 1981). Whether any behavior is sexual harassment depends on the perception of the parties involved: If the recipient sees the activity as harassment, it *is* sexual harassment.[7]

Most of the attention given to sexual harassment in recent years has been in the workplace (MacKinnon, 1979; Gutek et al., 1981). It is important to note, however, that sexual harassment can take place anywhere. The common male eyeballing of a woman's chest region is sexual harassment if she sees it as such, and this situation is hardly limited to the workplace.

The most insidious forms of sexual harassment (although in my own view no more and no less repulsive) involve coercion. These are situations in which persons confront the "unwanted imposition of sexual requirements in the context of a relationship of unequal power" (MacKinnon, 1979:1). This type of sexual harassment, most often taking place in the context of education and employment, is insidious because it affects the life chances of the recipient.

Sexual Harassment on the Job

We have only recently begun to pay research attention to sexual harassment. A central issue is how any form of social-sexual behavior is

---

[7]This means, of course, that social-sexual interaction between supervisors and employees or professors and students may be intended to be very sincere and not at all coercive, but actually be sexual harassment, since the recipient is either not interested or fearful of the consequences of not being interested.

perceived by the people involved. The initiator of the interaction may not view his or her behavior as sexual harassment, while it is perceived as such by the recipient. The opposite is also true. Gutek et al. (1981) obtained a random sample of individuals in Los Angeles in the fall of 1978 and, through telephone interviews, obtained data on the nature of sexuality in their workplace. The researchers examined five categories of social-sexual behaviors in order to study the extent to which each occurred, the extent to which each was seen as sexual harassment, and the characteristics of sexual harassment situations in the workplace:

1. Verbal comments of a sexual nature which are perceived by the recipient as positive
2. Verbal comments of a sexual nature which are perceived by the recipient as negative
3. Nonverbal behaviors of a sexual nature (looking, leering, making gestures, touching, brushing against)
4. Requests to socialize or date in which it is clear that the recipients' refusal will hurt her or his job situation and that his or her acceptance will enhance it.
5. Requests of sexual activity where it is clear that it will hurt the recipient's job situation if she or he refuses or enhance it if she or he accepts.

The proportion of males and females who thought that each form of social-sexual behavior in the workplace is sexual harassment is shown in Table 13-8. It is first evident that males are much less likely than females to view each of the five behaviors as harassment. Perhaps the most interesting finding in Table 13-7 is that fully 24 percent of the males and 14 percent of the females did not feel that socializing as a condition of work is harassment and that 19 percent of the males and 12 percent of the females did not see sexual activity as a condition of work as harassment. These percentages reflect the extent to which sexual harassment is expected to take place in American society.

In terms of the extent of sexual harass-

TABLE 13-8
The types of behaviors seen as sexual harassment in the workplace.

Social-Sexual Behavior	Persons Calling Behavior Sexual Harassment	
	Males (%)	Females (%)
Positive verbal comments	11	27
Negative verbal comments	48	63
Nonverbal sexual behaviors	35	65
Socializing as a condition of job	76	86
Sexual activity as a condition of job	81	88

Source: Gutek et al. (1981, table 1).

ment, it is obvious that sexual harassment in the workplace is not something that happens only to women. As shown in Table 13-9, women are more likely than men to receive negative verbal harassment, but the differences between males and females in the experience of other types of harassment are minimal.

Respondents were also asked about the characteristics of those who had initiated sexual harassment against them. Males described females who had harassed them as young, attractive, and not known by them for very long.

TABLE 13-9
Persons in Los Angeles sample who have experienced different types of sexual harassment in the workplace.

Type of Harassment	Persons Who Have Experienced Behavior	
	Males (%)	Females (%)
Positive verbal comments	45	47
Negative verbal comments	14	24
Nonverbal sexual behaviors	31	33
Socializing as a condition of job	6	9
Sexual activity as a condition of job	6	11

Source: Gutek et al. (1981, table 2).

Females, on the other hand, described male harassers as much older, not particularly attractive, and behaving this way toward other women. Due to the average differences in job position between men and women, females were much more likely to be sexually harassed by their supervisors than were men.

Sexual harassment frequently begins even before the first day of work. It is no secret that in many companies, one unwritten criterion for being hired is one's sexual attractiveness. The jokes in male-oriented magazines are legend and reflect a frequent reality. While the advantages on the job market for the young, sexually attractive woman may appear to be beneficial, they frequently turn into disadvantages. One of my friends who grew tired of having her body become the prime target of her boss's attentions took another position which offered a high salary and worldwide travel as an executive secretary. Her delight with the career opportunity suddenly turned to anger and frustration when she discovered, the first week on the job, that her scheduled trip to Italy involved more than secretarial skills. When she stated that she had no interest in being a traveling mistress, she was assigned a lower-paying position which involved never leaving the office.

While popular magazines extol the virtues of gaining the young, sexy, and single boss's sexual attention in the workplace, this romantic image is most frequently not what happens. In the *Redbook* study, the typical situation was a woman in her twenties being sexually sought by a male in his sixties (Safran, 1976).

The effects of sexual harassment on the job While many might respond that "a little fun never hurt anyone," there is no fun in sexual harassment. Usually the woman's initial reaction is one of anger and disbelief. Over time, severe emotional reactions develop which affect not only one's work, but life in general. Rightfully, suspicion of men in general may develop, the first thought being, "What does he want?" There is also a terrifying feeling of being alone and trapped, of being powerless with nowhere to turn. Reports to superiors may be laughed off or seized as an opportunity to instigate sexual harassment by the superior himself.

"I went to the personnel manager with a complaint that two men were propositioning me. He promised to take immediate action. When I got up to leave, he grabbed my breast and said, 'Be nice to me and I'll take care of you'." (Quoted by MacKinnon, 1979:49)

Perhaps even more damaging is that the female employee is left unsure about her job performance and ability. If she does concede to sexual activity as a condition of employment or promotion, she never knows if she could have made it on performance alone. If she does not agree to the sexual bargain, she may face massive assaults in her work performance evaluation regardless of her actual level of ability. Such processes serve, of course, to affect the long-range status of women in society, since they encourage the evaluation of one's worth on the basis of one's sexuality, not on the basis of one's nonsexual attributes.

One outcome of many instances of sexual harassment is that the person quits the job in order to escape. In 1981, the Merit Systems Board of the federal government conducted a study of sexual harassment among federal workers. It was found that approximately 18,000 women had left some federal job as a result of sexual harassment. Apart from the personal anguish it causes, such harassment and its consequences are estimated to cost the government $95 million a year in the replacement of workers who quit, loss of productivity, medical bills, and sick leave (*Seattle Times,* April 29, 1981).

The bases of sexual harassment Sexual harassment is still considered a legitimate form of conduct by many males. As part of the idea of sexual access rights, many men consider the verbal and staring forms of harassment as just "part of the job" and a compliment rather than an annoyance. A woman who raises objections may, in fact, be labeled sexually, if not socially, "abnormal." This tradition of sexual harassment makes it difficult to bring about changes since people have difficulty even defining it as a problem.

Sexual harassment is facilitated by the status of women in the world of work. They are overwhelmingly in low-status positions in any occupational area. They are therefore dependent upon the approval and good will of the males who tend to occupy the supervisor and managerial positions in order to maintain or advance their careers. This structure boils down to simple direct economic power over women in the workplace—power which a male superior can easily use in an attempt to obtain sexual access to an uninterested and unwilling female.

Legal changes The first case of sexual harassment came to court in the United States in the trial of Jane Corne and Adrienne Tomkins versus Bausch and Lomb in 1975; it was followed in 1976 with *Miller vs. Bank of America* (MacKinnon, 1979:59). In both cases, the charges were sex discrimination. In both cases, the court decided that sexual harrassment was not sex discrimination because the acts were not sufficiently connected to the workplace and the job. In the case of *Corne vs. Bausch and Lomb,* the sexual advances were seen by the court as "a personal proclivity, peculiarity or mannerism" (MacKinnon, 1979:59) and as not based on sex because Corne could just as easily have made the advances toward the male as the male toward her. This court attitude has largely remained intact. Cases of sexual harassment are now heard more often by the courts, but often in a superficial manner with the advances treated not as denial of equality under the law but as "personal whims" and "natural inclinations."

In more recent years, court decisions have moved in the direction of the legal issues involved, and in 1980 the Equal Employment Opportunities Commission of the federal government issued federal guidelines of what constitutes sexual harassment, based on the 1964 Civil Rights Act. Presently, organizations can be held liable for the sexual harassment activities of their employees and contractors.

Sexual Harassment in College

Even though the greatest concentration of researchers in this society is to be found in the colleges and universities, we have almost no published research on the sexual harassment of college students by professors or professors by students. Even though the "A's for lays" rumor has circulated for years, we have apparently been hesitant to look inside our own environment on this issue.

One of the very few inquiries is a study of persons completing graduate programs in psychology (Pope et al., 1979). This was a nationwide sample of the members of the Psychotherapy Section of the American Psychological Association. Thus, the extent to which it is representative of students in other fields or of undergraduates is unknown. More important, this study does not deal with sexual harassment, but only with sexual activity between professors and students. There is an obviously significant distinction between the two since consensual sexual activity is not sexual harassment. In this study, 10 percent of the respondents reported having sexual relations with their professors when they were students. This proportion had also increased over time. One-quarter of the most recent graduates in the study had sexual contact with their professors, but this was true of only 5 percent of those who had obtained their degrees more than twenty-one years ago.

Female students are more likely to have sexual contact with their professors than are male students. In the psychologists' study, 3 percent of the male and 17 percent of the female students reported sexual activity with their professors. Moving from overt sexual activity to more subtle forms of sexual interaction, 14 percent of the males and 60 percent of the females reported that they had experienced "seductive" attention from their professors, administrators, or supervisors. Such activities consisted of flirting, sexual joking, excessive attention, and touching.

Looking at the matter from the other side, 13 percent of the professors reported having sexual relationships with their students. The gender differences here are as expected: 19 percent of the male professors and 8 percent of the female professors had sexual relationships with their students. In an unpublished study by a student at California State

University-San Francisco in 1973 (cited by Pope et al., 1979), 50 percent of the faculty who answered a questionnaire said they would never have a sexual affair with a student. Another 25 percent reported they had engaged in sex with a student and 25 percent said they had never done so but would not turn down the opportunity.

In the most recent study of student-faculty sexual interaction, Skeen (1981) found that the largest number of such relationships involved a female student and a male professor but that sexual coercion was not the norm. Skeen found that only 1 percent of the relationships involved any sexual coercion. The majority of people involved (82 percent of the students and 64 percent of the professors) said they would be willing to become involved in such a relationship again. Quite the opposite of sexual coercion, the student-faculty relationships studied by Skeen were found to be characterized by strong affection and mutual respect between the partners.

The college environment has a number of characteristics which facilitate possible sexual interaction between students and professors. The intellectual excitement generated in the process of learning can be very stimulating and even romantic. Such excitement takes place at a point in the student's life when she (much more commonly than he) is expanding her freedom of behavior and thought and exploring her sexuality. The professor may well be a person she admires and respects on an intellectual and interpersonal level. The very nature of student-professor interaction frequently involves time for conversation, exploration, and idea exchange. Such a communicative environment maximizes the possibility of sexual attraction.

There is also, however, the possibility that what appears from the professor's viewpoint to be consensual sexual activity is actually a form of subtle coercion. A professor has a great deal of power and status. What may appear to be a consensual relationship between a student and a professor may involve the student's hesitation to not show interest for fear of endangering her intellectual relationship, academic standing, or professional opportunities. Professors have an ethical responsibility either to refrain from such relationships or to stand guard over the events to ensure that sexual coercion is not occurring. It is clear that a professor's trading grades and academic survival for sex is a violation of academic professional (and interpersonal) ethics. It is not clear, however, that two adults should be prohibited from developing a mature, responsible, nonmanipulative, and rewarding relationship simply because of their respective positions and occupations in society. Most college and university faculty would, however, probably take strong exception to this last statement.

STUDY GUIDE

TERMS TO KNOW

In this chapter it is more helpful if you test yourself by answering questions about certain concepts rather than by defining specific terms. The reason is that this chapter contains many important concepts that are not summarized by a single one-word term. You should be able to answer all the questions below. For those you have difficulty with, go back and review the relevant part of the chapter.

1. What is wrong with the term "date rape"?
2. Describe how each of the following is a social basis of rape: seeing victims and assailants; gender; the frequency of forced sex; the approval of forced sex.
3. Describe the concept of male sexual access rights and list the five conditions under which males are often assumed to have these rights to females in American society.

4. Describe some of the factors related to attributing responsibility to rape victims and the ways in which males and females differ in their views of rape and rape victims.
5. It was argued that the bases of rape are common in American society (question 2) and that it is more useful to think about what inhibits rape rather than what forces people to engage in rape. Describe the evidence for this contention.
6. Describe the continuum of the different types of rapes and rapists.
7. Describe the effects of rape on female sexuality, why these effects occur, and what processes are important (and why) in helping the rape victim make a successful reentry into sexuality.
8. Describe what is meant by proclivity to rape and what evidence there is for some males having a proclivity to rape.
9. Describe the different types of sexual coercion of children.

SELF-TEST

Part I: True-False Statements

1. In Giarrusso's research with high school students, a substantial minority of males, but almost no females, approved of rape under certain conditions.
2. Rape victims are judged to be responsible for the rape to the extent that they are seen as doing something to activate male sexual access rights.
3. Males and females do not differ in attributing responsibility to rape victims.
4. Malamuth, in a study of male college students, found that a majority of them said that they would be at least somewhat likely to rape a female If they could be assured of not being punished.
5. The expectancy effect of alcohol is found in male sexual arousal to rape depictions in that males who think they have consumed alcohol are as aroused by depictions of rape as by depictions of mutually consenting sexual activity.
6. The majority of female college students worry about being sexually assaulted.
7. The most important factor in how traumatic sexual coercion is for a child is the amount of force involved in the coercion.
8. Most children or young adolescents who have had a sexual experience with a brother or sister report that the experience was negative in nature.
9. Only a minority of all cases of incest involving a female child involve the father.
10. People who sexually harass persons of the other sex in the workplace have the same characteristics whether they are male or female.

Part II: Multiple-Choice Questions
Select the best of the three alternatives.

1. Those women most likely to be victims of stranger-stranger rape are between the ages of (a) 16 and 24; (b) 20 and 34; (c) 25 and 34.
2. The number of rapes that actually take place in the United States each year is approximately (a) 171,000; (b) 500,000; (c) 3.5 million.
3. The majority of convicted rapists are (a) anger rapists; (b) group rapists; (c) power rapists.
4. Rape trauma is (a) less severe for females who are more sexually experienced than for those with less sexual experience; (b) the most severe for those females who have never had intercourse prior to the rape; (c) not related in its severity to the victim's sexual experience.
5. Research on college students who report having been sexually coerced as children reveals that males are most likely to be sexually coerced by   and females are most likely to be sexually coerced by   .(a) an acquaintance/ a family member; (b) a stranger/ a stranger; (c) a family member/ an acquaintance.
6. In power rape the primary interest of the rapist is to (a) obtain sexual arousal and activity; (b) demonstrate to himself and the victim that he has more power and control than does a woman; (c) brutalize the victim physically.

7. The single most important factor in predicting which males will say that they would be likely to rape a female is *(a)* their perception of what other males would do; *(b)* the ease with which they become sexually aroused; *(c)* their marital status.

TOPICS FOR DISCUSSION

Design what you think would be the most effective program for the prevention of rape in the United States. Describe what, ideally, you would do, why you would do it, why it would prevent rape, and what obstacles would stand in the way of your making these changes.

In this chapter we have discussed the concept of male sexual access rights and how it is related to the existence of rape and to the approval of rape by a substantial minority of males and females. Discuss the sexual access rights conditions described in this chapter, citing specific examples of how individuals learn the view that males have sexual access rights to females under certain conditions.

SUGGESTED READINGS

Groth, A. N., *Men Who Rape.* New York: Plenum Press, 1979.

This is an excellent study of power and anger rapists and their characteristics. As in much research on rapists, it does not deal with those who were not caught and convicted, but discusses only a select type of rapist—the power and anger rapist.

Finkelhor, D., *Sexually Victimized Children.* New York: Free Press, 1979.

This, the single best study on sexually victimized children, is essential reading for anyone interested in this topic.

If you have an interest in studying the social bases of rape and the proclivity to rape in American society, you should consult the *Social Science Citation Index* in your library for the recent research in this area. This is an active field of research, and undoubtedly you will find more recent research than has been reviewed in this chapter.

KEY TO SELF-TEST

Part I: True-False Statements

1. F (Males were more likely to approve than were females, but a significant minority of both males and females approved of rape under certain male sexual access right conditions. Think back to our earlier discussion of sexual learning as a member of a society and a particular social group or category.)

2. T

3. F (While both males and females attribute responsibility to rape victims on the basis of question 2, males are much more likely to do so.)

4. T   **5.** T   **6.** T   **7.** T   **8.** F

9. T (These cases get the most publicity, but are a small proportion of all incest cases.)

10. F (What are the characteristics of the typical male and female who sexually harass others?)

Part II: Multiple-Choice Questions

1. *a*

2. *c* (Official estimates count only certain types of rapes.)

3. *c* (This is why studying convicted rapists gives biased information about the nature of rape.)

4. *c* (Rape trauma is not caused by the sex but by the fear and violence.)

5. *a*

6. *b* (What type of rapist is *a*? And *c*?)

7. *a* (This shows the importance of male peer support for various sexual acts.)

Chapter 14
The Sex Business

We have noted the tremendous diversity in the meanings, forms, and uses of sexuality among humans. A significant part of this diversity is that sex sells. Many types of sexuality can be a commodity—something that is bought and sold in the marketplace.

The world of commercial sex takes many different forms. The most common is selling a certain product which does not have sex as its basic meaning, purpose, or appearance by associating it with sexuality. Examples here are plentiful, including everything from designer jeans to automobiles. Of course, what is being sold here is the advertised product, but what is also subtly being sold is the sexual meaning the marketing efforts attach to the product. Thus consumers are encouraged to purchase the product because it is implied that the product will somehow make their lives more sexually rich, full, or satisfying.[1]

The term "commercial sex" is more often associated, however, with a more blatant purchasable sex, where one pays to obtain sexual stimulation in some direct form. In both these major forms of commercial sex, the primary purpose is the same: to make money. Few people are in the sex business (be it selling floor wax with sex appeal, detailed photographs of intercourse, or one's body) for philosophical reasons. This is an important point in understanding the structure and content of the world of commercial sex.

In this chapter, we shall discuss the major forms of commercial sex, which consist of sexually explicit materials ranging from magazines to live sex shows. In Chapter 15 we shall explore a specific part of the sex business, prostitution. In all these forms, the theme is basically the same. The product is marketed to create sexual stimulation. The difference in products is a matter of degree as well as kind. In products such as *Playboy,* many interests are tapped other than the sexual. In other magazines, the consumer's interest is purely to be sexually aroused, as is the case with films and other products of the sex business. The various sexual stimuli sold in the sex business also differ in explicitness and distance. With magazines, consumers largely purchase sexually arousing photographs. With films, they purchase moving photographs. With a live sex show, they purchase live actors. With prostitu-

[1] For a discussion of how the advertising industry developed males into sexual objects see: "Beefcake: How the Media Turned Men into Sex Objects," *Mademoiselle,* December 1981, pp. 126–128; 200.

Perhaps the most common form of commercial sex is using sexuality to sell a product.

tion, they purchase another person's body. In much of the more explicit sex business, the consumer also purchases the stimulus for the purpose of being aroused to the point of orgasm. The magazine may provide a stimulus during masturbation. The film may provide moving photographs for the same purpose, the live sex show real people, and prostitution a touchable person.

PORNOGRAPHY: WHAT IS IT?

The term "pornography" comes from the Greek *graphein* (writing about or writing of) and *porné* (prostitute). While this definition is precise, it is of little value since the term is rarely used today to refer to works of, or about, prostitutes.

The terms "pornographic" and "pornography" are most commonly attached to *hardcore* sexual material. The word "hardcore" usually means that the material leaves nothing to the imagination. Depending on the medium, hardcore material involves detailed discussions, photographs, or live presentations of sexual activity and the body parts involved in that activity. The second major category of sexual material is usually referred to as *softcore*. Softcore material, which is most often found on the newsstand magazine racks, shows nudity (most often female) and perhaps simulated or suggested sexual activity. R and X-rated films are softcore, XX and XXX films are hardcore.

It would be convenient to have a precise scientific definition of where pornography fits with respect to these two types of sexual materials. This, however, is not possible since what people define as pornographic varies greatly from one person to the next according to certain individual characteristics.

One of the best examples of the diversity in what people call pornography is found in a study by Brown et al. (1978a). In this research, a random sample of adults from a city in the western United States rated a series of photographs as to whether each was pornographic. As shown in Table 14-1, 79 percent agreed that two nude males petting was pornographic, but only 53 percent said that two nude females embracing was pornographic. At the other end, 13 percent said that one of Leonardo Da Vinci's paintings of Christ was pornography. What is one person's erotica (or art) is another person's smut.

In this chapter we shall not use the term "pornography" except to refer to material so called by the hardcore sex business itself. Instead, we shall use the term "sexually explicit material." Such material may take many forms, from the written or recorded word to still or moving pictures to objects and articles to live people. Some sexually explicit material may be defined by some as pornographic, by others as erotic, and by yet others as neither.

RESTRICTIONS ON SEXUALLY EXPLICIT MATERIAL

Throughout the history of American society, attempts have been made to deal with the question of restricting sexually explicit materials. They have consisted of legal debates and social movements, which are both still very much with us today.

TABLE 14-1
Adults rating various photographs as pornographic.

Picture Content	Adults Seeing Content as Pornographic (%)
Two nude males petting	79
Female performing fellatio on male	77
Male and female engaged in coitus, she on top, genitals showing	71
Two nude females embracing astride a third nude female	53
Male eating grapes in female genital area	52
Nude female on bed with genitals exposed	51
Nude male standing with genitals exposed	50
Female figurines in apparent sexual position	48
Nude male and female kissing and embracing	47
Male kissing breast of female with her shirt open	42
Nude female, side exposure with pubic hair visible	37
Nude male with pubic hair but not genitals showing	36
Nude female, frontal exposure of breasts	34
Rear exposure of three nude females jumping	32
Japanese print of dressed male and female in coital position	25
Male and female in bathing suits	25
Five males nude except socks and sunglasses, no genital exposure	22
Cartoon of knight urinating nuts and bolts	18
Drawing of infant with hand inside front of diaper	17
Rear exposure of nude male bathing, wife cooking and child playing	15
Female nursing infant	13
Leonardo Da Vinci's Christ	13
Renaissance painting of female nursing child by a stream	11
Couple kissing, faces only showing	11
Female in one-piece bathing suit	8

Source: Brown et al. (1978a, p. 88–89, table 2).

The Legal Debate

The first attempt to legally restrict sexually explicit material in America was a 1711 Massachusetts law which dealt with including sexual material in religious writings (Lipton, 1976). By the middle of the 1800s, most states had some type of law regarding sexually explicit material.

The Comstock Act Perhaps the single most important piece of legislation regarding sexually explicit material was the Comstock Act of 1873 (see Chapter 12). This law was widely used to censor sexually explicit materials of all types and in many states "little Comstock laws" are still being enforced.

The Supreme Court Beginning in the early 1950s, the Comstock Act and the "little Comstock laws" became increasingly controversial as the United States began to ease toward the so-called sexual revolution of the 1960s (see Chapter 1). This legal controversy reached a peak in 1957 when the Supreme Court gave its ruling on the case of *Roth vs. the United States.* In its decision, the Court attempted to provide the first federal ruling on what was obscene. It ruled that the test for obscenity was "whether, to the average person, applying contemporary community standards, the dominant theme of the material, taken as a whole, appeals to prurient (depraved or sick) interests." Slightly later, the Court added that the material must be "utterly without redeeming social importance."

As you might expect, this definition became the basis for numerous legal debates in obscenity trials. The problem, however, was that the terms could not be precisely defined. The result was a legal bog. Who is the "average person"? What exactly is "a community"? How do you determine "community standards"? What is "prurient" in terms of sexual interests? How do you measure the "social importance" of something?

On June 21, 1973, the Supreme Court gave its ruling on three separate obscenity cases. These rulings came to be known as the Miller decision (*Miller vs. California* was one of the cases). This decision slightly clarified some of the terms in the Roth decision, but further confused others. In a close (4 to 5) vote, the Court stated that the Roth ruling did not violate the First Amendment; the word "utterly" was removed and was replaced by "serious literary, artistic, political, or scientific value." The Court further ruled that a state falls in the category of "community," and thus states could devise their own obscenity laws. Such laws had to include, however, a statement on the kind of conduct portrayed in the sexually explicit material which qualified it as obscene. This same stipulation was also applied to city and county laws.

Effects of the Supreme Court decisions As you might expect, most conservatives saw the 1973 decision as too lenient. Given the earlier decision by the Supreme Court that year regarding abortion (Chapter 12), they were convinced that the morals of the country were in a state of ruin—with the aid of a liberal Supreme Court.

The principal outcome of these Court decisions was to "localize" the nature of obscenity and pornography. Whether one is charged, tried, and convicted depends largely on the sexual-political climate of the region in which the material is presented. For example, *Hustler* magazine is available on almost any newsstand in almost any city in the country. In 1976, however, Larry Flynt, the publisher of *Hustler,* was sentenced to thirteen months to twenty-five years in jail in Cincinnati, Ohio. Today, producers, distributors, and actors in hardcore films are often tried and convicted of obscenity in one city while their film is drawing crowds a few miles down the road. What is one person's erotica is another person's smut is clearly the legal status of obscenity laws today.

Social Movements

While the legal system has struggled with the question of obscenity in dealing with sexually explicit material, a number of social movements have attempted to limit, censor, or completely remove sexual materials from public access. In many cases, these movements have, in part, been responses to the frustration of some individuals with the legal system.

Based on politics and religion In the 1860s, California was experiencing the rise of the League of Deliverance. This organization, an outgrowth of the vigilante movement of the time, devoted its energy to stomping out what were seen as "vices" and "social evils" brought about by the gold rush of the 1850s. On the list of evils was sexually explicit material (as well as the Chinese and other minority groups) (Mauss, 1975). At about the same time this was taking place on the West Coast, Anthony Comstock and his followers were effectively managing to suppress sexual material in the East and Midwest.

As Mauss (1975) points out, some recent antipornography movements have their roots in these early efforts. In the 1950s, a number of large organizations appeared with the purpose of limiting sexually explicit material (often placing sex education in this category). American society saw the powerful and effective anti-Communist movement led by Senator Joseph McCarthy. Anyone suspected of aiding the "Communist conspiracy to overthrow America" was branded subversive and a threat to the American way of life. Sexually explicit material (and homosexuality, sex education, Alfred Kinsey, etc.) were labeled as part of this subversion—perhaps even as part of the Communist plot to undermine the moral fiber of the country. This fear of sexual material became organized through several nationwide, politically conservative groups, most of which had some connection with a conservative religious group or set of beliefs. Among the most active organizations was Citizens for Decent Literature—founded, as Larry Flynt should have known, in Cincinnati, Ohio. This organization, like many others, maintained a very large budget and a tax-exempt status. Other organizations that waged war against sexual materials included Morality in Media, the John Birch Society, and even the Ku Klux Klan.

These antipornography organizations lost their effectiveness in the 1960s when their attempts were not supported by Supreme Court decision or public sympathy. The Roth decision by the Supreme Court was a major defeat, and during the late 1950s and 1960s, Americans began to consume more, not less, sexual material (recall Chapter 1).

Without federal legal support or society-wide sentiment in their favor, these organizations were left with highly localized victories. Even these local victories, which infrequently appeared through the 1970s, were often seen as not worth the effort. For example, in 1980 a Federal District judge finally dismissed obscenity charges against ten individuals and five corporations for their involvement in the hardcore film *Deep Throat*. This was the end of a long series of trials which cost the state taxpayers 85 million (*Playboy,* February 1980: 57).

In recent years, we have seen the revitalization of conservative politics- and religion-based organizations against sexually explicit material in the form of the Moral Majority. While the long-term effectiveness of this new (but yet old) movement remains to be seen, its prognosis is dim. While being locally successful in some areas of the country and nationally successful in efforts such as television, the movement will fail for a variety of reasons. First, the Supreme Court rulings exist and the Court never changes its mind. It *is* the Supreme Court and the Supreme Court does not, by definition, make mistakes. Second, as many polls reveal, there is little public support for all the tenets of the Moral Majority. In the early 1980s, the organization was successfully riding a wave of popular conservatism and finding people who supported this or that point. Shortly, however, the same pattern will reappear, as it has since the 1800s. Conservatism will be replaced by more liberal views, and the universally conservative views of this organization will drive away most of its public support.

It is important to note that these organizations wage their war against sexually explicit material largely because it is a symbol of threat to a traditional social structure and lifestyle which they feel is endangered (Zurcher et al., 1973). Sexually explicit material is simply an easy target; it symbolizes a much larger set of concerns and discontents. (Note that the same has been found true of those who oppose sex education in the schools) (Richardson and Cranston, 1981).

One of the results of the feminist-based movement against pornography has been large-scale marches in protest against hardcore, sexually explicit material.

The feminist-based movement

During the late 1970s another major social movement rose up against sexually explicit material. Feminists began to speak out, charging that such material is sexist propaganda that humiliates and shows contempt for women while at the same time inspiring, or at least reinforcing, psychological degradation and physical danger of women (Morgan, 1978).

This movement has been highly splintered. Some feminists argue against any suppression of sexually explicit material. Other feminist leaders argue that strict controls should be levied on sexually explicit materials which depict violence against women or show women as sexual objects. Others argue that almost any material which provides sexually toned pictures of women should be suppressed because

they are male constructions and cast women as sexual objects.

Regardless of these differences, a number of organizations have developed to fight various forms of sexually explicit material: Women Against Violence Against Women, Women Against Violence in Pornography and Media, and Women for the Abolition of Pornography are but a few. The strategies of these various groups have differed greatly. Many publish newsletters and write articles describing their targets and the means to be used in fighting sexually explicit material. These suggested strategies have ranged from political action to boycotts of businesses selling magazines and records with offensive covers to taking photographs of customers to violence and vandalism. In 1979, for example, Marcia Womangold fired a rifle shot through a window of a respectable Harvard Square bookstore because it sold *Playboy, Penthouse,* and *Oui* magazines.

More peaceful actions have included "Take Back the Night" marches in the pornography districts of major cities. On October 10, 1979, for example, some 5,000 protesters marched into the Times Square area of New York City. Women Against Pornography routinely conducts tours of the Times Square area, pointing out the depictions of violence against women.

Effects of the feminist-based movement The feminist movement against sexually explicit material has raised a number of important issues, not the least of which has been the portrayal of women as sexual objects rather than sexual beings. However, since the 1950s no campaign against sexually explicit material has ever been able to produce anything more than sporadic irritation for the sex business and a great deal of public discussion. This appears to be the fate of this movement.

There have been some small victories for this movement but not in the hardcore sex industry. Hardcore businesses which sell magazines, books, films, and live sex shows are not influenced by protests, marches, posters, spray paint, or even rifle shots. They reap too much profit to let such minor irritations become an issue. Second, these businesses, and many of their customers, are not likely to be sympathetic to either the values of the women's movement in general or the ideology behind the attempts to suppress sexually explicit ma-

terial. Third, there is simply not enough widespread support among the American public for the suppression of sexually explicit material (Table 14-2). Fourth, what support does exist for the suppression of sexually explicit material is not friendly to the women's movement. When we examine, through national survey data, who in the general population is in favor of legal restrictions being placed on sexual material and who is supportive of the women's movement, we find that they are not the same people. Those most likely to favor restricting sexually explicit material do not favor the women's movement and those who favor the women's movement do not favor restricting sexually explicit material (Mahoney, 1981).

Issues in Restricting Sexually Explicit Material

In most of the products of the world of commercial sex, it is easy to see that women (and men to a considerable extent) are regarded as breasts, buttocks, genitals, hair, legs, and other body parts, but not as whole beings. Even the most respectable of popular magazines often present women as sexual objects and not sexual beings by fragmenting women (and men) into so many body parts carrying sexual meaning.

The real issue here is not whether such depictions exist (in many media forms), but what, if anything, should be done. At one ex-

TABLE 14-2
What Americans think about sexually explicit material.

Statement	Adult Americans Who Believe This Statement, %
Sexual materials provide information about sex.	63
Sexual materials lead to a breakdown in morals.	65
Sexual materials lead people to commit rape.	57
Sexual materials provide an outlet for bottled-up impulses.	69
There should be laws against the distribution of pornography whatever the consumer's age.	41
There should be laws against the distribution of pornography to persons under age 18.	53
There should be no laws forbidding the distribution of pornography.	6

Source: Data from Davis (1980), in a spring, 1980, probability sample of the United States population 18 or more years old not living in an institution.

treme, people argue that the First Amendment should not in any way be threatened because doing so would open the door for censoring anything those in power wish to censor. At the other extreme are those who argue that the intention of the First Amendment does not apply to hardcore sexual material and that the only moral and appropriate alternative is to censor such material.

The questions here are difficult and worth considering. It is very easy to agree with censorship when the target is something we personally find offensive. I assume that most of us would agree that pictures of women being strangled, beaten, and raped should be censored and that hardcore material featuring children is disgusting and should be abolished by law in any civilized society that values human dignity and rights. However, what else do we abolish? While you and your classmates may agree on the patent offensiveness of the above material, you will find that your consensus about what to censor suddenly disappears as you move toward more "acceptable" content. What about a hardcore film where a male and

female are obviously enjoying intercourse and oral sex? What about *Hustler* magazine? *Penthouse? Playboy? Cosmopolitan? Vogue?* What about makeup, lipstick, clothing, and automobile advertisements? What about movie magazines and gossip newspapers and popular television shows? You will find little agreement about where to draw the line or what the criteria for censorship should be.

Now, assuming that we cannot agree on where to draw the line, whom are we going to let draw it for us? Can I decide? Can the Moral Majority decide for us? How about your local pornography dealer? Who?

There is also the question of changing standards. What may be offensive to many today may well be perfectly acceptable in five years, or the other way around. For example, magazines containing photographs of female pubic regions were not sold in grocery stores ten years ago, but they are available in all but the most stodgy of supermarkets today. While a photograph of the bare female breast caused *Playboy* legal problems in the 1950s, magazines with photographs of women with their

Definitions of what is sexually explicit and what is acceptable change radically over time. These women are talking to Chicago policewomen about violating 1922 Chicago laws regarding the wearing of revealing bathing suits.

fingers in the vagina are now common in supermarket magazine racks.

Censorship is often regarded as a good thing as long as we can censor what we do not like and have those things we do like free from the censorship of others. Censorship, however, tends not to be so convenient or specific. Shea (1980) has made the point that in those cities in which sexually explicit businesses are allowed to operate, we are likely to find a strong women's movement. *Ms.* magazine has been the victim of censorship in the same cities in which you are not likely to find much sexually explicit material for sale. This censorship of *Ms.* is not being done by the local pornographers but by the censors, those who censor anything they do not agree with, be it equality for women or hardcore sex. What we are dealing with on this issue is basically freedom, the freedom to speak, print, and film no matter how much the content may be repulsive to some. There can be no doubt that *Ms.* magazine creates as much disgust in some Americans as hardcore sex does in others. One of the ironical aspects of the feminist-based debate on suppressing sexually explicit material is that the Comstock Act, which was used to persecute and censor Margaret Sanger and her followers, was the same law which led to obscenity convictions against hardcore films in the 1970s.

The Effects of Restricting Sexually Explicit Material

Zoning sex   Many cities have become concerned over the presence of hardcore sex businesses. In an effort to control such enterprises, they have created "combat zones," or areas of the city to which hardcore businesses are restricted. The experiment has generally been declared a failure since the result is most often to establish an area where a variety of illegal and socially undesirable activities gather. A new tactic has been to disperse hardcore business, but it has resulted in neighborhood resistance (perhaps most of the resistance is to a business painted dayglow orange).

Prohibition   Fromkin and Brock (1973) suggested that, according to commodity theory, restricting the availability of sexually explicit material would make it more desirable. Experimental research by Zellinger et al. (1975) and Jones and Joe (1980) supported this assumption. When you restrict sexually explicit material, individuals have more desire to view it.

Exposure   On the other side of the coin, research reveals that continual exposure to sexually explicit material results in the material's losing its intrigue and arousal value. This is the result of satiation. This appears to be what happened in Denmark on a national scale. When the legal restraints on sexually explicit material were lifted in Denmark, hardcore sales skyrocketed. After a short time, however, sales declined and have continued this trend. The result has been a significant drop in the number of pornography businesses.

TYPES OF SEXUALLY EXPLICIT MATERIAL

Within the sex business there are various types of sexually explicit material. The diversity, organization, and character of this business and its material are outlined here since it is important to gain an understanding of this aspect of sexuality in American society.

Magazines
The most common type of sexually explicit material appears in magazines. They cover a wide range of materials and they tend to be specialized around the diverse interests of the market. (For an interesting and humorous, but now dated, review of the different softcore magazines, see *Esquire,* November 1973, "The Skin Book Boom: What Have They Done to the Girl Next Door?") The content of magazines is largely governed by demand. What you see is what sells.

Softcore magazines   In the 1970s when the "skin book boom" took place, the market exploded with publications testing consumer interests. Currently, the market is large and diverse. There are magazines specializing in "pink" (close-ups of female genitals) and those which have built sales by favoring buttocks, legs, very large breasts, garter belts, and female homosexual activity. One recent variation in this market has been the "sex news" magazine. These publications feature photographic coverage of events in the world of sex, such as the nude this or that contest, the opening of a swingers club, amateur strip contests, wet T-shirt contests, sexually oriented parties, and the continual happenings at strip clubs and topless bars. Some publications have also become popular for sponsoring their own events. *Cheri,* for example, has its annual fellatio contest (using penis replicas for the softcore market). Other publications have specialized in telephoto nude photographs of famous women who would not otherwise pose for such publications.

The readership of many of these magazines is a steady one (repeat business is the mainstay of a publication). It is also an involved one. Many magazines have a staff of models who regularly appear and put forth the image of one big happy (and nude) family that the reader can come to know. Reader involvement in these publications is perhaps best shown by the "woman next door" photo sections in which readers send in nude photographs of women friends to be published in the magazine.

There is also a clear "star" phenomenon in the softcore magazine market. Readers often purchase an issue because of a photograph of a favorite model. They do so whether the model appears in *Playboy* or lesser known magazines.

In a small but important way, women have entered the softcore magazine field as both consumers of softcore magazines for women (*Playgirl*) and editors of magazines for males (see Deming, 1981, for a discussion).

The softcore magazine market in the United States is substantial. In 1981, the ten best-selling magazines had a total monthly circulation of over 16 million, and in 1979 they had brought in over $500 million in profit (Serrin, 1981). A large part of this profit is from a substantial mark-up, normally in the range of 100 percent.

Hardcore magazines   Within the hardcore magazine business there is even more diversity. There are few limits, other than demand, on the type of material which can be displayed on the "adult bookstore" shelf. Specialization here is even greater than for softcore magazines, covering consumer interests ranging from oral sex to ejaculation, anal sex, female and male homosexual activity, to group sex, different ethnic groups, sadomasochistic activity, bondage and discipline, animal-human sex, and many others.

The star phenomenon is also present and important in hardcore magazines but takes a different twist. Certain men and women achieve a star status which is often derived from their hardcore film appearances. A common magazine format is composed of stills from a film. In this way, the fan of a certain hardcore star can purchase the photographed fantasy that rapidly passed by on the screen in the hardcore theater.

The profit in hardcore magazines is even greater than in softcore, with mark-up as high as 600 percent and prices ranging up to $20 or more a copy. It is estimated that there are approximately 20,000 hardcore magazine stores in the United States. If run properly, such an establishment will have $150,000 to $200,000 a year in gross sales (Serrin, 1981).

It is important to note that the hardcore magazine business is firmly integrated with more legitimate and respectable business interests. The most explicit of hardcore magazines are printed by respected printers and almost all stores take bank credit cards. Thus, the credit card company and the local bank both profit from the sale.

Sexually Explicit Films

Full-time hardcore theaters in the United States attract approximately 2 to 3 million customers each week; their ticket revenues total at least $10 million (Serrin, 1981).

Some keen observers have argued that one of the reasons many citizens object to commercial sex establishments is that they seldom present themselves with much "class."

A brief history   Soon after Thomas Edison invented the movie camera in 1890, people began making sexually explicit films. The earliest known of such works was placed on the market for sale in 1915. These early films displayed sexual activity taking place in a highly contrived situation in a hurried manner; this pattern remained characteristic of the clandestine sexually explicit film until the mid-1970s. Compared with the hardcore films of today, the sexual activity was tame, quick, and even humorous. Over time, hardcore films remained technically low in quality and followed a standard script. Frequently the male would be dressed only in black socks and a mask. Burglars were a favorite male role since the mask could be worn to hide one's identity and

the film would not appear totally absurd. The sexual arousal of the woman was often depicted as coming about when she saw the male's wondrous organ—and rape myths were common fare. She would be lying on the bed. He would enter the room. She would resist and then become highly aroused.

None of the participants in these films appeared to be very enthusiastic; there was little foreplay and even less indication that people were engaging in enjoyable interaction with each other. This rather grim situation was rounded out by participants who were somewhat less than sexually attractive or skilled.

From the 1930s through the 1950s, hardcore films remained in the form of these "stag" films (so named because they were most often

Sex appeared in early twentieth-century films with regularity. The bath scene was a common element, and scenes such as this from the film *A Man's World* in 1918 resulted in the film industry imposing a strict code regarding sex in films.

purchased under the counter from someone who knew someone and shown to all-male groups or organizations—there were no hardcore theaters or peep shows as today). There were also a large number of films showing only female nudity.

In 1959, Americans received a sneak preview of what the future was to hold in sex films. Russ Meyer produced a movie entitled *The Immoral Mr. Teas.* This was a softcore color film that was technically rather well done and actually had a plot featuring attractive actors. The story focused on a shy man who comes to own a pair of glasses which allow him to see through walls and clothes. The rest is obvious. The significance of this film is that it applied some basics of the legitimate film (color, story, attractive actors, humor) to a sexually explicit—in this case, nudity only—film. The result was that the film was inexpen-

sive to make and turned a large profit. This was the first of a series of "nudie cuties," films which contained a great deal of nudity constructed around some cute gimmick.

In 1969 and 1970, the hardcore film industry began to emerge in its current form. The Mitchell brothers in San Francisco started to produce hardcore films with young and attractive performers, men and women who clearly enjoyed what they were doing. This business was not part of some back-alley production. Rather, it was an outcropping of the youth, antiestablishment movement of the late 1960s. The people involved were in touch with the counterculture movement and performers were readily available among young men and women interested in making money and doing what the 1950s establishment mentality feared most. The technical quality of these films was rather high and continued to improve; there

The modern hardcore pornography film is technically well produced and employs sexually attractive performers.

was a story line and interaction between the performers; and the diversity of sexual activity increased and became explicitly recorded on film, complete with varied camera angles, varied lighting, and close-ups.

In 1970, a foreign film, *I Am Curious Yellow,* served to partially set the stage for a revolution in hardcore movies. The film was a philosophical treatment which depicted a young couple having intercourse in a variety of public and private sites. *I Am Curious Yellow* attracted many young, educated, middle-class individuals and couples. Seeing the film was "in" even if you had no clue to its philosophical message. It was respectable to see the film because it was "not really" a sex film.

In 1973, the hardcore film industry came into its own with the production and distribution of the full-length film *Deep Throat.* There is no question that the film was sexist and oriented around male fantasies. The significance of the

film was, however, that it became very popular in respectable middle-class society and it made a great deal of money. With its humor and "novel" story, *Deep Throat* was reviewed in such publications as *Women's Wear Daily, The London Times,* the *New York Review of Books, Esquire,* and *Newsweek,* to mention a few. The featured performers became overnight stars, and for the first time, pornography performers became socially recognized. The female star, Linda Lovelace, appeared on the cover of *Esquire* magazine and was the subject of a photo layout in *Playboy.* Seeing the film became almost a requirement for residence in suburban America, and social gatherings often involved an avid discussion of the film. Lovelace had a successful talk-show tour, eventually wrote a book, and the nation discovered a new sexual technique.

Deep Throat was the beginning of "porno chic." Technically well-done films were produced in full length, with attractive performers (and today, even halfway talented actors) who left nothing to the imagination in acting out a sort of story line around a great deal of hardcore sex. *Deep Throat* revealed that America was ready for hardcore and that it was possible to make considerable money in hardcore films. The movie cost $25,000 to make, and it grossed $3 million in its first year and $50 million by 1979. Other films of this type quickly followed. *Behind The Green Door,* starring the Ivory Snow model, Marilyn Chambers, cost $45,000 to produce and grossed over $1 million in ten theaters in California alone. The hardcore film had clearly come out of hiding and into public acceptance. Today it is reported that most hardcore films will gross approximately $1.5 million to $2 million (Schipper, 1980).

The stars   Perhaps the most significant aspect of modern hardcore films is the hardcore sex star phenomenon. The hardcore film industry caters to a large clientele. In an effort to maintain and increase this market, advantage has been taken of fan enthusiasm for certain performers. As the quality of the films has improved dramatically, performers who meet certain physical or performance standards have become true stars. Many names are firmly lodged in the mind of the hardcore film customer. John Holmes (known for his 12-inch penis) had, for example, some thirty-eight fan clubs. In passing, it is interesting to note how Holmes's current name reflects the increasing respectability of hardcore films. Prior to the "porno chic" films of the 1970s, Holmes went by the name of Johnny Wadd, not exactly the type of name that allows one to be discussed seriously in reviews and respectable social gatherings.

The hardcore stars of today also have gained a kind of naughty, exciting respectability in certain segments of society. It is not uncommon to see them at socialite parties or to hear certain upper middle-class individuals speak with enthusiasm and pride about the hardcore star they met at a party or on vacation.

The importance of this star phenomenon is that satiation is a continual problem in the hardcore industry. Something has to be continually changed in the films to keep the customers coming back. It is very difficult to change the sex. As we shall see, the largest segment of the hardcore audience is mostly interested in "normal" sexual activities, and sex which reaches to the fringes of the sexual script is likely simply not to sell. The only thing you can change to attract large numbers of customers over and over again is the performers. Many men go to hardcore films for the same reason that people go to legitimate films: to see their favorite performer.

As part of this star process, certain performers now tour the country for the openings of their films. Again, the curious fascination and excitement, mixed with clear understanding that hardcore sex is "bad," are evident. When Marilyn Chambers came to Seattle for a film opening, she quickly received (and accepted) an invitation to appear on a very popular morning television talk show.

Loops In addition to full-length films, literally thousands of hardcore films are produced each year in the form of "loops." These are short (5- to 15-minute) films showing the maximum amount of sex in the shortest time with as little interference as possible from a story or dialogue. Loops involve a variety of sexual themes and are frequently specialized to tap a certain sexual interest. They often feature lesser known performers who are either working part-time or trying to enter the business.

Many loops are also produced by the businesses that show them, since it is not difficult to find performers and thus to make the profit that much greater. The loop film is usually set into a coin-operated projector in a private booth. The customer goes into the booth and as long as he places quarters in the slot, the film keeps running. (With the appearance of the new dollar coin, sometimes they are dollar machines—which emphasizes the fact that the hardcore industry has little ideological interest.) The booths are frequently located in adult bookstores and often serve as places for masturbation (Sundholm, 1977). A reel of loop film costs about $2 to make and will be sold to the store for between $20 and $30. One loop machine, costing about $600 initially, will bring in approximately $10,000 to $15,000 a year and will require almost no maintenance.

Home entertainment Both loops and full-length films are sold over the counter for home viewing. The prices of these films range from $15 to $100 each. The most recent product here has been video tapes of full-length hardcore films for home playback. In 1979, 1 million such videotapes were sold in the United States at a retail price ranging from $85 to $100 (Schipper, 1980). Cable television has also entered the lucrative sex business, but hardcore remains waiting in the wings. In many areas of the country, nudity has become the best-selling item for cable television. Dozens of cities have softcore cable stations and there are six pay-cable networks devoted entirely to sexually oriented material. The largest of these is Escapade which, at this writing, has over 100,000 subscribers on 45 cable systems, and another 100 cable systems, with over 5 million customers, have agreed to offer Escapade in the coming year (*Newsweek,* August 24, 1981). There is no question that there is an enormous market here. In Buffalo, New York,

Morality in Media demanded that the city council cancel the cable TV license of a cable company which offered Escapade. The newspapers and television news showed fleeting glimpses of what Escapade had to offer and the result was a dramatic increase in Escapade subscribers in the Buffalo area. The National Cable Television Association has urged cable companies to monitor themselves in terms of the type of material shown and not to broadcast hardcore material. Compliance with this request remains to be seen, given the market potential (*Newsweek,* August 24, 1981).

Overall content and changes Since 1973, the nature of hardcore films has changed somewhat. Technical improvements have continued and the star phenomenon has become ingrained. Plots have grown more important, efforts have been made to increase the acting ability, and women have started to produce major hardcore films. The industry has attempted to deal with the satiation problem by changing the content somewhat. There have been attempts to see what the consumer would buy. Films of blatant violence and even faked murder (the so-called snuff films, which most agree were a hoax) were attempted but without success. Only about 8 percent of the full-length and 12 percent of the loops produced today are aggressive or violent in character (Shea, 1980). There has also been a slight increase in activities such as bondage, discipline, and mild sadomasochism, but these films appear to be more a reflection of trends in the wider society than any independent inventiveness. The most recent variation has been the appearance of transsexuals with highly developed breasts and a penis. Child pornography has also been attempted but has remained on the outmost fringes of the industry. The market for such material is very small, given the characteristics of hardcore consumers and the tremendous legal risks. In its current relationship with the law, hardcore is doing just fine. It is not interested in gaining legal attention. Within the powers of the industry, there is also an exception to the "no values" rule: there is strong disapproval of child pornography, a stance reflected in the personal moral attitudes of most performers as well (Dudar, 1977).

Live Sex

Strippers have been a traditional part of the sex business in this country for many years. The folk-hero status of many strippers, as well as the existence of a strippers hall of fame and a national strippers union, attests to the traditional place of stripping in American male society.

While stripping lost popularity in the late 1960s and early 1970s with the topless craze and the growth of hardcore, it has recently made a comeback. There are strip clubs opening around the country and many establishments have recently become famous for their professional and amateur events.

The most recent addition to stripping has been male strippers for female audiences. While some establishments attempted to introduce nude male waiters and cocktail servers in 1978, interest was dim. In 1979 and 1980, however, male strip shows were a significant success in many areas.

As tolerance of the hardcore sex business has increased, the business has expanded to live sex shows involving everything from female homosexuality and heterosexual intercourse to bondage, discipline, and mild sadomasochism to "novelty" acts.

The Mail-Order Business

Another significant, but not often noted, aspect of the sexually explicit material industry is the mail-order business. This industry caters to those wishing to purchase any number of sex-related items ranging from hardcore films, inflatable dolls with water-filled and vibrating orifices, a machine you plug in a car cigarette lighter to stimulate the penis while driving, machines alleged to enlarge one's penis (which cannot be done), and "how to" books to any number of "sexual aids" in the form of vibrators, rubber penises, and leather goods.

Sex products other than films and books

(a)

find a larger market than most people suspect. Apart from individuals who buy specialized equipment for their sexual interests (leathers, bondage materials, and the like), there are many people who are searching for whatever it is they think is missing from their sex lives. A large portion of the mail-order business attempts to cater to these searchers.

One of the interesting features of the mail-order business is that it has a specific relationship with the softcore magazines. They are the only places through which to contact a large audience who might be interested in the products. The magazines also supply the motivation to purchase. I suspect that many males have sat and watched the so-called sexual revolution take place. They have read the softcore magazines which chronicle the events and suggest that almost every woman in the country is more than willing to spend most of her waking life fulfilling male sexual fantasies. Many of these men, however, are not participants in this fantasy world. The sexual revolution has not come to their neighborhood, much less to their lives. As they turn the last page of the softcore magazine with its photograph of a buxom young woman who purportedly says that she is very much into sex with any "guy who has the right equipment," they encounter

(a) Female strippers have long occupied a central place in the sexually explicit business world and are today making a comeback. (b) The most recent addition to stripping are male strippers for female audiences.

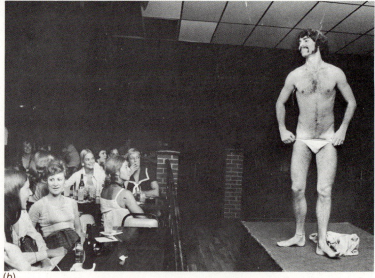

(b)

the mail-order ads. The magazine not only creates the image of a sexual world which never existed, but provides an obtainable alternative. For a significant number of males in our society, an inflatable plastic doll is the sexual revolution.

The demand for this aspect of the sex business is revealed by its success. In 1970, a factory making dildos (rubber objects shaped roughly like a penis and available in a variety of shapes, sizes, colors, movements, and functions) opened in North Hollywood. The annual sales of $5 million from 358 different products have increased an average of 28 percent a year since that time. Another firm employs eighteen people in a half-million-dollar-a-year business producing devices for sadomasochistic sex. Perhaps the best known of the mail-order businesses is the Pleasure Chest, which has a large catalog showing items ranging from edible underwear to genital jewelry to bondage masks. The Pleasure Chest has nine retail stores across the country and reportedly does an annual business of $10 million in an industry where the reported sales total over $100 million (Schipper, 1980).

Hardcore Newspapers

The most famous of the hardcore newspapers, *Screw,* has a circulation of over 125,000 as well as sales at adult bookstores and some newsstands. The paper is basically a means of communication about the world of hardcore sex. It contains articles, advertisements (for everything from films to prostitution), news about what is happening in the world of sex, reviews of hardcore films (which used to be rated on the "peter-meter"), and a consumers' guide to commercial sex in New York City. This last-mentioned section contains fascinating (and serious) reviews and ratings (from one to four erect penises) of the most recent hardcore films, live sex shows, sex emporiums, burlesque and strip shows, gay baths, swingers clubs, and leisure spas (which we will discuss). In short, *Screw* is the hardcore sex worlds' version of your local weekly entertainment review.

Business Consulting

Hardcore newspapers are not the only publications that attest to the organization and business character of the world of hardcore sex. The *Tab Report* is a sex-business publication containing purely business news relevant to the hardcore industry. It is a sophisticated publication that offers discussion of the business trends in the field and special guides for the budding business person. One can obtain refined and well-designed guides to aid one's hardcore business; these guides cover various topics from current laws and court cases to how to set up and run different sex businesses to advertising programs and packages. The existence and success of the *Tab Report* underscores the fact that hardcore sex is largely a rather sophisticated major business, complete with high-salaried executives, numerous full-time employees, and a clear business approach to the market. In fact, *Forbes* magazine described the hardcore business as one of the fastest-growing and highest-return industries today.

THE CHARACTER OF COMMERCIAL SEX

The character of commercial sex is rather straightforward. While we might assume that anything goes, this is not the case. Sex is portrayed in a very stylistic fashion. In a sense, it is all very conventional. There is a general script which most films follow, a consistent set of poses used by magazines, a common mode of operation and behavior used in live sex shows, and so on. The formula for success in commercial sex is not in complex and intriguing plots or eloquent line delivery, but simply in explicit displays of sex. The possible range of such displays is soon exhausted and the presentation which seems to be most acceptable is soon discovered.

There is also a general description of women as sexual objects. There is no question about that. Sexually explicit material is designed to attract and stimulate a male audience. In many cases, the women are clearly depicted as sexual beings who truly enjoy themselves. However, even here, what they do is for the pleasure of men and the satisfaction of male sexual fantasies. The goal of hardcore sexual material in whatever form is not to provide an in-depth analysis of an interpersonal relationship between sexual partners or to reveal two people's appreciation and respect for each other. The goal is to turn people on with pure, raw, physical sexual activity that will satisfy the fantasies of the male observers.

What takes place between the customer and the business is not the sex of everyday life. It is not interaction between people, but a male purchasing a female (or male) to achieve either sexual arousal, orgasm, or both. As such, the sex business communicates disembodiment and dissociation (Schulz, 1979:418) rather than whole persons interacting with each other. The sexual activity which the customer observes does not involve people. It involves genitals, breasts, buttocks, mouths, and other body parts and what they do to other body parts. The people just happen to be attached to these parts—attached without personalities, love, affection, feelings, or interaction other than physical sexual activities. The people to whom the parts belong are not important.

This dissociation and disembodiment are a central part of how commercial sex is conducted. Just as the photograph or film is an image, so is the live performer. He or she generally works in an almost trancelike state, knowing that the customer is interested only in his or her body parts and their motion. As long as these are displayed, then one is doing one's job.

It is not only women who are reduced to body parts having sexual meaning in the world of commercial sex. The customer is also reduced to a monetary object. Workers in the world of commercial sex do not care if the customer is a person, but only if he has money and spends it. The customer is often subjected to disdain, insults, and verbal abuse by those working in the hardcore field. This dislike for customers, apparent in much of the business, is not difficult to understand. If all you saw

while you were at work was a bunch of men in cubicles staring at your genitals and masturbating, you would probably soon develop the same perspective.

There are clearly parts of the sexually explicit business world where these descriptions do not apply. For example, sex boutiques and paraphernalia parties patterned after the Tupperware party are two notable exceptions. The primary difference between these two and what we have been describing is that the latter are oriented toward women customers, not toward men.

THE CUSTOMER

Many people probably envision the hardcore sex customer as some dirty, demented male in a raincoat. This is not the case. Dirty, demented men in raincoats do not have the cash required to feed a multimillion-dollar-a-year industry. Even if they did, there are not enough of them to go around. Rather, every study of the consumers of hardcore sex in America reveals that the average customer is an educated, middle-class male between the ages of 22 and 34.

Knowles and Poorrkaj (1974) conducted a study of commercial sex consumers in a probability sample of males in California in 1972. Of the adult males in the state, 24 percent had been to a sexually explicit film in the last year. In that year, 9 percent had been once, 10 percent between two and four times, and 5 percent five or more times. Of the adult males, 12 percent had been to see a live sex show in the last year, with 5 percent going once, 4 percent two to four times, and 3 percent five or more times. While the point has not been followed up by further research, Knowles and Poorrkaj also found that married males were more likely to attend sexually explicit films while single males were more likely to go to live sex shows. This suggests some interesting differences in the consumer interests of single and married males.

In regard to softcore material, male and female college students are not beyond participation as consumers. Houston (1981) found that among a sample of male and female college students at an eastern university, 36 percent of the white females and 59 percent of the white males said they went to X-rated movies or read "pornographic" books. Over 5 percent of the females and 9 percent of the males said they did so frequently or very frequently.

Houston (1981) also found significant differences in the consumer patterns of black and white college students. Black males and females were both more likely to attend X-rated movies or read pornographic books than their white peers. While slightly over 5 percent of the white females said they were consumers of this material frequently or very frequently, a similar interest was reported by slightly over 18 percent of the black females. Larger differences were found among males. Of the white males, 9 percent said they were consumers of such material frequently or very frequently, but 60 percent of the black male college students reported a similar tendency. The reasons for these differences are to be found in our earlier discussions of black and white differences in sexual learning.

It is interesting to note the contrast between potential male and female consumers of sexually explicit materials. Kenrick et al. (1980) found that among college students, those most likely to expose themselves to these materials were sex-typed, or traditional males and non-sex-typed, or nontraditional females. In the consumer world, this could make for a very strange combination of males and females in the sexually explicit marketplace.

THE EFFECTS OF EXPOSURE TO SEXUALLY EXPLICIT MATERIAL

Currently, sexually explicit materials are suggested to have two effects on the individuals who view them. First, such material is thought to lead people either to learn or to maintain a view of women as sexual objects. Second, sexually explicit material is believed to change behavior. The mild version of the behavior-change argument is that such material suggests possibilities and leads to experimentation. The extreme version is that exposure to this material leads men to commit acts of sexual violence against women and children.

Sanctioning a View of Women

Many people today argue that sexually explicit material encourages a view of women as simply sexual objects with so many body parts to be used by males for their sexual satisfaction. As we have noted, it is difficult to deny that this image characterizes most sexually explicit material. It does exist. However, to blame this material for this view is far too simple a solution to a general social problem.

The sex industry did not invent this view of women. The world of sexually explicit material merely used this image from what existed in the larger society, and sold it back at a profit. Sexually explicit materials provide a general image of women that has been characteristic of American society and much of Western culture long before the sex industry arose. Sexually explicit material does not differ in this respect from other "respectable" and socially accepted means of molding and reflecting images. It differs only in its explicitness. For example, it is difficult to see much difference between selling jeans, perfume, or automobiles by the use of sexually arousing photographs of women which focus on certain body parts and just selling sexually arousing photographs of women which focus on the same body parts. In fact, the advertising industry is probably much more efficient in communicating a view of women as sexual objects than is the sexually explicit industry. The advertising industry communicates through channels which are legitimate, esteemed, and noted by many millions of people. While most Americans would probably call a hardcore film gross, the same people would see an advertisement in a magazine which communicates the same sexual object message and say, "Oh, that is what is appropriate." It is also true that the sexually explicit industry has males as its primary target population. The legitimate media and the advertising industry, however, have largely females as their target populations. One could thus argue that the sexually explicit industry is making money chiefly by furnishing males with a rather common male image of women, and that the advertising industry is teaching women to view themselves in this manner.

To suggest that restricting or eliminating sexually explicit material will bring about any significant changes in the status of women is to attack a real problem with a false solution. It is not that one should not object to pornography if it violates one's personal standards. Rather, it should be understood that pornography is often attacked because it is an easy target. It is not socially respectable, it is usually without "class," and it does not maintain a position of power in American society. Major media presentations are not easy targets because they are respectable, have "class," and are powerful. Criticizing a business characterized by fluorescent-yellow store fronts having flashing neon signs reading "NUDE GIRLS" is easy. Criticizing a major women's magazine that sets trends in fashion and thought is almost un-American.

Influencing Sexual Behavior

It is also argued that exposure to sexually explicit material, especially hardcore material, results in changes in individual sexual behavior.

One interesting aspect of this argument is that people feel that such material affects others but not themselves. The *Presidential Commission Report on Obscenity and Pornography* found that 41 percent of the people surveyed nationally thought that sexually explicit material "makes men want to do new things with their wives." Only 7 percent said that such material affected them in this way. Of those surveyed, 56 percent said that sexually explicit material leads to a breakdown in morals, but only 1 percent said they were affected in this manner.

Overall, the research on how sexually explicit material affects people's sexual behavior suggests that the influence is minimal. Brown et al. (1976) exposed a group of males to photographic slides of this type. In the week fol-

lowing exposure, there was no increase in sexual activity over that of the week before exposure. There was a large increase in sexual activity on the same day as exposure to the material, most of which was in the form of masturbation. Howard et al. (1973) exposed a group of males to ninety minutes of sexually explicit material for fifteen consecutive days. Each day the researchers obtained data on sexual activity, sexual attitudes, and various other factors. Exposure to the material had no apparent effect on self-perception, ability to concentrate, interest in sex, sex drive, conservative attitudes toward sex, sexual frustration, sexual adjustment, neurotic conflicts over sex, or control of sexual impulses. Exposure to the material for the first five days was associated with spending more time thinking about sex and an increase in sexual feelings, but these apparent effects disappeared in the final ten days of exposure. One-quarter of the subjects reported slight increases in the sexual behaviors they usually engaged in, but these were short-lived. The most notable effects were that the subjects became more liberal in their attitudes toward sexually explicit material, the material became less sexually arousing, and they became increasingly bored with the material. In a study of married couples, Mann et al. (1973) found that exposure to sexually explicit films did not result in the couples' adding new sexual behaviors to their interaction, and there was no evidence of experimentation with different sexual behaviors as a result of seeing the films. One significant outcome, as reported in the Howard et al. study, was an increase in sexual activity on the night the couples saw the films. Even then, however, completing a questionnaire about sexual behavior appeared to have more effect on sexual activity than did viewing the films.

Overall, the research evidence suggests that exposure to sexually explicit material does not result in wild experimentation with new sexual behaviors. Further, exposure appears to have little effect on the sexual activity level. The influence it does have lasts for a very brief period and appears to be in the form of a slight increase in the person's usual sexual activities.

Exposure and Sex Offenses

One of the stronger charges against sexually explicit material is that it leads people to commit sex offenses. It is impossible to examine the exact cause-effect relationship between exposure to sexually explicit material and the commission of sex offenses. Most research on this question comes from survey research which allows us to note only correlation or relationships and not cause and effect. Some recent experimental research deals indirectly with this question, but does not actually measure the behavior of engaging in sex offenses.

The survey research on this question consistently suggests that sexual offenders have less experience with sexually explicit material than do nonoffenders (Cook and Fosen, 1971; Goldstein et al., 1971; Walker, 1971).

The most often cited data on this argument represent the closest situation to a societywide experiment. In 1969, legal changes in Denmark made sexually explicit hardcore material available to anyone over the age of 16. The effect of this legal change was a massive surge in the availability of such material. In an extensive review of the research on sex offenses following this change, Kutchinsky (1973) provided the clearest picture of what took place in Denmark. Overall, the amount of sex crime in Denmark after this change declined. It has been argued that this decrease is misleading because it was associated with two other factors: changes in the laws on sex offenses and changes in the willingness of people to report and police to record sex offenses. Kutchinsky (1973) clearly points out, however, that there were no changes in legislation or in police recording methods during this period which would account for even part of this decline in sex crimes. The conclusion drawn by Kutchinsky (who is often misquoted when this subject is discussed) is that the ready availability of sexually explicit hardcore material was not related to rape, but was perhaps associated with a marked decline in child molesting. The safest conclusion to be drawn from the Danish experience is that the availability of sexually explicit material is irrelevant as far as sexual offenses are concerned.

Effects on Interpersonal Aggression

Social psychologists and the public alike have, in recent years, had considerable interest in the relationship between exposure to sexually explicit material and aggression against other people following exposure. While the final word is by no means in, some strong tentative conclusions can be drawn.

The main emphasis in this research has been on the relationship between sexual arousal and interpersonal aggression. Since these studies have predominantly used sexually explicit material of the type purchased in adult bookstores, this research has a direct bearing on the effects of hardcore material on interpersonal aggression.

When experiencing mild or moderate levels of sexual arousal, individuals have been found to be less likely to aggress against another person than when they were not sexually aroused. When experiencing a high level of sexual arousal, individuals have generally been observed to be more likely to engage in aggression against another person than when they were not sexually aroused (Baron and Bell, 1973; Baron, 1974).

It was originally thought that mild or moderate arousal inhibited aggression because of *attention shift* in which a little sexual arousal drew the person's attention away from the possibility of being aggressive (Donnerstein et al., 1975). High sexual arousal, on the other hand, was thought to lead to a greater chance of interpersonal aggression through the *transfer of arousal*. Here it was thought that if the person was highly aroused sexually and cues of anger or hostility were presented, the arousal would likely transfer from sex to aggression.

The attention shift and transfer of arousal explanations for the observed relationship between sexual arousal and aggression both appear to be incorrect. In fact, current research strongly suggests that *sexual arousal itself is not related to aggressive or nonaggressive interpersonal behavior*. Rather than sexual arousal affecting aggression, the important factor appears to be what creates the arousal. Even though visual depictions of sexual activity are arousing to most people, sexual arousal is not always accompanied by good feelings. In fact, sexual arousal and feeling good or feeling bad are independent of each other. People may be aroused and feel good about what aroused them or they may be aroused and feel bad about what aroused them. Thus, when viewing sexually explicit material, some individuals react with arousal and good feelings (excited, curious, entertained) while others react with arousal and bad feelings (disgust, anger, depression) (Byrne et al., 1974). Feeling good, regardless of what the cause, tends to lead to kindness, while feeling bad, regardless of the cause, tends to result in aggression and hostility. When sexual arousal is created by stimuli which make one feel good, aggression is less likely. When sexual arousal is created by stimuli which make one feel bad, aggression is more likely (White, 1979; Zillman et al., 1981). *It is thus not sexual arousal which is associated with interpersonal aggression, but whether one feels bad or good as a result of exposure to the material which created the sexual arousal* (Figure 14-1). It just so happens that sexually explicit material which creates mild to moderate levels of sexual arousal is most likely to make people feel good, and sexually explicit material which creates high sexual arousal is most likely to make some people feel bad. In fact, since females generally have fewer positive and more negative responses when viewing sexually explicit material than do males, material which decreases aggression in males increases aggres-

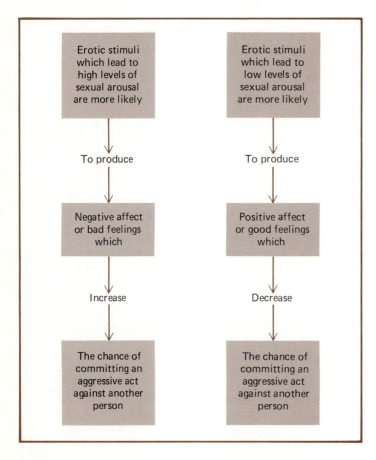

Erotic stimuli which lead to high levels of sexual arousal are more likely	Erotic stimuli which lead to low levels of sexual arousal are more likely
To produce	To produce
Negative affect or bad feelings which	Positive affect or good feelings which
Increase	Decrease
The chance of committing an aggressive act against another person	The chance of committing an aggressive act against another person

Figure 14-1 The relationship is really between feeling good or feeling bad and aggression. The only reason any relationship is ever found between sexual arousal itself and aggression is that stimuli which create high levels of arousal are more likely to create bad feelings than those which create low levels of arousal.

sion in females (Baron, 1979; Griffitt and Kaiser, 1978; Sapolsky and Zillman, 1981).

Thus, exposure to certain kinds of sexually explicit material probably increases the chance that people with certain characteristics are more likely to be aggressive. However, there is no evidence that this process is any different from any other process in which things which make people feel bad increase the chance of their engaging in aggressive behavior. Further, there are vast differences from individual to individual in the kind of sexually explicit material which makes them feel good or bad. What is one person's erotica is another person's smut.

SEXUAL AROUSAL AND SEXUALLY EXPLICIT MATERIAL

Supposedly, the purpose of producing sexually explicit material is to arouse the viewer sexually. How arousing are certain forms of sexually explicit material, and what are some of the factors associated with being aroused by sexually explicit stimuli?

Types of Visual Depictions That Are Arousing

One of the important findings from this line of research is that regardless of how powerful a sexual stimulant one may think sexually explicit material is, it cannot compete with one's imagination. Byrne and Lamberth (1971) had males and females either view photographs, read written descriptions, or imagine certain heterosexual sexual activities taking place. As shown in Figure 14-2, imagination is clearly superior in creating sexual arousal for both males and females. (One of the reasons that hardcore material is so susceptible to satiation is that it leaves nothing to imagine.)

If we were to guess what kinds of sexual activities depicted in sexually explicit material arouse people the most, we might name some typically prohibited and forbidden fruit behaviors. This is not the case. The more unusual or

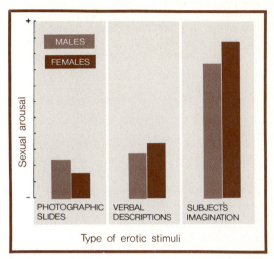

Figure 14-2 One's own imagination about sexual activities results in greater sexual arousal than either viewing photographs of these activities or reading descriptions of the behaviors.

extreme a sexual activity is seen as being, the less arousing is a photograph of that activity (Steele and Walker, 1974). The visual sexual material which is the most arousing (to heterosexuals) shows rather commonly experienced heterosexual activities and nudes of the other sex. Photographs of oral and group sex are only mildly arousing, and homosexuality, sadism, and nudes of the same sex are the least arousing (Steele and Walker, 1974).

The reason for these patterns is that we learn what kinds of sexual activities are sexually arousing and the largest part of this learning experience is focused on the more common sexual activities. We also learn by doing. By our own sexual experiences we learn to attach erotic meaning to certain behaviors. This learning process is, however, somewhat more interesting than we might think. For females, the more experience one has had with a particular sexual activity, the more aroused one is when viewing a picture of that activity (Griffitt, 1975). For males, the situation is very different; experience with a particular sexual activity is not related to arousal when viewing a picture of that activity. The important factor in the extent to which males are aroused by sexually explicit photographs is the extensiveness of masturbation experience. Males with more extensive masturbation experience are more aroused by *all forms of photographically depicted sexual activity* than are males with less extensive masturbation experience (Griffitt, 1975).

This gender difference is a reflection or outcome of gender differences in sexual learning. Since males learn to be more interested in physical sexual activity, a large part of their adolescent masturbation involves fantasizing about engaging in specific sexual acts. These fantasies during masturbation serve as an avenue for learning to attach erotic meaning to sexual activities even though one may never have experienced that activity. Males with extensive masturbation experience thus accumulate considerable sexual learning in this vein. For females, adolescent masturbation is much less common and frequent and, more important, tends to be less oriented toward physical activity in its fantasy component. Rather than learning through fantasy during masturbation, females are more likely to learn to attach erotic meaning to particular sexual activities by actually experiencing the activity in a situation which is defined as erotic. Thus, most commonly, females experience a sexual activity in a romantic situation and attach erotic meaning to that activity as a function of the situation in which it is experienced.

There are, of course, great individual differences here among both males and females, but the general pattern is still the basic gender difference in sexual learning and arousal to sexually explicit material.

Gender Differences in Arousal to Sexually Explicit Material

Consistent with the traditional Victorian concept of women as asexual, it has long been assumed that males are much more aroused by sexually explicit material, especially when visual, than are females. Survey reports have supported this idea in that women are not only less likely to view sexually explicit material, but also *report* being less aroused by it (Kinsey et al., 1953; Abelson et al., 1971).

There is good reason, however, to question these survey results. It has never been considered particularly appropriate for women to have an interest in sexually explicit material, and such material for women has only recently been available. Thus, women learned that they were not expected to be interested in such material, and if they were, the lack of availability of female-oriented material discouraged interest and experience with it.

When the question of gender differences in sexual arousal to sexually explicit material was placed under experimental scrutiny in which it could be observed how males and females reacted, there were some surprises. Early experimental research revealed that even though men were more sexually aroused by written or visual sexually explicit material than were women, most women were also sexually aroused by such material. More recent studies have revealed that these materials are as arousing to females as to males (Fisher and Byrne, 1978; Veitch and Griffitt, in press). Still, females are more likely than are males to have bad feelings when viewing such material (Byrne et al., 1974; White, 1979) and to rate it as being pornographic (Brown, 1979). However, there is some evidence that females have more interest than males in material rated as "more pornographic" (Brown, 1979). This is not unexpected, given both the traditional admonition for females not to view such material and the recent declines in the suppression of female sexuality.

Love versus lust It has traditionally been assumed that females are most aroused by sexually explicit material couched in a love theme while males are most sexually aroused by pure raw sex. This assumption has proven to be incorrect (Heiman, 1975). Fisher and Byrne (1978) had three groups of male and female subjects view the same film showing a male and female engaging in a variety of sexual activities, including oral sex, manual stimulation of genitals, and intercourse in various positions. The only difference between the three groups was what each one was told. One group was told that the context was love and that the couple were married and expressing their love for each other. The second group was told that the context was pure lust. The female was described as a prostitute and the male as her customer, and they were both said to be eager to have sex with each other. The third group was informed that the context was casual sex. The two people had met at a party, were sexually attracted to each other, and were going to enjoy their sexual exploration. As shown in Figure 14-3, the film was most arousing when the context was described as casual sex, and males and females did not differ on this point. Thus, males are not most aroused by lust and females are not most aroused by love. Rather, casual sex is the most arousing to both males and females. In a more recent study, Mosher and White (1980) specifically examined female sexual arousal as depending on an emotionally committed relationship versus casual sex. They found that when females imagined themselves in a sexual encounter, they became as aroused when they imagined they were emotionally committed to the male as when they imagined the situation to be a casual sexual experience.

As a result of differences in male and female sexual learning, the major difference between males and females is that females have more interest in *affectionate sexuality,* which includes such attitudes as feeling that affection with sex is important, that sex provides warmth and affection, and that it is important to have one's sexual partner hug one while engaging

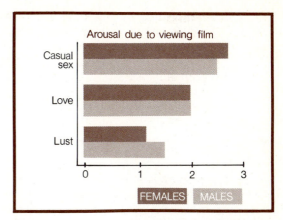

Figure 14-3 When male and female college students viewed a film of a man and woman engaging in intercourse, both males and females were most aroused when the situation was described as casual sex. (Based on data from Fisher and Byrne, 1978.)

in sexual activity (Libby and Strauss, 1980). Affection and love are not the same thing. Thus, while sexually explicit material does not have to be combined with love to be arousing to females, it more than likely must have an affection theme, as in casual sexual encounters described above. The presence of an affection theme is not, however, so important to males.

STUDY GUIDE

TERMS TO KNOW

Pornography

Roth vs. the United States

League of Deliverance

I Am Curious Yellow

Stars

Comstock Act

Social movements

Hardcore, softcore

Arousal and aggression

SELF-TEST

Part I: True-False Statements

1. The Supreme Court decisions on pornography and obscenity have provided clear legal guidelines for defining what is and what is not obscene material.
2. The conservative antipornography movements based in religion or politics have usually found societywide support for their views.
3. Zoning hardcore businesses into certain areas of a city has generally been a success in the United States.

4. There is rather solid evidence that the feminist-based movement against sexually explicit material will be successful.
5. The majority of the hardcore films today show explicit physical violence.
6. The hardcore business is a major and profitable industry in American society.
7. From the data available, it appears that less than 5 percent of the males in this country go to a sexually explicit film in any given year.
8. Exposure to sexually explicit material apparently makes people want to experiment with new sexual behaviors depicted in the material.
9. There is strong evidence from the Danish experience that the ready availability of hardcore material decreases sex offenses in a society.
10. Males are most sexually aroused by lust rather than by love or casual sex.

Part II: Multiple-Choice Questions
Select the best of the three alternatives.

1. When individuals are prohibited from viewing sexually explicit material, they *(a)* have less desire to view it than if they had not been prohibited; *(b)* have more desire to view it than if they had not been prohibited; *(c)* soon forget about it.
2. The most successful means the hardcore industry has found to avoid the problem of satiation is *(a)* revealing more and more nudity; *(b)* making child pornography; *(c)* creating stars.
3. The average customer of hardcore sexual material is *(a)* uneducated, white, over 50; *(b)* middle-class, educated; *(c)* low in social class, white, uneducated.
4. College females who are most likely to expose themselves to sexually explicit material are *(a)* traditional or sex-typed; *(b)* nontraditional or non–sex-typed; *(c)* high in sex guilt.
5. Studies of sex offenders indicate that their exposure to hardcore materials, compared with that of nonoffenders, is *(a)* more; *(b)* less; *(c)* the same amount.
6. The safest conclusion to be drawn from the Denmark experience is that hardcore material *(a)* has no relationship to sex crimes; *(b)* decreases sex crimes; *(c)* increases sex crimes.
7. When we examine the relationship between sexual arousal and aggression, we find that *(a)* increased aggression while aroused is caused by the transfer of arousal from sex to anger; *(b)* decreased aggression while aroused is caused by attention shift; *(c)* there is a relationship, not between arousal and aggression, but between aggression and feeling good or bad.
8. Of the following, which creates the most sexual arousal? *(a)* Viewing sexually explicit photographs; *(b)* reading descriptions of sexual activity; *(c)* imagining sexual activities taking place.
9. The kinds of sexual activities which create the most sexual arousal when depicted photographically are *(a)* those which are unusual and forbidden in the person's mind; *(b)* those which involve acceptable, but extreme, sexual behaviors; *(c)* those which are considered to be the least extreme and the most "normal" by the viewer.
10. With regard to gender differences in sexual arousal, when viewing sexually explicit material, *(a)* males are more aroused than females; *(b)* females are more aroused than males; *(c)* males and females are equally aroused.

TOPICS FOR DISCUSSION

This is an easy topic to get people to talk about once they get going. This chapter has tried to give you some idea of the nature of the world of commercial sex and to do so in an unbiased way. One way which is certain to start people exploring the issues here is for your class to attempt to get some consensus on what is and what is not acceptable in the world of commercial sex and why. An excellent preparation for such a discussion is to have a representative from the antiporn position speak to your class, and then to arrange a similar talk by a representative from the proporn side (someone who either works in the industry or is against the suppression of such material).

SUGGESTED READINGS

Ms., November 1978.
    This issue contains three articles on hardcore material from the feminist perspective. A must piece of reading to compare with the perspective of Shea (cited in the next entry).

Shea, R., "Women at War," *Playboy,* February 1980.
    A well-written article which takes the feminist-based attack on sexually explicit material to task.

Turan, K., and **S. F. Zito.,** *Sinema: American Pornographic Films and the People Who Make Them.* New York: Praeger, 1974.
    Although this is now somewhat dated, it is an interesting set of interviews on the hardcore and softcore industry in America.

Bryant, C. D. (Ed.), *Sexual Deviancy in Social Context.* New York: Franklin Watts, 1977.
    This is an excellent set of readings, many of which are rare and cover topics discussed in this chapter. See especially chapters 1, 3, 5, 7, 9.

Hurwood, B. J. (Ed.), *The Whole Sex Catalog.* New York: Pinnacle Books, 1975.
    A wealth of sex-related items, mainly of the softcore variety. Very interesting reading.

KEY TO SELF-TEST

Part I: True-False Statements

1. F (What has been the major legal outcome of these decisions?)
2. F (They have always gained much attention, but they have failed to gain societywide support for their entire set of views.)
3. F (What effect has this generally had?)
4. F (Those in favor of the values of feminism tend not to be in favor of suppression and those in favor of suppression tend not to be supportive of the feminist movement.)
5. F (This characterizes a minority of the films, and there is good reason for this. What is it?)
6. T (The business is *very* profitable.)
7. F (From studies in California, it seems to be closer to 24 percent.)
8. F (What does the effect appear to be?)
9. F (There is no evidence that it either increases or decreases.)
10. F (Males and females are most sexually aroused by depictions of casual sex.)

Part II: Multiple-Choice Questions

1. *b* (A finding which follows commodity theory. What happens when people are allowed all the viewing they want?)
2. *c* (This is the only aspect which can be varied with success and which will draw repeat customers.)
3. *b*
4. *b* (How about college males?)
5. *b*
6. *a*
7. *c* (You should be able to diagram this relationship.)
8. *c* (Perhaps one of the reasons is that the *most* sexually explicit material is the most prone to satiation.)
9. *c* (Learning. How does this learning differ for males and females?)
10. *c* (However, males and females are aroused by different depictions, their learning to be aroused by these is different, and their emotional reactions to the material is different.)

Chapter 15
Prostitution

FEMALE PROSTITUTION

When prostitution is mentioned, we most often think of women who sell sexual activity to men. Prostitution is, however, practiced by both males and females, and in recent years, greater attention has come to be focused on male prostitution, especially among children. While most of this chapter is devoted to female prostitution, we shall discuss male prostitutes to the extent that social scientists have accumulated data on the subject.

Prostitution is most often considered a deviant behavior, one which deviates from social norms. However, in a very real sense, prostitution is normal. Taken as a whole, it conforms in many ways to dominant patterns of sexuality and sexual learning in a society. As such, it is an important topic because it reveals one of the many different shades of the larger sexual picture in American society which we have discussed throughout this text.

What Is Prostitution?

While a definition of prostitution seems easy, the formal definitions vary considerably and appear to be rather arbitrary. The definition we shall employ is that of James (1976:2) as "any sexual exchange where the reward is neither sexual nor affectional."

An act of prostitution does not have to involve money. The reward for the sexual use of one's body may be anything which is neither sexual nor affectional, such as housing, clothes, or entertainment. Exchanges other than money seldom, however, get one legally (or even socially) labeled a prostitute. As James (1977) points out, four factors appear to lead to one's being so labeled: cash, number of sexual partners, knowledge of these sexual partners, and subtlety.

Money is seen as a purely nonemotional exchange and insinuates that the person is in the business of selling sex. The woman who exchanges commodities other than money for sex is safe from the law as long as she does so with few partners. A woman who has "too many" sexual partners is labeled promiscuous and one who has "far too many" is labeled a prostitute. One can violate all these first three conditions and still have relative impunity from the law as long as one is subtle. Invisible prostitutes who operate with class and keep their business from public view seldom have confrontations with the law. The prostitute who wears flashy clothes, uses blatant language, makes aggressive approaches to men, and generally makes her trade visible is certain to draw the attention of law enforcers and public disapproval.

A Brief History in Western Culture

The various forms of prostitution which have existed across time and cultures are too varied to be neatly summarized under the timeworn label "the world's oldest profession." (It is, in fact, no older than medicine or religion.) It is useful, however, to obtain some overview of prostitution as it existed in two of the major bases of Western civilization and to briefly examine its history in American society.

Ancient Greece In early Greece, women were not social equals of men. The only women who were trained as social equals of males were prostitutes. If a man wanted social interaction with a woman, he went to a prostitute. Prostitution was thus accepted as normal, and many Greek states had a standard prostitution tax. There were many types of prostitution and prostitutes in Greece, including brothels, streetwalkers, women who worked inns and taverns, and musicians and dancers. The highest class of prostitutes were the Hetairae, highly educated women with (unofficial) high status who catered to generals, politicians, and artists. The openness and acceptability of prostitution in ancient Greece are illustrated by a preserved shoe which has "follow me" engraved on the sole so that the prostitute's message was printed on the ground as she walked (Bullough and Bullough, 1978).

Ancient Rome As in all things sexual, the Romans did not romanticize prostitution. They viewed it as a necessary evil, and one which was in demand. The Romans had an idealized view of themselves. Just as the author Parson Weems erected the myth of George Washington and the cherry tree as a moral example of an ideal, so Roman historians created the legend of Rome as a virtuous, family-oriented society. Prostitution did not fit this idealized image and thus was held in low esteem. No senator, for example, was allowed to marry a prostitute or a woman who had descended from a prostitute (Bullough and Bullough, 1978).

There were several Latin words referring to prostitutes, but the one passed to the English language (prostitute) meant "to set forth in public," "expose for sale." Brothels were common, and many were located near the Circus Maximus where the games were held. Brothel prostitutes would sit or stand where they could be seen much as they do in many European countries today or as streetwalkers do in America. Prostitutes were originally required to wear a short, togalike gown to distinguish them from "respectable" women. Later, the dress requirements were relaxed, but many still wore brightly colored clothes and bleached their hair.

The status of prostitutes in Rome was generally quite low. They were considered to exist for sexual purposes alone, not for social company or interaction. Most of the brothel prostitutes were probably slaves from other countries (Bullough and Bullough, 1978). In addition, there were women who "worked" inns, public baths, and bakeries. The highest class of prostitutes in Rome were courtesans. These women were kept in the company of high political officials and regarded as more than merely sexual partners. Many of them occupy idealized places in the writings of the ancient Roman poets. There were also many part-time prostitutes who worked at certain times of the day or year and plied their trade in settings ranging from alleys to graveyards. Customers were also ranked in a status hierarchy, and a certain class of customer visited only a certain class of prostitute. Roman soldiers (who were not allowed to marry) and travelers went to one class of prostitute, while high-ranking officials went to another class, and slaves to yet another class. Even though prostitution was not esteemed in Rome, it reflected the structure of the large society, a not unusual condition.

Colonial America From the beginning of colonial America, prostitution has existed on this continent. Many prostitutes were, in fact, sent to America from Europe as part of their punishment. Many black and Indian slaves were unwilling participants in prostitution at the hands of their owners. Throughout the 1600s and 1700s, prostitution was common in the cities. Even though there were frequent moral outcries and attempts to curtail them, brothels were common and streetwalkers were apparent to the visitor (Bullough and Bullough, 1978). By 1680, a small path in New York behind Wall Street was known as Maiden Lane because of its many brothels and prostitutes. Prostitutes also worked in taverns (about half of which were owned and operated by women) as part of the entertainment available for male customers (Ryan, 1979:48).

The 1880s Up until the beginning of the 1800s, prostitution was unorganized in that it was mainly a free-lance business, scattered here and there without any real structure. As industrialization grew, large urban centers started to develop. These cities were rapidly filled with male immigrants and women working in the factories. There thus developed a large clientele for prostitution and a large number of women who could use the money.[1] In Victorian society, there was a clear dichotomy between "good" women and "bad" women. The proper Victorian woman was a wife and mother, protected in the home and the keeper of the family. She was also chaste and pure. This social division between middle-class and working women encouraged lower-status working women to enter prostitution because the social cleavage setting them apart as "bad" women was already part of society. Further, the double standard combined with the image of the proper middle-class Victorian woman to provide a demand for prostitution. Because of the sexual ideal (purity) for the middle-class female, men were almost encouraged to engage in premarital sex, and even sex while married, with prostitutes. This resulted in a system in which men could visit prostitutes without much social disapproval (if they were discreet), and certainly without legal interference. Women who were involved in prostitution, on the other hand, had very low social status and were subject to legal penalty.

In the West, the gold rush in California brought a massive migration of men into the

area. Since prostitution had by now come to be a central feature of the structure of society, these men were quickly followed by boatloads of prostitutes from Mexico and Central and South America (mainly Peru and Chile), as well as French and Chinese women (many Chinese were brought in to work the mines).

Most of the frontier prostitutes were young, white, unmarried, and welcome. The mere existence of a woman in a society in which there were fifty to a hundred men for every woman not only encouraged prostitution, but an image of the prostitute as well. It was during the frontier period that American society developed the idealized image of the prostitute as "the whore with the heart of gold." In the West, as elsewhere, it was not uncommon for the prostitute to occupy an ambiguous status in a community. On the one hand, she was held in low esteem because she was a "bad woman." On the other hand, particularly in frontier towns such as Virginia City, Nevada, she was esteemed as a friend, companion, adviser, and giver of social services (other than sex).[2] Most of the prostitution in the West was in the form of brothels run by a madam. Frequently these were in dance halls or saloons and thus were a central part of the male social life of the town (Blackburn and Ricards, 1979).

After the Civil War, many cities attempted to follow the European countries and confine prostitution to certain areas, make registration mandatory, and provide official periodic medical examinations. The only city successfully to do this was St. Louis from 1870 to 1874, with medical examinations being made at the Social Evil Hospital (Bullough and Bullough, 1978). Legal registration and medical examinations failed (having to go to the Social Evil Hospital probably did not aid the cause), and most cities resorted to confining prostitution to certain areas. These came to be known as red-light districts, a term derived from the red lanterns of train men who left them hanging on the front

---

[1]Have you ever wondered about the Rod Stewart hit song "Maggie May"? Maggie Mays were the prostitutes who worked the docks in England in the 1800s; most of them engaged in sex for a penny, a piece of bread, or a shot of gin (Bullough and Bullough, 1978:242).

[2]This is evidently still the case in some parts of Nevada. When Fran's Star Ranch (a legal house in Nevada, which we shall discuss) burned down, the V.F.W. Women's Auxiliary threw a "fire dance" and raised some $5,000. Fran is well known in the area for making generous contributions for local softball team uniforms, advertising in the high school yearbook, and donating to the local volunteer fire department.

Brothel prostitutes in Creede, Colorado, in the 1890s.

porch of a house while they visited a prostitute. Prostitution was, of course, generally against the law but, in a reflection of the American ambiguity about prostitution, it was tolerated; police and political pay-offs not to raid brothels were a common occurrence.

Out of this "zoning" of prostitution into certain areas grew many famous "sin centers" throughout the country; all these developments contributed to the lore and idealized image of prostitution. Bourbon Street and the French Quarter in New Orleans and the Barbary Coast in San Francisco became well-known centers of prostitution (Shumsky and Springer, 1981). The tacit approval of such centers and their activities is evidenced by the many city guidebooks published by restaurants and taverns, which gave detailed advertisements and descriptions of brothels in the city. Many prostitutes and brothels issued their own calling cards, which were freely distributed.[3]

[3]Some prostitutes also advertised as barbers. Therefore, around the turn of the century, many cities outlawed women barbers.

Out of this period, a number of women became infamous for their involvement in prostitution; their notoriety was all part of America's idealized image of the prostitute. Most of these women were madams in the pre-World War I period and operated "class houses." The Everleigh sisters of Chicago, for example, opened the Everleigh Club in 1900. The establishment consisted of a number of parlors designed richly in various themes (Moorish, Japanese, Gold Music, Red Rooms). Each parlor displayed expensive art and books, the brass beds contained marble inlay, and the ceilings were mirrored. There were barbers and masseurs in the establishment and a patron was admitted only with a letter of recommendation, an engraved business card from the club, or a formal introduction by someone known to the management. On October 24, 1911, the Everleigh sisters, having amassed considerable wealth, closed their posh brothel to retire respectably to New York City, where they lived until their deaths (Bullough and Bullough, 1978). While not all brothels were as luxurious and elite as the Everleigh Club, they were centers of male social activity. Unlike the houses of today, one could sit in the lounge with a group of male friends and drink, smoke cigars, and socialize in the company of friendly prostitutes. Prostitution was a significant part of many males' (almost) all-male social life.

This aspect of prostitution in America hides the less romantic aspects of the business. There is little doubt, for example, that many prostitutes would have preferred to be doing something else—if they had a choice. It also hides the very real enslavement of Chinese prostitutes in places where death and disease rates were very high and living conditions miserable by almost any standard. In the biographies of prostitutes, legend and idealized images have most often replaced the truth. One classic example is Martha Jane Cannary, an alcoholic at 24 and a prostitute in various Old West towns. Her fame came from her association with James Butler ("Wild Bill") Hickock, and her legendary nickname, "Calamity Jane," contains more truth than the fanciful legends would lead us to believe. This idealized image of the prostitute still remains with us today. While streetwalkers are arrested every day in the United States and it is commonplace for adolescents to enter the trade, prostitutes are portrayed as good-hearted fallen doves on *Gunsmoke, Hot I Baltimore, All in the Family, Laverne and Shirley, Laugh-In,* and major motion pictures.

The Extent of Prostitution

Today the open, publicly known brothel is much less common than it was in the 1800s and early 1900s. From a number of studies, it is also clear that a smaller proportion of the male population has experience with prostitutes than was the case fifty years ago. For example, Kinsey (1948) found that 69 percent of the males studied had experience with prostitutes by age 55, and that 37 percent had intercourse with a prostitute by age 18. This experience rate was much higher for males with only grade school education (74 percent) than either the high school (54 percent) or college-educated (28 percent). Among single

males age 16 to 20, Kinsey found that prostitutes provided 9 percent of their total sexual outlet (total orgasm experience), and among single males up to age 40, this figure was 39 percent. While experience with prostitutes was more common for single than for married males in the early 1900s, it was not absent for married men. Of those married males between the ages of 21 and 25, Kinsey (1948:250) estimated that 19 percent had intercourse with prostitutes. Of the males in this group who did have sex with prostitutes, such activity was not simply a once-in-a-lifetime event. For example, they had intercourse with prostitutes on an average of once a month (Kinsey, 1948:250), and all single males under the age of 30 had an average frequency of once every three weeks. Prostitution was frequently how a male had his first initial intercourse experience.

More recent studies point to a marked decline in the percentage of males having any experience with prostitutes. Hunt (1974) found that only 8 percent of the college-educated males under the age of 35 had ever had sex with a prostitute, and only 3 percent of the college-educated single males under 25 had had intercourse with a prostitute in the last year. Sorensen (1973), in a study of youth of high school age, found that only 1 percent of the males had ever had intercourse with a prostitute.

There are good reasons for this decline in the use of prostitution. As Gagnon (1977) points out, there has been a marked increase in competition in the last twenty years. Sexual attitudes and standards have liberalized considerably, particularly for and among unmarried women. Thus, male demand for premarital sexual activity with prostitutes has declined. Other forms of sexual entertainment have also increased or come into being, such as swinging, pornography, live sex shows, and topless and bottomless bars. All these factors have probably affected the prostitution market by decreasing the demand.

On the basis of these data, it seems safe to assume that prostitution on the whole has declined in American society in terms of the percentage of the population that participated as either customers or prostitutes. Other data also suggest this decrease. In 1859, Virginia City, Nevada, had a population of 7,064, of whom 138 were prostitutes (Blackburn and Ricards, 1979), or one prostitute for every fifty people in the town. It is highly unlikely that even the most wide-open of cities in the country today has one prostitute for every fifty residents.

Types of Prostitution

As James (1977) points out, the different types of prostitution and prostitutes are almost endless. In the United States, there are some major forms of prostitution which are important to discuss to gain some understanding of this aspect of the sex business.

Streetwalkers The way in which status is assigned in the larger society is reflected in a clear status structure in prostitution. The prostitutes with the lowest status are those with the poorest working conditions, the greatest visibility, the least control of their working environment and customers, and the greatest chance of physical violence and arrest. These are streetwalkers who literally work the streets ("on the block"). They may work independently, but more usually they work for a pimp (Exner et al., 1977). Streetwalkers tend to have the lowest level of education (and thus life chances) and make the least money of any prostitute. Exner et al. (1977) found that a streetwalker had an average education of eleven years and an average annual income of $8,000.

Bars Many prostitutes work one or several bars. This route is much safer from physical violence from a customer and the prostitute has more control over the nature of the customer as determined by the type of the bar itself. The important feature of bar prostitution is that it is one of the forms (hotels are another) of prostitution where the prostitute is tied into a network of individuals in order to be in business. She commonly pays any number of persons to allow her to do business in the establishment.

Massage parlors and erotic studios The brothel of yesteryear has been partially (but by no means entirely) replaced by the

Streetwalkers most commonly work with a pimp, whose visibility and style make the streetwalker highly vulnerable to arrest.

massage parlor and the erotic studio of to-day. Not all massage parlors offer prostitution, and the types of sexual activities they sell varies a great deal. Some parlors, for example, employ only "hand whores," who provide masturbation for the customer (a "local"). Other parlors offer a rather unlimited number of sexual activities.

A common type of massage parlor and erotic studio is the rip-off establishment. Here the customer is conned by being enticed into paying for sexual services and receiving a quick exit. For example, the business may advertise "oral sex." The customer first pays and is then escorted to a room where he is allowed to talk about sex (to himself). If he objects, there is little recourse. Burly bouncers escort him out the back door and few customers feel free to complain to the police or the better business bureau about not receiving the illegal services.

Even when massage parlors do offer sex for sale, the transaction is governed by a dominant theme. The purpose of the sex business is to make the most money with the least effort, not to offer satisfaction, communication, or enjoyment. Get 'em in, get 'em up, get 'em off, get 'em out is the general premise in this business.

Leisure spas   Found only in major cities, leisure spas are somewhat luxurious establishments much like the old high-class brothels of the early 1900s. Customers are often treated with great care, consideration, and apparent esteem. Baths, saunas, steam rooms, massage, and alcohol are offered to accompany almost any kind of sexual activity one wants. Depending on the services, such consumption costs between $50 and $200 an hour.

Conventions and circuits   Most prostitutes take advantage of conventions that bring many males to town. Other prostitutes travel a convention circuit from city to city. Still others (called "road whores" by those in the business) travel in groups of two or three and work a circuit of migrant labor camps, lumber camps, etc.

Escorts   One key to prostitution is freedom to advertise without risking the attention of the law. While not all escort services are fronts for, or allow, prostitution, such activity is common in larger cities. The male pays for the company of a woman for an evening of dinner and/or entertainment. It is generally up to the escort whether prostitution becomes a part of the evening activity and for how long and how much. As far as I am aware, this is the only form of prostitution available for female customers. In many major cities male escort services provide exactly the same customer services and options for females. The volume of business is unknown.

Call girls   Perhaps the best-known form of prostitution is that with the highest status. Call girls make initial contacts with customers only through a phone system. Their telephone numbers may be advertised and then answered through a madam working for a large number of call girls or passed to customers only by personal referral. The phone call serves to screen the customer and his request and to make an appointment. This form of prostitution is basically invisible, is almost totally free from arrest, and is reasonably safe from physical violence from the customer. The prostitute can also control the amount of business and the type of customer she deals with. Call girls have the highest level of education and make the most money. In the Exner et al. study (1977), the average education of call girls was two years of college and their average income was $77,000 a year.

The call girl sells more than sex. She sells physical attractiveness, certain physical characteristics, sexual technique, and frequently specialized sexual activities. These specialized activities may often be seen as desirable since the effort expended may be minimal, the time consumed short, and the price high. For example, to be paid $300 for a half-hour of throwing cream puffs at a nude male's genitals while yelling obscenities is considered by many call girls to be a reasonable exchange.

Nevada houses   Prostitution in Nevada is illegal in only two of the nineteen counties—those in which Reno and Las Vegas are located. There are approximately forty licensed brothels in the state which do an estimated annual business of $8 million. The popularity of these establishments is perhaps best illustrated by the existence of a guidebook to the brothels of Nevada (Engle, 1976), which provides descriptions, maps, and ratings. This volume is currently in its second edition.

The prostitutes in Nevada houses usually live in the houses three weeks a month, with one week off. They pay the house 50 to 60 percent of each "trick" in addition to room and board. The average Nevada house prostitute will net about $500 a week. Some women also work in the Nevada houses part-time. While their activity is often called a myth, some few female college students do in fact work weekends or holidays in the Nevada houses.

While the Nevada house work is steady and safe from violence and legal problems, it is also a take-what-comes-along proposition. Even though some houses refuse men they do not like, the hordes of smelly deer hunters from nearby states can be a bit much for even the most seasoned.

Even though prostitution is not legal in Clark and Washoe counties, it is readily apparent. The volume of potential customers and of money circulating the casinos and hotels is simply too lucrative for prostitution to ignore Reno and Las Vegas. In 1977, for example, the Clark County sheriff (Las Vegas) compiled dossiers on some 7,000 prostitutes and estimated there to be 3,000 of them working daily in the city (Bullough and Bullough, 1978). The key, however, is class and discretion. For many males, prostitution is part of the good time the Nevada cities offer and thus it is good for business—as long as it is done with distinction and subtlety.

Miscellaneous The miscellaneous forms of prostitution cover the range of one's imagination. Apparently not uncommon is the part-time prostitute who is also a housewife. Exner et al. (1977) apparently had no trouble locating a small sample of such part-time prostitutes. These women may work a couple of days a week or a "long lunch hour" or two. In many cases, their husbands may know and approve, but with 60 percent of these women in the Exner et al. sample, the husband did not know about her activity in prostitution.

CHILD AND TEENAGE PROSTITUTION

Child and teenage prostitution has recently gained some media and social service attention in the United States, but it is not new. In the 1800s child prostitution was common in Europe (Bullough and Bullough, 1978:246) as well as in major American cities. In 1852, for example, John Augustus reported taking seven girls between the ages of 10 and 13 out of brothels in New York. In 1850, the New York City police submitted a report to the mayor noting the existence of 3,000 young prostitutes in the city, two-thirds of whom were between the ages of 8 and 16 (Sanders, 1970, cited in Shoemaker, 1977).

Child and teenage prostitution in the United States today is engaged in by both males ("chickens") and females ("baby pros"). It is impossible to accurately estimate the number of such youth. Some researchers in this area have estimated that between 500,000 and 1.2 million males and females under the age of 16 are prostitutes in the United States either part- or full-time. This figure is estimated to double if 16- and 17-year-olds are included (Denson-Gerber, 1978, cited in *Tracy,* 1979).

Although these numbers may sound large, they are probably conservative even though some commonly quoted figures have to be taken with caution. It is often reported that in 1978, the Los Angeles Police Department had identified 30,000 child and adolescent males working as prostitutes in that city, 5,000 of whom were under age 14 and several hundred were as young as 8. Lemert (1978) has noted that these frequently cited figures were given a few days before the police department's annual budget hearing and a short time after the deputy mayor had been arrested for allegedly groping a vice officer in an adult theater—an incident which resulted in the vice squad's budget being reduced. The police reported that the figure of 30,000 was based on street estimates. Even so, the report was evidently sufficient to regain the losses to the vice squad budget.

Other studies suggest that regardless of the budget problems of the Los Angeles vice

Child and teenage prostitution involves both male and female youth.

squad, a large number of adolescents have at some time engaged in prostitution and that males are more likely to have done so than females. In one study of 822 students in a Midwestern urban high school, slightly over 5 percent of the males and 1 percent of the females reported that they had engaged in sex for money (Cornkovich and Giordano, 1980).

Exploitation

Many of the young prostitutes who have been studied have been found to be runaways (*Tracy,* 1979). These individuals, by their very age, are often susceptible to being coerced by adults and exploited in prostitution and pornography.

It has frequently been rumored that there are highly organized child and adolescent prostitution and pornography rings in various parts of the country. While there is little doubt that such efforts exist, the extent of this activity is unknown.

It also has to be noted that many of the children and youth involved in prostitution are quite capable when it comes to exploiting others. Although it is far removed from the personal experience of most of us, many of these young people are quite capable of "hustling" their way on the streets of a major city by prostitution without the aid of a coercing adult. Reiss (1960; 1961) noted that adolescent male prostitution was a rather common means of making money on the part of delinquent youth. Harris (1960) has described "baby pros" between the ages of 10 and 15 who worked alone and made $30,000 a year at that time. This does not negate the fact, however, that some young people wind up on the street for reasons that are not deliberate, totally free decisions about what they want to do with their childhood or adolescent years.

The Social Supports of Child and Teenage Prostitution

We should not be especially surprised that there are males who are interested in child or adolescent prostitutes, especially females. The child-woman figure has long been an image of innocence laced with forbidden and tantalizing sexuality in the minds of Americans. The clearest example are the young adolescent female models currently popular in advertising. As one editor of a leading fashion magazine put it (quoted in VerMeulen, 1981:4): "It's sex, you know? It's the child-woman look." "It's very provocative." ". . . they are still children, so the sex is forbidden. And that's provocative too, you know?" A photographer of these models (quoted in VerMeulen, 1981:4) states: "They're nymphs. And they have an innocence too! And if it's decadent innocence, it's just that much more exciting."

While the stardom of persons such as Brooke Shields may excite and intrigue the American public, there is a very thin line between posing nude at age 12 with one's mother's permission and selling jeans via sex at age 14 and encouraging the sexual attraction of some people to children and adolescents. It is not at all difficult to see how child and adolescent female prostitution is firmly grounded in what is considered by most to be a perfectly legitimate dimension of contemporary American society.

CUSTOMERS

The different types of men who go to adult female prostitutes are many and their reasons quite different. There are, however, some common characteristics of customers and prostitution which account for its attractiveness to many males.

Types of Customers

As James (1977) has described, not all customers of adult female prostitutes are attracted to prostitution out of pure lust. The traveler may not only be lonely when away from home, but he also has the anonymity he would not have in his hometown. Some *disabled* persons find that prostitutes do not apply the same standards of sexual acceptability as are maintained in the world of noncommercial sex. In most cases, the money is all that is required. During and after the Vietnam war, prostitutes served an important function in this regard for the many young males who returned home without arms or legs. The everyday world of noncommercial sex is relatively standardized in the form of a dominant sexual script prescribing appropriate and inappropriate sexual interests and activities. The *special* customer who has sexual interests which do not fit this script can find a willing partner in prostitution with no questions asked and the sexual activity conducted as if it were as common as kissing. The *impotent* male may find that a prostitute is nonthreatening, does not make him feel as if his lack of erection is a mark of masculine failure, and is more than willing to engage in a variety of sexual activities in which an erection is irrelevant. Some males go to prostitutes solely for *therapy* in the form of conversation. They may not want sex at all but just someone to talk to about their problems. The *uninvolved* male may go to a prostitute because she provides sex without any interpersonal commitments or because he lacks the time required to establish a sexual relationship in other kinds of cross-sex interaction.

Quantity, Variety, Quality

Prostitution is also attractive to many males because it contains elements which male sexual learning leads many men to define as "good sex" (James, 1977).

Males learn to place an emphasis on the quantity of sexual experiences. A man interested in the volume of sexual encounters can have sex with literally hundreds of prostitutes in the time it takes to develop a few sexual relationships outside of prostitution.

An aspect of this learned emphasis on quantity is an interest in variety. Many males use prostitution to obtain a variety of sexual experiences unlikely to be obtained elsewhere without considerable conscious effort. Regardless of what one desires, the variety is available in prostitution.

For many males, "good sex" is defined in terms of the physical activities involved. While prostitution is not noted for providing meaningful interpersonal relationships between sexual partners, it does offer raw sex and it is supplied by professionals. Quality is also provided in terms of satisfying the male's image of himself as a sexual being. Regardless of the size of his penis or the apparent ineptness of his sexual technique, he will be told by the prostitute that he is the "best lay in town."

ENTERING PROSTITUTION

Most of the women reading this would never even consider becoming a prostitute. For most of society, the "good woman"–"bad woman" dichotomy has been well learned. Even to be at the "bad" end of the continuum, let alone live the life, is repulsive to most women. How is it, then, that women become prostitutes? What are the factors responsible for selecting this lifestyle?

For many years, psychiatric models of deviance were employed to explain why women entered prostitution. These models basically argued that anyone who became involved in deviant behavior must themselves be deviant in some way. This assertion led to the reasoning that since prostitution is abnormal in terms of social acceptability, prostitutes must be psychologically abnormal. The end result of this rather long line of research was nothing. The reason for this failure is that prostitution is an occupation, and as such, must be understood just as we understand why a person selects to enter any other occupation. On the one hand, there are "push" forces in one's environment. On the other hand, there are "pull" forces in the occupation itself. Entering prostitution is not the result of some severe personality disorder, but rather, a quite easily understood process of drifting into a certain occupation

and lifestyle as a result of these push-and-pull forces.

The Female Gender Role

As James (1977) has pointed out, prostitution is easily understood as an exaggerated acting out of the traditional female role in American society. The prostitute learns, through a variety of slightly different learning experiences than most women, that being sexually enticing and providing males with sexual activity will result in rewards. "All women in our culture must somehow come to terms with the fact that their personal value is inseparable from their sexual value" (James, 1976:40). The prostitute merely carries this one step further and comes to see "sex as a status tool [which is] exploited to gain male attention" (Davis, 1978:304). In the choice to enter prostitution, she simply realizes that "carrying out the implications of the 'normal' female role can pay off not only in a certain sort of social status, but also in cold cash" (James, 1976:40).

This view is not so far removed from what many Americans consider perfectly reasonable uses of female sexuality. On the NBC special, *Women Who Rate a 10* on February 15, 1981, many of the women who are well known for their physical appeal said that one of the things they liked about being attractive was that they obtained certain privileges from men they would not get if they were unattractive (e.g., parking-lot spaces, faster services from male store clerks). Recalling our discussion in Chapter 5 regarding the sexually arousing qualities of female physical attractiveness, it is clear how this traditional element of the female role is not different in kind from exchanging sexual activity for money, but rather, only different in degree.

Early Sexual Experiences

One way in which the prostitute comes to her occupation is through early sexual experiences which differ from those normally experienced by adolescent females in this society. Prostitutes have intercourse much earlier than most women usually do. In James's (1976) research, for example, 57 percent had had intercourse between ages 15 and 17 and 92 percent by age 19, a significantly higher proportion than their peers at that time. This early sexual experience is frequently superficial and not emotionally charged, as it is for most adolescent women. James (1976) found that the average number of partners a prostitute had before entering the occupation was twenty-three, only five of which had been meaningful relationships. This type of early sexual experience enables one to separate sex from affection and emotional involvement.

Sex as a Commodity

Aiding in developing the view that sex can be easily detached from interpersonal involvement are the types of early sexual experiences that prostitutes tend to have (James, 1976). Prostitutes are much more likely than nonprostitutes to have early and initial sexual experiences that are negative in nature. In James's sample, 23 percent first experienced intercourse through physical force. Further, 65 percent had a forced or "bad" sexual experience before age 15, 57 percent had been raped—36 percent of them more than once and 8 percent by more than one person at a time. Such experiences not uncommonly involve a close relative. In James's study, 25 percent of the prostitutes had had intercourse with their father or close relative; sexual advances by a man at least 10 years older than themselves were much more common than among nonprostitutes.

These kinds of early sexual experiences all aid the prostitute to see sex not as an avenue of emotional and affectional exchange, but as something divorced from close relationships and affection. It is not unusual for prostitutes to view sex as a commodity which can be exchanged for some type of reward during this learning process. These early experiences also mean that the prostitute does not go through the usual pattern of extensive petting before experiencing intercourse at a later age. This omission is important in that prostitutes tend not to learn the typical patterns of "technical

virginity" and thus do not learn to place the same social and psychological values on males' sexual access to their bodies as do nonprostitutes. Rather, they learn to see sexual access to their bodies as a commodity.

Parental interaction In addition to the pattern of frequent sexual abuse by fathers and other relatives, prostitutes are much more likely to have serious disputes with their family, to obtain little parental sexual guidance, and to leave home at an early age. In James's research, the average prostitute left home at age 16 and entered prostitution at age 18.

Labeling Processes

The "good girl"–"bad girl" dichotomy arising out of the Victorian view of male and female sexuality is still very much with us. It is something which most adolescent males and females are well aware of as they begin to construct a socially learned image of sexuality. Once the "bad girl" label is attached, it is very difficult to remove, in the eyes of both others and oneself. A distinguishing characteristic of prostitutes is that they tend to get into trouble with juvenile authorities because of adolescent sexual activity. Once one starts along this path of being labeled a "bad girl," the avenues into "acceptable" society become rapidly closed and the avenues into "unacceptable" society open wider. To turn this drifting process around is a difficult process indeed.

Attraction to Prostitution

When asked, prostitutes also report that the occupation has certain attractions (James, 1976). Money ranks high on the list. Given that the occupational skill levels and educational attainment of most prostitutes are low, there are few, if any, jobs available to women that provide the possibility of such high pay. Prostitution is also attractive because it is seen as glamorous, as the fast life, as exciting. It provides social opportunities and experiences (at least in the mind of the young woman drifting in this direction) that are not available elsewhere. For example, in a very realistic sense, the occupational opportunities available to women who wish to have excitement, high pay, glamour, and a fast life without having particular job skills or education are nil. For men, there are many such opportunities under such conditions. Being a construction worker, for example, provides this type of lifestyle if one desires it to do so. For women, however, prostitution is the only easily accessible occupation that meets these requirements under these conditions.

These early learning experiences, placed in the context of the traditional female role, supported by a lack of parental influence, and bearing a negative label on the basis of sexual activity, combine well with a pattern of likely associates and a narrow set of occupational alternatives to make prostitution an easy choice. No special set of personality characteristics are needed for these push-pull factors to operate. James (1976) administered a number of personality inventories to prostitutes and a control sample of nonprostitutes. The only difference she was able to discern between the groups is that prostitutes scored slightly higher on the IQ tests. Exner et al. (1977) compared streetwalkers, house prostitutes, and call girls with nonprostitute women of the same age, marital status, and education. Call girls and house prostitutes were found not to differ from the nonprostitute controls in personality characteristics. Streetwalkers were less mature and more dependent than their controls and no group had any signs of psychopathology. Exner et al. did find one group of prostitutes which were characterized by significantly different personality characteristics than either their controls or the other types of prostitutes. Housewives who were part-time prostitutes revealed significant patterns of psychological maladjustment. This finding is not unexpected since this group fits into neither the "normal" world of prostitution nor that of nonprostitution.

In this same vein, it is a myth that prostitutes hate men. Their attitudes toward men vary greatly and display no standard pattern. The important thing to understand is that occupationally, the male must be viewed in a certain manner. He is the "john" and the prostitute's goal is to "turn a trick." If the prostitute is good, she does this without getting beaten up or arrested and for as much money and little effort as possible. The john is a member of the "straight" world and not in the "trade." In a very real sense, he is seen as a sucker to be paying for the prostitute's services in the first place. Additionally, much of prostitution involves a very real "con" in which the woman gets the john off and out for more money than she really believes she is worth. This is how she makes money and survives. Charity is not an important element of prostitution. Such an occupational structure is not likely to lead to having endearing feelings toward one's clients, regardless of the front that might be presented as part of the "con" during sexual activity. Such an attitude is common in much of commercial sex and is to be expected as an outcome of the occupation, not a requirement for entry.

Another common myth is that prostitutes are incapable of sexual responsiveness and that they get no pleasure from sex with the customers. An opposing, and equally incorrect, view is that prostitutes are "oversexed:" As for sexual responsiveness, prostitutes in general have orgasm as frequently as do nonprostitutes in their unpaid intercourse experiences. Call girls, in fact, tend to be more orgasmic than their nonprofessional counterparts (Exner et al., 1977). In the Exner study, it was further found that orgasm during paid intercourse varied widely, depending on the type of prostitute. While call girls experienced orgasm in 65 percent of their occupational intercourse, house prostitutes did so only 35 percent of the time and streetwalkers only 10 percent of the time. Major contributing factors here are undoubtedly the degree to which customers can be selected, the nature of the sexual activity, and the situation itself.

THE PIMP

"The Man" (prostitutes dislike the term "pimp") is a person who acts as a prostitute's agent for a percentage of her earnings. Not all prostitutes, and especially not call girls, work through a pimp. Streetwalkers and those who work hotels and bars without a pimp are referred to as "outlaws."

The pimp plays a more important role in the life of the prostitute than being merely a business agent. His role is a reflection and an exaggeration of the traditional male-female relationship in American society. He is "The Man." Traditionally, women learn that in order to be complete, they need a man to take care of them, to handle their business. The pimp fills all these roles within the context of a deviant lifestyle. The prostitute and the pimp share the values of the fast life. He protects her from arrest and bails her out when she is arrested. He (presumably) takes care of her when she is sick. If she goes to jail, he looks out for her property and her children. He handles the bills, provides clothing, housing, medical care, transportation, and entertainment. He also provides her with intimacy and emotional support and a sense of belonging. Additionally, the pimp provides her with status. Just as the status of a married woman is largely determined by the occupational status of her husband (Mahoney and Richardson, 1979), the status of most prostitutes in the world of prostitution is determined by the status of their pimp.

Status for the pimp comes through the only available option in this life; symbols denoting success in making money. Thus, dress, car, jewelry, and lifestyle are important in determining the status of the pimp. It is also determined by how well he handles his business interests.

In the larger cities, pimps tend to be blacks, and the black hustler serves as a general model for white pimps as well. The historical foundation of this situation is found in the frequent prostitution of black women in America and the limited opportunities for status for a black male in a racist society. Being a hustler has long been one of the few ways a black man could get ahead—symbolically, at least (James, 1976). Even though racist social patterns have changed considerably over time, the idealized role of the pimp is still very real.

The group of prostitutes a pimp has working for him is called a "stable," which may range in size from two to ten women. Each woman in a stable may be a partner with the pimp in an emotional and sexual sense as long as he fulfills his obligations to her. Most pimps have, however, a "main lady" who is a favorite and who takes on a managerial role. Each woman in the stable may believe that she will eventually be the "main lady" and that when she and the pimp have it made, they will retire from the world of prostitution together. Others, however, are interested only in a short-term business relationship. In actuality, few prostitutes realize this goal even though they may stay with a pimp for a number of years. Few pimps leave the life before they are consumed by violence or drugs or condemned to prison (James, 1976).

Pimps tend to be older than prostitutes since age is not an important economic factor. Given that they share a common set of lifestyle values with prostitutes, pimps also tend to have similar levels of education (eleven years) (James, 1976). The pimp commonly enters the life by simply being in close proximity to prostitution and taking the traditional male role into a business form. While pimps do recruit prostitutes into their stables, they do not recruit women into prostitution, as often thought. In fact, pimps may actually be recruited into the life by an older prostitute (James, 1976).

It is also generally thought that pimps force adolescent women into prostitution through force or drugs. They do do so, but not as the norm. First, dealing with an underage person involves great risk. Adolescent women are not only not responsible, but they present a rash of legal problems the pimp can do without. Addicting women to drugs and then forcing them into prostitution is also largely a myth. This is not the usual pattern. An addict is of little use to the pimp because she works for the drugs, not for him, and having to supply her with drugs is expensive (James, 1976).

It is also a myth that the pimp-prostitute relationship is founded on physical brutality. Not only is psychological coercion more effective when needed, but a prostitute who is beat-

The prostitute-pimp relationship takes on many of the dependency characteristics of the traditional male-female role. It is, therefore, the prostitute who is dependent on the pimp.

en up is of less economic value. In fact, the most common source of physical brutality to prostitutes is the customer—one reason why prostitutes categorize customers in terms of their potential for violence (as well as their ability to pay and the service desired) (James, 1976).

Enticing a prostitute away from a pimp can be a risky business—not because he is upset that she is leaving, but because his reputation can be damaged. If the prostitute and the pimp share a common set of values and get along well, she may leave when she wants without causing a problem. The break-up is much like a break-up in a dating relationship. On the other hand, if she has "done him wrong" and then attempts to leave, she is probably going to face physical brutality. The most important factor in such a process is the pimp's pride.

SOCIETY, LAWS, AND MORALS

The history of prostitution in modern times is largely the history of legal and moral attempts to eradicate the occupation. Throughout the history of the United States, there have been moral reform movements against prostitution. These movements were attempted in the colonial period but first took hold after the Civil War. They were initially concerned with prostitution, but later turned to the purification of the entire society (Bullough and Bullough, 1978). At the turn of the century, there were numerous investigations of prostitution in many cities and even on a national level.

One of the first attempts to deal with prostitution legally and on a national level was the request of President Grant for Congress to ban the importation of Chinese women for the purpose of prostitution. In 1875, Congress replied with a law banning the importation of any woman for prostitution. In 1907, this law was amended to include importation for any "immoral" purpose "for hire or without hire" (Bullough and Bullough, 1978). At the same time, Representative James Mann of Illinois introduced a bill aimed at the interstate commerce in prostitution. Given the federal action regarding any "immoral" purpose, the Mann Act quickly became applicable not only to the legal attempt to curtail prostitution but to the legislation of morals. It dealt with the transportation of any woman across any state line for any "immoral" purpose. Such is the history of the legal handling of prostitution.

Prostitution, like the sexually explicit materials industry, is a business of male fantasy. In the legal system's attempts to deal with prostitution, it has been a history of attempting to place moral judgments into law—judgments not about male fantasies and motivations, but about proper female sexual behavior. Legal action on prostitution has historically been directed toward the prostitute, not her customers. This has, of course, resulted in both discrimination and hypocrisy. While the pillars of a community join in bemoaning the evils of prostitution, many of them are often property owners in areas housing prostitution and even customers.

Recently, "anti-john" laws have been enacted in some jurisdictions; under these laws, the customer can be arrested. The law in New York perhaps reveals the often half-hearted nature of this effort. Going to a prostitute under the age of 11 carries a maximum sentence of seven years (*Time,* October 2, 1978). In some parts of the country, volunteers have attempted to discourage customers. Chicago had the Broadway Hookers Parade in which flashlights were shone in the faces of embarrassed male customers and their license-plate numbers recorded. In Joliet, Illinois, the local newspaper printed the names of arrested customers, including a priest and judge (*Time,* October 2, 1978). Even these tactics, however, are discriminatory on the basis of status. Just as it is the streetwalker who is most likely to be arrested, it is the customer of the streetwalker who is the most likely to be known. Call girls and their customers remain free of arrest and harassment. Vancouver, British Columbia, Canada, has recently enacted legislation which at least honestly states the government's position. The new anti-hooker law (as it is called) specifically prohibits only publically visible soliciting for prostitution and applies equally to both customer and prostitute and males and females.

It is clear that, regardless of what one thinks of adult female prostitution, it is not going to disappear through legal or moral action. Many individuals, really beginning with Margo St. James and the prostitute organization Coyote ("call off your old tired ethics"), have argued for decriminalization. Unlike legalization, which would involve only greater legal involvement, decriminalization would remove prostitution from legal concern. There are laws on the books to deal with the prostitution of minors, and business licenses could be required for some form of regulation. (Even that, however, is not necessary from many points of view.) It is clear that most of the cases involve consenting adults, that drawing the line at the exchange of money for sex is arbitrary if not difficult, that the current laws are discriminatory, and that the illegal nature of the activity only aids in its being associated with other illegal activities. It is also obvious that the legal systems have never been able to curtail prostitution. The reason for this is that there is a high demand and a ready supply, a demand and supply created not by the inherent immorality of prostitute and customer. Rather, the demand and supply are created by the very structure of male and female roles and male and female sexual learning. Until changes come about in the social and psychological bases of prostitution, legal efforts are simply efforts to satisfy complaints about the moral character of society by symbolically arresting those involved in the activity who are at the bottom of the class and status structure, streetwalkers and their customers.

MALE PROSTITUTION

There are two major types of male prostitution: males who sell sex to males and males who sell sex to females. It is clear that the latter do exist and even though the exact extent of this form of prostitution is unknown, it is safe to assume that it is very rare.

The most common form of male prostitution involves the sale of sex to other males. Because male prostitution lacks the traditional glamour and tacit social approval of female prostitution, social scientists, the public, and the law have given it little attention in the United States. This picture is beginning to change, however, with the recent concern about child and teenage prostitution; a large part of which involves male prostitution.

Types of Male Prostitution

Just as the world of female prostitution is diverse, so is there variety in the world of male prostitution. While delineating all the types of male prostitution is impossible, there do appear to be some major forms. Allen (1980), in a study of male prostitutes, has described four major types: full-time professionals, call boys and kept boys, part-time hustlers, and delinquents.[4]

Full-time professionals These are males who conduct the prostitution activity on a full-time basis by operating off the street or through pickups in bars. They usually do not work constantly but make a pickup when they need some money or feel like working. Even though they frequently share a residence with another male prostitute, they tend to live from day to day, with some of the full-time professionals following the warm weather around the country. Most of these men are masculine in appearance and have some female relationships or are married. Some even support a family through prostitution. They are not homosexuals in the sense that they prefer sex with men or identify themselves as gay.

While it is common for full-time professionals to brag about making $50 to $100 a customer, $15 to $20 is the actual income. Full-time professionals, knowing and associating with other male prostitutes, were found by Allen (1980) to maintain an informal association in which customers who did not pay were

physically assaulted, as were prostitutes who cheated customers.

Call boys and kept boys The males in this category are either call boys or kept by another male. Call boys are the male equivalent of call girls. They frequently advertise and list their phone numbers. They may also have a pimp or a madam. Allen (1980) points out that modern technology has an influence here. One pimp for male prostitutes had a 24-hour answering service and carried a beeper at all times to alert him to calling customers. Either the call boy will have a client come to him or he will go to the client's home or hotel room. The normal fee is $50 in the customer's residence, or $30 in the prostitute's; in both cases, 30 to 50 percent goes to the pimp. The call boy, like the call girl, is more physically attractive, socially presentable, and sexually versatile. He may often be a paid companion for dinner, the theater, or other evening-out activity with sex as part of the process. A kept boy is the male equivalent of a mistress. He is paid and cared for to live with another male. While some maintain long-term relationships of this nature, most are houseboys; they have no strong emotional attachment to their keeper, and when they tire of being a sexual servant, they move on.

Part-time hustlers This is the largest category of male prostitutes and consists of males who work part-time either off the streets and bars or as call boys. They tend to work only when they need the money. They enjoy the life of the gay subculture on the streets and many enjoy having sex with men. This group tends to be more particular about the characteristics of the customer. They are engaging in the activity for other than purely monetary reasons.

Delinquents These are most often males between the ages of 14 and 17 who live the life of a delinquent on the streets. Part of this life for them involves exploiting vulnerable male homosexuals from time to time. Their strategy is to pick up a male looking for a male prostitute and then threaten, assault and rob, or blackmail him. Their sexual activities tend not to be versatile. They are not gay and most

---

[4]Allen (1980) identified these four types as groups I through IV. I have taken the liberty of attaching nonnumerical names to the groups.

frequently only allow the customer to fellate them for a fee.

Houses While most male prostitutes work independently, those who work for a pimp or madam most often work as call boys. There are, however, a few male houses of prostitution (Pittman, 1977). These establishments usually offer a wide range of services based on individual specialties but social scientists and the public know very little about them.

Entry into Male Prostitution

In Allen's (1980) study, the ages of the male prostitutes compared closely with the ages reported in other studies. The average age of all the male prostitutes he studied was 17, with kept boys and call boys the oldest (average age, 18) and delinquents the youngest (average age, 16). The average age at entry into prostitution tends to be younger for males (14) than for females. This difference is most likely due to the greater freedom of movement and less restriction of males in American society (Allen, 1980).

Entry into male prostitution is quite similar to entry into female prostitution in that both involve a process of *drift*. Entry is not an abrupt occupational and lifestyle decision made on some Saturday morning or a process of being captured and enslaved in prostitution. Rather, entry is a gradual movement toward prostitution as a result of certain psychological and situational characteristics which make entry more probable and plausible than for the average reader of this text. Usually the male is introduced to prostitution by a male friend over a period of months, a fact which suggests the prior association with peers and a lifestyle not far removed from prostitution.

While the research on factors associated with this drift into male prostitution has not received nearly as much attention as in the case of female prostitutes, Allen (1980) provided some data that are suggestive. As among females, early sexual experience plays some part. Two-thirds of the males in the Allen study had their first sexual experience with a male at the average age of 13.5 years. The one-third who had their first sexual experience with a female did so at an average age of 12. It must

be kept in mind that this early age at first sexual experience may not mean much since all these males are sexually experienced, and if we were to compute the age at first sexual experience for males who are sexually experienced by age 14 (the average age of first prostitution for male prostitutes), it would probably be close to 12 or 13. Allen does point out that early sexual experience and an enthusiasm about sex were evident among the males studied. He also found that being seduced in one's first sexual experience seemed to be characteristic of male prostitutes. Here again, caution must be exercised in drawing conclusions. If one has one's first sexual experience at 12 or 13, one almost has to be seduced, since the average 12- or 13-year-old simply has not learned enough about the world of sexuality to be a seducer.

The most abrupt entry into prostitution perhaps occurs among runaways. It is here that the youth (either male or female) may decide on prostitution as a means of making some money while living off the street.

It should also be kept in mind that the average 14-year-old male prostitute may not live the life you and I find attractive, but he is also not necessarily an innocent victim of enslavement in commercial sex. It is clear that the independence and toughness of the adolescent hustler are at a level of adaptation to this life that would astonish many Americans (Ginzburg, 1967).

TRANSSEXUAL AND TRANSVESTITE PROSTITUTION

Transsexual and transvestite prostitution also exists. In both cases, the female prostitute is imitated. Transsexual prostitutes are often males who have undergone a partial male-to-female sex change procedure, so that they have female breasts and other secondary sexual characteristics as well as a penis. Transvestite prostitutes are males who dress as females and seek male clients as part of their playing out a female sexual role. Both transsexual and transvestite prostitution appear to be relatively rare but have become more common in recent years.

STUDY GUIDE

TERMS TO KNOW

Defining prostitution

Entering prostitution

Types of prostitution

Child and teenage prostitution

Male prostitution

Customers

SELF-TEST

Part I: True-False Statements

1. In order for a sexual act to be prostitution, the sex must be exchanged for money.
2. In the Old West, the frontier prostitute was universally looked down on as a "bad woman."
3. As many males today have sex with prostitutes as did males in Kinsey's time.
4. The pimp is the person most likely to harm the prostitute physically.
5. Prostitution on the part of females is an exaggerated acting out of the traditional female role.
6. Most female prostitutes are not capable of sexual response in terms of high levels of arousal and orgasm.
7. Males are more likely than females to be child or teenage prostitutes.
8. Entry into prostitution by both males and females is usually abrupt rather than a slow process of moving ever closer to this lifestyle.

Part II: Multiple-Choice Questions
Select the best of the three alternatives.

1. The type of female prostitution with the highest risk of physical brutality to the prostitute, the lowest pay, and the worst working conditions is that engaged in by *(a)* the call girl; *(b)* the Nevada house prostitute; *(c)* the streetwalker.
2. Female child prostitution *(a)* has appeared in the United States in only the last ten years; *(b)* is known to have been rather common in this country in the 1800s; *(c)* is more common today than male child prostitution.
3. Being sexually attracted to female prostitutes who are children or young adolescents is *(a)* associated with mental illness; *(b)* not far removed from the use of children as sexually provocative models in advertising; *(c)* most common among married males over the age of 50.
4. Males' attraction toward female prostitutes is based on *(a)* the forbidden nature of prostitution, *(b)* male sexual learning about what constitutes "good sex"; *(c)* prostitutes being sexual mother figures for many males.
5. Female prostitutes tend to *(a)* have more personality disturbances than nonprostitutes; *(b)* be less sexually responsive than nonprostitutes; *(c)* have earlier and more superficial sexual experiences than nonprostitutes.
6. Drifting into female prostitution is associated with *(a)* a series of negative childhood sexual experiences which push one into this life; *(b)* being attracted to prostitution because of the characteristics the occupation is seen as having; *(c)* certain "push" factors in the form of learning experiences and certain "pull" factors such as the attractive aspects of the occupation.

7. The relationship between the pimp and the prostitute is *(a)* based on fear and physical abuse; *(b)* one in which the prostitute is enslaved by the pimp; *(c)* an exaggeration of the traditional male-female relationship in the larger society.

TOPICS FOR DISCUSSION

Discuss *exactly* what it is about prostitution that disturbs you the most. Different people are disturbed by different characteristics of prostitution, but make a list among yourselves which is very specific. When you have your individual list, discuss (1) how the characteristics you have named are disturbing because of the sexual script you have learned as a member of this society and of a particular social group or category, and through individual learning experiences, and (2) whether each characteristic is really an aspect of prostitution. It is very important here that females talk about female prostitution and males talk about male prostitution, and that you compare the opinions of males and females.

Should prostitution be decriminalized, or should there be more strict and effective legal suppression? Does your answer apply to all kinds of prostitution? Why do you think these changes should be made? Would they work?

SUGGESTED READINGS

Bullough, V., and **B. Bullough,** *Prostitution: An Illustrated Social History.* New York: Crown Publishers, Inc., 1978.
This is an excellent history of female prostitution from its origin to the present. An easily read, scholarly work with interesting and informative photographs and illustrations.

James, J., "Prostitutes and Prostitution," in E. Sagarin and F. Montanino (eds.), *Deviants: Voluntary Actors in a Hostile World.* Morristown, N.J.: General Learning Press, 1977.
James's research in female prostitution is perhaps the best available today and this excellent chapter summarizes her research findings in an easily readable manner.

KEY TO SELF TEST QUESTIONS

Part I: True-False Statements

1. F (The exchange of money is certain to get one labeled a prostitute, but any exchange which is neither sexual nor affectional is prostitution.)
2. F (She was frequently a respected member of the community in the eyes of males.)
3. F (In terms of percentage of males, there has been a dramatic decline.)
4. F (Who is most likely to do so?)
5. T (Can you describe the evidence for this statement in terms of the nature of female prostitution and factors related to entering prostitution?)
6. F (This is a myth. How does this vary by type of prostitute?)
7. T
8. F (The process is one of drifting into the activity. You should be able to describe the factors associated with this drift for females.)

Part II: Multiple-Choice Questions

1. *c*
2. *b* (We have only recently started to pay attention to it.)
3. *b*
4. *b* (What aspects of male sexual learning are directly related to seeing female prostitutes as attractive sexual partners?)
5. *c* (The statements *a* and *b* are myths.)
6. *c* (Can you describe these "push" and "pull" factors for females?)
7. *c* (Describe some of the ways in which this is evident.)

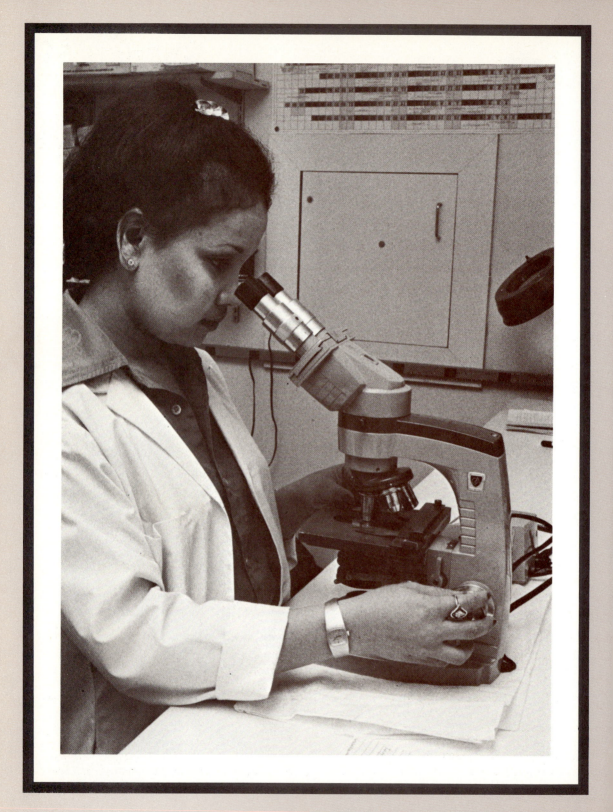

Chapter 16
Sexually Transmitted Diseases

In this chapter we shall discuss the ways in which sexuality can lead to changes in health status. In the next chapter we shall explore some of the more common ways in which a change in health status leads to changes in sexuality.

Traditionally, the discussion of sexually transmitted diseases has been couched in preventive terms. Specifically, how can negative health outcomes as a result of sexual activity be prevented? Discussions of this nature are quite consistent with the view that sex is bad or that "sexual excess" results in physical damage. In many ways, this Victorian view of sexually transmitted diseases is still with us today. It is still popular to think that sexually transmitted diseases are contracted by "promiscuity." While it is true that if you never had any sexual contact with anyone, your chances of getting such a disease would be near zero, the view that promiscuity is the major factor in transmitting such diseases has little to do with reality.

In fact, such a view of sexually transmitted diseases is a major factor in their growth and continuation. The term "VD" (venereal disease) carries very negative connotations, particularly about one's sexual patterns and partners. These images have a great deal to do with people's not discussing and practicing preventive health care in regard to sexually transmitted diseases.

KNOWLEDGE ABOUT SEXUALLY TRANSMITTED DISEASES

One outcome of the stigma attached to sexually transmitted diseases is that people do not talk about them. No talk means that no information is exchanged. No information exchanged means little knowledge within the general population.

Levels of Knowledge

Arafat and Allen (1977) found that among college students, the overall level of knowledge about sexually transmitted diseases is quite low. Reichelt and Werley (1975), in a study of Michigan teenagers, found that one-quarter of the people sampled thought that these diseases could be normally contracted from sources other than sexual contact, 14 percent thought that the disappearance of symptoms means the disease is cured, one-quarter thought that once you had a sexually transmitted disease you were immune to infection in the future, and

BOX 16-1
THE FACTS ABOUT VENEREAL DISEASE

The quotes below are statements taken from a United States Public Health Service publication in 1922 entitled *The Facts about Venereal Disease*. At this point, you should find this interesting reading. I have taken the liberty of making comments. The material is abbreviated from the original publication, but the order of the statements is exactly as it appeared in print and I have not altered the thrust of the communication in any way. The first thing to note is that the Public Health Service was part of the Department of Treasury in 1922. Remember the connection between sex and economy?

> The Government wants every man in the United States to know about venereal diseases (gonorrhea and syphilis) and how to avoid them.

The government was not interested in women having this knowledge.

> Gonorrhea in a man always causes temporary illness . . . this [the symptoms] happens about three to ten days after contact with a diseased woman.

Men evidently never gave the infection to women.

> It [a syphilis symptom] usually appears from two to eight weeks after going with a loose woman who has the disease.

Now that the concept of "loose women" has brought up the moral issue, the moral crusade against the social evils of the day begins by using the fear of venereal disease as a weapon.

> Most prostitutes and loose women have either syphilis or gonorrhea or both. Prostitutes are the chief carriers of these diseases . . . a loose woman is sure to get the germs of one or both diseases sooner or later . . . girls who permit intercourse "on the quiet" and those who do not charge (charity girls) are just as dangerous as public prostitutes. . . . Prostitution cannot be made safe. The only way to keep from getting

one-third did not know that a condom helps prevent such diseases.

Sources of Knowledge
While many parents say that topics such as sexually transmitted disease should not be taught in the public schools, we consistently find that teachers are the most important source of information about the subject and that parents are the least important source.

Thornburg (1981) obtained data on the source of *first information* that people obtained about a variety of sexual topics, including sexually transmitted disease. Only 9 percent of a large sample of high school students said they gonorrhea or syphilis is to keep away from all loose women and prostitutes.

Now that you are utterly scared to death of "loose women" and prostitutes, the argument begins to build toward its real goal.

Some men believe that a clean girl can be picked by her looks. . . . The nice girl who saves her charms for the men she likes and says she has only had one other lover in her life may have caught syphilis from that one.

Now that no woman is to be trusted, the government builds its case. Have you guessed what the next part of the argument will be?

A man may keep from sex intercourse without hurting himself. . . . Athletic trainers [are you ready?] insist that their men keep from all sex activity in order that they may be in the best physical condition for important contests. Polar explorers have been months away from women and at these times have performed some of the greatest feats of endurance.

And here we go, with a little medical mumbo jumbo to really set the stage:

The testicles make an "internal secretion," a substance which can not be seen, but which is absorbed into the blood and carried through the body, giving added strength to the nerves, and power to the brain and muscles.

Now that you know how we made it to the North Pole, you get the grand finale.

Masturbation or self-abuse is harmful. Athletics, abundant outdoor life, wholesome companions, lots of good fun, constant employment will help one break the habit called "self abuse" . . . and recover from any harm it may have done.

And these, they said, are *The Facts About Venereal Disease*.

first learned about such disease from their mothers and 2 percent from their fathers. The school was the most frequently mentioned first source of information, followed by peers and literature.

The same results appear when we ask people the most important overall source of information about sexually transmitted disease.

Bennett and Dickinson (1980) found that among college students, 67 percent of the males and 75 percent of the females listed their teachers as their most important source. Only 5 percent of the males and 4 percent of the females said that parents were their major source of information, and only about 27 percent of both males and females said they had obtained *any* information about sexually transmitted disease from their parents.

GONORRHEA

Gonorrhea is the oldest known sexually transmitted disease. It was first described, and originally named, by the Greek physician Galen in 140 B.C. He mistook the early symptoms of gonorrhea for semen flowing from the penis and labeled the disease from the Greek words *gonos,* meaning "seed," and *rhoia,* meaning "flow."

In the Middle Ages, gonorrhea and syphilis were thought to be the same disease. This idea became particularly popular in 1767 when John Hunter inoculated himself with gonorrhea bacteria from a patient. Unfortunately, the patient also had syphilis and Hunter developed the symptoms of both diseases. He thus mistakenly convinced himself that gonorrhea and syphilis were the same thing. In 1830, syphilis and gonorrhea were distinguished as separate

diseases by Philip Ricord. In 1879, Neisser identified the bacteria (which is named after him) that cause gonorrhea; in 1943, it was demonstrated that penicillin is an effective medication (Blau, 1961).

Incidence of Gonorrhea
As shown in Figure 16-1, the proportion of the United States population having gonorrhea declined sharply from 1946 to 1957 with the use of penicillin after World War II. From that time until 1975, gonorrhea infections increased dramatically, reaching epidemic proportions. From 1975 until 1981, the disease has shown a slight, but significant, decline.

This small decline in recent years is assumed to be the result of two factors: the National Gonorrhea Control Program and changes in treatment (Brown and Weisner, 1980; Rein, 1981). The National Gonorrhea Control Program, implemented in 1972, consists of three stages. The first stage was designed to reduce the incidence of gonorrhea and to re-

Figure 16-1 Rates of syphilis and gonorrhea in the United States, 1946–1977.

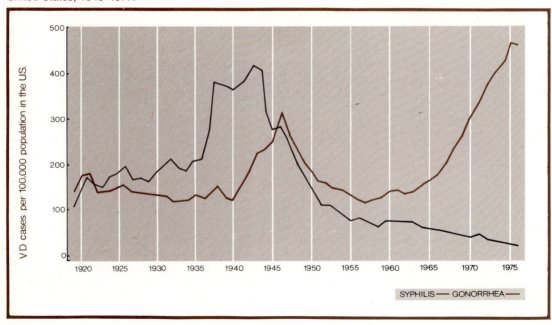

duce the resistance of gonorrhea bacteria to antibiotics (Brown and Weisner, 1980). In the late 1960s, the normal treatment was just enough antibiotics to kill the bacteria. This, however, resulted in producing stronger, more antibiotic-resistant bacteria, since weaker organisms were killed and those strong enough to survive the minimal dose reproduced. These stronger bacteria thus produced even stronger strains of gonorrhea bacteria and the disease became increasingly resistant to treatment. The initial phase of the national control program involved administering overly large doses of antibiotics. This overkill approach stopped the "survival of the fittest" process and inhibited the increasing resistance of gonorrhea bacteria to antibiotics (Rein, 1981). By 1975, nationwide testing for gonorrhea was also established in all state and local health offices, resulting in some 9 million tests a year. Currently, the national control program is involved in attempts to locate transmitters who may be "core infectors" (Brown and Weisner, 1980; Phillips et al., 1980).

Gonorrhea is still a major health problem. With more than 1 million *reported* cases each year, it is more prevalent than the common cold (chicken pox is the fourth most common disease, with only 154,000 cases a year). Translated into rates, there are currently 468 people with gonorrhea among every 100,000 individuals. The real rates of gonorrhea are known, however, to be considerably higher than these reported rates. It is estimated that as few as 25 percent of all gonorrhea cases are actually reported to the National Center for Disease Control in Atlanta, Georgia, where national health statistics are accumulated.

Incidence Patterns

The incidence of gonorrhea differs greatly by age. As shown in Table 16-1, the infection rate is much higher for those age 20 to 24 than for any other age group. The rate is also higher in cities than rural areas and differs by state. With the exception of our nation's capital (with a rate of 2,445 per 100,000 population compared with a nationwide rate of 468), Alaska

TABLE 16-1
Gonorrhea rates by age in the United States, 1978.

Age Group	Males (Number of cases per 100,000 population)	Females
0–14	11	37
15–19	978	1,482
20–24	2,409	1,569
25–29	1,648	669
30–39	661	191
40–49	196	43
50+	33	6

Source: Center for Disease Control: *Reported Morbidity and Mortality in the United States, 1978; Morbidity and Mortality Weekly Report 27 (54th Annual Supplement),* 1979.

has the highest gonorrhea rate and Vermont the lowest. Vast differences also exist by city. San Francisco (which we will discuss in detail) has the highest rate of any major city (2,756 cases per 100,000 population) while Yonkers, New York, has the lowest (138). As noted in Table 16-1, males also have significantly higher rates than do females.

Transmission

The main means by which gonorrhea is transmitted from one person to the next is by genital-to-genital contact. It may also be spread by oral-to-genital or anal-to-genital contact. In oral-genital activity, the female is much more likely to contract the infection from the male's penis than the male is to contract the infection from the woman's vagina. Of course, the major problem in controlling gonorrhea is that people keep infecting one another. If one person gets the infection and has it treated without having all of his or her sexual contacts treated also, the person's chances of being reinfected by them is quite high.

When genital-genital contact is made with a person who has gonorrhea, it is not certain that that person will become infected. Nationally, one-third of those individuals who have intercourse with an infected individual become infected themselves (*Sexually Transmitted Disease Newsletter,* 1978).

While getting sexually transmitted diseases, especially ones such as gonorrhea, from a toilet seat has always been a common joke, recent research indicates that even though it is not likely, it is possible. Gilbaugh and Fuchs (1979) found that gonococci bacteria when placed on a toilet seat or paper remained viable enough to be picked up by an individual for up to two hours afterwards. In a moist environment such as a towel, these bacteria remain viable for up to twenty-four hours.

Core transmitters Yonke et al. (1978) suggested that a major proportion of all gonorrhea infections may be spread and maintained by a core of individuals who have sexual contact with a relatively large number of people who, in turn, then pass it to others. Phillips et al. (1980) have support for this "core transmitters" concept. They found that in a given period of time a core group of 323 women with gonorrhea had a total of 1,008 male sexual contacts. This means slightly over 3 sexual contacts per infected woman, as compared with 0.92 sexual contacts per infected person nationally (*Sexually Transmitted Disease Newsletter,* 1978).

Male Symptoms

In males, the bacteria invade the urethra and produce inflammation. The first symptoms may appear anywhere between the first day and two weeks following contact with a carrier, but usually, they are evident within three to five days.

First, a clear, thin fluid seeps from the urethral opening. Within a day or two, the fluid becomes thicker and white, yellow, or yellowish-green in color. The glans of the penis then becomes swollen around the urethral opening and there is a burning sensation when urinating. One may also pass pus and/or blood in the urine. If not treated, the infection spreads up the urethra to the prostate, seminal vesicles, bladder, epididymis, and local lymph glands. The infection may also move into the

bloodstream and produce inflammation of the joints, heart, or spine.

Female Symptoms

The reason we earlier mentioned females in the research on core transmitters is that in 50 to 80 percent of the cases of female infection, there are no symptoms in the early stages of gonorrhea. This is sometimes true for the male as well, but is much more common for females (Bicher et al., 1977). A female is therefore very likely not to know when she has gonorrhea. The reason for the frequent lack of obvious symptoms is that the bacteria invade the cervix and pus is discharged from the infected area into the vagina and may thus go unnoticed. The infection may—but not always—spread to the urethra and cause pain when urinating.

The usual lack of obvious symptoms makes it extremely important that a male who becomes infected notify all his sexual contacts so that they may obtain medical care. He may have contracted the disease from a woman who does not know that she has it, or he may spread the disease to a partner who will not know she has been infected. Not notifying a partner is a serious ethical issue.

Female Outcomes

If gonorrhea is left untreated in a female, it has about a 50 percent chance of moving into the uterus and oviducts. If this occurs and there is no treatment, there is a strong chance of permanent damage which may result in sterility. The bacteria may also enter the bloodstream and cause damage to the joint, spine, or heart. At one time, almost a third of all cases of blindness in children were due to the infant's being infected with gonorrhea by the mother as it passed through the cervix in birth (Schulz, 1979). Today this is rare, thanks to gonorrhea tests and proper medication for infected infants.

Perhaps the major health outcome for women who get gonorrhea today is salpingitis (also known as pelvic inflammatory disease, a term no longer accepted as the correct name). We shall discuss salpingitis in detail later, but it is important to note here that this is the most frequent and serious complication of gonorrhea in women (St. John et al., 1981; Curran, 1980).

When gonorrhea is transmitted by oral contact with the infected individual's genitals, there are few, if any symptoms. A sore throat may be the only clue to infection. Many cases of rectal gonorrhea infections also exhibit no symptoms, although itching and discharge may develop in the early stages.

Treatment

In the early 1980s, there is no blood test to check for gonorrhea. The only means of diagnosis is by chemical examination of the discharge associated with the infection. The current treatment recommended by the Center for Disease Control is two large injections of penicillin at two separate body sites (one in each buttock) and oral medication. Tetracycline may also be taken orally—in daily doses for five days. Since many patients never return to the physician after the initial diagnostic visit, this treatment procedure can be ineffective (Kroger, 1979). A follow-up examination should be made three to seven days after completion of treatment to make certain the disease has been controlled (*Center for Disease Control, Recommended Treatment Schedules,* 1979).

Several researchers are currently working on the development of a gonorrhea vaccine. It will probably be forthcoming, but at present such insurance is not available.

SYPHILIS

The exact origin of syphilis is unknown even though its history has been marked by one country's placing the blame on another. The English called it the "French disease" and the "Spanish pox" and the French passed the favor by calling it the "Naples disease." The dominant theory has been that Columbus and his crew brought syphilis to Europe upon his

return from the New World. A second theory suggests that syphilis is one of many diseases caused by a single common organism and that it took on special characteristics as it evolved in the human species over time and in various geographical regions.

The name "syphilis" comes from the Italian poet and physician Fracastoro who, in 1530, wrote a poem in which a swineherd or shepherd, Syphilis, had the disease. The origin of the term is from the Greek meaning "swine" or "love." In 1905, the organism causing syphilis was discovered by two German scientists and in 1906 Wasserman, Neisser, and Bruck developed a blood test (the Wasserman test) for the infection. Today, the Wasserman test for syphilis has been replaced by a number of more effective blood-testing procedures.

Incidence

From shortly after World War II until the late 1950s, the rate of syphilis infection in the United States declined dramatically. From the late 1950s until the mid-1960s, the rate again increased and since that time has more or less leveled off (Figure 15-1). Today, gonorrhea is a much more serious health problem than syphilis.

In 1978, there were 21,656 cases of primary- and secondary-stage syphilis in the United States. Another 434 cases were congenital (transmitted to the infant by the mother) and some 40,000 cases were third-stage syphilis. In 1978, the syphilis rate (primary and secondary stages) in the United States was 10 per 100,000 population. As shown in Table 16-2, the rate of infection is highest for those aged 20 to 29 and for males.

Symptoms

There are four stages in syphilis and each stage has a different set of symptoms. The initial or *primary stage* is characterized by a sore called a chancre (pronounced shank-er) which appears at the point where the infection enters the body. This usually develops three to four weeks after sexual contact with an infect-

TABLE 16-2
Syphilis rates by age in the United States, 1978.

Age Group	Males (Number of cases per 100,000 population)	Females
0–14	0.2	0.4
15–19	17.0	13.0
20–24	46.0	16.0
25–29	47.0	12.0
30–39	29.0	6.0
40–49	14.0	2.0
50+	2.0	0.3

Source: Center for Disease Control: *Reported Morbidity and Mortality in the United States, 1978; Morbidity and Mortality Weekly Report 27 (54th Annual Supplement),* 1979.

ed person (but may be as soon as ten days or as long as three months). In males, the chancre can appear anywhere on the penis or scrotum, but usually develops on the glans or between the glans and the penis shaft. Generally, only one chancre appears, but multiple sores are known. Rarely, chancres may appear on the fingers, lips, mouth, breast, or anus. In women, the chancre is often not visible, since it develops on the cervix or inner vaginal walls. It may also appear, however, on the vaginal lips, clitoris, or urethral opening. Again owing to the lack of visibility of early symptoms in women, it is important that a male notify each of his partners so that they may obtain treatment.

At first the chancre is a dull red bump

A chancre on the penis is a symptom of the primary stage of syphilis.

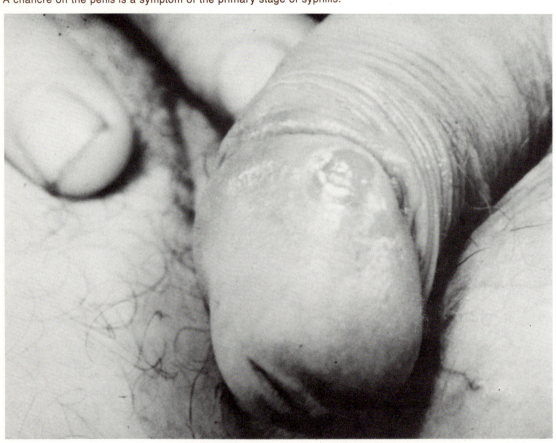

about the size of a pea. The surface then breaks down and becomes an open, indented sore. The chancre is painless, and if not treated, will heal itself in one to five weeks. Even though this symptom disappears when left untreated, the infection continues to develop within the body and the person can still transmit the disease to sexual partners. If left untreated, syphilis moves into the *secondary stage.* Approximately six weeks after the first appearance of a chancre, a generalized rash develops on the skin. This rash is highly variable in its characteristics and location, but it does not itch or cause pain. In about 25 percent of all cases, the secondary stage is also accompanied by frequent headaches, loss of appetite, nausea, constipation, pain in the bones, muscles, or joints, and a low and persistent fever. One of the problems of diagnosis at this stage is that these symptoms are characteristic of many other illnesses. If left untreated, these symptoms will usually disappear in about two to six weeks.

While one may feel better, the condition has actually become more dangerous, however, as the disease moves into the *latent* (hidden) *stage.* After about one year in this stage, the infected person can no longer pass the disease to a sexual partner. A pregnant woman can, however, transmit the disease to an unborn fetus. In about 25 percent of all cases in the latent stage, however, the person reenters the primary and secondary stages. A chancre may reappear at the original site, a rash may again develop, and the disease may then go into its hidden form again. Approximately two-thirds of those individuals who enter the latent stage live the rest of their lives without any further problems. The other one-third, however, develop the serious complications of *late-* or *tertiary-stage* syphilis.

There are three major types of late-stage syphilis: benign and cardiovascular late syphilis and neurosyphilis. In *benign late syphilis,* the skin, muscles, digestive organs, liver, lungs, eyes, and endocrine glands may be affected. The characteristic effect of this type of late-stage syphilis is a gumma or large destructive ulcer on the affected area. If treated

promptly, the ulcer will heal and, in most cases, the person will recover without ill effects. If not treated, the ulcer will destroy the affected area. Benign late-stage syphilis develops in about 17 percent of the untreated cases in about three to seven years after the beginning of the original infection. *Cardiovascular late syphilis* attacks and injures the heart and major blood vessels. This form of late syphilis develops between ten and forty years after the original infection in about 10 percent of the cases left untreated. *Neurosyphilis* affects the spinal cord and brain, resulting in paralysis and insanity, and the end result is usually death. This form develops between ten and twenty years after the original infection in approximately 8 percent of the untreated cases.

Congenital syphilis Syphilis during pregnancy often results in the woman's having fewer and less severe symptoms than if she were not pregnant. If the mother has syphilis, the infection can travel through her blood supply and enter the placenta and infect the fetus. If the placenta has not developed, the transfer is not possible. Thus, if a woman's syphilis infection is detected and treated before the fourth month of pregnancy, the child will not develop the disease. If the mother is in the primary or secondary stage of syphilis, the child will almost certainly contract the disease and most often will die either before or shortly after birth. If the mother is in the latent stage, the child may escape infection or develop the symptoms later. In these latter cases, the disease does not immediately threaten the child's life.

Diagnosis and Treatment

While the symptoms characteristically associated with syphilis may suggest infection, they are not dependable enough to be the basis of a firm diagnosis. The only way to diagnose the disease with any degree of certainty is by means of a blood test. The basis of any blood test for infection is the presence of *antibodies.* An antibody is a chemical produced by the body when it is invaded by disease-causing organisms. The body produces different types of antibodies for different kinds of disease-causing organisms, and therefore the blood test examines for the normal presence of syphilis antibodies.

As noted earlier, one problem with the blood tests for syphilis is that the same organism can cause syphilis and other very similar, but not venereal, diseases, such as yaws. The blood tests cannot tell these diseases apart.

The most common test is the VDRL. These letters stand for Venereal Disease Research Laboratory of the U.S. Public Health Service, where the test was developed. This is a reasonably accurate test, and it is cheap and easy to perform. It does, however, have some limitations. It cannot produce accurate results unless the disease has been present in the body for four to six weeks. Even after that, it produces a "false negative" result (it says no when it really means yes) in 24 percent of the cases. Thus, a negative result with a VDRL does not always mean that a person does not have primary-stage syphilis. In the secondary stage, however, the VDRL is 100 percent accurate. The VDRL will also produce a "false positive" (it says yes when it really means no) in some people who have recently had chicken pox, measles, mononucleosis, or infectious hepatitis. False positives are also very common (60 percent) in heroin users.

If there is a suspected false positive or false negative result with the VDRL, the fluorescent treponemal antibody absorption test (FTA-ABS for short) is used. This test is far more accurate than VDRL, but it is also more difficult and requires expensive equipment.

The most common form of unusual bump on the genitals is a simple pimple. Many people mistake a chancre for a pimple (perhaps often from wishful thinking), and when the "pimple" disappears, the problem is out of sight and out of mind. Don't try and fool yourself. If you have anything unusual on your genitals, go to your Public Health Office and have a blood test. Also, if you think you have syphilis and are in the primary stage and the result is negative, ask to have a FTA-ABS run. You will feel better and the health staff will be impressed with your knowledge.

Visual diagnosis of syphilis in the secondary stage is also not very reliable, even when performed by a physician. In one study (Chapel, 1981), only 40 percent of the patients who actually had secondary-stage syphilis were diagnosed as having it by a physician. Part of the reason for this is more general than just secondary-stage syphilis. Sexually transmitted disease diagnosis receives little attention in most medical training. Textbook descriptions of symptoms are often inadequate for real-life practice, and frequently, medical students have only one lecture on sexually transmitted diseases in four years of medical school. Few medical school students ever see a real patient with a sexually transmitted disease (Felman, 1981).

HERPES

There are five viruses which cause the herpes type of infections. The two most commonly known ones are herpes simplex Type I and herpes simplex Type II (Tummon et al., 1981). There are several forms of herpes virus infection, not all of which are sexually transmitted diseases. These include cold sores, the most common form of infection and affecting some 30 million people; herpes encephalitis, a rare but deadly brain disease; neonatal herpes, transmitted during pregnancy or birth; herpes of the eyes, the leading cause of infectious blindness in young adults; and the well-known genital herpes (McKean, 1981).

Actually, a very large percentage of the American population has at some time been exposed to some type of herpes virus. Ninety-five percent of all blood samples taken reveal some herpes antibody, indicating that the person was exposed to the virus but the immune systems rejected the infection (McKean, 1981).

Herpes Simplex Type I

Herpes Type I is the cause of most cold sores and usually infects the head region. Type I can also infect the genital region if it is transmitted by oral-genital contact (McKean, 1981). Type I also takes on a recurring form by the same processes described below for herpes simplex Type II, although recurrence is more common for herpes Type II (Tummon et al., 1981).

Herpes Simplex Type II

Herpes Type II generally infects the individual below the waist and only on the genitals. As in Type I, Type II herpes can be transmitted to the head region by means of oral-genital contact.

The first known record of Type II or genital herpes, as it is often called, was made in 1736 by Jean Astruc, and the name "herpes" was applied to genital skin eruptions in 1814 by Thomas Bateman. It was not until 1912 that the herpes simplex virus itself was discovered, and in 1946 the virus was isolated in the female vaginal tract (Tummon et al., 1981).

Transmission and Infection   The initial herpes II infection is transmitted by direct contact with an individual who has the disease. The transmission can be genital-genital, genital-oral, genital-anal, or oral-anal. After initial infection, there is an incubation period of between two and twenty days with an average of six days. When herpes Type II results in genital infection, as it customarily does, the virus travels through the peripheral nerves to the ganglia in the spinal cord located in the sacral region. Here in the sacral ganglia, the virus become latent. It presents no symptoms, cannot be seen by even an electron microscope, and cannot be destroyed by the body's immune system.

The herpes virus, like all viruses, is a small organism which invades the nucleus of a cell and then "instructs" it to produce virus molecules. The herpes virus, once located in the sacral ganglia cells, reproduces itself while being free from attack. Periodically, the virus becomes reactivated (a process known as viral shedding) and moves back along the nerve pathway to the skin, where it causes a recurrent infection in the form described in the following subsection. This is the insidious nature of the disease. Once one has herpes Type II, he or she has it for life and will suffer the

symptoms when it undertakes a recurrence (Tummon et al., 1981).

The name "herpes" comes from *herpein,* "to creep," an unfortunately accurate title. Eighty percent of all herpes II patients have recurrent infection episodes, but the longer one has the disease, the less frequent the recurrences (Tummon et al., 1981). There is no single factor or set of factors which has been scientifically shown to be associated with these recurrent episodes. Reports from patients suggest that recurrence may be more likely when the person is under emotional or physical stress, has a fever, engages in sexual activity, menstruates, or goes into the sun.

General symptoms   The symptoms of herpes Type II infection begin with an ache or itch followed by visible blisters resembling cold sores on the skin about 1 or 2 millimeters in diameter. These sores then rupture and form an erosion in the center. The erosions crust over and heal. Once healed, there is no scar although there may be a slight darkening of the skin (Tummon et al., 1981). In the initial infection, this process takes an average of twenty days. In recurrent infections, the average is approximately ten days (Tummon et al., 1981). The initial infection also usually results in more severe symptoms than in recurrent infections, and it may be accompanied by fever and tenderness and swelling of the lymph nodes.

Female symptoms   In females, the sores are usually multiple and located on the labia minora, labia majora, or both. They may also appear on the clitoris, buttocks, thigh, or cervix. Research indicates that the cervix is the most common site of herpes II in females, meaning that one may have the disease and not know it (Adam et al., 1980). If the sores are located on the dry skin, they will crust over before healing, as described above. However, in many females the sores are located on a moist region and will not crust over before healing. Patients may also suffer from pain in the region of the perineum, difficult or painful urination, or painful intercourse (Tummon et al., 1981). It is not uncommon for women to be treated for vulva pain or irritation as if it were

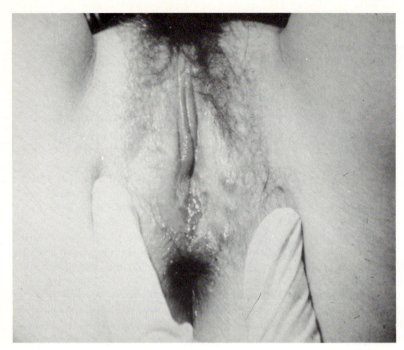

Blisters resembling cold sores on the vulva are symptoms of the herpes type II infection.

caused by a vaginal infection when the actual cause is herpes II. Diagnosis by a physician is usually visual, but there are laboratory tests as well.

Male symptoms   In males, the penis is the most common site of the blisterlike sores, but they may also appear on the general pubic area, the buttocks, thighs, or anal region. Since the skin is dry, the sores usually crust over before healing.

Treatment   Presently, there is no cure for herpes II. Therefore, once one contracts the virus he or she has it for life and must contend with recurrent infections. While there are numerous home remedies reported to be effective in treating the painful blisters of herpes II outbreaks, the only effective medication available in the United States is acyclovir (created and marked by Burroughs Wellcome Company under the trade name Zovirax). This ointment is applied every three hours, for seven days. Several clinical trials indicate that the medication is effective in reducing the pain,

healing time, and duration of the blister outbreak. The major problem in finding a cure for herpes II is that the cure has to be able to kill the virus while it is in the cells of the ganglia without damaging the cells in which it has taken up residence—a difficult task. Research is also examining a vaccine against herpes II, and preliminary reports indicate that several drugs show promise (Skinner et al., 1980; McKean, 1981).

Additional health complications· At present, an exact cause-and-effect relationship between herpes II and certain forms of cancer has not been established. A relationship between cervical cancer and herpes II was first noted in 1966 (Tummon et al., 1981), and even though that relationship is clear today (Kumar et al., 1980), herpes II remains to be established as a cause of cervical cancer (Seth and Balachandran, 1980). It may well be a contributor to cervical cancer by causing cervical infections and abnormalities which later increase the chance of cervical cancer. There is also a relationship between prostate cancer and herpes II, but here too, no cause-and-effect has been established (Baker et al., 1981).

Fetal and neonatal herpes II

Without a doubt, the greatest serious health risk with herpes II which is presently established is infection of the fetus and the newborn by the mother. This risk is not confined to herpes II, but also exists for herpes I (American Academy of Pediatrics, 1980). Both forms of herpes can fatally affect the unborn fetus, but 75 percent of these deaths are due to herpes II. At least 50 percent of the children born to mothers with herpes II have serious neurological or vision problems, and 60 percent die (American Academy of Pediatrics, 1980). The most severe risk is to infants whose mothers have herpes II and whose fetal membranes rupture more than four to six hours before birth. This allows the herpes virus to enter the fetus directly. If the mother has herpes II, the current practice is a cesarean section so as not to risk infection from this source or from an unknown active infection in the cervix (American Academy of Pediatrics, 1980). Some recent evidence indicates that a vaginal delivery is safe if the herpes II is not active at the time of birth. Grossman et al. (1981) reported vaginal delivery of 60 infants in 58 pregnancies, 58 of whom survived even though the mother had herpes II in its latent form. On the other hand, Hain et al. (1980) found that herpes II can invade even the intact placenta and that a cesarean section cannot therefore prevent all cases of infant infection.

Incidence Herpes II is a serious health problem in the United States. With more than 20 million victims and approximately 300,000 to 500,000 new cases each year, herpes II constitutes 13 percent of all sexually transmitted disease infections (Altman, 1979; Smith, 1981; McKean, 1981).

Life effects Given that once one has herpes II and that it cannot be cured, the individual's life often is severely restricted. The infection may become active at any time, the factors which cause recurrence are unknown, and there is presently no cure. If one finds that some condition, such as stress or sunshine, seems to activate recurrence of the symptoms, one's life can become extremely confined and guarded in order to avoid the painful outbreaks. Additionally, if one has any moral responsibility, one is not willing to be a sexual partner with a person who does not have herpes II. If you have the virus and tell a person about it, you are unlikely to find that person much interested in sex. In response to these life problems, HELP, a nationwide herpes group, has been formed by the American Social Health Association in Palo Alto, California. The organization currently has some 40 chapters and 25,000 members. HELP sponsors discussion groups, hotlines, lectures, and a newsletter for herpes II victims which aid them in dealing with the disease, including the location of other herpes II victims as potential sexual partners (McKean, 1981).

CHLAMYDIA

Chlamydia are microorganisms closely related to bacteria which cause a variety of infections, including genital ones (Schachter, 1978). Chlamydial infections appear to be in epidemic proportions in the United States, being over twice as common as gonorrhea. In 1981, for example, 8 to 9 percent of the women attending prenatal clinics in Seattle and Denver had chlamydial infections, compared with 2 percent having gonorrhea (Handsfield et al., 1981).

Chlamydia are mainly transmitted by sexual contact but can also be contracted by nonsexual contact (Handsfield et al., 1981). The connections the infection appears to have with other disorders make it a major health problem in both the United States and the rest of the world. It has been linked to stillbirth and newborn death; it is the world's leading cause of preventable blindness and the predominant cause of several types of cervical infections; and it is the most common cause of pneumonia in children one to three months in age (Handsfield et al., 1981; Schachter, 1978).

Chlamydial infection is also strongly implicated in salpingitis, a major sexually transmitted disease having serious health outcomes (Handsfield et al., 1981; Holmes et al., 1980; Paavoner, 1980).

The symptoms of chlamydial infection are varied and ill-defined but commonly involve an infection of the urogenital tract. Many individuals have no symptoms. Therefore, the only way to identify the infection is by examining a tissue culture. It is currently thought that most cases of this infection go undiagnosed until some aftereffect is noticeable.

SALPINGITIS

Previously labeled ambiguously as pelvic inflammatory disease, or PID, salpingitis takes two major forms: *gonococcal,* when gonorrhea viruses are found in the lower genital tract, and *nongonococcal,* when gonorrhea viruses are not located (Westrom, 1980). The disease itself is an infection which can appear in any part of the female reproductive system, and it is caused by gonococcal or nongonococcal infections located in the cervix (St. John et al., 1981). Salpingitis has been clearly linked with prior gonorrhea and chlamydial infection (St. John et al., 1981; Curran, 1980). However, salpingitis caused by nongonoccal infections can come from any infection source in the genital tract or even from a nearby pelvic organ such as the appendix (Westrom, 1980). Thus, in many, but not all cases, the original cause is some other sexually transmitted infection. It is here, of course, that the line between sexually transmitted and other diseases becomes thin at best.

While salpingitis can be caused by any source of infection anywhere in the genital tract, reproductive organs, or even pelvic region, by far the most cases begin with an infection in the lower genital tract. From this location, the infection ascends to the cervix. How this ascent takes place is not exactly known, but some normal cervical resistance factor is thought to protect against an infection ascending from the lower genital tract up to and into the cervix. This resistance is believed to disappear at ovulation and menstrual bleeding (Westrom, 1980). From the cervix, the infection may spread to any reproductive organ as salpingitis.

Symptoms

Salpingitis is often difficult to diagnose because the symptoms are frequently unclear (Jacobson, 1980). Common symptoms may include tenderness in the pelvic organs, abdominal pain, painful urination, vaginal discharge, abnormal menstrual bleeding, severely increased menstrual cramps, or even chills and fever (Eschenbach and Holmes, 1975; Golden, 1980). Given these vague symptoms, diagnosis of salpingitis is indeed a serious problem (Golden, 1980).

Incidence

The exact incidence of salpingitis in the United States is unknown, but it is increasingly clear that it is a major health problem. The most recent estimate as of this writing is that there are about 200 cases per 100,000 women (St. John et al., 1981), or almost 1 million cases annually in the United States. These 1 million cases result in 2.5 million physician visits, 250,000 hospital admissions involving 1.5 million days of hospitalization, 150,000 surgical procedures, and 900 deaths annually (Curran, 1980). It is estimated that if these rates continue until the year 2000, 50 percent of all women who were 15 years old in 1970 will have salpingitis. Of these women, 15 percent will require hospitalization, over 50 percent of whom will require major gynecologic surgery (Curran, 1980).

Treatment

If salpingitis has not caused a major complication, it can be effectively treated with antibiotics (Cooperman and Ruiz, 1980; Rees, 1980). However, quite often the disease is not diagnosed until some rather serious, or potentially serious, complication has taken place. In these cases, the required treatment may be surgery in addition to medication for the original infection. Further, as mentioned earlier, the difficulty of early diagnosis and the relatively high rates of gonorrhea and chlamydial infections make treatment at the origin difficult.

Complications

The most serious complication of salpingitis is infection of an ovary or oviduct, resulting in an abscess which then ruptures. Mortality in these cases is between 50 and 90 percent (Ginsburg et al., 1980). Salpingitis also frequently results in less life-threatening, but still serious, damage to the ovaries and oviducts (St. John et al., 1981). As a consequence, it has been implicated as the cause of approximately 50 percent of all ectopic pregnancies; and the risk of an ectopic pregnancy is 6 to 10 times greater than normal for those women who have had salpingitis (Curran, 1980). When the disease is caused by a gonorrhea infection, infertility results in more than 20 percent of the cases (Curran, 1980). Clearly, this is among the most dangerous of all sexually transmitted diseases.

Risk Factors

The factors which increase the risk of getting salpingitis are rather clear since major research attention has been focused here. In summary, these risk factors are related to contracting a sexually transmitted disease in general. Having more than one current intercourse partner increases one's risk of salpingitis 2.6 times over that of having only one current partner; having coitus more than five times a week increases one's risk 1.9 times; and being under 25 increases one's risk 1.9 times (Burkman and Woman's Health Study, 1981). These are all important risk factors since they increase the chance one will contract some initial sexually transmitted infection which will ascend to the cervix and cause salpingitis. There is some evidence that younger women (ages 15 and 16) may be more prone to salpingitis because at these ages the cervical mucus

may have hormonal characteristics which weaken the resistance to ascent (Holmes et al., 1980).

Use of the interuterine device (IUD) has been clearly associated with the chance of salpingitis (Osser et al., 1980). Vessey et al. (1981c) found that the incidence of acute salpingitis was 10 times greater among IUD users than among women who had never used this device. The duration of IUD use and the type of IUD appear unrelated to the chance of salpingitis (Burkman and Woman's Health Study, 1981).

NONGONOCOCCAL URETHRITIS (NGU)

All inflammations of the urethra that have not been caused by gonorrhea are called NGU. This is a bit of a catch-all term since the exact causes have not been isolated. It is relatively clear, however, that chlamydia is one, if not the only, major cause. Occurring in both males and females, the symptoms are a clear, thin, white discharge from the urethra. The treatment is with antibiotics, but some patients do not respond well to treatment and the infection may recur quickly. NGU is thought to be much more common than gonorrhea and is clearly implicated in salpingitis.

GENITAL WARTS

Venereal or genital warts are caused by a virus similar to that which causes common skin warts outside the genital area of the body. It is thought that this virus is usually transmitted by sexual contact, but this is not always so. The probability of contracting the virus after sexual contact with an infected partner is, however, between 60 and 70 percent. Uncircumcised males are more apt to get genital warts than circumcised males.

The warts appear some one to three months after sexual contact with an infected partner. In men, they most often appear on the glans and foreskin, the urethral opening, the penile shaft, and the scrotum—in that order of frequency. They may also appear in the anus through anal intercourse. In women, they most frequently appear on the bottom of the vaginal opening, but also occur on the labia, deep in the vagina, and the cervix.

Diagnosis is visual. If the warts are small, they can be removed by applying a chemical derived from the mandrake plant (podophyllin). The instructions for its use must be followed closely or chemical burns will result. If the warts are large, they must be removed surgically.

PEDICULOSIS (PUBIC LICE) "CRABS"

Pubic lice are small parasitic lice which affect the pubic region and adhere to the hair shafts. In their drawing blood from the body, they cause severe itching, often at night. This reaction, however, does not appear in all people. Although pubic lice are sexually transmitted by the touching of genital areas, they can be contracted in other ways, including—are you ready?—the infamous toilet seat or any other physical contact. Pubic lice are often visible, being as large as the size of this o. They can be easily killed with drugs available without a prescription. (Kwell in the United States or Kwellada in Canada and A-200 Pyrinate are two major brand names.)

SCABIES

Scabies are extremely small mites about the size of a pin head. They are generally not visible to the naked eye. They burrow beneath the skin and feed on liquid. This invasion creates a small, wavy, slightly elevated line or lines on the skin which can be seen with a magnifying glass. The same cure as for pubic lice can be used effectively.

VAGINITIS

Vaginitis is vaginal inflammation or irritation. While it is not strictly a sexually transmitted disease, it is a very common genital problem for women. Vaginitis is not dangerous, but it can be very uncomfortable and deserves immediate medical attention. There are three common kinds of vaginitis and all three have very similar symptoms. They can be distinguished by microscopic examination of a drop of vaginal secretion. If you have vaginitis, you should demand that this microscopic analysis be performed before a diagnosis is made and treatment prescribed. All too often, medication is prescribed on the basis of guesswork rather than precise testing. *Just because you do not have one of the ten major life-threatening diseases of the world does not mean that you should settle for less than first-quality medical care. It is your body.*

Yeast Infection

Yeast infection (also called candidiasis, moniliasis, or fungus) is caused by a yeast fungus. Yeast organisms normally reside in the vagina, but a yeast infection is due to a greater-than-normal growth of such organisms. This growth is aggravated by changes in hormones during pregnancy which cause the cells of the vagina to store more sugar and thus to make for a good growth environment for the yeast. Diabetes creates the same condition. Birth control pills having a high dose of estrogen (more than .05 milligrams per pill) make a woman more susceptible, and antibiotics reduce the number of other organisms in the vagina and enhance the growth environment for yeast. Also, anything which in general lowers the body's resistance to disease can aid the growth process of yeast organisms.

The organisms can also move to the vagina from the anus. After anal intercourse, the penis should always be completely washed before being inserted in the vagina. The anus should always be wiped from the vagina back rather than toward the vagina. The organisms may also travel under the foreskin of the penis and be transmitted during intercourse.

The symptoms include itching, which may be very severe, a redness of the vulva, a dryness and redness of the vagina, painful sexual intercourse, and a thick, curdlike vaginal discharge which is white (in general, it resembles cream cheese).

Treatment is best given in the form of an antibiotic that is administered in tablets which are inserted into the vagina before going to bed. The symptoms usually disappear within forty-eight hours and treatment should continue for about four weeks. This treatment can be messy since the medication leaks out of the vagina while the woman is sleeping. Stopping the treatment before the designated time period results, however, in a return of the infection.

Trichomonas

Trichomonas ("trich") is caused by a microscopic, single-celled organism. Sexual contact is probably the most common form of transmission, but the trichomonads (the organism) can survive at room temperature on moist objects for several hours. Thus, one may contract the organism by a washcloth, towel, or even the infamous toilet seat. In some men, the organisms can enter the penis, move up the urethra, and terminate in the prostate gland. When the male ejaculates (remember that 60 percent of the ejaculate comes from the prostate), the organisms can be deposited in the vagina.

Most often, the symptom is an abundant vaginal discharge which is frothy, thin, white or yellow, and unpleasant in odor. A few women patients have no symptoms. The discharge irritates the vagina and vulva, commonly causing redness, pain, and itching. These symptoms can become very severe. Over a long term (months or years), the walls of the cervix can become damaged, making one more susceptible to cervical cancer.

In the female, trichomonas invades the vagina and cervix, the Skene's and Bartholin's glands, the urethra, and the bladder. In males, there are seven possible sites of infection in the genitourinary tract.

Topical treatments are generally considered ineffective and a common effective medication is Flagyl, which must be taken by both sexual partners or they will pass the infection back and forth.

Diagnosis is initially made by the observation of red, raised spots on the vagina and cervix and is confirmed by microscopic examination of a drop of vaginal discharge. If you suspect trichomonas, do not douche before going to the doctor. The douche would change the appearance of the discharge and reduce the number of trichomonads, making accurate diagnosis more difficult. Embarrassment about the discharge and odor is not the appropriate response; these are natural symptoms of the infection and should be regarded in a medical, not a social, manner.

Bacterial

Bacterial forms of vaginitis used to be called "nonspecific" since the specific infection agents were not isolated. Bacterial infections result in a yellow or greenish vaginal discharge and perhaps an unpleasant odor, itching, and pain during urination or intercourse. These infections arise spontaneously or through intercourse, and diagnosis is confirmed by microscopic examination of vaginal discharge.

Treatment is somewhat problematic. The common medication, ampicillin, is only about 50 percent effective, and there is some concern over the safety of other effective drugs. In any case, both sexual partners must take the medication to avoid passing the infection back and forth in a never-ending cycle.

CYSTITIS

Cystitis is the most common of the many urinary tract infections caused by bacteria entering the bladder. Cystitis occurs almost exclusively among women, perhaps because of the longer trek the bacteria (E.coli) must make up the urethra of the male to reach the bladder.

These bacteria are present in large numbers in the large intestine of all perfectly healthy men and women, so why it infects some women and not others is unknown. There are, however, a number of factors which make a woman more susceptible to this infection. The urethral opening is located directly under the clitoris and during sexual intercourse is continually rubbed. If intercourse is quite vigorous or is repeated often in a short period, the urethral opening may be slightly irritated and the tissue is more susceptible to the bacteria entering. For this reason, this was once called "honeymoon cystitis." However, with changes in patterns of sexual interaction which have diminished the sexual marathon nature of the wedding night, this term has become less relevant.

The symptoms of cystitis often develop rapidly and include burning pain during urination, a frequent need to urinate, cloudy urine, and sometimes pain in the lower abdomen or back and a fever.

Diagnosis is made by a urine test, and treatment is important since continuation of the bladder infection could spread to the kidneys, creating serious problems. The normal treatment is by means of sulfa drugs or any number of antibiotics. *Black males and females should, however, refuse to take sulfa medication unless a test is made for G6PD enzyme deficiency.* Approximately 10 to 14 percent of American blacks have an inherited deficiency of the blood enzyme G6PD. In such cases, sulfa drugs cause a serious form of anemia (death of red blood cells) which can be fatal.

If one has chronic (repeated) cystitis and cautions have been taken to avoid infection, one should consult a physician for tests of the proper functioning of the urinary system.

SEXUAL PREFERENCE AND SEXUALLY TRANSMITTED DISEASES

With the increasing recognition of homosexuality, medical researchers have started to attend to the patterns and problems of sexually transmitted diseases that vary by sexual preference. At present, it appears that one of the factors most strongly related to the likelihood of contracting one of these diseases is sexual preference.

Gender Differences

In our earlier discussion of homosexuality, the point was made that gender was the single most important factor in understanding homosexualities. The same principal applies to homosexuality and sexually transmitted diseases. In the general population, males are more likely than females to contract either syphilis or gonorrhea (Morton et al., 1979). This difference is due to males' having a larger number of sexual partners and being more willing to engage in coitus with someone they know only casually. The same is true—to a much greater extent—among homosexuals. Specifically, homosexual males have much higher rates of sexually transmitted disease than do homosexual females. Bell and Weinberg (1978) found that two-thirds of the homosexual males, but none of the homosexual females, had ever contracted a sexually transmitted disease from a same-sex sexual contact. In a recent study of homosexual women, Robertson and Schachter (1981) found not one existing case of gonorrhea, syphilis, herpes simplex virus, or chlamydial infection.

These differences between male and female homosexuals are due to the same factor that creates differences in sexually transmitted disease rates between heterosexual males and females: different patterns of sexual behavior, which are the result of male and female differences in sexual learning. Specifically, Darrow et al. (1981) found, in a study of over 4,000 gay males, that the single best predictor of the life history of sexually transmitted disease was a person's total number of sexual partners, with the frequency of anal intercourse and sex with complete strangers also important.

Given that gay males have more sexual contacts than heterosexual males and that, in general, more body sites are potentially affected because of anal intercourse, gay males are much more likely than heterosexual males to contract gonorrhea, syphilis, anal warts, and genital and rectal herpes virus (Judson et al., 1980; Handsfield, 1981).

On the other hand, gay males are apparently less likely than heterosexual males to contract other sexually transmitted diseases, such as NGU, scabies, and genital warts (Judson et al., 1980). The lower incidence of these diseases is due to less susceptibility of the mucous lining of the anus to the infectious agents and lower rates of pubic-pubic contact.

With closer examination of sexually transmitted disease patterns among gay men, a wide range of diseases are being discovered and classified as sexually transmitted which have never been so classified for heterosexual populations. Owen (1980) identified ten such diseases which were sexually transmitted in homosexual males, including typhoid fever, amebiasis (a parasite spread by anal sexual activity, which is very difficult to treat and causes infection of the internal organs), and hepatitis A and B. As Handsfield (1981) has pointed out, these discoveries require somewhat of a redefinition of the range of sexually transmitted diseases.

STUDY GUIDE

TERMS TO KNOW

Gonorrhea	Salpingitis
Syphilis	Nongonococcal urethritis
Chancre	Vaginitis
Herpes	Cystitis
Chlamydia	Trichomonas

SELF-TEST

Part I: True-False Statements

1. If the mother has syphilis, the only way the infant can get the disease is by it coming into contact with a chancre during birth.
2. Gonorrhea can be transmitted only by genital-genital contact.
3. A person who has intercourse with an individual who has gonorrhea has a 95 percent chance of getting the disease.
4. If the symptoms of primary-stage syphilis disappear without any medical treatment, the disease has been cured by the body's immune system.
5. Once one has contracted herpes Type II, one always has the disease.
6. Recurrent herpes Type II outbreaks are less severe than the initial outbreak.
7. When the mother has herpes Type II, the infant has no chance of being infected unless normal birth takes place by the fetus passing through the cervix.
8. When the mother has herpes Type II, the virus can invade the placenta.
9. Chlamydial infections have been closely linked with salpingitis.
10. The symptoms of salpingitis are most often unclear and ambiguous.
11. IUD use is associated with an increased risk of salpingitis.
12. Trichomonas is a form of vaginitis.
13. Cystitis occurs almost exclusively among females.
14. Yeast organisms are not normally found in the vagina.
15. Cystitis can be brought on by vigorous intercourse.

Part II: Multiple-Choice Questions
Select the best of the three alternatives.

1. The vast majority of salpingitis cases begin with *(a)* an infection in the uterus which travels to the lower genital tract; *(b)* an infection in the lower genital tract which ascends to the cervix; *(c)* pregnancy.

2. The recurrence of herpes Type II outbreaks is caused by *(a)* stress; *(b)* sexual activity; *(c)* a factor or condition not yet known.

3. One's first and most important source of information on sexually transmitted diseases is one's *(a)* parents; *(b)* teachers and school; *(c)* peers.

4. The initial or primary stage of syphilis is characterized by the symptom of *(a)* a thick puslike fluid seeping from the urethral opening; *(b)* painful blisters on the genital area; *(c)* one or more painless chancres on the part of the body where the infection entered.

5. Small mites or lice are involved in *(a)* salpingitis and NGU; *(b)* vaginitis and cystitis; *(c)* scabies and pediculosis.

6. The best predictor of whether gay males have had sexually transmitted disease is *(a)* age; *(b)* the number of different sexual partners; *(c)* whether the person is bisexual or strictly homosexual in sexual preference.

7. Gonorrhea is *(a)* more common among males than females; *(b)* more common among females than males; *(c)* equally common among males and females.

8. In recent years, the percentage of people with gonorrhea has shown *(a)* a slight increase; *(b)* a large increase; *(c)* a slight decrease.

9. Chlamydia is transmitted *(a)* only by sexual contact; *(b)* only by nonsexual contact; *(c)* by either sexual or nonsexual contact.

TOPICS FOR DISCUSSION

One fact about sexually transmitted disease is that it is rarely discussed either in general or with sexual partners. Why do you think this is so? Consider the ideal image we have of sexuality in American society and how sexually transmitted diseases fit with this image; think also of our image of sexually transmitted diseases in terms of what they mean about the infected person's sexuality, and the general view that sex is "good" but sex is "bad" (Chapter 1).

We have seen that females are more likely than males to be the victims of certain serious sexually transmitted diseases, such as salpingitis, and that for many sexually transmitted diseases, females are unlikely to have obvious symptoms. What kind of unwritten code of ethics do you think now exists among people you know with regard to protecting sexual partners from sexually transmitted disease? What kind of male-female code of ethics do you think should exist in order to protect sexual partners, especially women? What kinds of things would make implementing this code easy or difficult?

SUGGESTED READINGS

The best sources of new and increasing information regarding sexually transmitted diseases are the professional journals where research on this topic appears. New knowledge about various sexually transmitted diseases is rapidly accumulating, yet is slow to reach the general public. If you have a further interest in new information, you should go directly to these journals. Some of the technical language may be a mystery, but from reading this chapter, you should have enough knowledge to make sense of the journal articles. The most informative journals are *Sexually Transmitted Diseases, American*

Journal of Obstetrics and Gynecology, and *Obstetrics and Gynecology.* The Center for Disease Control in Atlanta, Georgia, also publishes a series of reports on sexually transmitted diseases. Your reference librarian can help you find these reports.

KEY TO SELF-TEST QUESTIONS

Part I: True-False Statements

1. F (Syphilis can be transmitted to the fetus from the mother through the interchange of blood supply between the mother and the placenta. See the discussion in Chapter 3 for a description of this interchange.)
2. F
3. F (Approximately one-third of those who have intercourse with a person who has gonorrhea contract the disease themselves.)
4. F (The disease has only gone into the secondary stage and become more dangerous to one's health.)
5. T (At present, there is no known cure. Where does the virus reside when there is not an outbreak?)
6. T
7. F (The infant's chance of getting herpes either during birth or while still in the placenta is currently being debated, but it is clear that birth can take place without herpes infection being transmitted to the infant and that the fetus can contract herpes before birth.)
8. T (But the conditions for its doing so are not clear.)
9. T (They are perhaps the most common form of sexually transmitted disease among women.)
10. T (Not only is the disease very serious, but it is difficult to diagnose accurately.)
11. T
12. T (What are the other two forms of vaginitis?)
13. T (Why do researchers think this is so?)
14. F
15. T (The urethral opening is irritated.)

Part II: Multiple-Choice Questions

1. *b* (It is thought that younger females may be more susceptible to salpingitis. Why?)
2. *c* (People report that many different things bring outbreaks, but nothing has been scientifically shown to be associated with recurrent outbreaks.)
3. *b* (Think, however, about the status of sex education in the schools in the United States.)
4. *c* (What disease is characterized by the symptoms in *a*? How about *b*?)
5. *c*
6. *b* (Sexually transmitted diseases are sexually transmitted.)
7. *a* (What age group has the highest rates of gonorrhea in the United States?)
8. *c* (Why?)
9. *c* (But transmission is much more often by sexual contact.)

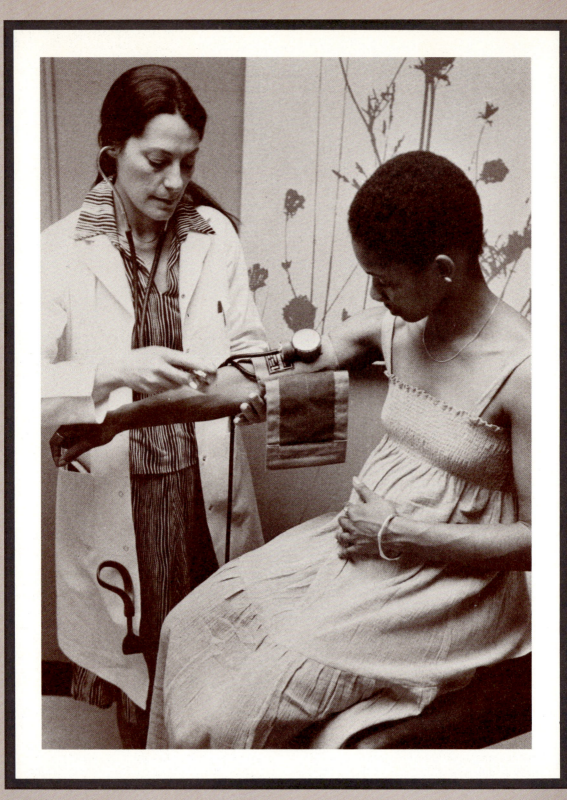

Chapter 17
Health, Sexuality, and Treatment

Health is not just the absence of illness, but the presence of an optimal state of mental and physical existence. While the relationship between sexuality and health has usually been thought of with prevention as the goal, this approach is rapidly changing.

Historically, the relationship between health and sexuality was seen in terms of preventing sexually transmitted diseases while being sexually active. As the changes in sexual attitudes brought more open discussion and recognition of sexuality in the 1960s and 1970s, we have seen the emergence of another view of sexuality and health. This is the view that a satisfactory sexual existence is important to a person's entire life and that sex is not limited to the young and vigorous. This has stimulated discussion, research, and help in the area of sexual problems related to (1) chronic illness or injury and (2) physical, social, and psychological problems.

In this chapter, we shall first discuss the relationship between sexuality and certain chronic illnesses and then the nature of sexual therapy.

SEXUALITY AND CHRONIC ILLNESS

Since we associate sex with youth, vigor, and vitality and illness with a loss of these charac-teristics, chronic illness is frequently seen as resulting in a loss of sexuality in both a physical and psychological sense. In recent years health professionals have challenged this view. The result has been not only a greater understanding of how certain chronic illnesses affect sexuality, but also the development of means of dealing with these sexual problems and of aiding the patient in maintaining or establishing a full sexual life as part of routine medical practice and health care (see Hogan, 1980, as an example).

Female Breast Cancer
Breast cancer is the most common form of cancer among women and is the leading cause of female cancer death in the United States. One out of every eleven women in the United States will have breast cancer at some time in her life. There are approximately 111,000 new cases each year and 37,000 deaths annually (Langone, 1981; Schottenfeld, 1981).

Risk factors   While the cause of breast cancer is not known, certain factors are associated with a greater risk of developing the disease. These risk factors are not causes, but correlates. Women who have *menarche before the age of 12* have a 1.1 to 1.5 times greater risk of breast cancer than women who have menarche after the age of 12. *Menopause after age 35* carries a 1.3 to 2 times greater

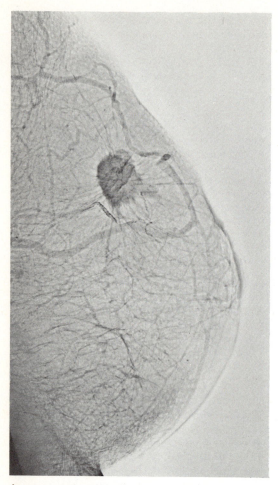

An x-ray mammogram showing a malignant tumor.

such family history of breast cancer. If a relative has had breast cancer before she reached menopause, your risk is tripled. If a relative of yours had breast cancer in both breasts, your risk of breast cancer increases 5 times and if a relative has had cancer of both breasts before she reached menopause, your risk is increased 9 times (Carlile, 1981).

Breast cancer is relatively rare in women under the age of 25, but risk increases for every age group after that, with about 75 percent of all new cases appearing in women over the age of 40 (*Nursing*, 78:20).

Risk is two to four times greater for upper-social-class women than lower-social-class women, and white females have 1.1 to 1.9 times greater risk than black females (Kelsey, 1979).

Breast cancer risk is also associated with country of residence. North American and northern European women have 4 or more times greater risk than Asian and African women, a factor thought largely due to the amount of fat in the diet (Kelsey, 1979; Moore, 1980). There is no evidence at all for the common misconception that sexual activity, breast fondling, breast feeding, bruises, bites, or blows to the breast increases the risk of developing breast cancer (*Nursing*, 78:20). One national survey found that 50 percent of the women sampled thought that bumps or bruises cause breast cancer, and 10 percent (30 percent of the blacks and 20 percent of the Hispanics) thought that breast fondling causes it (*Journal of the American Medical Association*, 1981).

Type of breast cancer   Female breast cancer is usually one of the following more common forms (*Nursing*, 78:20):

- *Intraductal carcinoma.* This is the most common form, accounting for about 50 percent of all cases. The tumor affects the inside of the epithelial tissue (one of the four types of tissues in the body) of the milk ducts leading to the nipple. (As we shall discuss, this is why squeezing the nipple is an important part of a breast self-examination.)

risk than menopause before age 35 (Carlile, 1981). 2 times greater means twice as great; 3 times greater means the risk is tripled, etc. The risk (2 times, etc.) refers to risk over not having the risk factor. Menarche and menopause appear to be risk factors because of the increased time the woman is exposed to estrogen. Thus, an *oophorectomy* (surgical removal of the ovaries) lowers breast cancer risk if it takes place before menopause (Miller, 1981).

A *family history* of breast cancer dramatically increases risk. If a grandmother or an aunt has breast cancer, one's risk is increased 2 times over that of the person who has no

- *Lobular carcinoma.* This begins on the milk glands and is often a small cancer that does not invade other parts of the breast or surrounding body tissues.
- *Mammary sarcoma.* This is a rare form which arises from the ligaments, muscles, and tendons that support the breast.
- *Paget's disease.* This first appears as an irritation on the nipple either with or without an accompanying mass. It develops from the large ducts in the nipple and often spreads to the milk ducts.
- *Inflammatory carcinoma.* This is a rare form which involves the skin and lymph system of the breast.

About half of all breast cancers start in the upper, outside one-fourth of the breast and spread to the axillary lymph nodes (those in the armpit). About 25 percent of all breast cancers start in the central area of the breast and spreads to the mammary lymph nodes (*Nursing,* 78:20). Only 1 percent of all breast cancers involves both breasts at the same time, and the left breast is more often afflicted than the right (Kelsey, 1979). Of all women who get cancer in one breast, 16 percent eventually get cancer in the other breast. Of all women who get breast cancer only 8 to 9 percent have cancer in both breasts at the same time (Leis et al., 1981).

Breast self-examination Evidence clearly favors self-examination of one's breasts (BSE) as important in the early detection of breast cancer, even though there is some controversy among physicians and medical researchers as to its value. BSE has two major advantages: it involves no expense, and it can be done conveniently at home (Paterson, 1981). One of the concerns about BSE is that it causes needless anxiety. A woman finds a lump or other abnormality in her breast and then worries about breast cancer until she can see a physician. Another, somewhat more severe, concern is that a woman may avoid routine examination by a physician because she does BSE (Paterson, 1981). However, women who use BSE are also more likely to make more use of mammography (breast x-ray for cancer) than are women who do not do BSE (Hugely and Brown, 1981). Further, the weight of the research evidence shows that among those women who are unlikely to use other breast cancer detection methods, *BSE is an important means of early breast cancer detection* (Paterson, 1981). In fact, 80 percent of all breast tumors are detected by patients themselves, rather than by an examining physician (Senie et al., 1981).

The tremendous importance of doing BSE each month is that frequent medical examination, including physical examination of the breasts, is strongly related to early breast cancer detection (Senie et al., 1981). The importance of early detection is without doubt. In patients, for example, 55 years old and older, there is a three- to fourfold increase in the risk of death between early and late diagnosis of breast cancer, the difference being whether the tumor is localized or has spread (Jacques et al., 1981).

One important result of doing BSE is that you become familar with your breasts and know what is normal for you. This makes it possible to detect any abnormality in the early stages. While the whole process of BSE may create some anxiety because you are made aware of the fact you are checking for a dangerous disease, the risk of late detection is worth a little anxiety (which will disappear if the process becomes a normal monthly routine).

For the majority of women in American society, BSE is not a monthly routine. A 1979 national survey conducted by the National Cancer Institute (*Journal of the American Medical Association,* 1981) found that even though 76 percent of the women questioned said that cancer is the greatest health concern of women today and 44 percent specifically mentioned breast cancer, few did BSE.

Ninety-six percent of American women have heard of BSE, but only 83 percent have done a self-examination in the last year and only 29 percent do a BSE each month. Worse yet, of this 29 percent who say they do a BSE each month, many cannot describe the steps

BOX 17-1
HOW TO DO A BREAST SELF-EXAMINATION

The examination should be done once a month about one week after the end of your period. This is the best time to detect breast abnormalities. *First,* while in the shower (when your skin is wet and slick), glide your hands over your skin. With the fingers flat, use your right hand to examine your left breast and your left hand to examine the right, moving over every part of the breast. Check for any lump, thickening, or hard knot. *Second,* in front of a mirror inspect your breasts with your arms at your sides. Then raise your arms high overhead. Look for any changes in the contour of each breast—a swelling, a dimpling of skin, changes in the nipple. Next, rest your palms on your hips and flex your chest muscles. Your left and right breasts will not match (very few women's do). If you do this regularly, you will become familiar with what your breasts look like and any change will be noticeable. *Third,* lying down, examine your right breast by placing a pillow under

your right shoulder. Place your right hand behind your head while lying on your back (this distributes the breast tissue more evenly on the chest wall, rather than letting it partly fall along the rib cage). With your fingers flat, press your left hand gently in small circular motions. Start at the outermost part of your breast at the top (12 o'clock) and move to 1 o'clock and so on all around the breast (a ridge of firm tissue is normal in the lower curve of each breast). Now move in toward the nipple 1 inch and repeat the circle. Keep circling the breast until each inch is covered, including the nipple. Now repeat this procedure on the left breast, with the pillow under your left shoulder and using your right hand. The important thing here is to become familiar with your breast structure so changes can be detected. *Fourth,* gently squeeze each nipple between the thumb and index finger. Any discharge should be reported to your physician immediately.

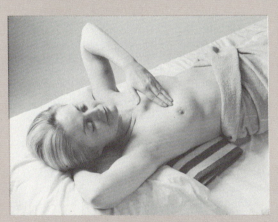
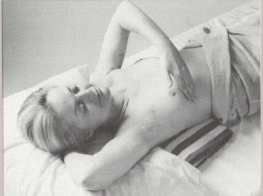
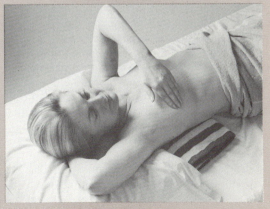

taken in making this examination (*Journal of the American Medical Association,* 1981).

Research indicates that a majority of women have a positive attitude toward BSE, but a significant proportion do not feel comfortable talking to someone about breast cancer or touching their own breasts (Howe, 1981). It is also apparent to most health professionals that many women feel that if you ignore the possibility of breast cancer, you will not get it. While this is a nice theory for your cat which thinks that when its head is covered you cannot see its body either, it is a poor excuse for responsible health care.

The consequences of not practicing simple preventive health care in the form of a monthly BSE are simply too severe (like death, for example). Every women age 20 and over should do a BSE each month.

Physician breast examination In addition to BSE, other methods of detection of breast cancer should be carried out on a regular basis. Between the ages of 20 and 40, a woman should have a trained nurse or physician conduct a breast examination once every two to three years. If you have a family history of breast cancer, this examination should take place more frequently.

Mammography Mammography has been the only way to detect breast cancer before it is large enough to be felt by BSE or a physician examination. This x-ray of the breast is not necessary for younger women, but women 50 years of age should begin to have a mammography routinely unless there is a personal or family history of breast cancer. If a woman's sister or mother has had breast cancer, she should begin annual mammography examinations at age 40. New equipment now allows lower doses of radiation than before. In any event, you should insist that the dose be less than one rad (a measure of radiation exposure) per breast.

There is no question as to the absolute value of mammography in terms of saving life. The research indicates that screening of entire populations of women with x-ray mammography results in a 40 percent reduction in breast cancer deaths for women over 50 years of age (Shapiro, 1977). New low-dose mammography has a high life-saving value and very few risks due to exposure to radiation (Howe et al., 1981).

The major problem with mammography is not that radiation may have some minor health risk, but that it is very expensive. A standard mammogram requires two shots of each breast and this, in addition to the office examination fee, cost approximately $150 to $200 in 1981. While some health insurance plans cover the cost of mammograms, many others only do so when breast cancer is suspected. Moreover, a great many women have no medical insurance. Thus, mammography is simply not an effective means of routinely testing for breast cancer. Additionally, it is not widely accepted among women (because of the radiation exposure) and is relatively inaccurate in women with a breast tissue structure which appears to be higher in risk for breast cancer; breasts with dense tissue and heavy duct pattern.

Ultrasound By the time you read this, a virtual revolution will have taken place in the means of detecting breast cancer in women. This is the development of ultrasound mammography. Following the basic techniques of sonar, ultrasound uses sound waves to obtain data on the internal structure of the breast. Recently, these techniques have been all but perfected and combined with visualization such that a still or moving picture of the breast is directly obtained. Ultrasound breast examination is made in two ways. In one, the patient lies prone on a table and full ultrasound visualizations are taken of both breasts. In the second, a smaller, hand-held device is used to examine particular segments of the breast structure. The value of ultrasound is that it is totally noninvasive. There is no exposure to anything other than harmless sound waves. Also, ultrasound is apparently more accurate in detecting breast abnormalities than is x-ray mammography (Cole-Beuglet et al., 1980; Frazier et al., 1980; DeGezzelle et al., 1981). At the present, it appears that ultrasound will make possible the safe, accurate, and economical testing for breast cancer in the general population.

Other testing methods There is a great deal of interest in developing a method of testing for breast cancer as part of a routine blood or urine examination. If *cancer markers* (substances which appear in the blood or urine in the presence of cancer) could be isolated, it would be easy to detect and treat many forms of cancer in the early stages. Recently, a method was tested in several countries which involved measuring the immune complexes as they circulated through the blood. International tests of this method revealed, however, that it was not yet accurate enough to be implemented as a standard testing procedure (Herberman et al., 1981). Such research continues, however, in almost every major medical research facility in the world.

Treatment of Breast Cancer

There are a number of different treatments for breast cancer, depending on the size, type, location, and stage of tumor development, as well as the characteristics of the patient.

Nonsurgical methods involve radiation therapy, chemotherapy, hormone therapy, and radiation implants at the site of the tumor (Moore, 1980).

Surgery The traditional treatment for breast cancer has been surgery combined with either chemotherapy or radiation therapy, or both. The issue in surgery has always been how drastic the surgery should be. The answer to this question has generally been guided by the assumption that it is better to do more drastic surgery than may be minimally necessary in order to make sure that the malignancy is completely removed. There are basically four forms of surgery for breast cancer, each differing in severity in the extent of tissue removal (Langone, 1981):

- *Lumpectomy* is the least severe, involving a single small incision and the removal of the tumor and surrounding tissue.

- *Quadrantectomy* involves an incision from under the arm downward to the nipple and removal of one-quarter of the breast containing the tumor and the lymph nodes as well as some muscle tissue.

- *Modified radical mastectomy* involves two major incisions starting under the arm and traveling downward around the nipple and joining below the breast. The entire breast is removed, as well as the lymph nodes and some chest muscle tissue.

- *Radical mastectomy* is the most severe form of breast surgery, involving two major incisions which start under the arm and travel downward around the breast, joining well under the breast. The entire breast is removed, as well as the lymph nodes and all layers of chest muscle underneath the lymph nodes and armpit (referred to as the Halsted method after its inventor, Dr. William Stewart Halsted of John Hopkins Hospital).

The debate over mastectomy Recently, there has been considerable debate within the medical profession regarding the wisdom of frequently performing radical mastectomy in the treatment of breast cancer. Surgeons who argue for the use of radical mastectomy contend that breast cancer is most often multi-centered (see editorial in the *British Medical Journal,* 1981; Langone, 1981; Urban, 1980), and thus effective removal of the dangerous tissues requires this severe surgical method. Multicentered breast cancers actually appear in 9 to 44 percent of all breast cancer cases (*British Medical Journal,* 1981). This means that an extensive examination must be conducted to determine the existence and extent of multicentric breast cancers in any given patient. Given this, it is argued that a radical mastectomy is the only truly effective means of maximizing survival and bringing about local control of the cancer (*British Medical Journal,* 1981).

The long-time use of the Halsted radical mastectomy without much apparent questioning is interesting. Halsted introduced this surgical procedure for breast cancer in an article published in 1894 (Halsted, 1894), and it has remained the traditional treatment since that time (Moxley et al., 1980). However, Halsted introduced the method for the treatment of *locally advanced* tumors and *devised it on the basis of his understanding of tumor growth in 1894*. He thought that tumors in the breast spread contiguously. That is, the malignancy spread out from a single central tumor to cover an increasingly larger area. Thus, he recommended the removal of a large bloc of tissue surrounding the actual tumor as a safe method of stopping the disease. We now know, however, that not all tumors grow in this manner, a fact which makes the radical mastectomy a procedure that is often based on an inaccurate, and more than slightly dated, theory.

Recent evidence on surgery   There are, however, two components to survival: duration of life and quality of life. The radical mastectomy involves removal of considerable amounts of chest and muscle tissue, which often affects use of the arm for some time and also involves significant disfigurement (especially from the patient's own view of self). Many physicians are suggesting, on the basis of recent research, that too many radical mastectomies are performed. Several recent studies suggest that more conservative treatments (one of the other less severe forms of surgery, combined with radiation therapy) result in survival rates comparable with those for radical mastectomy in some types of breast cancers (Calle et al., 1978; Harris et al., 1978; Pierquin et al., 1976; Carbell and Goodman, 1981).

The most definitive study to date is that of Veronesi et al. (1981). In this research, conducted in Milan, Italy, 701 breast cancer patients with a tumor less than ¾ inch in size and having no apparent (to touch) axillary node involvement were randomly assigned to one of two treatment conditions. Half the women received radical mastectomies and the other half received quadrantectomies and dissection of the axillary nodes, combined with radiation therapy. These 701 women were then followed for up to five years to check on survival. There

were no significant differences between the two groups in the duration of survival. The quality of survival was, however, much greater in the women who had not had the radical mastectomy. Veronesi et al. (1981) conclude (along with many others) that radical mastectomy appears to involve unnecessary mutilation if the patient has a cancer less than ¾ inch in size and if there is no tangible evidence of axillary node involvement.

The estrogen approach   As mentioned earlier, women who have early menarche or late menopause have a higher risk of breast cancer. This is thought to be due to the fact that some types of tumors contain estrogen receptors (Samaan et al., 1981; Bird et al., 1981). For these types of tumors, estrogen promotes tumor growth in the form of breast cancer. A surgical method infrequently used as an alternative to mastectomy, or in addition to it in advanced cases, is to remove the source of endogenous (produced by the body) estrogen. This is done by oophorectomy (removal of the ovaries) and/or adrenalectomy (removal of the adrenal gland) (Boova et al., 1981). These methods are employed only when the cancer is in an advanced stage and when the tumor is an estrogen receptor. These operations have only a 50 percent chance of success in stopping tumor growth and carry a 5 percent chance of death from the operation itself (Check, 1980a). These estrogen receptor processes may open the way, however, for more effective diagnosis and treatment of breast cancer. Some studies have found that certain chemicals can be used to block the synthesis of estrogen by the body, thus possibly blocking these estrogen receptor tumors from taking in estrogen and growing (Check, 1980).

Mastectomy and Sexuality

Even though mastectomy itself is not as psychologically and emotionally difficult for a woman as is her discovery of a lump in her breast (Jamison et al., 1978), it is most often problematic for the patient. In a breast-oriented culture where women clearly learn that their sexual image and value are closely related to

BOX 17-2

THE BREAST PATTERN, CANCER RISK CONTROVERSY

Dr. John Wolfe (1976; 1979) has proposed and developed a scheme which is rather widely used to identify breast tissue patterns from x-ray mammograms and to associate these with the risk of *developing* breast cancer. Wolfe identifies four breast pattern categories: N1, which is a dense, fatty tissue breast; P1, which is dense with predominant ducts; P2, which is even more dense, with more predominant ducts; and DY, which is the most dense breast tissue, composed of benign (not malignant) fibrocystic changes in structure. On the basis of his research, Wolfe contends that the N1 breast pattern has the lowest risk of developing breast cancer and P1 the next greatest risk, followed by greater risk with P2 and highest risk with DY. According to Wolfe, women with N1 breast tissue have almost a zero chance of developing breast cancer, while women with a DY pattern have 20 to 30 times more chances of developing breast cancer. The focus of the debate over Wolfe's system is that many women have apparently had a breast surgically removed when they had a high-risk breast pattern (DY) and other high-risk characteristics, even though they were young and did not actually have a malignant tumor in the breast. Recent studies have begun to dispute the validity of the Wolfe system in terms of its accuracy of predicting breast cancer. Two recent studies found no relationship between breast cancer and breast patterns.

Egan et al. (1977) found that the only significant breast pattern identified by mammography was one that was not included in the Wolfe scheme. More recently, Egan (1980) pointed out that given the proportion of women with P2 and DY patterns (high risk, according to Wolfe) who actually develop breast cancer, one would have to perform mastectomies on twenty-one women to prevent one case of cancer. Wolfe (1980) argues, however, that these researchers have not read the mammograms correctly and that considerable training is required to be able to identify the four breast patterns accurately. Even though one study sent him a series of mammograms and he and the researchers agreed on the pattern in 83 percent of the cases, Wolfe (1980) argues that 95 percent agreement is necessary for his scheme to be tested. It is worth noting in passing that between 27 and 37 percent of all women have the low-risk N1 and P1 breast patterns, while 63 to 73 percent have the high-risk P2 and DY patterns (Egan, 1980).

their breasts, a woman's sexual self-view is a very critical concern to her when she knows she has to have a mastectomy. It is more important, in fact, than her concern about death from the cancer (Witkin, 1978).

This concern, however, does not appear to be brought out in preoperation discussion with medical professionals. In one recent study, it was found that only 7 percent of the women who had mastectomies discussed how the operation might affect their sexuality with either a nurse or physician before or immediately after the surgery (Dornbusch et al., 1978). The women did not do so even though 50 percent of them wanted such a discussion. They thought it was an inappropriate topic since the medical professional did not bring it up.

While there is some disagreement in the

research on how mastectomy affects sexuality, it is clear that a substantial proportion of women experience negative effects. One study found that the majority of women who had had mastectomies said that there was no change in their sexuality after the surgery. One-fifth to one-quarter of these women said, however, that orgasm was less frequent, sexual satisfaction was less, and the frequency of intercourse had declined after surgery (Jamison et al., 1978). Another study found that in the three months following mastectomy, significant changes in sexual behavior took place. While 40 percent of the women resumed coitus within one month after discharge from the hospital, one-third had not resumed coitus by six months after discharge. For those who had resumed coitus, the frequency of intercourse and the frequency of initiating intercourse both declined (Dornbusch et al., 1978).

Other aspects of sexuality also appear to be frequently affected by mastectomy. For example, Dornbusch et al. (1978) found that frequency of stimulation of the remaining breast declined, as did complete nudity during coitus and the use of the female superior position in intercourse. A significant factor in these changes is that the man and the woman do not know how to react to such an operation. This is revealed in the decline both in nudity and in use of positions in which the breasts are highly visible, as well as in the fact that by three months after the operation 38 percent of the male mates of mastectomy patients had not viewed the incision site (Dornbusch et al., 1978). The woman's sexual adjustment following mastectomy is, not unexpectedly, strongly related to the attitude of her sexual partner (Watkin, 1978).

Men appear to be slightly more affected by mastectomy than do women themselves. While no studies have directly compared patients and their partners, Wellisch et al. (1978) found negative reactions in males to be common. Of the men whose partners had had a mastectomy, 14 percent said the effect of the surgery on their sexual relationship was "bad." Another 21 percent said it was "somewhat bad," and 53 percent said it had no effect.

Uterine (Endometrial) Cancer

There are three types of uterine cancer, depending on the exact location of the tumor or tumors: endometrial, cervical, and ovarian. In precise terms, cancer of the uterus is referred to as "endometrial" or "cancer of the endometrium" or of "the mucous lining of the uterine cavity." Often, however, endometrial cancer is inaccurately called uterine cancer.

Of the three forms of uterine cancer, endometrial is the most common, and its incidence has shown sharp increases in the last five to six years (Barber, 1981). Currently, the incidence of endometrial cancer is 22.4 per 100,000 women, with a death rate of 3.8 per 100,000 women (Schottenfeld, 1981). Given that most endometrial cancer, owing to its location, is contained within the uterus, this form of uterine cancer has the highest survival rate (81 percent over a five-year period, Schottenfeld, 1981). Treatment normally involves removal of the uterus and oviducts and perhaps the ovaries.

Ovarian Cancer

The second most common form of uterine cancer in the United States is cancer of the ovaries. With 17,000 new cases each year, ovarian cancer is associated with a high death rate of 11,000 deaths annually (Schottenfeld, 1981; Hreshchyshyn et al., 1980), and only a 36 percent survival rate over five years after treatment (Schottenfeld, 1981). The reason for this high death rate is that ovarian cancer easily spreads to other organs in the abdominal area and late detection is the rule. While some physicians are becoming more aware of the possibility of ovarian cancer, the symptoms commonly presented by a patient are nonspecific. Diagnosis is therefore difficult and catching the cancer in the early stages is problematic (Hreshchyshyn et al., 1980). Treatment is by means of surgical removal of the ovaries and other affected tissues followed by chemotherapy or radiotherapy.

Cervical Cancer

Cancer of the cervix is the least common of the three forms of uterine cancer with an inci-

BOX 17-3
BREAST CANCER HOTLINE

Rose Kushner runs the only known breast cancer hotline service in the United States, if not the world. Ms. Kushner, a medical writer by profession, developed breast cancer in 1974. She searched library sources for information for victims of breast cancer and found literally nothing. She then wrote an article for women on what it is like to be a breast cancer patient. The article was rejected by major newspapers because breast cancer was a taboo topic. On September 27, 1974, Betty Ford had breast cancer surgery. Suddenly, the disease was not only a topic suitable for print, but one which sold a lot of newspapers and newsmagazines. This was followed on October 10, 1974, by Happy Rockefeller's breast cancer surgery. Suddenly Kushner's article was fit to print.*

After the appearance of her article, she started getting phone calls and letters from women all over the United States and as far away as Spain. Kushner saw an obvious need, and out of her own conviction to provide information to women, she set up a breast cancer hotline in her home. The letters poured in and the calls came day and night. In order to keep her family from being driven crazy, she has now moved the service to a rented office where she works with no outside support except volunteers and small contributions, both of which are sparse because people still do not want to think about breast cancer. (Those who have not had it do not want to be reminded that they might get it and those who have had it want to forget that they had it.) Regardless of the fact that this service is now totally supported and run by Kushner, she urges you to call if you have questions about breast cancer (calling is better than writing because it is difficult for her to find the time to answer letters and communication is better over the phone). The phone number of this amazing person is 301-984-1020. The address is: *Rose Kushner's Breast Cancer Advisory Service,* 11426 Rockville Pike, Rockville, Maryland 20852

*When I interviewed Rose Kushner, she argued that her article was allowed to get into print because two famous women got breast cancer and had surgery. The media coverage of Mrs. Ford and Mrs. Rockefeller thus provided the definition of breast cancer as an acceptable topic for print and discussion. There is evidence to support this idea: In a study of women voluntarily participating in a breast cancer screening program in a major health plan program, Fink et al. (1978) found that the Ford and Rockefeller events precipitated dramatic increases in the number of women coming in to be screened for the disease.

dence of 10.7 cases and 4.2 deaths per 100,000 women annually, making up only 4 percent of all female cancer in the United States (Schottenfeld, 1981). While cervical cancer, like any other cancer, is indeed a serious health risk, it has been somewhat overemphasized in recent years. One result of this emphasis has been earlier detection and thus a decreasing death rate due to cervical cancer (Moore, 1980). As we shall discuss, there are easy tests for cervical cancer and the frequency of such tests is now well established.

Risk factors   While the causes of cervical cancer remain unknown, several factors are associated with a higher risk of this form of uterine cancer. Black females are twice as likely as white females to get it (Moore, 1980). Greater risk of cervical cancer is also associated with lower socioeconomic status (Moore, 1980). While some would like to suggest that this statement is a myth, cervical cancer risk is also associated with poor hygiene and intercourse with uncircumcised males, especially those with poor hygiene practices (Moore, 1980). Perhaps for this reason, cervical cancer is rare among orthodox Jewish women who practice strict hygiene codes (Moore, 1980). Risk is also greater for women who have had a larger number of children, perhaps due to damage to the cervix in birth. The one factor with the clearest relationship to the risk of cervical cancer is sexual activity. An early age at first coitus and many sexual partners have been repeatedly associated with a greater risk of cervical cancer (Barber, 1981; Swan and Brown, 1981). It is thought that these are the reasons that cervical cancer is very rare in nuns and women with no coital experience (Barber, 1981).

The relationship between cervical cancer and sexual activity, hygiene, and other sexually related factors has prompted the hypothesis that cervical cancer is caused by a virus that may be sexually transmitted in some manner. Rotkin (1973) even suggested that cervical cancer be classified as a sexually transmitted disease. The direct evidence for the sexually transmitted virus notion is, however, still lacking.

Detection   Cervical cancer can be effectively detected by means of a PAP (Papanicolaou) test. In this test a smear is taken from the cervix and examined in a laboratory. The test is simple and inexpensive and should be a routine part of every woman's health care. In the past, a PAP smear was recommended annually. However, given that cervical cancer is easily detected and grows slowly, the American Cancer Society has now revised the recommended period between PAP tests.

All females should have their first PAP test shortly after they first begin having coitus. The test should be conducted two years in a row. If both these annual tests are negative the test should be done every three years to age 35, then every five years to age 60, and then every three years after age 60. However, if one has

some of the characteristics associated with higher risk of cervical cancer, the PAP test should be more frequent than every three years; specifically, having a large number of intercourse partners or having herpes simplex II.

Hysterectomy and Sexuality

All three types of uterine cancer are most commonly treated by means of surgery in which the uterus and cervix are removed (*hysterectomy*). If the ovaries are removed, the procedure is called an *oophorectomy;* if any portion of the vagina is removed, the additional procedure is called a *vaginectomy.*

Hysterectomy is the single most common major operation performed in the United States today, even though only females are eligible (Moore, 1980). With over three-fourths of a million hysterectomies performed each year in this country, one-fourth of the women reaching menopause in the United States today do so through surgical means (Moore, 1980; Zussman et al., 1981).

There are, of course, other medical reasons for performing hysterectomies, such as the uterus failing to remain in its normal position, fibroid tumors on the uterus, excessive uterine bleeding, or severe pelvic infection which does not respond to medication (Moore, 1980). Also, the earlier detection of cervical cancer has led to more hysterectomy operations among younger women (Seibel et al., 1981).

Given the frequency of such surgical procedures and the fact that the reproductive organs involved are assumed to play some role in sexual response, considerable research attention has been given to the effects of hysterectomy on sexuality.

At the outset, we must understand that the issues here are complex and that this complexity is not at all reflected in the existing research. First, almost no research separates the effects of surgery itself from other treatment effects such as radiotherapy or chemotherapy. These different procedures may have very different physical and psychological effects. Second, almost none of the research details the exact nature of the surgical procedures employed. For example, a hysterectomy involving removal of only the uterus and cervix differs vastly from a hysterectomy involving partial removal of the vagina (vaginectomy). Third, none of the existing research has taken into consideration the fact that women experience sexual sensations differently. For example, as we noted in Chapter 5, some women are more sensitive to clitoral stimulation and some women are more sensitive to stimulation of the cervix and uterus by pressure from the penis in the vagina. Fourth, there is an almost universal ignoring of psychological and learning factors in examining the effects of gynecological surgery on sexual response. In almost all research, the assumption is made that the body parts are all that one need consider. Last, the measures of sexuality are weak. Usually, subjects are asked to compare postsurgery sex with presurgery sex rather than actually taking presurgery measurements and comparing them with postsurgery measures. What measures are taken generally fail to deal with anything but the most blatant of sexual behaviors (most frequently, how often one has intercourse).

Be that as it may, this research does suggest the way in which major gynecological surgery may affect female sexuality.

In terms of its physical effects on sexual activity, there are several factors which are important. Amias (1975) has made the following significant findings: In most cases, coitus can be resumed within six weeks after hysterectomy, but it may be three to four months before normal coital pressure can be enjoyed. After any hysterectomy, the vagina undergoes some temporary shrinkage and may thus be tighter than normal, and postoperative infections may occur. If the upper part of the vagina has been removed because of cancer of the cervix, the vagina will be shorter than normal. The careful resumption of coitus will, however, stretch the vagina to its original length, since it is a very flexible organ. Radiation treatment for cancer actually has more of an effect than surgery. Radiotherapy, Amias explains, lessens

vaginal lubrication and length, and expansion of the vagina is rarely possible after a full course of radiation therapy.

While not all studies agree, most of the research indicates that hysterectomy, oophorectomy, or both have little or no effect on female sexuality. One of the early studies in this area found that 37 percent of the women who had had both hysterectomy and oophorectomy said their sexual relationships had deteriorated following surgery. For 29 percent however, no change occurred after surgery, and fully 34 percent said their sexual relationship improved after surgery (Dennerstein et al., 1977). Somewhat more recent studies reveal even less negative effects of gynecological surgery. Chapman (1978) found that women who had a hysterectomy showed no postoperative change in orgasm regularity, a slight increase in the frequency of coitus, and a significant increase in precoital foreplay. Many of the women in the Chapman research said they felt "changed" after the operation, some reporting that they "felt like virgins again." Martin et al. (1980) did a one-year follow-up on forty-four women who had a hysterectomy. They found no significant difference between before and after surgery in the percentage of women experiencing sexual indifference, no sexual response, or painful intercourse. Further, only 12 percent of the women who were living with a sexual partner experienced less frequent intercourse after surgery, while 56 percent had no change and 32 percent experienced more frequent intercourse. More recently, Seibel et al. (1981) found that for forty-four women who had a hysterectomy for cancer (thirty-six of whom had a partial vaginectomy also), the average frequency of coitus did not change after surgery and the average percentage of the times orgasm was experienced was not reduced for any patient. For the sample as a whole, the actual enjoyment of coitus increased following surgery, and 93 percent of the sample desired coitus as often as, or more often than, they did before surgery.

The current evidence thus suggests that women report no necessary decline in either sexual interest or activity following gynecological surgery, even when it is in the more radical form (vaginectomy).

There are perhaps many factors related to sexual patterns after such surgery, and these have only been touched on by existing research. For example, Seibel et al. (1981) suggest that not having an abdominal scar is important for one's sexual self-image and thus for sexuality (hysterectomy can be by vaginal incision). Perhaps the reason the oft-cited Dennerstein study found such relatively high rates of deteriorated sexual relationships after surgery was the psychological status of the patients prior to surgery. In this particular study, 47 percent of the women were anxious about being sexually altered by the surgery. Dennerstein et al. (1977) also found that there was a significant relationship between postoperative decline in sexual desire and an increase in painful intercourse and anxiety over deterioration of sexuality. Further, the overall sexual outcome following surgery was worse for those women who had a low frequency of coitus prior to surgery. Thus, factors such as overall knowledge about sexual functioning and overall preoperation patterns of sexuality appear to be important in the sexual outcome of gynecological surgery (Dennerstein et al., 1977; Krueger et al., 1979).

The change in interpersonal sexuality In all research on the effects of illness and surgery on sexuality, especially cancer, it has been assumed that more is better and less is worse. Thus, this research typically examines some aspect of sexuality that is physical, such as the actual, or even the desired, frequency of intercourse. If there is less frequent sexual activity, it is assumed that the sexual relationship has diminished; if there is no change or increased frequency, it is assumed that the sexual relationship has not been altered or has actually been improved. This is, of course, a very narrow view of what human sexuality is and can be.

Leiber et al. (1976) point out that the decrease in the frequency of physical-sexual acts may not mean that the relationship has declined in quality. Rather, other forms of intimacy may have replaced physical-sexual acts. In a study of cancer patients and their spouses, Leiber et al. found evidence to support such a suggestion. In general, it was found that both patients and their spouses experienced a decline in the desire for intercourse and an increase in the desire for affection and physical closeness. On the average, these couples engaged in less sexual intercourse and more conversation with each other as a direct result of one of the partners' illness.

Again, however, we see the tremendous importance of gender differences in sexual learning. While a decline in the desire for coitus was related to an increase in the desire for physical closeness, males and females differed on both these desires. Women, whether they were patients or spouses of patients, were more likely than men to desire less coitus and more physical closeness.

Testicular Cancer

Cancer of the testis affects between 2.8 and 4.4 men per 100,000 each year in the United States (Muir and Nectoux, 1979; Conklin et al., 1978). Even though testicular cancer accounts for only 1 percent of all male cancer in this country, it is responsible for approximately 1,000 deaths annually (Schottenfeld et al., 1980). Deaths from testicular cancer peak between the ages of 25 and 34 and after 70 (Schottenfeld et al., 1980) and 80 percent of the males who get testicular cancer are under the age of 40 (Conklin et al., (1978).

The risk of testicular cancer is 4 to 5 times lower for black than for white males (Muir and Nectoux, 1979; Conklin et al., 1978) and this form of cancer is rare in Asian males (Conklin et al., 1978). White males also are more likely to have more serious forms of testicular cancer than are black males (Daniels et al., 1981). While sexual activity is not related to the risk of testicular cancer (Schottenfeld et al., 1980), undescended testes are. Malignancy in a testicular tumor is 48 times more likely in an undescended testis (Conklin et al., 1978). For this reason, undescended testes should be corrected before the age of 5 (Conklin et al., 1978).

Treatment Testicular cancer is among the most curable cancers known. If caught in the early stages, the long-term survival rates reach 90 percent. If caught in the later stages, the survival rates range from 32 to 95 percent, depending on the extent of the malignancy (Faley et al., 1979). Treatment most often includes surgical removal of the affected testis. However, chemotherapy alone has a 70 percent cure rate, and where it does not produce complete remission, many cases can be cured with follow-up surgery (Einhorn et al. 1981). Since survival rates are very high for early-stage testicular cancer, self-examination is an important health care practice for males.

Self-examination Males should become familar with self-examination for testicular cancer and carry out the procedure monthly. The best time to do a self-examination is immediately after a shower or bath because the warm temperature causes the dartos muscle to relax and the testes to hang away from the body wall. Hold the scrotum in the palm of your hand and feel the testicle with the thumb and forefinger. Apply a slight amount of pressure—if it hurts, you are applying too much pressure—and move over the entire surface. The testis should feel slippery and smooth and the consistence slightly rubbery. Any lumps or irregularities in the surface should be reported to your physician. As in the case of breast self-examination, it is important that you become familar with the structure of your testes so that changes are noted easily (Murray and Wilcox, 1978).

Effects of treatment Not all lumps in the testes are cause for concern, Frequently, these are natural contours of the testis or an infection which can be treated with antibiotics. This, however, is for a physician to determine. Even if radical surgery is needed in the case of testicular cancer, erection and orgasm remain unaffected. If the lymph nodes located in the inquinal area have to be removed on account of the spread of the tumor, there is usually surgical destruction of a nerve chain which closes the bladder sphincter during ejaculation. This sphincter closes off entry to and exit from the bladder and keeps ejaculate from going inside the bladder rather than out through the penis. If this sphincter ceases to operate upon ejaculation, a condition known as *retrograde ejaculation* occurs; that is, the ejaculate passes into the bladder rather than out of the penis. This, however, affects only ejaculation and not orgasm.

For cosmetic purposes a gel-filled testicular prosthesis can be placed in the scrotal sac when a testis is removed so that the genitals will not be altered in appearance (Murray and Wilcox, 1978).

Male Breast Cancer

Breast cancer among males is 100 times less common than among females. Making up only 0.2 percent of all male cancer, there are 900 new cases of male breast cancer each year and 300 resulting deaths in the United States (Kelsey, 1979; Schottenfeld et al., 1980; Yap et al., 1979). Black males and Jewish males have a higher risk of breast cancer than white and non-Jewish males and far more risk than Japanese males. As in females, male breast cancer is more common in the left than the right breast (Kelsey, 1979).

Kaposi's Sarcoma

Kaposi's sarcoma is a form of malignancy which is uncommon in the United States with rates of 0.02 people per 100,000. Primarily affecting the elderly, it can take any number of forms from a skin lesion to extensive internal involvement. Recently, however, the disease has appeared with inexplainable frequency among homosexual males in New York and California, with twenty-six reported cases and eight deaths. The reason for this apparently high incidence in these two populations remains unknown (Center for Disease Control, July 3, 1981).

Prostate Cancer

Cancer of the prostate is the second most common form of male cancer, making up 17 percent of all male cancer in the United States. Each year, there are 64,000 new cases of prostate cancer and 21,000 resulting deaths (Schottenfeld, 1981). Prostate cancer is rare below age 50, but is increasingly more likely after that age (Schottenfeld, 1981). While testicular cancer is rare among black males, the opposite is the case for prostate cancer, with black males more at risk than white males. In fact, in the United States, black males have the highest rate of prostate cancer of all ethnic groups—a rate 20 times that of white males (Schottenfeld et al., 1980). For reasons not understood, the lowest rates in the world for this cancer are in Japan (perhaps because of diet), and it is rare in Central and South America and parts of Africa (Schottenfeld et al., 1980). Married males are more likely to get prostate cancer, as are males who have many sexual partners (Schottenfeld, 1981; Baker et al., 1981). Males with herpes simplex virus Type II also have a higher risk (Baker et al., 1981).

Treatment   There are several modes of treatment for prostate cancer, but by far the most common is surgery in which some or all of the prostate gland is removed (prostatectomy). Other treatment methods involve radiation or chemotherapy with or without surgery. A method receiving recent attention is the use of radioactive 125 iodine implants. These implants are placed in or near the tumor and removed after a short time.

Effects on sexuality   The aspect of sexuality which has received the most attention with regard to prostatectomy is erection. The actual effects of prostate surgery are still not firmly established. One major factor affecting erection after surgery appears to be the manner in which the surgery is done. Depending on the extent of the surgery, loss of erection is reported to range from 6 percent (Herr, 1979) to nearly 50 percent (Finkle and Taylor, 1981). In general, the more radical the prostate surgery, the more likely the loss of erection following surgery. Other factors, however, are clearly important in this loss of erection ability. Zohar et al. (1977) found that certain psychological factors are significant. Specifi-

cally, if the patient is clearly told what to expect, loss of erection is less, thanks to a reduction in anxiety over impotence. Further, being generally high in life satisfaction is associated with no sexual after-effects of prostate surgery (Zohar et al., 1976). The influence of these psychological factors is illustrated by the fact that many men who cannot obtain an erection following prostate surgery routinely have erections during their sleep (Madorsky et al., 1976). The sexual effects of 125 iodine treatment appear to be less than surgery. Fowler et al. (1979) found that only 7 percent of the males treated for prostate cancer in this manner have erection loss after treatment. Herr (1979) found that only 2 percent of the males treated with 125 iodine implants had erection loss and 50 percent of those who had erection problems before treatment did not have them after treatment.

Prostate problems other than cancer are also common in older males. The most common is enlargement in which the prostate places pressure on the urethra, making urination difficult or impossible. Most often, this is treated with medication, or in extreme cases, with surgery.

Cardiovascular Disease

Cardiovascular disease is the number one health problem in the United States today, particularly among males. As such, the relationship between this disease and sexuality affects a significant proportion of the population.

Postcoronary sexual concerns
Several studies reveal that many males have significant sexual concerns following a heart attack. Krop et al. (1979), for example, found that only 34 percent of the male heart-attack patients they studied had no concern about their postcoronary sexual behavior. As shown in Table 17-1, these concerns range from worrying about how one's partner feels about having sex with a person who has had a heart attack to chest pains during sexual activity.

One of the major concerns of both patients and physicians is the effect on the heart of the physiological activity during sexual arousal.

TABLE 17-1
Sexual concerns of males after a heart attack.

Sexual Concern	Heart-Attack Patients Having This Concern (in %)
Chest pain or other discomfort might occur during sex.	43
Might have erection problems.	41
Sex might be difficult for self or partner.	34
Desire for sex may decrease.	28
Won't be able to have sex for a while.	29
Premature ejaculation.	24
Problems reaching orgasm.	23
Partner will feel guilty about having sex.	18
Partner's desire for sex might decrease.	17
Resuming sex may be harmful.	49

Source: Krop et al. (1979:95, table 2).

This concern appears to have increased after Masters and Johnson (1966) reported that the heart rate during intercourse increases to as high as 180 beats per minute. The research of Hellerstein and Friedman (1970) suggests, however, that 180 beats per minute may not be typical during sexual activity. Specifically, Masters and Johnson obtained their data while subjects engaged in coitus in a laboratory. Merely being observed by others and/or measured with a variety of devices may increase the heart rate. Hellerstein and Friedman equipped male heart-attack patients with a portable EKG (electrocardiograph) to measure heart activity during sexual activity. The sexual activity took place with the patients' spouses and in the privacy of their own homes in a normal pattern. The EKG results revealed that the average maximum heart rate for these men during intercourse was 117 beats per minute, with a range from 90 to 144. Within two minutes after orgasm, the heart rate dropped back down to an average of 85 beats per minute. These data suggest that there is little inherent danger in heart-attack patients engaging in intercourse as far as accelerated heart rate is concerned, since the average heart rate while walking up stairs or doing normal work is 120 beats per minute.

Johnson and Fletcher (1979) have found, however, that post–heart-attack and surgery patients do routinely experience heartbeat irregularities (arrhythmia) during sexual activity, a pattern certainly not desirable in patients.

Coital coronary One of the most common concerns of postcoronary patients is actually having a heart attack due to sexual activity—a "coital coronary." Massie et al. (1969) report that this is very rare. The only study I know of on the subject is that of Ueno (1963), who studied 5,559 sudden deaths from records of the Tokyo Medical Examiners Office. Of these, only 0.6 percent were precipitated by sexual activity. One physician reportedly tells his patients that sex is all right as long as it is with one's wife. This appears to be an accurate prescription. Ueno found that 77 percent of the deaths precipitated by sexual activity occurred during extramarital sexual activity and that 34 percent took place in hotel rooms.

Sexual and heart problems It is also worth noting that some research suggests that sexual problems may be present among males who have heart attacks *before* the heart attack. Wabek and Burchell (1980) found that two-thirds of the males hospitalized for a heart attack had some significant sexual problem prior to the attack. The most common problem was erection difficulty and the second most common was a decrease in sexual desire. In one of the rare studies of sexuality and heart illness among women, Abramov (1976) found that a majority of the women heart-attack patients studied had experienced problems of sexual arousal before the attack.

This in no way means that sexual problems cause heart attacks. What these findings may reflect is that the physiological or socio-psychological factors which precipitated the heart attack also affected sexuality. Stress is an obvious example. As we shall see, certain personality characteristics which appear to be related to heart-attack risk are also related to a person's seeking professional help for sexual problems.[1]

Enhanced sexuality As we have noted, a major illness does not automatically mean a decline in one's sexuality. This is also true for heart patients. Brenton (1968) reported that some couples become less sexually inhibited following the male's heart attack. Having special requirements placed on their sexual activity by a physician may force the couple to discuss and experiment with their sexuality—something they have not done before.

Stroke

It is estimated that 500,000 people a year suffer stroke and that 200,000 of these people survive with some varying degree of impairment due to damage to some part of the brain blood supply (Bray et al., 1981). Stroke patients tend to be especially affected sexually since neither males nor females experience a decrease in sexual interest or desire compared with before the stroke, but they do experience a considerable decrease in sexual response at the physiological level (Bray et al., 1981;

---

[1]See Derogatis and King (1981) for a recent review of the effects of sexual activity on heart-attack patients.

Allsup-Jackson, 1981). Comparing behavior before and after stroke, Bray et al. (1981) found that males declined dramatically in their ability to obtain an erection and ejaculate and females experienced a significant decline in the likelihood of orgasm and changes in menses.

Diabetes

It is often stated that diabetic males experience complete loss of erection ability (impotence) approximately one year after the onset of the disease (e.g., Sandler et al., 1980; Woods, 1979). This impotence is thought to be due to brain pathology brought about by diabetes (Jensen, 1981a; Kolodny et al., 1974) rather than vascular changes in the genitals (Kaplan, 1974). The fact is that *the actual incidence of impotence among diabetic males is not known.* Some studies suggest that at least half of all diabetic males are impotent (Podolsky, 1980; Kolodny et al., 1974; Rubin and Babbott, 1958). During uncontrolled diabetes, especially during the first five years, impotence has been found to come and go and after this period to be chronic (Karacan et al., 1978). Even in the case of chronic (persistent and long-term) impotence the cause is not clear. While Kolodny et al. state that it is due to brain pathology, Karacan et al. state that it is due to changes in autonomic nerve fibers in the corpora cavernosa of the penis.

A recent study (Jensen, 1981a) has questioned the inevitability of impotence within one year after the onset of diabetes. Following insulin-treated diabetic male patients for two years, he found that even though sexual interest and erection ability deteriorated, only 10 percent were impotent at the end of this period. Jensen (1981a), also argues that the idea that impotence in diabetes is organic is highly suspect and that psychological factors may play as major a role as organic factors. Such things as fear of complications of the illness, depression, and life restrictions may well have a negative effect on sexual functioning.

Perhaps the clearest research to date is

that of Jensen (1981b) in which male diabetics were compared to male nondiabetics of the same age. Jensen found that 44 percent of the diabetics had some problem with sexual functioning, compared with 13 percent of the nondiabetic males. This strongly suggests that the actual effect of diabetes on sexual functioning over and above a nondiabetic condition is much less than has been assumed. Jensen (1981b) found that the most common sexual problems diabetic men faced were erection and sexual interest, with ejaculation difficulty being rare.

While there has been much less research on the effects of diabetes on sexual functioning in women, there is rather consistent evidence of negative effects. A decrease in orgasm regularity appears to begin within one year of the onset of the disease (Kolodny, 1971; Ellenberg, 1977). Even though it is argued that this is due to neurological factors (Kolodny, 1971), not enough was known about female orgasm in 1971 to state this with certainty. Certain forms of vaginitis and dyspareunia (painful intercourse) are also diabetic in origin (Krosnick and Pedolsky, 1981). Dyspareunia is especially common in diabetic women in middle and later ages due to inflammation from estrogen deficiency (Krosnick and Podolsky, 1981), and diabetic women are more likely to get vaginal infections (Mims and Swenson, 1980).

As in the case of males, recent research appears to question these previous findings of sexual problems as a direct result of diabetes. Jensen (1981b) also compared diabetic and nondiabetic women and found that while 27 percent of the diabetic women had some problem with sexual functioning, this was also true for 25 percent of the nondiabetic women. Further, the major sexual problem reported by the two groups was the same—a lack of interest in sex.

Kidney Failure
Both males and females with kidney failure tend to experience sexual problems (Woods,

1979). There are, however, greater individual differences in the appearance of sexual problems with kidney failure and it is not clear whether these problems are physiological or psychological in origin. Unlike other illnesses, kidney failure requires continual reliance upon others and a machine for survival. The patient must deal with both having a fatal disease and being dependent upon medical personnel and a dialysis machine. These conditions also entail severe disruptions in work and family life. It is reasonable to assume that all these factors, as well as physiological changes, play some part in the sexual problems of persons with kidney failure. Steele et al. (1977) found that overall sexual satisfaction, the frequency of coitus, sexual arousal, and orgasm were common problems for dialysis patients who were married. For example, in this small sample, 78 percent of the male patients had problems with erection, 56 percent had ejaculation difficulty, and 53 percent did not have orgasm. Among the female patients, 57 percent experienced problems in sexual arousal, 57 percent had orgasm difficulty, and 14 percent had no orgasm. The occurrence of these sexual problems was clearly related to the degree of depression the patient experienced due to the illness. One very significant finding of the Steele et al. research was that female spouses were more affected sexually by their husband's illness than male spouses were by their wife's illness. The importance of this is that females learn, more than males, to connect interpersonal and emotional factors to sexuality. Males, on the other hand, are more likely to see sex in a physical light and therefore to be less affected by existing interpersonal and emotional conditions. Thus, wives of patients had their sexuality much more affected by the existing interpersonal climate of a fatal illness than did husbands of patients.

Spinal Cord Injury
Spinal cord injury can have a significant effect on the sexuality of certain members of the population. Of all spinal cord injuries, 69 per-

cent happen to males and 30 percent to males between the ages of 15 and 24, with the greatest risk being between the ages of 20 and 34 (Bracken et al., 1981).

In Chapter 5, we reviewed the relationship between the brain and the genitals in terms of sexual arousal and orgasm. We noted the complex feedback systems involved and the processes of interpretation. Recall that, at least for males, erection and ejaculation are controlled by nerve centers in the lower part of the spinal cord and that both these processes may take place as a reflex action. Tactile stimulation of the penis, or anywhere else, results in a message of touch being sent through the spinal cord to the brain, where the touch is *interpreted* (on the basis of other information) as sexual or not. If interpreted as sexual, the message is relayed to the erection center and on to the blood vessels, and erection results. The same process may begin in the brain with a sexual thought or a visual or auditory stimulus.

The key to all this is that in order for the erection to be more than a reflex action, information must pass to and from the brain through the spinal cord. If the information cannot get to the brain through the spinal cord— because of injury to the latter—the interpretation process in the brain cannot take place and there is no sexual sensation but just a physiological erection. The same applies to ejaculation. Ejaculation may take place as a reflex action without any pleasurable sensation or psychological experience. The importance of spinal cord injury to sexual functioning is thought to be physiological since a damaged or completely severed spinal cord results in an impaired and nonexistent transfer of signals to and fro between the brain and the erection and ejaculation centers. As we shall see, however, much of the research on the sexuality of males and females with spinal cord injuries calls these basic assumptions into question.

Males Most of the research on spinal cord injury and sexuality has been with males. It may be argued (perhaps with more than a kernel of truth) that a major reason for this focus is that females are not expected to be as sexual as males and thus they are seen as losing less if they lose some sexual capacity. But the major reason that most of the research has been done on males is that they are more than twice as likely to suffer a spinal cord injury owing to occupational patterns in American society.

Higgins (1979) has recently reviewed the research on sexual functioning and spinal cord injury. He points out that for males, the level and type of sexual functioning after injury vary greatly. The varied research in this area reports that between 49 and 92 percent of males are able to have erections after spinal cord injury (Higgins, 1979). In general, the research indicates that erection is more likely when the injury is high in the spinal cord and thus above the erection center. Erection is also apparently more likely when the injury does not completely sever the spinal cord. We must keep in mind that two types of erections may take place: a reflex erection, which is simply a reflex action generated from the erection center without any signal passing to or from the brain; and a psychogenic erection, where the erection response is due to a psychological stimulus. From what we have already discussed, it should be the case that psychogenic erections should be impossible when the spinal cord is completely severed. However, several studies (reviewed by Higgins, 1979) found that males with completely severed spinal cords had psychogenic erections. Some studies also report that males who do not even have reflex erections have psychogenic erections.

Among the studies reviewed by Higgins, the percentage of males with spinal cord injury able to engage in intercourse ranges from 5 to 56 percent. In many cases, reflex, but not psychogenic, erection may be possible. This means that even though one can experience an erection, one may not be able to do so when it is possible to engage in coitus.

Ejaculation in males with spinal cord injuries is much less common than erection. For males with complete lesions of the spinal cord, the reported percentage having ejaculation ranges from zero to 7 percent and 27 to 50 percent for those males with incomplete severing (Higgins, 1979). Orgasm experiences are reportedly more rare, with between 2 and 16 percent of the injured males studied have orgasmic sensations.

Females   As mentioned, much less data are available on females with spinal cord injuries. What is available, however, raises some very interesting questions about the nature of sexual response and the nervous system.

There is no research reporting on the genital responses of females with spinal cord injuries (Higgins, 1979). There are, however, a few studies which deal with female sexual response following injury to the spinal cord. Weiss and Diamond (1966), in a study of twenty-one women, found *increased sexual sensations, sexual desire, and sexual activity following spinal cord injury.* Fitzpatrick (1974) reported on two women with such injury. One of the women experienced no arousal, orgasm, or coitus after her accident. The other women experienced arousal, orgasm, and coitus once a month following her injury. Bregman (1975) reported on thirty-one women who had suffered spinal cord injury. Seven of them said they had a "full sexual life" following injury, six said they experienced less satisfaction, and one said she experienced more satisfaction after the injury. Clearly, we have a great deal to learn about not only the sexual effects of spinal cord injury, but the physiological processes involved in sexual response.

Reorientation   Not all sexual pleasure need revolve around erections and orgasms. Even though the dominant view (particularly among males) of "good sex" in American society can rather accurately be characterized as goal- and performance-oriented, it is entirely possible to learn that sexual satisfaction and enjoyment can come in many forms through many means. Currently many therapy programs are underway in the United States in which patients with spinal cord injuries learn to have less of a performance- and goal-oriented view of sexuality.

Chronic Pain

Among couples where one of the partners suffers from chronic pain (pain not related to any malignant disease which does not respond to traditional pain treatment, and which exists for an extended period of the time) the patterns of sexuality are much the same as those in other chronic illness relationships. Both males and females with chronic pain report less interest in sex and greater difficulty in becoming sexually aroused, as well as less frequency of sexual activity (Maruta et al., 1981).

The majority of the patients studied by Maruta et al. reported that these sexual effects were due to pain after (not during) sexual activity. He and his associates further suggested that chronic pain, as well as other chronic illnesses, may often be accompanied by certain interpersonal problems stemming directly from the illness of one of the partners. They suggest that many illnesses such as this result in the spouses feeling the obligation and need to care for the other person. This situation, they suggest, often results in a kind of "superficial harmony" or "pseudo mutuality" in which there is apparent closeness and harmony in the relationship but with ever-increasing conflicts and guilt-accompanied resentment. Thus, the illness and its symptoms and physiological outcomes may be less important in negatively affecting sexuality than these underlying interpersonal dynamics; such dynamics are not easily discussed in any relationship, especially one where one of the partners is seriously ill.

Rectal Surgery

Rectal problems and surgery are not the kinds of topics frequently discussed at cocktail parties. While Betty Ford and Happy Rockefeller may have brought breast cancer and surgery out of the closet in 1974, many other forms of major surgery remain shrouded in secrecy, embarrassment, and silence. Such major surgical procedures are, however, relatively common in cases of rectal or colon cancer. In fact, there is an association for people who have had rectal and colon surgery involving removal of these organs in Great Britain, Ireland, and the United States.

There are certain surgical and adaptive procedures performed when removal of the colon, the rectum, or both is required. An *ileostomy* is where the large intestine is removed and the small intestine is connected to an opening in the abdomen (called a *stoma*). The contents of the small intestine then drain into a bag worn by the patient. A *colostomy* is a procedure where the colon (the lower part of the large intestine) is connected to a stoma, and the rectum and anus are bypassed or surgically removed.

Given the severe body modification involved in such surgical procedures, it is not difficult to see how sexual problems of adaptation may result. In a sample of married couples where one of the partners had had an ileostomy, Burnham et al. (1977) found that 50 percent of the patients said they were embarrassed by the stoma. These feelings, however, were largely not shared by the patients' partners. This type of surgery is so severe and obvious that it may actually not contain as many sexual problems as other forms of cancer surgery. For example, Burnham et al. (1977) found that 90 percent of the married couples they studied said that they could freely discuss the sexual problems with each other. Sexual problems that are centered on such major body modifications and the traditional taboos regarding excretion are more severe for unmarried persons who do not have a steady sexual partner. Brouillette et al. (1981) found that embarrassment with new sexual partners was a major and frequent problem for ileostomy patients. Dlin et al. (1959) noted that among single individuals, the patterns of petting remained unchanged, but how and when to reveal the fact of the ileostomy to a new partner was a serious concern.

The actual sexual effects of such surgery are not, however, great. In the Burnham et al. (1977) study, the married couples showed no change in sexual interest. Brouillette et al. found that most patients resumed coitus within six months of the operation. If the surgery does not involve the rectum, there is little damage to sexual activity. When rectal excision (removal) is required, the results are less satisfactory. More than half the rectal excision patients in the Brouillette et al. study said that the perineal wound (incision in the perineum)

resulted in sexual problems, and only 15 percent of the females in the Burnham et al. research said there was any discomfort in coitus when the rectum was left intact. For males, there is no automatic loss of erection function when there is no rectal excision, and even when the rectum is removed, only a small proportion experience erection problems (Burnham et al., 1977). The extent to which erection problems are experienced is physiologically dependent on damage to important nerves in the perineal area (between the anus and testicles) and on the person's age (Hogan, 1980). In the Burnham et al. research, only 8 percent of both the males and females said that the presence of a stoma made coitus difficult.

There are, however, important differences between males and females in how this surgery affects sexuality. These differences are the result of traditional gender disparities in sexual behavior patterns and expectations. Females are much more likely than males to be concerned about the stoma and the bag being unattractive, while males are more concerned about the bags' being a hinderance to physical sexual activity. The male's traditional sexual role is to be the physically active agent, and the female's traditional sexual role is to be sexually attractive (Burnham et al. 1977). When these problems are overcome, this type of surgery may even have a beneficial sexual effect. Brouillette et al. (1981) found that many ileostomy patients reported an improvement in their sexuality due to improved communication with their sexual partners that was necessitated by the physical effects of the surgery.

Multiple Sclerosis

While there are many diseases which affect the person's neurologic and muscular functioning, multiple sclerosis is of particular importance with regard to lifetime sexuality. Not only are the causes of the disease not known, but it strikes young individuals, with the highest incidence in those 30 to 35 years old. The affected individuals can therefore expect to experience the sexual effects for the remainder of their lives.

The disease directly affects the nerves and results in both motor and sensory disturbances in which deterioration continues until permanent damage and eventually death occur in the majority of cases. (Hogan, 1980). These changes in physical condition generally come during the person's most active years of life and thus require major alterations in living.

Sexual dysfunction is common for both males and females with multiple sclerosis. Problems of erection appear for 26 percent (Ivers and Goldstein, 1963) to 80 percent (Lilitus et al., 1976) of male patients. The majority of males report lessened sexual desire and no sex life, or an unsatisfactory one, in the advanced stages (Lilius et al., 1976). Females in the advanced stages frequently report decreased or no interest in sex, decreased or no sensitivity in the clitoris, and orgasm difficulty (Lilius et al., 1976). A minority of women patients report that the low level of their sexual satisfaction is caused by spasticity of muscles, a disinterested partner, weakness, problems of vaginal lubrication, or no partner available (Lilius et al., 1976). Other studies have found that women patients with even mild multiple sclerosis have frequent sexual problems, such as decreased sexual interest, orgasm difficulty, painful intercourse, and problems of vaginal lubrication (Lundberg, 1978).

While it is clear that impairment of certain muscle structures and nerve networks (such as those to the genitals) could be responsible for these often reported sexual problems, not all experts in the field agree. Many regard these problems as psychological in origin (Kolodny et al., 1979:268-269). This debate of course points to what we have repeatedly discussed as the major issue in human sexuality: the extent to which sexual behavior is physiologically or psychologically determined. As we have seen many times, this debate comes to the front in research and treatment in sexuality and chronic illness.

THE TREATMENT OF SEXUAL PROBLEMS

Since the early 1970s we have witnessed increased concern given to the identification and treatment of sexual problems. This concern has spanned the range from helping persons with chronic illness deal with sexuality to aiding in the solution of everyday sexual problems encountered by those who have no physical illness or impairment.

The treatments of sexual problems encountered by the chronically ill and the seriously injured are largely within the field of nursing. It is not possible in the space limitation here to describe these treatments, but for an exceptional summary discussion, one should see R. Hogan's *Human Sexuality: A Nursing Perspective* (1980). Within this perspective of treating the sexual problems of the chronically ill, the assumption is most often made that any existing sexual problems are physical in nature, that they are caused by the illness itself or one of its physical outcomes. Thus, the primary treatments here involve alternative patterns of sexuality when coitus is not possible or when physical adjustments must be made in such situations as paralysis, ileostomy, or arthritis. While the nursing and medical professions acknowledge at present that psychological factors may be somewhat important in the sexual problems encountered by the chronically ill, the dominant point of view is that these problems are mainly physiological in origin and that their treatment is therefore physical in nature.

As is perhaps apparent from our previous discussion, there is some reason to doubt the pervasiveness of physical causes of sexual problems among the chronically ill. I suspect that as research and understanding grows in this area, we shall find that psychological factors play a much more influential part in the development of sexual problems than has previously been thought.

It is also very important to note that the reason chronically ill persons have sexual problems is largely due to the limited definition of sexuality in American society. It has probably become apparent by now that most of the research discussed in the first section of this chapter assumed that a sexual problem exists when the genitals do not work in the manner normally expected (lack of erection, painful intercourse, no orgasm response, no ejaculation, etc.). As has been pointed out, this is a very limited view of sexuality. In almost all but the most severe cases of chronic illness, people can think about, touch, love, communicate with, and appreciate another person. These core characteristics of sexuality do not require an erection, a moist vagina, erect clitoris, orgasm, or the ability to position two bodies in a particular fashion so that they may move in unison in a certain manner. Thus, a very large part of what are considered sexual problems of the chronically ill is the result of placing all one's sexual eggs in a basket that is very much physically, coitally, and orgasmically oriented. The extent to which low levels of sexual satisfaction encountered by the chronically ill are the result of not being able to maintain some socially defined level of *physical* performance remains unknown. It is a safe bet, however, that this is an extremely important consideration.

SEXUAL THERAPY

Since 1970, American society has seen the creation of an entirely new occupation—sex therapy. To be certain, there were people with what we today call sexual problems before 1970, but after the 1970 publication of Masters and Johnson's reports on sexual therapy, the field of sexual therapy spread like wildfire.

Generally, sexual therapy is a term used to refer to treating the sexual problems of individuals other than the chronically ill, or persons having some identifiable physiological basis for whatever sexual problems they have.

In general, sexual therapy involves identifying the type of the individual's sexual problem, identifying what is thought to be the cause of the problem, and administering treatment to solve the problem. The major difference between sexual therapy and sexual treatment for the chronically ill is that sexual therapy seeks to cure the problem by dealing with its cause, while sexual treatment attempts to adapt the individual to the problem by alternative modes of sexual activity.

Types of Sexual Therapy

It is impossible to summarize all the specific sexual therapy techniques currently in use for various sexual dysfunctions. There are, however, some major methods which are employed and from which many slight modifications have developed.

Before Masters and Johnson Before the extremely popular techniques of Masters and Johnson (which we shall discuss), sexual therapy did exist. It was not, however, a full-scale occupation and was not widely known to the American public. Some of the methods utilized in those earlier days were effective (apparently) and are still in use today. One such technique is the Semans or "start-stop" technique for the treatment of premature ejaculation (Seamans, 1956). It involves masturbating to the point of near-ejaculation and then stopping until the feeling that one is going to ejaculate ceases. Then masturbation starts again and the procedure is repeated. With each repetition of this start-stop exercise, the male is able to engage in longer periods of sexual stimulation before the feeling that ejaculation is inevitable is reached. This procedure was later modified by Masters and Johnson, but is used by many therapists today.

A second early technique was Kegel's exercise used in the treatment of orgasmic dysfunctions. One of the central physiological processes in heightened sexual arousal and orgasm is myotonia or muscle tension. This exercise concentrates on the woman's developing strength in the pubococcygeal muscle which runs along the sides of the vaginal opening. One can become aware of this muscle and develop strength and control by voluntarily stopping the flow of urination. After this awareness is developed, the woman practices tightening and relaxing the muscles several times a day. Since vaginal muscle strength has been linked in a correlational manner to orgasm, this method may be an effective means of treating orgasm response that is less frequent than desired (Perry and Wipple, 1981).

Masters and Johnson To the average person, the names Masters and Johnson are strongly linked to sex therapy. Masters and

Johnson were the leaders in developing a comprehensive sexual therapy program for men and women that is feasible and that appears to have a low failure rate. Masters and Johnson view sexual dysfunction as a learned response to certain types of sexual situations. Thus their program focuses on relearning. The basic treatment involves both partners, consists of initial screening and measurement, followed by two weeks of information and homework exercises practiced by the couple under the guidance of a counselor. A central tenet of the program is that sex is a form of communication and that if interaction between two people is impaired outside the bedroom, it will be impaired sexually as well (Masters and Johnson, 1976). It is assumed that communication consists of three elements; one partner's self-representation to the other, vulnerability in interaction, and problem solving (Tullman et al., 1981). Efforts are focused on improving communication between the partners by "neutrality," in which the couple learns not to predict the present on the basis of past feelings or behaviors (Tullman et al., 1981).

Kaplan approach Helen Singer Kaplan has expanded the work of Masters and Johnson and she takes a much more psychological approach to therapy. The emphasis of her approach is that sexual dysfunctions cannot be divorced from personality problems and interpersonal conflicts. Her treatment is oriented toward the dynamics of the individual person and the nature of the relationship between partners. Thus, this program takes more than two weeks depending on the couple. The basic assumption is that deep-seated fears may be the cause of most sexual problems, perhaps the most common of which is fear of intimacy (Kaplan, 1974; 1980). It is assumed that considerable time may be required to deal with these deep-seated fears before the actual sexual problem can be approached directly. The Kaplan approach thus combines psychoanalysis with relearning.

Heiman and LoPiccolo's program In direct contrast to the Masters and Johnson (1970) and Kaplan (1974;1980) approaches, which deal with couples, Heiman

and LoPiccolo's approach deals with single people. The method focuses on learning about one's body, what one's genitals look like, how to strengthen certain muscles, and most important, how to give oneself pleasure. Through such approaches as learning about one's anatomy and sexual responses by means of masturbation, a woman, for example, learns to have orgasm and experience sexual pleasure.

Do These Sex Therapies Work?

The model for most programs of sex therapy has been the Masters and Johnson treatment. While not all programs using this treatment follow Masters and Johnson to the letter, many programs are rooted in the basic program, its assumptions, and its modes of treatment.

Part of the enthusiasm about this program has been due to its being quick. While the Kaplan model is time-consuming and laborious, the Masters and Johnson program can reportedly be conducted to completion in a two-week period. Another important reason for its popularity among sex therapists is its apparent success. Masters and Johnson reported that after two weeks of therapy, only 20 percent of their patients failed to improve.

Recently, however, the Masters and Johnson program in particular, and sex therapy in general, have encountered some serious criticism. This criticism has raised questions challenging much of the field of sex therapy as it exists today.

The most widely read and controversial criticism has been directed toward Masters and Johnson and comes from Zilbergeld and Evans (1980). They summarize their evaluation of Masters and Johnson's methods of evaluating the success and failure of sex therapy as follows (1980:29): "Masters and Johnson's research is so flawed by methodological errors and slipshod reporting that it fails to meet customary standards—and their own—for evaluation research." Basically, Zilbergeld and Evans argue that from Masters and Johnson's published materials, one cannot determine a success from a failure and that, in many respects, it is not possible to accurately evaluate the effectiveness of their treatment program on the basis of published data.

Kolodny (1981) has answered most of the criticisms raised by Zilbergeld and Evans (1980). A couple of points about this debate are, however, important for our discussion. First, Zilbergeld and Evans are correct in pointing out that from Masters and Johnson's published works, one cannot tell precisely what is done in the program and how the effectiveness of the treatment is measured. It is significant that Kolodny has to publish a response and clarification with regard to the questions raised by Zilbergeld and Evans. This clarification of important matters comes some eleven years after Masters and Johnson first published their book on sexual therapy. One of the central tenets of science is that it is public and capable of replication. Clarity and detail should have appeared long before criticism. As we shall see, the field of sexual therapy has not been noted for its clear definitions and precise data. Second, the Zilbergeld and Evans criticism has itself been criticized because it was harsh and it appeared in the popular magazine *Psychology Today*. Many have argued that there was no need to be so harsh and that the criticism should have appeared in an established professional journal rather than a popular magazine. It is worth keeping in mind, however, that Masters and Johnson have become household names and that the average person does not read the staid professional journals found only in a university library. Since Masters and Johnson and their work have become widely known to the public through such communication channels as the popular press, television talk shows, and magazine articles, it seems more than a little dishonest to hide any criticism from public view.

It should also be pointed out, however, that Masters and Johnson are not the only sex therapists who have reported on a program and failed to provide scientifically precise definitions. This problem characterizes most of the field of sex therapy (Kilmann, 1978).

Kaplan (1980) has offered additional criticisms of the Masters and Johnson approach. She argues that the sexual problems people

report are only excuses for real underlying fears. Thus, if one treats only the excuse and not the underlying fear, the real sexual problem is never dealt with. Apart from the fact that it may be enough to treat only the excuse if that is what makes people happy, Kaplan's method presents other problems.

While Kaplan (1980) does not report any direct success rates, it is insinuated that the success rate for the problems she deals with is about 50 percent.

Apart from whatever the success rates of the Kaplan approach may be, this form of sexual therapy apparently has more serious problems—problems which are characteristic of all sex therapy. Unless one is going to capitalize on a lot of accident, one cannot solve a sexual problem without knowing what *causes* the problem. All sex therapies assume that the causes of sexual problems are known. This assumption explains why the methods differ; they have different ideas about what causes the problem. It can be stated without doubt that *we do not have enough knowledge about human sexuality to say with any degree of certainty what definitely causes certain sexual problems*. A field of study which cannot decide whether the absence of erection is due to physiological or psychological factors has no business talking about cause and effect in a global sense.

While not knowing enough about human sexuality to devise precise methods of curing or solving sexual problems affects all sexual therapy, it is perhaps most serious in the case of the Kaplan method. This method rests on psychoanalytic theory about human behavior. While there is hardly room here to detail the problems with psychoanalytic theory, it is sufficient to say that there is very little evidence in support of it. Ellis (1981) has pointed out some of the more glaring errors in Kaplan's psychoanalytic approach with regard to human sexuality. Kaplan assumes that adult sexual problems are the result of childhood conflicts and experiences where the child is "traumatized." Not only is this assumption very debatable, but the idea that having the individual realize this will cure the problem is simply not supported by clinical psychology. Kaplan apparently ignores the mounds of research which indicate that not all the cognitions which affect one's sexuality are logical and rational. She relies heavily on the "unconscious," a concept which is by definition not measurable and thus not subject to scrutiny as a factor in sexual problems. In many cases, she apparently confused which factor came first. For example, she states that the focus on the unattractive or unacceptable aspects of a sexual partner leads to such things as anger. There is ample evidence suggesting that, to the contrary, such things as anger lead to focusing on the undesirable aspects of another rather than the other way around.

Interestingly, the LoPiccolo method has received the least attention in the media and the field, yet it may appear to be the most effective. While there are no absolutely solid data on the success rates of this method, it is at least logical. As we have seen, the assumptions underlying this method are based (perhaps purely accidentally and not owing to research) on established scientific observation in the study of human sexuality. As we discuss various types of sexual problems and their correlates, we shall see how this is specifically the case.

WHAT IS A SEXUAL PROBLEM?

Any therapy or treatment must first have a problem or problems which it treats. Without problems, there is no need for treatment. From some important studies, it is apparent that sexual problems are relatively common in American society.

In a *Psychology Today* questionnaire, respondents were asked if they had any sexual problems. Of the men responding, 19 percent said they had a problem ejaculating too quickly, 8 percent reported trouble reaching orgasm, 6 percent had difficulty becoming sexually aroused, 5 percent cited a problem with getting or maintaining an erection, and 1 percent had a problem with pain during intercourse. Of the women, 38 percent said they had trouble

reaching orgasm, 20 percent had difficulty in becoming aroused, and 10 percent had a problem with painful intercourse.

In a 1978 study of 100 couples who were not in treatment for sexual problems (average age 37 for females, 35 for males, predominately white, college-educated, middle-class), Frank et al. (1978) found many with sexual problems, as shown in Table 17-2.

Both these studies suggest that self-reported sexual problems are relatively common for both males and females. A relatively large proportion of people report not only that they or their relationships have characteristics which they see as sexually problematic, but also that these problems are important. In the *Psychology Today* study, for example, "sex life" was rated between the fourth and the sixth (depending on the respondent's marital status and sex) most important contributor to overall life happiness (Shaver and Freedman, 1976).

It is essential to realize that in large part, these sexual problems originate from social definitions of acceptable or expected sexual behavior. A person or a couple has a certain characteristic in their sexual activity. Whether or not this characteristic is defined as a problem depends on each of the persons involved having learned that there is some performance standard that is considered appropriate, expected, and "normal." One person may not see anything at all problematic about having orgasm in half his or her sexual encounters, while another person will see anything less than 100 percent a problem. Many sexual problems have probably been created in this way by the widespread discussion of sexual problems and therapy. As such topics become more widely debated, people are more likely to look at their own behavior, define it as "not good enough," and then say they have a problem.

Types of Sexual Problems
In the field of sexual therapy, sexual problems are usually referred to as *sexual dysfunctions*. The very term reveals our performance-

TABLE 17-2
Married males and females reporting sexual problems.

Sexual Problem	Females Reporting This Problem (%)	Males Reporting This Problem (%)
Difficulty in getting sexually excited	48	*
Difficulty in maintaining sexual excitement	33	*
Difficulty in reaching orgasm	46	*
Reaching orgasm too quickly	11	*
Inability to reach orgasm	15	*
Difficulty in getting an erection	*	7
Difficulty in maintaining erection	*	9
Difficulty in ejaculating	*	4
Ejaculating too quickly	*	36
Partner choosing inconvenient time for sex	31	16
Inability to relax	47	12
Disinterested in sex	35	16
Turned off	28	10
Not enough foreplay	38	21

*Respondents not asked to rank this problem.
Source: Frank et al. (1978, p. 113, table 3).

oriented and physically biased view of sexuality. *Function* means that something does something. *Dysfunction* means that something does not do what it is supposed to or that it fails to function. There are, as we have seen, a set of rather common sexual dysfunctions.

Erection Problems

Impotence, or erectile dysfunction, is assumed to be a relatively common problem for males, but in any precise sense this is impossible to verify with existing data. The reason is that there is no clear definition of what impotence (note the power and lack of power connotations of the term) or erectile dysfunction means. The *Psychology Today* and Frank et al. research suggests that somewhere around 5 to 9 percent of all males have erection problems of some kind.

Erectile dysfunctions are generally classified as *primary impotence* and *secondary impotence.* Primary impotence is used some-

times to refer to the man's never having an erection sufficient to accomplish coitus (although he may have an erection with masturbation). At other times, the term refers to a man's never having an erection sufficient to accomplish coitus with a given partner although he may do so with other partners or in masturbation. Secondary impotence most often refers to having successfully completed intercourse at least once but now being unable to have an erection sufficient to engage in coitus, or, to having intercourse at least once with a given partner and then not being able to obtain an erection with that partner.

Without belaboring the fact, it is apparent that there are massive problems of definition here. For example, the entire definition that this is a problem is centered on coitus. There are literally thousands of forms of sexual activity which do not require an erection (among them, fellatio) and thus are situations in which the absence of erection is not a problem. The definition of secondary impotence has been further defined by Masters and Johnson as occurring when the male does not obtain an erection sufficient for coitus in at least 25 percent of his coital opportunities. Why 25 percent? There is nothing magical about this number, and I suspect that from the viewpoint of men themselves, anywhere between 10 and 25 percent would be defined as a "problem."

Erection problems also vary between being more or less permanent and situational or transitory. Permanent lack of erection increases with age, and the incidence of this permanent lack is much less than for situational or temporary lack of an erection. Kinsey, for example, found that in over 4,000 males, those who were totally and permanently without erection by age were as follows: 1.3 percent by age 35; 6.7 percent by age 50; 18.4 percent by age 60; 27 percent by age 70; and 55 percent by age 75.

The causes of erection problems are usually divided into *organic* and *psychological*. Organic impotence refers to impotence caused by some physiological or biochemical factors. Jehu (1979) lists twenty causes of organic impotence, including chemicals, surgery, and various diseases and disorders of the endocrine, nervous, and vascular systems. Psychological impotence refers to impotence caused by other than physical factors. Some argue that almost all impotence is psychological in nature, while others contend that much impotence is organic. While it has been traditionally assumed that most impotence is organically based, evidence is mounting that psychological fctors are more important. For many of the chronic illnesses, such as diabetes and spinal cord injury, more and more research suggests that the basis of erection problems in many of these cases is the psychological reaction to the illness situation, not the illness itself. The fact that many males who have been diagnosed as having organic impotence obtain erections during sleep raises further questions about the extent of organic impotence (Marshall et al., 1981), but the issue remains hotly debated (Schumacher and Lloyd, 1981).

There is not much more agreement about what psychological factors are responsible for impotence when there is no organic basis of the problem. It has been customary to assume that anxiety over sex is an important factor. However, while one-time inability to get an erection the first time one has sex with a given person may be related to performance anxiety, there is little evidence that sexual anxiety is a major factor when the problem persists (Cooper, 1969). Some forms of anxiety do appear to be important in impotence problems. Rosenheim and Neumann (1981) found, for example, that the male's anxiety about interaction with others and his tendency to experience frequent guilt were related to impotence. They reported that males with persistent erection problems were ill at ease in interpersonal situations, cautious, unassertive, sensitive to the disapproval of others, self-conscious, self-critical, and self-punishing. These characteristics, combined with the fact that the wives of impotent males tended to be more outwardly aggressive, suggests an interesting hypothesis. Males tend to see the erect penis as a sign of masculinity and power. Impotence may really mean lack of power, at least from the point of view of the male who experiences this life situation.

Premature Ejaculation

There are even greater problems in defining what is meant by premature ejaculation. Most sex therapists have recognized this difficulty, and many in the field have debated when an ejaculation should be considered "premature." Masters and Johnson (1970) define premature ejaculation as occurring when the man cannot postpone ejaculation while the penis is in the vagina long enough to satisfy the woman in at least 50 percent of his coital encounters. While this definition does take into account the interaction and mutuality involved in coitus, it does not consider that many women never have orgasm via penile penetration of the vagina, that those women who do have such orgasm differ widely in how much stimulation they require, that how long vaginal penetration takes to result in orgasm in a woman is a function of stimulation prior to penile insertion, and most

BOX 17-4
SURGICAL SOLUTIONS TO SEXUAL DYSFUNCTIONS

While most sexual dysfunctions appear to be psychological in origin rather than physiological, some few individuals experience problems that are organic in nature. The most common of these is male erectile dysfunction (impotence). In cases where the cause is organic, a penile prosthesis may be used. This is a mechanical device which is placed inside the penis to make erection possible. Such devices were first introduced in 1952 in the form of semirigid rods surgically inserted into the penis. There are currently many different types of rods and many different surgical procedures employed in their location (Sotile, 1979). All rods are permanent and provide a semi-rigid penis at all times, so that intromission is possible. A second, and more recent, method is the use of an inflatable hydraulic penile prosthesis. It consists of a 3/8-inch cylinder inserted the full length of the penis with an inflate-deflate pump inserted in the scrotum and a fluid reservoir located in the nearby tissue (Sotile, 1979; Malloy et al., 1979). The man activates the pump himself and the pump mechanism fills the cylinder with fluid, creating erection. The rod procedure is easier to insert surgically, costs less to the patient, and has fewer complications because of its simplicity. The hydraulic prosthesis, however, allows for a more normal erection and provides control of erection. The outcome of such devices appears to be positive in most cases. Sotile (1979) reports that rod implants have a satisfactory outcome in 89 percent of the cases and hydraulic devices are satisfactory in 96 percent of the cases. Nevertheless, some problems do emerge. Approximately 17 percent of all rod implants result in some complication, and in 40 percent of these cases, the rod must be removed because of infection (Sotile, 1979). Hydraulic devices have historically had a higher complication rate (31 percent) because they are indeed more complex (Sotile, 1979), but in recent years this rate has declined considerably (Malloy et al., 1979). As of 1981, more than twenty thousand semirigid rod implant operations had been performed and over seventy-one thousand inflatable prostheses had been implanted in males in the United States (Kaufman et al., 1981). On the psychological level the majority of males with penile implants report an improvement in their self-concept, an increased interest in sex, a decline in the frequency of coitus relative to the past but an increase in the satisfaction with coitus, and an improvement in their overall relationship with their partner (Kaufman et al., 1981). There has been little research, but it appears that a small minority of women have some concern about the semirigid penile implant. (I know of no research on women's feelings about the inflatable implants.) Kramarsky-Binkhorst (1978) found that 16 percent of the female partners of men with semirigid penile implants worried about hurting the penis, refused to touch the penis after the implant, thought the penis was too short, or thought the penis was too inflexible.

important, that the woman's satisfaction may or may not mean orgasm on her part and may involve anything from thirty seconds to thirty minutes of penile insertion.

Kaplan (1974) argues that premature ejaculation is the absence of voluntary control over the ejaculation reflex after the man attains heightened sexual arousal. This definition seems more concrete than that of Masters and Johnson, and one which might be pointed more toward what a person would consider a "problem." However, with this definition, all males might be considered to be premature ejaculators, since once a certain level of sexual arousal is reached, the voluntary control of ejaculation is not possible. On the other hand, we could say that no male has premature ejaculation since ejaculation cannot take place (normally) unless this level of arousal is reached. Again, we are left with no concrete definition of this sexual dysfunction. The fact is that premature ejaculation is ejaculating "too quickly." What constitutes "too quickly" is a matter of personal preference and opinion which are established by what the individual learns is the appropriate amount of sexual stimulation prior to ejaculation. If American males were suddenly to find themselves in Mangaia, it is quite likely that even the most long-lasting men would suffer from premature ejaculation, since Mangaian males are expected to (and do) engage in constant coital thrusting for a long period while the female has several orgasms.

Retarded Ejaculation

Retarded ejaculation is generally defined as the inability to ejaculate during penis-vagina contact. As might be expected, this is a relatively rare form of male sexual dysfunction, but one which is still subject to problems of definition. If a male wants to ejaculate during intromission and never does, the definition of this as a problem is reasonably clear. However, if retarded ejaculation is a "sometimes" affair, it becomes less clear when it is and when it is not a problem. Again, the basis for its being defined as a problem is an emphasis on penis-

vagina contact as an important—if not the most important— form of heterosexual stimulation. The inability to ejaculate during anal or oral intercourse is not considered retarded ejaculation.

Orgasmic Dysfunction

Again this dysfunction is broken into primary and secondary categories. *Primary orgasmic dysfunction* is the inability of a woman to have orgasm at any time in her life through any form of sexual stimulation. *Secondary orgasmic dysfunction* is the inability to have orgasm in some situations. Perhaps in no other area is the social basis of sexual dysfunctions more apparent. It was not until public discussion involved the topic of female orgasm that the lack thereof became defined by many women as a problem. The greater the discussion about the right of women to orgasmic response, the more cases there are of this particular sexual dysfunction.

It is very interesting to note that males may have the dysfunction of retarded ejaculation but not of orgasmic dysfunction, while females may experience orgasmic dysfunction but not retarded ejaculation. Why the male response is defined as ejaculation and not orgasm escapes me, since even though they are separate physiological responses, they do almost always appear at the same time. Why females do not have ejaculatory dysfunction is clear. Up until 1980, it was thought that females did not ejaculate. However, the recent work of Perry and Whipple (1980) make it clear that some females do ejaculate. I suspect that once this new knowledge becomes widespread throughout the public realm we may have another female sexual dysfunction— retarded ejaculation. This expectation assumes, of course, that women will come to feel that the ejaculatory response is one they should experience.

The reasons why some women experience difficulty in reaching orgasm or having no orgasm at all are relatively well understood. The causes can be psychological in origin, in which some factor inhibits the woman's reaching that level of sexual arousal where vasocongestion creates sufficient muscle tension for the orgasmic response to occur. The basis of the problem can be in learning, wherein the woman simply never learned what an orgasm is or how to be sensitive to bodily changes that take place in high levels of arousal leading to orgasm. The basis of the problem can be physiological in terms of muscle strength and tension ability in the orgasmic platform. The basic cause can also be the use of an inappropriate form of sexual stimulation. As we have discussed, there are two types of female orgasm. Some women are more sensitive to clitoral stimulation, while others are more sensitive to deep vaginal-uterine pressure involved in coitus. If the "wrong" type of sexual stimulation takes place for a particular woman, orgasm is unlikely, or at best difficult. The root of the problem may also be organic in that brainstem, nerve, vascular, or muscle damage may inhibit the physiological processes that take place in orgasm.

Without question, however, learning is the single most important factor. In understanding its importance, one must clearly face the fact that orgasm difficulty is predominately a female, not a male, problem. This difference lies not in physiological differences, but in differences in sexual learning. On a somewhat larger scale, it should be kept in mind that there are cultures where all women reportedly have orgasm in all intercourse encounters and where the lack of female orgasm is unheard of.

Vaginismus

Other sexual dysfunctions are more concrete and thus have clearer definitions than those discussed above. Vaginismus is one such dysfunction. This is the condition where the muscles in the lower one-third of the vagina contract involuntarily so that penile insertion is not possible, or is at least difficult and painful. Kaplan (1974) suggests that this is a learned response associated with previously experienced pain or fear in attempts at coitus. Masters and Johnson (1970) relate the condition to a highly religious and restricted sexual learning

environment. Again, it is important to note what is excluded from this category of sexual dysfunction. Vaginismus applies only to the vagina, not to the anus or the mouth. Yet, a great many women cannot relax the anal muscles for anal intercourse, and many women have a learned and uncontrollable revulsion to a penis in the mouth. These responses might be considered by some to be "uptight," but not as sexual dysfunctions. The reason is that anal, and to a lesser extent, oral intercourse is avant garde, while vaginal-penile contact is the traditionally standard and accepted form of heterosexual interaction. It is expected in this society. Not to be able to do it is therefore a problem. The other forms of coitus are still seen as "extras," and thus their absence is not a problem.

Dyspareunia

Dyspareunia is painful intercourse. While this is usually a female problem, it is (infrequently) seen in males as well. Interestingly, there is some confusion of the terms used in North America and England. British authors apply the term "dyspareunia" to all coital pain and the term "vaginismus" to all painful coitus that does not have an organic cause. North American literature uses the term "dyspareunia" for all coital pain regardless of its cause and "vaginismus" when talking about involuntary spasms of the levator, animuscles, and perineal muscles (Lamont, 1980). Here we shall adhere to the North American usage.

As with other sexual problems, dyspareunia may be based on either physical or psychological problems. Lamont's research indicates that approximately 43 percent of the women with dyspareunia have the problem because of *intrapersonal* factors, such as fear of sex-related activity, pain, or intimacy, or some traumatic sexual experience, ignorance of bodily functions, or strongly traditional sexual attitudes. Lamont reports that for another 27 percent, the basis of the problem is *interpersonal,* such as conflicts over having more children, contraception disagreements, sexual disagreements, and other interpersonal sexual prob-

BOX 17-5

CHANGING DEFINITIONS OF SEXUAL PROBLEMS

It is interesting to note that the federal government made a distinct effort to inhibit sexual desire in the early 1920s. At that time what is now considered a sexual problem was considered a personal virtue. The following posters were made available to schools by the federal government.

WHAT THE TESTICLES DO FOR A MAN

The Testicles make a secretion that goes into the blood.

The blood takes the secretion to the brain and muscle.

This secretion gives a man
MUSCLE TONE
BRAIN POWER
NERVE STRENGTH

THE CONTROL of the AIRPLANE

To be an aviator a man must be in the very best condition, and pass a strict physical examination. To control an airplane a man must have self-control.

"Sexual intercourse is not necessary to preserve health and manly vigor. The natural sexual impulse can be kept under control by avoiding associations, conversations and thoughts of a lewd character."

Manual of Military Training (Moss)
Section 1466, page 522

The Secret of Strength

The secretion from the testicles helps greatly in giving one

Courage	Strength
Energy	Endurance
Will Power	

Courage   Strength
Energy   Endurance
WILL POWER

Sometimes a man does not fully possess these qualities because he is ignorant and abuses his sex organs
(Self abuse or masturbation)

If a man has this habit and stops at once and absolutely, nature will come to his rescue and assist him in regaining these qualities lems, all of which are characterized by a lack of communication with one's partner and special difficulty in discussing sex. Lastly, Lamont suggests that approximately 30 percent of the dyspareunia cases are rooted in physical causes.

These different bases for discomfort in intercourse have varying chances of treatment. While Lamont (1980) reports a cure rate of between 89 percent and 95 percent, women with intrapersonal and interpersonal problems are the least likely to accept treatment.

For males it is generally agreed that the problem of dyspareunia is most usually due to irritations or infections of the penis or foreskin or to the foreskin perhaps being too tight to retract upon erection (this is really a problem of painful erection and not coitus).

Inhibited Sexual Desire

Perhaps more than any other sexual difficulty, the problem of sexual desire is subject to social definition. Not everyone can have this "problem." Nuns and priests cannot have it, those past a certain age cannot have it, those under a certain age cannot have it, and whether or not you can have it has certainly varied over time. While we have heard some shrouded discussion of the "new celibacy," not wanting to engage in sex is not a popular choice in American society today.

Whether or not a person has a lack of sexual desire is a matter of that person's definition of how much he or she thinks is right to have and how much the partner thinks the person should have. As we have noted in our discussions of topics ranging from the sexual behavior of heterosexual college students, to the patterns of intercourse frequency in marriage, to the descriptions of the Mangia and Inis Beag, to the differences between male and female homosexuals, to the sexual desires of cancer patients and their spouses, there are enormous differences among individuals in their interest in sexual activity, the frequency with which they prefer to engage in sexual activity, and what they see as sexual activity. Any effort to define the point at which the de-

gree of sexual desire is or is not a problem without considering such factors as sexual expectations and individual preferences is totally futile.

Sexual aversion There are, however, many cases in which the persons in a relationship see a problem in the amount of desire one or both of them has for sexual activity. Given the average American's expectations of how much sexual interest a person should show, it is safe to say that most people regard *sexual aversion* as having a good chance of being problematic. Sexual aversion is defined here as an unwillingness to be involved in any sexual activity and an avoidance of any touching or communicating that might lead to sexual activity (Murphy et al., 1979).

Interestingly, sexual aversion tends to appear in relationships where the people care deeply for each other, want to please each other, and need the approval of each other. These factors, of course, make the problem worse, and it is usually these couples who seek help; relationships not having this pattern may simply dissolve without seeking professional help (Murphy and Sullivan, 1981).

Murphy et al. (1979) have found that women who experience sexual aversion tend to have acute anxiety in many areas of their lives, including the sexual. They suffer from self-concept and self-acceptance problems and tend to see their body and genitals as unattractive. They also experience considerable pressure from their partner for sexual activity (this is at least partly a perception problem), and report that 50 percent of the time they engage in intercourse to avoid a marital hassle (Murphy et al., 1979).

THE FUTURE OF SEXUAL THERAPY AND PROBLEM SOLVING

You started studying this text by reading a discussion of the history of sexuality. In a very real sense, this final chapter is our most recent history. As we have emerged from the changes in sexual attitudes and behaviors which took place through the 1970s and early 1980s, increased attention has been given to solving sexual problems. As all the excitement of the "sexual revolution" of the 1970s dies down to a routine glow in which we find it hard to remember what it "used to be like," greater attention will be given to dealing with and solving sexual problems. The future of these efforts rests on a number of factors having to do with what we now call sex therapy.

Accurate Diagnosis and Understanding

Any program of sexual therapy must be able to make accurate diagnosis and classification of sexual problems. This ability must be based on an understanding of the nature of sexual problems. It is simply not possible to hope for any degree of success in sexual therapy unless one first understands the basis of a particular behavior which is defined by the person as a problem. *It is patently clear that we do not have this kind of knowledge.* Within the field of human sexuality, there is a clear distinction (as there is in almost any field) between pure research and application. It is the nature of the beast that the professional with applied interest pays small heed to what the pure researcher is doing and the researcher spends little effort in examining applied problems (there are some notable individual exceptions to this rule). As the situation now stands, we currently do not have sufficient understanding of human sexuality to be able to rationally devise a sexual therapy program that is scientifically grounded.

A good example of this problem is the recent research of Cole et al. (1979). In sexual therapy for a couple, it is common practice to label one partner as dysfunctional in some way and the other partner as not dysfunctional. One person is thus symptomatic and the other asymptomatic. Cole et al. (1979) compared symptomatic and asymptomatic males and symptomatic and asymptomatic females who had been categorized as such under a commonly used set of sexual therapy criteria. Among the males, they found no difference between those labeled symptomatic and those labeled asymptomatic on the following points:

- Mother's attitude that sex is beautiful
- Mother's attitude that sex is not discussed
- Father's attitude that sex is beautiful
- Father's attitude that sex is not discussed
- Age at first dating
- Guilt about petting
- A wide range of adolescent sexual behaviors from petting to intercourse
- Perception of partner's sex knowledge
- Current masturbation
- Attitude that sex problems affected their marriage
- Ability to view self in the nude
- Ability to view partner in the nude
- Initiation of sexual activity with partner
- Any desired changes in sexual behavior

When symptomatic and asymptomatic women were compared with one another, the almost identical pattern of no differences emerged. The important point here is that these are the factors which are typically seen by sex therapists as the primary causes of the sexual dysfunction of couples. This research strongly suggests that they are not.

Treatment and Knowledge

One of the characteristics of nonmedical efforts to help people has been that the treatment methods have always been used before there was an adequate understanding of the behavior being treated. This is no more true of sexual therapy efforts than other social programs. We have seen this tendency in desegregation, civil rights, the woman's movement, welfare programs, and so forth. If one reviews all the efforts in the field of sex therapy, one sees many programs established on the basis of some assumptions about human sexuality, but very few programs that are based on solid scientific knowledge about human sexual functioning. There are good reasons for this. One reason, of course, is that sex therapists are seldom social scientists and thus have generally not been trained to think in terms of "What do we know scientifically?" A second reason is that most therapists probably feel an urgent need to help people with their sexual problems and are personally dedicated to doing that. With such a humanistic orientation, the last thing one wants to think about or hear is the mumbling of some social scientist about "a lack of data on the subject."

This is not to say that some methods of sex therapy are not vitally in tune with what we know about human sexuality. For example, many programs treating orgasmic dysfunctions of women use a masturbation-teaching process. This work is very much in agreement with what we know about female arousal and orgasm as a learned response, and it is no great surprise that these programs appear to be quite effective in teaching women to experience orgasm (LoPiccolo and Lobitz, 1972; Heiman et al., 1977; McMullen and Rosen, 1979). The same is true for the treatment of male premature ejaculation (Zeiss, 1978; Zeiss et al., 1978; Kinder and Blakeney, 1977). However, even these programs apparently happened upon successful treatment by accident or good guesses rather than by scientific knowledge produced by good research. We find that masturbation therapy programs were introduced *before* the role of masturbation in the learning of orgasm was clearly understood through research. On the other side of the coin, major sexual therapy programs exist today where the assumptions underlying the treatment actually contradict what is scientifically known about human sexual behavior.

It is becoming increasingly clear to the field of sex therapy that many sexual problems cannot, as Kaplan (1974) has argued for years, be treated apart from the whole person. While sex therapists have long recognized that most sexual problems are psychological rather than physiological in origin, there has been little attempt to define which sexual problems involve how much of the person's psychological existence. Even more important, there must be, and is, more attention given to the

fact that sexual interaction between two people involves just that: interaction between two people. In Chapter 6, we noted that sexual satisfaction is not a matter of genitals and what they do, but is a function of the nature of the overall relationship between two people. Increasingly, the field of sex therapy is coming to note that many sexual problems are not problems of the genitals at all. Rather, the problems that appear in the genitals are based in problems of the interaction taking place between two people and the psychological bases of these problems. For example, Cole et al., (1979) found that one of the major factors which distinguishes symptomatic from asymptomatic individuals is the nature of their marital relationship. Sewell and Abramowitz (1979) have found that personal flexibility and the ability to change are major factors in who will and who will not even stay in a program of sexual therapy. Zilbergeld and Ellison (1979) point out that many single men and women simply lack the essential social skills for developing and maintaining a relationship or sexual interaction within that relationship. Clement and Pfafflin (1980) recently found that sexually dysfunctional patients *and their partners* lack self-confidence and self-assurance, see themselves as unattractive, are easily irritated and depressed, and describe themselves as obstinate and uncooperative. Additionally, it was found that females with sexual problems or females whose male partners had sexual problems tended to be shy, inhibited, turned into themselves, distrustful of others, and desirous of hiding their feelings.

Measurement and Evaluation

Most sex therapists followed the lead of Masters and Johnson in evaluating the success of treatment. It is now abundantly clear that more precise evaluation methods are needed. It is absolutely impossible to evaluate the effectiveness of a treatment program unless one has scientifically solid measures of pre- and posttreatment sexual behavior and response. It is perhaps here, more than anywhere else, that the unfortunate division between pure research and applied areas in human sexuality becomes clear. In general, sex therapists are not trained scientists and thus do not know how to devise and implement the precise scientific measures needed to evaluate therapy. Given the model supplied by Masters and Johnson, adequate evaluation was thought to be properly conducted without all the bother of precise scientific measures.

We are now observing, however, attempts by a number of therapists to construct precise definitions and measures of sexual function and dysfunction (Derogatis and Melisaratos, 1979; Derogatis and Meyer, 1979; LoPiccolo and Steger, 1974).

In short, sexual problems are not located in the genitals alone. Rather, they are rooted in the individual's own psychology and in the interaction which takes place between two individuals. While there has been great enthusiasm for quick and easy treatment of sexual problems, again, largely following from the work of Masters and Johnson, it is apparent that human sexuality is more complicated than, as one prominent sex therapist once said, "taking candy from a baby." As we have seen, human sexuality is a complex phenomenon. To think that sexual problems are more easily solved than any other human problem is to be naive about both humans and sex.

STUDY GUIDE

TERMS TO KNOW

Breast self-examination	Prostate cancer
Mammography	Coital coronary
Ultrasound	Diabetes
Radical mastectomy	Ileostomy
Breast patterns	Sexual therapy
Uterine cancer	Dyspareunia
Ovarian cancer	Cervical cancer
Hysterectomy	Stoma
	Vaginismus

SELF-TEST

Part I: True-False Statements

1. The risk of female breast cancer is greater the later one has menopause and the earlier one has menses.
2. Bruises on the breasts, bumps to the breasts, and fondling of the breasts are associated with an increased risk of breast cancer for females.
3. A majority of American women do a BSE each month.
4. Males do not get breast cancer.
5. Cervical cancer is associated with poor sexual hygiene.

6. While not all the studies agree, the majority of research indicates that hysterectomy and oophorectomy have little or no adverse effect on female sexuality.
7. One of the dangers with sexual activity after a heart attack is that the heart rate becomes much higher during sexual activity than it is during other daily activities.
8. Male diabetics almost always experience a loss of ability to have an erection after having the disease for approximately one year.
9. There is an increasing amount of evidence that the most common cause of impotence in males is organic.
10. Most dyspareunia is due to some organic or physiological problem.

Part II: Multiple-Choice Questions
Select the best of the three alternatives.

1. The safest and most effective means of female breast cancer detection is *(a)* breast self-examination; *(b)* mammography; *(c)* ultrasound.
2. The most recent research indicates that *(a)* in all cases, the best treatment for female breast cancer is radiation therapy; *(b)* in all cases, the only truly effective treatment for female breast cancer is radical mastectomy so that all the affected tissue has surely been removed; *(c)* in some female breast cancer cases, quadrantectomy and dissection of the axillary lymph nodes with radiation treatment is as effective as radical mastectomy.
3. The most common form of uterine cancer is *(a)* ovarian; *(b)* endometrial; *(c)* cervical.
4. After a female has become sexually active by starting to engage in intercourse, she should *(a)* have a PAP test annually; *(b)* have a PAP test annually for two years in a row, and if these are negative, every three years until age 35; *(c)* have a PAP test every three years until age 35.
5. In gynecological surgery, it is found that *(a)* most women experience less sexual response and satisfaction following the surgery because of the removal of reproductive organs that govern sexual response; *(b)* for some persons, the patterns of sexual interaction change from physical-sexual activities (such as intercourse) to interpersonal intimacy and communication; *(c)* orgasm response almost always declines when the surgery involves removal of the ovaries.
6. The field of sexual therapy is characterized by *(a)* high success rates in curing sexual problems; *(b)* difficulty in providing precise definitions of sexual problems and inadequate measures of success in treatment; *(c)* clear definitions of two types of symptoms that make up a sexual problem but a lack of people working as sex therapists.
7. It is clear that the field of sexual therapy has *(a)* little scientifically established knowledge about the exact causes of behavior that are called sexual dysfunctions; *(b)* a solid understanding of the factors which cause psychologically based sexual problems but not adequate knowledge about the factors that cause physiologically based sexual problems; *(c)* sufficient understanding of the causes of sexual problems to be able to conduct successful treatment in most cases.

TOPICS FOR DISCUSSION

In this chapter we have relied upon the knowledge you have gained from the previous sixteen chapters of the text. Thus, for many of the discussions about the effects of chronic illness on sexuality, you probably understood much more about why these patterns exist than was actually explained in that particular section. Review the effects of chronic illness on sexuality and discuss how sexual learning in American society (Chapter 3) is reflected in these effects.

In our discussion of sex therapy, a major point was made that the definitions of sexual problems are direct reflections of the dominant sexual script in American society in that behaviors which do not fit the script well are defined as problems. Other than the commonly discussed sexual problems we have listed in this chapter, devise your own list of what you think are sexual problems from your own point of view. As a group, discuss the lists you have come up with, why you listed something as a sexual problem, and how the list of problems differs for males and females.

SUGGESTED READINGS

Kolodny, R. C., W. H. Masters and **V. E. Johnson,** *Textbook of Sexual Medicine.* Boston: Little, Brown, 1979.
This is a comprehensive introductory coverage of many of the issues discussed in this chapter. The first author is one of the leading researchers in the field of sexual medicine and sexual therapy, and the perspective is somewhat different from that taken in this chapter.

LoPiccolo, J., and **L. LoPiccolo** (Eds.), *Handbook of Sex Therapy.* New York: Plenum Press, 1978.
Although this book is now getting somewhat dated, it is a standard reference volume reviewing the many approaches and aspects of sexual therapy.

Masters, W. H. and **W. H. Johnson,** *Human Sexual Inadequacy.* Boston: Little, Brown, 1970.
Although this book is now considerably dated and suffers many of the problems we have discussed regarding the field of sexual therapy, it is the book that was responsible for the growth of the sexual therapy field, written by the people largely responsible for its development.

KEY TO SELF-TESTS

Part I: True-False Statements

1. T (This is thought to be due to the higher levels of body-produced estrogen to which the individual is exposed.)
2. F (This is a myth that research reveals is believed by many women.)
3. F (Even among the small number who say they do a BSE each month, a substantial proportion cannot describe how to do the examination.)
4. F (Breast cancer is much more rare among males, but it does occur.)
5. T (You will find that many people say that this is a myth, but research reveals otherwise.)
6. T (In fact, in many cases the effect is positive in terms of how the woman feels and the changes which take place in sexual interaction patterns.)
7. F (The data reported by Masters and Johnson regarding heart rate during sexual activity led people to believe this, but more recent and accurate research has shown that the heart rate during sexual activity is actually lower than that while doing moderate work.)
8. F (This has long been thought to be true, but research reveals that many males do not experience this loss of ability and many diabetic males have erections during sleep.)

9. F (The other way around. There is increasing evidence that learning and physiological factors are the most important.)
10. F (The research reveals that the largest number of cases are due to intra- or interpersonal problems.)

Part II: Multiple-Choice Questions

1. *c* (Ultrasound is more accurate and safer than mammography.)
2. *c* (Recent research reveals that far too many radical mastectomies are performed.)
3. *c* (Which is the least common?)
4. *c* (Cervical is the least common form of cancer and it develops slowly. Thus, the recommendations have been lowered for the frequency of PAP tests.)
5. *b*
6. *b*
7. *a*

Bibliography

Abel, G. G. "Women's Vaginal Responses during REM Sleep," *Journal of Sex and Marital Therapy,* 1979, **5:**895–903.

Abelson, H., R. Cohen, E. Keaton, and C. Suder. "National Survey of Public Attitudes toward and Experience with Erotic Materials," in *Technical Report of the Commission on Obscenity and Pornography,* vol. 6. Washington: U.S. Government Printing Office, 1971.

Abplanalp, J. M., A. F. Donnelly, and R. M. Rose. "Psychoendocrinology of the Menstrual Cycle, II: The Relationship between Enjoyment of Activities, Moods, and Reproductive Hormones," *Psychosomatic Medicine,* 1979, **8:**605–615.

Abramov, L. A. "Sexual Life and Sexual Frigidity among Women Developing Myocardial Infarction," *Psychosomatic Medicine,* 1976, **38:**418–425.

Abramson, P. R. "Ethical Requirements for Research on Human Sexual Behavior: From the Perspective of Participating Subjects," *Journal of Social Issues,* 1977, **33:**184–193.

———, and I. W. Handschumacher. "The Mosher Sex Guilt Scale and the College Population: A Methodological Note," *Journal of Personality Assessment,* 1978, **42:**635.

———, P. Michalak, and C. Alling. "Perceptions of Parental Sex Guilt and the Sexual Behavior and Arousal of College Students," *Perceptual and Motor Skills,* 1977, **45:**337–338.

———, and D. L. Mosher. "Development of a Measure of Negative Attitudes toward Masturbation," *Journal of Consulting and Clinical Psychology,* 1975, **43:**485–490.

———, ———, L. M. Abramson, and B. Woychowski. "Personality Correlates of the Mosher Guilt Scales," *Journal of Personality Assessment,* 1977, **41:**375–382.

———, L. B. Perry, T. T. Seeley, D. M. Seeley, and A. B. Rothblatt. "Thermographic Measurement of Sexual Arousal: A Discriminant Validity Analysis," *Archives of Sexual Behavior,* 1981, **10:**171–176.

Adam, E., G. D. Dreesman, R. H. Kaufman, and J. L. Melnick. "Asymptomatic Virus Shedding after Herpes Genitalis," *American Journal of Obstetrics and Gynecology,* 1980, **137:**827–830.

————, R. H. Kaufman, J. L. Melnick, A. H. Levy, and W. E. Rawls. "Seroepidemiologic Studies of Herpes Virus Type 2 and Carcinoma of the Cervix, III, Houston, Texas," *American Journal of Epidemiology,* 1972, **96:**427–442.

Adamson, J. D., J. A. Burdick, C. L. Corman, and F. S. Chebib. "Physiological Responses to Sexual and Unpleasant Film Stimuli," *Journal of Psychosomatic Research,* 1972, **16:**153–162.

Addiego, F., E. G. Belzer, J. Comolli, W. Moger, J. D. Perry, and B. Whipple. "Female Ejaculation: A Case Study," *Journal of Sex Research,* 1981, **17:**13–21.

Albrecht, S. L. "Correlates of Happiness among the Remarried," *Journal of Marriage and the Family,* 1979, **41:**857–867.

Albro, J. C., and C. Tully. "A Study of Lesbian Lifestyles in Homosexual Micro-Culture and Heterosexual Macro-Culture," *Journal of Homosexuality,* 1979, **4:**331–344.

Allen, C. *A Textbook of Psychosexual Disorders,* 2d ed. London: Oxford University Press, 1969.

Allen, D. M. "Young Male Prostitutes: A Psychosocial Study," *Archives of Sexual Behavior,* 1980, **9:**399–426.

Allgeier, A. R., E. R. Allgeier, and T. Rywick. "Orientations toward Abortion: Guilt or Knowledge," *Adolescence,* 1981, **16:**273–280.

Allgeier, E. R. "The Influence of Androgynous Identification on Heterosexual Relations," *Sex Roles,* 1981, **7:**321–330.

————, A. R. Allgeier, and T. Rywick. "Abortion: Reward for Conscientious Contraceptive use?" *Journal of Sex Research,* 1979, **15:**64–75.

————, and A. F. Fogel. "Coital Position and Sex Roles: Response to Cross-Sex Behavior in Bed," *Journal of Consulting and Clinical Psychology,* 1979, **46:**588–589.

Allsup-Jackson, G. "Sexual Dysfunction of Stroke Patients," *Sexuality and Disability,* 1981, **4:**161–168.

Altman, J. K. "First Apparent Success Reported in Treatment of a Form of VD," *New York Times,* June 27, 1979, 136.

Altschuler, M. "Cayapa Personality and Sexual Motivation," in D. S. Marshall and R. C. Suggs (eds.), *Human Sexual Behavior.* Englewood Cliffs, N.J.: Prentice-Hall, Inc., 1972.

Alzate, H. "Sex Behavior of Columbian Female University Students," *Archives of Sexual Behavior,* 1978, **7:**43–54.

American Academy of Pediatrics, Committee on Fetus and Newborn, Committee on Infectious Diseases. "Perinatal Herpes Simplex Virus infections," *Pediatrics,* 1980, **66:**147–149.

Amias, A. G. "Sexual Life after Gynecological Operations, I," *British Medical Journal,* June 14, 1975, 608–609.

Amir, M. *Patterns of Forcible Rape.* Chicago: The University of Chicago Press, 1971.

Aquirre, B. E. "Repeat Induced Abortion: Single, Married and Divorced Women," *Journal of Biosocial Science,* 1980, **12:**275–286.

Arafat, I., and D. E. Allen. "Venereal Disease: College Students' Knowledge and Attitudes," *Journal of Sex Research,* 1977, **13:**223–230.

————, and W. L. Cotton. "Masturbation Practices of Males and Females," *Journal of Sex Research,* 1974, **10:**293–307.

———, and B. Yorburg. "On Living Together without Marriage," *Journal of Sex Research,* 1973a, **9:**97–106.

———, and ———. "Drug Use and the Sexual Behavior of College Women," *Journal of Sex Research,* 1973b, **9:**21–29.

Asayama, S. "Sexual Behavior in Japanese Students: Comparisons for 1974, 1960, and 1952," *Archives of Sexual Behavior,* 1976, **5:**371–390.

Athanasiou, R., P. Shaver, and C. Tavris. "Sex," *Psychology Today,* January 1970, 37–52.

Atkeson, B. M., K. S. Calhoun, P. A. Resick, and E. M. Ellis. "Victims of Rape: Repeated Assessment of Depressive Symptoms," *Journal of Consulting and Clinical Psychology,* 1982, **50:**96–102.

Avery, A. W., and C. A. Ridley. "Sexual Intimacy among College Students: A Look at Interpersonal Relationship," *College Student Journal,* 1975, **9:**199–205.

Baker, L. H., W. K. Mebust, T. D. Y. Chin, D. Chapman, D. Hinthorn, and D. Towle. "The Relationship of Herpes Virus to Carcinoma of the Prostate," *The Journal of Urology,* 1981, **125:**370–347.

Baker, S. W., and A. A. Ehrhardt. "Prenatal Androgen, Intelligence, and Cognitive Sex Differences," in R. C. Friedman, R. M. Richart, and R. L. Vande Wiele (eds.), *Sex Differences in Behavior.* New York: John Wiley & Sons, 1974.

Barbaree, H. E., W. L. Marshall, and R. D. Lanthier. "Deviant Sexual Arousal in Rapists," *Behavior Research and Therapy,* 1979, **17:**215–222.

Barber, H. R. K. "Uterine Cancer (Prevention)," *Cancer,* 1981, **47:**1126–1132.

Barker-Benfield, B. "Sexual Surgery in Late Nineteenth-Century America," *International Journal of Health Services,* 1975, **5:**279–298.

Barker-Benfield, G. L. "The Spermatic Economy: A Nineteenth-Century View of Sexuality," in M. Gordon (ed.), *The American Family in Social-Historical Perspective,* 2d ed. New York: St. Martin's Press, 1978.

Barker, W., and D. Perlman. "Volunteer Bias and Personality Traits in Sexual Standards Research," *Archives of Sexual Behavior,* 1975, **4:**161–171.

Baron, R. A. "The Aggression-Inhibiting Influence of Heightened Sexual Arousal," *Journal of Personality and Social Psychology,* 1974, **30:**318–322.

———. "Heightened Sexual Arousal and Physical Aggression: An Extension to Females," *Journal of Research in Personality,* 1979, **13:**91–102.

———, and P. A. Bell. "Effects of Heightened Sexual Arousal on Physical Aggression," Summary. *Proceedings of the 81st Annual Convention of the American Psychological Association,* 1973, **8:**171–172.

Barrera, M. E., and D. Maurer. "The Perception of Facial Expressions by Three-Month Old," *Child Development,* 1981, **52:**203–206.

Barrett, C. J. "Intimacy in Widowhood," *Psychology of Women,* 1981, **5:**473–487.

Bartell, G. *Group Sex.* New York: Peter H. Wyden, 1971.

Bauman, K. E., and R. R. Wilson, "Sexual Behavior of Unmarried University Students in 1968 and 1972," *Journal of Sex Research,* 1974, **10:**327–333.

Beals, C. "Sex Life in Latin America," in A. Ellis and A. Abarbanel (eds.), *Encyclopedia of Sexual Behavior,* Vol. 2. New York: Hawthorn Books, Inc., 1961.

Beck, L. R., A. R. Ramon, C. E. Flowers, G. Z. Lopez, Jr., D. E. Lewis, and D. R. Cowsar. "Clinical Evaluation of Injectable Biodegradable Contraceptive System," *American Journal of Obstetrics and Gynecology,* 1981, **140:**799–806.

Beck, S. B., C. I. Ward-Hull, and P. M. McLear, "Variables Related to Women's Somatic Preferences of the Male and Female body." *Journal of Personality and Social Psychology,* 1976, **34:**1200–1210.

Beer, A. E., J. F. Quebbeman, J. W. T. Ayers, and R. F. Haines. "Major Histocompatibility Complex Antigens, Maternal and Paternal Immune Responses, and Chronic Habitual Abortion in Humans," *American Journal of Obstetrics and Gynecology,* 1981, **141:**987–999.

Bell, A. P., and M. S. Weinberg. *Homosexualities: A Study of Diversity among Men and Women.* New York: Simon & Schuster, 1978.

Bell, R. R. "Religious Involvement and Marital Sex in Australia and the United States," *Journal of Comparative Family Studies,* 1974, **5:**109–116.

————, and J. B. Chaskes. "Premarital Sexual Experience among Coeds, 1958 and 1968," *Journal of Marriage and the Family,* 1970, **32:**81–84.

————, S. Turner, and L. Rosen. "A Multivariate Analysis of Female Extramarital Coitus," *Journal of Marriage and the Family,* 1975, **37:**375–384.

Belzer, E. G., Jr. "Orgasmic Expulsion of Women: A Review and Heuristic Inquiry," *Journal of Sex Research,* 1981, **17:**1–12.

Bender, L., and A. Blau. "The Reaction of Children to Sexual Relations with Adults," *American Journal of Orthopsychiatry,* 1937, **7:**500–518.

Benditt, J. M. "Current Contraceptive Research," *Family Planning Perspectives,* 1980, **12:**149–152, 154–155.

Benjamin, H. "Response to Dedication of Fourth International Conference on Gender Identity," *Archives of Sexual Behavior,* 1978, **7:**247–248.

Benjamin, H. *The Transsexual Phenomenon.* New York: Julian Press, 1966.

Benkert, O., W. Witt, W. Adam, and A. Leitz. "Effects of Testosterone Undecanoate on Sexual Potency and the Hypothalamic Pituitary-Gonadal Axis of Impotent Males," *Archives of Sexual Behavior,* 1979, **8:**471–479.

Bennett, S. M., and W. B. Dickinson, "Student-Parent Rapport and Parent Involvement in Sex, Birth Control, and Venereal Disease Education," *Journal of Sex Research,* 1980, **16:**114–130.

Bentler, P. M., and M. D. Newcomb, "Longitudinal Study of Marital Success and Failure," *Journal of Consulting and Clinical Psychology,* 1978, **46:**1053–1070.

————, and W. H. Peeler, "Models of Female Orgasm," *Archives of Sexual Behavior,* 1979, **8:**405–423.

Berger, R. M. "Psychological Adaptation of the Older Homosexual Male," *Journal of Homosexuality,* 1980, **5:**161–175.

Bicher, M., D. Cherniak, A. Feingold, and S. Gardner (eds.). *V. D. Handbook,* 3d ed. Montreal: Montreal Health Press, 1977.

Bird, C. E., B. Houghton, W. Westenbrink, M. Tenniswood, E. E. Sterns, and A. F. Clark. "Estradiol Receptor Levels in Human Breast Carcinomas," *Canadian Medical Association Journal,* 1981, **124:**1010–1012.

Blackburn, O. M., and S. L. Ricards, "The Prostitutes and Gamblers of Virginia City, Nevada: 1870," *Pacific Historical Review,* 1979, **58:**239–258.

Blair, J. J. "The Public Health of Contraceptives: Open Forum," *Medical Journal and Record.* cxxxvii, 1933, 7–9.

Blake, J. "The Pill and the Rising Costs of Fertility Control," *Social Biology,* 1977, **24:**267.

Blau, S. "Venereal Diseases," in A. Ellis and A. Abarbanel (eds.), *Encyclopedia of Sexual Behavior,* Vol. 2. New York: Hawthorn Books, Inc., 1961.

Blum, R. H. *Students and Drugs.* San Francisco: Jossey-Bass, 1969.

Blumenstein, B. A., M. B. Douglas, and W. D. Hall, "Blood Pressure Changes and Oral Contraceptive Use: A Study of 2,676 Black Women in the Southeastern United States," *American Journal of Epidemiology,* 1980, **112:**5339–5552.

Boova, R., A. Carabasi, D. Scotti, C. Kuroda, and F. E. Rosato. "Transvenous Adrenalectomy for Advanced Carcinoma of the Breast," *Surgery, Gynecology and Obstetrics,* 1981, **152:**627–632.

Borders, J. A., and P. Cutright. "Community Determinants of U.S. Legal Abortion Rates," *Family Planning Perspectives,* 1979, **11:**227–233.

Boston Women's Health Book Collective. *Our Bodies, Ourselves.* New York: Simon & Schuster, 1976.

Bower, D. W., and V. A. Christopherson. "University Students' Cohabitation: A Regional Comparison of Selected Attitudes and Behavior," *Journal of Marriage and the Family,* 1977, **39:**447–453.

Bracken, M. B., D. H. Freeman, Jr., and K. Hellenbrand. "Incidence of Acute Hospitalized Spinal Cord Injury in the United States, 1970–1977," *American Journal of Epidemiology,* 1981, **113:**615–622.

Bray, C. P., R. S. DeFrank, and T. L. Wolfe. "Sexual Functioning in Stroke Survivors," *Archives of Physical Medicine and Rehabilitation,* 1981, **62:**286–288.

Breasted, M. *Oh! Sex Education!* New York: Praeger, 1970.

Bregman, S. *Sexuality and the Spinal Cord Injured Woman.* Minneapolis: Sister Kenney Institute, 1975.

Brenton, M. *Sex and Your Heart.* New York: Coward-McCann, 1968.

Briddell, D. W., D. C. Rimm, G. E. Caddy, G. Krawitz, D. Sholis, and R. J. Wunderlin. "Effects of Alcohol and Cognitive Set on Sexual Arousal to Deviant Stimuli," *Journal of Abnormal Psychology,* 1978, **87:**418–430.

Brim, O., and S. Wheeler, *Socialization after Childhood.* New York: John Wiley & Sons, 1966.

Brinton, L. A., M. P. Vessey, R. Flavel, and D. Yeates. "Risk Factors for Benign Breast Disease," *American Journal of Epidemiology,* 1981, **113:**203–214.

Brissett, D., and L. S. Lewis. "The Big Toe, Armpits, and Natural Perfume: Notes on the Production of Sexual Ecstacy," *Society,* 1979, **16:**63–73.

British Medical Journal. "Breast Cancer: A Case for Conservatism," editorial. 1981, **282:**759.

Broderick, C. B. *Marriage and the Family.* Englewood Cliffs, N.J.: Prentice-Hall, Inc., 1979.

Broude, G. J., and S. J. Green. "Cross Cultural Codes on Twenty Sexual Attitudes and Practices," *Ethology,* 1976, **15:**409–429.

Brouillette, J. N., E. Pryor, and T. A. Fox. "Evaluation of Sexual Dysfunction Following Rectal Resection and Intestinal Stoma," *Diseases of the Rectum and Colon,* 1981, **24:**96–102.

Brown, C., J. Anderson, L. Burggraf, and N. Thompson. "Community Standards, Conservatism, and Judgments of Pornography." *Journal of Sex Research,* 1978, **14:**81–95 (a).

Brown, J. J., and D. H. Hart. "Correlates of Females' Sexual Fantasies," *Perceptual and Motor Skills,* 1977, **45:**819–825.

Brown, M. "Viewing Time of Pornography," *Journal of Psychology,* 1979, **102:**83–95.

———, D. M. Amoroso, and E. E. Ware. "Behavioral Effects of Viewing Pornography," *Journal of Social Psychology,* 1976, **98:**235–245.

Brown, S. T., and P. J. Wiesner. "Problems and Approaches to the Control and Surveillance of Sexually Transmitted Agents Associated with Pelvic Inflammatory Disease in the United States," *American Journal of Obstetrics and Gynecology,* 1980, **138:**1096–1100.

Brown, W. A., P. M. Monti, and D. P. Corriveau, "Serum Testosterone and Sexual Activity and Interest in Men," *Archives of Sexual Behavior,* 1978, **7:**97–103 (b).

Brownmiller, S. *Against Our Will: Men, Women and Rape.* New York: Simon & Schuster, 1975.

Bullough, V. L. "Transsexualism in History," *Archives of Sexual Behavior,* 1975, **4:**561–571.

———. *Sexual Variance in Society and History.* New York: John Wiley & Sons, 1976.

———. *Homosexuality: A History.* New York: New American Library, 1979.

———. "Technology and Female Sexuality and Physiology: Some Implications," *Journal of Sex Research,* 1980, **16:**59–71.

———, and B. Bullough. *Sin, Sickness and Sanity: A History of Sexual Attitudes.* New York: Meridian, 1977.

———, and ———. *Prostitution: An Illustrated Social History.* New York: Crown Publishers, Inc., 1978.

Burgess, A. W., A. N. Groth, and M. P. McCausland. "Child Sex Initiation Rings," *American Journal of Orthopsychiatry,* 1981, **51:**110–119.

———, and L. L. Holmstrom. "Rape Trauma Syndrome," *American Journal of Psychiatry,* 1974, **131:**981–986.

———, and ———. "Recovery from Rape and Prior Life Stress," *Research in Nursing and Health,* 1978, **1:**165–174.

———, and ———. "Rape: Sexual Disruption and Recovery," *American Journal of Orthopsychiatry,* 1979, **49:**648–657.

Burgess, E. W., and P. Wallin. *Engagement and Marriage.* New York: Lippincott, 1953.

Burkman, R. T., and The Woman's Health Study. "Association between Pelvic Inflammatory Disease and the Intrauterine Device: Findings from a Large Cohort Study," *British Medical Journal,* 1981, **282:**855–857.

Burnham, W. R., J. E. Lennard-Jones, and B. N. Brooke. "Sexual Problems among Married Ileostomists: Survey conducted by the Ileostomy Association of Great Britain and Ireland," *Gut,* 1977, **18:**673–677.

Burr, W. A., and K. F. Schulz. "Delayed Abortion in an Area of Easy Accessibility," *Journal of the American Medical Association,* 1980, **244:**44–48.

Burt, M. R. "Cultural Myths and Supports for Rape," *Journal of Personality and Social Psychology,* 1980, **38:**217–230.

———, and R. E. Estep. "Apprehension and Fear: Learning a Sense of Sexual Vulnerability," *Sex Roles,* 1981, **7:**511–522.

Butler, C. A. "New Data about Female Sexual Response," *Journal of Sex and Marital Therapy,* 1976, **2:**40–46.

Byrne, D. "The Imagery of Sex," in J. Money and H. Husaph (eds.), *Handbook of Sexology.* New York: Excepta Medica, 1977.

———, F. Cherry, J. Lamberth, and H. E. Mitchell. "Husband-Wife Similarity in Response to Erotic Stimuli," *Journal of Personality,* 1973, **41:**385–394.

———, and J. Lamberth. "The Effect of Erotic Stimuli on Sex Arousal, Evaluative Responses, and Subsequent Behavior," in *Technical Report of the Commission on Obscenity and Pornography,* Vol. 8. Washington: U.S. Government Printing Office, 1971.

———, J. D. Fisher, J. Lamberth, and H. E. Mitchell. "Evaluations of Erotica: Facts or Feelings?" *Journal of Personality and Social Psychology,* 1974, **29:**111–116.

Calhoun, L., J. Selby, and L. Warring. "Social Perception of the Victim's Causal Role in Rape: An Exploratory Examination of Four Factors," *Human Relations,* 1976, **29:**517–526.

———, ———, A. Cann, and G. T. Keller. "The Effects of Victim's Physical Attractiveness and Sex of Respondents on Social Reactions to Victims of Rape," *The British Journal of Social and Clinical Psychology,* 1978, **17:**191–192.

———, ———, and H. E. King. "The Influence of Pregnancy on Sexuality: A Review of the Current Literature," *Journal of Sex Research,* 1981, **17:**139–151.

Califia, P. "Lesbian Sexuality," *Journal of Homosexuality,* 1979, **4:**255–266.

Calle, R., J. P. Pilleron, P. Schlienger, and J. R. Vilcoq. "Conservative Management of Operable Breast Cancer: Ten Years' Experience at the Foundation Curie," *Cancer,* 1978, **42:**2045–2053.

Cantor, J. R., D. Zillman, and J. Bryant. "Enhancement of Sexual Arousal in Response to Erotic Stimuli through Misattribution of Unrelated Residual Excitation," *Journal of Personality and Social Psychology,* 1975, **32:**69–75.

Caprio, F. "Fetishism," in A. Ellis and A. Abarbanel (eds.), *Encyclopedia of Sexual Behavior,* Vol. I. New York: Hawthorn Books, Inc., 1961.

Carbell, S. C., and R. L. Goodman. "Radiation Therapy: An Alternative to Mastectomy," *The Female Patient,* 1981, **6:**47–50.

Cargan, L. "Singles: An Examination of Two Stereotypes," *Family Relations,* 1981, **30:**377–385.

Carlile, T. "Breast Cancer detection," *Cancer,* 1981, **47:**1164–1169.

Carlson, E. R., and C. E. K. Coleman, "Experimental and Motivational Determinants of an Induced Sexual Fantasy," *Journal of Personality,* 1977, **45:**528–542.

Carns, E. E. "Talking about Sex: Notes on First Coitus and the Double Sexual Standard," *Journal of Marriage and the Family,* 1973, **35:**677–688.

Casey, W. C., and J. J. Kaufman. "Penile Revascularization for Erectile Disability," *International Surgery,* 1980, **65:**175–178.

Cates, W. "The Hyde Amendment in Action," *Journal of the American Medical Association,* 1981, **246:**1109–1112.

Catlin, N., J. F. Keller, and J. W. Croake. Sexual History and Present Behavior of Unmarried Cohabitating College Couples," *College Student Journal,* 1976, **10:**253–259.

CBS Special. *Gay Power, Gay Pride,* with H. Reasoner, April 26, 1980.

Center for Disease Control. "Reported Morbidity and Mortality in the United States, 1978," *Morbidity and Mortality Weekly Report,* No. 27 (54th Annual Supplement), 1979(a).

———. "Recommended Treatment Schedules, Gonorrhea, 1979," *Morbidity and Mortality Weekly Report,* Jan. 19, 1979(b), No. 2.

———. "Kaposi's Sarcoma and Pneumocyctis Pneumonia among Homosexual Men—New York City and California," *Morbidity and Mortality Weekly Report,* 30, July 3, 1981, No. 25.

Cerny, J. A. "Biofeedback and the Voluntary Control of Sexual Arousal in Women," *Behavior Therapy,* 1978, **9:**847–855.

Chapel, T. A. "Physician Recognition of the Signs of Secondary Syphilis, *Journal of the American Medical Association,* 1981, **246:**250–251.

Chapman, J. D. "Sexuality: The Mature or Childbearing Years and the Effect of Gynecologic Surgery." Paper presented at the 45th Annual Convention of the American College of Osteopathic Obstetricians and Gynecologists, Phoenix, Ariz., Feb. 17, 1978.

Chappell, D., and J. James. "Victim Selection and Apprehension from the Rapist's Perspective: A Preliminary Investigation." Paper presented at the 2d International Symposium on Victimology, Boston, 1976.

Check, W. A. "Medical Adrenalectomy May Replace Surgery for Advanced Breast Cancer," *Journal of the American Medical Association,* 1980a, **244:**9–10.

———. "Folate for Oral Contraceptive Users May Reduce Cervical Cancer Risk," *Journal of the American Medical Association,* 1980b, **244:**633–634.

Chou, S., J. G. Gallagher, T. C. Merigan. "Controlled Clinical Trial of Intravenous Acyclovir in Mucocutaneous Herpes Simplex Virus Infections," *Lancet,* June 27, 1981, 1391–1394.

Christensen, H. T., and C. F. Gregg. "Changing Sex Norms in America and Scandinavia," *Journal of Marriage and the Family,* 1970, **32:**616–627.

———, and L. B. Johnson. "Premarital Coitus and the Southern Black: A Comparative View," *Journal of Marriage and the Family,* 1978, **40:**721–731.

Christianson, R. E. "The Relationship between Maternal Smoking and the Incidence of Congenital Anomalies," *American Journal of Epidemiology,* 1980, **112:**684–695.

Clark, A. L., and P. Wallin. "Women's Sexual Responsiveness and the Duration and Quality of Their Marriages," *American Journal of Sociology,* 1965, **71:**187–196.

Clarkson, T. B., and N. J. Alexander. "Does vasectomy increase the Risk of Artherosclerosis?" *Journal of Cardiovascular Medicine,* 1980, **15:**999–1008.

Clayton, P. J., and P. E. Bornstein. "Widows and Widowers," *Medical Aspects of Human Sexuality,* 1976, **10:**27–53.

Clayton, R. R., and H. L. Voss. "Shacking Up: Cohabitation in the 1970's," *Journal of Marriage and the Family,* 1977, **39:**273–283.

Clement, U., and F. Pfafflin. "Changes in Personality Scores among Couples Subsequent to Sex Therapy," *Archives of Sexual Behavior,* 1980, **9:**235–244.

Clifford, R. E. "Subjective Sexual Experience in College Women," *Archives of Sexual Behavior,* 1978, **3:**183–197.

Clinch, T. A. "Margaret Sanger: Rebel in the Midst of Victorian Moralism," in J. R. Barber (ed.), *Human Sexuality: 80–81, Annual Editions.* Guilford, Conn.: Duskin Publishing Corp., 1980.

Cochran, S. D., and L. A. Peplau. "Interplay of Attachment and Autonomy in Love Relationships: A Comparison of Men and Women." Paper presented at the Annual Meeting of the Western Psychological Association, San Diego, Calif., April 1979.

Cochran, W. G., F. Mosteller, and J. W. Tukey. *Statistical Problems of the Kinsey Report on Sexual Behavior in the Human Male.* A report of the American Statistical Association Committee to advise National Research Council, Committee for Research in Problems of Sex. Washington: American Statistical Association, 1954.

Coffman, D. M. "Rape in Black and White: The Effects of Victim and Offender Race on Attributions to Rape Victims and Offenders." Unpublished master's thesis, Western Washington University, Department of Sociology, 1981.

Cole, C. M., P. E. Blakeney, F. A. Chan, A. P. Chesney, and D. L. Cresen. "The Myth of Symptomatic versus Asymptomatic Partners in the Conjoint Treatment of Sexual Dysfunction," *Journal of Sex and Marital Therapy,* 1979, **5:**79–89.

Cole-Beuglet, C., A. B. Kurtz, C. S. Rubin, and B. B. Goldberg. "Ultrasound Mammography," *Radiologic Clinics of North America,* 1980, **18:**133–143.

Collins, J. K. "Self-Recognition of the Body and Its Parts during Late Adolescence," *Journal of Youth and Adolescence,* 1981, **10:**243–254.

Comfort, A. (Ed.). *Sexual Consequences of Disability.* Philadelphia: George F. Stickley Co., 1978.

Conchar, J. "Social Injuries of the Rectum," *American Journal of Surgery,* 1977, **134:**611–612.

Condry, J., and S. Condry. "Sex Differences: A Study of the Eye of the Beholder," *Child Development,* 1976, **47:**812–819.

Conklin, M., K. Klint, A. Morway, J. R. Sawyer, and R. Shepard. "Should Health Teaching Include Self-Examination of the Testes?" *American Journal of Nursing,* 1978, **78:**2073–2074.

Constantine, L. L. "Multilateral Relations Revisited: Group Marriage in an Extended Perspective," in B. I. Murstein (ed.), *Exploring Intimate Lifestyles.* New York: Springer, 1978.

———, and J. M. Constantine. "Sexual Aspects of Group Marriage," in R. W. Libby and R. N. Whitehurst (eds.), *Marriage and Alternatives.* Glenview, Ill.: Scott, Foresman and Co., 1977.

Cook, R. F., and R. H. Fosen. "Pornography and the Sex Offender: Patterns of Exposure and Immediate Arousal Effects of Pornographic Stimuli," in *Technical Reports of the Commission on Obscenity and Pornography,* Vol. 7. Washington: U.S. Government Printing Office, 1971.

Cooper, A. J. "A Clinical Study of 'coital anxiety'," *Journal of Psychosomatic Research,* 1969, **13:**143–147.

Cornkovich, S. A., and P. C. Giordano. "A Comparative Analysis of Male and Female Delinquency," in D. A. Kelly (ed.), *Criminal Behavior: Readings in Criminology.* New York: St. Martin's Press, Inc., 1980.

Cosby, B. "The Regular Way," *Playboy,* December 15, 1968, 115, 288–289.

Cott, N. F. "Passionlessness: An Interpretation of Victorian Sexual Ideology, 1790–1850," *Signs,* 1978, **4:**219–237.

Crepault, C., and M. Couture. "Men's Erotic Fantasies," *Archives of Sexual Behavior,* 1980, **9:**565–581.

Curran, J. P., S. Neff, and S. Lippold. "Correlates of Sexual Experience among University Students," *Journal of Sex Research,* 1973, **9:**124–131.

Curran, J. W. "Economic Consequences of Pelvic Inflammatory Disease in the United States," *American Journal of Obstetrics and Gynecology,* 1980, **138:**848–851.

Current Population Reports, *Marital Status and Living Arrangement,* Series P-20, No. 388, May 1979.

Cvetkovich, G., and B. Grote. "Psychosocial Maturity and Teenage Contraceptive Use: An Investigation of Decision-Making and Communication Skills," *Population and Environment,* 1981, **4:**211–226.

———, ———, A. Bjorseth, and J. Sarkissich. "On the Psychology of Adolescent's Use of Contraceptives," *Journal of Sex Research,* 1975, **11:**256–269.

Daniels, J. L., R. E. Stutzman, and D. G. McLeod. "A Comparison of Testicular Tumors in Black and White Patients," *The Journal of Urology,* 1981, **125:**341–342.

Darrow, W. W., D. Barrett, K. Jay, and A. Young. "The Gay Report on Sexually Transmitted Diseases," *American Journal of Public Health,* 1981, **71:**1004–1011.

D'Augelli, J. F., and H. J. Cross. "Relationship of Sex Guilt and Moral Reasoning to Premarital Sex in College Women and Couples," *Journal of Consulting and Clinical Psychology,* 1975, **43:**40–47.

Davidson, J. M. "Biological Determinants of Sex: Their Scope and Limitation," in H. A. Katchadourian (ed.), *Human Sexuality: A Comparative and Developmental Perspective.* Berkeley: University of California Press, 1979.

Davies, J. M. "Testicular Cancer in England and Wales: Some Epidemiological Aspects," *Lancet,* April 25, 1981, **8226:**928–931.

Davies, R. "Representing the Lesbian Mother," *Family Advocate,* 1979, **1:**21–24.

Davis, G. L., and H. J. Cross. "Sexual Stereotyping of Black Males in Interracial Sex," *Archives of Sexual Behavior,* 1979, **8:**269–279.

Davis, H. P., and Z. Matejcek. "Children Born to Women Denied Abortion: An Update," *Family Planning Perspectives,* 1981, **13:**32 34.

Davis, J. A. *General Social Surveys, 1972-1980: Cumulative Data.* Principal Investigator, James A. Davis; Associate Study Director, Tom W. Smith; Research Assistant, C. Bruce Stephenson. Chicago: National Opinion Research Center, 1980. New Haven, Conn.: Yale University, Roper Public Opinion Research Center.

Davis, K. B. *Factors in the Sex Life of Twenty-two Hundred Women.* New York: Harper & Brothers, 1929.

Davis, N. "The Prostitute: Developing a Deviant Identity," in J. M. Henslin (ed.), *Studies in the Sociology of Sex,* 2d ed. New York: Appleton-Century-Crofts, 1978.

Dawson, D. A., D. J. Meny, and J. C. Ridley. "Fertility Control in the United States before the Contraceptive Revolution," *Family Planning Perspectives,* 1980, 12, 76–78, 80–86.

DeGezelle, H., A. Vanpeperstraete, P. DeFoort, R. Serreyn, and D. Vandekerckhove. "Comparison of Breast Tumors Evaluated by Ultrasound, Mammography and Clinical Investigation," *Archives of Gynecology,* 1981, **230:**219–223.

Deitz, S. R., and L. E. Byrnes. "Attribution of Responsibility for Sexual Assault: The Influence of Observer Empathy and Defendant Occupation and Attractiveness," *Journal of Psychology,* 1981, **108:**17–29.

DeJong, W., and T. M. Anabile. "Rape and Physical Attractiveness: Judgments concerning the Likelihood of Victimization." Paper presented at the Annual Meeting of the American Psychological Association, New York, September 1979.

Delamater, J. D. "Methodological Issues in the Study of Premarital Sexuality," *Sociological Methods and Research,* 1974, **3:**30–61.

———, and P. MacCourquodale. "The effects of Interview Schedule Variations on Reported Sexual Behavior," *Sociological Methods and Research,* 1975, **4:**215–236.

———, and ———. *Premarital Sexuality: Attitudes, Relationships, Behavior.* Madison: University of Wisconsin Press, 1979.

Delaney, J., M. J. Lupton, and E. Toth. *The curse: A Cultural History of Menstruation.* New York: E. P. Dutton & Co., 1976.

Deming, A. "The Sex Editor is a Lady," *Cosmopolitan,* March 1981, 244–247, 260.

Denfield, D. "Dropouts from Swinging: The Marriage Counselor as Informant," in J. R. Smith and L. R. Smith (eds.), *Beyond Monogamy.* Baltimore: John Hopkins University Press, 1974.

Dennerstein, L., C. Wood, and G. D. Burrows. "Sexual Response following Hysterectomy and Oophorectomy," *Obstetrics and Gynecology,* 1977, **49:**92–96.

Denson-Gerber, J. "Sexual and Commercial Exploitation of Children. Legislative Responses and Treatment Challenges." Unpublished report, 1978.

Dermer, M., and T. A. Pyszczynski. "Effects of Erotica upon Men's Loving and Liking Responses for Women They Love," *Journal of Personality and Social Psychology,* 1978, **36:**1302–1309.

Derogatis, L. R., and K. M. King. "The Coital Coronary: A Reassessment of the Concept," *Archives of Sexual Behavior,* 1981, **10:**325–336.

———, and N. Melisaratos. "The DFSI: A Multidimensional Measure of Sexual Functioning," *Journal of Sex and Marital Therapy,* 1979, **5:**244–281.

———, and J. K. Meyer. "A Psychological Profile of the Sexual Dysfunctions," *Archives of Sexual Behavior,* 1979, **8:**201–223.

———, ———, and P. Boland. "A Psychological Profile of the Transsexual, II: The Female," *Journal of Nervous and Mental Disease,* 1981, **169:**157–168.

———, ———, and N. Vazquez. "A Psychological Profile of the Transsexual, I: The Male," *Journal of Nervous and Mental Disease,* 1978, **166:**234–254.

Diamont, L. "Attitude, Personality and Behavior in Volunteers and Nonvolunteers for Sexual Research," Summary. *Proceedings of the 78th Annual Convention of the American Psychological Association,* 1970, **5:**423–424.

Dingfelder, J. R. "Primary Dysmenorrhea Treatment with Prostaglandin Inhibitors: A Review," *American Journal of Obstetrics and Gynecology,* 1981, **140:**874–877.

Dion, K. K., E. Berscheid, and E. Walster. "What is Beautiful Is Good," *Journal of Personality and Social Psychology,* 1972, **24:**285–290.

Dion, L. "Expectations and Aspirations for Marriage among College Students." Unpublished Master's Thesis, Department of Sociology, Western Washington University, 1981.

DiVasto, P. V., D. Pathak, and W. R. Fishburn. "The Interrelationship of Sex Guilt, Sex Behavior and Age in an Adult Sample," *Journal of Sex Research,* 1981, **10:**119–122.

Dixon, G. W. J. J. Schlesselman, H. W. Ory, and R. P. Blye. "Ethinyl Estradiol and Conjugated Estrogens as Postcoital Contraceptives," *Journal of the American Medical Association,* 1980, **244:**1336–1339.

Djerassi, C. *The Politics of Contraception.* New York: W. W. Norton, 1979.

Dlin, B. M., A. Perlman, and E. Ringold. "Psychosexual Response to Ileostomy and Colostomy," *AORN Journal,* 1969, **10:**80–81.

Doane, B. K., and B. G. Quigley. "Psychiatric Aspects of Therapeutic Abortion," *Canadian Medical Association Journal,* 1981, **125:**427–432.

Dodson, B. *Liberating Masturbation.* New York: Bodysex Designs, 1974.

Donnerstein, E., and G. Barrett. "Effects of Erotic Stimuli on Male Aggression toward Females," *Journal of Personality and Social Psychology,* 1978, **36:**180–188.

———, M. Donnerstein, and R. Evans. "Erotic Stimuli and Aggression: Facilitation or Inhibition," *Journal of Personality and Social Psychology,* 1975, **32:**237–244.

———, and J. Hallam. "Facilitating Effects of Erotica on Aggression against Women," *Journal of Personality and Social Psychology,* 1978, **36:**1270–1277.

Dornbusch, F. D., R. L. Webster, and R. C. Kolodny. "Mastectomy and Sexual Behavior: A Pilot Study," *Sexuality and Disability,* 1978, **1:**16–26.

Dornbusch, S. M., J. M. Carlsmith, J. T. Gross, J. A. Martin, A. Rosenberg, and P. Duke. "Sexual Development, Age, and Dating: A Comparison of Biological and Social Influences upon One Set of Behaviors," *Child Development,* 1981, **52:**179–185.

Doty, R. L., M. Ford, G. Preti, and G. R. Huggins. "Changes in the Intensity and Pleasantness of Human Vaginal Odors during the Menstrual Cycle," *Science,* 1975, **190:**1316–1317.

Dowies, M. "The Corporate Crime of the Century," *Mother Jones,* November 1979, 23–25, 37–38, 49.

Dressler, J. "Study of Law Student Attitudes Regarding the Right of Gay People to Be Teachers," *Journal of Homosexuality,* 1979, **4:**313–340.

Dudar, H. "America Discovers Child Pornography," *Ms.,* August 1977, 45–47, 80.

Dutton, D. G., and A. P. Aron, "Some Evidence for Heightened Sexual Attraction under Conditions of High Anxiety," *Journal of Personality and Social Psychology,* 1974, **30:**510–517.

Dytrych, Z., Z. Matejcek, V. Schuller, H. P. David, and H. L. Friedman. "Children Born to Women Denied Abortion," *Family Planning Perspectives,* 1975, **7:**165.

Edwards, A. E., and J. R. Husted. "Penile Sensitivity, Age, and Sexual Behavior," *Journal of Clinical Psychology,* 1976, **3:**7–14.

Edwards, D. D., and J. S. Edwards. "Marriage: Direct and Continuous Measurement," *Bulletin of the Psychonomic Society,* 1977, **10:**187–188.

Edwards, J. N. and A. Booth. The Cessation of Marital Intercourse," *American Journal of Psychiatry,* 1976a, **133:**1333–1336.

———, and ———. "Sexual Behavior In and Out of Marriage: An Assessment of Correlates," *Journal of Marriage and the Family,* 1976b, **38:**73–81.

Edwards, M. S. "Venereal Herpes: A Nursing Overview," *Journal of Obstetric Gynecologic and Neonatal Nursing,* 1978, **7:**7–14.

Egan, R. L. "Mammographic Patterns and Breast Cancer Risk," *Journal of the American Medical Association,* 1980, **244:**287.

———, R. C. Mostellar, C. D. Steven et al., "High Risk Breast Tumor Patients," *Acta Radiological Therapy Physics Biology,* 1977, **16:**337–351.

Ehrenreich, B., M. Dowie, and S. Minkin. "The Charge: Genocide. The Accused: The U.S. Government," *Mother Jones,* November 1979, 26–37.

Ehrhardt, A. A. "Maternalism in Fetal Hormonal and Related Syndromes," in J. Zubin and J. Money (eds.), *Contemporary Sexual Behavior: Critical Issues in the 1970's.* Baltimore: John Hopkins University Press, 1973.

———. "Prenatal Hormonal Exposure and Psychosexual Differentiation," in E. J. Sachar (ed.), *Topics in Psychoendocrinology.* New York: Grune & Stratton, 1975.

———, and S. W. Baker. "Fetal Androgens, Human Central Nervous System Differentiation and Behavior Sex Differences," in R. C. Friedman, R. M. Richart, and R. L. Van de Wiele (eds.), *Sex Differences in Behavior,* New York: John Wiley & Sons, 1974.

———, R. Epstein, and J. Money. "Fetal Androgens and Female Gender Identity on the Early-Treated Adrenogenital Syndrome," *John Hopkins Medical Journal,* 1968a, **122:**160–167.

———, K. Evers, and J. Money. "Influence of Androgen and Some Aspects of Sexually Dimorphic Behavior in Women with the Late Treated Adrenogenital Syndrome," *John Hopkins Medical Journal,* 1968b, **123:**115–122.

Ehrmann, W. W. "Student Cooperation in a Study of Dating Behavior," *Marriage and Family Living,* 1952, **14:**322–326.

———. "Male and Female Reports on Premarital Coitus," *Social Problems,* 1954, **1:**155–159. Reprinted as "Social Class and Premarital Coitus among Male and Female College Students," in J. Himelhoch and S. S. Fava (eds.), *Sexual Behavior in American Society,* New York: W. W. Norton, 1955.

Elias, J. E., and V. D. Elias. "Sexual World of the Adolescent," *Counseling Psychologist,* 1975, **5:**92–97.

———, and P. Gebhard. "Sexuality and Sexual Learning in Childhood," *Phi Delta Kappan,* 1969, **50:**401–405.

Ellenberg, M. "Sexual Aspects of the Female Diabetic," *Mount Sinai Journal of Medicine,* 1977, **44:**495–500.

Ellis, A. "Review of Disorders of Sexual Desire by E. S. Kaplan," *Archives of Sexual Behavior,* 1981, **10:**395–397.

Ellis, E. M., B. M. Atkeson, and K. S. Calhoun. "An Assessment of Long-Term Reaction to Rape," *Journal of Abnormal Psychology,* 1981, **90:**263–266.

Ellison, C. R. *Sexuality Today,* 1980, Sept. 15, 1980, 3.

Elman, D. T., T. J. Killebrew, and C. Oros. "How Sexual Orientation and Physical

Attractiveness Affect Impressions of Males," *Personality and Social Psychology Bulletin,* 1978, **4:**352–362.

Engle, R. *Brothels of Nevada.* Los Angeles: Halloway House, 1976.

Erhman, W. W. "Premarital Dating Behavior and Fertility," *Social Biology,* 1978, **25:**94–101.

Erikson Paige, K. "Sexual Pollution: Reproductive Taboos in American Society," *Journal of Social Issues,* 1977, **33:**144–165.

Eschenbach, D. A., and K. K. Holmes. "Acute Pelvic Inflammatory Disease: Current Concepts of Pathogenesis, Etiology, and Management," *Clinical Obstetrics and Gynecology,* 1975, **18:**35–56.

Evans, D., and D. Skeen. "The Dynamics of Sexuality among Mentally Retarded Persons." Paper presented at the 52d Annual Meeting of the Pacific Sociological Association, Portland, Ore., March 18–20, 1981.

Evans, I. M., and L. A. Distiller. "Effects of Luteinizing Hormone-Releasing Hormone on Sexual Arousal in Normal Men," *Archives of Sexual Behavior,* 1979, **8:**385–395.

Evans, J. R., G. Selstad, and W. H. Welcher. "Teenagers' Fertility Control Behavior and Attitudes before and after Abortion, Childbearing, or Negative Pregnancy Test," *Family Planning Perspectives,* 1976, **8:**192–200.

Everett, G. M. "Amyl Nitrate (poppers) as an Aphrodisiac," in M. Sandler and G. L. Gessa (eds.), *Sexual Behavior: Pharmacology and Biochemistry.* New York: Raven, 1975.

Exner, J. E., Jr., J. Wylie, A. Leura, and T. Parrill. "Some Psychological Characteristics of Prostitutes," *Journal of Personality Assessment,* 1977, **41:**474–485.

Falbo, T., and L. A. Peplau. "Power Strategies in Intimate Relationships," *Journal of Personality and Social Psychology,* 1980, **38:**618–628.

Family Planning Perspectives. "Supreme Court Upholds Right of Mature Minor to Obtain Abortion without Parental Consent." 1979a, **11:**252.

———. "Contraceptive Tubal Sterilization Rate Increases More than Twice during the Period 1970–1976. 1979b, **11:**253–255.

———. "School Sex Education Required in Three States and D.C., but Most States Allow Local Districts to Decide." 1980. **12:**307–309.

Farkas, G. M. "Comments on Levin et al. and Rosen and Kopel: Internal and External Validity Issues," *Journal of Consulting and Clinical Psychology,* 1978, **46:**1515–1516.

———, and R. C. Rosen. "Effect of Alcohol on Elicited Males' Sexual Response," *Journal of Studies on Alcohol,* 1976, **37:**265–272.

———, L. F. Sine, and I. M. Evans. "Personality, Sexuality, and Demographic Differences between Volunteers and Nonvolunteers for a Laboratory Study of Male Sexual Behavior," *Archives of Sexual Behavior,* 1978, **7:**513–520.

———, ———, and ———. "The Effects of Distraction, Performance Demand, Stimulus Explicitness and Personality on Objective and Subjective Measures of Male Sexual Arousal," *Behavior Research and Therapy,* 1979, **17:**25–32.

Farrell, R. A., and J. F. Nelson. "A Causal Model of Secondary Deviance: The Case of Homosexuality," *Sociological Quarterly,* 1976, **17:**109–120.

Feigelman, W. "Peeping: The Pattern of Voyeurism among Construction Workers," in C. D. Bryant (ed.), *Sexual Deviancy in Social Context.* New York: New Viewpoints, 1977.

Feldman-Summers, S., and K. Lidner. "Perceptions of Victims and Defendants in Criminal Assault Cases," *Criminal Justice and Behavior,* 1976, **3:**135–149.

——, P. Gordon, and J. R. Meagher. "The Impact of Rape on Sexual Satisfaction," *Journal of Abnormal Psychology,* 1979, **88:**101–105.

Felman, Y. M. "Physician's Recognition of the Signs and Symptoms of Secondary Syphilis," *Journal of the American Medical Association,* 1981, 246, 252.

Fink, R., R. Roeser, W. Venet, P. Strax, L. Venet, and M. Lacher. "Effects of New Events on Responses to a Breast Cancer Screening Program," *Public Health Reports,* 1978, **93:**318–327.

Finke, N. "Sex Education in Moscow Schools," *Seattle Post-Intelligencer,* Oct. 14, 1979, A12.

Finkelhor, D. *Sexually Victimized Children.* New York: Free Press, 1979.

——, "Sex Among Siblings: A Survey of Prevalence, Variety, and Effects," *Archives of Sexual Behavior,* 1980, **9:**171–194.

Finkle, A. L., and T. G. Meyers. "Sexual Potency in Aging Males. IV.: Status of Private Patients before and after Prostatectomy," *The Journal of Urology,* 1960, **84:**152.

——, and S. P. Taylor. "Sexual Potency after Radical Prostatectomy," *The Journal of Urology,* 1981, **1215:**350–352.

Finkle, M. L., and D. S. Finkle. "Sexual and Contraceptive Knowledge, Attitudes, and Behavior of Male Adolescents," *Family Planning Perspectives,* 1975, **7:**256–260.

Fisch, I. R., and J. Frank. "Oral Contraceptives and Blood Pressure," *Journal of the American Medical Association,* 1971, **137:**2499–2503.

Fisher, J. L. "Transitions in Relationship Style from Adolescence to Young Adulthood," *Journal of Youth and Adolescence,* 1981, **10:**11–24.

Fisher, C., J. Gross, and J. Zuch. "Cycle of Penile Erection Synchronous with Dreaming (REM) Sleep: Preliminary Report," *Archives of General Psychiatry,* 1965, **12:**29–45.

Fisher, S. *The Female Orgasm.* New York: Basic Books, Inc, 1973.

Fisher, W. A., and D. Byrne. "Sex Differences in Response to Erotica? Love or Lust," *Journal of Personality and Social Psychology,* 1978, **36:**117–125.

——, ——, M. Edmunds, C. T. Miller, K. Kelley, and L. A. White. "Psychological and Situation-Specific Correlates of Contraceptive Behavior among University Women," *Journal of Sex Research,* 1979, **15:**38–55.

Fitz-Gerald, M., and D. Fitz-Gerald. "The Potential Effects of Deafness upon Sexuality," *Sexuality and Disability,* 1980, **3:**177–181.

——, and ——. "Sexuality and Deafness in America: An Overview," *British Journal of Sexual Medicine,* In press.

Fitzpatrick, W. F. "Sexual Function in the Paraplegic Patient," *Archives of Physical and Medical Rehabilitation,* 1974, **55:**221–227.

Fleming, M. Z., S. R. Jenkins, and C. Bugarin. "Questioning Current Definitions of Gender Identity: Implications of the Bem Sex-Role Inventory for Transsexuals," *Archives of Sexual Behavior,* 1980, **9:**13–26.

Ford, K., M. Zelnik, and J. F. Kantner. "Sexual Behavior and Contraceptive Use among Groups of Young Women in the United States," *Journal of Biosocial Science,* 1981, **13:**31–45.

Forrest, J. D., E. Sullivan, and C. Tietze. "Abortion in the United States 1977–1978," *Family Planning Perspectives,* 1979, **11:**329–341.

Fowler, J. E., Jr., W. Barzell, B. S. Hilaris, and W. F. Whitmore, Jr. "Complications of 125 Iodine in the Implantation and Pelvic Lymphadectomy in the Treatment of Prostatic Cancer," *The Journal of Urology,* 1979, **121:**447–451.

Fox, G. L. "Sex Role Attitudes as Predictors of Contraceptive Use among Unmarried University Students," *Sex Roles,* 1977, **3:**265–283.

Fraley, E. E., P. H. Lange, and B. J. Kennedy. "Germ-Cell Testicular Cancer in Adults," *New England Journal of Medicine,* 1979, **301:**1420–1426.

Frank, E., C. Anderson, and D. Rubinstein. "Frequency of Sexual Dysfunction in 'Normal' Couples," *New England Journal of Medicine,* 1978, **299:**111–115.

———, ———, and ———. "Marital Role Strain and Sexual Satisfaction," *Journal of Consulting and Clinical Psychology,* 1979, **47:**1096–1103.

Frazier, T. G., S. M. Ryan, C. Cole-Beuglet, A. B. Kurtz, and B. B. Goldberg. "Dysplastic Breasts by Mammography: Further Evaluation by Ultrasound." Paper presented at the Annual Meeting of the American Radium Society, April 28, 1980.

Freedman, D. S., and A. Thornton. "The Long-Term Impact of Pregnancy at Marriage on the Family's Economic Circumstances," *Family Planning Perspectives,* 1979, **11:**6–20.

Freud, S. "'Civilized' Sexual Morality and Modern Nervous Illness," in *Complete Psychological Works of Sigmund Freud,* standard ed. London: Hogarth Press, 1959.

Friedrich, E. G., Jr. "Tampon Effects on Vaginal Health," *Clinical Obstetrics and Gynecology,* 1981, **24:**395–406.

Fritz, G. S., K. Stoll, and N. N. Wagner. "A Comparison of Males and Females Who Were Sexually Molested as Children," *Journal of Sex and Marital Therapy,* 1981, **7:**54–59.

Fromkin, H. L., and T. C. Brock. "Erotic Materials: A Commodity Theory Analysis of the Enhanced Desirability which May Accompany Their Unavailability," *Journal of Applied Social Psychology,* 1973, **3:**219–231.

Frumkin, R. M. "Early English and American Sex Customs," In A. Ellis and A. Abaranel (eds.), *Encyclopedia of Sexual Behavior.* New York: Hawthorn Books, Inc., 1961.

Fuchs, A-R., P. Husslein, and F. Fuchs. "Oxytocin and the Initiation of Human Parturition, II. Stimulation of Prostaglandin Production in Human Decidua by Oxytocin," *American Journal of Obstetrics and Gynecology,* 1981, **141:**694–697.

Furstenberg, F. F. "The Social Consequences of Teenage Parenthood," *Family Planning Perspectives,* 1976, **8:**148–151, 155–164.

Gagnon, J. H. "Female Child Victims of Sex Offenses," *Social Problems,* 1965, **13:**176–192.

———. "Scripts and the Coordination of Sexual Conduct," in R. Dienstbier and J. K. Cole (eds.), *Nebraska Symposium on Motivation.* Lincoln: University of Nebraska Press, 1974.

———. *Human Sexualities.* Glenview, Ill.: Scott, Foresman and Co., 1977.

———, and C. S. Greenblat. *Life Designs: Individuals, Marriages and Families.* Glenview, Ill.: Scott, Foresman and Co., 1978.

———, and W. S. Simon. *Sexual Conduct: The Social Sources of Human Sexuality.* Chicago: Aldine, 1973.

Galbraith, G. G., and D. L. Mosher. "Associative Sexual Responses in Relation to Sexual Arousal, Guilt and External Contingencies," *Journal of Personality and Social Psychology,* 1968, **10:**142–147.

———, and ———. "Effects of Sex Guilt and Sexual Stimulation on the Recall of Word Associations," *Journal of Consulting and Clinical Psychology,* 1970, **34:**67–71.

Gallagher, N. "The San Francisco Experience," *Playboy,* January 1980, 117–118.

Gallup Poll Report No. 156, July, 1978.

Garfield, R. E., and R. H. Hayashi. "Appearance of Gap Junctions in the Myometrium of Women during Labor," *American Journal of Obstetrics and Gynecology,* 1981, **140:**254–260.

Garner, B., and R. W. Smith. "Are There Really Any Gay Male Athletes? An Empirical Survey." Paper presented at the Society for the Scientific Study of Sex Convention, San Diego, Calif., June 1976.

Garris, L., A. Steckler, and J. C. McIntire, "The Relationship between Oral Contraceptives and Adolescent Sexual Behavior," *Journal of Sex Research,* 1976, **12:**135–146.

Gebhard, P. H. "Factors in Marital Orgasm," *Journal of Social Issues,* 1966, **22:**88–95.

———. "Postmarital Coitus among Widows and Divorcees," in P. Bohannan (ed.), *Divorce and After.* New York: Doubleday & Co., 1970.

———. "Fetishism and Sadomasochism," in D. Byrne and L. A. Byrne (eds.), *Exploring Human Sexuality.* New York: Crowell, 1977a.

———. "The Acquisition of Basic Sex Information," *Journal of Sex Research,* 1977b, **13:**148–169.

———, J. H. Gagnon, W. B. Pomeroy, and C. V. Christensen. *Sex offenders.* New York: Harper & Row, 1965.

———, and A. B. Johnson. *The Kinsey Data: Marginal Tabulations of the 1938–1963 Interviews Conducted by the Institute for Sex Research.* Philadelphia: W. B. Saunders, 1979.

Geer, J. H., and R. Fuhr. "Cognitive Factors in Sexual Arousal: The Role of Distraction," *Journal of Consulting and Clinical Psychology,* 1976, **44:**238–243.

———, P. Morokoff, and P. Greenwood. "Sexual Arousal in Women: The Development of a Measurement Device for Vaginal Blood Volume," *Archives of Sexual Behavior,* 1974, **3:**559–564.

Geis, G. "Group Sexual Assaults," *Medical Aspects of Human Sexuality,* 1971, **5:**101–113.

———, R. Wright, T. Garret, and P. R. Wilson. "Reported Consequences of Decriminalization of Consensual Adult Homosexuality in Seven American States," *Journal of Homosexuality,* 1976, **1:**419–426.

Gelles, R. J. "Power, Sex and Violence: The Case of Marital Rape," *The Family Coordinator,* 1977, **26:**339–347.

Gerrard, M. "Sex Guilt in Abortion Patients," *Journal of Consulting and Clinical Psychology,* 1977, **45:**708.

Giambra, L. M., and C. E. Martin. "Sexual Daydreams and Quantitative Aspects of Sexual Activity: Some Relations for Males across Adulthood," *Archives of Sexual Behavior,* 1977, **6:**497–505.

Giarrusso, R., P. Johnson, J. Goodchilds, and G. Zellman. "Adolescents' Cues and Signals: Sex and Assault." Paper presented at the Western Psychological Association Meeting, San Diego, Calif., April 1979.

Gibbons, F. X. "Sexual Standards and Reactions to Pornography: Enhancing Behavioral Consistency through Self-Focused Attention," *Journal of Personality and Social Psychology,* 1978, **36:**976–987.

Gilbaugh, J. H., Jr. and P. C. Fuchs. "The Gonococcus and the Toilet Seat," *New England Journal of Medicine,* 1979, **301:**91–93.

Gilbert, A. N. "Doctor, Patient, and Onastic Diseases in the Nineteenth Century," *Journal of the History of Medicine and Allied Sciences,* 1975, **30:**217–234.

———. "Buggery and the British Navy 1700–1861," *Journal of Social History,* 1976–1977, **10:**72–98.

Gilmartin, B. G. "Sexual Deviance and Social Networks: A Study of Social, Family, and Marital Interaction Patterns among Co-Marital Sex Participants," in J. R. Smith and L. R. Smith (eds.), *Beyond Monogamy.* Baltimore: John Hopkins University Press, 1974.

———. "Swinging: Who Gets Involved and How?" in R. W. Libby and R. N. Whitehurst (eds.), *Marriage and Alternatives.* Glenview, Ill.: Scott, Foresman and Co., 1977.

———. Unpublished tables on a sample of swingers and controls, 1972. Cited in B. I. Murstein, "Swinging," in B. I. Murstein (ed.), *Exploring Intimate Lifestyles.* New York: Springer Publishing Co., 1978.

Ginsberg, L. H. "The Institutionalized Mentally Disabled," in H. L. Gochros and J. S. Gochros (eds.), *The Sexually Oppressed.* New York: Association Press, 1977.

Ginsburg, D. S., J. L. Stern, K. A. Hamod, R. Genadry, and M. R. Spence. "Tubo-Ovarian Abscess: A Retrospective Review," *American Journal of Obstetrics and Gynecology,* 1980, **138:**1055–1058.

Ginsburg, K. N. "The 'Meat-Rack': A Study of the Male Homosexual Prostitute," in C. D. Bryant (ed.), *Sexual Deviancy in Social Context.* New York: New Viewpoints, 1977.

Gjorgon, A. N. *Barrier Contraception and Breast Cancer: Contributions to Gynecology and Obstetrics,* Vol. 8, P. J. Keller (Series Ed.). Basel, Switzerland: S. Karger, 1980.

Gladwin, L. A. "Tobacco and Sex: Some Factors Affecting Nonmarital Sexual Behavior in Colonial Virginia," *Journal of Social History,* 1978 (Fall), **12:**57–75.

Glass, S. P., and T. L. Wright. "The Relationship of Extramarital Sex, Length of Marriage, and Sex Differences of Marital Satisfaction and Romanticism: Athanasiou's Data Reanalyzed," *Journal of Marriage and the Family,* 1977, **39:**691–703.

Glick, P. C., and A. J. Norton. "Marrying, Divorcing, and Living Together in the United States Today," *Population Bulletin,* 1977, **32:**3–41.

———, and G. B. Spanier, "Married and Unmarried Cohabitation in the United States," *Journal of Marriage and the Family,* 1980, **42:**19–30.

Gochros, H. L., and J. S. Gochros (Eds.). *The Sexually Oppressed.* New York: Association Press, 1977.

Gold, F. M., and R. S. Hotchkiss. "Sexual Potency following Simple Prostatectomy," *New York State Journal of Medicine,* December 1969, 2987–2989.

Gold, R. B., and P. D. Wilson. "Depo-Provera: New Developments in a Decade-Old Controversy," *Family Planning Perspectives,* 1981, **13:**35–39.

Golden, W. E. "Better Diagnosis Could Aid Battle against Pelvic Inflammatory Disease," *Journal of the American Medical Association,* 1980, **243:**2471–2472.

Goldsmith, S., M. O. Gabrielson, J. Gabrielson, V. Mathews, and L. Potts. "Teenagers, Sex and Contraception," *Family Planning Perspectives,* 1972, **4:**32–38.

Goldstein, M. J., H. S. Kant, L. L. Judd, C. J. Rice, and R. Green. "Exposure to Pornography and Sexual Behavior in Deviant and Normal Groups," *Technical Report of the Commission on Obscenity and Pornography,* Washington: U.S. Government Printing Office, 1971.

Goode, E., and L. Haber. "Sexual Correlates of Homosexual Experience: Exploratory Study of College Women," *Journal of Sex Research,* 1977, **13:**12–21.

———, and R. R. Troiden. "Amyl Nitrate Use among Homosexual Men," *American Journal of Psychiatry,* 1979, **136:**1067–1069.

Gosselin, C., and G. Wilson. *Sexual Variations: Fetishism, Sadomasochism, and Transvestism.* New York: Simon & Schuster, 1980.

Gough, H. G. "Some Factors Related to Men's State Willingness to Use a Male Contraceptive Pill," *Journal of Sex Research,* 1979, **15:**27–37.

Graber, B. "Circumvaginal Musculature and Female Sexual Function; The Past, Present, and Future," *Journal of Sex and Marital Therapy,* 1981, **7:**31–36.

Graham, C. A., and W. C. McGrew. "Menstrual Synchrony in Female Undergraduates Living in a Coeducational Campus," *Psychoneuroendocrinology,* 1980, **5:**245–252.

Granberg, D. "The Abortion Activitists," *Family Planning Perspectives,* 1981, **13:**157–163.

———, and B. W. Granberg. "Pro-Life versus Pro-Choice: Another Look at the Abortion Controversy in the U.S.," *Sociology and Social Research,* 1981, **65:**424–430.

Green, R. "One-Hundred Ten Feminine and Masculine Boys: Behavioral Contrasts and Demographic Similarities," *Archives of Sexual Behavior,* 1976, **5:**425–446.

———. "Biological Influences on Sexual Identity," in H. A. Katchadourian (ed.), *Human Sexuality: A Comparative and Developmental Perspective.* Berkeley: University of California Press, 1979a.

———. "Childhood Cross-Gender Behavior and Subsequent Sexual Preference," *American Journal of Psychiatry,* 1979b, **135:**692–697.

Griffitt, W. "Response to Erotica and the Projection of Response to Erotica in the Opposite Sex," *Journal of Experimental Research in Personality,* 1973, **6:**330–338.

———. "Sexual Experience and Sexual Responsiveness: Sex Differences," *Archives of Sexual Behavior,* 1975, **4:**529–540.

———. "Sexual Stimulation and Sociosexual Behaviors," In M. Cook and G. Wilson (eds.), *Love and Attraction: An International Conference.* New York: Pergamon Press, 1979.

———. "Sexual Intimacy in Aging Marital Partners." Unpublished manuscript prepared for the National Council Commission on Aging: Stability and Change in the Family, 1980.

———, and D. L. Kaiser. "Affect, Sex Guilt, and the Rewarding-Punishing Effects of Erotic Stimuli," *Journal of Personality and Social Psychology,* 1978, **36:**850–858.

———, J. May, and R. Veitch. "Sexual Stimulation and Interpersonal Behavior: Heterosexual Evaluative Responses, Visual Behavior, and Physical Proximity," *Journal of Personality and Social Psychology,* 1974, **30:**367–377.

Gross, A. E. "The Male Role and Heterosexual Behavior," *Journal of Social Issues,* 1978, **34:**87–107.

Grosskurth, P. *Havelock Ellis: A Biography.* New York: Alfred A. Knopf, 1980.

Grossman, J. H., W. C. Waller, and J. L. Sever. "Management of Genital Herpes Simplex Virus during Pregnancy," *Obstetrics and Gynecology,* 1981, **58:**1–4.

Groth, A. N. "The Adolescent Sexual Offender and His Prey," *International Journal of Offender Therapy and Comparative Criminology,* 1977, **21:**249–254.

———. *Men Who Rape: The Psychology of the Offender.* New York: Plenum Press, 1979.

———, and H. J. Birnbaum. "Adult Sexual Orientation and Attraction to Underage Persons," *Archives of Sexual Behavior,* 1978, **7:**175–181.

———, and A. Burgess. "Sexual Dysfunction during Rape," *New England Journal of Medicine,* 1977, **297:**764–766.

———, ———, and L. L. Holmstrom. "Rape: Power, Anger and Sexuality," *American Journal of Psychiatry,* 1977, **134:**1239–1243.

Grunert, G. M., T. S. Drake, and K. Takaki. "Microsurgical Reanastomosis of the Fallopian Tubes for Reversal of Sterilization," *Obstetrics and Gynecology,* 1981, **58:**148–151.

Gutek, A., C. Y. Nakamura, M. Gahert, I. Handschumacher, and D. Russell. "Sexuality in the Workplace," *Basic and Applied Social Psychology,* 1981, **1:**255–265.

Haeberle, E. J. *The Sex Atlas: A New Illustrated Guide.* New York: Seabury Press, 1978.

Haims, L. J. *Sex Education and the Public Schools.* Lexington, Mass.: Lexington Books, 1973.

Hain, J., N. Doshi, and J. H. Harger. "Ascending Transcervical Herpes Simplex Infection with Intact Fetal Membranes," *Obstetrics and Gynecology,* 1980, **56:**106–109.

Halstead, M. M., and L. S. Halstead. "A Sexual Intimacy Survey of Former Nuns and Priests," *Journal of Sex and Marital Therapy,* 1978, **4:**83–90.

Halsted, W. S. "The Results of Operations for the Cure of Cancer of the Breast Performed at the Johns Hopkins Hospital from June 1889 to January 1894," *John Hopkins Hospital Report,* 1894, **4:**297–350.

Hamer, J. "Sexual Harassment Is Now a Serious Business," *Seattle Times,* Dec. 17, 1981, A14.

Hamilton, G. V. *A Research in Marriage.* New York: Medical Research Press, 1929.

Hammond, B. E., and J. A. Ladner. "Socialization into Sexual Behavior in a Negro Slum Ghetto," in C. B. Broderick and J. Bernard (eds.), *The Individual, Sex and Society.* New York: Johns Hopkins Press, 1969.

Handsfield, H. H. "Sexually Transmitted Diseases in Homosexual Men," *American Journal of Public Health,* 1981, **71:**989–990.

———, W. E. Stamm, and K. K. Holmes. "Public Health Implications and Control of Sexually Transmitted Chlamydial Infections," *Sexually Transmitted Diseases,* 1981, **8:**85–86.

Hanson, F. W., and J. W. Overstreet. "The Interaction of Human Spermatazoa with Cervical Mucous in Vivo," *American Journal of Obstetrics and Gynecology,* 1981, **140:**173–177.

Hansson, R. O., M. E. O'Connor, W. H. Jones, and T. J. Blocker. "Maternal Employment and Adolescent Sexual Behavior," *Journal of Youth and Adolescence,* 1981, **10:**55–60.

Haring, M., and L. Meyerson. "Attitudes of College Students toward Sexual Behavior of Disabled Persons," *Archives of Physical Medicine and Rehabilitation,* 1979, **60:**257–260.

Hariton, E. B., and J. L. Singer. "Women's Fantasies during Sexual Intercourse: Normative and Theoretical Explanations," *Journal of Consulting and Clinical Psychology,* 1974, **42:**313–322.

Harlap, S., and A. M. Davies. "Late Sequelae of Induced Abortion: Complications and Outcome of Pregnancy and Labor," *American Journal of Epidemiology,* 1975, **102:**217–224.

Harris, J. R., M. B. Levene, and S. Hellman. "Results of Treating Stages I and II Carcinoma of the Breast with Primary Radiation Therapy," *Cancer Treatment Reports,* 1978, **62:**985–991.

Harris, R. W. C., L. A. Brinton, R. H. Cowdell, D. C. G. Skegg, P. G. Smith, M. P. Vessey, and R. Doll. "Characteristics of Women with Dysplasia or Carcinoma in Situ of the Cervix Uteri," *British Journal of Cancer,* 1980, **42:**359.

Harris, S. *They Sell Sex.* Greenwich, Conn.: Fawcett Publications, 1960.

Harry, J. "On the Validity of Typologies of Gay Males," *Journal of Homosexuality,* 1976–1977, **2:**143–152.

——. "The 'Marital' Liasons of Gay Men," *The Family Coordinator,* 1979, **28:**622–629.

——. "Fag Bashing." Paper presented at the Annual Meeting of the American Sociological Association, 1980.

Harvey, S. M. "Trends in Contraceptive Use at One University: 1974–1978," *Family Planning Perspective,* 1980, **12:**301–304.

Hass, A. *Teenage Sexuality: A Survey of Teenage Sexual Behavior.* New York: Macmillan Co., Inc., 1979.

Hassell, J., and E. W. L. Smith. "Female Homosexuals' Concepts of Self, Men and Women," *Journal of Personality Assessment,* 1975, **39:**154–159.

Hasting, D., and C. Markland. "Post-Surgical Adjustment of twenty-five Transsexuals (Male-to-Female) in the University of Minnesota Study," *Archives of Sexual Behavior,* 1978, **7:**327–336.

Hatch, J. P. "Vaginal Photoplethysmography: Methodological Consideration," *Archives of Sexual Behavior,* 1979, **8:**357–374.

Hatcher, R. A., G. K. Stewart, F. Stewart, F. Guest, P. Stratton, and A. H. Wright. *Contraceptive Technology 1978–1979.* New York: Irvington Publishers, 1978.

Hatfield, E., D. Greenberger, J. Traupmann, and P. Lambert. "Equity and Sexual Satisfaction in Recently Married Couples," *Journal of Sex Research,* 1982, **18:**18–32.

——, S. Sprecher, and J. Traupmann. "Men's and Women's Reactions to Sexually Explicit Films: A Serendipitous Finding," *Archives of Sexual Behavior,* 1978, **7:**583–592.

Hayes, J., and J. H. Littlefield. "VD Knowledge in High School Seniors," *Journal of School Health,* 1976, **9:**546–547.

Hayes, S. W., and L. J. Oziel. "Homosexuality: Behavior and Attitude," *Archives of Sexual Behavior,* 1976, **5:**283–289.

Hedblom, J. H., and J. J. Hartman. "Research on Lesbianism: Selected Effects of Time, Geographic Location, and Data Collection Technique," *Archives of Sexual Behavior,* 1980, **9:**217–234.

Heider, K. G. "Dani Sexuality: A Low Energy System," *Man,* 1976, **11:**187–201.

Heim, N. "Sexual Behavior of Castrated Sex Offenders," *Archives of Sexual Behavior,* 1981, **10:**11–19.

Heiman, J. R. "Women's Sexual Arousal," *Psychology Today,* 1975, **8:**90–94.

———, L. LoPiccolo, and J. LoPiccolo. *Becoming Orgasmic: A Sexual Growth Program for Women.* Englewood Cliffs, N.J.: Prentice-Hall, Inc., 1976.

Hellerstein, H. K., and E. H. Friedman. "Sexual Activity and the Postcoronary Patient," *Archives of Internal Medicine,* 1970, **125:**987–999.

Henderson, S. R. "Reversal of Female Sterilization: Comparison of Microsurgical and Gross Surgical Techniques for Tubal Anastomosis," *American Journal of Obstetrics and Gynecology,* 1981, **139:**73–79.

Henshaw, S., J. D. Forrest, E. Sullivan, and C. Tietze. "Abortion in the United States, 1978–1979," *Family Planning Perspectives,* 1981, **13:**6–18.

———, ———, ———, and ———. "Abortion Services in the United States, 1979 and 1980," *Family Planning Perspectives,* 1982, **14:**5–15.

Henshel, A. M. "Swinging: A Study of Decision Making in Marriage," *American Journal of Sociology,* 1973, **73:**885–891.

Henson, D. E., and H. B. Rubin. "Voluntary Control of Eroticism," *Journal of Applied Behavior Analysis,* 1971, **4:**37–44.

———, and ———. "A Comparison of Two Objective Measures of Sexual Arousal in Women," *Behavior Research and Therapy,* 1979, **16'**143–151.

Henze, L. F., and J. W. Hudson. "Personal and Family Characteristics of Cohabitating and Noncohabitating College Students," *Journal of Marriage and the Family,* 1974, **36:**722–727.

Herberman, R. B., M. Bordes, P. H. Lambert, H. S. Luthra, R. A. Robins, P. Sizaret, and A. Theofilopoulos. "Report on International Comparative Evaluation of Possible Value of Assays for Immune Complexes for Diagnosis of Human Breast Cancer," *International Journal of Cancer,* 1981, **27:**569–576.

Hernton, C. *Sex and Racism in America.* New York: Doubleday & Co., 1965.

Herold, E. S. "Contraceptive Embarrassment and Contraceptive Behavior Among Young Single Women," *Journal of Youth and Adolescence,* 1981, **10:**233–242.

———, and M. S. Goodwin. "Adamant Virgins, Potential Nonvirgins and Nonvirgins," *Journal of Sex Research,* 1981a, **17:**97–113.

———, and ———. "Premarital Sexual Guilt and Contraceptive Attitudes and Behavior," *Family Relations,* 1981b, **30:**247–253.

———, D. Mantle, and O. Zemitis. "A Study of Sexual Offenses against Females," *Adolescence,* 1979a, **14:**65–72.

———, J. Mottin, and Z. Sabry. "Effect of Vitamin E on Human Sexual Functioning," *Archives of Sexual Behavior,* 1979b, **8:**397–403.

Herr, H. W. "Preservation of Sexual Potency in Prostatic Cancer Patients after 125 I Implantation," *Journal of the American Geriatrics Society,* 1979, **27:**17–19.

Heslinga, K. "Psychosexual Problems of the Motor Disabled," in J. Money and H. Musaph (eds.), *Handbook of Sexology.* New York: Excerpta Medica, 1977.

Hicks, S. "Relationship and Sexual Problems of the Visually Handicapped," *Sexuality and Disability,* 1980, **3:**165–176.

Higgins, G. E. "Sexual Response in Spinal Cord Injured Adults: A Review of the Literature," *Archives of Sexual Behavior,* 1979, **8:**173–196.

Himes, N. E. *Medical History of Contraception.* New York: Gamut Press, Inc., 1963. Originally published, 1936.

Hirschfield, M., *Sexual Anomalies.* New York: Emerson Books, 1948.

Hite, S. *The Hite Report.* New York: The Macmillan Co., 1977.

Hobart, C. W. "Trial Marriage among Students: A Study of Attitudes and Behavior." Unpublished manuscript, University of Alberta, 1972.

Hoeffer, B. "Children's Acquisition of Sex-Role Behavior in Lesbian-Mother Families," *American Journal of Orthopsychiatry,* 1981, **51:**536–544.

Hogan, R. *Human Sexuality: A Nursing Perspective.* New York: Appleton-Century-Crofts, 1980.

Hohman, L. B., and B. Shaffner. "The Sex Lives of Unmarried Men," *American Journal of Sociology,* 1947, **52:**501–507.

Holmes, K. K., D. A. Eschenbach, and J. S. Knapp, "Salpingitis: Overview of Etiology and Epidemiology," *American Journal of Obstetrics and Gynecology,* 1980, **138:**893–900.

Holmstrom, L. L. and A. W. Burgess. "Sexual Behavior of Assailants during Reported Rapes," *Archives of Sexual Behavior,* 1980, **9:**427–439.

Hoon, E. F., and P. W. Hoon. "Styles of Sexual Expression in Women: Clinical Implications of Multivariate Analysis," *Archives of Sexual Behavior,* 1978, **7:**105–116.

Hoon, P. W., J. P. Wincze, and E. F. Hoon. "Physiological Assessment of Sexual Arousal in Women," *Psychophysiology,* 1976, **13:**196–205.

———, ———, and ———. "A Test of "Reciprocal Inhibition: Are Anxiety and Sexual Arousal in Women Mutually Inhibitory?" *Journal of Abnormal Psychology,* 1977, **86:**65–74.

Hottois, J., and N. A. Milner. *The Sex Education Controversy,* Lexington, Mass.: Lexington Books, 1975.

Houston, L. N. "Romanticism and Eroticism among Black and White College Students," *Adolescence,* 1981, **16:**263–272.

Howard, J. L., M. B. Liptzin, and C. B. Reifler. "Is Pornography a Problem?" *Journal of Social Issues,* 1973, **29:**133–145.

———, C. B. Reifler, and M. B. Liptzin. "Effects of Exposure to Pornography," in *Technical Report of the Commission on Obscenity and Pornography,* Vol. 8. Washington: U.S. Government Printing Office, 1971.

Howe, G. R., G. J. Sherman, R. M. Semenciw, and A. B. Miller. "Estimated Benefits and Risks of Screening for Breast Cancer," *Canadian Medical Association Journal,* 1981, **124:**339–403.

Howe, H. L. "Social Factors Associated with Breast Self-Examination among High Risk Women," *American Journal of Public Health,* 1981, **71:**251–255.

Hoyenga, K. B. and K. T. Hoyenga. *The Question of Sex Differences.* Boston: Little-Brown, 1979.

Hreshchyshyn, M. M., R. C. Park, J. A. Blessing, H. J. Norris, D. Levy, L. D. Lagasse, and W. T. Creasman. "The Role of Adjuvant Therapy in Stage I Ovarian Cancer," *American Journal of Obstetrics and Gynecology,* 1980, **138:**139–145.

Hudson, W. W., D. F. Harrison, and P. C. Crosscup. "A Short-Form Scale to Measure Sexual Discord in Dyadic Relationships," *Journal of Sex Research,* 1981, **17:**157–174.

Hudson, W. W., and W. A. Ricketts. "A Strategy for the Measurement of Homophobia," *Journal of Homosexuality,* 1980, **5:**357–372.

Huey, C. J., G. Kline-Graber, and B. Graber. "Time Factors and Orgasmic Response," *Archives of Sexual Behavior,* 1981, **10:**111–118.

Huguley, C. M., and R. L. Brown. "The value of Breast Self-Examination," *Cancer,* 1981, **47:**989–995.

Hulka, B. S., L. E. Chambless, D. G. Kaufman, W. C. Fowler Jr., and B. G. Greenberg. "Protection against Endometrial Carcinoma by Combination-Product Oral Contraceptives," *Journal of the American Medical Association,* 1982, **247:**475–477.

Hunt, M. *Sexual Behavior in the 1970's.* Chicago: Playboy Press, 1974.

Hurlock, B. *Adolescent Development,* 2d ed. New York: McGraw-Hill Book Co., 1955.

Husslein, P., A-R. Fuchs, and F. Fuchs. "Oxytocin and the Initiation of Human Parturition I: Prostaglandin Release during Induction of Labor by Oxytocin," *American Journal of Obstetrics and Gynecology,* 1981, **141:**688–693.

Hyde, J. S. *Understanding Human Sexuality.* New York: McGraw-Hill Book Co., 1979.

Intercom, "New Contraceptive Cap Custom-Made for Cervix," May 1979, **7:**2.

Irwin, P., and N. L. Thompson. "Acceptance of the Rights of Homosexuals: A Social Profile," *Journal of Homosexuality,* 1977, **3:**107–121.

Istvan, J., and W. Griffitt. "Effects of Sexual Experience on Dating Desirability and Marriage Desirability: An Experimental Study," *Journal of Marriage and the Family,* 1980, **42:**377–385.

Ivers, P. R., and N. P. Goldstein. "Multiple Sclerosis: A Current Appraisal of Symptoms and Signs," *Mayo Clinic Proceedings,* 1963, **38:**457–466.

Jacobs, J. A., and W. H. Tedford. "Factors Affecting the Self-Esteem of the Homosexual Individual," *Journal of Homosexuality,* 1980, **5:**373–382.

Jacobson, L. "Differential Diagnosis of Acute Pelvic Inflammatory Disease," *American Journal of Obstetrics and Gynecology,* 1980, **138:**1006–1011.

Jacques, P. F., S. C. Hartz, R. W. Tuthill, and C. Hollingsworth. "Elimination of Lead Time Bias in Assessing the Effect of Early Breast Cancer Diagnosis," *American Journal of Epidemiology,* 1981, **113:**93–97.

James, J. "Prostitution." Unpublished manuscript, University of Washington, Seattle, Washington, 1976.

———. "Prostitutes and Prostitution," in E. Sagarin and F. Montanino (eds.), *Deviants: Voluntary Actors in a Hostile World.* Morristown, N.J.: General Learning Press, 1977.

James, W. H. "The Honeymoon Effect on Marital Coitus," *Journal of Sex Research,* 1981, **17:**139–151.

Jamison, K. R., D. K. Wellisch, and R. O. Pasnau. "Psychosocial Aspects of Mastectomy, I: The Woman's Perspective," *American Journal of Psychiatry,* 1978, **135:**432–436.

Janda, L. H., and K. O'Grady. "Development of a Sex Anxiety Inventory," *Journal of Consulting and Clinical Psychology,* 1980, **48:**169–175.

———, ———, O'Grady, K. E., and S. A. Barnhart. "Effects of Sexual Attitudes and Physical Attractiveness on Person Perception of Men and Women," *Sex Roles,* 1981, **7:**189–199.

———, ———, J. Nichelous, D. Harsher, C. Denny, and K. Denner. "Effects of Sex Guilt on Interpersonal Pleasuring," *Journal of Personality and Social Psychology,* 1981, **40:**201–209.

Jansen, R. P. S. "Cyclic Changes in the Human Fallopian Tube Isthmus and Their Functional Importance," *American Journal of Obstetrics and Gynecology,* 1980, **136:**292–308.

Jedlicka, D. "Sequential Analysis of Perceived Commitment to Partners in Premarital Coitus," *Journal of Marriage and the Family,* 1975, **37:**385–390.

Jehu, D. *Sexual Dysfunction: A Behavioral Approach to Causation, Assessment, and Treatment.* New York: John Wiley & Sons, 1979.

Jensen, S. B. "Sexual Function in 20 Younger Insulin-Treated Diabetic Out Patients: A Two-Year Follow-Up Study," *Sexuality and Disability,* 1981a, **3:**61 67.

———. "Diabetic Sexual Dysfunction: A Comparative Study of 160 Insulin Treated Diabetic Men and Women and an Age-Matched Control Group," *Archives of Sexual Behavior,* 1981b, **10:**493–504.

Jessor, S. L., and R. Jessor. "Transition from Virginity to Nonvirginity among Youth: A Social-Psychological Study over Time," *Developmental Psychology,* 1975, **11:**473–484.

Jick, H., A. M. Walker, R. N. Watkins, D. C. Dewart, J. R. Hunter, A. Danford, S. Madsen, B. J. Sinan, and K. J. Rothman. "Oral Contraceptives and Breast Cancer," *American Journal of Epidemiology,* 1980, **112:**577–585; "Replacement Estrogens and Breast Cancer," ibid., 586–594.

———, ———, K. J. Rothman, J. R. Hunter, L. B. Holmes, R. N. Watkins, D. C. D'Ewart, A. Danford, and S. Madsen. "Vaginal Spermicides and Congenital Disorders," *Journal of the American Medical Association,* 1981, **245:**1329–1332.

Joe, V. C., C. R. Brown, and R. Jones. "Conservatism as a Determinant of Sexual Experiences," *Journal of Personality Assessment,* 1976, **40:**516–521.

———, R. N. Jones, and A. S. Noel. "Birth Control Practices and Conservatism," *Journal of Personality Assessment,* 1979, **43:**536–540.

———, and S. Kostyla. "Social Attitudes and Sexual Behaviors of College Students," *Journal of Consulting and Clinical Psychology,* 1975, **43:**430.

Johnson, B. L., and G. F. Fletcher. "Dynamic Electrocardiographic Recording during Sexual Activity in Recent Post-Myocardial Infarction and Revascularization Patients," *American Heart Journal,* 1979, **98:**736–741.

Johnson, R., N. Stephen, N. Horowitz, and P. Frost. "Disseminated Kaposi's Sarcoma in a Homosexual Man," *Journal of the American Medical Association,* 1982, **247:**1739–1741.

Johnson, S. R., S. M. Guenther, D. W. Laube, and W. C. Keettel. "Factors Influencing

Lesbian Gynecological Care: A Preliminary Study," *American Journal of Obstetrics and Gynecology,* 1981, **140:**20–25.

Johnson, W. T., and J. D. DeLamater. "Response Effects in Sex Surveys," *Public Opinion Quarterly,* 1976, **40:**165–181.

Jones, C., and E. Aronson. "Attribution of Fault to a Rape Victim as a Function of Respectability of the Victim," *Journal of Personality and Social Psychology,* 1973, **26:**415–419.

Jones, E. F., J. R. Beniger, and C. F. Westoff. "Pill and IUD Discontinuation in the United States, 1970–1975: The Influence of the Media," *Family Planning Perspectives,* 1980, **12:**293–300.

Jones, R. N., and V. C. Joe. "Pornographic Materials and Commodity Theory," *Journal of Applied Social Psychology,* 1980, **10:**311–322.

Journal of the American Medical Association, "The 'Pill' Receives Mixed Reviews in Latest Report," Walnut Creek Study. 1981, **246:**1071–1072.

Judson, F. N., K. A. Penley, M. E. Robinson, and J. K. Smith. "Comparative Prevalence Rates of Sexually Transmitted Diseases in Heterosexual and Homosexual Men," *American Journal of Epidemiology,* 1980, **112:**836–843.

Kaas, M. J. "Sexual Expression of the Elderly in Nursing Homes," *Gerontologist,* 1978, **4:**372–378.

Kaats, G. R., and K. E. Davis. "Effects of Volunteer Biases in Studies of Sexual Behavior and Attitudes," *Journal of Sex Research,* 1971, **7:**26–34.

Kaffman, M. "Sexual Standards and Behavior of the Kibbutz Adolescent," *American Journal of Orthopsychiatry,* 1977, **47:**207–217.

Kahn, E., and C. Fisher. "Some Correlates of Rapid Eye Movement in the Normal Aged Male," *Journal of Nervous and Mental Disease,* 1969, **148:**495–505.

Kalin, R. "Social Drinking in Different Settings," in D. C. McClelland, W. N. Davis, R. Kalin, and E. Wanner (eds.), *The Drinking Man.* New York: The Free Press, 1972.

Kanekar, S., and M. B. Kolswalla. "Factors Affecting Responsibility Attributed to a Rape Victim," *Journal of Social Psychology,* 1981, **113:**285–286.

Kanin, E. J. "Male Aggression in Dating-Courtship Relations," *American Journal of Sociology,* 1957, **63:**197–204.

———. "Reference Groups and Sex Conduct Norm Violations," *Sociological Quarterly,* 1967, **8:**495–504.

———, and D. H. Howard. "Postmarital Consequences of Premarital Sex Adjustments," *American Sociological Review,* 1958, **23:**556–562.

———, and S. R. Parcell. "Sexual Aggression: A Second Look at the Offended Female," *Archives of Sexual Behavior,* 1977, **6:**67–76.

Kaplan, H. S. *The New Sex Therapy.* New York: Brunner-Mazel, 1974.

———. *Disorders of Sexual Desire.* New York: Brunner-Mazel, 1980.

Karacan, I., C. J. Hursch, R. L. Williams, and J. I. Thorby. "Some Characteristics of Nocturnal Penile Tumescence in Young Adults," *Archives of General Psychiatry,* 1972, **26:**351–356.

———, P. J. Salis, J. C. Ware, B. Dervent, R. L. Williams, F. B. Scott, S. L. Attia, and L. E.

Beutler. "Nocturnal Penile Tumescence and Diagnosis in Diabetic Impotence," *American Journal of Psychiatry,* 1978, **135:**191–197.

Katchadourian, H. A. (ed.). *Human Sexuality: A Comparative and Developmental Perspective.* Berkeley: University of California Press, 1979.

———, and D. T. Lunde. *Fundamentals of Human Sexuality.* New York: Holt, Rinehart & Winston, 1975.

Kaufman, J. J., R. J. Boxer, B. Boxer, and M. Quinn. "Physical and Psychological Results of Penile Prostheses: A Statistical Survey," *The Journal of Urology,* 1981, **126:**173–175.

Kay, C. "Breast Cancer and Oral Contraceptives: Findings in the Royal College of General Practicioners Study," *British Medical Journal,* 1981, **282:**2089–2093.

Kee, P., and R. K. Darroch. "Perception of Methods of Contraception: A Semantic Differential Study," *Journal of Biosocial Science,* 1981, **13:**209–218.

Kelly, J. "The Aging Male Homosexual: Myth and Reality," *Gerontologist,* 1977, **17:**328–332.

Kelsey, J. L. "A Review of the Epidemiology of Human Breast Cancer," *Epidemiologic Reviews,* 1979, **1:**74–109.

Kempton, W. "The Mentally Retarded Person," in H. L. Gochros and J. S. Gochros (eds.), *The Sexually Oppressed.* New York: Association Press, 1977.

Kenrick, D. T., and S. E. Gutierres. "Contrast Effects and Judgments of Physical Attractiveness: When Beauty Becomes a Social Problem," *Journal of Personality and Social Psychology,* 1980, **38:**131–140.

———, W. L. Wagenhal, D. O. Stringfield, H. J. Ransdel, and R. H. Dahl. "Sex Differences, Androgyny, and Approach Responses to Erotica: A New Variation on the Old Volunteer Problems," *Journal of Personality and Social Psychology,* 1980, **38:**517–524.

Kiernan, K. E. "Teenage Motherhood-Associated Factors and Consequences, the Experience of a British Cohort," *Journal of Biosocial Science,* 1980, **12:**393–405.

Kilmann, P. R. "The Treatment of Primary and Secondary Orgasmic Dysfunction: A Methodological Review of the Literature since 1968," *Journal of Sex and Marital Therapy,* 1978, **4:**155–176.

———, R. L. Wanlass, R. F. Sabalis, and B. Sullivan. "Sex Education: A Review of Its Effects," *Archives of Sexual Behavior,* 1981, **10:**177–206.

Kilpatrick, D. G., L. J. Veronen, and P. A. Resick. "The Aftermath of Rape: Recent Empirical Findings," *American Journal of Orthopsychiatry,* 1979, **49:**658–669.

Kinder, B. N., and P. Blakeney. "Treatment of Sexual Dysfunction: A Review of Outcome Studies," *Journal of Clinical Psychology,* 1977, **33:**523–530.

King, W. "New Contraceptive Uses Skin Implants," *Seattle Times,* Aug. 11, 1981.

Kinghorn, G. R., and M. A. Walsh. "Oral Contraceptive Use and Prevalence of Infection with Chlamydia Trachomatis in Women," *British Journal of Venereal Diseases,* 1981, **47:**187–190.

Kinsey, A. C., W. B. Pomeroy, and C. E. Martin. *Sexual Behavior in the Human Male.* Philadelphia: W. B. Saunders Co., 1948.

———, ———, ———, and P. Gebhard. *Sexual Behavior in the Human Female.* Philadelphia: W. B. Saunders Co., 1953.

Kirby, D., J. Alter, and P. Scales. "An Analysis of U.S. Sex Education Programs and Evaluation Methods, Bethesda, Md.: Mathech Inc., 1979" (CDC Contract No. 200-78-0804). Available from Center for Disease Control, Bureau of Health Education, Atlanta, Ga.

Kirkpatrick, M., C. Smith, and R. Roy. "Lesbian Mothers and Their Children: A Comparative Survey," *American Journal of Orthopsychiatry,* 1981, **51:**545–551.

Kleine, C. L., and R. A. Staneski. "First Impressions of Female Bust Size," *Journal of Social Psychology,* 1980, **110:**123–134.

Knab, D. R. "Estrogen and Endometrial Carcinoma," *Obstetrical and Gynecological Survey,* 1977, **32:**267–281.

Knapp, J. "Co-Marital Sex and Marriage Counseling: Sexually Open Marriages and Related Attitudes and Practices of Marriage Counselors." Doctoral dissertation, University of Florida, 1974.

———. "Some Non-Monogamous Marriage Styles and Related Attitudes and Practices of Marriage Counselors," *The Family Coordinator,* 1975, **24:**505–514.

Knapp, J. J., and R. N. Whitehurst. "Sexually Open Marriage and Relationships: Issues and Prospects," in R. W. Libby and R. N. Whitehurst (eds.), *Marriage and Alternatives.* Glenview, Ill.: Scott, Foresman and Co., 1977.

Knowles, L., and H. Poorrkaj. "Attitudes and Behavior on Viewing Sexual Activities in Public Places," *Sociology and Social Research,* 1974, **58:**130–135.

Knox, D., and K. Wilson. "Dating Behaviors of University Students," *Family Relations,* 1981, **30:**255–258.

Koff, W. C. "Marihuana and Sexual Activity," *Journal of Sex Research,* 1974, **10:**194–206.

Kolarsky, A., J. Madlafousek, and V. Novotna. "Stimuli Eliciting Sexual Arousal in Males Who Offend Adult Women: An Experimental Study," *Archives of Sexual Behavior,* 1978, **7:**79–87.

Kolodny, R. C. "Sexual Dysfunction in Diabetic Females," *Diabetes,* 1971, **20:**557–559.

———. "Evaluating Sex Therapy: Process and Outcome at the Masters and Johnson Institute," *Journal of Sex Research,* 1981, **17:**301–318.

———, C. B. Kahn, and H. H. Goldstein. "Sexual Dysfunction in Diabetic Men," *Diabetes,* 1974, **23:**306–309.

———, W. H. Masters, V. E. Johnson, and M. A. Biggs. *Textbook of Human Sexuality for Nurses.* Boston: Little-Brown, 1979.

Komarovsky, M. *Dilemmas of Masculinity: A Study of College Youth.* New York: W. W. Norton, 1976.

Kopp, M. E. *Birth Control in Practice: Analysis of Ten Thousand Case Histories of Birth Control.* New York: McBride, 1933.

Kramarsky-Binkhorst, S. "Female Partner Perception of Small-Carion Implant," *Urology,* 1978, **12:**545–548.

Kraybill, W. G., R. Kaufman, and D. Kinne. "Treatment of Advanced Male Breast Cancer," *Cancer,* 1981, **47:**2185–2189.

Kroener, W. F. "Surgical Sterilization by Fimbriectomy," *American Journal of Obstetrics and Gynecology,* 1969, **104:**247.

Kroger, F. "Compliance Strategies in a Clinic for Treatment of Sexually Transmitted Diseases," *Sexually Transmitted Diseases,* 1979, **7:**178–182.

Krop, H., D. Hall, and J. Mehta. "Sexual Concerns after Myocardial Infarction," *Sexuality and Disability,* 1979, **2:**91–97.

Krosnick, A., and S. Podolsky. "Diabetes and Sexual Dysfunction: Restoring Normal Ability," *Geriatrics,* 1981, **36:**92–100.

Krueger, J. C., J. Hassell, D. B. Goggins, T. Ishimatsu, M. R. Pablico, and E. J. Tuttle. "Relationship between Nurse Counseling and Sexual Adjustment after Hysterectomy," *Nursing Research,* 1979, **28:**145–150.

Krulewitz, J. E., and E. Johnson-Payne. "Attributions about Rape: Effects of Rapist Force, Observer Sex, and Sex-Related Attitudes," *Journal of Applied Social Psychology,* 1978, **8:**291–305.

————, and J. E. Nash. "Effects of Rape Victim Resistance, Assault Outcomes and Sex of Observer on Attributes about Rape," *Journal of Personality,* 1979, **47:**557–576.

————, and ————. "Effects of Sexual Attitudes and Similarity on Men's Reaction to Male Homosexuals," *Journal of Personality and Social Psychology,* 1980, **38:**67–74.

Kumar, A., M. S. Selin, D. L. Madden, et al. "Humoral- and Cell-Mediated Immune Responses to Herpes virus Antigens in Patients with Cervical Carcinoma," *Gynecological Oncology,* 1980, **14:**18–25.

Kunin, C. M., and R. E. Ames. "Methods of Determining the Frequency of Sexual Intercourse and Activities of Daily Living in Young Women," *American Journal of Epidemiology,* 1981, **113:**55–61.

Kutchinsky, B. "The Effect of Easy Availability of Pornography on the Incidence of Sex Crimes; The Danish Experience," *Journal of Social Issues,* 1973, **29:**163–181.

Lamont, J. A. "Female Dyspareunia," *American Journal of Obstetrics and Gynecology,* 1980, **136:**282–285.

Lancer, W. C. *The Mind of Adolf Hitler: The Secret Wartime Report.* New York: Basic Books, Inc., 1972.

Lancet, M., B. Modan, S. Kavenaki, H. Antonovski, and I. Shoham. "Sexual Knowledge and Practices of Israeli Adolescents," *American Journal of Public Health,* 1978, **68:**1083–1089.

Laner, M. R. "Permanent Partner Priorities: Gay and Straight," *Journal of Homosexuality,* 1977, **3:**21–39.

————, and R. H. Laner. "Sexual Preference or Personal Style—Why Lesbians are Disliked," *Journal of Homosexuality,* 1980, **5:**339–356.

Lang, A. R., J. Searles, R. Lauerman, and V. Adesso. "Expectancy, Alcohol and Sex Guilt as Determinants of Interest in and Reaction to Sexual Stimuli," *Journal of Abnormal Psychology,* 1980, **89:**644–653.

Langevin, R., D. Paitich, C. Anderson, J. Kamrad, S. Pope, G. Geller, L. Pearl, and S. Newman. "Experimental Studies of the Etiology of Genital Exhibitionism," *Archives of Sexual Behavior,* 1979, **8:**307–331.

Langone, J. "Breast Cancer: Debate over Surgery," *Discover,* 1981, **2:**24–28.

Langston, R. D. "Stereotyped Sex Role Behavior and Sex Guilt," *Journal of Personality Assessment,* 1975, **39:**77–81.

Lansky, D., and G. T. Wilson. "Alcohol, Expectations, and Sexual Arousal in Males: An Information Processing Analysis," *Journal of Abnormal Psychology,* 1981, **90:**35–45.

Larsen, K. S., M. Reed, and S. Shoffman. "Attitudes of Heterosexuals toward Homosexuality: A Likert-Type Scale and Construct Validity," *Journal of Sex Research,* 1980, **16:**245–257.

LaTorre, R. A. "Devaluation of the Human Love Object—Heterosexual Rejection as a Possible Antecedent to Fetishism," *Journal of Abnormal Psychology,* 1980, **89:**295–298.

——, and K. Kear. "Attitudes toward Sex in the Aged," *Archives of Sexual Behavior,* 1977, **6:**203–213.

Lauersen, N. H., T. Den, J. Scher, C. Iliescu, and K. H. Wilson. "A New Abortion Technique: Intravaginal and Intramuscular Prostaglandin," *Obstetrics and Gynecology,* 1981, **58:**96–100.

Laws, D. R., and H. B. Rubin. "Instructional Control of an Automatic Sexual Response," *Journal of Applied Behavior Analysis,* 1969, **2:**93–99.

Laws, J. L., and P. Schwartz, (Eds.). *Sexual Scripts: The Social Construction of Female Sexuality.* Hinsdale, Ill.: Dryden Press, 1977.

Layde, P. M., V. Beral, and C. R. Kay. "Further Analysis of Mortality in Oral Contraceptive Users: Royal College of General Practicioners Oral Contraception Study," *Lancet,* March 7, 1981, **1:**541–546.

——, H. W. Ory, H. B. Peterson, M. S. Scally, J. R. Greenspan, J. C. Smith, and D. Fleming. "The Declining Length of Hospitalization for Tubal Sterilization," *Journal of the American Medical Association,* 1981, **245:**714–718.

Leiber, L., M. M. Plumb, M. L. Gerstenzang, and J. Holland. "The Communication of Affection between Cancer Patients and Their Spouses," *Psyhosomatic Medicine,* 1976, **38:**379–389.

Leis, H. P., Jr., A. Cammarata, R. LaRaja, L. Reed, J. Cleary, and E. Makoon-Singh. "Bilateral Breast Cancer," *Breast, Diseases of the Breast,* 1981, **7:**13–17.

Lemert, E. This is book review in *Contemporary Sociology* Jan. 1978, **7:**37–39.

Lester, D. "Telephone Counseling and the Masturbator," in C. D. Bryant (ed.), *Sexual Deviancy in Social Context.* New York: Franklin Watts, 1977.

Levin, R. J., and A. Levin. "Sexual Pleasure: The Surprising Preferences of 100,000 Women," *Redbook,* September 1975, 51–58.

Levine, M. P. "Gay Ghetto," *Journal of Homosexuality,* 1979, **4:**363–377.

Levinger, G. "Systematic Distortion in Spouses' Reports of Preferred and Actual Sexual Behavior," *Sociometry,* 1966, **29:**291–299.

Levitt, E. E., and A. D. Klassen, Jr. "Public Attitudes toward Homosexuality," *Journal of Homosexuality,* 1974, **1:**29–43.

Lev-Ran, A. "Sex Reversal as Related to Clinical Syndromes in Human Beings," in J. Money and H. Musaph (eds.), *Handbook of Sexology.* New York: Excerpta Medica, 1977.

Lewis, L. S., and D. Brissett. "Sex as Work," *Social Problems,* 1967, **15:**8–18.

Lewis, R. A., and W. R. Burr. "Premarital Coitus and Commitment among College Students," *Archives of Sexual Behavior,* 1975, **4:**73–79.

Libby, R. W., and M. A. Strauss. "Make Love Not War? Sex, Sexual Meanings, and Violence in a Sample of University Students," *Archives of Sexual Behavior,* 1980, **9:**133–143.

————, and R. N. Whitehurst. *Marriage and Alternatives.* Glenview, Ill.: Scott, Foresman and Co., 1977.

Lilius, H. G., E. J. Valtonen, and J. Wikstrom. "Sexual Problems in Patients Suffering from Multiple Sclerosis," *Journal of Chronic Diseases,* 1976, **29:**643–647.

Lipton, M. A. "Pornography," in B. J. Saddock, H. I. Kaplan, and A. M. Freedman (eds.), *The Sexual Experience.* Baltimore: Williams & Wilkins, 1976.

LoPiccolo, J., and W. C. Lobitz. "The Role of Masturbation in the Treatment of Orgasmic Dysfunction," *Archives of Sexual Behavior,* 1972, **2:**163–171.

————, and J. C. Steger. "The Sexual Interaction Inventory: A New Instrument for Assessment of Sexual Dysfunction," *Archives of Sexual Behavior,* 1974, **3:**585–595.

Lothstein, L. M. "The Postsurgical Transsexual: Empirical and Theoretical Considerations," *Archives of Sexual Behavior,* 1980, **9:**547–564.

Lowe, G. D. O., M. M. Drummond, C. D. Forbes, and J. C. Barbenel. "Increased Blood Viscosity in Young Women using Oral Contraceptives," *American Journal of Obstetrics and Gynecology,* 1980, **137:**840–842.

Luginbuhl, J., and C. Mullin. "Rape and Responsibility: How and How Much Is the Victim Blamed?" *Sex Roles,* 1981, **7:**547–560.

Lundeberg, P. O. "Sexual Dysfunction in Patients with Multiple Sclerosis," *Sexuality and Disability,* 1978, **1:**218–222.

MacDonald, A. P., and R. G. Games. "Some Characteristics of Those Who Hold Positive and Negative Attitudes toward Homosexuals," *Journal of Homosexuality,* 1974, **1:**9–27.

Macdonald, J. M. *Indecent Exposure.* Springfield, Ill.: Charles C Thomas, 1973.

Macdougal, J. C., and S. Morin. "Sexual Attitudes and Self-Reported Behavior of Congenitally Disabled Adults," *Canadian Journal of Behavioral Science,* 1979, **11:**189–204.

Mackinnon, C. A. *Sexual Harassment of Working Women.* New Haven, Conn.: Yale University Press, 1979.

MacMahon, B., P. Cole, and J. Brown. "Etiology of Human Breast Cancer: A Review," *Journal of the National Cancer Institute,* 1973, **50:**21–42.

Madore, C., W. E. Hawes, F. Many, and A. C. Hexter. "A Study of the Effects of Induced Abortion on Subsequent Pregnancy Outcome," *American Journal of Obstetrics and Gynecology,* 1981, **139:**516–521.

Madorsky, M. L., M. G. Ashamalla, I. Schussler, H. R. Lyons, and G. H. Miller, Jr. "Post-Prostatectomy Impotence," *The Journal of Urology,* 1976, **115:**401–403.

Mahoney, E. R. "Patterns of Sexual Behavior among College Students." Unpublished research report, Department of Sociology, Western Washington University, 1979a.

————. "Sex Education in the Public Schools: A Discriminant Analysis of Pro and Anti Individuals," *Journal of Sex Research,* 1979b, **15:**264–275.

————. "Premarital Coitus and the Southern Black—A Comment," *Journal of Marriage and the Family,* 1979, **41:**694–695.

————. "Religiosity and Sexual Behavior among Heterosexual College Students," *Journal of Sex Research,* 1980, **16:**97–113.

————. "Attitudes toward the Women's Movement and Attitudes toward Sexually Explicit Materials." Unpublished research report, Department of Sociology, Western Washington University, 1981.

————, and J. G. Richardson. "Perceived Social Status of Husbands and Wives: The Effects of Labor Force Participation and Occupational Prestige," *Sociology and Social Research,* 1979, **63:**364–374.

Malamuth, N. M., and J. V. P. Check. "Sexual Arousal to Rape and Consenting Depictions: The Importance of the Women's Sexual Arousal," *Journal of Abnormal Psychology,* 1980, **89:**763–766.

————, S. Haber, and S. Feshbach. "Testing Hypotheses regarding Rape: Exposure to Sexual Violence, Sex Differences, and the Normality of Rapists," *Journal of Research in Personality,* 1980a, **14:**121–137.

————, S. Heim, and S. Feshbach. "Sexual Responsiveness of College Students to Rape Depictions: Inhibitory and Disinhibitory Effects," *Journal of Personality and Social Psychology,* 1980a, **38:**399–408.

————, and B. Spinner. "A Longitudinal Content Analysis of Sexual Violence in the Best-selling Erotica Magazines," *Journal of Sex Research,* 1980, **16:**226–237.

Malatesta, V. J., R. H. Pollack, W. A. Wilbanks, and E. E. Adams. "Alcohol Effects on the Orgasmic-Ejaculatory Response in Human Males," *Journal of Sex Research,* 1979, **15:**101–107.

Malloy, T. R., A. J. Wein, and V. L. Capiniello. "Further Experience with the Inflatable Penile Prosthesis," *The Journal of Urology,* 1979, **122:**478–480.

Mancini, J. A., and D. K. Orthner. "Recreational Sexuality Preferences among Middle-Class Husbands and Wives," *Journal of Sex Research,* 1978, **14:**96–106.

Mann, J., L. Berkowitz, J. Sidman, S. Starr, and S. West. "Satiation of the Transient Stimulating Effect of Erotic Films," *Journal of Personality and Social Psychology,* 1974, **30:**729–735.

————, J. Sidman, and S. Starr. "Evaluating Social Consequences of Erotic Films; An Experimental Approach," *Journal of Social Issues,* 1973, **29:**113–131.

Margolis, H. F., and P. M. Rubenstein. *The Group Sex Tapes.* New York: David McKay & Co., 1971.

Markowski, J. W., J. W. Croake, and J. F. Keller. "Sexual History and Present Sexual Behavior of Cohabiting and Married Couples," *Journal of Sex Research,* 1978, **14:**27–39.

Marshall, P., D. Surridge, and N. Delva. "The Role of Nocturnal Penile Tumescence in Differentiation between Organic and Psychogenic Impotence: The First Stage of Differentiation," *Archives of Sexual Behavior,* 1981, **10:**1–10.

Martin, C. E. "Sexual Activity in the Aging Male," in J. Money and H. Musaph (eds.), *Handbook of Sexology.* New York: Excerpta Medica, 1977.

Martin, R. L., W. V. Roberts, and P. J. Clayton. "Psychiatric Status after Hysterectomy: A One-Year Follow-up," *Journal of the American Medical Association,* **244:**350–353.

Maruta, T., D. Osborne, D. W. Swanson, and J. M. Halling. "Chronic Pain Patients and Spouses' Marital and Sexual Adjustment," *Mayo Clinic Proceedings,* 1981, **56:**307–310.

Massie, E., E. Rose, J. Rupp, and R. Whelton. "Sudden Death during Coitus: Fact or Fiction?" *Medical Aspects of Human Sexuality,* March 1969, 22–26.

Masters, W. H., and V. E. Johnson. *Human Sexual Response.* Boston: Little, Brown, 1966.

————, and ————. *Human Sexual Inadequacy.* Boston: Little, Brown, 1970.

————, and ————. "Principles of the New Sex Therapy," *American Journal of Psychiatry,* 1976, **133:**548–554.

Matejcek, Z., Z. Dytrych, and V. Schuller. "Children from Unwanted Pregnancies," *Acta Psychiatrica Scandinavia,* 1978, **57:**67–90.

————, ————, and ————. "The Prague Study of Children Born from Unwanted Pregnancies," *International Journal of Mental Health,* 1979, **7:**63–77.

————, ————, and ————. "Follow-up Study of Children Born from Unwanted Pregnancies," *International Journal of Behavioral Development,* 1980, **3:**243–251.

Mathes, E. W., and L. I. Edwards. "Physical Attractiveness as an Input in Social Exchanges," *Journal of Psychology,* 1978, **98:**267–275.

Maugh, Y. H., III. "Male "Pill" Blocks Sperm Enzyme," *Science,* 1981, **22:**314.

Mauss, A. L. *Social Problems as Social Movements.* Philadelphia: J. B. Lippincott, 1975.

McCauley, C., and C. P. Swann. "Male-Female Differences in Sexual Fantasy," *Journal of Research in Personality,* 1976, **12:**76–86.

————, and ————. "Sex Differences in the Frequency and Functions of Fantasies during Sexual Activity," *Journal of Research in Personality,* 1980, **14:**400–411.

McClean, P. D. "Brain Mechanisms of Elemental Sexual Functions," in B. J. Saddock, H. I. Kaplan, and A. M. Freedman (eds.), *The Sexual Experience.* Baltimore: Williams & Wilkins, 1976.

McClintock, M. K. "Menstrual Synchrony and Suppression," *Nature,* 1971, **229:**244–245.

McDermott, J. *Rape Victimization in 26 American Cities.* Washington: U.S. Department of Justice, Law Enforcement and Assistance Administration, 1979.

McKean, K. "Closing In on the Herpes Virus," *Discover,* October 1981, 74–78.

McMullen, S., and B. C. Rosen. "Self-Administrated Masturbation Training in the Treatment of Primary Orgasmic Dysfunction," *Journal of Consulting and Clinical Psychology,* 1979, **47:**912–918.

McMurty, J. "Monogamy: A Critique," in R. W. Libby and R. N. Whitehurst (eds.), *Marriage and Alternatives.* Glenview, Ill.: Scott, Foresman and Co., 1977.

Mead, M. *Sex and Temperament in Three Primitive Societies.* New York: W. W. Norton, 1935.

Mednick, R. A. "Gender-Specific Variances in Sexual Fantasy," *Journal of Personality Assessment,* 1977, **41:**248–254.

Meigs, A. S. "Male Pregnancy and the Reduction of Sexual Opposition in a New Guinea Highlands Society," *Ethology,* 1976, **15:**393–407.

Melnick, J. L., and E. Adam. "Epidemiological Approaches to Determining Whether Herpes virus Is the Etiological Agent of Cervical Cancer," *Progress in Experimental Tumor Research,* 1978, **21:**49–69.

Mendelsohn, M. J., and D. L. Mosher. "Effect of Sex Guilt and Premarital Sexual Permissiveness on Role-Played Sex Education and Moral Attitudes," *Journal of Sex Research,* 1979, **15:**174–183.

Meyer, J., and D. Reter. "Sex Reassignment Follow-Up," *Archives of General Psychiatry,* 1979, **36:**1010–1015.

Meyer-Bahlburg, H. F. L. "Sex Hormones and Male Homosexuality in Comparative Perspective," *Archives of Sexual Behavior,* 1977, **6:**297–235.

———. "Sex Hormones and Female Homosexuality: A Critical Examination," *Archives of Sexual Behavior,* 1979, **8:**101–120.

Meyerwitz, J. H. "Sex and the Mentally Retarded," *Medical Aspects of Human Sexuality,* 1971, **5:**94–118.

Micheal, R. P., R. W. Bonsall, and P. Warner. "Human Vaginal Secretions: Volatile Fatty Acid Content," *Science,* 1974, **186:**1217–1219.

Miller, A. B. "Breast Cancer," *Cancer,* 1981, **47:**1109–1113.

Miller, P. Y., and W. Simon. "Adolescent Sexual Behavior: Context and Change," *Social Problems,* 1972, **20:**59–76.

Miller, W. R., and H. I. Lief. "Masturbatory Attitudes, Knowledge, and Experience: Data from Sex Knowledge and Attitudes Tests (SKAT)," *Archives of Sexual Behavior,* 1976, **5:**447–467.

Mims, F. H., and M. Swenson. *Sexuality: A Nursing Perspective.* New York: McGraw-Hill Book Co., 1980.

Mitchell, C. D., B. Bean, and S. R. Gentry. "Acyclovir Therapy tor Mucocutaneous Herpes Simplex Infections in Immunocompromised Patients," *Lancet,* June 27, 1981, 1389–1392.

Mitchell, K. R., D. M. Mitchell, and R. J. Kerby. "Note on Sex Differences in Student Drug Usage," *Psychological Reports,* 1970, **27:**116.

Mohl, P. C., R. Adams, D. M. Greer, and K. A. Sheley. "Prepuce Restoration Seekers: Psychiatric Aspects," *Archives of Sexual Behavior,* 1981, **10:**383–394.

Mohr, J. C. *Abortion in America: The Origins and Evolution of National Policy, 1800–1900.* New York: Oxford University Press, 1978.

Mohr, J. W., R. E. Turner, and M. B. Jerry. *Pedophilia and Exhibitionism.* Toronto Press, 1964.

Money, J. "Determinants of Human Gender Identity/Role," in J. Money and H. Musaph (eds.), *Handbook of Sexology.* New York: Excerpta Medica, 1977.

———, and J. Dalery. "Iatrogenic Homosexuality: Gender Identity in Seven 46XX Chromosomal Females with Hyperadrenocortical Hermaphroditism Born with a Penis," *Journal of Homosexuality,* 1976, **1:**357–371.

———, and A. A. Ehrhardt. *Man and Woman, Boy and Girl.* Baltimore: John Hopkins University Press, 1972.

———, and V. Lewis. "IQ, Genetics and Accelerated Growth: Adrenogenital Syndrome," *Bulletin of the John Hopkins Hospital,* 1966, **118:**365–373.

Monge, R. H., J. B. Dusek, and J. Lawless. "An Evaluation of the Acquisition of Sexual Information through a Sex Education Class," *Journal of Sex Research,* 1977, **13:**170–184.

Moore, E. C. "Woman and Health, United States, 1980," *Public Health Reports,* Special Supplement to September–October 1980 issue.

Moreault, D., and D. R. Fallingstad. "Sexual Fantasies of Females as a Function of Sex Guilt and Experimental Responses Cues," *Journal of Consulting and Clinical Psychology,* 1978, **46:**1385–1393.

Morgan, A. J., Jr. "Psychotherapy for Transsexual Candidates Screened out of Therapy," *Archives of Sexual Behavior,* 1978, **7:**273–284.

Morgan, R. "How to Run the Pornographers out of Town (and Preserve the First Amendment)," *Ms,* November 1978, **55:**78–80.

———, and G. Steinem. "The International Crime of Genital Mutilation," *Ms,* March 1980, 65–67, 98, 100.

Morin, S. F., and F. M. Garfinkle. "Male Homophobia," *Journal of Social Issues,* 1978, **34:**29–47.

Morris, N. M. "The Biological Advantages and Social Disadvantages of Teenage Pregnancy," *American Journal of Public Health,* 1981, **71:**796.

———, and J. R. Udry. "Pheromonal Influences on Human Sexual Behavior: An Experimental Research," *Journal of Biosocial Science,* 1978, **10:**147–157.

Morton, W. E., H. B. Horton, and H. W. Baker. "Effects of Socioeconomic Status on Incidences of Three Sexually Transmitted Diseases," *Sexually Transmitted Diseases,* 1979, **6:**206–210.

Mosher, D. L. "The Development and Validation of a Sentence Completion Measure of Guilt." Unpublished doctoral dissertation, Ohio State University, 1961.

———. "The Development and Multitrait-Multimethod Matrix Analysis of Three Measures of Three Aspects of Guilt," *Journal of Consulting and Clinical Psychology,* 1966, **30:**25–29.

———. "Measurement of Guilt in Females by Self-Report Inventories," *Journal of Consulting and Clinical Psychology,* 1968, **32:**690–695.

———. "Sex Guilt and Sex Myths in College Men and Women," *Journal of Sex Research,* 1979, **15:**224–234.

———, and P. R. Abramson. "Subjective Sexual Arousal to Films of Masturbation," *Journal of Consulting and Clinical Psychology,* 1977, **45:**796–807.

———, and H. J. Cross. "Sex Guilt and Premarital Sexual Experiences of College Students," *Journal of Consulting and Clinical Psychology,* 1971, **36:**27–32.

———, and K. E. O'Grady. "Homosexual Threat, Negative Attitudes toward Masturbation, Sex Guilt, and Males' Sexual and Affective Reactions to Explicit Sexual Films," *Journal of Consulting and Clinical Psychology,* 1979, **47:**866–873.

———, and B. B. White. "Effects of Committed or Casual Erotic Guided Imagery on Females' Subjective Sexual Arousal and Emotional Response," *Journal of Sex Research,* 1980, **16:**273–299.

Mostofi, F. K. "Testicular Tumors: Epidemiologic, Etiologic, and Pathologic Features," *Cancer,* 1973, **32:**1186–1201.

Mould, D. E. "Neuromuscular Aspects of Women's Orgasms," *Journal of Sex Research,* 1980, **16:**197–201.

Moxley, J. H., J. C. Allegra, J. Henney, and F. Muggia. "Treatment of Primary Breast Cancer: Summary of the National Institutes of Health Consensus Development Conference," *Journal of the American Medical Association,* 1980, **244:**797–800.

Muir, C. S. and J. Nectoux. "Epidemiology of Cancer of the Testis and Penis," *National Cancer Institute Monograph,* 1979, No. 53.

Murphy, C., and M. Sullivan. "Anxiety and Self-Concept Correlates of Sexually Aversive Women," *Sexuality and Disability,* 1981, **4:**15–26.

———, ———, and M. Leland. "Sexual Aversion," *Sexuality and Disability,* 1979, **2:**148–154.

Murray, B. L. S., and L. J. Wilcox. "Testicular Self-Examination," *American Journal of Nursing,* 1978, **78:**2074–2075.

Murstein, B. I. *Love, Sex, and Marriage.* New York: Springer Publishing Co., 1974a.

———. "Sex Drive, Person Perception, and Marital Choice," *Archives of Sexual Behavior,* 1974b, **3:**331–347.

——— (ed.). *Exploring Intimate Lifestyles.* New York: Springer Publishing Co., 1978.

———, "Swinging." In B. I. Murstein (ed.), *Exploring Intimate Lifestyles.* New York: Springer Publishing Company, 1978.

National Center of Health Statistics, *Annual Summary of Births, Deaths, Marriages, and Divorces: United States, 1980,* vol 29, No. 13, Monthly Vital Statistics Report, Sept. 17, 1981.

Nawy, H. "In the Pursuit of Happiness?: Consumers of Erotica in San Francisco," *Journal of Social Issues,* 1974, **29:**147–161.

Neuman, R. P. "Masturbation: Madness and the Modern Concepts of Childhood and Adolescence," *Journal of Social History,* 1975, **8:**1–27.

Newsweek. "Cable TV: Coming of Age," Aug. 24, 1981, 44–49.

New York State Department of Public Health, Office of Biostatistics. "Effects of Induced Abortion on Subsequent Reproductive Function." Albany, N.Y.: April 18, 1980 (mimeo). Reviewed in *Family Planning Perspectives,* 1981, **13:**80–81.

Nezhat, C., A. E. Karpas, R. B. Greenblat, and V. B. Mahesh. "Estradiol Implants for Conception Control," *American Journal of Obstetrics and Gynecology,* 1980, **138:**1151–1156.

Noe, J., R. Sato, C. Coleman, and D. R. Laub. "Construction of Male Genitalia: The Stanford Experience," *Archives of Sexual Behavior,* 1978, **7:**297–303.

Nowinski, J., J. R. Heiman, and J. LoPiccolo. "Factors Related to Sexual Behavior in Nondysfunctional Couples," *American Journal of Family Therapy,* 1981, **9:**14–23.

Nursing, 78. "Pathophysiology: What You Should Know (about Breast Cancer). Breast self-examination." Jan. 20, 1978, 23.

Oaks, R. F. "Things Too Fearful to Name: Sodomy and Buggery in Seventeenth-Century New England," *Journal of Social History,* 1978, **12:**268–281.

———. "Perceptions of Homosexuality by Justices of the Peace in Colonial Virginia," *Journal of Homosexuality,* 1979–1980, Special Issue on Homosexuality and the Law, **5:**35–41.

Offer, D., and W. Simon. "Stages of Sexual Development," in B. J. Sadock, H. I. Kaplan, and A. M. Freedman (eds.), *The Sexual Experience.* Baltimore: Williams & Wilkins, 1976.

Ohlmeyer, P., H. Brilmayer, and H. Hullstrung. "Periodische vorange in schlaf," *Pflueger Archives of General Physiology,* 1944, **248:**559–560.

O'Neill, N., and G. O'Neill. *Open Marriage: A New Lifestyle for Couples.* New York: M. Evans & Co., 1972.

Ory, H., P. Cole, B. MacMahon, and R. Hoover. "Oral Contraceptives and Reduced Risk of Benign Breast Diseases," *New England Journal of Medicine,* 1976a, **294:**419–422. (b)

———, Z. Naib, S. B. Conger, R. A. Hatcher, and C. W. Tyler. "Contraceptive Choice and Prevalence of Cervical Dysplasia and Carcinoma in Situ," *American Journal of Obstetrics and Gynecology,* 1976b, **124:**573.

———, A. Rosenfield, and L. C. Landman. "The Pill at 20: An Assessment," *Family Planning Perspectives,* 1980, **12:**278–283.

———, and The Women's Health Study. "Ectopic Pregnancy and Intrauterine Contraceptive Devices: New Perspectives," *Obstetrics and Gynecology,* 1981, **57:**137–144.

Osser, S., P. Liedholm, and N-O. Sjoberg. "Risk of Pelvic Inflammatory Disease among Users of Intrauterine Devices, Irrespective of Previous Pregnancy," *American Journal of Obstetrics and Gynecology,* 1980, **138:**864–867.

Ostrander, L. D., Jr., D. E. Lamphiear, W. D. Block, G. W. Williams, and W. J. Carmen. "Oral Contraceptives and Physiological Variables," *Journal of the American Medical Association,* 1980, **244:**677–679.

Overstreet, J. W., J. E. Gould, D. F. Katz, and F. W. Hanson. "In Vitro Capacitation of Human Spermatazoa after Passage through a Column of Cervical Mucous," *Fertility and Sterility,* 1980, **34:**604–606.

Owen, W. F., Jr. "Sexually Transmitted Diseases and Traumatic Problems in Homosexual Men," *Annals of Internal Medicine,* 1980, **92:**805–808.

Paavoner, J. "Chlamydia Trachomatis in Acute Salpingitis," *American Journal of Obstetrics and Gynecology,* 1980, **138:**957–959.

Pagano, M., and N. M. Kirschner. "Sex Guilt, Sexual Arousal, and Urinary Acid Phosphatase Output," *Journal of Research in Personality,* 1978, **12:**68–75.

Parlee, P., and C. Werner. "Lonely Losers: Stereotypes of Single Dwellers," *Personality and Social Psychology,* 1978, **4:**292–295.

Patrick, A. "Men in Love," *Essence,* February 1979, 57.

Pauly, I. B. "Female Transsexualism: Part I," *Archives of Sexual Behavior,* 1974, **3:**487–526.

Payne, E. C., A. R. Kravitz, M. T. Notham, and J. V. Anderson. "Outcome following Therapeutic Abortion," *Archives of General Psychiatry,* 1976, **33:**725–733.

Pearl, R. "Contraception and Fertility in 4,945 Married Women: A Second Report on a Study in Family Limitation," *Human Biology,* 1934, **6:**355–401.

Pennebaker, J. W., M. A. Dyer, S. Caulkins, D. L. Litowitz, P. L. Ackreman, D. B. Anderson, and K. M. McGraw. "Don't the Girls Get Prettier at Closing Time: A Country and Western Application to Psychology," *Personality and Social Psychology Bulletin,* 1979, **5:**122–125.

Peplau, L. A., Z. Rubin, and C. T. Hill. "Sexual Intimacy in Dating Relationships," *Journal of Social Issues,* 1977, **33:**86–109.

Peritz, E., S. Ramcharan, J. Frank, W. L. Brown, S. Huang, and R. Ray. "The Incidence of Cervical Cancer and Duration of Oral Contraceptive Use," *American Journal of Epidemiology,* 1977, **106:**462–469.

Perry, G., M. Glezerman, and V. Insler. "Selective Filtration of Abnormal Spermatazoa by the Cervical Mucous in Vitro," in V. Insler and G. Bettendorf (eds.), *The Uterine Cervix in Reproduction.* Stuttgart, W. Germany: George Thiem Verlag, 1977.

Perry, J. D., and B. Whipple. "Two Devices for the Physiological Measurement of Sexual 'activity.'" Paper presented at the Eastern Regional Conference of the Society for the Scientific Study of Sex, Philadelphia, April 27, 1980.

——, and ——. "Pelvic Muscle Strength and Female Ejaculation," *Journal of Sex Research,* 1981, **17:**22–39.

Persky, H., N. Charney, H. I. Lief, C. P. O'Brien, W. R. Miller, and D. Strauss. "The Relationship of Plasma Estradoil Level to Sexual Behavior in Young Women," *Psychosomatic Medicine,* 1978a, **40:**523–535.

——, H. I. Lief, D. Strauss, W. R. Miller, and C. P. O'Brien. "Plasma Testosterone Level and Sexual Behavior of Couples," *Archives of Sexual Behavior,* 1978b, **7:**157–173.

Persson, G. "Sexuality in a 70-Year-Old Population," *Journal of Psychosomatic Research,* 1980, **24:**335–342.

Peterman, D. J., C. A. Ridley, and S. M. Anderson. "A Comparison of Cohabitating and Noncohabitating College Students," *Journal of Marriage and the Family,* 1974, **36:**344–354.

Peterson, H. B., J. R. Greenspan, F. Destephano, F. W. Ory, and P. M. Layde. "The Impact of Laparoscopy on Tubal Sterilization in the United States Hospitals, 1970 and 1975 to 1978," *American Journal of Obstetrics and Gynecology,* 1981, **140:**811–814.

Peterson, O. L. "Breast Self-Examination: An Adjuvant to Early Cancer Detection," *American Journal of Public Health,* 1981, **71:**572–576.

Petras, J. W. *Sexuality and Society.* Boston: Allyn & Bacon, Inc., 1973.

Pettiford, P. "Pregnancy and Welfare Dependency: A Research Note." *The City of New York Human Resources Administration,* New York, February 1981 (mimeo). Reviewed in *Family Planning Perspectives,* 1981, **13:**189.

Pfeiffer, E., and G. C. Davis. "Determinants of Sexual Behavior in Middle and Old Age," in E. Palmore (ed.), *Normal Aging II: Reports from the Duke Longitudinal Studies, 1969–1973.* Durham, N.C.: Duke University Press, 1974.

——, A. Verwoerdt, and H-S Wang. "Sexual Behavior in Aged Men and Women," in E. Palmore (ed.), *Normal Aging: Reports from the Duke Longitudinal Study, 1955–1969.* Durham, N.C.: Duke University Press, 1970.

——, ——, and C. G. Davis. "Sexual Behavior in Middle Life," in E. Palmore (ed.), *Normal Aging II: Reports from the Duke Longitudinal Studies, 1970–1973.* Durham, N.C.: Duke University Press, 1974.

Phillips, L., J. J. Potterat, R. B. Rothenberg, C. Pratts, and R. D. King. "Focused Interviewing in Gonorrhea Control," *American Journal of Public Health,* 1980, **70:**705–708.

Pierquin, B., I. Baillet, and J. F. Wilson. "Radiation Therapy in the Management of Primary Breast Cancer," *American Journal of Roentgenology,* 1976, **127:**645–648.

Pietropinto, A., and J. Simenauer. *Beyond the Male Myth.* Chicago: Signet-New American Library, 1977.

Pittman, D. J. "The Male House of Prostitution," in J. M. Henslin (ed.), *Deviant Lifestyles.* New Brunswick, N.J.: Transaction Books, 1977.

Playboy. "Forum Newsfront." February 1980, 27, 57.

——. "The Great Playboy Sex Aids Road Test," March 1978, 135–137.

Pocs, O., and A. G. Godow. "Can Students View Parents as Sexual Beings?" *The Family Coordinator,* 1977a, **26:**31–36.

——, ——, W. L. Tolone, and R. H. Walsh. "Is There Sex after 40?" *Psychology Today,* June 1977b, **11:**54+.

Podolsky, S. "Sexual Impotence in the Aging Diabetic Male: Organic or Psychogenic Etiology?" *Gerontologist,* 1980, **20:**181.

Pomeroy, W. B. *Dr. Kinsey and the Institute for Sex Research.* New York: Harper & Row, 1972.

Pope, K. S., H. Levenson, and L. R. Schover. "Sexual Intimacy in Psychology Training," *American Psychologist,* 1979, **34:**682–689.

Population Reports: Oral Contraceptives. Series A, No. 5, January 1979.

Population Reports: Barrier Methods. Series H. No. 5, September 1979.

Population Reports: Population Information Program, Reversing Female Sterilization. Series C, No. 8, September 1980.

Prescott, J. W., and D. Wallace. "Abortion and the 'Right to Life': Facts, Fallacies, and Fraud, II—Psychometric Studies," *The Humanist,* November–December 1978, 36–42.

Presser, H. B. "Age at Menarche, Sociosexual Behavior and Fertility," *Social Biology,* 1978, **25:**94–101.

Prince, V. "Transsexuals and Pseudotranssexuals," *Archives of Sexual Behavior,* 1978, **7:**263–272.

——, and P. M. Bentler. "Survey of 504 Cases of Transvestism," *Psychological Reports,* 1972, **31:**903–917.

Qian, S. Z., G. W. Jing, X. Y. Wu, Y. Xu, Y. Q. Li, and Z. H. Zhou. "Gossypol Related Hypokalemia: Clinicopharmacologic Studies," *Chinese Medical Journal,* 1980, **93:**477.

——, Y. Xu, Z. C. Chen, L. M. Cao, S. G. Sun, X. C. Tang, Y. E. Wang, L. Y. Shen, and M. K. Zhu. "The Influence of Gossypol on the Potassium Metabolism of Rats and the Effect of Some Possible Contributing Factors (Low-K and Low-Mg Intake)," *Acta Phramaceutica Sinica,* 1979, **14:**514–520.

Rabkin, J. G. "Epidemiology of Forcible Rape," *American Journal of Orthopsychiatry,* 1979, **49:**634–647.

Rachman, S. "Sexual Fetishism: An Experimental Analogue," *Psychological Record,* 1966, **16:**293–296.

——, and R. J. Hodgson. "Experimentally-Induced 'Sexual Fetishism': Replication and Development," *Psychological Record,* 1968, **18:**25–27.

Rainwater, L. *Family Design: Marital Sexuality, Family Size, and Contraception.* Chicago: Aldine, 1965.

Ramey, J. "Intimate Groups and Networks: Frequent Consequences of Sexually Open Marriage," *The Family Coordinator,* 1975, **24:**515–530.

Ray, R. E., and C. E. Walker. "Biographical and Self-Report Correlates of Female Guilt Responses to Visual Erotic Stimuli," *Journal of Consulting and Clinical Psychology,* 1973, **41:**93–96.

Reevy, W. R. "Premarital Petting Behavior and Marital Happiness Prediction," *Marriage and Family Living,* 1959, **21:**349–355.

Reichelt, P. A. "Changes in Sexual Behavior among Unmarried Teenage Women Utilizing Oral Contraception," *Journal of Population,* 1978, **1:**57–68.

———, and H. H. Werley. "Contraception, Abortion and Venereal Disease: Teenagers' Knowledge and the Effect of Education," *Family Planning Perspectives,* 1975, **7:**83–87.

Reid, J. *From Private Vice to Public Virtue: The Birth Control Movement in America since 1830.* New York: Basic Books, Inc., 1978.

Rein, M. F. "Therapeutic Decisions in the Treatment of Sexually Transmitted Diseases: An Overview," *Sexually Transmitted Diseases,* 1981, **8:**93–99.

Reiss, A. J. "The Social Integration of Queers and Peers," *Social Problems,* 1961, **9:**102–120.

Reiss, H. T., J. Nezlek, and L. Wheeler. "Physical Attractiveness in Social Interaction," *Journal of Personality and Social Psychology,* 1980, **38:**604–617.

Reiss, I. L. *The Social Context of Premarital Sexual Permissiveness.* New York: Holt, Rhinehart & Winston, 1967.

———. *Family Systems in America,* 2d ed. New York: Holt, Rhinehart & Winston, 1976.

———, A. Banwart, and H. Foreman. "Premarital Contraceptive Usage: A Study and Some Theoretical Explorations," *Journal of Marriage and the Family,* 1975, **37:**619–630.

Rhyne, D. "Bases of Marital Satisfaction among Men and Women," *Journal of Marriage and the Family,* 1981, **43:**941–955.

Richardson, J. A., and G. Dixon. "Effect of Legal Termination on Subsequent Pregnancy," *British Medical Journal,* 1976, **1:**1303–1304.

Richardson, J. G., and J. E. Cranston. "Social Change, Parental Values, and the Salience of Sex Education," *Journal of Marriage and the Family,* 1981, **43:**547–558.

Riddle, D. I. "Relating to Children: Gays as Role Models," *Journal of Social Issues,* 1978, **34:**38–58.

Robbins, J. M. "Objective versus Subjective Responses to Abortion," *Journal of Consulting and Clinical Psychology,* 1979, **47:**994–995.

Robbins, M., and G. D. Jensen. "Multiple Orgasm in Males," *Journal of Sex Research,* 1978, **14:**21–26.

Robertiello, R. C. "The Clitoral versus Vaginal Orgasm Controversy and Some of Its Ramifications," *Journal of Sex Research,* 1970, **6:**307–311.

Robertson, P., and J. Schachter. "Failure to Identify Venereal Disease in a Lesbian Population," *Sexually Transmitted Diseases,* 1981, **8:**75–76.

Roht, L. H., and H. Aoyama. "Induced Abortion and Its Sequelae: Prematurity and Spontaneous Abortion," *American Journal of Obstetrics and Gynecology,* 1974, **120:**868–874.

Roothe, G. "Exhibitionism outside Europe and America," *Archives of Sexual Behavior,* 1973, **2:**351–363.

Rorhbaugh, J., and R. Jessor. "Religiosity in Youth: A Personal Control against Deviant Behavior," *Journal of Personality,* 1975, **43:**136–155.

Rosen, E., R. Fox, and I. Gregory. *Abnormal Psychology.* Philadelphia: W. B. Saunders, 1972.

Rosen, R. C. "Suppression of Penile Tumescence by Instrumental Conditioning," *Psychosomatic Medicine,* 1973, **35:**509–514.

———, D. Shapiro, and G. E. Schwartz. "Voluntary Control of Penile Tumescence," *Psychosomatic Medicine,* 1975, **6:**479–483.

Rosen, R. H., J. W. Ager, and L. J. Martindale. "Contraception, Abortion, and Self-Concept," *Journal of Population,* 1979, **2:**118–139.

Rosenberg, L., C. H. Hennekens, B. Rosner, C. Belanger, K. J. Rothman, and F. E. Speizer. "Oral Contraceptive Use in Relation to Nonfatal Myocardial Infarction," *American Journal of Epidemiology,* 1980, **111:**59–66.

Rosenheim, E., and M. Neumann. "Personality Characteristics of Sexually Dysfunctional Males and Their Wives," *Journal of Sex Research,* 1981, **17:**124–138.

Ross, M. W., L. J. Rogers, and H. McCullough. "Stigma, Sex, and Society: A New Look at Gender Differentiation and Sexual Variation," *Journal of Homosexuality,* 1978, **3:**315–330.

Rothenberg, P. B., and P. E. Varga. "The Relationship between Age of Mother and Child Health and Development," *American Journal of Public Health,* 1981, **71:**810–817.

Rothstein, R. "Authoritarianism and Men's Reactions to Sexuality and Affection in Women," *Journal of Abnormal and Social Psychology,* 1960, **61:**329–334.

Rotkin, I. D. "A Comparison Review of Key Epidemiological Studies in Cervical Cancer related to Current Searches for Transmissible Agents," *Cancer Research,* 1973, **33:**1353–1300.

Roviaro, S. E., and D. S. Holmes. "Arousal Transfer: The Influence of Fear Arousal on Subsequent Sexual Arousal for Subjects with Low and High Sex Guilt," *Journal of Research in Personality,* 1980, **14:**307–320.

Roy, R., and D. Roy. "Is Monogamy Outdated?" in R. W. Libby and R. N. Whitehurst (eds.), *Marriage and Alternatives: Exploring Intimate Relationships.* Glenview, Ill.: Scott, Foresman and Co., 1977.

"Royal College of General Practicioners Oral Contraceptive Study: Mortality among Oral Contraceptive Users," *Lancet,* 1977, **2:**727–731.

Rubin, A., and D. Babbott. "Impotence and Diabetes Mellitus," *Journal of the American Medical Association,* 1958, **168:**498–500.

Rubin, H. B., and D. E. Henson. "Voluntary Enhancement of Penile Erection," *Bulletin of the Psychonomic Society,* 1975, **6:**158–160.

———, and ———. "Effects of Alcohol on Male Sexual Responding," *Psychopharmacology,* 1976, **47:**123–134.

Rubin, L. "The Marriage Bed," *Psychology Today,* 1976, **10:**44+.

Russ-eft, P., M. Sorenger, and A. Beever. "Antecedents of Adolescent Parenthood and Consequences at Age 30," *The Family Coordinator,* 1979, **28:**173–180.

Russell, M. J., G. M Switz, and K. Thompson. "Olfactory Influences on the Human Menstrual Cycle." Paper presented at the meeting of the American Society for the Advancement of Science, San Francisco, June 1977.

Ryan, M. P. *Womanhood in America: From Colonial Times to the Present,* 2d ed. New York: Franklin Watts, 1979.

Safran, C. "What Men Do to Women on the Job: A Shocking Look at Sexual Harassment," *Redbook,* November 1976, 148–149, 229.

St. John, R. K., O. G. Jones, J. H. Blount, and A. A. Zaidi. "Pelvic Inflammatory Disease in the United States: Epidemiology and Trends among Hospitalized Women," *Sexually Transmitted Diseases,* 1981, **8:**62–66.

Salmon, U. J., and S. H. Geist. "Effects of Androgens upon Libido in Women," *Journal of Clinical Endocrinology,* 1943, **3:**325.

Samaan, N. A., A. U. Buzdar, K. A. Aldinger, P. N. Schultz, K-P Yang, M. M. Romsdahl, and R. Martin. "Estrogen Receptor: A Prognostic Factor in Breast Cancer," *Cancer,* 1981, **47:**554–560.

Sanders, W. B. (Ed.). *Juvenile Offenders for a Thousand Years: Selected Readings from Anglo-Saxon Times to 1900.* Chapel Hill: University of North Carolina Press, 1970.

Sandler, J., M. Myerson, and B. N. Kinder. *Human Sexuality: Current Perspectives.* New York: Mariner Publishing Co. 1980.

Sapolsky, B. S., and D. Zillman. "The Effect of Soft-Core and Hard-Core Erotica on Provoked and Unprovoked Hostile Behavior," *Journal of Sex Research,* 1981, **17:**319–343.

Sarafino, E. P. "An Estimate of Nationwide Incidence of Sexual Offenses against Children," *Child Welfare,* 1979, **58:**127–134.

Sartwell, P. E., T. Alfonse, T. Masi, F. R. Arthes, G. R. Greene, and H. E. Smith. "Thromboembolism and Oral Contraceptives: An Epidemiologic Case-Controlled Study," *American Journal of Epidemiology,* 1969, **90:**365–380.

Savolainen, E., E. Saksela, and L. Saxen. "Teratogenic Hazards of Oral Contraceptives Analyzed in a National Malformation Register," *American Journal of Obstetrics and Gynecology,* 1981, **140:**521–524.

Scales, P. *Sex Education and the Prevention of Teenage Pregnancy: An Overview of Policies and Programs in the United States.* Family Impact Seminar, Washington, D. C., George Washington University, Institute for Educational Leadership, 1979.

Schachter, J. "Chlamydial Infections," *New England Journal of Medicine,* 1978, **298:**428–435+.

Schafer, R. B., and R. Braito. "Self-Concept and Role Performance Evaluation among Marriage Partners," *Journal of Marriage and the Family,* 1979, **41:**801–810.

Schein, J. D., and M. Delk. *The Deaf Population of the United States.* Silver Spring, Md: National Association of the Deaf, 1974.

Scheiner-Engel, P., R. C. Schiavi, H. Smith, and D. White. "Sexual Arousability and the Menstrual Cycle," *Psychosomatic Medicine,* 1981, **43:**199–214.

Schill, T. R., and J. Chapin. "Sex Guilt and Males' Preference for Reading Magazines," *Journal of Consulting and Clinical Psychology,* 1972, **39:**516.

Schipper, H. "Filthy Lucre: A Tour of America's Most Profitable frontier," *Mother Jones,* April 1980, 31–33, 60–62.

Schmidt, G. and V. Sigusch. "Sex Differences in Responses to Psychosexual Stimulation by Films and Slides," *Journal of Sex Research,* 1970, **6:**268–283.

Schottenfeld, D. "The Epidemiology of Cancer: An Overview," *Cancer,* 1981, **47:**1095–1108.

———, M. E. Warshauer, S. Sherlock, A. G. Zauber, M. Leder, and R. Payne. "The Epidemiology of Testicular Cancer in Young Adults," *American Journal of Epidemiology,* 1980, **112:**232–246.

Schulz, D. A. *Human Sexuality.* Englewood Cliffs, N.J.: Prentice-Hall, Inc., 1979.

Schwartz, M. A. "A Study of the Attitudes, Sex Knowledge, and Sources of Sex Information of 87 Ninth Grade Lower-Class Boys." Unpublished doctoral dissertation, Columbia University, 1968.

Schwartz, S. "The Effects of Arousal on Appreciation for Varying Degrees of Sex-Relevant Humor," *Journal of Experimental Research in Personality,* 1973b, **41:**61–64.

———. "Effects of Sex Guilt and Sexual Arousal on the Retention of Birth Control Information," *Journal of Consulting and Clinical Psychology,* 1973a, **41:**61–64.

Scott, F. B., W. E. Bradley, and G. W. Timm. "Management of Erectile Impotence: Use of Implantable Prosthesis," *Urology,* 1973, **2:**80–82.

Scroggs, J. R. "Penalties for Rape as a Function of Victim Provocativeness, Damage, and Resistance," *Journal of Applied Social Psychology,* 1976, **6:**360–368.

Seaman, B., and G. Seaman. *Women and the Crisis in Sex Hormones.* New York: Rawson Associates, 1977.

Seattle Times. "Sexual Harassment Costs U.S. $95 Million a Year," April 29, 1981.

Sebold, H. "Patterns of Interracial Dating and Sexual Liason," *Journal of Comparative Family Studies,* 1974, **4:**23–36.

Seibel, M., M. G. Freeman, and W. L. Graves. "Hysterectomy for Carcinoma in Situ and Sexual Function," *Gynecologic Oncology,* 1981, **11:**195–199.

Seiler, J. S., M. Roland, J. R. Snyder, and R. C. Post. "Tubal Sterilization by Bipolar Laparoscopy: Report of 232 Cases," *Obstetrics and Gynecology,* 1981, **58:**92–95.

Selby, J. W., L. G. Calhoun, and T. A. Brock. "Sex Differences in the Social Perception of Rape Victims," *Personality and Social Psychology Bulletin,* 1977, **3:**412–415.

Seligman, C., J. Brickman, and D. Koulack. "Rape and Physical Attractiveness: Assigning Responsibility to Victims," *Journal of Personality,* 1977, **45:**554–563.

Semans, J. "Premature Ejaculation: A New Approach," *Southern Medical Journal,* 1956, **49:**353–358.

Senanayake, P., and D. G. Kramer. "Contraception and the Etiology of Pelvic Inflammatory Disease: New Perspectives," *American Journal of Obstetrics and Gynecology,* 1980, **138:**852–860.

Senie, R. T., P. R. Rosen, M. L. Lesser, and D. W. Kinne. "Breast Self-Examination and Medical Examination Related to Breast Cancer Stage," *American Journal of Public Health,* 1981, **71:**583–590.

Serrin, W. "Sex Is a Growing Multimillion Dollar Business," *New York Times,* Feb. 9, 1981, B1–B6.

Seth, P., and N. Balachandran. "Elution of Herpes Simplex Virus-Specific Cytoxic Antibodies from Squamous Cell Carcinoma of Uterine Cervix," *Nature,* 1980, **286:**613–615.

Sevely, J. L. and J. W. Bennett. "Concerning Female Ejaculation and the Female Prostate," *Journal of Sex Research,* 1978, **14:**1–20.

Sewell, H. H., and S. I. Abramowitz. "Flexibility, Persistence, and Success in Sex Therapy," *Archives of Sexual Behavior,* 1979, **8:**497–506.

Sewell, R. A., V. Braren, S. K. Wilson, and R. K. Rhamy. "Extended Biopsy Followup after Full Course Radiation for Resectable Prostatic Carcinoma," *The Journal of Urology,* 1975, **113:**371–3 .

Sexuality and Deafness: Precollege Programs, Gallaudet College. Washington, D.C.: Kendall Green, May 1979.

Sexually Transmitted Disease (STD) Statistical Newsletter, 1978, No. 128. Washington: U.S. Department of Health, Education, and Welfare, Public Health Service, Center for Disease Control.

Shapiro, S. "Evidence on Screening for Breast Cancer from a Randomized Trial," *Cancer,* 1977, **39** (Sup. 6), 2772–2782.

Shaul, S., J. Bogler, J. Hale-Harbaugh, and A. D. Norman. *Toward Intimacy: Family Planning and Sexuality Concerns of Physically Disabled Women,* 2d ed. New York: Human Sciences Press, 1978.

Shaver, P., and J. Freedman. "Your Pursuit of Happiness," *Psychology Today,* August 1976, 26+.

Shea, R. "Woman at War," *Playboy,* February 1980, 27+.

Shoemaker, D. J. "The Teeniest Trollops: 'Baby Pros', 'Chickens,' and Child Prostitutes," in C. D. Bryant (ed.), *Sexual Deviancy in Social Context.* New York: New Viewpoints, 1977.

Shorter, E. *The Making of the Modern Family.* New York: Basic Books, Inc., 1975.

———. "Writing the History of Rape," *Signs,* 1977, **3:**471–482.

Shumacher, S., and C. W. Lloyd. "Physiological and Psychological Factors in Impotence," *Journal of Sex Research,* 1981, **17:**40–53.

Shumsky, N. L., and L. M. Springer. "San Francisco's Zone of Prostitution, 1880–1934," *Journal of Historical Geography,* 1981, **7:**71–89.

Silverman, I. J. "A Survey of Cohabitation on Two College Campuses," *Archives of Sexual Behavior,* 1977, **6:**11–20.

Silverman, L. T., J. N. Sprafkin, and E. A. Rubenstein. "Physical Contact and Sexual Behavior on Prime-Time TV," *Journal of Communication,* 1979, **29:**33–43.

Simon, W., A. Berger, and G. H. Gagnon. "Beyond Anxiety and Fantasy: The Coital Experiences of College Youth," *Journal of Youth and Adolescence,* 1972, **1:**203–222.

Simon, W., and J. H. Gagnon. *Sexual Conduct: The Social Sources of Human Sexuality.* Chicago: Aldine, 1973.

Singer, J., and I. Singer. "Types of Female Orgasm," *Journal of Sex Research,* 1972, **8:**255–267.

Skeen, D. "Unequal Status in Sexual Relationships: An Examination of Tabooed Sexual Contact between Students and Professors." Paper presented at the 52d Annual Meeting of the Pacific Sociological Association, Portland, Ore., March 18–21, 1981.

Skinner, G. R., D. R. Williams, A. W. Moles, and A. Sargent. "Prepubertal Vaccination of Mice against Experimental Infection of the Genital Tract with Type 2 Herpes Simplex Virus," *Archives of Virology,* 1980, **64:**329–338.

Skrapec, C., and K. R. MacKenzie. "Psychological Self-Perception in Male Transsexuals, Homosexuals, and Heterosexuals," *Archives of Sexual Behavior,* 1981, **10:**357–370.

Small, M. P. "The Small-Clarion Penile Prosthesis," *Urologic Clinics of North America,* 1978, **5:**549–562.

Smelser, N. J. *Theory of Collective Behavior.* New York: Free Press, 1962.

Smith, D. S. "The Dating of the American Sexual Revolution: Evidence and Interpretation," in M. Gordon (ed.), *The American Family in Social History,* 2d ed. New York: St. Martin's Press, 1978.

———, and M. S. Hindus. "Premarital Pregnancy in America 1640–1971: An Overview and Interpretation," *Journal of Interdisciplinary History,* 1975, **4:**537–570.

Smith, E. S. O., C. S. Defve, and J. R. Miller. "An Epidemiological Study of Congenital Reduction Deformities of the Limbs," *British Journal of Preventive Medicine,* 1977, **31:**39–41.

Smith, J. W., J. E. Torres, and N. D. Holmquist. "Association of Herpes Simplex Virus (HSV) with Cervical Cancer by Lymphocyte Reactivity with HSV-1 and HSV-2 Antigens," *American Journal of Epidemiology,* 1979, **110:**141–147.

Smith, M. S. "The Deaf," in H. L. Gochros and J. S. Gochros (eds.), *The Sexually Oppressed.* New York: Association Press, 1977.

Smith, R. E., J. P. Keating, R. K. Hester, and H. E. Mitchell. "Role and Justice Considerations in the Attribution of Responsibility to a Rape Victim," *Journal of Research in Personality,* 1976, **10:**346–357.

Smith, R. J. "Drug Shows Promise against Herpes," *Science,* 1981, **213:**524.

Smith, R. S. "Voyeurism: A Review of the Literature," *Archives of Sexual Behavior,* 1976, **5:**585–608.

Smith, R. W. "Research and Homosexuality," *The Humanist,* 1979, (March-April), 20–22.

Smithyman, S. D. "Characteristics of 'undetected' rapists," in W. H. Parsonage (ed.), *Perspectives on Victimology.* Beverly Hills, Calif.: Sage, 1979.

Sohn, N., M. A. Weinstein, and I. Conchar. "Social Injuries of the Rectum," *American Journal of Surgery,* 1977, **134:**611–612.

Sorensen, R. *Adolescent Sexuality in Contemporary America.* New York: World Publishing, 1973.

Sotile, W. M. "The Penile Prosthesis: A Review," *Journal of Sex and Marital Therapy,* 1979, **5:**90–102.

Spanier, G. B. "Perceived Sex Knowledge, Exposure to Eroticism and Premarital Sexual Behavior: The Impact of Dating," *Sociological Quarterly,* 1976a, **17:**247–261.

Spanier, G. B. "Formal and Informal Sex Education as Determinants of Premarital Sexual Behavior," *Archives of Sexual Behavior,* 1976b, **1:**39–67.

Spanier, G. B. "Sources of Sex Information and Premarital Sexual Behavior," *Journal of Sex Research,* 1977, **13:**73–88.

———. "Sex Education and Premarital Sexual Behavior among American College Students," *Adolescence,* 1978, **13:**659–674.

———, and C. L. Cole. "Mate Swapping: Perceptions, Value Orientations, and Participation in a Midwestern Community," *Archives of Sexual Behavior,* 1975, **4:**143–159.

Spengler, A. "Manifest Sadomasochism of Males: Results of an Empirical Study," *Archives of Sexual Behavior,* 1977, **6:**441–456.

Spreitzer, E., and L. Riley. "Factors Associated with Singlehood," *Journal of Marriage and the Family,* 1974, **36:**533–543.

Staples, R. *The Black Woman in America.* Chicago: Nelson-Hall, 1973.

———. "Race, Liberalism, Conservatism and Premarital Sexual Permissiveness: A Bi-Racial Comparison," *Journal of Marriage and the Family,* 1978, **40:**733–742.

Steele, D. G., and C. E. Walker. "Male and Female Differences in Reaction to Erotic Stimuli as Related to Sexual Adjustment," *Archives of Sexual Behavior,* 1974, **3:**459–470.

Steele, T. E., S. H. Finkelstein, and F. O. Finkelstein. "Hemodialysis Patients and Spouses: Marital Discord, Sexual Problems, and Depression," *Journal of Nervous and Mental Disease,* 1976, **162:**225–237.

Stein, P. *Single.* Englewood Cliffs, N.J.: Prentice-Hall, Inc., 1976.

Stephan, W., E. Berscheid, and E. Walster. "Sexual Arousal a Heterosexual Perception," *Journal of Personality and Social Psychology,* 1971, **20:**93–101.

Stewart, F., F. Guest, G. Stewart, and R. Hatcher. *My Body, My Health: The Concerned Woman's Guide to Gynecology.* New York: John Wiley & Sons, 1979.

Stone, H. M. *Contraceptive Methods: A Clinical Survey.* Clinical Research Department of the American Birth Control League, 1925. Cited in Himes (1936).

Storms, M. D. "Attitudes toward Homosexuality and Femininity in Men," *Journal of Homosexuality,* 1978, **3:**257–263.

———. "Theories of Sexual Orientation," *Journal of Personality and Social Psychology,* 1980, **38:**783–792.

———. "A Theory of Erotic Orientation Development," *Psychological Record,* 1981, **88:**340–353.

———, M. L. Stivers, S. M. Lambers, and C. A. Hill. "Sexual Scripts for Women," *Sex Roles,* 1981, **7:**699–707.

Story, M. "A Longitudinal Study of a University Human Sexuality Course on Sexual Attitudes," *Journal of Sex Research,* 1979, **15:**184–204.

Strobino, B., J. Kline, and Z. Stein. "Exposure to Contraceptive Creams, Jellies, and Douches and Their Effect on the Zygote." Paper presented at the 13th Annual Meeting of the Society for Epidemiologic Research, Minneapolis, June 19, 1980.

Strong, L. D. "Alternative Marital and Family Forms: Their Relative Attractiveness to College Students and Correlates of Willingness to Participate in Nontraditional Forms," *Journal of Marriage and the Family,* 1978, **40:**493–503.

Sue, D. "Erotic Fantasies of College Students during Coitus," *Journal of Sex Research,* 1979, **15:**299–305.

Sundholm, C. A. "The Pornographic Arcade: Ethnographic Notes on Moral Men in Immoral Places," in C. D. Bryant (ed.), *Sexual Deviancy in Social Context.* New York: New Viewpoints, 1977.

Sussman, N. "Sex and Sexuality in History," in B. J. Saddock, H. I. Kaplan, and A. M. Freedman (eds.), *The Sexual Experience.* Baltimore: Williams & Wilkins, 1976.

Svanberg, L., and U. Ulmsten. "The Incidence of Primary Dysmenorrhea in Teenagers," *Archives of Gynecology,* 1981, **230:**173–177.

Swan, S. H., and W. L. Brown. "Oral Contraceptive Use, Sexual Activity, and Cervical Carcinoma," *American Journal of Obstetrics and Gynecology,* 1981, **139:**52–57.

Swieczkowski, J. B., and C. E. Walker. "Sexual Behavior Correlates of Female Orgasm and Marital Happiness," *Journal of Nervous and Mental Disease,* 1978, **166:**355–342.

Tanner, J. M. *Growth at Adolescence,* 2d ed. Oxford, England: Blackwell, 1962.

Tavris, C. "Men and Women Report Their Views on Masculinity," *Psychology Today,* 1977, (January) 35–38; 42; 82.

———, and S. Sadd. *The* Redbook *Report on Female Sexuality.* New York: Delacorte Press, 1977.

Templar, D. I., and E. Eberhardt. "Necrophilia: A Review," *Essence,* 1980, **4:**63–67.

Terman, L. M. *Psychological Factors in Marital Happiness.* New York: McGraw-Hill Book Co., Inc., 1938.

———. "Correlates of Orgasm Adequacy in a Group of 556 Wives," *Journal of Psychology,* 1951, **32:**115–172.

Thompson, L., and G. B. Spanier. "Influence of Parents, Peers, and Partners on the Contraceptive Use of College Men and Women," *Journal of Marriage and the Family,* 1978, **40:**481–492.

Thomson, P., and A. Templeton. "Characteristics of Patients Requesting Reversal of Sterlization," *British Journal of Obstetrics and Gynaecology,* 1978, **85:**161–164.

Thorman, G. "Cohabitation: A Report on the Married-Unmarried Lifestyle," *Futurist,* 1973, 250–254.

Thornburg, H. D. *Development in Adeolescence.* Monterey, Calif.: Brooks/Cole Publishing Co., 1975.

———. "Adolescent Sources of Information on Sex," *Journal of School Health,* 1981, **51:**274–277.

———, and C. M. Mistretta. "Tactile Sensitivity as a Function of Age," *Journal of Gerontology,* 1981, **36:**34–39.

Tietze, C. *Induced Abortion: 1979,* 3d ed. New York: The Population Council, 1979.

Time. "Unhappy over Hookers," Oct. 2, 1978, 48.

Tolor, A., and P. V. DiGrazia. "Sexual Attitudes and Behavior Patterns during and following Pregnancy," *Archives of Sexual Behavior,* 1976, **5:**539–551.

Tordjman, G., R. Thierree, and J. R. Michel. "Advances in the Vascular Pathology of Male Erectile Dysfunction," *Archives of Sexual Behavior,* 1980, **9:**391–398.

Tracy. *The Sexual Exploitation of Children: An Initial Study.* June 1979. 8140 Park Road, Richmond, British Columbia V6Y 1T1.

Troiden, R. R., and E. Goode. "Variables Related to the Acquisition of a Gay Identity," *Journal of Homosexuality,* 1980, **5:**383–392.

Trussell, S. T. "Economic Consequences of Teenage Childbearing," *Family Planning Perspectives,* 1976, **8:**184–190.

Tullman, G. M., F. H. Gilner, R. C. Kolodny, R. L. Dornbusch, and G. D. Tullman. "The Pre- and Post-Therapy Measurement of Communication Skills of Couples Undergoing Sex Therapy at the Masters and Johnson Institute," *Archives of Sexual Behavior,* 1981, **10:**95–109.

Twichell, J. "Sexual Liberality and Personality: A Pilot Study," in J. R. Smith and L. G. Smith (eds.), *Beyond Monogamy.* Baltimore: Johns Hopkins University Press, 1974.

Udry, J. R. "Age at Menarche, Age at First Coitus, and Age at First Pregnancy," *Journal of Biosocial Science,* 1979, **11:**483–541.

———, and N. M. Morris. "A Method of Validation of Reported Sexual Data," *Journal of Marriage and the Family,* 1967, **29:**442–446.

———, and ———. "Relative Contribution of Male and Female Age to the Frequency of Marital Intercourse," *Social Biology,* 1978, **25:**128–134.

Ueno, M. "The So-Called Coition Death," *Japanese Journal of Legal Medicine,* 1963, **17:**333–340.

Ugerer, J. C., R. J. Harford, F. L. Brown, and H. D. Kleger. "Sex Guilt and Preferences for Illegal Drugs among Drug Abusers," *Journal of Clinical Psychology,* 1976, **32:**891–895.

Upchurch, M. L. "Sex Guilt and Contraceptive Use," *Journal of Sex Education and Therapy,* 1978, **4:**27–31.

Urban, J. A. "Treatment of Primary Breast Cancer: Management of Local Disease: A Minority Report," *Journal of the American Medical Association,* 1980, **244:**800–803.

Uttal, W. R. *The Psychobiology of Mind.* Hillsdale, N.J.: Erlbaum, 1978.

Valins, S. "Cognitive Effects of False Heart Rate Feedback," *Journal of Personality and Social Psychology,* 1966, **4:**400–409.

Vance, E. B., and N. N. Wagner. "Written Descriptions of Orgasm: A Study of Sex Differences," *Archives of Sexual Behavior,* 1976, **5:**87–98.

Vander, A. J., J. H. Sherman, and D. S. Luciano. *Human Physiology: The Mechanism of Body Function.* New York: McGraw-Hill Book Co., 1980.

Veitch, R., W. Griffitt. "The Perception of Erotic Arousal in Men and Women by Their Same and Opposite Sex Peers," *Sex Roles,* in press.

Vener, A. M., and C. S. Stewart. "Adolescent Sexual Behavior in Middle America Revisited: 1970–1973," *Journal of Marriage and the Family,* 1974, **36:**728–735.

VerMeulen, M. "Turning Kids into Sex Symbols," *Parade,* 1981, March 8, 1981, 4–6.

Veronen, L. J., D. G. Kilpatrick, and P. A. Resick. "Treating Fear and Anxiety in Rape Victims: Implications for the Criminal Justice System," in W. H. Parsonage (ed.), *Perspectives on Victimology.* Beverly Hills, Calif.: Sage, 1979.

Veronesi, U., R. Saccozzi, M. Del Vecchio. "Comparing Radical Mastectomy with Quadrantectomy, Axillary Dissection, and Radiotherapy in Patients with Small Cancers of the Breast," *New England Journal of Medicine,* 1981, **305:**6–11.

Vessey, M. P., R. Doll, K. Jones, K. McPherson, and D. Yeates. "An Epidemiological Study of Oral Contraceptives and Breast Cancer," *British Medical Journal,* 1979, **1:**1757–1760.

———, K. McPherson, and R. Doll. "Breast Cancer and Oral Contraceptives: Findings in Oxford-Family Planning Association Contraceptive Study," *British Medical Journal,* 1981a, **282:**2093–2094.

———, ———, and D. Yeates. "Mortality in Oral Contraceptive Users," *Lancet,* 1981b, March 7, 549–550.

———, D. Yeates, R. Flavel, and K. McPherson. "Pelvic Inflammatory Disease and the Intrauterine Device: Findings from a Large Cohort Study," *British Medical Journal,* 1981c, 282, 855–857.

Voget, F. W. "The Sex Life of American Indians," in A. Ellis and A. Abarbanel (eds.), *Encyclopedia of Sexual Behavior.* New York: Hawthorn Books, Inc., 1961.

Voigt, K. D., and H. Schmidt. "Sex and the Involution of the Genitals in the Aging Male," in J. Money and H. Musaph (eds.), *Handbook of Sexology.* New York: Excerpta Medica, 1977.

Wabek, A. J., and R. C. Burchell. "Male Sexual Dysfunction Associated with Coronary Heart Disease," *Archives of Sexual Behavior,* 1980, **9:**69–75.

Wachowiak, D., and H. Bragg. "Open Marriage and Marital Adjustment," *Journal of Marriage and the Family,* 1980, **42:**57–62.

Wade, M. E., P. McCarthy, J. R. Abernathy, G. S. Harris, H. C. Danzer, G. D. Braunstein, and W. A. Uricchio. "A Randomized Prospective Study of Two Methods of Natural Family Planning: An Interim Report," *American Journal of Obstetrics and Gynecology,* 1979, 134, 268.

Wade, M. E., P. McCarthy, G. D. Braunstein, J. R. Abernathy, C. M. Suchindran, G. S. Harris, H. C. Danzer, and W. A. Uricchio. "A Randomized Prospective Study of the Use-Effectiveness of Two Methods of Natural Family Planning," *American Journal of Obstetrics and Gynecology,* 1981, **141:**368–376.

Walker, C. E. "Erotic Stimuli and the Aggressive Sexual Offender," in *Technical Report of the Commission on Obscenity and Pornography,* (V. 6). Washington, D. C.: U.S. Government Printing Office, 1971.

Walker, A. M., J. R. Hunter, R. N. Watkins, H. Jick, A. Danford, L. Alhadeff, and K. J. Rothman. "Vasectomy and Non-Fatal Myocardial Infarction," *Lancet,* 1981a, Jan. 3, 13–15.

———, H. Jick, J. R. Hunter, A. Danford, and K. Rothman. "Hospitalization Rates in Vasectomized Men," *Journal of the American Medical Association,* 1981b, **245:**2315–2317.

Wallin, P., and A. Clark. "Religiosity, Sexual Gratification, and Marital Satisfaction in the Middle Years of Marriage," *Social Forces,* 1964, **42:**303–309.

Walsh, R. H., M. Z. Ferrell, and W. L. Tolone. "Selection of Reference Group, Perceived Reference Group Permissiveness, and Personal Permissiveness Attitudes and Behavior: A Study of Two Consecutive Panels (1967–1971; 1970–1974)," *Journal of Marriage and the Family,* 1976, **38:**495–507.

———, and W. M. Leonard. "Usage of Terms for Sexual Intercourse by Men and Women," *Archives of Sexual Behavior,* 1974, **3:**373–376.

Walster, E., J. Traupmann, and G. W. Walster. "Equity and Extramarital Sexuality," *Archives of Sexual Behavior,* 1978, **7:**127–142.

———, G. W. Walster, and J. Traupmann. "Equity and Premarital Sex," *Journal of Personality and Social Psychology,* 1978, **36:**82–92.

Walters, J., P. C. McHenry, and L. H. Walters. "Adolescents' Knowledge of Childbearing," *Family Coordinator,* 1979, **28:**163–171.

Warburton, D., Z. Stein, and J. Kline. "Environmental Influences on Rates of Chromosome Anomalies in Spontaneous Abortions," abstr. in *American Journal of Human Genetics,* 1980, **32:**92.

Wasow, M. "Sexuality and the Institutionalized Mentally Ill," *Sexuality and Disability,* 1980, **3:**3–16.

———, and M. B. Loeb. "Sexuality in Nursing Homes," *Journal of the American Geriatrics Society,* 1979, **27:**73–79.

Weidner, G., J. Istvan, and W. Griffitt. "Beauty in the Eye of the Horny Beholderess: Evaluation of Attractive, Medium Attractive, and Unattractive Men by Sexually Aroused Women." Paper presented at the Annual Meeting of the Midwest Psychological Association, Chicago, 1979.

Weinberg, M. S. "Sexual Embourgeoisment: Social Class and Sexual Activity—1938–1970," *American Sociological Review,* 1980, **45:**33–48.

————, and C. J. Williams. "Gay Baths and the Social Organization of Impersonal Sex," *Social Problems,* 1975a, **23:**124–136.

————, and ————. *Male homosexuals: Their Problems and Adaptations.* New York: Penguin, 1975b.

Weinberger, L. E., and J. Millham. "Attitudinal Homophobia and Support of Traditional Sex Roles," *Journal of Homosexuality,* 1979, **4:**237–246.

Weir, R. J., E. Briggs, A. Mack, L. Naismity, L. Taylor, and E. Wilson. "Blood Pressure in Women Taking Oral Contraceptives," *British Medical Journal,* 1974, **1:**533–535.

————, D. L. Davies, and R. Fraser. "Contraceptive Steroids and Blood Pressure," *Journal of Steroid Biochemistry,* 1975, **6:**961–964.

Weiss, A., and D. Diamond. "Sexual Adjustment, Identification, and Attitudes of Patients with Myelopathy," *Archives of Physical Medicine and Rehabilitation,* 1966, **47:**245–250.

Wellisch, D. K., K. R. Jamison, and R. O. Pasnau. "Psychosocial Aspects of Mastectomy: II. The Man's Perspective," *American Journal of Psychiatry,* 1978, **135:**543–546.

Westoff, C. F. "Coital Frequency and Contraception," *Family Planning Perspectives,* 1974, **6:**136–141.

————. "Trends in Contraceptive Practice: 1965–1973," *Family Planning Perspectives.* 1976, **8:**54–57.

————, J. S. DeJung, N. Goldman, and J. D. Forrest. "Abortion Preventable by Contraceptive Practice," *Family Planning Perspectives,* 1981, **13:**218–223.

————, and E. F. Jones. "Contraception and Sterilization in the United States, 1965–1975," *Family Planning Perspectives,* 1977, **9:**153–157.

————, and J. McCarthy. "Sterilization in the United States," *Family Planning Perspectives,* 1979, **11:**147–152.

Westrom, L. "Incidence, Prevalence, and Trends of Acute Pelvic Inflammatory Disease and Its Consequences in Industrialized Countries," Part 2, *American Journal of Obstetrics and Gynecology,* 1980, **138:**880–892.

White, C. B. "Sexual Interest, Attitudes, Knowledge, and Sexual History in Relation to Sexual Behavior in the Institutionalized Aged," *Archives of Sexual Behavior,* 1982, **11:**11–21.

White, L. A. "Erotica and Aggression: The Influence of Sexual Arousal, Positive Affect, and Negative Affect on Aggressive Behavior," *Journal of Personality and Social Psychology,* 1979, **37:**591–601.

Whitehurst, N. N. "Open Marriage: Problems and Prospects." Paper presented at the Annual Meeting of the National Council on Family Relations. St. Louis, October 1974.

Wicklund, R. A. "Objective Self-Awareness," in L. Berkowitz (ed.), *Advances in Experimental Social Psychology.* New York: Academic, 1975.

Wiggins, J. S., N. Wiggins, and J. C. Conger. "Correlates of Heterosexual Somatic Preference," *Journal of Personality and Social Psychology,* 1968, **10:**82–92.

Wildman, R. W., R. W. Wildman, II, A. Brown, and C. Trice. "Note on Males' and Females' Preference for Opposite Sex Body Parts, Bust Sizes, and Bust Revealing Clothing," *Psychological Reports,* 1976, **38:**485–486.

Willcox, R. R. "Sexual Behavior and Sexually Transmitted Disease Pattern in Male Homosexuals," *British Journal of Venereal Diseases,* 1981, **57:**167–169 (a).

——. "The Rectum as Viewed by the Venerealogist," *British Journal of Venereal Diseases,* 1981, **57:**1–6 (b).

Wilsnack, S. C. "The Effects of Social Drinking on Women's Fantasy," *Journal of Personality,* 1974, **42:**43–61.

Wilson, G. D. *The Psychology of Conservatism.* London: Academic Press, 1973.

Wilson, G. T., and D. M. Lawson. "Expectancies, Alcohol, and Sexual Arousal in Male Social Drinkers," *Journal of Abnormal and Social Psychology,* 1976, **85:**587–594.

——, and ——. "Expectancies, Alcohol and Sexual Arousal in Women," *Journal of Abnormal Psychology,* 1978, **87:**358–367.

——, ——, and D. B. Abrams. "Effects of Alcohol on Sexual Arousal in Male Alcoholics," *Journal of Abnormal Psychology,* 1978, **87:**609–616.

Wincze, J. P., E. F. Hoon, and P. W. Hoon. "Physiological Responsivity of Normal and Sexually Dysfunctional Women during Erotic Stimulus Exposure," *Journal of Psychosomatic Research,* 1976, **20:**445–451.

Witkin, M. H. "Psychosexual Counseling of the Mastectomy Patient," *Journal of Sex and Marital Therapy,* 1978, **4:**20–28.

Wolchik, S. A., V. E. Beggs, J. P. Wincze, D. K. Sakheim, D. H. Barlow, and M. Mavissakalian. "The Effect of Emotional Arousal on Subsequent Sexual Arousal in Men," *Journal of Abnormal Psychology,* 1980, **89:**595–598.

Wolfe, J. N. "Risk for Breast Cancer Development Determined by Mammographic Parenchymal Pattern," *Cancer,* 1976, **37:**2486–2492.

——. "Breast Parenchymal Patterns: Prevalent and Incident Carcinomas," *Radiology,* 1979, **131:**267–268.

——. "Response to Egan," *Journal of the American Medical Association,* 1980, **244:**221–224.

Woods, N. F. *Human Sexuality in Health and Illness.* St. Louis: C. V. Mosby, 1979.

Wulf, D. "Female Sterilization: A Centennial Conference," *Family Planning Perspectives,* 1981, **13:**24–28.

Yap, H. Y., C. K. Tashima, G. R. Blumenschein, and N. E. Eckles. "Male Breast Cancer: A Natural History Study," *Cancer,* 1979, **44:**749–754.

Yonke, J. A., H. W. Hethcote, and A. Nold. "Dynamics and Control of the Transmission of Gonorrhea," *Sexually Transmitted Diseases,* 1978, **5:**51–56.

Zabin, L. S., and S. D. Clark, Jr. "Why They Delay: A Study of Teenage Family Planning Clinic Patients," *Family Planning Perspectives,* 1981, **13:**205–217.

Zdeb, M. "The Probability of Developing Cancer," *American Journal of Epidemiology,* 1977, **106:**6–16.

Zeiss, R. A. "Self-Directed Treatment for Premature Ejaculation," *Journal of Consulting and Clinical Psychology,* 1978a, **46:**1234–1241.

——, A. Christensen, and A. G. Levine. "Treatment for Premature Ejaculation through Male-Only Groups," *Journal of Sex and Marital Therapy,* 1978b, **4:**139–143.

——, and A. M. Zeiss. "The Role of Sexual Behavior in the Post-Divorce Adjustment Process." Paper presented at the annual meeting of the Western Psychological Association, San Diego, California, April 1979.

Zellinger, P. A., H. L. Fromkin, D. E. Speller, and C. A. Kohn. "A Commodity Theory Analysis of the Effects of Age Restrictions upon Pornographic Materials," *Journal of Applied Psychology,* 1975, **60:**94–99.

Zelnik, M. "Sex Education and Knowledge of Pregnancy Risk among U.S. Teenage Women," *Family Planning Perspectives,* 1979, **11:**355–357.

————, and J. F. Kantner. "Sexual Experience of Young Unmarried Women in the United States," *Family Planning Perspectives,* 1972, **4:**9–18.

————, and ————. "The Resolution of Teenage First Pregnancies," *Family Planning Perspectives,* 1974, **6:**74–80.

————, and ————. "Sexual and Contraception Experience of Young Unmarried Women in the United States, 1976 and 1971," *Family Planning Perspectives,* 1977, **9:**55–71.

————, and ————. "Reasons for Nonuse of Contraception by Sexually Active Women Aged 15–19," *Family Planning Perspectives,* 1979a, **11:**289–296.

————, and ————. "Sexual Activity, Contraceptive Use and Pregnancy among Metropolitan-Area Teenagers: 1971–1979," *Family Planning Perspectives,* 1980b, **12:** 230–237.

————, Y. J. Kimm, and J. F. Kantner. "Probabilities of Intercourse and Contraception among U.S. Teenage Women, 1971 and 1976," *Family Planning Perspectives,* 1979c, **11:**177, 179–183.

Zilbergeld, B., and M. Evans. "The Inadequacy of Masters and Johnson," *Psychology Today,* August 1980, 29–43.

————, and C. Rinkleib-Ellison. "Social Skills as an Adjunct to Sex Therapy," *Journal of Sex and Marital Therapy,* 1979, **5:**340–350.

Zillman, D., J. Bryant, and R. A. Carveth. "The Effect of Erotica Featuring Sadomasochism and Bestiality on Motivated Intermale Aggression," *Personality and Social Psychology Bulletin,* 1981, **7:**153–159.

Zohar, J., D. Meiras, B. Maoz, and N. Durst. "Factors Influencing Sexual Activity after Prostatectomy: A Prospective Study," *The Journal of Urology,* 1976, **116:**332–334.

Zuckerman, M. "Physiological Measures of Sexual Arousal in the Human," *Psychological Bulletin,* 1971, **75:**297–329.

————, R. N. Bone, R. Neary, D. Mangelsdorff, and B. Brustman. "What Is the Sensation Seeker? Personality Trait and Experience Correlates of the Sensation-Seeking Scales," *Journal of Consulting and Clinical Psychology,* 1972, **39:**308–321.

————, R. Tushup, and S. Finner. "Sexual Attitudes and Experience: Attitude and Personality Correlates and Changes Produced by a Course in Sexuality," *Journal of Consulting and Clinical Psychology,* 1976, **44:**7–9.

Zurcher, L. A., Jr., R. G. Kirkpatrick, R. G. Cushing, and C. K. Bowman. "Ad Hoc Antipornography Organizations and Their Active Members: A Research Summary," *Journal of Social Issues,* 1973, **29:**69–94.

Zussman, L., S. Zussman, R. Sunley, and E. Bjornson. "Sexual Response after Hysterectomy-Oopphorectomy: Recent Studies and Reconsideration of Psychogenesis," *American Journal of Obstetrics and Gynecology,* 1981, **140:**725–729.

CHAPTER-OPENING PHOTO CREDITS

Chapter 1   Bettmann Archives
Chapter 2   Dellenback/Kinsey Institute for Sex Research
Chapter 3   Erika Stone/Photo Researchers
Chapter 4   Leonard Freed/Magnum
Chapter 5   Doug McMullin
Chapter 6   Joel Gordon
Chapter 7   Joel Gordon
Chapter 8   Chester Higgins, Jr./Photo Researchers
Chapter 9   Kagan/Monkmeyer Press Photo
Chapter 10 Bettye Lane/Photo Researchers
Chapter 11 Elliot Erwit/Magnum
Chapter 12 Les Mahon/Monkmeyer Press Photo
Chapter 13 Arthur Trees/Magnum
Chapter 14 Edo Koenig/Black Star
Chapter 15 Wide World Photos
Chapter 16 Erika Stone/Photo Researchers
Chapter 17 Paul Conklin/Monkmeyer Press Photo

PHOTO CREDITS

Chapter 1
p. 4   Museo Nazionale, Tarquinia
p. 11   New York Public Library Picture Collection
p. 14   Culver Pictures

Chapter 2
p. 38   Bettmann Archive
p. 39   Kinsey Institute for Sex Research: (a) Varies Fisher and (c) Wallace Kirkland

Chapter 3
p. 70   Carnegie Institution of Washington, Department of Embryology, Davis Division

Chapter 4
p. 93   Abigail Heyman/Archive Pictures
p. 96   Joel Gordon
p. 111 Playboy Magazine, © 1970

Chapter 5
p. 136 Elliot Erwitt/Magnum
p. 137 Otto Lang
p. 141 Playboy Magazine, © 1977
p. 143 J. R. Heiman

Chapter 6
p. 168 Reproduced by permission of G. P. Putnam's Sons from Philip Rawson, *Erotic Art of the East*. New York: Putnam, 1968. Copyright © 1968 by Philip Rawson
p. 179 Charles Gatewood
p. 181 Rafael Macia/Photo Researchers

Chapter 7
p. 197 Rick Smolan/Stock, Boston
p. 198 Burk Uzzle/Magnum
p. 203 Burk Uzzle/Magnum
p. 216 Henri Cartier-Bresson/Magnum

Chapter 8
p. 242 Copyright © 1979, Jules Feiffer
p. 248 Bill Aron/Editorial Photocolor Archives

Name Index

Subject Index

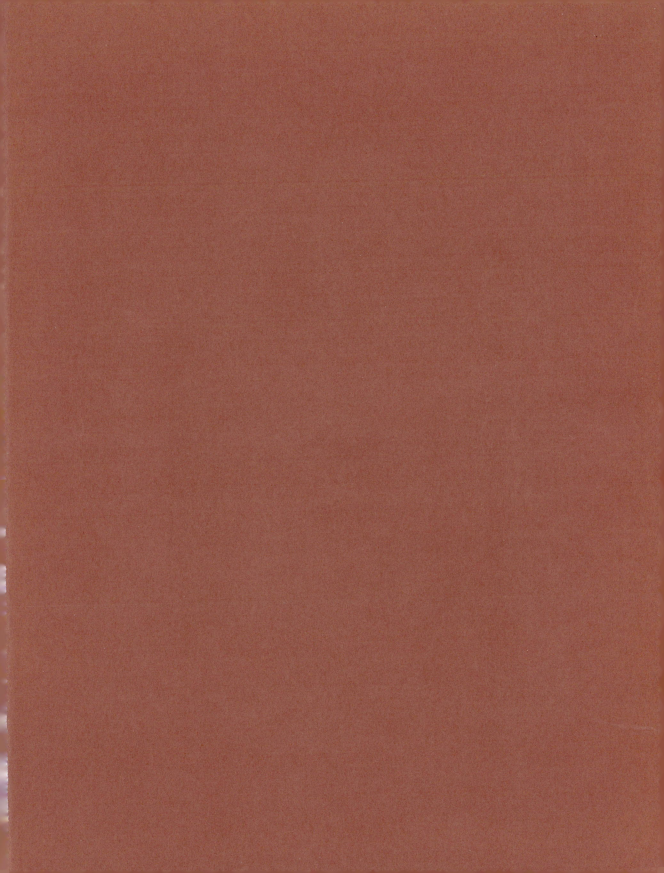